The Economics of Legal Minimum Wages

*A Conference Sponsored by the
American Enterprise Institute for Public Policy Research*

The Economics of Legal Minimum Wages

Edited by Simon Rottenberg

American Enterprise Institute for Public Policy Research
Washington and London

Library of Congress Cataloging in Publication Data

Main entry under title:

The Economics of legal minimum wages.

    (AEI symposia ; 81A)
    Papers presented at a conference held at the
American Enterprise Institute, Washington, D.C.,
Nov. 1 and 2, 1979.
      1. Wages—Minimum wage—United States—Congresses.
2. Labor supply—United States—Congresses. 3. Human
capital—United States—Congresses. I. Rottenberg,
Simon. II. American Enterprise Institute for Public
Policy Research. III. Series: American Enterprise
Institute for Public Policy Research. AEI symposia;
81A.
HD4918.E26   331.2′3′0973   80–26563
ISBN 0–8447–2197–2
ISBN 0–8447–2198–0 (pbk.)

AEI Symposia 81A

Printed in the United States of America

Contents

Contributors

Professor Nabeel Al-Salam
Department of Economics
University of California—Los Angeles

Professor Carolyn Shaw Bell
Department of Economics
Wellesley College

Professor Barry R. Chiswick
Department of Economics
University of Illinois at Chicago Circle

Professor Marshall R. Colberg
Department of Economics
Florida State University

Professor Vittorio Corbo
Faculty of Economic Sciences
University of Chile
Santiago, Chile

Dr. Philip Cotterill
Health Care Financing Administration
Office of Research
Demonstrations and Statistics
American Medical Association
Chicago, Illinois

Professor Robert F. Cotterman
Department of Economics
University of California—Los Angeles

Professor James C. Cox
Department of Economics
University of Arizona

Professor James Cunningham
Department of Economics
University of Houston

Professor Ronald G. Ehrenberg
School of Industrial and Labor Relations
Cornell University

Professor Isaac Ehrlich
Department of Economics
State University of New York at Buffalo

Dr. William Fellner
Resident Scholar
American Enterprise Institute
Washington, D.C.

Professor Bruce Gardner
Department of Agricultural Economics
Texas A & M University

Professor Robert S. Goldfarb
Department of Economics
George Washington University

Professor Kenneth Gordon
Department of Economics
Smith College

Professor Peter Gregory
Department of Economics
University of New Mexico

Professor Thomas J. Kniesner
Department of Economics
University of North Carolina

Professor Keith B. Leffler
Department of Economics
University of Washington

Professor Linda Leighton
Department of Economics, Dealy Hall
Fordham University

Professor J. Peter Mattila
Department of Economics
Iowa State University

Professor J. Huston McCulloch
Department of Economics and Finance
Ohio State University

Professor Jacob Mincer
Department of Economics
Columbia University

Professor J. R. Moroney
Department of Economics
Tulane University

Professor Ronald L. Oaxaca
Department of Economics
University of Arizona

Professor Llad Phillips
Department of Economics
University of California, Santa Barbara

Professor Solomon William Polachek
Department of Economics
University of North Carolina

Professor Aline Quester
Department of Economics
State University of New York
College at Cortland

Professor James F. Ragan, Jr.
Department of Economics
Kansas State University

Professor Jean-Jacques Rosa
Institut d'Etudes Politiques et
Fondation pour la Nouvelle
Economie Politique
Paris, France

Professor Sherwin Rosen
Department of Economics
University of Chicago

Professor Simon Rottenberg
Department of Economics
University of Massachusetts

Professor Paul L. Schumann
Department of Economics
Cornell University

Professor John M. Trapani
Department of Economics
Tulane University

Professor Finis Welch
Department of Economics
University of California, Los Angeles

*This conference was held
on November 1 and 2, 1979
at the American Enterprise Institute
Washington, D.C.*

Introduction

Simon Rottenberg

The Fair Labor Standards Act was adopted by the Congress in 1938. The act has been amended a number of times since then, most recently in 1977. Its main provision is to establish, for the employments it covers, legal minimum wages. No employer may legally pay, in covered employments, less than $3.10 per hour, and that sum will ratchet, by law, to $3.35 per hour at the beginning of 1981. The federal minimum wage law is complemented by state minimum wage laws.

A very large proportion of private-sector nonsupervisory employees is employed in occupations that are covered by minimum wage laws. Of 59 million such workers in 1977, 52 million were covered by the Fair Labor Standards Act and an additional 5 million by state minimum wage laws.

Those who promote minimum wage laws do so because, it is said, they believe that such laws alleviate poverty and improve the conditions of life of the working poor. Upon closer analytical examination, however, it can be seen that such laws have perverse effects—they intensify poverty and diminish the living standards of the poor.

We begin by examining the standard textbook prescriptions about wage making and the consequences of wages in competitive labor markets in which there are no public policy constraints affecting the terms of employment. In such markets, there is a supply schedule of labor to an occupation that shows the quantity of labor services that will be offered at all possible hypothetical prices and a demand schedule of labor to the occupation that shows the quantity of labor services that will be taken up at all possible hypothetical prices.

Offers of labor services, in response to given prices, will depend upon the value of alternative uses of time; bids for labor services, in response to given prices, will depend upon the demand for the commodities and services that require labor of the relevant occupational class for their production, and it will depend upon the quality of substitutes for labor in the production of those commodities and services. The two price-quantity relationships—offers of labor and price and bids

1

for labor and price—will cause a price or wage rate to occur in the market.

Workers, who are owners of their own services, and employers, who seek to secure those services for some period of time, engage in consensual exchange transactions. Neither workers, who have alternative uses for time, nor employers, who can substitute other factors of production for workers, are coerced to engage in exchange. If transactions do occur—that is to say, if employers' bids are accepted by workers and workers' offers are accepted by employers—there are advantages to both parties to the transaction and both are made better off. If such were not the case, in the absence of coercion they would not have consented to participate.

The services of labor are a factor of production that firms combine with the services of other factors to produce output of commodities and services. Factors of production will be substitutable for one another. Successful firms that survive in their product markets will have combined factors of production in such a way that their output will be produced at the lowest possible cost.

Just as the competitive labor market for the relevant occupation will generate a price for the services of labor of that class, other labor markets for other occupations will generate a price for each of them, and markets for each of the other, nonlabor factors will generate prices for them.

The set of prices of factors of production will express their relative social-scarcity value. The more scarce a factor is, relative to the community's demand for it, the higher will be its price. The different prices of different production factors signal to users the uses to which they should be put. Firms seeking out cost-minimizing factor combinations will husband relatively scarce and socially more valuable resources and will be more profligate in the use of relatively more abundant and socially less valuable resources.

Firms will serve the social purpose without giving it explicit attention. Given the price of labor in an occupation, that quantity of it will be employed by a firm such that the contribution to the output of the firm of the last unit of labor of that class that is employed will be equal in value to the wage rate in that occupation. Each worker is paid a claim on the output of others equal to the contribution he makes to the community's output; exploitation does not occur. Every firm that desires to employ a unit of labor services must pay the market price for that service; any that sought to pay less would find its labor moving to other employments or other uses of time. The competitive market disciplines firms to pay the market price for labor.

2

Wage rates will be different in different occupations. Some occupations require, for their successful performance, higher skills than do others. The labor market will cause payments to be made for labor services that will compensate those who have incurred investment costs in the learning of the relevant skills. The existence of skill differentials in wages will provide incentives for the learning of a skill; the magnitudes of the skill differentials will be just sufficient to secure the quantity of investment in the acquisition of skill that serves the community's purposes. Wage differences among occupations will also compensate workers for hazards, dirt, and other discommodities they encounter at work.

Adjusting for other advantages and disadvantages in different employments, wages will be equal in all employments.

The production of some commodities and services requires more labor-intensive factor combinations than does the production of other commodities and services. Different regions of the country have different resource endowments; labor is relatively more abundant in some regions than in others. Other things being equal, competitive markets will see to it that commodities requiring much labor in their production will be produced in regions where labor is relatively abundant, because labor services are cheaper there. The location of producing facilities and producing activities will be responsive to the principle of comparative advantage. Commodities will exchange among regions in ways that cause them to be produced in regions in which it is relatively more efficient to produce them.

In competitive markets, those that discriminate against some classes of the population are compelled to pay a price for the discriminatory properties of their preference sets. The market will require them to pay a higher price for labor services than the price at which the members of the dispreferred population class make their services available. The price they pay for labor will be higher than what they would have paid if they had not discriminated.

Thus, if competitive labor markets are permitted to establish the wages of labor, the community tends to get the basket of commodities and services that it desires, produced by cost-minimizing input combinations in places that are appropriate to their production, when determined on a standard of efficiency; and the output of the community is distributed among its members in proportions that maximize the community's welfare, because exploitation does not occur and an efficient set of incentives instructs and guides economic behavior and choice.

Suppose, now, that a set of minimum wages is introduced that is enforced by law. The level of the legal minimum wages could be, in principle, set lower than the wages that would prevail in the market in the absence of the law. In that case, the legal minimum wages would be superfluous. They would not govern. The wages that will be paid would be those that would occur if there were no minimum wage law.

We shall suppose a nonsuperfluous legal minimum wage set at a level higher than the level that would prevail in a competitive market, and we shall assume that the law is complied with or enforced. The minimum wage law will, in that case, distort the relative price set. The signaling system instructing socially efficient resource use becomes malformed. Relative prices no longer express the relative social scarcities of resources. Inefficient input combinations occur. Less output is squeezed from the resources that are employed in production. The diminution of output tends to intensify poverty and to make people, on average, less well off.

The quantity that buyers want to buy of any commodity or service, including the services of labor, is inversely related to its price; the higher the price, other things being equal, the smaller is the quantity that buyers want to buy. This is the law of demand in the language of the economics profession; demand schedules are downward-sloping on conventionally drawn graphs.

If, therefore, government intervenes to enforce a price for labor higher than would appear in competitive markets, a smaller quantity of labor is employed in the production vector in which the higher price is enforced. If there is a vector of the economy that is not covered by the minimum wage law, some of those released by diminished hiring in the covered vector will take up employment in the uncovered vector and employment there will increase. This, however, moves an increment of workers to what is for them second-best employment opportunity; they are made worse off. If that were not so, they would have chosen employment in the uncovered vector, preferentially, without having to be forced into that vector by the loss of employment in the covered vector— a loss of employment precisely produced by the enforcement of the minimum wage there.

The smaller the fraction of the economy left uncovered by the minimum wage law, the larger will be the fraction of diminished employment produced by that law that will be moved into the state of unemployment.

Those who will be most adversely affected by a legal minimum wage law will be low-wage workers. It is they who are most intensively and most immediately touched by such laws; those in high-wage employments are either unaffected by minimum wage laws or affected trivially. Low-wage workers who will be forced into second-best employment or into unemployment by minimum wage laws systematically include young people, minorities, the elderly, the handicapped, and those without skill.

Resource endowments differ among the states and regions. Competitive markets cause prices to reflect these variant conditions. In competitive markets, labor-intensive commodities tend to be produced in regions where labor is low in price and abundant, and labor-extensive commodities are produced in regions where labor is high in price and scarce. There is efficient specialization and division of labor among regions and efficient exchange among them. As a result, aggregate output is enlarged. Where the state enforces a uniform price for labor of a class, as by a legal minimum wage system, this efficient division-of-labor arrangement tends to be frustrated; the spatial distribution of economic activity is distorted, and output is diminished. Where a price for labor is enforced that is higher than the competitive price, the market does not clear. The number who want to be employed in the relevant occupation at that price exceeds the number who will be employed. There is an excess supply of labor to that occupation at that price. Physical rationing must occur. Physical rationing is an inefficient and frequently inequitable system for allocating economic activity and opportunity for employment among aspirants for it.

Legal minimum wages are frequently an instrument employed by privileged classes of workers to enforce their privileged positions by preventing other classes of workers from entering their occupations and competing with them. South African white trade unionists have, for decades, promoted the principle of "equal pay for equal work." They have insisted that black workers may be permitted to work in occupations mainly held by white workers only if the blacks are paid the same wage rates as are white workers. Because white workers are relatively scarce and black workers are relatively abundant in South Africa, an unconstrained competitive market would establish differential wages for them. Thus, the equal-pay-for-equal-work rule enforces a wage for black workers that is higher than their competitive wage. The rule dilutes the incentive given employers to employ blacks rather than whites in the relevant occupations, and it deprives black workers of opportunities for employment that some of them would prefer, at competitive wage rates, to alternative occupational employment. The white workers' rule does not and is not intended to improve the conditions of work of black workers; rather, it enforces and entrenches the privileged position of white workers.

Minimum wage laws often have the same effect. They are regressive. They redistribute income and wealth from those worse off to those who are better off. They enforce the privileged positions of some workers at the expense of other workers who are in less privileged positions.

Similarly, legal minimum wages are frequently employed as an instrument to prevent the reallocation of economic activity among regions by compelling labor in poorer regions to offer their services at a price not less than the price at which labor is offered in richer regions. This impedes the employment and occupational progress of workers in the poorer regions and gives an advantage to better-off workers at the expense of worse-off workers.

Legal minimum wages may compress the structure of wages and, therefore, suboptimally alter the system of incentives for the acquisition of skills. Differences in wages and earnings among workers at different levels of skill provide an incentive system for investment in skill acquisition. The larger those differences, the larger is the incentive to invest in the formation of human capital. There is some socially optimal spread of wage rates among occupations. If minimum wages compress that spread and cause the differences between the wage rates in unskilled and skilled occupations to be too small, the return on investment in skill acquisition is reduced, less investing is done, the average quality of the labor force is diminished, output is lower, and poverty tends to be intensified.

The distorted structure of wages paid for the services of labor in different occupations and trades as a result of the enforcement of legal minimum wage laws not only produces a socially inappropriate incentive system for investment in the formation of human capital but also causes socially inappropriate signals to be emitted that guide the movement of labor from place to place and from trade to trade. Workers transact for the sale of their services in places and in occupations where they are less productive and, therefore, where their earnings are less than would have occurred if the proper signaling system of competitive labor markets had been permitted to prevail. This might have transpired, of course, if the minimum wage laws had not been applied in those markets.

Thus, minimum wage laws can be perverse in their effects. On the surface, they will appear to many to raise the wages of the working poor. Scratch the surface, and it can be seen that such laws can have opposite consequences. They can move low-wage workers to unemployment and to less desirable employments; they can diminish the output of the economy; they can generate inefficient combinations of factors of production and an inefficient distribution of economic activity among regions; they can regressively redistribute income from poorer workers to those who are better off; they can reduce the stock of skill commanded by the working class. These are standard expectations that are analytically derived by the application of textbook principles of economics.

The papers of this volume, which were produced for a Conference on Legal Minimum Wages held in Washington, D.C., in late 1979, examine diverse aspects of the economics of minimum wages. Some are theoretical constructs, but most are assays at the empirical measurement of minimum wage effects. Taken together, they constitute a significant contribution to the professional literature.

Papers

The Effect of a Legal Minimum Wage on the Pay and Employment of Teenage Students and Nonstudents

James F. Ragan, Jr.

Introduction

Minimum wage legislation appears to be undergoing a reassessment. Although some concern was voiced at an early stage,[1] criticism of this law has intensified in recent years. Over the past two decades, coverage under the federal minimum wage law has been extended to more and more of the less skilled work force. This period has also seen a deterioration of the youth labor market.[2] According to a large body of studies,[3] these two forces are intimately related. Given the growing awareness that the legal minimum wage has adverse effects on the employment of low-productivity workers, an increasing number of individuals of various political and social backgrounds have spoken out against this law. Indicative of this trend, a *New York Times* editorial argues that liberals should no longer embrace the minimum wage.[4]

NOTE: I would like to thank Gail Ragan for computer assistance.

[1] One of the classic essays on minimum wage was published over thirty years ago. See George Stigler, "The Economics of Minimum Wage Legislation," *American Economic Review* 36 (June 1946):358–65.

[2] Throughout this paper, the terms "youth" and "teenager" are used interchangeably. Both refer to sixteen- to nineteen-year-olds. Workers younger than sixteen are ignored for data reasons and also because few of them are in the labor market.

[3] Robert S. Goldfarb, "The Policy Content of Quantitative Minimum Wage Research," *Proceedings of the Industrial Relations Research Association,* December 1974, pp. 261–68, surveys many of the early studies. More recent work includes that of Jacob Mincer, "Unemployment Effects of Minimum Wages," *Journal of Political Economy* 84 (August 1976): S87–S104; Finis Welch, "Minimum Wage Legislation in the United States," in Orley Ashenfelter and James Blum, eds., *Evaluating the Labor Market Effects of Social Programs: Industrial Relations Section* (Princeton: Princeton University Press, 1976), pp. 1–38; Edward M. Gramlich, "Impact of Minimum Wages on Other Wages, Employment, and Family Incomes," *Brookings Papers on Economic Activity* 2 (1976): 430–51; and James F. Ragan, Jr.,"Minimum Wages and the Youth Labor Market," *Review of Economics and Statistics* 59(May 1977): 129–36.

[4] The following is an excerpt taken from the editorial, entitled "The Minimally Useful Minimum Wage": "Since the Depression, liberals have favored higher minimum wages while conservatives have resisted. But this debate has become sterile. Whatever the merits of minimum wages in the past, they make little economic sense today." See *New York Times,* March 21, 1977, for the full editorial.

Claims that a minimum wage is necessary "to provide families with a standard of living approaching the nonfarm poverty level" and to "protect them [low-wage workers] from exploitation" are being scrutinized and found to be fallacious.[5] Economists have pointed out that a minimum wage by itself provides no income—income depends on hours of work as well as on a wage rate. Numerous researchers find that the minimum wage law results in job loss for some workers, and, as shown by Edward Gramlich,[6] this law also reduces the average number of hours worked by teenagers, some of whom are forced from full-time work to part-time. Income for many is therefore reduced. It is also being asked why teenagers, generally supplemental workers rather than breadwinners, should be denied jobs that pay wages below those full-time workers require to support a family.

Some workers unquestionably benefit from a minimum wage through the receipt of higher income. Their gains, however, come at the expense of other workers. The gains and losses are not shared equally by all segments of the population. Groups with the lowest levels of productivity suffer the greatest loss. Where discrimination prevails, the minimum wage merely replaces wage discrimination (paying lower wages) with employment discrimination (not hiring). Thus, those experiencing the greatest losses tend to be those in greatest need.

Concern has especially focused on youths. Although some adults are also denied jobs as a consequence of the minimum wage, a disproportionate share of the burden is borne by youths. This has more than a temporary effect. Because a job confers experience, sharpens various skills, and accustoms one to the routine of work, those denied jobs as teenagers may find themselves worse off throughout their working lives. Some recent studies find that for youths future earnings and employment are indeed affected by current employment status. Given the twin evils of lost employment and lost experience, some have advocated a lower minimum wage for teenagers than for adults. In fact, the House of Representatives in 1977 defeated such a proposal by a single vote. Opposition to this proposal was based on the understanding that, although a lower minimum for teenagers would expand their employment, employment of low-productivity adults would suffer (although by a lesser amount). Of course, employment of low-productivity adults could also

---

[5] The specific quotations came from a publication by the U.S. Department of Labor, "Statement of the Secretary," in *Minimum Wage and Maximum Hours Standards under the Fair Labor Standards Act,* Washington, D.C., 1978, pp. 1–4, but these are common arguments in support of the minimum wage. For a critical discussion of these views, see James F. Ragan, Jr., "Minimum Wage Legislation: Goals and Realities," *Nebraska Journal of Economics and Business* 17 (Autumn 1978): 21–28.

[6] Gramlich, "Impact of Minimum Wages."

be expanded if they too could be hired at a lower minimum wage. Indeed, total employment would be maximized if the minimum wage law were repealed. Most congressmen are not yet ready, however, to discard the concept of a minimum wage.

The trick then is to determine how high to set the minimum wage. Why not raise it to the average wage rate in the economy? No one should be expected to work for less than anyone else receives. If that seems too generous, why not set an hourly minimum of four dollars or five dollars? Clearly, the costs of setting a minimum wage too high are more, in terms of lost jobs and production, than society is willing to pay. The minimum wage must be kept low enough so that the costs are acceptable. Those supporting a minimum wage then have responsibility for selecting the "optimal" value of this minimum. But, as George Stigler asked, how does one come up with a minimum wage that is optimal for all occupations and industries?[7] And would not the optimal minimum, if such a thing existed, change frequently over time in response to economic growth and fluctuations? If so, this increases the risks that the damage done by the minimum wage may prove to be more severe than anticipated. It is hoped that, as the problems and deleterious effects of a legal minimum wage become more apparent, reassessment of minimum wage legislation will continue.

This study attempts to provide further evidence concerning the impact on teenage employment of the federal minimum wage. In the process, a second question is addressed: How does the minimum wage affect teenage wage rates, both in real terms (net of inflation) and relative to the wages of other workers? Although the pattern of results is not uniform across teenage groups, our findings are that the minimum wage has an adverse effect for many segments of the teenage population, most notably for nonwhite males and males not in school. An increase in the minimum wage is found to raise relative costs of employing young workers, causing employers to cut back on teenage employment.

An Overview

The theory of minimum wages is both simple and complex. Complications arise for several reasons.[8] First, while some companies are covered by the Fair Labor Standards Act, others are exempt. Thus, the economy

---

[7] Stigler, "Economics."

[8] Various complications are discussed by Mincer, "Unemployment Effects"; Welch, "Minimum Wage Legislation," in Ashenfelter and Blum, *Labor Market Effects;* and Alan A. Fisher, "The Problem of Teenage Unemployment" (Ph.D. diss., University of California, Berkeley, 1973).

consists of two sectors: "covered," where companies are required to pay the minimum wage, and "uncovered." Within both the youth and adult populations, productivity differences exist among workers. Moreover, the productivity distributions by age (and other characteristics) overlap; some youths are more productive than some adults. Finally, if employers have substantial control over wages (that is, "monopsony power"), certain ambiguities arise concerning the minimum wage's effect on employment.[9]

Despite these complicating factors, the basis for the economic prediction that a minimum wage reduces teenage employment is rather simple. If forced to pay higher wages for low-productivity workers, employers will reduce employment of such workers. The contributions of some workers to a company's revenues will, at the higher wage, no longer be substantial enough to allow the company to profitably employ them. Although some of these workers will find employment in companies exempt from the legal minimum wage, others will not. Some of those denied jobs in the covered sector will, now unemployed, continue to search for jobs there. Others, discouraged by reduced job prospects in the covered sector and possibly lower wages in the uncovered sector,[10] will withdraw from the labor force. Thus, total employment of low-productivity workers will decline, the magnitude of decline being greater the more pervasive is the coverage of the Fair Labor Standards Act. Given their limited skills, experience, and maturity, the productivity of teenagers is, on average, low vis-à-vis the productivity of adults. As a consequence, the decline in employment induced by the minimum wage will fall heavily on teenagers.

Most studies have attempted to capture the effect of a legal minimum wage with some version of the following variable:[11]

$$MIN = \frac{MW \times COV}{AHE}$$

where:

MW = nominal value of the minimum wage,

[9] These issues are examined by Stigler, "Economics," and James F. Ragan, Jr., "The Theoretical Ambiguity of a Minimum Wage," *Atlantic Economic Journal*, March 1977, pp. 56–60.

[10] Wages in the uncovered sector can be expected to fall if an increase in the minimum wage shifts workers out of the covered sector (as a consequence of decreased employment there) and into the uncovered sector.

[11] This variable was popularized by Thomas W. Gavett, in U.S. Department of Labor, Bureau of Labor Statistics, *Youth Unemployment and Minimum Wages*, Bulletin 1657 (1970), pp. 1–29; and Hyman B. Kaitz, "Experience of the Past: The National Minimum," in the same volume, pp. 30–54.

COV = fraction of either total population or teenage population covered by minimum wage legislation,[12]

AHE = some broad measure of average earnings, for example, average hourly earnings in either manufacturing or the private economy.

The minimum wage is deflated by average hourly earnings to take into account that the minimum wage is not important per se but is important in relation to other wage rates. A minimum wage of $1.00 would obviously have a more pronounced effect in 1960 when average hourly earnings in the private economy were $2.09 than in 1978 when average hourly earnings were $5.69. Hourly earnings rise over time due to increases in both worker productivity and prices. What is relevant is the minimum wage relative to other wage rates. But there is something else to consider. The minimum wage should have a bigger bite, the greater the number of workers covered by the law. For this reason, the minimum wage variable is weighted by the fraction of workers subject to minimum wage legislation.

This study will first examine the link between teenage employment and a MIN variable. This is the standard, direct approach. The second part of the paper consists of a novel, indirect technique.[13] According to the previous discussion, the basic reason a minimum wage affects youth employment is that (1) the minimum wage alters youth wages, and (2) as youth wages are raised above market levels, youth employment declines, that is, youth employment is inversely related to youth wages. The minimum wage raises youth wage rates in companies covered by the legal minimum, and, although this may be mitigated somewhat by reduced wages in uncovered companies, if youth employment declines it is because the increased wages and reduced employment in the covered sector dominate any opposite effects in the uncovered sector. A limitation of the direct approach is that it sheds no light on either of the above two propositions. It attempts to measure only the ultimate impact of the minimum wage.

---

[12] Conceptually, the fraction of the teenage population covered is superior. This is because the effect of changes in coverage depends on where they occur. A change in a teenage-intensive industry, such as retail trade, should have a larger impact on teenage employment than a change in an adult-intensive industry, such as manufacturing. Actual teenage coverage is not known, but it can be estimated. Indeed, the coverage variable of this study is based on estimated teenage coverage.

[13] This approach is novel in the sense that no comparable studies have been published. A similar analysis was undertaken, however, in my dissertation. See James F. Ragan, Jr., "The Impact of Minimum Wage Legislation on the Youth Labor Market" (Ph.D. diss., Washington University, 1975).

The indirect approach will first test whether, despite incomplete coverage, the minimum wage raises youth wage rates—both in absolute terms and relative to other wages. Next, the relationship between relative youth wages and youth employment will be examined. This two-step technique provides another test of whether an increase in the minimum wage reduces youth employment. If such a relationship can be established under the indirect approach as well as under the direct approach, the credibility of our results will be enhanced. More important, examining the role of youth wage rates should yield a deeper understanding of the link between the minimum wage and youth employment.

The Direct Approach

Specification of the Model. The basis of the direct approach presented here is an earlier model examining the effect of the minimum wage over the time period 1963 I–1972 IV.[14] The effect was studied for sixteen separate demographic groups. Youths were categorized by age (sixteen to seventeen, eighteen to nineteen); race (white, nonwhite); sex; and school enrollment status (major activity, school; major activity, other). Results are again analyzed for these sixteen demographic groups, but estimates can now be performed for a more extended sample period, ending in 1978 IV. Except for an additional set of manpower variables, based on public service employment, the employment equation estimated here is similar to the earlier equation.

Teenagers are studied on the basis of narrowly defined subgroups to allow for the possibility that a particular factor may have a differential effect across subgroups. For instance, one would expect nonwhites to be more susceptible to minimum wage legislation than whites. Whether because of less investment in themselves (for example, less and often inferior education), discrimination, or some other factors, the market wage rates of nonwhites tend to be lower than those of whites. Consequently, wages of nonwhites will be forced up to a greater extent than wages of whites, leading to a disproportionate decline in nonwhite employment. As Peter Mattila found,[15] the minimum wage may also have a different impact on students than it does on nonstudents.

In this paper the dichotomy between students and nonstudents is based on "major activity." Students are those whose major activity, according to the monthly Current Population Survey, is going to school.

---

[14] See Ragan, "Minimum Wages and Youth."

[15] J. Peter Mattila, "Youth Labor Markets, Enrollments, and Minimum Wages," *Proceedings of the Thirty-first Annual Meeting of the Industrial Relations Research Association, August 29–31, 1978* (1979), pp. 134–40.

Those attending school but whose major activity is working would not be counted among the in-school group. An alternative enrollment classification would be to consider as students all those who attend school, regardless of the number of hours in school. Data are also available according to this broader classification, but only for the month of October. Studying employment fluctuations across the year seemed preferable because the minimum wage value, manpower enrollment, cyclical conditions, and other factors vary throughout the year. To take advantage of quarterly data, the "major activity" enrollment classification was used. Reference will be made, however, to Mattila's work, which utilizes the October data.

Conceivably, enrollment status itself depends on the value of the minimum wage and other variables. Lack of time prevented testing of this hypothesis, but in earlier work this possibility was explored. For the sample period ending in 1972 IV, the quarterly school enrollment rate (defined as the percentage of the teenage group whose major activity was school) was estimated as a function of the minimum wage and other potentially important variables. There was no tendency for these variables to be statistically significant or even to assume the expected sign. As noted in the previous research:

> [E]nrollment relationships may have been masked by a variable response pattern: the decision to enter or leave school may not be carried out until the next semester or next academic year. But whatever the case, no systematic relationship was found between market variables and the enrollment rate—which justifies treating the enrollment decisions as given.[16]

To the extent schooling decisions are made at the beginning of the academic year, annual (October) enrollment data would be more suited for examining the enrollment response. Therefore, lack of a discernible statistical relationship between the minimum wage variable and quarterly enrollment should not be construed as proof that the enrollment response is independent of minimum wage legislation. Investigation of this question is left for other researchers.

The employment equation to be estimated attempts to explain movements over time in the fraction of a particular teenage group with jobs. A central hypothesis is that these movements are related to the minimum wage variable. This variable is defined as the applicable minimum wage deflated by average hourly earnings in the private economy and weighted by the estimated fraction of the teenage group covered by the legal minimum wage. More specifically:

[16] See Ragan, "Minimum Wages and Youth," n. 17.

17

$$MIN \equiv \sum_i [I_i(p_i MP + n_i MN)]/AHE$$

where:

MN = minimum wage for newly covered workers (workers covered by the most recent minimum wage amendment),

MP = minimum wage for previously covered workers,

AHE = average hourly earnings of nonsupervisory employees in the private, nonfarm economy,

I_i = fraction of youth employment coming from industry i,

n_i = fraction of nonsupervisory workers in industry i covered by the most recent minimum wage amendment,

p_i = fraction of nonsupervisory workers in industry i covered by previous minimum wage legislation,

i = major industry division (wholesale trade and retail trade considered separate divisions).

This variable is lagged one quarter.[17]

Youth employment can also be expected to exhibit cyclical and seasonal fluctuations. Recognized as one of the better measures of labor market tightness, the unemployment rate of males from twenty-five to fifty-four years of age, lagged one quarter, is the cyclical variable included in our equation. As the labor market strengthens, and the adult male unemployment rate falls, employment prospects for teenagers should improve; as the labor market deteriorates, youth employment can be expected to decline. Because the employment data are not seasonally adjusted, a set of seasonal dummies is appropriate. For both students and nonstudents, employment patterns vary across the year.

Employment may also be sensitive to relative supply of the particular group. As the population of a youth group rises relative to total population, do members of that group experience greater difficulty finding jobs? The answer depends in part on the substitutability of members of this group for members of other groups. The greater the substitutability, the less likely it is that an increase in relative supply will reduce the group's rate of employment. If a reduction does occur, the magnitude involved will depend on the degree of wage rigidity, which in turn is

---

[17] From 1961 until 1977 establishments brought into compliance by the most recent minimum wage amendment were in most years permitted to pay a lower minimum wage than establishments covered by previous amendments. For example, the minimum wage in 1968 was $1.60 for previously covered workers but only $1.15 for newly covered workers. The latter minimum wage was raised annually through 1971, when both newly covered and previously covered workers were subject to the $1.60 minimum wage.

The fraction of youth employment coming from industry i, I_i, refers to 1960 census employment. To keep this term exogenous, it was necessary to use the employment distribution in a year prior to 1963, when our sample period begins.

influenced by the level of the minimum wage and the extent of coverage. When wage flexibility is restricted, the decline in employment will be more severe, but even with wage flexibility some decline in the rate of employment is possible, because a reduction in wage rates is likely to make work less attractive for some individuals. The basic question is whether a bulge in relative youth population has led to a reduced rate of youth employment or whether, alternatively, youth employment has kept stride with population growth.

The final factor taken into account is youth enrollment in government manpower programs. Because most enrollees are classified as employed, an expansion of these programs might be expected to increase employment. There are actually a myriad of manpower programs, both past and present. Though not readily available for all series, quarterly data do exist for the two major programs affecting youths: the Neighborhood Youth Corps (NYC) and public service employment. Separate variables were formed from these two sets of data.

The Neighborhood Youth Corps started in 1965 and was phased out in 1974. Over this period, more than 5 million youths participated. Separate programs were established for youths in school and out of school, allowing us to examine the impact of the in-school youth corps program on student employment and the impact of the out-of-school youth corps program on nonstudent employment. Participation in the program was not random. For example, a disproportionate number of nonwhites were involved. Moreover, participant characteristics (race, sex, age) displayed some variation over this period. For these reasons, it is appropriate to examine how employment of a particular demographic group is affected by NYC enrollment of that group rather than by total Neighborhood Youth Corps enrollment. Characteristics data are available by age, race, and sex, but there is no information on the fraction of enrollees from a particular age-race-sex subgroup. Assuming the distributions of age, race, and sex characteristics are independent of one another, that fraction can be reasonably estimated as the product of three separate numbers: fraction of NYC enrollees of that age, fraction of that race, and fraction of that sex. This is the method employed. Our first manpower variable is based on the estimated percentage of the particular group enrolled in the Neighborhood Youth Corps.

Public service employment (PSE) serves as the basis for the other manpower variable. This variable is defined to include enrollment in the Public Employment Program (PEP), which survived from late 1971 through 1974, plus enrollment in programs under the Comprehensive Employment and Training Act of 1973. These were Titles II and VI of the act and the PSE component of Title I as well as the summer youth employment program. Quarterly enrollment data were available for all programs except summer youth employment. As this program was centered around the months of June, July, and August, it was assumed that two-thirds of the enrollment occurred in the third quarter of the year and one-third in the second quarter.

Unlike the Neighborhood Youth Corps program, data are not available separately for students and nonstudents. Because the impact of PSE programs on student/nonstudent employment is likely to vary across the year, our basic PSE variable is multiplied by a set of seasonal dummies. In other words, we allow for the possibility that aggregate (student plus nonstudent) PSE enrollment may have a differential effect on student employment and nonstudent employment for each quarter of the year. As was the case with the NYC variable, our PSE variables are deflated by population; that is, they refer to the percentage of a particular group enrolled in PSE programs.

Based upon the preceding discussion, an employment rate equation was estimated for the various teenage groups over the sample period 1963 I–1978 IV. A log-linear specification was selected, which necessitated adjusting the manpower variables to take on only positive values. (Unadjusted values were zero in those quarters where manpower enrollment was zero.) This was accomplished by adding the value "one" to the unadjusted variable. The equation estimated is presented below:

$$\frac{N}{P} = a_0 + a_1 U = a_2 MIN + a_3 POP + a_4 NYC$$
$$+ \sum_{i=5}^{8} a_i PSE_{i-4} + \sum_{i=9}^{11} a_i\ SEAS_{i-8} + \varepsilon \qquad (1)$$

where:

N/P = log of the employment ratio (fraction of the youth subgroup employed),

U = log of cyclic variable (unemployment rate of males aged twenty-five to fifty-four, lagged one quarter),

MIN = log of minimum wage variable,

POP = log of supply variable (population of youth group relative to total population aged sixteen and older),

NYC = log of first manpower variable (one plus the percentage of the youth group enrolled in the Neighborhood Youth Corps),

PSE_i = log of one plus the percentage of the youth group enrolled in public service employment programs in quarter i,

$SEAS$ = seasonal dummy (which assumes value one in quarter i and value zero in other quarters),

ε = error term (assumed to be normally distributed).

For female groups a time trend was also included. The labor force participation rate of females has risen over time, something true for teenagers as well as adults. Inclusion of the time trend improves the fit of the estimated equation, as measured by R^2 and Durbin-Watson statistics. There is no corresponding trend in labor force participation of males, and when a time trend is added it is statistically insignificant. Therefore, the time trend is included in the equation only for female groups.

The Findings. Equation (1) was estimated by the ordinary least squares regression technique. Results are presented in table 1, for males, and table 2, for females. Although coefficients of the manpower variables were generally positive, their performance was uneven. Frequently, their t-values were low. In the results reported here, the NYC variable was deleted unless significant at the 10 percent level, and the set of PSE variables was deleted unless one or more of these variables was significant. Regression results were very similar whether or not all manpower variables were retained, although the minimum wage coefficient for nonwhite sixteen- to seventeen-year-old females not in school switched from an insignificant negative value to an insignificant positive value once the manpower variables were dropped.

There is evidence that, at least for some teenage groups, a legal minimum wage reduces employment. With the inclusion of all manpower variables, the minimum wage coefficient is negative for eleven of sixteen groups. When the manpower variables with low t-values are excluded, the minimum wage coefficient remains negative ten times, statistically significant (at the 5 percent level) in half of these cases.

The detrimental employment effect is most conspicuous for certain male teenagers. In three of four cases, the minimum wage coefficient for males not in school is statistically less than zero at the 1 percent level. Although the minimum wage coefficient is also negative for most student groups, the associated t-values are low and the estimated coefficients much smaller in absolute terms. This is consistent with the findings of Peter Mattila, even though he estimated an annual employment equation (based on October data) over a different sample period and even though his enrollment classification counted all attending school as students, not just those whose major activity was school. For all four of his nonstudent teenage groups, Mattila found that the minimum wage had an adverse effect on employment.[18] For teenage students the effect was unclear; none of their coefficients was statistically significant. Our findings, as well as his, indicate that males not in school suffer disproportionately from a minimum wage when compared with their counterparts attending school.

[18] Mattila, "Youth Labor Markets," p. 138.

TABLE 1

MALE EMPLOYMENT REGRESSION

Group[a]	U	MIN	POP	NYC	PSE1	PSE2	PSE3	PSE4	C	SEAS1	SEAS2	SEAS3	R^2	DW
MEA	−.28 (11.32)	−.034 (.59)	.16 (1.18)		1.70 (5.94)	.42 (5.68)	.35 (7.62)	2.26 (7.05)	−1.05 (9.86)	−.089 (4.14)	.087 (2.03)	.11 (.78)	.819	1.20
MNA	−.088 (3.65)	.047 (.80)	.37 (10.33)	.066 (2.19)	−.071 (.25)	.13 (1.90)	.15 (3.17)	−.27 (.92)	.19 (3.14)	−.078 (3.89)	−.47 (11.42)	−.83 (12.45)	.849	2.19
MEB	−.51 (4.77)	−.24 (.73)	−.89 (2.20)						−2.54 (5.78)	−.15 (3.79)	−.28 (2.52)	−1.08 (2.76)	.600	C.O.[b]
MNB	−.12 (2.03)	−.57 (4.34)	−.12 (.70)	.083 (3.09)					−1.22 (2.30)	−.11 (2.33)	−.10 (.66)	−.08 (.29)	.559	1.32
MEC	−.22 (5.07)	.12 (1.10)	.066 (.73)		.56 (3.51)	.34 (3.02)	.12 (1.40)	.52 (2.99)	−.88 (12.14)	−.009 (.26)	.11 (2.85)	−.15 (1.40)	.816	1.40
MNC	−.099 (9.76)	−.13 (4.57)	−.008 (.36)		.11 (2.16)	.15 (4.65)	.11 (4.91)	.18 (3.40)	−.17 (9.71)	−.036 (3.96)	−.030 (3.03)	−.050 (3.19)	.752	1.52
MED	−.41 (5.25)	−.39 (1.13)	−.48 (3.19)						−2.38 (7.88)	−.032 (.43)	−.094 (1.18)	−.77 (4.81)	.579	1.44
MND	−.22 (10.79)	−.28 (3.29)	−.27 (4.44)						−.82 (7.32)	−.079 (4.20)	−.037 (1.92)	.029 (.92)	.812	1.24

NOTES: (1) Variables except the constant (C), seasonal dummies, and (for females) time trend are in natural logarithms. Sample period is 1963 I–1978 IV. (2) Absolute values of t-statistics are in parentheses. See text for description of variables. Critical t-values are 1.68 for $\alpha = .05$ and 2.40 for $\alpha = .01$. For a one-tailed test with fifty-one degrees of freedom, critical t-values are 1.68 for $\alpha = .05$ and 2.40 for $\alpha = .01$.

[a] M = male, F = female; E = enrolled in school, N = not enrolled; A = white 16–17-year-old, B = nonwhite 16–17-year-old; C = white 18–19-year-old, D = nonwhite 18–19-year-old.

[b] Cochrane-Orcutt adjustment for first-order autocorrelation was performed. In the unadjusted equation, $DW = 0.83$.

TABLE 2

FEMALE EMPLOYMENT REGRESSION

Group	U	MIN	POP	NYC	PSE1	PSE2	PSE3	PSE4	TIME	C	SEAS1	SEAS2	SEAS3	R^2	DW
FEA	-.24 (9.44)	-.16 (2.48)	.34 (1.85)		1.49 (2.93)	.33 (3.53)	.29 (4.96)	1.57 (2.92)	.0086 (10.06)	-1.66 (11.07)	-.13 (5.86)	-.068 (1.36)	.16 (.86)	.932	1.57
FNA	-0.30 (.98)	2.8 (3.07)	.75 (9.87)	.17 (2.60)					.0050 (5.06)	.005 (.04)	-.068 (2.67)	-.70 (10.95)	-1.24 (10.56)	.920	1.65
FEB	-.42 (3.69)	-.11 (.53)	-.72 (1.56)		2.87 (3.49)	.39 (3.30)	.23 (2.79)	2.73 (3.23)	.0001 (.02)	-3.12 (4.64)	-.17 (2.00)	-.33 (2.48)	-.78 (1.77)	.535	1.76
FNB	-.19 (2.77)	.026 (.16)	.51 (2.44)						.0033 (1.77)	.19 (.32)	-.050 (.91)	-.46 (3.03)	-.73 (2.48)	.318	2.37
FEC	-.093 (2.31)	.087 (.76)	-.008 (.06)		-.29 (.94)	.051 (.26)	.26 (.192)	-.12 (.37)	.0086 (8.25)	-1.45 (17.34)	-.007 (.21)	.018 (.47)	-.39 (3.12)	.905	1.74
FNC	-.086 (9.81)	-.054 (1.77)	.17 (2.79)		.17 (2.28)	.23 (5.14)	.13 (3.94)	.18 (2.28)	.0025 (7.39)	-.53 (27.17)	-.044 (5.23)	-.096 (10.30)	-.13 (5.41)	.939	1.27
FED	-.40 (3.55)	-.11 (.40)	-.95 (4.02)		.82 (2.01)	.47 (2.59)	.59 (4.33)	1.09 (2.72)	-.0006 (.12)	-3.53 (6.05)	.008 (.07)	-.14 (1.36)	-1.29 (5.40)	.586	1.41
FND	-.21 (4.97)	.13 (1.25)	-.72 (4.93)		.029 (.19)	.055 (.83)	.071 (1.43)	-.064 (.44)	.0035 (2.17)	-1.83 (7.22)	-.12 (3.31)	-.079 (2.15)	.12 (2.12)	.532	1.47

NOTE: See notes to table 1.

23

Why has the brunt of the minimum wage law been felt by those out of school rather than by students? Mattila offers some insights. First, employment distributions diverge. Because students are disproportionately concentrated in those industries having low rates of coverage, they are more likely to find jobs exempt from the minimum wage. In addition, student learner certificates enable some employers covered by the law to hire students at a wage rate 15 percent below the minimum wage. Thus, students have apparently been more successful in evading the minimum wage law. If the 15 percent differential were extended to all teenagers, employment prospects for those not in school would undoubtedly brighten. The effect of a differential youth minimum wage is, however, outside the scope of this study.

The effect of a legal minimum wage also varies by race. Job loss is most conspicuous for nonwhites. Not only is the minimum wage coefficient negative for all four nonwhite male categories, but each of these coefficients is more negative than the coefficients for white males.

As was true in my earlier research, the effect of a minimum wage is less clear-cut for females.[19] Evidence of a statistically significant adverse effect appears for only two groups. It is not clear whether the minimum wage is less important for females or simply more difficult to discern. Consistent with the former view, the data indicate that teenage females are more likely than males to work in industries with low minimum wage coverage. The alternative view is that the minimum wage relationship for females has been obscured, perhaps by the upward trend in labor force participation and employment.

Earlier we referred to a previous study by this author over a shorter time period (1963 I–1972 IV). How do minimum wage results of the two studies compare? They are similar, but somewhat stronger results were obtained for the shorter sample period. What has happened between 1972 and 1978 that may have modified the observed relationship between the minimum wage variable and employment?

Coverage was slightly expanded as a consequence of the 1974 and 1977 amendments to the Fair Labor Standards Act but cut back in 1976 by the Supreme Court ruling in *National League of Cities et al.* v. *Usery.* This ruling removed from coverage most state and local government employees. These subtle changes in coverage may not have been picked up by our minimum wage variable. Of particular concern, even though coverage was legally cut back by the *National League of Cities* case, it may have been difficult for employers, especially certain governmental employers, to stop paying their employees the minimum wage. In that event, effective coverage late in the sample period may have exceeded

---

[19] Ragan, "Minimum Wages and Youth."

measured coverage. Although it is possible that these recent changes could have been more readily discerned with a more complicated lag structure, insufficient time prevented experimentation with lags for the minimum wage variable.

Another problem pertains to youth manpower enrollment. The Youth Employment and Demonstration Projects Act, signed by President Carter on August 5, 1977, added four new programs to the Comprehensive Employment and Training Act: (1) Youth Employment and Training Programs, (2) Young Adult Conservation Corps, (3) Youth Incentive Entitlement Pilot Projects, and (4) Youth Community Conservation and Improvement Projects. Funded at $1 billion for fiscal 1977, these programs undoubtedly expanded youth employment in 1978, but I was unable to obtain data on youth enrollment in these programs. This expansion in 1978 in manpower enrollment corresponded with an increase in the minimum wage. Therefore, some of the job loss that would have been expected to arise as a consequence of the minimum wage may have been offset by these new manpower programs. This would bias downward the equation's estimate of employment loss due to the minimum wage. According to this argument, our equation should underpredict actual employment in 1978. Indeed, there was a definite pattern of positive residuals that year.

Another potential problem pertains to an apparent shift in the "major activity" enrollment series vis-à-vis the total enrollment series. According to Mattila, the gap between the two series widened in the 1970s.[20] By implication, there has been an increase in the portion of students who view work, not schooling, as their major activity. Perhaps for those attending school, hours of work have increased relative to hours of schooling. Whether or not this is a problem here depends on which of these two enrollment series one wishes to use. In any case, the divergence of the two series would be expected to lead to somewhat different empirical results.

Before estimating the effect of a minimum wage via the indirect approach, a discussion of other variables in our employment equation is in order. As tables 1 and 2 indicate, teenage employment is highly cyclical. The coefficient of the adult male unemployment rate is negative for all sixteen groups and significant at the 5 percent level for fifteen. In every instance, the cyclical effect is more pronounced for students than for nonstudents of the same age, race, and sex, perhaps due to students' lesser attachment to the labor force. This differential response further indicates the appropriateness of decomposing the youth population into student and nonstudent categories. The common view that

---

[20] Mattila, "Youth Labor Markets," pp. 71–76.

nonwhites tend to be the last hired, first fired, is also supported. True in all eight cases, the cyclical sensitivity of nonwhites is greater than that of whites of the same age, sex, and enrollment status. Of course, this difference may be attributable in part to the minimum wage. Even if nonwhite teenagers have less education (in terms of both quality and quantity) and skills or face discrimination, their employment fluctuations will be diminished if their wage rates adjust to keep them competitive with other workers. The minimum wage may have impeded such an adjustment of relative wages.

The increase in relative population has been associated with employment problems for nonwhite teenagers but not for white teenagers. For nonwhites the coefficient of *POP* is negative seven of eight times, significant at the 1 percent level four times and at the 5 percent level one additional time. On the other hand, there is no tendency for the population coefficient to be negative for white teenagers.

Our first manpower variable, which captures enrollment in the Neighborhood Youth Corps, is significant only three times, in each instance for sixteen- to seventeen-year-olds. This program had no perceptible impact on older teenagers and apparently had a limited impact on younger teenagers. The public service employment variable performed more strongly, displaying a pattern of statistical significance except for nonwhite males.

The Indirect Approach

Specification of the Model. This section focuses on two questions: (1) Does an increase in the minimum wage raise youth wages? (2) Is youth employment inversely related to youth wages? If both statements are true, the implication is that any wage reduction and employment gain in the uncovered sector is insufficient to offset the wage hike and employment loss in the covered sector.

These questions have not previously been addressed in time series analysis. The only time series studies dealing with wage rates have focused on the link between some industrial wage series and industrial employment. For example, Albert Zucker estimated employment in the low-wage, nondurable manufacturing sector as a function of mean wages there, uncovering a negative relationship.[21] Within a cross-sectional setting, the relationship between youth wages and youth employment has been examined by Arnold Katz and by Alan Fisher.[22] Both find an

---

[21] Albert Zucker, "Minimum Wages and the Long-Run Elasticity of Demand for Low-Wage Labor," *Quarterly Journal of Economics* 87 (May 1973): 267–77.

[22] Arnold Katz, "Teenage Employment Effects of State Minimum Wages," *Journal of Human Resources* 8 (Spring 1973): 250–56; Alan A. Fisher, "The Minimum Wage and Teenage Unemployment: A Comment on the Literature," *Western Economic Journal* 11 (December 1973): 514–24.

inverse relationship, generally significant. The drawback of cross-sectional work is that it does not enable us to study the impact of changes in the federal minimum wage.

The reason there have been no time series studies dealing with youth wage rates is that no youth wage series exist over time. That would indeed appear to be a formidable obstacle, but it will prove not to be insurmountable if a proxy can be found. The proxy selected is the mean wage rate in that sector of the economy where employment of the particular subgroup is concentrated. For each youth subgroup, y_i, we obtained the list of y_i-intensive industries—those three- and four-digit industries having the highest ratio of y_i employees relative to total employees. Averaging the wage series of these industries, weighted by the y_i employment in each, we obtain W_{y_i}, the mean wage of the y_i-intensive sector. This is our wage proxy.

For example, the youth-intensive industries for white, sixteen- to seventeen-year-old females are grocery stores, eating and drinking establishments, department stores, mail order houses, variety stores, shoe stores, and drugstores. In 1970, 37.15 percent of employed, white, sixteen- to seventeen-year-old females worked in one of these industries, but only 7.96 percent of all employees worked there; that is, the youth intensity of this sector was $37.15/7.96 = 4.66$.[23] The expectation is that, because youths are so heavily concentrated in the youth-intensive sector, movements in youth wages will be captured by movements in the proxy, W_{y_i}. This author is aware of the limitations of the proxy, but the complete absence of time series studies based on youth wage rates would appear to justify the current experiment.

[23] Following are the youth-intensive industries for the other youth groups, the percentage of the group employed in these industries, and (in parentheses) the youth intensity. Nonwhite females (16–17): hotels and motels, eating and drinking establishments, department stores, mail order houses, variety stores, and switchboard operation—18.24 (2.58); white females (18–19): banking, eating and drinking establishments, department stores, mail order houses, variety stores, shoe stores, drugstores, and switchboard operation—23.68 (3.00); nonwhite females (18–19): hotels and motels, banking, department stores, mail order houses, switchboard operation, and yarn and thread mills—16.20 (3.00); white males (16–17): grocery stores, eating and drinking establishments, variety stores, shoe stores, and drugstores—30.00 (4.92); nonwhite males (16–17): hotels and motels, grocery stores, eating and drinking establishments, shoe stores, and general retail trade—25.02 (3.56); white males (18–19): motor vehicle dealers, grocery stores, eating and drinking establishments, shoe stores, and drugstores—16.15 (2.40); nonwhite males (18–19): hotels and motels, grocery stores, yarn and thread mills, lumber and wood products, and beverages—10.78 (2.35). The distribution of youth employment by industry was obtained by averaging data from U.S. Department of Commerce, Bureau of the Census, *Census of Population: 1960 Subject Reports, Industrial Characteristics* (Washington, D.C., 1967), tables 2, 4, 6; and idem, *Census of Population: 1970 Subject Reports, Industrial Characteristics* (Washington, D.C., 1973), tables 32, 34, 35. The source of the industrial wage series (average hourly earnings) was U.S. Department of Labor, Bureau of Labor Statistics, *Employment and Earnings, 1909–75*, Bulletin 1312–10 (Washington, D.C., 1975).

The first question is whether a change in the minimum wage variable is associated with a change in W_{y_i}. We predict a positive relationship. An increase in the minimum should force up youth wages, W_i, and therefore average wages in the youth-intensive sector. The higher minimum may also put upward pressure on the wages of others, W_o, which would further raise W_{y_i}. Any increase in W_o will be relatively small, however. Because youths are low-productivity workers, their wage distribution will be lower than that of other workers; that is, for any given wage in the distribution, W', the fraction of youths earning less than W' will exceed the fraction of other workers earning less than W'. The fraction of youths affected by a minimum wage hike will therefore exceed the fraction of other workers affected. Hence, youth wages will rise more than the wages of other workers.[24]

Another potential source of increase in W_{y_i} relates to a change in employment shares. If relative wages of youths are raised, other workers, higher paid but more productive, may be substituted for youths.[25] This too would increase W_{y_i}.[26] Any such increase is secondary, however; it reinforces the effect of a change in W_i. If W_i does not rise, there will

---

[24] W_{yi} can be written as the weighted average of youth wages and the wages of others:

$$W_{yi} = aW_i + (1-a)W_o$$

where:

W_i = mean wages of youths employed in the youth-intensive sector,
W_o = mean wages of others employed in the youth-intensive sector,
a = youth employment share in the youth-intensive sector.

Thus,

$$\frac{\partial W_{yi}}{\partial MIN} = a\frac{\partial W_i}{\partial MIN} + (1 - a)\frac{\partial W_o}{\partial MIN} + (W_i - W_o)\frac{\partial a}{\partial MIN}$$

If an increase in the minimum raises youth wages, $\partial W_i/\partial MIN > 0$. The wages of others may also be forced up; but, because their wage distribution is higher than youths', W_o will rise by a lesser amount, namely, $\partial W_o/\partial MIN < \partial W_i/\partial MIN$.

From the above identity for W_{yi}, it is obvious that the variable W_i could be solved for indirectly if values of a and W_o were known. Indeed, Finis Welch recommended solving for W_i and then using this variable for the youth wage series in place of W_{yi}. Conceptually, that approach would be superior, but data limitations appear overwhelming. Even if estimates for W_o could be derived, we would still face the task of estimating the youth employment share, a. Detailed census data on youth employment share by industry are available, but time series data are not. Since minimum wage changes alter youth employment shares across industries, it would not be legitimate to treat a as constant over time. Consequently, without better data, we do not feel that reliable estimates of W_i can be obtained.

[25] Empirical work by Welch ("Minimum Wage Legislation," in Ashenfelter and Blum, *Labor Market Effects*, p. 30) confirms that, at least at a very aggregative level, youth employment shares do vary with the minimum wage variable. In response to an increase in the minimum wage, Welch finds a reduction in the youth employment shares for manufacturing, retail trade, and services and an increase for "other industries" (the residual category).

[26] The effect of a reduced employment share is captured in n. 24 by the term $(W_i - W_o)\partial a/\partial MIN$.

be no substitution away from youths. Whenever substitution does occur, its magnitude will be positively related to the increase in W_i. Thus, increases in W_{y_i} stemming from either an increase in W_o or a reduction in the youth employment share merely augment the increase that resulted from W_i being raised; these effects come into play only if W_i is increased. We can infer, therefore, that if the minimum wage raises W_{y_i}, it raises W_i.

Does a change in the minimum wage alter wages in the youth-intensive sector? To find out, the following wage-change equation was estimated:

$$WP_t - WP_{t-1} = b_o + b_1 (MINP_t - MINP_{t-1})$$
$$+ b_2 U_t + b_3 POP_t + \sum_{i=4}^{6} b_i SEAS_{i-3} + \varepsilon \quad (2)$$

where:

WP = log of nominal wage rate of youth-intensive sector deflated by the consumer price index (CPI),

$MINP$ = log of nominal minimum wage variable deflated by CPI (same as the MIN variable of the direct approach except that deflator is CPI),

U = log of unemployment rate of males aged twenty-five to fifty-four, lagged one quarter,

POP = log of fraction of total population aged sixteen and older coming from the particular youth subgroup,

$SEAS$ = seasonal dummy.

If an increase (decrease) in the real minimum wage variable raises (lowers) real wages in the youth-intensive sector, b_i should be positive. U is a market tightness variable designed to capture changes in WP due to cyclical fluctuations. POP is a relative supply variable (identical to the one used in the direct approach). It allows us to determine whether, other things equal, the rate of wage increase in the youth-intensive sector diminishes as the fraction of y_i employees increases. Equations are also run without POP. Because youth employment is highly seasonal, a set of seasonal dummies is also included. As the youth employment share changes from quarter to quarter, so should WP (because mean wages of youths and mean wages of other workers differ).

To see how minimum wage legislation changes wages of the youth-intensive sector relative to other wages, a second version of equation (2) was estimated. Wages of the youth-intensive sector and the minimum wage variable were both deflated by average hourly earnings of private nonfarm employees instead of by the consumer price index.

$$RELW_t - RELW_{t-1} = c_o + c_1 (MIN_t - MIN_{t-1})$$
$$+ c_2 U_t + c_3 POP_t + \sum_{i=4}^{6} c_i SEAS_i + \varepsilon \quad (2')$$

where:

$RELW$ = log of relative wage rate of youth-intensive sector (W_{y_i} deflated by average hourly earnings),

MIN = minimum wage variable deflated by average hourly earnings.

The sample period for equations (2) and (2') is 1963 I–1975 II. This is because consistent wage series, obtained from *Employment and Earnings, United States, 1909–75*, were available only through 1975 II. Although industrial series since 1975 II are also available in the monthly Department of Labor publication *Employment and Earnings*, there are breaks in some of the key industrial series, which prevent us from coming up with a consistent wage series over a longer sample period.

Coefficients of the change-in-minimum-wage variables for the equation without *POP* are presented in table 3. These coefficients, positive all sixteen times and statistically significant twelve times, demonstrate quite convincingly that an increase in the minimum wage raises wages in the youth-intensive sector—both in real terms and relative to other wages. This provides evidence, therefore, of the link between the minimum wage and wages of youths. Although coefficient values are low, the implication is not that an increase in the minimum wage leads to only a minor increase in youth wages. A small increase in average wages in the youth-intensive sector is compatible with a substantial increase in youth wages, as long as wages of other workers are raised by a lesser amount.[27] Without additional information, the relationship between an increase in wages of the youth-intensive sector and an increase in youth wages cannot be determined.

Because coefficient values of the other variables may also be of interest, results from estimating equation (2'), both with and without *POP*, are displayed in tables 4 and 5. The low *t*-values (generally less than unity) and minuscule coefficients for U imply that market tightness is not an important determinant of the change in relative wages. Relative supply does not appear to be important either, although results were a bit stronger in equation (2). Coefficient values of *POP* were negative all eight times there, compared to five times in equation (2'), but statistical significance was attained only twice, both times for nonwhites.

---

[27] This can be seen by referring back to n. 24. Because the youth employment share, a, is small, $\partial W_y / \partial MIN$ could be sizable even though $\partial W_{y_i} / \partial MIN$ is not. What is required is that $\partial W_o / \partial MIN$ and $\partial a / \partial MIN$ be small relative to $\partial W_y / \partial MIN$.

TABLE 3

MINIMUM WAGE ELASTICITIES, WAGE CHANGE EQUATION

Group[a]	$MINP_t - MINP_{t-1}$	$MIN_t - MIN_{t-1}$
MA	.047	.035
	(3.34)	(2.78)
MB	.039	.026
	(2.89)	(2.20)
MC	0.50	0.35
	(2.77)	(2.96)
MD	.051	.032
	(2.81)	(2.13)
FA	.043	.033
	(3.14)	(2.84)
FB	.028	.021
	(1.84)	(1.55)
FC	.029	.022
	(1.70)	(1.47)
FD	.024	.016
	(1.10)	(.84)

NOTES: (1) $MINP$ = Log of minimum wage variable deflated by consumer price index. MIN = Log of minimum wage variable deflated by average hourly earnings. The sample period is 1963 I–1975 II. (2) Numbers in parentheses are t-statistics. Critical values for a one-tailed test are 1.68 for α = .05 and 2.42 for α = .01.
[a] M = male, F = female; A = white 16–17-year-old, B = nonwhite 16–17-year-old; C = white 18–19-year-old, D = nonwhite 18–19-year-old.

The seasonal dummies are frequently significant, supporting our claim that wages in the youth-intensive sector vary with the youth share of employment. Especially noteworthy is the performance of *SEAS3*. Its coefficient is negative all eight times and significant six. In all but two instances, it is more negative than coefficients of the other seasonal dummies. This is what we would expect, as the youth share of employment is highest in the summer.

The next question is what relationship, if any, exists between wages of the youth-intensive sector and youth employment. To learn the answer, equation (1) was reestimated replacing *MIN* with the relative wage variable, *RELW*, lagged one quarter.[28] Results appear in tables 6 and 7.

[28] The significance of seasonal dummies in the wage change equation indicates that the wage series should be seasonally adjusted; but, because of the low coefficients of the seasonal dummies, it does not matter empirically whether or not this is done. Based on the seasonal coefficients of our wage change equation, we constructed a seasonally adjusted wage variable. Its coefficient in the employment equation and the coefficient of the unadjusted wage variable were identical to the first three decimal places.

TABLE 4
MALE WAGE CHANGE REGRESSION

Group	MIN	U	POP	C	SEAS1	SEAS2	SEAS3	R^2	DW
MA	.034 (2.68)	.0002 (.13)	-.0097 (.43)	.013 (.69)	-.0008 (.50)	-.0061 (3.97)	-.011 (6.93)	.641	1.70
	.035 (2.78)	.0002 (.10)		.0049 (2.47)	-.0007 (.47)	-.0061 (3.99)	-.011 (6.99)	.640	1.69
MB	.026 (2.16)	-.0016 (.90)	-.0032 (.48)	.0049 (.70)	-.0026 (1.68)	-.0076 (4.99)	-.013 (8.80)	.702	1.78
	.026 (2.20)	-.0015 (.85)		.0082 (4.12)	-.0026 (1.67)	-.0076 (5.03)	-.013 (8.87)	.700	1.77
MC	.035 (2.91)	-.00002 (.01)	-.0012 (.24)	.0043 (1.04)	-.0010 (.75)	-.0003 (.19)	-.010 (7.35)	.681	2.00
	.35 (2.96)	.00007 (.04)		.0034 (1.93)	-.0010 (.75)	-.0003 (.19)	-.010 (7.43)	.680	2.00
MD	.032 (2.13)	.0002 (.09)	.0036 (.78)	.0072 (1.30)	-.0043 (2.65)	-.0013 (.81)	-.0034 (2.13)	.235	2.48
	.032 (2.13)	-.0001 (.05)		.0032 (1.56)	-.0043 (2.68)	-.0013 (.80)	-.0034 (2.15)	.224	2.44

NOTE: See notes to tables 1 and 3. Sample period is 1963 I - 1975 II.

TABLE 5
FEMALE WAGE CHANGE REGRESSION

Group	MIN	U	POP	C	SEAS1	SEAS2	SEAS3	R^2	DW
FA	.031 (2.72)	−.0003 (.15)	−.042 (1.73)	.034 (1.69)	.0081 (4.98)	.0010 (.61)	−.0020 (1.23)	.629	1.76
	.033 (2.84)	−.0008 (.42)		−.0007 (.30)	.0084 (5.05)	.0011 (.69)	−.0020 (1.20)	.603	1.66
FB	.020 (1.52)	−.0005 (.21)	−.0069 (.78)	−.0033 (.36)	.0030 (1.46)	−.0044 (2.18)	−.0072 (3.54)	.468	2.16
	.021 (1.55)	−.0003 (.12)		.0035 (1.30)	.0031 (1.50)	−.0044 (2.18)	−.0072 (3.53)	.460	2.13
FC	.022 (1.44)	.0016 (.57)	.0016 (.13)	−.0034 (.30)	.0077 (3.61)	−.0022 (1.05)	(1.10)		
	.022 (1.47)	.0014 (.57)		−.0020 (.74)	.0076 (3.65)	−.0022 (1.06)	−.0023 (1.11)	.456	1.88
FD	.015 (.80)	.0059 (1.69)	.0095 (1.11)	.0088 (.93)	.0010 (.35)	−.0080 (2.77)	−.0070 (2.40)	.322	2.08
	.016 (.84)	.0053 (1.53)		−.0008 (.21)	.0009 (.32)	−.0080 (2.76)	−.0070 (2.42)	.303	2.02

NOTE: See notes to tables 1 and 3. Sample period is 1963 I – 1975 II.

TABLE 6

MALE EMPLOYMENT REGRESSION BASED ON RELATIVE YOUTH WAGES

Group	U	RELW	POP	NYC	PSE1	PSE2	PSE3	PSE4	C	SEAS1	SEAS2	SEAS3	R^2	DW
MEA	-.30 (12.13)	-.87 (1.29)	.10 (.69)		1.52 (3.41)	.43 (4.17)	.012 (.04)	1.17 (2.11)	-1.24 (5.73)	-.096 (4.55)	.070 (1.58)	.056 (.36)	.855	1.36
MNA	-.091 (3.31)	1.30 (1.56)	.38 (7.84)	.050 (1.53)	-.35 (.68)	.077 (.69)	.32 (1.14)	-1.01 (1.50)	.60 (2.44)	-.085 (3.92)	-.49 (9.13)	-.86 (9.57)	.866	2.45
MEB	-.44 (3.24)	-1.89 (.49)	-.89 (1.76)						-3.21 (2.75)	-.14 (2.73)	-.24 (1.54)	-1.06 (2.10)	.557	C.O.
MNB	-.050 (.80)	-6.73 (5.01)	-.039 (.18)	.10 (3.39)					-3.29 (4.91)	-.082 (1.76)	-.12 (.67)	-.20 (.62)	.549	1.44
MEC	-.25 (5.46)	-1.25 (1.12)	.11 (1.26)		.85 (2.84)	.34 (1.91)	-.43 (2.02)	.85 (1.98)	-1.26 (4.14)	-.013 (.38)	.13 (3.39)	-.061 (.54)	.846	1.67
MNC	-.078 (6.21)	-1.25 (3.03)	.062 (1.85)		-.14 (1.25)	.063 (1.03)	.084 (1.17)	-.031 (.19)	-.44 (4.11)	-.028 (2.55)	-.041 (3.22)	-.087 (3.88)	.696	1.52
MED	-.32 (2.83)	-7.87 (2.53)	-.22 (.99)						-3.24 (8.03)	-.009 (.13)	-.006 (.08)	-.48 (2.08)	.617	1.51
MND	-.12 (5.00)	-2.82 (3.00)	-.007 (.06)						-.78 (7.90)	-.049 (2.67)	-.061 (2.93)	-.082 (1.78)	.748	1.34

NOTE: $RELW$ = relative youth wage rate. Sample period is 1963 I – 1975 II. See notes to tables 1 and 3.

TABLE 7
Female Employment Regression Based on Relative Youth Wages

Group	U	RELW	POP	NYC	PSE1	PSE2	PSE3	PSE4	TIME	C	SEAS1	SEAS2	SEAS3	R^2	DW
FEA	−.28 (8.73)	−1.82 (2.77)	.34 (1.69)		1.39 (1.20)	.35 (2.27)	−.008 (.01)	−.44 (.26)	.0082 (8.62)	−2.27 (6.83)	−.14 (5.97)	−.069 (1.27)	.16 (.78)	.916	1.68
FNA	.042 (.95)	2.77 (3.55)	.78 (8.12)	.19 (2.71)					.0062 (5.67)	.97 (2.63)	−.071 (2.42)	−.76 (9.27)	−1.31 (8.51)	.915	1.87
FEB	−.39 (3.07)	−.70 (.23)	−.79 (1.61)		3.66 (2.74)	.57 (3.28)	−1.13 (1.04)	−.63 (.32)	.0010 (.18)	−3.49 (2.24)	−.23 (2.69)	−.39 (2.79)	−.85 (1.80)	.613	1.83
FNB	−.094 (1.12)	.84 (.44)	.33 (1.39)						.0044 (1.75)	.006 (.01)	−.13, (2.23)	−.39 (2.30)	−.51 (1.55)	.448	2.68
FEC	−.053 (.88)	1.07 (.65)	.016 (.11)		−.67 (.74)	−.017 (.04)	.34 (.43)	−.77 (.52)	.0094 (6.76)	−1.21 (2.41)	−.011 (.26)	.008 (.16)	−.38 (2.34)	.880	1.75
FNC	−.078 (5.44)	−.086 (.21)	.24 (3.42)		.049 (.23)	.13 (1.32)	.19 (.96)	.090 (.26)	.0021 (6.18)	−.54 (4.55)	−.040 (3.84)	−.10 (8.58)	−.15 (5.43)	.913	1.25
FED	−.48 (3.50)	−9.55 (1.31)	−1.15 (3.61)		.23 (.24)	1.08 (2.20)	.67 (.93)	.30 (.20)	.0013 (.25)	−6.12 (3.02)	.065 (.55)	−.13 (.106)	−1.45 (4.77)	.656	1.44
FND	−.23 (6.21)	−4.92 (2.68)	−.13 (.80)		.17 (.67)	.37 (2.93)	−.005 (.03)	−.30 (.80)	.0011 (.83)	−2.04 (4.15)	−.087 (2.80)	−.092 (2.92)	−.044 (.78)	.710	1.88

NOTE: See note to table 6.

The coefficient of *RELW* is negative twelve of sixteen times and significant at the 1 percent level six times, mostly for male subgroups. This supports our claim that an increase in relative wages is associated with a decline in youth employment. Moreover, in both the wage-change equation and the employment equation based on relative wages, results were more robust for male subgroups. It is no surprise then that the performance of the minimum wage variable in equation (1) was stronger for males. Also consistent with the results from equation (1), the detrimental employment effect of higher wages is most conspicuous for nonwhite males and males not in school. Results of the other variables in the employment equation are similar whether the minimum wage or the relative wage variable is used.

The relative wage variable discussed above is a proxy for youth wages relative to average wages in the private sector of the economy. For comparative purposes, an alternative relative wage proxy was also tried: youth wages relative to adult wages, where the adult wage rate was proxied by average hourly earnings in manufacturing. Tables 8 and 9 contain coefficient estimates for the new relative wage variable, *RELM,* as well as for *RELW.* In addition, the minimum wage coefficient

TABLE 8

COEFFICIENTS AND *t*-STATISTICS OF WAGE VARIABLES IN MALE
EMPLOYMENT EQUATION

Group	RELW	RELM	MIN
MEA	− .87	− .56	− .11
	(1.29)	(1.61)	(1.86)
MNA	1.30	.76	.046
	(1.56)	(1.57)	(.68)
MEB	− 1.89	− 4.76	− .14
	(.49)	(2.14)	(.40)
MNB	− 6.73	− 4.40	− .52
	(5.01)	(5.65)	(3.32)
MEC	− 1.25	− .87	.0028
	(1.12)	(1.67)	(.03)
MNC	− 1.25	− .58	− .13
	(3.03)	(2.36)	(3.86)
MED	− 7.87	− 5.67	− .53
	(2.53)	(3.42)	(1.66)
MND	− 2.82	− 1.34	− .23
	(3.00)	(2.16)	(3.09)

NOTE: *RELW* is the youth wage rate deflated by average hourly earnings in the private sector. *RELM* is the youth wage rate deflated by average hourly earnings in manufacturing. *MIN* is the minimum wage variable. Sample period is 1963 I – 1975 II.

TABLE 9

COEFFICIENTS AND *t*-STATISTICS OF WAGE VARIABLES IN FEMALE
EMPLOYMENT EQUATION

Group	RELW	RELM	MIN
FEA	−1.82	−1.59	−.21
	(2.77)	(2.86)	(2.99)
FNA	2.77	2.16	.31
	(3.55)	(3.53)	(3.12)
FEB	−.70	−.62	−.24
	(.23)	(.24)	(1.08)
FNB	.84	.70	−.0063
	(.44)	(.50)	(.04)
FEC	1.07	.88	.10
	(.65)	(.69)	(.71)
FNC	−.086	.13	−.051
	(.21)	(.47)	(1.15)
FED	−9.55	−6.31	−.22
	(1.31)	(1.04)	(.69)
FND	−4.92	−3.25	−.017
	(2.68)	(2.44)	(.19)

NOTE: See note to table 8.

of equation (1), reestimated over the common sample period 1963 I–1975 II, is included. Overall, results of the three wage variables are comparable. Although coefficients of the relative wage variables are larger in absolute value, it should be remembered that any change in the minimum wage will be larger than the consequent change in relative wages. The difference in magnitude of the coefficient values was therefore anticipated.

There are potential problems involved in using a proxy for the relative youth wage rate. Moreover, even if a proxy were not necessary, the limited variability of a relative wage variable would raise concern about the prospects of measurement error. For such reasons, results of the indirect approach, by themselves, should be interpreted with caution. But, when supported by the findings of the direct approach, confidence in the indirect results is enhanced. The indirect results are indeed consistent with the direct results of the previous section. In terms of statistical significance, they actually perform a bit better. Taken together, these results and those of the previous section support the view that an increase in the minimum wage raises youth wages relative to other wages, inducing firms to substitute other workers for youths. The result is a loss in employment for many segments of the youth population. We conclude that any wage reduction and employment gain in the uncovered sector of the economy is insufficient to offset opposite changes in the covered sector. Finally, within the constraints of data availability, results of this section justify future research linking minimum wage legislation and wage rates.

Concluding Remarks

The legal minimum wage has been effective in raising teenage wage rates, both in real terms (that is, deflated by the consumer price index) and relative to the wages of adults. This, in turn, has caused firms to reduce their employment of teenagers. Whether measured directly, by a minimum wage variable, or indirectly, by a proxy for relative teenage wages, a higher minimum wage leads to job loss among teenagers. This is most evident for nonwhite males and males not in school.

Manpower programs expand teenage employment. To the extent these programs are deemed necessary to mitigate the job loss induced by the minimum wage, the billions of dollars spent on youth manpower programs can be viewed as a cost of the minimum wage. Where successful, these programs are to be welcomed. But their benefits have frequently been found to be low relative to costs. Perhaps this is why these programs are justified in the *Employment and Training Report of the President* with the comment that, "cost-benefit calculations aside," these programs have been "largely successful."[29] The goal here is not to evaluate government manpower programs but simply to point out that the size and costs of these programs are apparently related to minimum wage legislation.

Some of the flaws inherent in minimum wage legislation have already been cited in the introduction to this chapter. These will not be reexamined here, but in conclusion let me express my hopes that reevaluation of the minimum wage law will continue. A strong case can be made that, although the goals of a minimum wage, such as a higher standard of living for low-income families, are laudable, the actual outcome is less felicitous. Teenagers (as well as other low-productivity workers) are denied jobs and the experience that comes with being employed.

Appendix: Sources and Description of the Data

Student employment and population data, unpublished, were obtained from the U.S. Department of Labor. Although there are hazards in

---

[29] See U.S. Department of Labor and U.S. Department of Health, Education, and Welfare, *Employment and Training Report of the President* (Washington, D.C.: 1978), p. 79.

using unpublished data,[30] errors can likewise be found in published data.[31] The finer disaggregation available through use of unpublished data generates more detailed information and, of most interest, enables us to separately examine behavior of students and nonstudents. Data on total employment (student plus nonstudent) and total population came from table A–3 in *Employment and Earnings*. Nonstudent employment (population) was calculated as the difference between total employment (population) and student employment (population). Quarterly observations were obtained by averaging monthly data.

The employment and population series were both adjusted on an a priori basis to maintain consistency throughout the sample period. Starting in January 1972, data from the monthly Current Population Survey were based on 1970 census benchmarks rather than on 1960 benchmarks. Then, in January 1974, the Census Bureau introduced a new adjustment technique to lessen the problem of population undercount.[32] Both of the above changes led to slight alterations in the employment and population series. For example, these adjustments raised the population figures of nonwhite female teenagers by 10,000 (0.92 percent) in January 1972 and by an additional 4,000 (0.34 percent) in January 1974. To obtain a consistent population series, these adjustments were netted out. In other words, published population figures for this group were reduced by 0.92 percent starting in January 1972 and by another 0.34 percent starting in January 1974. Because the adjustments were relatively minor and because employment and population changes tended to be in the same direction, thereby leaving the employment-population term little changed, the data revisions turned out to be unimportant. After the empirical work of this paper was concluded, our employment regression for males was reestimated with unadjusted data. Results were very similar to those obtained using adjusted data. Future researchers directing their efforts along these lines apparently need not worry about these adjustments.

The unemployment rate for adult males and the population term,

---

[30] Data for the years 1963–1973 and 1978 came directly from the Department of Labor. Data for 1974–1977 were kindly supplied by Peter Mattila, who had obtained them from the Department of Labor. For a discussion on problems associated with unpublished data, see Frederic B. Siskind, "Minimum Wage Legislation in the United States: Comment," *Economic Inquiry* 15 (January 1977): 135–38; and Welch, "Minimum Wage Legislation," in Ashenfelter and Blum, *Labor Market Effects*.

[31] In the July 1976 issue of U.S. Department of Labor, Bureau of Labor Statistics, *Employment and Earnings*, for example, the June population of sixteen- to seventeen-year-olds is incorrectly reported to be 558,000. Based on various identities and on the population figure for the preceding and subsequent months, the correct figure is 608,000. The error arises because the civilian labor force figure reported, 227,000, is 50,000 too low.

[32] These adjusted techniques are described in ibid., February 1972 and February 1974.

used in constructing the relative supply variable, came from *Employment and Earnings*. Unpublished data on manpower enrollment were provided by the U.S. Department of Labor, Employment and Training Administration. The data used in constructing the minimum wage variable are described in the text.

Bibliography

Fisher, Alan A. "The Problem of Teenage Unemployment." Ph.D. dissertation, University of California, Berkeley, 1973.

———. "The Minimum Wage and Teenage Unemployment: A Comment on the Literature." *Western Economic Journal* 11 (December 1973): 514–24.

Gavett, Thomas W. Introduction to U.S. Department of Labor, Bureau of Labor Statistics, *Youth Unemployment and Minimum Wages,* Bulletin 1657, pp. 1–29. Washington, D.C. 1970.

Goldfarb, Robert S. "The Policy Content of Quantitative Minimum Wage Research." *Proceedings of the Industrial Relations Research Association,* December 1974, pp. 261–68.

Gramlich, Edward M. "Impact of Minimum Wages on Other Wages, Employment, and Family Incomes." *Brookings Papers on Economic Activity* 2 (1976): 430–51.

Kaitz, Hyman B. "Experience of the Past: The National Minimum." In U.S. Department of Labor, Bureau of Labor Statistics, *Youth Unemployment and Minimum Wages,* Bulletin 1657, pp. 30–54. Washington, D.C., 1970.

Katz, Arnold. "Teenage Employment Effects of State Minimum Wages." *Journal of Human Resources* 8 (Spring 1973): 250–56.

Mattila, J. Peter. "Youth Labor Markets, Enrollments, and Minimum Wages." *Proceedings of the Thirty-first Annual Meeting of the Industrial Relations Research Association, August 29–31, 1978,* 1979, pp. 134–40.

Mincer, Jacob. "Unemployment Effects of Minimum Wages." *Journal of Political Economy* 84 (August 1976): S87–S104.

Ragan, James F., Jr. "The Impact of Minimum Wage Legislation on the Youth Labor Market." Ph.D. dissertation, Washington University, 1975.

———. "The Theoretical Ambiguity of a Minimum Wage." *Atlantic Economic Journal* 5 (March 1977): 56–60.

———. "Minimum Wages and the Youth Labor Market." *Review of Economics and Statistics* 59 (May 1977): 129–36.

———. "Minimum Wage Legislation: Goals and Realities." *Nebraska Journal of Economics and Business* 17 (Autumn 1978): 21–28.

Siskind, Frederic B. "Minimum Wage Legislation in the United States: Comment." *Economic Inquiry* 15 (January 1977): 135–38.

Stigler, George. "The Economics of Minimum Wage Legislation." *American Economic Review* 36 (June 1946): 358–65.

U.S. Department of Commerce, Bureau of the Census. *Census of Population: 1960 Subject Reports, Industrial Characteristics.* Washington, D.C., 1967.

———, Bureau of the Census. *Census of Population: 1970 Subject Reports, Industrial Characteristics.* Washington. D.C. 1973.

U.S. Department of Labor, Bureau of Labor Statistics. *Employment and Earnings*. Washington, D.C., various issues.

———. Bureau of Labor Statistics. *Employment and Earnings, 1909–75*, Bulletin 1312–10. Washington, D.C., 1975.

———. "Statement of the Secretary." In *Minimum Wage and Maximum Hours Standards under the Fair Labor Standards Act*, pp. 1–4. Washington, D.C., 1978.

———. *Minimum Wage and Maximum Hours Standards under the Fair Labor Standards Act*. Washington, D.C., various issues.

———, and U.S. Department of Health, Education, and Welfare. *Employment and Training Report of the President*. Washington, D.C., 1978.

Welch, Finis. "Minimum Wage Legislation in the United States." In Orley Ashenfelter and James Blum, eds., *Evaluating the Labor Market Effects of Social Programs: Industrial Relations Section*, pp. 1–38. Princeton: Princeton University Press, 1976.

———. "Minimum Wage Legislation in the United States: Reply." *Economic Inquiry* 15 (January 1977): 139–42.

Zucker, Albert. "Minimum Wages and the Long-Run Elasticity of Demand for Low-Wage Labor." *Quarterly Journal of Economics* 87 (May 1973): 267–77.

The Effects of Federal Minimum Wages on the Industrial Distribution of Teenage Employment

Robert F. Cotterman

The subject of this paper is an investigation into the distribution of teenage employment across industries and, in particular, the role that minimum wages may play in explaining the observed distributions. My focus in this paper is solely on eighteen- to nineteen-year-old males; females and other groups of young males show equally interesting behavior that will, I hope, be analyzed in the future.

My own interest in the subject of patterns of teenage employment across industries arose from viewing data such as that presented in table 1. This table provides the industrial breakdown of employment for two groups of teens and for a reference group of adult white males. Each row of the table gives, for a particular demographic group and a particular year, the proportion of the employed members of that group who were working in various industries.

It is clear from table 1 that at each point in time there were among the industries some fairly substantial differences of employment between the racial groups of teens and between each teenage group and the adult group. For both groups of teens there were sizable changes over time in these distributions, with the magnitude, and sometimes even the direction of change, differing by race, whereas changes over time typically appear to be much smaller for the reference group of adults. The share of black teen employment devoted to agriculture, for example, far exceeds the white teen share in both 1950 and 1960, and both teen shares exceed the adult share. Over time, the decline in the share is so large for black teens, however, that by 1970 the shares in agriculture are virtually the same for black and white teens. In manufacturing, on the other hand, the share for white teens exceeds the share for black teens in 1950 and 1960, and the shares for both groups of teens are less than the adult share. The shares for the teenage groups have moved in opposite directions over time, with black teen employment moving to-

NOTE: A portion of this research was funded by a grant from the Rockefeller Foundation. I wish to thank Finis Welch and Nabeel Al-Salam for helpful discussions. Tom Means performed the computations. I retain responsibility for all errors.

42

TABLE 1

Percentage Distribution of Employment by Industry

Demographic Group and Year	Agriculture, Forestry, Fisheries	Manufacturing	Retail Trade	Services Other than Personal	Personal Services	Others
White males, 18–19 years old						
1950	22.4	27.3	19.8	7.0	2.1	19.4
1960	10.8	26.3	26.7	10.4	2.3	18.0
1970[a]	5.7	23.9	34.3	14.6	2.1	19.0
Nonwhite males, 18–19 years old						
1950	40.0	18.6	13.2	6.1	6.8	13.4
1960	20.6	17.9	21.4	11.1	7.0	13.8
1970[b]	5.6	30.2	21.3	17.8	3.2	21.1
White males, 25–54 years old						
1950	12.6	28.5	13.3	9.3	2.2	33.1
1960	7.1	32.6	11.6	10.6	1.8	33.4
1970[a]	4.4	31.5	11.3	14.6	1.6	36.7

NOTE: For 1950 and 1960, the cross-column sums fall short of 100 percent by the percentage of employed individuals who fail to report their industry of employment.

[a] In 1970, white data include all those not classified as Negro.

[b] In 1970, nonwhite data exclude all those not classified as Negro.

SOURCES: Department of Commerce, Bureau of the Census, *Census of Population: 1950 Special Reports, Industrial Characteristics*, Report PE–1D, tables 3, 5; and vol. 2, *Characteristics of the Population*, pt. 1, *United States Summary*, table 96. Idem, *Census of Population: 1960 Subject Reports, Industrial Characteristics*, Final Report PC(2)–7F, tables 4, 6; and vol. 1, *Characteristics of the Population*, pt. 1, *United States Summary*, table 46. Idem, *Census of Population: 1970 Subject Reports, Industrial Characteristics*, Report PC(2)–7B, tables 34, 35; and vol. 1, *Characteristics of the Population*, pt. 1, *United States Summary*, sec. 1.

43

ward manufacturing and white teen employment shifting away. By 1970 the proportion of black teen employment located in manufacturing exceeds the proportion for white teens and is nearly equal to that of the adult group. Both groups of teens typically show rising shares of their employment devoted to the retail trade and service (other than personal services) sectors, whereas the adult share in retail trade declines until by 1970 it is far below the teen shares. The white teen share in retail trade continues to rise between 1960 and 1970, however, while the black teen share remains roughly constant.

There are undoubtedly a substantial number of factors, aside from minimum wages, involved in producing the employment patterns noted above. A large portion of the downward movement in agricultural employment for teens probably reflects both a decline in the agricultural industry as a whole and the increasing urbanization of the population, both of which are reflected in the declines for the adult group. The rising share of black teen employment in manufacturing is presumably in part a result of the expansion of manufacturing activity in the South. The fact that employed white teens are more likely to be employed in the retail sector than are blacks may reflect differences in the degree of proximity to retail outlets. Minimum wages may also be part of the story, however, as suggested in previous work by Finis Welch.[1] Because I shall focus on minimum wage effects, it may be helpful to consider some of the potential effects in more detail.

The Role of Minimum Wages

To see the role that minimum wages may play in determining the industrial distribution of teen employment, first consider a single, competitive labor market in which numerous firms in various industries are doing their hiring. Suppose that in the absence of minimum wage laws the wage rate for some group of teenage workers (assumed to be homogeneous from the firms' perspectives) would be w. Now let a strictly enforced legal minimum wage of w_m be imposed on some but not all of the firms in this market, where w_m is assumed to be larger than w. Firms that are now covered by the minimum wage will find that the cost of using this type of teenage labor has risen, and, therefore, they will reduce the number of teens they employ.

What happens next depends upon how jobs in the covered firms are rationed and what the alternatives to covered-sector employment are perceived to be. One possibility is that jobs in covered firms are

[1] Finis Welch, "Minimum Wage Legislation in the United States," *Economic Inquiry* 12 (September 1974): 285–318.

rationed strictly on the basis of luck. All of those willing to work at the minimum wage have an equal chance of obtaining employment at that wage. With regard to alternatives to covered-sector employment, it seems reasonable to assume that the group of teenage workers is heterogeneous with regard to the value they place on nonmarket alternatives. That is, the "reservation wage"—the lowest wage rate at which the individual would enter the market—varies across teens, so that a higher wage rate would result in more teens wishing to work.

Under these assumptions, the minimum wage rate will result in both a contraction of employment in covered firms and a reshuffling of workers. Some teens who were unwilling to work at the wage rate, w, will enter the market at the minimum wage, w_m, and some of these teens will be lucky enough to obtain jobs at the minimum wage. As a consequence, the number of workers displaced by the minimum wage will be larger than the reduction in employment in the covered firms.

Teens who were previously employed in the covered firms but who have lost their former jobs would all be willing to work in the uncovered firms at their old wage rate, w. However, the attempts of these workers to obtain such jobs will put downward pressure on the wage rate in the uncovered firms. Downward movement of the wage in uncovered firms will serve to increase the number of workers that the latter firms wish to hire and to decrease the number of workers who seek employment in these firms as nonmarket alternatives become relatively more attractive. As a result, in the new equilibrium the wage in uncovered firms is now lower than w and employment is larger than before.

This analysis bears implications for the industrial distribution of teenage employment. If a minimum wage is introduced into a portion of some industry, we should observe a decline in employment in the covered sector of that industry. We should also, however, observe an increase in employment in the uncovered sectors of all industries. Hence, the introduction of minimum wages in one industry has spillover effects on the uncovered sectors of both that industry and all other industries.

The existence of these spillover effects may go partway toward explaining the high and rising shares of teenage employment in the retail trade sector. This sector had much lower coverage rates than average in both 1959 and 1960. By 1970 coverage had increased substantially but was still lower than in many other industries. This sector was therefore a likely recipient of workers displaced by minimum wages in other industries.

An Empirical Specification

To test for the existence of these sorts of minimum wage effects, it is necessary to be more explicit about their nature. In my empirical specification, I assume that the effect of minimum wage w_m on employment in industry i has two components. The first arises from the effects of the minimum wage imposed on industry i itself, an effect that is assumed to be proportional to

$$C_{im}\left(\frac{w_m}{\overline{w}}\right) \tag{1}$$

where C_{im} is the proportion of industry i covered by the minimum wage w_m, and $\overline{w}$ is the average manufacturing wage. This particular variable, or some variant of it, has appeared frequently in minimum wage studies.[2] The intuition behind it may be briefly explained as follows. The term $w_m/\overline{w}$ is the ratio of the minimum wage to the average manufacturing wage. As such, it is designed to measure the size of the minimum wage relative to the price of a standardized bundle of labor services that could be purchased at the wage $\overline{w}$. The larger w_m is relative to $\overline{w}$, the larger is the anticipated negative effect of the minimum wage on covered-sector employment in industry i. The coverage rate C_{im} enters because the net disemployment effects on the ith industry should rise with increases in coverage. Increases in coverage place more firms under the minimum and leave fewer uncovered firms available to pick up workers who are disemployed by the minimum. Although workers who are disemployed by the minimum wage in industry i may obtain work in the uncovered sector, these reemployed workers are dispersed among the uncovered sectors of all industries. Hence, I expect the variable reflecting "own" minimum wages, as measured by expression (1), to be negatively related to employment in industry i.

The second minimum wage component in industry i arises from effects of minimum wages imposed in other industries. This effect is assumed to be proportional to

$$(1 - C_{im})\left\{\overline{C}_{im}\left(\frac{w_m}{\overline{w}}\right)\right\} \tag{2}$$

where $\overline{C}_{im}$ is the average coverage rate *outside* of industry i. The term enclosed in braces in expression (2) is analogous to the first minimum wage component given by expression (1). The difference is that in this case, we compute the net disemployment effects in industries outside, rather than inside, of the ith industry. Hence, the term in braces is designed to measure the net displacement of workers in other industries— workers who become candidates for hire by the expanding firms in the uncovered sector of industry i. The term $(1 - C_{im})$ in expression (2) is the fraction of industry i that is uncovered and therefore available to pick up the displaced workers from other industries. Thus, I expect

[2] See, for example, ibid., or Jacob Mincer, "Unemployment Effects of Minimum Wages," *Journal of Political Economy* 84 (August 1976): S87–S104.

that the variable reflecting minimum wages imposed in other industries, as measured by expression (2), will be positively related to employment in industry i.

The analysis to this point has assumed that, in the absence of minimum wages, the workers under consideration would all earn less than the minimum wage that is later imposed. In a group of workers as heterogeneous as eighteen- to nineteen-year-old males, however, there will certainly be many individuals who would otherwise earn more than the minimum wage. For such individuals the effects may be quite different.

Consider, therefore, a group of workers who would earn more than w_m (even in the absence of minimum wage laws), and suppose that these workers are good substitutes in production for the less productive workers who would otherwise earn less than w_m. The imposition of a minimum wage of w_m into a portion of industry i will induce covered-sector employers to substitute some of these more productive workers for the less productive workers whose wage has risen. In the uncovered sectors of all industries, firms will substitute away from these highly productive workers and toward the less productive workers displaced by the minimum, because the wage rate for the latter will have fallen in the covered sector.

For these more productive workers, the imposition of minimum wages on firms outside of industry i may also have different effects on employment in industry i than those discussed above (for the case of less productive workers), for suppose that these highly productive workers in industry i would also be highly productive in other industries. The imposition of minimum wages in these other industries may result in a contraction of employment in industry i as covered-sector employers outside of industry i seek to hire these highly productive workers to replace the less productive workers whose wage has risen.

In terms of expressions (1) and (2), the implications of considering more productive workers are the following. For less productive workers (those who would otherwise earn less than w_m), I argued that expression (1), which reflects minimum wages imposed in the "own" industry, should be negatively related to employment in industry i. For more productive workers, on the other hand, this effect may well be positive. Similarly, I stated that for less productive workers the variable given by expression (2), which reflects minimum wages imposed in other industries, should be positively related to employment in industry i. For more productive workers, this relationship may instead be negative.[3]

---

[3] Expression (2) also appears less attractive as a specification for picking up the "other" industry effects on more productive workers. In particular, one might want to delete the term $(1 - C_{im})$. Because of the method used to compute the variables (discussed below), this change would simply rescale the estimated coefficients.

The upshot of this discussion is that we no longer have clear predictions of minimum wage effects for minimum wages imposed either in the own industry or in other industries. Whether the effects for highly productive workers or the effects for less productive workers dominate may depend upon the distribution of productivity of teens and others within the various industries, and on the position of the minimum wage relative to the productivity distributions.

One may be able to go a bit further, however. Some industries, such as manufacturing, tend to be high-wage industries with correspondingly high productivity distributions. Other industries, such as retail trade and agriculture, tend to be low-wage industries. If the effects for highly productive workers dominate anywhere, they would be expected to do so in the high-wage industries rather than in the low-wage industries. Conversely, if the effects for less productive workers dominate anywhere, they would be expected to do so in the low-wage rather than in high-wage industries.

Empirical Analysis

In order to see whether minimum wage effects are of any help in explaining industrial distributions, I have computed some cross-sectional estimates for various industries in 1960 and 1970. The purpose of the analysis is therefore to gain understanding of the industrial employment patterns existing at each of two points in time.

I have chosen in this analysis to measure the industrial pattern of employment in a somewhat different way from the method used in table 1. Rather than dividing the number of teens employed in a given industry by the total number of teens employed, I have instead divided by the population of the teenage group. The resulting set of numbers may be termed the "industry-specific employment rates." The advantage of using these industry-specific employment rates is that population is exogenous whereas total employment is not. Minimum wages may affect the total level of employment of a group, as well as the allocation of a given level of employment across industries. Industry-specific employment rates therefore seem to be of more substantive interest, because they deal directly with the question of how the probability of employment in an industry is altered as a consequence of minimum wages rather than with the question of how a given level of employment is reshuffled across industries.

Industry-specific employment rates for four industries—agriculture, manufacturing, services (other than private-household workers), and retail trade—were computed within "local" labor markets. These local labor markets were obtained by drawing a sample of twenty-six states from the 1960 and 1970 Public Use Samples of the U.S. *Census of Population*.[4] These states may be rather crudely characterized as "North" or "South."[5] Within northern states, areas were further classified as central cities of standard metropolitan statistical areas (SMSAs), other urban areas of SMSAs, and the state remainder. Within the states classified as South, areas are broken down into central cities of SMSAs, other urban areas, and rural areas. Each type of area within each state constituted one of the local labor markets used as a unit of observation.

Many of the variables used in the analysis were computed at the local labor market level. One exception to this rule deserves explicit mention, however. In computing the federal minimum wage variables using expressions (1) and (2), national coverage rates were used for the C_{im}. Thus the terms C_{im} and $(1 - C_{im})$ are national constants within each cross-section, and they serve no purpose other than to make cross-year and cross-industry comparisons somewhat easier. In expression (2), the sources of variation in each cross-section come from interarea variation in the average manufacturing wage ($\overline{w}$) and from differences in industry mix across areas that produce interarea variation in $\overline{C}_{im}$. In expression (1), on the other hand, the sole source of interarea variation is differences in the average manufacturing wage. A uniform federal minimum wage would be expected to have more adverse effects in regions in which nominal wage rates are lower, and it is this type of effect that expression (1) attempts to capture. In an empirical specification as parsimonious as the one employed here, however, the average manufacturing wage may well proxy other things. As a consequence, a great deal of care is required in interpreting the estimates.

In estimating the impact of minimum wages in each cross-section, I have, of course, attempted to control for some other factors. The list of control variables includes the industry-specific employment rate of adult white males (twenty-five to fifty-four years old), the growth rate of the industry within each state, the school enrollment rate of the teen group, and, for the retail trade regressions, a variable reflecting state minimum wages in the retail sector.

The first variable in this list—the industry-specific employment rate of adult males—controls for variation across areas in the size of different industries; for example, one would expect city dwellers to be very un-

---

[4] These twenty-six states contained over 95 percent of the census sample of black males aged eighteen to nineteen and the vast majority of white males in this age group as well.

[5] Classified as South were Florida, Kentucky, Tennessee, Alabama, Mississippi, Arkansas, Louisiana, Oklahoma, Texas, Maryland, District of Columbia, Virginia, West Virginia, North Carolina, South Carolina, and Georgia. States classified as North included Pennsylvania, New York, New Jersey, Ohio, Michigan, Illinois, Indiana, Wisconsin, Missouri, and California. The North-South distinction was used only in grouping types of areas within states and is otherwise of no consequence.

likely to work in the agricultural sector, and the adult industry-specific employment rate should pick up this type of effect. It is also assumed that the adult rates are themselves fairly insensitive to minimum wages and are therefore suitable proxies for what the teen employment rates would be in the absence of minimum wages (aside from the effects of school enrollment).

The growth rate of the industry within each state[6] is included because the young are expected to have little in the way of industry-specific skills that would bind them to particular industries. Consequently, their employment should be especially sensitive to the growth of particular industries, with unusually large (small) employment in rapidly growing (declining) industries.

The school enrollment rate is used as a control only with some misgivings. On the one hand, one might wish to control for the lower employment probability and differing industry choice for students as opposed to nonstudents. On the other hand, the serious question of the endogeneity of the enrollment decision is ignored in using the enrollment rate as a control variable—that is, the enrollment decision and the work decision are presumably made jointly, and this "jointness" could pose problems in using the enrollment rate as a control variable.

Finally, in analyzing retail trade, I have included a variable to reflect state minimum wage coverage of the retail sector. This variable is computed in a manner identical to that given in expression (1).[7] With this exception, I have completely ignored state minimum wage laws in the belief that these laws have had small effects, given the existence of federal coverage. The reason that I have made an exception in the case of retail trade is that federal coverage of retail trade was extremely small in 1960, whereas a few states had minimum wage laws covering at least a portion of the retail sector.

With these caveats in mind, consider the regression evidence presented in tables 2 and 3. Each column gives, for a particular year, industry, and group (white or black) of eighteen- to nineteen-year-old males, the effects of the listed variables on the industry-specific employment rate of that group. Because my primary interest is in minimum wage effects, I shall confine my discussion to the minimum wage variables. The first row of coefficients gives the effects of minimum wages in the "own" industry, and the second row of coefficients gives the effects of minimum wages introduced into other industries.

---

[6] This variable was computed by regressing a time series of Bureau of Labor Statistics employment data (in logs) for each state and industry on time and time squared.

[7] For this computation I have assumed, no doubt incorrectly, that if any portion of the retail sector was covered by a state law, then the whole retail sector was covered (except that portion already covered by federal law).

Notice first the minimum wage effects in the services and retail trade sectors—two industries that are relatively low-wage (for eighteen- to nineteen-year-olds). As might be expected, the story for less productive workers typically appears to dominate here. The effect of own federal minimum wages leads to contraction of teen employment in these industries. The effect of federal minimum wages imposed outside of these industries is generally to increase teenage employment in these industries, presumably as teens displaced elsewhere by minimum wages seek employment in the uncovered sectors in retail trade and services.

Notice, however, that I appear to have identified negative own-industry effects in the retail trade sector in 1960; yet the federal coverage rate in retail trade was a mere 3 percent in 1960, hardly enough to produce a measurable own-industry effect. In view of the proviso I injected earlier concerning the source of variation in the own-industry minimum wage variable, I would suggest that this 1960 effect is probably not due to minimum wages at all. Instead, this variable is probably proxying other area effects that determine the size of the retail sector. That is, those areas with higher average manufacturing wages have a larger retail trade sector for reasons unrelated to minimum wages.[8]

Now consider the minimum wage effects in manufacturing, a high-wage industry. The story for highly productive workers generally appears to hold here. Federal minimum wages within the manufacturing industry lead to increased employment of eighteen- to nineteen-year-old males, presumably as covered-sector employers substitute toward this group and away from less productive workers (perhaps slightly younger males).[9] The effect of minimum wages imposed outside of manufacturing is generally to decrease the probability of manufacturing employment for eighteen- to nineteen-year-old males. Presumably, covered-sector employers outside of manufacturing are then substituting the highly productive manufacturing workers for some of their (now more expensive) less productive workers.

Minimum wage effects in the agricultural sector are more puzzling. In 1970 for whites and in 1960 for blacks, the minimum wage effects are similar to those found in the other low-wage industries, services and retail trade. The estimates for blacks in 1970, though measured with little precision, and the estimate for whites in 1960 go in the opposite direction.

One possible explanation for the 1960 results is that in 1960 black teens may have suffered greater disemployment than whites as a con-

---

[8] This same problem may have contaminated the own-industry estimates for other industries as well.

[9] An alternative explanation for this own-industry effect is that I have succeeded in "identifying" the labor demand curve in manufacturing.

TABLE 2

REGRESSION ESTIMATES OF THE EFFECTS OF MINIMUM WAGES ON THE PROPORTIONS OF BLACK MALES 18–19 YEARS OLD EMPLOYED IN VARIOUS INDUSTRIES

(t-statistics in parentheses)

Variable	Agriculture[a]		Manufacturing		Services[b]		Retail Trade	
	1960	1970	1960	1970	1960	1970	1960	1970
Federal minimum wages in own industry[c]	—[d]	0.778 (0.96)	0.108 (0.98)	0.578 (1.86)	-2.10 (2.72)	-0.284 (0.88)	-8.06 (1.81)	-1.11 (3.13)
Federal minimum wages in other industries[e]	0.817 (4.24)	-0.253 (0.43)	5.56 (0.67)	-25.0 (1.56)	0.642 (1.64)	0.745 (0.66)	-0.26 (1.06)	1.01 (1.65)
Adult industry-specific employment rate	1.06 (10.15)	0.588 (3.64)	0.178 (2.25)	0.50 (5.64)	0.553 (1.72)	0.332 (1.40)	1.49 (4.39)	-0.258 (0.84)
Enrollment rate (proportion enrolled)	-0.13 (2.46)	-0.003 (0.06)	-0.214 (3.91)	-0.188 (2.47)	0.074 (1.14)	-0.014 (0.25)	-0.011 (0.18)	-0.043 (0.88)
Rate of employment growth in industry[f]	0.97 (2.63)	0.102 (0.44)	-0.741 (1.32)	0.747 (1.66)	0.099 (0.11)	0.317 (0.74)	1.01[g] (1.18)	-0.087[g] (0.26)
State minimum wages in retail trade[h]	—	—	—	—	—	—	0.002 (0.026)	-0.328 (3.22)

Intercept	−0.047 (1.03)	−0.053 (1.12)	0.079 (1.26)	0.069 (0.97)	0.039 (0.37)	0.039 (0.38)	0.075 (1.11)	0.25 (4.53)
R^2	0.86	0.45	0.37	0.44	0.26	0.10	0.45	0.34
Sample size (number of local labor markets)	71	76	71	76	71	76	71	76

NOTE: Estimates are obtained from weighted regressions. The dependent variable is the number of teens (in the demographic group) employed in the given industry, divided by the civilian, noninstitutional population of the demographic group. The square root of the population of the demographic group was used to weight each observation.

a Includes forestry and fisheries.

b Excludes workers in private households.

c Constructed as in expression (1) in the text. For 1970 the variable is constructed by summing across the minimum wages for newly covered and previously covered workers.

d Agricultural workers were not covered by federal minimum wages in 1960.

e Constructed as in expression (2) in the text. For 1970 the variable is constructed by ignoring the agricultural minimum wage and summing across minimum wages for newly covered and previously covered workers. Adult white male weights are used in constructing the coverage rate outside of industry i.

f Percentage growth rate per year, divided by 100.

g Retail trade and wholesale trade were merged in computing growth in employment.

h See text for the method of computation.

SOURCE: Author.

TABLE 3

REGRESSION ESTIMATES OF THE EFFECTS OF MINIMUM WAGES ON THE PROPORTIONS OF WHITE MALES 18–19 YEARS OLD EMPLOYED IN VARIOUS INDUSTRIES

(t-statistics in parentheses)

Variable	Agriculture[a] 1960	Agriculture[a] 1970	Manufacturing 1960	Manufacturing 1970	Services[b] 1960	Services[b] 1970	Retail Trade 1960	Retail Trade 1970
Federal minimum wages in own industry[c]	[d]	−0.483 (2.27)	0.161 (1.33)	0.524 (4.15)	−0.192 (0.67)	−0.275 (2.19)	−17.12 (−4.98)	−0.912 (3.52)
Federal minimum wages in other industries[e]	−0.182 (1.77)	0.421 (2.48)	−4.24 (0.81)	−17.78 (3.08)	0.154 (1.13)	0.248 (0.60)	0.28 (1.44)	−0.030 (0.06)
Adult industry-specific employment rate	0.693 (14.64)	0.638 (16.98)	0.478 (7.75)	0.522 (15.09)	0.382 (2.76)	0.195 (1.93)	0.427 (1.38)	−0.090 (0.33)
Enrollment rate (proportion enrolled)	−0.061 (1.24)	0.063 (2.45)	−0.23 (2.97)	−0.188 (3.55)	0.097 (2.27)	−0.003 (0.08)	−0.0 (0.0)	0.008 (0.12)
Rate of employment growth in industry[f]	0.162 (0.80)	0.173 (2.39)	0.594 (1.29)	0.387 (2.20)	0.085 (0.32)	0.029 (0.16)	0.836[g] (1.57)	1.14[g] (3.91)
State minimum wages in retail trade[h]	—	—	—	—	—	—	−0.023 (0.46)	−0.099 (1.34)

Intercept	0.088 (2.23)	−0.032 (1.39)	0.094 (1.23)	0.046 (0.85)	−0.040 (1.10)	0.100 (2.28)	0.22 (3.69)	0.337 (5.54)
R^2	0.85	0.87	0.58	0.81	0.40	0.36	0.43	0.59
Sample size (number of local labor markets)	71	76	71	76	71	76	71	76

NOTES: See notes to table 2.

55

sequence of federal minimum wages imposed outside of agriculture. Some blacks and whites who would otherwise have worked in agriculture in 1960 may not have done so as a consequence of the decline in the agricultural wage brought about by the influx of disemployed workers from other sectors. If these disemployed workers, some of whom entered agriculture, were largely black, then we may obtain, on net, a positive other-industry effect for blacks in agriculture but a negative effect for whites. More work is needed to see whether this explanation will hold up under additional scrutiny.

Although these results provide some insight, one may gain additional perspective on the order of magnitude of net minimum wage effects by considering the following hypothetical experiment. Suppose that all federal minimum wages in 1970 were twenty-five cents higher than their actual 1970 levels.[10] All else the same, what would the effect have been on the industry-specific employment rates of teens? Table 4 uses the regression estimates from table 2 and table 3 to answer this question.

The first two columns of numbers in table 4 give the actual industry-specific employment rates for teens in 1970 (in the twenty-six-state sample). The next two columns give the estimated change in these employment rates that would have occurred under the hypothesized increase in the minimum wage levels. The final two columns express the change as a percentage of the original industry-specific employment rate.

Notice that the estimated effects on employment of eighteen- to nineteen-year-old males are negative for both racial groups and for all industries except manufacturing. Although a twenty-five-cent increase in minimum wages might seem to be fairly small, estimated disemployment effects are sometimes quite large, particularly in agriculture for blacks and in retail trade for teens of both races.

It is worth emphasizing that the results in table 4 are derived from regression estimates. These estimates will, at best, provide reasonable predictions of the effects of "small" changes in the independent variables and are likely to be wide of the mark for "large" changes. For example, the regression estimates would predict that *any* increase in federal minimum wages in 1970 would have increased the employment of this age group in manufacturing. It seems highly unlikely, however, that this relationship would in fact hold for extremely large increases in minimum wages. The assumption implicit in constructing table 4 is that a twenty-five-cent increase in minimum wages is small enough for the regression model to be appropriate.

---

[10] Federal minimum wage levels in 1970 were $1.60 (the basic minimum), $1.45 for "newly covered" nonagricultural workers, and $1.30 for agricultural workers.

TABLE 4

ESTIMATED EFFECTS OF TWENTY-FIVE-CENT INCREASE IN ALL FEDERAL MINIMUM WAGES ON THE PROPORTIONS OF 18–19-YEAR-OLD MALES EMPLOYED IN VARIOUS INDUSTRIES

(computed at 1970 mean for all variables)

Industry	Actual Proportion Employed in Industry in 1970[a]		Estimated Change in Proportion Employed as Result of $0.25 Increase in Federal Minimum Wages		Estimated Percentage Change in Proportion Employed	
	Blacks	Whites	Blacks	Whites	Blacks	Whites
Agriculture	0.022	0.026	−0.014 (1.55)	−0.002 (0.84)	−62.4	−6.9
Manufacturing	0.137	0.134	0.001 (0.07)	0.006 (1.63)	0.5	4.8
Services	0.087	0.081	−0.002 (0.24)	−0.008 (2.36)	−2.4	−9.5
Retail trade	0.072	0.185	−0.019 (4.31)	−0.030 (6.85)	−25.9	−16.4

NOTE: Figures in parentheses are *t*-statistics.
[a] Based on the sample of twenty-six states. These values are industry-specific employment rates.
SOURCE: Author.

TABLE 5
SAMPLE MEANS OF VARIABLES

Variable	Sample	Agriculture		Manufacturing		Services		Retail Trade	
		1960	1970	1960	1970	1960	1970	1960	1970
Industry-specific employment rate of 18–19-year-old males	Black	0.1144	0.0225	0.1031	0.1374	0.0940	0.0869	0.1075	0.0723
	White	0.0555	0.0264	0.1658	0.1337	0.0688	0.0814	0.1583	0.1847
Federal minimum wages in own industry	Black	0.0	0.1362	0.3767	0.3602	0.0753	0.2487	0.0119	0.2091
	White	0.0	0.1301	0.3435	0.3439	0.0687	0.2375	0.0108	0.1996
Federal minimum wages in other industries	Black	0.2273	0.1586	0.0064	0.0079	0.1811	0.0820	0.2272	0.1192
	White	0.2146	0.1536	0.0061	0.0076	0.1735	0.0791	0.2152	0.1145
Adult industry-specific employment rate	Black	0.0693	0.0270	0.2916	0.2831	0.1121	0.1486	0.1168	0.1101
	White	0.0653	0.0334	0.3177	0.3068	0.1121	0.1442	0.1098	0.1042
Rate of employment growth in industry	Black	−0.0438	−0.0466	0.0195	0.0220	0.0403	0.0510	0.0185	0.0394
	White	−0.0446	−0.0395	0.0133	0.0169	0.0392	0.0488	0.0170	0.0371

State minimum wages in retail trade									
	Black	—	—	—	—	—	—	0.0309	0.0364
	White	—	—	—	—	—	—	0.0594	0.0514

		1960	1970
Employment rates (proportion enrolled)	Black	0.4189	0.5256
	White	0.5111	0.6611

NOTE: Each sample mean is a weighted average of means for the local labor markets in the twenty-six states. The weight for each local market is the (sample) proportion of the appropriate teenage population located in that local market.
SOURCE: Author.

Summary and Conclusions

The empirical work in this paper suggests that federal minimum wages have altered the industrial distribution of teenage employment. For eighteen- to nineteen-year-old males, the effects of federal minimum wages imposed in high-wage industries, such as manufacturing, may be to increase the probability of their employment in these industries. Conversely, imposition of federal minimum wages outside of one of these industries may decrease the probability of their employment in that industry. On the other hand, in a low-wage industry, such as retail trade or services, the own-industry effect may be to decrease the employment probability of this group in this industry, whereas the other-industry effect may be to increase the employment probability of this group in this industry.

The results presented above are surely consistent with other studies that find that minimum wages have a negative net employment effect on teenage males. My findings supplement these studies by showing some of the interindustry shifts that occur and by demonstrating that there may be some groups of teens, such as highly skilled manufacturing workers, whose employment prospects are enhanced by minimum wages.

Appendix

The sample means of variables are presented in table 5.

Bibliography

Mincer, Jacob. "Unemployment Effects of Minimum Wages." *Journal of Political Economy* 84 (August 1976): S87–S104.

Welch, Finis. "Minimum Wage Legislation in the United States." *Economic Inquiry* 12 (September 1974): 285–318.

The Impact of Minimum Wages on Teenage Schooling and on the Part-Time/Full-Time Employment of Youths

J. Peter Mattila

Both academic economists and policy makers have shown a great deal of interest in the impact of minimum wages on young people. Much of this interest has focused on the employment difficulties and the unemployment experience of teenagers. Little or no attention has been paid to the impact of minimum wages on other characteristics of youths, such as school enrollment—yet there is good reason to believe that school enrollment may be affected. If minimum wages create barriers to employment, then additional schooling may be one strategy for overcoming that barrier, and as we shall argue, teenagers may attempt to work part-time while they continue their education.

Looked at from this perspective, minimum wage legislation may have effects far beyond the often mentioned impact on unemployment. The laws may indirectly alter the size and composition of classroom enrollments and thereby affect the quality of education. Minimum wages may indirectly shift the supply of part-time labor and, as a consequence, alter the economics of the retail and service industries. Of most importance, the substitution of additional schooling for work experience and job training may have long-run effects on the incomes and well-being of those youths adversely affected by the minimum wage law.

Youth Activities and Adjustment Patterns

Minimum wage laws constrain only covered employment in the youth's opportunity set. To the extent that job opportunities are limited in industries covered by the law, the teenager has four major alternatives to consider: queuing for covered-sector jobs, taking a job in the noncovered sector, investing in additional schooling or training, and undertaking other nonmarket activities. Let us discuss each of these options.

NOTE: The research reported in this paper was supported in part by the U.S. Employment and Training Administration, although the opinions, conclusions, and policies discussed do not necessarily represent the official opinion or policy of the Department of Labor.

Although fewer jobs will be available in industries covered by the law, some positions will open as normal turnover occurs. One plausible strategy might be for the youth to queue for these openings as an unemployed job searcher. In practice, this would involve making job applications, being very patient, and maintaining one's availability to start a job quickly if necessary. Presumably, this approach will be more attractive the higher the job separation rate and the lower the opportunity cost of waiting.

There are at least two reasons why teenagers might not consider this an attractive strategy by itself. First, more experienced adults who are also in the queue (having been displaced by minimum wages) may be preferred to teenagers when job vacancies do arise. Teenagers may frequently be passed over by covered-sector employers. Second, there is an opportunity cost to simply waiting. This cost is the forgone education and training that might lead to improved employment prospects. Although some youths might attempt to take courses while they waited for a job offer, such a strategy limits one's availability for work.

A second response to the minimum wage constraint is to take a job in the noncovered sector. Although Congress legislated major expansions in coverage in the 1961, 1967, and 1974 amendments to the Fair Labor Standards Act, approximately 13 percent of all private-sector jobs and the majority of state and local government jobs still remain exempt from the minimum wage provisions.[1] As seen in table 1, most of the exempt jobs are in industries where teenagers work: agriculture, services, and retail trade.

As table 2 indicates, a substantial proportion of teenage workers do hold jobs that pay less than the minimum wage. Approximately one-tenth of full-time teenage workers (those working thirty-five or more hours per week) earn low wage rates. Subminimum rates are even more common among part-time workers.

Jacob Mincer has shown that although it is theoretically possible for labor to flow on net from the noncovered to the covered sector and thereby raise wage rates in the noncovered sector (which induces labor-force entry), empirical evidence suggests that the opposite occurs;[2] that is, Mincer estimates that increases in minimum wages induce labor-force exit. This suggests that wage rates in the noncovered sector have deteriorated as a result of the law and that, on net, labor has flowed from the covered to the noncovered sector.

[1] Approximately one-half of those private-sector workers who are not covered by the federal law have some coverage under state laws or orders, although there is a great deal of variation in rates and enforcement among states. Only one-fourth of state and local government workers are similarly covered by state laws or orders.

[2] Jacob Mincer, "Unemployment Effects of Minimum Wages," *Journal of Political Economy* 84 (August 1976): S87–S104.

TABLE 1

PERCENTAGE OF NONSUPERVISORY, NONPROFESSIONAL WAGE AND
SALARY WORKERS COVERED BY THE FEDERAL MINIMUM WAGE
LAW

	1953	1960	1964	1967	1972	1977
Agriculture	0	0	0	31	40	39
Domestic service	0	0	0	0	0	64
Other services	18	19	22	68	71	74
Retail trade	3	3	32	58	62	79
Wholesale trade and contract construction	45	56	75	87	99	99
All other private industries	91	90	93	95	99	99
Total private sector	55	54	63	77	82	87
State and local government	0	0	0	44[a]	46[a]	5[a]

[a] State and local government coverage, extended under the 1967 and 1974 amendments, was invalidated by the Supreme Court in 1976 (*National League of Cities* v. *Usery*).
SOURCE: U.S. Department of Labor, Employment Standards Administration estimates.

TABLE 2

PERCENTAGE OF 16–19-YEAR-OLD WAGE AND SALARY WORKERS
REPORTING HOURLY EARNINGS LESS THAN THE MINIMUM WAGE

	Minimum Wage	Survey Range: Workers Earning Less than	% below Minimum Wage	
			Full-time workers	Part-time workers
May 1973	$1.60	$1.60	5	22
May 1974	2.00	2.00	13	43
May 1975	2.10	2.00[a]	7+	26+
May 1976	2.30	2.25[a]	13+	44+
May 1977	2.30	2.25[a]	7+	24+

[a] Workers were categorized into the following wage ranges: under $1.60, $1.60–$1.99, $2.00–$2.24, $2.25–$2.49, and so on. Hence, our percentages are underestimates for 1975, 1976, and 1977.
SOURCE: Unpublished tabulations supplied by the U.S. Department of Labor, Bureau of Labor Statistics.

Mincer's analysis and empirical results suggest that minimum wages have induced some youths to pursue non–labor market alternatives. Conceivably, some teenagers may undertake housework or child-care duties while others become part of the "street culture."

It is the thesis of this paper that many of those who withdraw from the labor force do so in order to continue or resume their formal education. There are several reasons why additional schooling may be a reasonable response to a minimum wage constraint. First, to the extent that forgone earnings decline, the rate of return to additional education will rise. Further investments in human capital should raise the value of the teenager's productivity and help the youth to escape eventually from the low-paying jobs of the noncovered sector. Second, to the extent that employers use education as a screening device, continued enrollment may signal potential employers that he/she is a good prospect, is motivated, and is reliable. In this case the individual attempts to move ahead in the queue for the better covered-sector jobs. Third, the Fair Labor Standards Act provides some direct incentives. Covered firms may hire certain students for 15 percent less than the prevailing minimum wage rate through the Department of Labor's certification programs. In addition, student employees, like all employees of public schools, colleges, and universities, are not covered by the law. A nonrandom telephone survey of several southern colleges by the author indicates that most paid their student employees 20 percent less than the $2.90 minimum wage in 1979.

Of course, not all youths will adopt this strategy of continued schooling. We would expect more able youths from high-income families to be most likely to enroll. The more able youths should be better able to convert schooling into productive human capital and to convince firms of their employability. Those who derive much disutility from school will be less likely to enroll. From this point of view, it is the average student rather than the below average student who is likely to adopt this strategy. Minimum wages may induce the average student to complete high school and perhaps begin at a community college or university rather than drop out of high school.

Those from higher-income families should be better able to finance their schooling than those from poor families. Traditionally, human capital investments were financed primarily by the student's family or from the student's own earnings. Only since the 1960s have government grants and guaranteed loan programs been available to help the poor finance their education. These observations suggest that school enrollment may be a more important response to minimum wage laws for white teenagers than for less affluent nonwhite teenagers, and they suggest that joint part-time work and school enrollment might be a frequently adopted strategy.

Even though minimum wages may limit the availability of jobs in general, there may be counterforces at work that tend to increase the numbers of enrolled students in the labor force. Students who need part-time work in order to help finance their educations will necessarily experience some unemployed job search simply while they look for work. And because students require jobs that are compatible with their school schedules, their transportation constraints, and their wage aspirations, they may experience more frequent spells and possibly longer duration of search. This suggests that minimum wages may have increased enrolled unemployment.

In addition to the need to finance an education, the youth may have other incentives for adopting a joint work-study program. From the point of view of the screening hypothesis, potential employers may favor those who signal having both formal schooling and practical work experience. For the average student with mediocre grades (who we feel is most likely to extend his/her education), some work experience may be as important as is additional education.

Some jobs may be available to students that are not available to others. We have already pointed out that the Fair Labor Standards Act provides exemptions for certain students working in covered jobs and for students employed by public schools. Hence, some may find it easier to obtain jobs simply by enrolling. As table 2 indicates, subminimum wage rates are both available and acceptable to many part-time teenage workers.

In summary, we argue that minimum wage laws have limited job opportunities in the covered sector and have forced teenagers into alternative activities. Additional schooling is one way to overcome the minimum wage barrier. We argue, too, that there are incentives to look for part-time work while in school. This implies that minimum wages should raise unemployment among the enrolled. Whether enrolled employment rises or falls depends upon the number of new subminimum wage jobs that are created in noncovered industries relative to the number of covered-sector jobs that are lost.

Data on Youth Activities

Questions on school enrollment have been asked each October since 1947 as a supplement to the regular Current Population Survey.[3] Youths are classified into two categories, those enrolled in school and those not enrolled. Persons within each category are further subdivided by their labor force status.

---

[3] In addition to the usual questions on unemployment, employment, and hours of work, the survey interviewer asks, for each member of the family, "Is ——— attending or enrolled in school?" If so, the next question is, "What grade or year is ——— attending?" (Current Population Survey questionnaire for October 1967, Form CPS-1, 8–9–67). Those enrolled in special schools such as trade schools, business colleges, and barber schools are *not* included with the enrolled.

Table 3 summarizes the October distribution of enrollment and labor force activity averaged over the past three decades by age and sex. It is not surprising that 90 percent of the fourteen- to seventeen-year-olds were enrolled or that more eighteen- to nineteen-year-olds worked than were in school. Somewhat more interesting is the fact that so many of the younger students were in the labor force. Although they worked relatively few hours each week, 14 percent of the female and 20 percent of the male population aged fourteen to seventeen simultaneously worked at part-time jobs and attended classes. (Part-time workers are defined as those who worked less than thirty-five hours during the survey week.) Considerably smaller proportions reported working full-time or seeking work while enrolled. Among those not in school, most worked full-time or were homemakers.

Figures 1 and 2 illustrate how these proportions have been changing over time. Figure 1 indicates that for males aged fourteen to seventeen school enrollments increased until the late 1960s and declined slightly until 1974. Since the early 1960s, most of the growth in enrollments has been associated with the growth of enrolled part-time workers and enrolled job seekers rather than full-time students not in the labor force.

TABLE 3

DISTRIBUTION OF YOUTHS BY TYPE OF ECONOMIC ACTIVITY: AVERAGE, OCTOBER 1947–OCTOBER 1977

(as percentage of cohort population)

	Youths Age 14–17		Youths Age 18–19	
	Male	Female	Male	Female
Enrolled in school	90	89	40	32
Labor force	24	17	15	9
Employed	22	15	14	9
Full-time	2	1	3	2
Part-time	20	14	11	7
Unemployed	2	2	1	1
Not in labor force	66	72	25	22
Not enrolled[a]	10	11	60	68
Labor force[a]	8	5	56	42
Employed[a]	7	4	51	37
Full-time[a]	5	3	44	29
Part-time[a]	2	1	7	8
Unemployed	1	1	5	5
Not in labor force	2	6	4	26

[a] Includes those in the armed forces.
SOURCE: October Current Population Survey.

Data are not plotted for females in this age group, as they are very similar to the data in figure 1.

It is particularly interesting to note in figure 1 that enrolled un-employment (solid line) has increased by a considerable amount relative to not-enrolled unemployment (broken line). Although there has been considerable discussion of the problem of rising youth unemployment, it has not always been made clear that, at least for fourteen- to seventeen-year-olds, this is a problem of rising *student* unemployment. This is an important observation because in formulating policy one should take into account the time and location constraints faced by students.

Figure 2 plots comparable data for females from eighteen to nine-teen. Enrollment has increased steadily over the three decades, appar-ently at the expense of not-enrolled employment and household activ-ities. As with the younger group, part-time employed students have increased during the last decade relative to students who are not in the labor force. Note, too, the more rapid growth of unemployed students relative to unemployed nonstudents.

Data are not plotted for males from eighteen to nineteen. If they were, they would differ in three major ways from the series for females. First, enrollment among males of this age declined in the early 1970s and remained low through 1977. Apparently the depression in higher education has affected men more than women. Second, male activities were disrupted by the draft in the early 1950s and late 1960s whereas female activities were not. Third, few males have ever been in the not-enrolled, not-in-the-labor-force category.

The October Current Population Survey is the primary source of time series data with which we may test the hypotheses raised in the section on adjustment patterns.[4] The major shortcoming of these data is that they are available only for October of each year. This makes it impossible to exploit the information we have on the seasonal timing of minimum wage increases. This also reduces our sample size to the thirty-one observations available over these three decades.

On the other hand, there are some definite advantages to this data set. First, this sample spans nine general increases in the minimum wage

---

[4] A second time series on the "major activity" of youths has been available quarterly since 1963 from the Current Population Survey. Youths who were going to school most of the survey week are classified as "major activity, school." Youths who were attending school but who were devoting more hours to either work or other activities are classified as "major activity, other." Because an increasing proportion of students are working and working longer hours, more and more youths are being classified as "major activity, other." Hence, the major-activity series does not record many students as students and is not useful for our purposes. For further analysis, see J. Peter Mattila, "The Impact of Minimum Wages on School Enrollment and Labor Force Status of Youths," Final Report to the U.S. Employment and Training Administration, Grant no. 91–19–78–32, June 1979.

FIGURE 1
Enrollment and Labor Force Status of Males Age 14–17 as a Proportion of Their Population, 1947–1977

Proportion of Population

Enrolled

Enrolled, Not in Labor Force

Enrolled, Employed Part-Time

Not Enrolled, Employed (Includes Armed Forces)

Enrolled, Unemployed

Not Enrolled, Unemployed

Source: October Current Population Surveys.

FIGURE 2
ENROLLMENT AND LABOR FORCE STATUS OF FEMALES AGE 18–19 AS A PROPORTION OF THEIR POPULATION, 1947–1977

Proportion of Population

SOURCE: October Current Population Surveys.

as well as the major expansions of coverage in 1961, 1967, and 1974. This provides variation in the crucial explanatory variable that may more than offset the lack of quarterly variation. Many other time series studies have spanned a much shorter period. Second, the larger time period allows for more secular and cyclical variation in enrollment ratios, which may help to offset the lack of quarterly variation. If we were to obtain data on enrollments in January 1978 to supplement our presently available data on October 1977 enrollments, would we double our independent information? To the extent that students enroll for school years rather than for school months or quarters, quarterly data may not add as much information as would an equivalent number of additional October observations. This is not to say that we would not prefer having quarterly data 1947–1976, but its absence may not be as costly as it might seem.

The major problem with time series analysis is collinearity; that is, several of the variables tend to follow similar patterns over time. This frequently makes it difficult to determine the impact of any one explanatory variable on the dependent variable. Fortunately, collinearity is less of a problem for us because of a ratchet pattern of our most important explanatory variable, the minimum wage index.

We use the same minimum wage index as constructed by the U.S. Employment Standards Administration and as used in many other time series studies. Basically, it is computed as the ratio of the minimum wage rate to average hourly earnings, with this ratio multiplied by the proportion covered by the law.[5] The resulting index is plotted in figure 3. The index follows a ratchet pattern, rising sharply each time Congress legislated major increases in the rate (1950, 1956, 1961, 1967–1968, and 1974–1977) and declining between rate increases as average hourly earn-

---

[5] To be more precise, the minimum wage index is calculated as

$$MW = \sum_i \frac{E_i}{E_t} \left(p_i \frac{MP_i}{AHE_i} + n_i \frac{MN_i}{AHE_i} \right)$$

where E is employment, AHE is average hourly earnings of production workers, MP is the basic minimum for previously covered workers, MN is the minimum for newly covered workers, p is the fraction of nonsupervisory workers previously covered, n is the fraction of nonsupervisory workers newly covered (by the most recent amendment), i indexes major industries, and t refers to the total nonfarm economy. Because it is available back through 1947 and because earlier work suggested it made little difference, we used the index weighted by all industry employment rather than weighted by teenage employment (which is available only since 1954). Taking into account the month in which this minimum wage increased in any given year, we interpolated to obtain quarterly estimates. The fourth-quarter figure was used in regressions that utilized October enrollment data. See U.S. Department of Labor, Bureau of Labor Statistics, *Youth Unemployment and Minimum Wages*, Bulletin 1657, Washington, D.C., 1970, pp. 12–13.

FIGURE 3
MINIMUM WAGE INDEX, 1947–1977

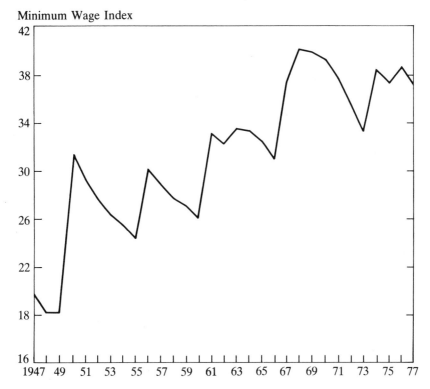

Minimum Wage Index

SOURCE: Adjusted by author to October value as based on U.S. Department of Labor, Employment Standards Administration index.

ings rose because of general inflation and productivity increases. Whatever upward trend does occur in the index occurs because of the extension of coverage in 1961, 1967–1969, and 1974 (see table 1).

This ratchet pattern distinguishes our minimum wage variable from several of the other important variables that influence school enrollments and labor force status. These other variables tend to be more smoothly trending variables or variables that rise and fall with the business cycle. This gives us more confidence that we can, in fact, isolate and estimate the impact of minimum wage legislation.

Control Variables

As discussed earlier, youths are assumed to choose among the activities that are available: school, work, unemployed job search, and others.

71

In order to estimate the impact of minimum wages alone, we have attempted to control for other major variables that influence the teenage decision process.

School enrollment is likely to increase as the rate of return to the investment in education increases and it becomes easier to finance such investments. Hence, we control for variation in the rate of return to school (*ROR*) and for average real after-tax family income (*INCOME*). A detailed description of the sources and construction of the variables is provided in the appendix, but we will mention a few interesting characteristics of these variables here. The *INCOME* variable basically trends upward throughout the 1950s and 1960s, reflecting the growth in real productivity and income of the teenager's parents. After 1972, real after-tax income declines by 7 percent through the 1975 recession, with a slight recovery in 1976 and 1977.

The rate of return to completing high school (*RORH*) is estimated to have risen until the early 1960s. Thereafter it declines slightly until the 1970s, which we interpret as reflecting the impact of the maturing "baby boom" generation upon the labor market for high school graduates. Since the early 1970s, the rate of return to high school seems to have increased. A time series was also constructed to reflect trends in the rate of return to college (*RORC*). This was necessary in order to control for the propensity of eighteen- to nineteen-year-old youths to enter college. Our estimates suggest that there was a slight decline in the rate of return in the late 1940s, reflecting the graduation of World War II veterans under the GI bill program. Thereafter, *RORC* increases until the early 1970s. For males, the payoff from college appears to have declined steadily since 1971, reflecting the widely discussed depression in higher education of the 1970s.[6] For females, our estimates suggest little downturn in *RORC* until 1974–1975. This may reflect better opportunities for college-trained women due to affirmative action plans, and it appears to reflect an increasing number of hours and weeks worked per year during the 1970s for women with some college education relative to those with high school educations.

A teenager's major alternative to schooling is market work. Two variables, *SERVICE* and *AGRI*, were created to control for shifting employment opportunities. Because it is well known that the service sector has been growing steadily over several decades at the expense of the goods-producing sector and because many young people find employment in service-type jobs (which frequently are sufficiently flexible

---

[6] Not all agree that the decline was so prolonged. For the more pessimistic view, see Richard B. Freeman, *The Over-educated American* (New York: Academic Press, 1976). For a more optimistic view, see J. P. Smith and Finis Welch, "Local Labor Markets and Cyclic Components in Demand for College Trained Manpower" (Santa Monica, Calif.: Rand Corporation, February 1978).

to allow joint schooling and work), we have attempted to control for this growth in demand. Our *SERVICE* variable measures the upward trend in the proportion of jobs found in the service or sales occupations.[7] This variable was computed over all age groups so as to minimize endogeneity with teenage workers. The *AGRI* variable controls for considerable variation in the demand for agricultural laborers. This was particularly true in the 1940s and 1950s when several of the Census Bureau's studies of student employment reported that employment would be high in October one year and low in another October due to the timing of the harvest. The basic trend of the *AGRI* variable is negative.

Unemployed job search by teenagers is assumed to vary with the business cycle. Because one of our tasks is to explain the growth in youth unemployment, we do not want to include teenage unemployment in an aggregate measure of cyclical variation. As a consequence, we adopt the unemployment rate of men aged thirty-five to fifty-four (*U*). This rate has the feature that, unlike the aggregate unemployment rate, it rose no higher in the 1975 recession than it did in the 1958 and 1961 recessions.

Finally, we turn to other (nonschooling, non–labor market) activities. These are more likely the more productive they are and the more readily available are other sources of income. Our *INCOME* variable controls in part for the latter. The most common other activity is child care and housework, particularly for females aged eighteen to nineteen. We control for this with the proportion of women in this age group who have children (*KIDS*). This variable trends upward from 1947 to 1960, reflecting the baby boom of those years, and trends down thereafter.

Substantial numbers of young men from eighteen to nineteen years old have served in the armed forces. We control for variation in the numbers drafted into the military by including a control variable *AF*, the proportion of all men of this age in the armed forces. Because men fourteen to seventeen years old and women were not subject to the draft, those few who enlisted were included with the not-enrolled, full-time employed categories within their respective age groups.

Empirical Estimates

For males aged fourteen to seventeen and for females aged fourteen to seventeen, the following equation was utilized in order to estimate the impact of a change in the minimum wage rate:

---

[7] In the regressions for females eighteen to nineteen years old, the *SERVICE* variable includes clerical workers as well as service and sales workers.

$$Y_i = a_0 + a_1 MW_t + a_2 MW_{t-1} + a_3 RORH + a_4 INCOME$$
$$+ a_5 SERVICE + a_6 AGRI + a_7 U$$

Here Y_i refers to the proportion of teenagers in the ith enrollment/labor force category. For males from fourteen to seventeen, a regression equation was estimated for each of fourteen such categories, six of which are plotted in figure 1. An additional fourteen regressions were estimated for females in the same age group. Because Mincer found some evidence of a lagged response to a change in the minimum wage law, we include both the current October value of the minimum wage index (MW_t as plotted in figure 3) and the previous year's October index (MW_{t-1}). We compute the total minimum wage impact as the sum of the current and lagged impacts. In each equation, we control for all of the other explanatory variables discussed in the section on control variables. The explanatory variables were identical in each of the regressions. All regressions were adjusted for autocorrelation of residuals and were estimated independently of one another.[8]

The estimated equation differed slightly for eighteen- to nineteen-year-olds. The rate of return to a college education ($RORC$) replaces the rate of return to high school ($RORH$). The proportion of males of this age in the armed forces (AF) was included as an additional control variable.[9] And for females of the same age we added the presence-of-children variable ($KIDS$) in order to control for variation in child-care activity.

[8] Because our categories Y_i cover all possible states and because the eight fundamental categories (full-time employed, part-time employed, unemployed, and not in labor force for the enrolled and for the not-enrolled) are mutually exclusive, the impacts of minimum wages on the categories should be linearly related; that is, because employment and unemployment sum to the labor force, so should the respective minimum wage coefficients. They would sum if we had estimated our equations using ordinary least squares. Because we adjusted for autocorrelated residuals and did not impose any constraints, the estimated coefficients do not sum precisely. As seen in table 4, however, the basic relationships still hold approximately. Among males aged fourteen to seventeen enrolled, for instance, the employment impact (.0079) and the unemployment impact (.0020) sum to .0099, which is not too different from the .0091 estimate for the labor force. Because several categories were close to 0 or close to 1, we transformed the dependent variable using the logit transformation. The estimated coefficients were then retransformed for presentation in table 4.

[9] Originally, we had not included AF in the regressions for eighteen- to nineteen-year-old females. However, upon examining the residuals, it was apparent that during the Korean War years (1950–1956) we were substantially and consistently *underestimating* the proportion of females in the labor force and not enrolled and *overestimating* the proportion of females not in the labor force and not enrolled. Although smaller and less consistent, the residuals during the peak years of the Vietnamese War were similar. We interpret this as being a result of the shortage of males, which increased wage rates for females and induced women to work more. The AF variable was included to control for this phenomenon.

In table 4, we report our estimates of the minimum wage impact. Each entry in that table can be interpreted as the estimated impact of a 10 percent increase in the minimum wage rate (holding the other control variables constant) on the proportion of teenagers in the relevant

TABLE 4

ESTIMATES OF THE IMPACT OF A 10 PERCENT INCREASE IN THE MINIMUM WAGE INDEX ON THE PROPORTION OF TEENAGERS IN AN ENROLLMENT/LABOR FORCE CATEGORY

	Youths Age 14–17		Youths Age 18–19	
	Males	Females	Males	Females
Enrolled in school	.0076	.0069	.0133	.0126
	(2.70)**	(2.95)**	(1.96)*	(3.07)**
Labor force	.0091	.0072	.0077	.0077
	(2.10)*	(1.79)*	(1.85)*	(2.14)*
Employed	.0079	.0056	.0062	.0062
	(1.99)*	(1.56)	(1.67)	(1.80)*
Full-time	.0016	.0011	.0007	.0005
	(1.72)*	(1.44)	(.45)	(.27)
Part-time	.0058	.0044	.0064	.0059
	(1.65)	(1.26)	(1.86)*	(2.22)*
Unemployed	.0020	.0018	.0009	.0012
	(2.03)*	(1.70)	(.98)	(1.30)
Not in labor force	.0016	.0032	.0061	.0036
	(.34)	(.55)	(1.31)	(.93)
Not enrolled	− .0076[a]	− .0069[a]	− .0133	− .0126[a]
	(2.70)**	(2.95)**	(2.07)*	(3.07)**
Labor force	− .0069[a]	− .0051[a]	− .0112	− .0082[a]
	(2.80)**	(3.07)**	(1.83)*	(2.18)*
Employed	− .0058[a]	− .0052[a]	− .0105	− .0070[a]
	(2.84)**	(3.40)**	(2.07)*	(1.75)*
Full-time	− .0050[a]	− .0031[a]	− .0091	− .0090[a]
	(2.97)**	(2.64)**	(2.09)*	(2.01)*
Part-time	− .0005	− .0018	− .0002	.0026
	(.76)	(3.10)**	(.19)	(.94)
Unemployed	− .0014	− .0002	− .0017	− .0016
	(2.59)**	(.51)	(.67)	(.74)
Not in labor force	− .0003	− .0015	− .0018	− .0046
	(.75)	(1.37)	(1.13)	(1.31)

NOTE: t-ratios in parentheses.
[a] Those in the armed forces are included among those not enrolled, employed full-time.
* Significant at .05 level.
** Significant at .01 level.
SOURCE: Author.

enrollment/labor force category; for instance, a 10 percent increase in the minumum wage rate lowered the proportion of males aged fourteen to seventeen who were not enrolled but employed full-time by 0.0050. Comparing this to the observation from table 3 that on average the proportion of males of this age in the same category was 0.052, we estimate a 9.6 percent reduction in full-time employment. Hence, for fourteen- to seventeen-year-olds, the elasticity of response appears to be approximately -0.96. This elasticity is reported in table 5. The corresponding elasticities for eighteen- to nineteen-year-olds are also negative, although smaller in magnitude.

Among the not-enrolled, the adverse effect of legal minimums is much stronger on full-time employment than on part-time employment. This is consistent with our observation that part-time jobs are more likely to be in the noncovered sector and to pay subminimum wage rates. It is also interesting that we do not observe any increase in unemployment or in "other activities" among those not enrolled. In fact, all of these coefficients in table 4 are negative, although only one is statistically significant.

Table 4 provides considerable support for our thesis that minimum wages have increased school enrollments. All of the enrollment coefficients are positive and statistically significant. The total magnitude of

TABLE 5

EMPLOYMENT AND LABOR FORCE ELASTICITIES WITH RESPECT TO THE MINIMUM WAGE

	Youths Age 14–17		Youths Age 18–19	
	Males	Females	Males	Females
Enrolled in school				
Labor force	.37	.42	.50	.75
Employed	.36	.36	.45	.67
Full-time	.80	1.10	.24	.29
Part-time	.29	.30	.58	.79
Unemployed	.83	2.00	.60	1.09
Not enrolled				
Labor force	$-.86$	-1.02	$-.27$	$-.19$
Employed	$-.84$	-1.24	$-.28$	$-.19$
Full-time	$-.96$	-1.03	$-.30$	$-.30$
Part-time	$-.31$	-1.50	$-.03$	.31
Unemployed	-1.27	$-.25$	$-.37$	$-.33$

NOTE: All elasticities are computed at the means of the dependent variable and the minimum wage index.
SOURCE: Author.

the increase in enrollment is similar to (if not slightly larger than) the magnitude of the decrease in the not-enrolled labor force. This suggests that the major adjustment made by displaced teenagers is to continue their schooling rather than to drop out or to join the ranks of the full-time employed.

Most of these additional students do remain in the labor force as they continue their schooling. We expected that many would desire jobs in order to help finance their educations. As a consequence, minimum wages have tended to increase enrolled unemployment. In fact, we conclude that if minimum wages have increased unemployment at all the increase has occurred within the student unemployment category. We find no evidence that minimum wages have increased nonstudent unemployment, at least among teenagers. Our interpretation is that minimum wages raise unemployment indirectly. By shifting more youths into school, student unemployment rises because of the natural time and location constraints faced by students.

In our earlier discussion, we were not able to predict whether minimum wages would increase or decrease enrolled employment. Our statistical estimates suggest that enrolled employment increases, primarily because of a rise in part-time employment rather than full-time employment, as seen in table 4. This indicates that students may have an easier time getting work than nonstudents—or at least it suggests that they may be more willing to lower their aspirations and accept subminimum rate jobs.

One implication of tables 4 and 5 is that minimum wage studies that aggregate students and nonstudents are probably underestimating the size of the disemployment and labor force effects. Those studies may not count as displaced youths who are forced out of full-time jobs but who return to school and take part-time jobs. As a result, we find employment elasticities for nonstudents of approximately -1.0 for fourteen- to seventeen-year-olds and -0.3 for eighteen- to nineteen-year-olds. In contrast, Mincer's estimate was only -0.2 for white sixteen- to nineteen-year-olds when students and nonstudents were combined.[10] Of course, we are also underestimating the size of the displacement effect, as data do not allow us to estimate how many youths took jobs in the noncovered sector after being forced out of covered-sector employment.

The October survey data divide the enrolled into those in high school and those in college. This was not of much interest for fourteen- to seventeen-year-olds because so very few are in college. However, on

---

[10] Mincer, "Unemployment Effects," used quarterly data 1954–1968, controlled for other influences using a time trend, time squared, and the unemployment rate, and estimated an eight-quarter Almon distributed lag minimum wage effect.

average from 1947–1977, 30 percent of eighteen- to nineteen-year-old students were in high school, and 70 percent were enrolled at the college level. Regressions were run for eighteen- to nineteen-year-old high school students alone, and although the minimum wage elasticities were positive (0.14 for males and 0.17 for females), they were not statistically significant. The elasticities were much larger (0.42 for males and 0.53 for females) for college students of this age group and were statistically significant.

This strong impact on college enrollments may surprise many who view minimum wages as having adverse effects only on high school dropouts. We do not deny that these youths may be the most severely affected group; we simply point out that they are more likely to be forced into subminimum rate jobs in noncovered industries. We interpret our results as indicating that even some high school graduates lacking work experience and job training are priced out of jobs by a rising minimum wage. Because the law does not allow employees to cut the wage rate and thereby shift training costs onto the shoulders of the youths, these displaced youths may opt to pay for additional training themselves by going on to a junior or community college or a university. This impact appears to induce only an additional year or two of college training. When similar regressions were run for those aged twenty to twenty-four enrolled in college, the minimum wage elasticities were smaller and not statistically significant. Hence, we find little evidence that minimum wages have increased the number of bachelor's degrees appreciably.

Because our interest is primarily in the minimum wage variable, we will not reproduce in this paper the many pages of tables that contain our estimated coefficients for the control variables.[11] For the interested reader, however, we will briefly mention a few of our results. The important rate-of-return-to-high-school ($RORH$) variable was positively and significantly related to school enrollments for fourteen- to seventeen-year-olds as was the payoff of college ($RORC$) for males aged eighteen to nineteen. For eighteen- to nineteen-year-old females the $RORC$ coefficient was essentially zero. As discussed earlier, the $RORC$ variable did not turn down during the early 1970s for females as it did for males. Hence, it was hard to distinguish our female $RORC$ variable from some of our other trending control variables. Rising $INCOME$ increased high school level enrollments significantly among all groups (except females aged eighteen to nineteen) and reduced employment among the not-enrolled.

An increasing number of jobs in the service ($SERVICE$) industries

---

[11] These are reported in Mattila, "Impact of Minimum Wages."

and agriculture (*AGRI*) were associated with higher not-enrolled employment in each age-sex category. These variables were also positively related to enrolled employment (except for eighteen- to nineteen-year-old males) and negatively related to the not-in-the-labor-force enrolled. Adult unemployment (*U*) was positively associated with both enrolled and not-enrolled teenage unemployment and negatively related to not-enrolled employment.

More *KIDS* had a positive, although not significant, impact on the proportion of women aged eighteen to nineteen who were not in the labor force or enrolled. An increase in the proportion in the armed forces (*AF*) reduced school enrollment and not-enrolled employment among males in this age group.

Overall, our control variables usually had the expected signs and were frequently significant. As is true with many time series analyses, our model fit the data very well. Of the fifty-six regressions run (each corresponding to one entry in table 4), more than one-half had R^2s exceeding .90. These results give us considerable confidence in our minimum wage estimates.

Robustness of Empirical Estimates

We would feel even more confident in our conclusions if our estimates were not sensitive to the choice of data set or to changes in the specification of the control variables.

We have performed several sensitivity tests using the October survey data. In order to determine whether inclusion of the earlier years made a difference, we reestimated our regressions over the 1959–1977 period. Our results did not change much except for the labor force categories within the enrolled group. The 1947–1977 regressions indicated that minimum wages shift youths primarily into the enrolled labor force and only secondarily into the enrolled, not-in-the-labor-force status. The 1959–1977 regressions suggest just the opposite. The latter indicate that minimum wages have primarily increased enrolled, not-in-the-labor-force status, slightly increased enrolled unemployment, and reduced enrolled employment (including part-time employment).

This is an interesting change and suggests a possible explanation. Prior to 1961, the service, sales, and agricultural industries were not usually covered by the Fair Labor Standards Act (see table 1). During the 1940s and 1950s, any youths who were displaced from covered jobs and who turned to schooling would have had an easier time finding jobs in these service industries. However, the 1961 and 1967 amendments, which substantially extended coverage, may have raised barriers to student employment.[12] Whatever the explanation, we conclude that our results on the employment status of students are sensitive to the time period analyzed. We emphasize, however, that the positive impact of minimum wages on total enrollment still was observed over the shorter time period.

Our results are somewhat less stable when the time series is shortened to the 1963–1977 period. The impact of minimum wages on school enrollments falls to zero for males aged fourteen to seventeen but increases in magnitude for eighteen- to nineteen-year-olds. However, all school enrollment coefficients become statistically insignificant over the 1963–1977 period. Although the shrinking number of degrees of freedom may contribute to this, the loss of significance is more likely due to the elimination of the important 1961 amendments that extended coverage of the Fair Labor Standards Act to many retail trade jobs for the first time.

Another test was made in order to determine whether our results were sensitive to the 1967 changes in the definition of employment and unemployment.[13] We reran all of the regressions with the addition of a binary control variable that takes on the value 1 over the period 1967–1977. The magnitude of minimum wage impact on school enrollment and the other labor force categories was virtually unchanged, and, if anything, the size of the t-ratios increased.

One additional test was performed in order to determine whether our results are sensitive to the specification and construction of our set of control variables. Following Mincer, we reran the regressions using only a time trend, time squared, the unemployment rate, and the proportion in the armed forces (for males aged eighteen to nineteen) as control variables. Although our results differed slightly in magnitude and significance from those in table 4, the basic conclusions were not altered.[14]

There are not very many other bodies of time series data with which we may test the hypotheses raised in this paper. Edward Gramlich uses data from 1963 to 1975 that are *not* disaggregated by enrollment status but that are available by hours of work. Like us, he finds evidence that the minimum wage law seems to have shifted teenagers out of full-time

---

[12] Finis Welch reports evidence that minimum wages shifted youths out of manufacturing into service industries after the Fair Labor Standards Act was passed in 1938 and discussess trends since then. Finis Welch, *Minimum Wages: Issues and Evidence* (Washington, D.C.: American Enterprise Institute, 1978), pp. 29–31.

[13] This and the preceding paragraph were inserted in response to suggestions made by Sherwin Rosen (see his Commentary, herein).

[14] See J. Peter Mattila, "Youth Labor Markets, Enrollments, and Minimum Wages," *Proceedings of the Thirty-first Annual Meeting of the Industrial Relations Research Association, August 29–31, 1978* (1979), pp. 134–40.

jobs into part-time jobs.[15] James F. Ragan, Jr., analyzes the quarterly "major activity" data, 1963–1978, that divide teenagers into those having "major activity, school" and those having "major activity, other."[16] Unfortunately, an increasing proportion of part-time students are not classified as being in school in this data set so that it is of limited use to us (see note 4 to this chapter). However, the less pronounced impact of minimum wages on major-activity schooling found by Ragan suggests that any induced students still continue to be heavily involved in labor-market and other activities. Many of these induced students may be part-time and night students.

Recently some cross-section empirical analysis has been undertaken by Ronald Ehrenberg and Alan Marcus and by James Cunningham.[17] Cross-section work relies on interstate variation in wage levels at a point in time, relative to a uniform national minimum wage rate. Using 1970 *Census of Population* data, Ehrenberg and Marcus generally find evidence that high relative minimum wages increase school enrollments, although generally not significantly. Their results using 1966 National Longitudinal Survey data are somewhat contradictory. Cunningham attempts to use 1960 *Census of Population* data by state to predict what school enrollments would have been in 1970 had minimum wages not increased. He concludes that rising minimums depressed school attendance

We are surprised by both the differing results among these cross-section studies and their seeming inconsistency with our time series findings. It is hoped that future research will be able to explain these differences. For now, we would suggest that it is difficult to control in the cross-section for interstate variation in the other determinants of school enrollment, such as the payoff and opportunity costs of schooling. As Mincer has pointed out, it is more difficult to control for variation in state and local minimum wage laws, for the extent of legal compliance, and for variation in the extent of legal exemptions issued by the Department of Labor.[18] Until economists have successfully dealt with these

---

[15] Edward M. Gramlich, "Impact of Minimum Wages on Other Wages, Employment, and Family Incomes," *Brookings Papers on Economic Activity* 2 (1976): 409–51.

[16] James F. Ragan, Jr., "Minimum Wages and the Youth Labor Market," *Review of Economics and Statistics* 59 (May 1977): 129–36; and idem, "The Effect of a Legal Minimum Wage on the Pay and Employment of Teenage Students and Nonstudents," herein.

[17] Ronald G. Ehrenberg and Alan Marcus, "Minimum Wage Legislation and the Educational Decisions of Youths: Perpetuation of Income Inequality across Generations?" draft of paper dated February 1979; James Cunningham, "The Impact of Minimum Wages on Youth Employment, Hours of Work, and School Attendance: Cross-sectional Evidence from the 1960 and 1970 Censuses," herein.

[18] Jacob Mincer, "Effects of Minimum Wages on Employment, Unemployment, and Skill Formation of Youths," draft of paper dated September 1978.

problems, we feel that time series data will be our most reliable base for empirical analysis.

Conclusions and Implications

We have argued that although teenagers are displaced by minimum wages it is not likely that many would passively accept unemployed job search while waiting for jobs to open. Rather, we have argued that there are incentives for teenagers to continue their education. And we feel that we have presented reasonably strong time series evidence that school enrollments have increased during the past three decades whenever minimum wage rates and coverage increased. It remains to be seen whether cross-section evidence will also support this hypothesis.

Our analysis also indicates that minimum wages raise teenage unemployment primarily through raising school enrollments. Students have always had higher unemployment rates because of the constraints placed on their time and location. By increasing school enrollments, minimum wages have indirectly increased teenage unemployment.

The results indicate that minimum wages have shifted youths away from full-time work as they continue their education. It is less certain whether this increased schooling takes the form of full-time schooling or joint schooling and part-time work. Further research will be necessary in order to clarify this.

We conclude that minimum wage effects extend well beyond the narrow issue of unemployment, which was the focus of research in the 1960s. By inducing more average and marginal students to continue their education, minimum wage laws may have raised the average class size and lowered the quality of the median student. We might speculate that the law has contributed to the rapid growth in community college enrollments during the last two decades and may have contributed to the widely discussed drop in the median score on the college entrance examinations.

Policies aimed at reducing whatever unemployment was caused by the minimum wage law should recognize that most of this unemployment occurs among students. These policies should recognize that students have time and location constraints that limit their flexibility. Although such "natural" unemployment may be very difficult to reduce, expansion of the number of part-time jobs available to youth might help. One obvious way of achieving this would be to maintain or expand the number of sales, service, and agricultural jobs that are exempt from the Fair Labor Standards Act. A lower minimum wage rate for teenagers would also help.

These comments apply to the school year, as our data relate to the month of October. We have not considered explicitly the problem of youth unemployment in the summer. We expect that few would go to school in the summer as a consequence of the employment barriers created by minimum wages.

In the absence of the law, more youths would have held full-time jobs and been involved in on-the-job training programs.[19] Schooling is undertaken in a second-best attempt to compensate for this shortfall in job training. Although perhaps a more productive strategy than un-employed search, education is likely to be less productive than training for such individuals. In this sense, minimum wages may not only lower income while the displaced youth is a teenager but may also lower income throughout the individual's lifetime.

Appendix

The dependent variables on school enrollment and employment status are from the "Employment of School Age Youths" of the U.S. Department of Commerce, Bureau of the Census, *Current Population Reports: Labor Force*, ser. P–50, 1947–1959; and from U.S. Department of Labor, Bureau of Labor Statistics, *Special Labor Force Reports*, 1959–1978. All proportions are computed relative to the total population, including youths in the armed forces. Armed forces data are from data supplied by the Bureau of Labor Statistics and as estimated from data published in Bureau of the Census, *Current Population Reports: Population Estimates and Projections*, series P–25.

Real disposable mean family income (*INCOME*) was based upon Bureau of the Census, *Current Population Reports: Consumer Income*, ser. P–60, 1947–1978. From this annual estimate of mean total money income, federal taxes (after deductions for the personal exemption and the standard deduction) were estimated for an assumed four-person family. Tax rates and other tax rules were taken from Joseph Pechman, *Federal Tax Policy* (Washington, D.C.: Brookings Institution, 1977). An average state and local income tax rate was estimated by dividing total state and local income tax revenues from Bureau of the Census, *Governmental Finances*, by the number of families in the United States. Estimates of federal, state, and local income taxes and social security taxes were deducted from mean family income. Disposable income was then adjusted to constant dollars by use of the consumer price index.

The *SERVICE* and *AGRI* variables are computed from data on

[19] Several of our comments in this paragraph were stimulated by Mincer, "Effects of Minimum Wages"; also see Linda Leighton and Jacob Mincer, "Effects of Minimum Wages on Human Capital Formation," herein.

employment by occupation published by the Bureau of the Census, *Current Population Reports: Monthly Report on the Labor Force*, ser. P–57, 1947–1959, and the Bureau of Labor Statistics, *Employment and Earnings and Monthly Report on the Labor Force*, 1959–1970. *SERVICE* is the proportion of all persons aged fourteen and over employed in the service or sales occupations. For regression involving females over age eighteen, *SERVICE* is defined to be the proportion of all persons fourteen and over employed in clerical, service, or sales occupations. We defined the variable *AGRI* to be the proportion of all persons fourteen and over employed as farm laborers or foremen. In the case of both the *SERVICE* and the *AGRI* variables, it was our hope that they would be sufficiently exogenous so as not to compete with the minimum wage variable; that is, when coverage of the minimum wage law was extended to cover some agricultural workers in the 1960s, we would expect that our measure of *AGRI* would decline somewhat at the same time that our minimum wage variable increased. Presumably each would compete with the other to explain any related decline in youth employment. In this sense, our estimate of the impact of minimum wages may be somewhat smaller than it would be. Similar comments apply with respect to the *SERVICE* variable. Both variables were computed for the month of October.

The variable *KIDS* is defined as the ratio of women ever married with children ever born to the population of all women by age bracket. By excluding women having children out of wedlock who never married and by including a few women who gave birth but whose only child died thereafter, this measure will be somewhat biased at a point in time. The important question is whether or not there is any important bias in the fundamental underlying trends in this measure over time. Unfortunately, there is little reliable information on trends in birth out of wedlock. *KIDS* is constructed by multiplying two series together. The first is the number of ever-married women with children ever born divided by ever-married women. This is available for selected years from the "fertility studies" of the Bureau of the Census, *Current Population Reports: Population Characteristics*, ser. P–20, for women aged fifteen to nineteen. Missing years were estimated by interpolation. This variable from the fertility studies was multiplied by the ratio of women ever married to all women. The latter ratio is available annually, 1947–1977, from the Marital Status Studies of the same *Population Characteristics* series for women eighteen to nineteen.

Our cyclical variable *U* is calculated for the fourth quarter of each year as the ratio of the number of males aged thirty-five to fifty-four who were unemployed to the number of males aged thirty-five to fifty-four in the labor force. Seasonally unadjusted data were supplied by the Bureau of Labor Statistics. The minimum wage variable (MW) was defined in note 5 to this chapter.

Discussion of the estimated rates of return to schooling have been postponed until now because they were the most complicated to construct, requiring a considerable number of man-hours. Although far from ideal, we feel that the resulting series adequately reflects the major trends in the payoff from school and is broadly consistent with the human-capital literature. In particular, our series on the payoff from college follows a pattern similar to that constructed by John Bishop, using a different data set, as presented in "The Impact of Public Policy on the College Attendance of Women," paper presented to the American Economic Association, New York, December 28, 1977.

Our estimates rely heavily upon annual income data by age, sex, and educational attainment as published in Bureau of the Census, *Current Population Reports: Consumer Income*, ser. P–60, 1947–1978. The benefits of going to college were estimated in a particular age bracket (*a*) as the difference between the mean (median) annual income of those having one or more years of college (I_a^C) and the mean (median) annual income of those who completed their education after four years of high school (I_a^{HS}). Such data are available from 1956 (or 1958) to 1977 for males and from 1963 to 1977 for females. For any given age bracket, this differential was divided by the consumer price index (P), and the resulting ratio was smoothed by regressing it on time (T), time squared (T^2), time cubed (T^3), and the adult male unemployment rate (U). This was done to eliminate cyclical variation and random noise in the series, as we wanted a series that picked up only changes in the long-run payoff from school. A smoothed time series, $B_a^{C-HS} = I_a^C - I_a^{HS}/P$, was constructed for each age bracket for which data are published (a = 25–34; 35–44; 45–54; 55–64; 65 +).

The costs of schooling were divided into the opportunity costs of forgone earnings and the tuition costs (of college). Opportunity costs of those in college were estimated from the median annual income of persons aged twenty to twenty-four who worked year-round, full-time, during the year. Such data are available from the Consumer Income Series annually from 1955 to 1977 for men and for women. As above, each series was adjusted by the consumer price index and smoothed, yielding a series I_{20-24}. The annual cost of college tuition and fees net of student aid per full-time equivalent student (Tu) is taken from estimates made by June A. O'Neill, *Sources of Funds to Colleges and Universities* (Berkeley, Calif.: Carnegie Commission on Higher Education, 1973) and U.S. Center for Education Statistics, *Financial Statistics of Institutions of Higher Education* (Washington, D.C., 1968–1977), annual issues. It was assumed that because of summer and part-time

85

work a student would incur only 75 percent of the opportunity cost each year, and it was assumed that the typical student would attend college 3.5 years, as some drop out before finishing. The expected cost of a college investment is then $C = 3.5(0.75 I_{20-24} + Tu)$.

For any given year, the internal rate of return of college (i) was computed by solving the following equation for i:

$$C = \frac{10B_{25-34}^{C-HS}}{(1 + i)^7} + \frac{10B_{35-44}^{C-HS}}{(1 + i)^{17}} + \frac{10B_{45-54}^{C-HS}}{(1 + i)^{27}} + \frac{10B_{55-64}^{C-HS}}{(1 + i)^{37}} + \frac{7B_{65+}^{C-HS}}{(1 + i)^{46}} \quad (2)$$

Because of the lack of more detailed data, this implicitly assumes that the mean real income differential for those in the twenty-five-to-thirty-four age bracket existed for each of the ten years in that bracket (and so on for the other age brackets) and that all of that benefit was received midway through each respective age bracket (that is, at ages twenty-nine, thirty-nine, forty-nine, fifty-nine, and sixty-eight). In spite of these various data limitations, our results seem to be broadly consistent with those estimated using better data and more sophisticated methodology. For instance, in 1959 we estimate the rate of return from one or more years of college for males to be 9.1 percent, which is not dissimilar to Giora Hanoch's estimates of 7.1 percent (9.3 percent) for one-to-three years of college and 9.6 percent (10.1 percent) for four years of college for northern (southern) whites. Of course, our interest is not in the actual level of the rate at a point in time but rather in how it varies over time.

The internal rate of return was computed using equation (2) for each year for which data were available. For males, this provided a time series 1958–1977. For years prior to this, our estimates are less reliable. In order to have a consistent series since the late 1940s, we relied heavily upon comparisons between the 1950 and 1960 *Census of Population* data and comparisons between 1946, 1956, and 1958 Consumer Income Survey data. By computing the internal rate of return from college for each of these years, we were able to fix estimated levels in 1946 and 1949 in comparison to the years 1958 and 1959 from our previously estimated series. By interpolating and with some additional information from a comparison of median earnings of professional workers (having a median four years of college) versus clerical and sales workers (having a median four years of high school), we extended the rate of return series back to 1947.

For females, the difficulties were greater as we had a longer period (1947–1963) to estimate back and virtually no information from the 1946 Consumer Income Survey of the 1950 *Census of Population*. As a consequence, we extrapolated by relying heavily on relative changes in the difference between median annual female professional income (median four years of college) and median annual female clerical and salesworker income (median four years of high school).

Time series for men and for women were also constructed to reflect trends in the rate of return to finishing high school (*RORH*). The methodology used is identical to that described above except that the benefits were computed as the difference between mean (median) annual incomes of those completing four years of high school and those completing only one to three years of high school. The costs were estimated using median income of persons aged fourteen to nineteen by sex who worked year-round, full-time. No tuition was included. Extrapolation of the series back to 1947 was based in part on trends in the relative differences between median earnings of clerical and sales workers (median four years of high school) and laborers (median eight to nine years of grade school).

The Impact of Minimum Wages on Youth Employment, Hours of Work, and School Attendance: Cross-sectional Evidence from the 1960 and 1970 Censuses

James Cunningham

This paper investigates the effect of a legislated minimum wage upon the employment and schooling decisions of young people. Previous studies in this area have indicated consistently that the employment of young, unskilled workers falls in response to a minimum wage. It has never been demonstrated, however, that reduced overall employment is, in fact, the result of worker displacement among firms that are covered by minimum wage laws. The present study verifies this relationship. As part of the employment/schooling problem, changes between full-time and part-time employment and nonemployment are also measured.

The decomposition of employment into "covered" and "uncovered" components reveals some interesting relationships not readily apparent at the aggregate level. In particular, supply responses seem now to be more involved than was previously perceived. Evidence is presented that suggests that among some groups of teenagers a minimum wage drives out less productive workers but induces more productive workers to enter jobs covered by minimum wage laws. In explaining such processes an important distinction is made between full-time and part-time employment. Wages among part-time jobs are lower than among full-time jobs. It is further argued that the same is generally true for an *individual's* wage opportunities in the two job categories. The existence of such wage differentials has two major ramifications. First,

NOTE: This project initially began as a joint undertaking with Finis Welch. Though his name is not included as an author, his input was significant, and the end product is better as a result. He, of course, shares no blame for errors. The author also benefited from discussions with Lou Stern, Jeff Moore, and John Raisian of the University of Houston. Tom Means, Huey-Juan Hsieh, and Dean Gold provided excellent research assistance along the way. Partial funding was received through grants from the Rockefeller Foundation, the Foundation for Research in Economics and Education (Los Angeles), and the Office of Research Development, University of Houston.

a minimum wage will have a greater impact upon part-time employment, and second, school decisions, as they depend upon employment opportunities, will be influenced by changing full-time/part-time wage differentials resulting from the minimum wage. In support of this hypothesis, consider table 1. Panel A gives the proportion of sixteen- to twenty-four-year-old workers who worked (part-time) less than thirty-five hours per week in 1970. The industries are ranked in descending order of the proportion of all workers covered by federal minimum wage laws in 1970. Ninety-nine percent of all workers in manufacturing and mining were covered, for example, whereas coverage was lowest for agriculture (approximately 40 percent). Proportions are computed separately by school status and sex. The most striking feature is that industries with high coverage employ a smaller fraction of part-time, young workers. It is interesting that this pattern is less convincing for males out of school. Note also the decline in part-time workers among nonstudent workers.

Panel A suggests the relative substitution of full-time for part-time youth in covered industries. Panel B indicates the overall displacement of youth from covered jobs because of low average productivity or unwillingness to accept full-time positions. Each number is an index. It measures the proportion of all part-time workers in the particular industry as compared with the fraction of adult part-time workers in the industry. This index is based on the notion that youth and adult part-time employment would be distributed in approximately the same way in the absence of minimum wage effects. These data reveal clearly the anticipated shift in part-time youth employment from covered to uncovered establishments. The difference is somewhat stronger for students than for nonstudents. Our findings indirectly verify these relationships to be minimum wage effects.

In the section "Theoretical Considerations," a very brief review of certain theoretical aspects is made to provide a framework within which to interpret empirical results. The emphasis is not on completeness but on establishing a set of priors. The section "Empirical Results" develops an empirical approach designed to measure minimum wage effects on employment and schooling decisions. Estimates are discussed for both black and white cohorts. Because of relatively limited data for blacks, however, the estimates for these groups do not appear to be especially robust. Thus, discussion is confined primarily to the results for whites.

Theoretical Considerations

The purpose of anticipating minimum wage effects on a priori grounds is to permit more intelligent evaluation and interpretation of empirical findings. A full theoretical treatment is not within the scope of this

TABLE 1
PROPORTION OF WORKERS AGE 16–24 EMPLOYED PART TIME BY INDUSTRY IN 1970

	Above-Average Coverage				Below-Average Coverage		
	Manufacturing and mining	Construction	Transportation and communication	Finance	Services	Wholesale and retail trade	Agriculture
Panel A: Unweighted							
Male							
In school	.508	.607	.535	.504	.778	.806	.784
Out of school	.102	.177	.097	.079	.150	.116	.209
Female							
In school	.550	.657	.523	.535	.797	.873	.829
Out of school	.153	.192	.136	.104	.234	.282	.361
Panel B: Weighted							
Male							
In school	49	61	44	62	158	192	174
Out of school	65	121	52	56	128	107	221
Female							
In school	59	305	77	55	94	115	223
Out of school	72	397	85	44	100	140	421

SOURCE: Author.

paper, however. Instead, a brief sketch is presented of a theoretical framework that should draw out key possibilities and establish some priors.

An individual will not be hired if the wage that must be paid exceeds the worth of the worker to the employer. Worth, or the value of a worker's product, is influenced, in turn, by skill level and by the *relative* employment of workers of similar makeup as compared with other "types" of labor performing other functions. The value of each worker in a particular job/skill class can therefore be increased, other things equal, by laying off some of the workers. To illustrate, an employer who is suddenly confronted with having to pay a minimum wage of $3.00 to employees currently earning $2.50 will be inclined to lay off some of these workers until the contribution of each remaining worker has risen to the $3.00 level imposed by the wage floor. At the same time, an effort will be made to replace the less productive employees with individuals who can perform similar tasks but who possess superior skills. Thus, a substitution process takes place as employers attempt to substitute toward higher-quality labor. In addition, however, costs of production are very likely to be increased, despite the substitution. Higher costs lead to reduced output and lower demand for all labor groups, including the highly skilled. The net change in demand for workers who originally earn a wage above the minimum is indeterminant. In practice, though, one suspects that output effects are comparatively small in view of the limited number of low-productivity workers that would actually be hired by most firms in the absence of a wage floor.

The schooling decision is influenced by the relative earnings expected from continuing one's education as opposed to terminating it. A decision must also be made whether to work while in school, and this will be based upon the wage expected from working as a student versus the reward from hastening the completion of one's education.[1] A minimum wage can potentially alter the structure of wages over these various activities and, hence, the return to schooling and the incentive to work while in school.

A minimum wage law applies to employers who deal directly in interstate trade, produce a good or service essential to interstate trade, or do a given minimum (dollar) volume of business each year. Thus, within a given industry there are covered and uncovered establishments. Aggregated over industries, these groups are referred to as the covered and uncovered sectors. Recognition of the distinction between these two types of employers adds a new dimension and greater complexity

---

[1] Wages determine the returns to current employment and investment activity. Interacting with both of these is the value placed upon leisure time.

to the problem. As before, covered employers attempt to escape the minimum wage by using more capable workers in place of inexperienced or otherwise less productive labor. Low-productivity workers are thus displaced from covered jobs. They may choose to work in the uncovered sector, leave the labor force, or become unemployed as they queue for a covered job at the minimum wage. The latter option presupposes some turnover in these positions. On the other hand, highly productive workers tend to be attracted to covered establishments and away from uncovered establishments or nonemployment activities (for example, school).

Other things equal and in the absence of a minimum wage, workers belonging to a particular skill class should receive the same wage from any employer willing to hire at least one of its members. A minimum wage obviously increases the wage of anyone who is able to retain a covered job and who previously earned below the minimum. If there are enough high-quality substitutes available to replace all subminimum workers, then it is possible that no further wage effects would occur. The wage paid to low-skilled workers in uncovered jobs would be unchanged. Only high-productivity workers would be observed in covered jobs. In practice this does not happen. First, skilled workers are not scale replicas of low-skilled workers. Differences in skill mix make them imperfect substitutes. Second, the covered sector is very large and would demand too much uncovered skilled labor to avoid wage adjustment. As a result, the wage of skilled labor is expected to be bid up and the wage of unskilled labor to fall as displaced workers try to gain employment in uncovered jobs. This is what we expect intuitively, but there is another story. Low-skilled wages can rise if the return to waiting (that is, as an unemployed worker) for scarce covered jobs is high enough to attract workers away from uncovered jobs.

Some individuals will probably wait for covered jobs, so we expect unemployment to rise in any case. Labor force participation of each skill group will move directly with the change in opportunity wage. Thus, if low-productivity labor is paid a lower wage, some individuals will drop out and undertake other activities, such as schooling.[2]

With regard to schooling, the effect of a minimum wage is strictly ambiguous. Because education and skill are associated positively, an increase in wages would raise the return to human investment. If wages paid to low-skilled labor also rise, then an offsetting force is introduced. Otherwise, and in general, one expects people in low-skilled groups to acquire more schooling and other forms of training.[3]

---

[2] An equilibrium is that wages paid in the uncovered sector must be equal to the *expected* wage from pursuing covered employment. If one is lowered, then so is the other.

[3] The theoretical possibilities are numerous. Only the more likely events have been mentioned here. A formal treatment of the issues is available from the author upon request.

Unfortunately, the world is somewhat more complicated than the above discussion suggests. When a person chooses to attend school, concurrent employment is typically limited to part-time jobs. Upon completion of school many, especially males, take full-time jobs. An important distinction must be made between full- and part-time employment of a particular individual. A person's part-time wage offer will very often be below his full-time offer. Moreover, part-time workers generally earn less per hour than do full-time workers.[4] These observations have two important implications. Displacement of part-time employees from covered firms is likely to be greater than that of full-timers within a specific skill class. In addition, if the minimum wage exceeds the ex ante part-time wage level but falls at or below the full-time wage, a large shift in demand can be expected from part-time to full-time labor. In general, the full-time wage will be bid up relative to the part-time wage.[5] What this means is that the cost of remaining in school and not working full time rises. It is most likely that the cost of not working while attending school will fall with a minimum wage hike, provided the part-time wage also falls. Fewer employed students should be observed unless the student population increases overall, in which case the response is ambiguous. If the full-time wage is increased, we would predict that students would leave school, contrary to the expectations derived from the simpler model above.

The introduction of a full-time/part-time wage differential appears to increase the possibility that a minimum wage will discourage schooling and, through supply effects, suggests a way by which a skill class that appears less productive based on wage data can actually increase employment in covered establishments.

The discussion so far has been in terms of a particular skill class. People do not identify themselves by skill class, however. Instead, individuals are grouped by demographic characteristics, and one is left to

---

[4] Donald Parsons, "The Cost of School Time, Forgone Earnings, and Human Capital Formation," *Journal of Political Economy* 82 (March 1974):251–66, for example, found that young males out of school earn 25–35 percent more per hour than their counterparts in school. Theoretically, such a difference could be expected based upon the effect of fixed periodic costs associated with each worker. The hourly wage reflects these costs. The shorter the work period the greater the (hourly) deduction required to meet these costs. Similarly, it can be argued that a worker's productivity, that is, efficiency and effort, rises over the initial hours of work in each period of employment. Both factors suggest employers will pay lower part-time wages for the same work.

[5] A case to the contrary can be made, however. Suppose you own a business that experiences large demand increases periodically during the day. Sales are slack much of the day. (Restaurants operate in this fashion.) Now a minimum wage requires that many of your workers be paid more. The business is more expensive to run, and to economize you shut down part or all of the operation during slack periods. The demand for part-time workers has risen, and you may have to pay higher wages to part-timers to maintain a desired work force. Although this case is certainly plausible, it is felt that the situation described in the text is more common and dominates the data.

infer the average productivity and skill composition of each "cohort." Within any group are likely to be individuals with both superior and inferior skills vis-à-vis the minimum wage floor. Obviously, cohorts whose members are on average more experienced and have greater schooling tend to have more individuals at the upper productivity levels and *proportionately* fewer (though not necessarily in absolute terms) at the lower levels. Thus, an older cohort would be more productive than a younger cohort of the same race and sex.

Recognition of the fact that cohorts do not contain a homogeneous group of people with respect to skills and market productivity raises interesting possibilities concerning the availability of "superior" individuals to assume positions in covered firms and hence the relative change in cohort employment in such jobs. This issue receives considerable attention later in this chapter.

In summary, young cohorts are expected to experience net displacement from covered jobs. Some of these individuals will turn up in the uncovered sector as others drop out of the labor force or wait for a covered job. The response of school attendance is ambiguous. Part-time employment should generally fall relative to full-time employment.

Empirical Results

Methodology. The objective of our empirical work is to measure the net or reduced form effects of a minimum wage upon the distribution of employment (and nonemployment) across schooling choices (that is, "in" or "out") and, separately, across full-time/part-time categories. An attempt is made also to identify relative employment changes between jobs covered by minimum wage law and those not covered. Unlike most studies, the present effort follows Finis Welch and James Cunningham (and, recently, Ronald Ehrenberg and Alan Marcus) in using a cross-sectional model in which the unit of observation is the state.[6] The main advantage of this approach is that it avoids the problem of collinearity among explanatory variables and permits access to several rich sources of data not maintained on an annual basis. Variation in the real minimum wage is quite large due to substantial differences in hourly wages across

---

[6] Finis Welch and James Cunningham, "The Effects of Minimum Wages on the Level and Age Composition of Youth Employment," *Review of Economics and Statistics* 60 (February 1978): 140–45; Ronald G. Ehrenberg and Alan Marcus, "Minimum Wage Legislation and the Educational Decisions of Youths: Perpetuation of Income Inequality across Generations?" manuscript, February 1979.

states and the inclusion of measures of state minimum wages and coverage rates. Also avoided to a large extent is the question of how markets adjust to a change in the wage floor and the problem of disentangling long-term from short-term effects. In particular, cross-section estimates reflect long-run adjustments, thus obviating consideration of appropriate lag structure.

A problem with cross-section models, however, is the means of controlling for ex ante patterns of employment and schooling choices. Previous studies have implicitly assumed either that structural differences across regions are uncorrelated with the minimum wage (or any other variable of interest) or that such differences would not exist in the absence of a wage floor. It seems quite obvious that significant and permanent structural differences do exist across states and that these cannot be attributed solely to real minimum wage effects. Some of the explanatory variables included in previous research no doubt capture part of the structural variation, but one must suspect that part remains at large. The crucial question is whether structural differences are related systematically to measures of the real minimum wage. Plausible arguments can be made that suggest such a relationship may well exist. Consider the following case.

The impact of a particular nominal level of the minimum wage is determined by the distribution of productivity evaluated in nominal terms. A natural measure of the real, or effective, minimum wage is the ratio of these two quantities. Productivity is typically measured by an average hourly wage rate that is presumably free of minimum wage effects. Nominal wages reflect both the price level and the real productivity of labor in a particular state, however. Low wages may thus indicate higher relative demand for unskilled labor. Such a state could also be expected to experience a relatively high dropout rate from school in the absence of a wage floor and probably higher labor force participation and employment rates of teenagers; yet this state would be subject to a high *real* minimum wage upon the introduction of a uniform wage floor for all states. If the true minimum wage impact were, in fact, nil, *measured* effects would indicate that a high minimum causes greater employment and dropout rates among young cohorts. To avoid the biases suggested by this example, explicit efforts have been made to control for structural differences between regions.

In general terms, our approach is to compare the schooling and employment choices of a cohort in each state at two points in time and then to isolate that part of the overall change attributable to change in the minimum wage during the interim. The results of a person's decisions can be characterized by one of ten "outcomes" derived from the following cross-partition, J, of the separate choice categories:

$$J = \begin{bmatrix} \text{out of school} \\ \text{in school} \end{bmatrix} \times \begin{bmatrix} \text{employed full time} \\ \text{employed part time} \\ \text{------------} \\ \text{not employed} \end{bmatrix}$$

$$\times \begin{bmatrix} \text{covered employment} \\ \text{uncovered employment} \end{bmatrix}$$

A person may be in school and working full time in a covered establishment, for example. The two combinations involving nonemployment and choice of either covered or uncovered sector employment are undefined. The term "choice" is used loosely here because of the market restrictions imposed by the minimum wage laws. A person who chooses to work in a covered establishment may have to wait as one of the unemployed ("not employed"), for example, until a position opens up.

The objective is to determine how changes in the minimum wage affect the probability of observing someone in each of the various categories. To do this, an explicit functional form must be chosen that parametrically links the minimum wage, and other variables, to these outcome probabilities. A reasonable choice is the widely used conditional polytomous logit function, which in the present context may be written in logarithmic form as:

$$\ln(P_{il}) = \gamma \ln(P_{il}^{*}) + \alpha_i W_l + \beta_i' X_l + D$$

for the ith outcome and region l. D is the logarithm of the normalizing factor:

$$D = \ln[\sum_{j \epsilon J} \exp(\gamma \ln(P_{jl}^{*}) + \alpha_j W_l + \beta_j' X)]$$

P_{il} is the probability of outcome i at a point in time. P_{il}^{*} is an estimate of the probability of outcome i prior to a change in the minimum wage. The variable W_l measures the minimum wage change, and X_l is a vector of variables (plus a constant) that control for other factors not captured by P^{*} or W that may affect change in the probabilities. The parameters of this system, γ, α_i, β_i, are estimated using the maximum likelihood technique.[7]

---

[7] The interested reader is referred to James Cunningham, "The Impact of Minimum Wages on Youth Employment, Hours of Work, and School Attendance: Cross-sectional Evidence from the 1960 and 1970 Censuses," mimeographed, October 1979, for a detailed discussion of the estimation technique. See Henri Theil, "A Multinational Extension of the Linear Logic Model," *International Economic Review* 10 (October 1969): 251–59, for a full exposition of the polytomous function.

Data and Implementation of the Model. The basic sources of data on employment, enrollment, and wages are the large 1960 and 1970 1/100 censuses of population; 1960 data is used to provide preliminary estimates of employment and schooling patterns as they *would have appeared* in 1970 had not minimum wages changed during the decade (that is, P_i^*'s). These estimates are adjusted for national trends (1960–1970) in school attendance, labor force participation, and industry-specific employment for each of the eight cohorts. These results, in turn, are adjusted for state-specific changes in the industrial distribution of employment: Changes in the proportional employment of adults (twenty-five to fifty-four years old) between 1960 and 1970 are applied to the employment figures of each age group (by race and sex) so as to maintain the employment of that cohort relative to its adult counterpart at the (nationally revised) 1960 levels. With the exception of national trends, it is therefore assumed that young and adult workers will be found in fixed proportions within a region over time. Thus, relative wages are implicitly assumed to be constant in the absence of minimum wage changes.

The adjusted 1960 data and unadjusted 1970 data are thus partitioned according to the scheme (J) above. Because it is not known whether a specific employee is covered, we must determine the probability that a worker, in general, will be found in a covered firm in a particular industry; that is, the federal and state "coverage rates" must be calculated for each industry. Department of Labor estimates of 1970 federal coverage rates are used. These are national averages but are assumed to apply to each state and for each cohort.[8] State coverage rates are computed for each industry and by sex and age where differences occur—based upon each state law as of 1970.[9] Account is also taken when a state law exempts students, part-time workers, or employees of specific occupations.

Computing covered employment is basically a matter of weighting industry employment by the sum of the federal coverage rate and the outcome/cohort-specific state coverage rate and then summing over industries. Uncovered employment is simply the balance. Thus, when 1970 coverage rates are applied to adjusted 1960 data the result is an estimate of what employment would have been, ex ante, in 1970. Calculating proportions based upon the above partition and the 1960 data yields the P_i^*'s. The left-hand side Ps are similarly derived from the 1970 census data.

---

[8] U.S. Department of Labor, Employment Standards Administration, Division of Evaluation and Research, unpublished table dated March 7, 1977.
[9] See Welch and Cunningham, "Effects of Minimum Wages," for additional information on this procedure.

Differences between each P_i and P_i^* may arise in response to changes in the effective minimum wage between 1960 and 1970. People are reshuffled among industries, employment rate, and school status. The pressure exerted by a minimum wage law upon employment in a particular industry is not only a function of the nominal minimum wage as compared with the average productivity level but also of the extent of coverage.[10] The effective minimum wage in a given year uses a measure of overall coverage interacted with the simple "real" minimum wage. As both federal and state laws are taken into account, a sum is formed of the respective interactions. For present purposes, an appropriate minimum wage variable is an index of the proportionate *change* in the effective minimum wage that occurred during the 1960s. Thus,

$$MW = \left[\frac{C_{70}^f W_{70}^f + C_{70}^s W_{70}^s}{W_{70}^h} \right] \div \left[\frac{C_{60}^f W_{60}^f + C_{60}^s W_{60}^s}{W_{60}^h} \right]$$

where:

C_t^s = proportion of the employed covered by state law in year t,

W_t^s = average state minimum wage applicable to cohort in year t,

C_t^f, W_t^f = same for federal coverage,[11]

W^h = average hourly earnings of adult white males (twenty-five to fifty-four) in manufacturing.[12]

Six control variables are introduced in addition to MW. These include proportionate decimal changes in: proportion of work force unionized ($UNION$), unemployment rate of white adult males ($UNEMP$), proportion living in central city by race ($CITY$), median years of schooling of adults aged twenty-five and over by race and sex ($MEDYRS$), and median family income by race ($FAMINC$). Also included is a measure of schooling quality change (Q).

The intent and interpretation of these variables is fairly straightforward. A word of explanation may be in order with respect to Q,

[10] More correctly, the wage floor must be applied to the distribution of productivity, not just its mean. Relative mean productivities are here assumed to adequately characterize the relative position and shape of this distribution as it changes over time.

[11] In 1970 there were two federal wage levels: $1.60, applicable to previously covered employment, and $1.45 on newly covered employment. W_{70}^f is computed as a weighted average of the two over industries where the weights are relative coverage rates—old to new. The state minimum wage is similarly computed when the applicable wage varies from industry to industry. The weight is an industry coverage rate times the proportion of adult employment in the industry. The weights are normalized to sum to one.

[12] The average wage was computed from census annual earnings data. Annual earnings are divided by weeks × 40. Weekly hours are available only for the survey week and so are subject to large sampling variance. Although it is assumed that a forty-hour week errs in the other direction, the error is probably quite small with respect to white adult males. The manufacturing wage was selected to limit composition effects across states.

however. The question of how to measure the demand for low-skilled workers (cross-sectionally in particular) has received little serious consideration in the literature. Some measure of average hourly wages is typically used. This study does not attempt to fill this gap but does recognize that the relative productivity of new labor market entrants, our subjects here, and the experienced work force is a function not only of average education levels but also of the relative quality of education provided to or acquired by the two groups. As a crude measure of this difference, a ratio is computed of current (for example, in 1960) per student capita expenditures in public schools to the average expenditure level during the preceding thirty years as measured at the decenniums (for example, 1950, 1940, 1930). The difference of ratios based upon 1970 and 1960 was used in estimation:

$$Q_{60}^{70} = \frac{\exp_{70}}{\overline{\exp}_{40-50}} - \frac{\exp_{60}}{\overline{\exp}_{30-50}}$$

Using the difference form, as opposed to a proportionate change, limits the effect of nominal expenditure changes to biasing the constant—provided each region has experienced similar patterns of price fluctuation. Means and standard deviations for all variables are reported in appendix A.

The results are reported in the "Estimates" section. By race, schooling estimates are discussed first, followed by the full-time/part-time results.

Estimates. For each cohort two sets of estimates are made. The first allows us to study changes in school attendance and employment decisions, but the full-time/part-time choice is subsumed. The following six-way classification is derived from the partition, J, above:

$$J_s = \begin{bmatrix} \text{out of school} \\ \text{in school} \end{bmatrix} \times \begin{bmatrix} \text{employed in covered establishment} \\ \text{employed in uncovered establishment} \\ \text{not employed} \end{bmatrix}$$

The second set of estimates subsumes the schooling choice and yields the following five-way classification:

$$J_r = \begin{bmatrix} \text{employed full time} \\ \text{employed part time} \\ \text{not employed} \end{bmatrix} \times \begin{bmatrix} \text{employed in covered establishments} \\ \text{employed in uncovered establishments} \end{bmatrix}$$

Both the semielasticity and full elasticity of each outcome probability with respect to the minimum wage are used to measure the minimum wage impact. A semielasticity is the absolute change in a specific probability relative to a 100 percent change in the effective minimum wage. The full elasticity is the *proportionate* probability change relative to a minimum wage change.[13] The semielasticities must sum to zero since the sum of outcome probabilities is always one. Taken together, these values tell us how people alter their choices. The full elasticity gives an indication of whether the change in the number of people making a given set of decisions is important relative to the number originally making those same decisions. That is, will the change be noticeable?

The results for white cohorts are discussed first, followed by the results for blacks. Tables 2 and 5 provide a summary for white and black cohorts, respectively. They present results with regard to composite outcomes that are of special interest. For example, does a minimum wage hike reduce school attendance? Tables 3, 4, 6, and 7 give detailed results.

Whites. All groups experience net displacement from covered establishments (refer to table 2, panel B, line 1a). This reflects the fact that groups of relatively young people contain many recent labor market entrants who, as yet, have gained little marketable skill. Even the youngest group contains highly capable individuals whose productivity exceeds the minimum wage level. These individuals may be sought by firms as they attempt to circumvent the costs created by minimum wage laws and may be attracted to covered firms by higher wage offers. Thus, as discussed earlier, this substitution process consists of a positive component as well as the displacement, or negative, component. In the case of young white cohorts, the latter dominates.[14]

---

[13] The semielasticity of outcome i evaluated at mean probabilities ($\overline{P}$) is written:

$$W_m \frac{\partial P_i}{\partial W_m} = MW \frac{\partial P_i}{\partial MW} = \overline{MW}\, \overline{P}_i\, [\hat{\Pi}_i - B],$$

where

$$B = \sum_{j \in J} \hat{\Pi}_j\, \overline{P}_j,$$

and the Π's are parameter estimates, $\hat{\Pi}_k = (\alpha_k - \alpha_1)$. For identification purposes α_1 is assumed to be zero. The full elasticity is simply $(W_m/P_i)(\partial P_i/\partial W_m)$.

[14] Panel A also presents estimates of the displacement effect. Technically, these estimates should be very close to those in panel B. In fact, the correspondence is generally very close among the eight cohorts with the exception of sixteen- to nineteen-year-old white males. In the latter case, the estimates are of the same size but differ substantially in magnitude (the semielasticities from panels A and B, respectively, are $-.002$ and $-.027$ for the young male group). At this time a satisfying explanation cannot be offered for this difference. It is the writer's opinion, however, that panel B offers the more accurate picture because of the relative consistency of these estimates across cohorts.

100

In absolute terms the older group experiences greater displacement than the corresponding younger group for each sex. This relationship is eliminated for females and actually reversed for males when proportionate changes are considered. There are simply far fewer young people to displace from covered jobs than is true of the older cohorts. Still, some readers may be surprised that twenty- to twenty-four-year-olds are not less adversely affected as compared with teenagers. This issue is explored in greater depth below with regard to the detailed results.

An increase in the minimum wage reduces employment in the covered sector. How do persons who are displaced from covered establishments redistribute themselves over the remaining alternatives?[15] Our finding is that a large majority of males who are displaced from the covered sector take jobs with employers not covered by a minimum wage law; very few become disemployed (see panel B, lines 1*b* and 2). Females, on the other hand, more or less evenly relocate in the uncovered sector and out of the work force. The impact upon uncovered employment for males and both disemployment and uncovered employment for females is, in each case, statistically significant and fairly large. The influx of women to the uncovered sector would be particularly noticeable. A 10 percent rise in the wage floor, for example, would increase employment there by 3.5 percent.

It is interesting to speculate briefly as to why women are less likely to remain employed than men. Recall that (positive or negative) disemployment caused by a minimum wage is comprised of two components: unemployed members of the labor force who are searching for covered jobs, and individuals who enter or exit the labor force. Because of the latter, net disemployment can be negative but is most likely positive. It was conjectured above that the wage of high-skilled persons is bid up, especially in relation to those whose productivity is below the minimum. Productive individuals should tend to be drawn into the labor force while some of the less productive members exit, given that their opportunity wage probably falls.[16] Labor force participants tend to have more marketable skill relative to the opportunity cost (that is, the sac-

---

[15] Recall that the alternatives include taking an uncovered job or becoming "not employed." If not employed, an individual chooses either to remain in the labor force for the purpose of waiting for a scarce covered job or to leave the labor force completely. When reference is made to displacement of persons, this is a probabilistic statement because some of the waiters ultimately land a covered job. More accurately, "slots," not specific individuals, have been eliminated.

[16] The possibility of increased wages for low-productivity workers cannot be ruled out. The evidence here supports a decline, however. Unless aggregate (uncovered) demand for labor from cohorts of young people increases significantly, one cannot observe both employment and wage increases in the uncovered sector. Because such a demand shift is improbable and uncovered employment rises, it must be concluded that expected wages have fallen, especially for low-productivity workers.

TABLE 2

MEASURED IMPACT OF THE EFFECTIVE MINIMUM WAGE ON SELECTED OUTCOME PROBABILITIES FOR WHITE YOUTHS

	Males Age 16–19		Males Age 20–24		Females Age 16–19		Females Age 20–24	
	D	E	D	E	D	E	D	E
Panel A: Schooling choice model (tables)								
1. Employed								
(a) covered	-.002	-.005	-.045*	-.079	-.039*	-.148	-.058*	-.136
	(.007)		(.012)		(.007)		(.013)	
(b) uncovered	-.000	-.001	.044*	.288	.022*	.376	.029*	.361
	(.005)		(.009)		(.004)		(.007)	
(c) not in school	.012*	.090	-.006	-.010	.012*	.087	-.032*	-.073
	(.005)		(.012)		(.005)		(.013)	
(d) in school	-.014*	-.049	.004	.027	-.029*	.161	.002	.033
	(.007)		(.009)		(.006)		(.006)	
2. Not employed	.002	.003	.001	.005	.017*	.025	.029*	.060
	(.007)		(.011)		(.007)		(.013)	
3. Not in school	.019*	.092	.003	.005	.015*	.052	.004	.005
	(.006)		(.011)		(.007)		(.009)	
Panel B: Employment rate model (tables)								
1. Employed								
(a) covered	-.027*	-.084	-.035*	-.061	-.035*	-.133	-.058*	-.134
	(.007)		(.012)		(.007)		(.013)	

	D	E	D	E	D	E	D	E
(b) uncovered	.024* (.004)	.272	.035* (.009)	.232	.021* (.004)	.357	.028* (.007)	.354
(c) full-time	.025* (.005)	.163	.005 (.012)	.009	.013* (.005)	.098	-.021 (.012)	-.055
(d) part-time	-.029* (.007)	-.114	-.005 (.009)	-.034	-.027* (.006)	-.147	-.008 (.008)	-.062
2. Not employed	.003 (.007)	.006	-.000 (.011)	-.001	.014* (.007)	.021	.029* (.013)	.060

NOTES: (1) Column D gives the semielasticity of the logit function for P_i with respect to (proportionate changes in) the effective minimum wage evaluated at mean probabilities. Column E gives the full elasticity. (2) Asymptotic standard errors are in parentheses.
*Significant at .05 level.
SOURCE: Author.

rifice) of working than those who do not enter, however. One therefore expects nonparticipants to be generally less productive than participants. This should be particularly true of the older cohorts, where formal education is no longer pursued exclusively by a significant share of the members. We conclude that entry of high-productivity (high opportunity cost) workers is likely to be limited. Shifts in labor force status should, therefore, be dominated by the exit of low-productivity workers.

It is difficult a priori to predict relative changes either by skill class across sex-age cohorts or by cohort across skill classes. This task is not undertaken here as a means of explaining disemployment effects. It is, however, a well-established fact that the labor force participation rate of women is more sensitive to changes in employment incentives than it is for men. Other things equal, a drop in expected wage will produce a greater withdrawal of women than men from the job market. Disemployment will accordingly increase more for women, provided that an opposite and offsetting relationship does not exist for unemployment.[17]

With regard to full-time/part-time employment, a pattern similar to that observed for sector-specific outcomes emerges for males and younger females (refer to panel B, lines 1c and 1d). A definite shift has occurred from part-time to full-time work. Based upon our priors regarding the relative productivity of these two groups, the expectation was that relatively more part-time workers would be displaced from covered jobs. In fact, for these three cohorts full-time employment is actually increased. For the older females both categories (full-time/part-time) are reduced, but the changes are not statistically significant. Note that, although the absolute reduction is greater for full-time employment in their case, the part-time response is proportionately slightly larger. Discussion of these issues is continued below.

School attendance is reduced somewhat by minimum wages among teenage males and females (panel A, lines 3, 1c, and 1d). The older cohorts exhibit no net response. Lower attendance among teenagers is associated with reduced employment of students, and this, as is indicated below, is due to displacement of students from jobs covered by minimum wage laws.

We turn now to examine some interesting questions that arise in light of the detailed results in tables 3 and 4.[18]

It has been mentioned that covered employment falls for all cohorts,

---

[17] There seems to be no reason to expect unemployment to behave in this fashion. In fact, unemployment could rise by more among female cohorts. A factor that determines how many people queue for covered jobs (that is, become unemployed temporarily) is the probability each period of being offered a position. Because employment turnover appears lower for males, it follows, ceteris paribus, that the probability of being made an offer is lower for them. Hence, fewer males, relative to females, will stick around waiting for a job in a covered establishment.

[18] These tables have the same basic format as table 2. In fact, table 2 is derived from tables 3 and 4; for example, the semielasticity of covered employment, line 1a of panel A, is the

but the impact upon younger sets was not as large as expected, a priori, compared with the young adults. Examination of tables 3 and 4 (first two lines) reveals the source of this surprise. Employment of teenagers among covered establishments, either full time or out of school, *increases,* whereas the same activities shrink for young adults! The increases are significantly different from zero for young males. What can account for this surprising and admittedly anomalous result? We shall sketch an argument that consists of two parts. The first reviews the conditions necessary to observe increased covered employment of teenagers working full time or not attending school. The second part explains why twenty- to twenty-four-year-olds may experience a decline in these cells *as compared with their teenage counterparts* (that is, absolute changes may be positive or negative).

Full-time employment of covered workers will rise if firms decide to hire enough of the more productive members of the cohort to offset layoffs of the less productive members. Of course this means that the full-time wage is bid up by these employers and/or that the alternatives facing these more productive individuals become less attractive—for example, the expected wage in part-time employment.[19] Where the additional workers come from is not certain. They may have left jobs with uncovered firms, or they may have left, or been displaced from, covered part-time jobs and now choose full-time employment.[20] Either way, teenagers shift away from part-time work and, not coincidentally, away from school attendance.

In any group of young workers there are undoubtedly some whose productivity is at, or only slightly above, the current minimum wage level. Some of these individuals would be laid off if the minimum wage were raised. There are also those individuals, *not* employed full time in the covered sector, whose productivity exceeds the minimum by a wider margin. Some of these individuals will *select* full-time covered employment, given that employment incentives change in the manner we have described.[21] Change in full-time covered employment is simply the net of these two flows, of course.

---

sum of the semielasticities (column D) from the first two lines of table 3, namely, .010 = −.002, for white males sixteen to nineteen years old. Full elasticities are computed as a weighted average of the corresponding entries in column E.

[19] Because the argument seems not to require any special distinction between student and nonstudent employees from the employers' point of view, this argument will focus on the full-time/part-time distinction. The schooling and full-time choices go hand in hand, however. As noted earlier, most full-time workers are not in school, so the decision to work full-time excludes school attendance for most individuals.

[20] Recall the observation that in many types of jobs a full-time worker is more productive than the part-time counterpart. It is thus possible for a person to qualify for a full-time position even though he is among those displaced from part-time jobs.

[21] Although these arguments refer to a minimum wage increase, the same line of reasoning applies to an extension of coverage.

TABLE 3

MEASURED IMPACT OF THE EFFECTIVE MINIMUM WAGE ON JOINT SCHOOL ATTENDANCE AND SECTOR-SPECIFIC EMPLOYMENT PROBABILITIES FOR WHITE YOUTHS

	Males Age 16–19		Males Age 20–24		Females Age 16–19		Females Age 20–24	
	D	E	D	E	D	E	D	E
EMP/COV/OUT	.010*	.091	−.039*	−.087	.003	.024	−.057*	−.157
	(.005)		(.012)		(.005)		(.012)	
EMP/COV/IN	−.012*	−.054	−.006	−.050	−.041*	−.287	−.001	−.014
	(.006)		(.008)		(.005)		(.006)	
EMP/NCOV/OUT	.002	.082	.033*	.280	.009*	.408	.026*	.361
	(.002)		(.008)		(.002)		(.006)	
EMP/NCOV/IN	−.002	−.031	.010*	.319	.012*	.356	.003	.360
	(.004)		(.004)		(.003)		(.002)	
NEMP/OUT	.007**	.097	.009	.075	.003	.019	.036*	.090
	(.004)		(.008)		(.006)		(.012)	
NEMP/IN	−.005	−.010	−.008	−.048	.014	.026	−.006	−.064
	(.007)		(.008)		(.008)		(.007)	

NOTES: (1) For outcomes: EMP = employed, $NEMP$ = not employed, COV = covered employment, $NCOV$ = not covered, OUT = out of school, IN = in school, $FULL$ = full-time employment, $PART$ = part-time employment. (2) Column D gives the semielasticity of the logit function for P_i with respect to (proportionate changes in) the effective minimum wage evaluated at mean probabilities. Column E gives the full elasticity. (3) Asymptomatic standard errors are in parentheses.
*Significant at .05 level.
**Significant at .01 level.
SOURCE: Author.

TABLE 4

MEASURED IMPACT OF THE EFFECTIVE MINIMUM WAGE ON JOINT EMPLOYMENT RATE AND SECTOR-SPECIFIC EMPLOYMENT PROBABILITIES FOR WHITE YOUTHS

	Males Age 16–19		Males Age 20–24		Females Age 16–19		Females Age 20–24	
	D	E	D	E	D	E	D	E
EMP/COV/FULL	.013* (.005)	.100	−.018 (.012)	−.040	.005 (.005)	.041	−.042* (.012)	−.130
EMP/COV/PART	−.040* (.006)	−.205	−.017* (.008)	−.140	−.039* (.006)	−.265	−.016* (.008)	−.143
EMP/NCOV/FULL	.013* (.002)	.449	.023* (.008)	.196	.008* (.002)	.406	.021* (.006)	.336
EMP/NCOV/PART	.011* (.004)	.188	.012* (.004)	.369	.012* (.003)	.330	.008* (.003)	.412
NEMP	.003 (.007)	.006	−.000 (.011)	−.001	.014** (.007)	.021	.029* (.013)	.059

NOTE: See notes to table 3 for detailed information.
SOURCE: Author.

107

TABLE 5

MEASURED IMPACT OF THE EFFECTIVE MINIMUM WAGE ON SELECTED OUTCOME PROBABILITIES FOR BLACK YOUTHS

	Males Age 16–19		Males Age 20–24		Females Age 16–19		Females Age 20–24	
	D	E	D	E	D	E	D	E
Panel A: Schooling choice model (tables)								
1. Employed								
(a) covered	−.028*	−.148	−.029**	−.059	.005	.035	.030*	.085
	(.012)		(.015)		(.005)		(.013)	
(b) uncovered	.014*	.206	.040*	.279	−.003	−.067	.011	.091
	(.007)		(.008)		(.005)		(.009)	
(c) not in school	−.031*	−.228	.006	.011	−.002	−.022	.047*	.113
	(.012)		(.015)		(.006)		(.014)	
(d) in school	.016**	.130	.005	.086	.003	.040	−.007	−.135
	(.009)		(.006)		(.004)		(.007)	
2. Not employed	.015	.020	−.012	−.031	−.001	−.001	−.041*	−.076
	(.013)		(.014)		(.007)		(.014)	
3. Not in school	−.036*	−.122	−.016**	−.019	−.022*	−.068	.007	.008
	(.014)		(.009)		(.010)		(.010)	
Panel B: Employment rate model (tables)								
1. Employed								
(a) covered	−.026*	−.135	−.031*	−.064	.003	.025	.032*	.092
	(.012)		(.015)		(.004)		(.013)	

(b) uncovered	.012**	.184	.040*	.280	−.004	−.072	.019*	.163
	(.007)		(.008)		(.005)		(.009)	
(c) full-time	−.023*	−.168	.011	.022	−.001	−.008	.045*	.123
	(.011)		(.015)		(.005)		(.013)	
(d) part-time	.010	.083	−.002	−.022	.000	.003	.007	.064
	(.009)		(.009)		(.004)		(.009)	
2. Not employed	.014	.018	−.009	−.024	.000	.001	−.051*	−.097
	(.013)		(.014)		(.006)		(.014)	

NOTE: See notes to table 3.
SOURCE: Author.

TABLE 6

MEASURED IMPACT OF THE EFFECTIVE MINIMUM WAGE ON JOINT SCHOOL ATTENDANCE AND SECTOR-SPECIFIC EMPLOYMENT PROBABILITIES FOR BLACK YOUTHS

	Males Age 16–19		Males Age 20–24		Females Age 16–19		Females Age 20–24	
	D	E	D	E	D	E	D	E
EMP/COV/OUT	-.033*	-.322	-.030**	-.069	.002	.026	.033*	.104
	(.011)		(.016)		(.004)		(.013)	
EMP/COV/IN	.005	.055	.002	.038	.003	.046	-.003	-.066
	(.008)		(.005)		(.003)		(.006)	
EMP/NCOV/OUT	.003	.082	.036*	.286	-.004	-.147	.015**	.139
	(.005)		(.008)		(.005)		(.009)	
EMP/NCOV/IN	.011*	.315	.004	.226	.001	.024	.004	-.388
	(.005)		(.003)		(.003)		(.004)	
NEMP/OUT	-.005	-.034	-.022	-.078	-.020*	-.087	-.041*	-.090
	(.011)		(.013)		(.010)		(.014)	
NEMP/IN	.020	.035	.011	.117	.019**	.032	.000	.001
	(.015)		(.007)		(.010)		(.007)	

NOTE: See notes to table 3 for detailed information.
SOURCE: Author.

TABLE 7

Measured Impact of the Effective Minimum Wage on Joint Employment Rate and Sector-Specific Employment Probabilities for Black Youths

	Males Age 16–19		Males Age 20–24		Females Age 16–19		Females Age 20–24	
	D	E	D	E	D	E	D	E
EMP/COV/FULL	-.027*	-.251	-.023	-.058	.003	.036	.025*	.090
	(.010)		(.015)		(.003)		(.012)	
EMP/COV/PART	.001	.009	-.008	-.095	.001	.012	.004	.098
	(.008)		(.009)		(.003)		(.008)	
EMP/NCOV/FULL	.003	.096	.035*	.300	-.003	-.129	.020*	.226
	(.005)		(.007)		(.005)		(.008)	
EMP/NCOV/PART	.009**	.270	.005	.200	-.000	-.016	-.001	-.024
	(.005)		(.004)		(.003)		(.005)	
NEMP	.014	.018	-.009	-.024	.000	.001	-.051*	-.097
	(.013)		(.014)		(.006)		(.014)	

NOTE: See notes to table 3 for detailed information.
SOURCE: Author.

Age is usually associated positively with experience and schooling and hence with skill and productivity. Although older workers are typically not expected to experience as strong a negative impact from a minimum wage hike as younger workers, two conditions are discussed below that can diminish or even reverse the anticipated pattern.[22]

Condition 1: For a small increase in the minimum wage the number of workers displaced from full-time covered jobs in a given age group increases with the number employed.

Underlying this condition is the observation that full-time covered employment increases with age; approximately threefold for whites between the ages of sixteen to nineteen and twenty to twenty-four. The growth stems from three sources: new labor force entrants, transfers from uncovered and covered part-time jobs, and reduced unemployment with age. To some extent the growth reflects employment of individuals who are finally gaining access to covered jobs as their skills have developed sufficiently—through schooling or on-the-job training—to push them above the productivity threshold created by the minimum wage. To some extent, however, the growth consists of individuals whose skills had been adequate but who had chosen not to work at a full-time job— for example, while they completed postsecondary education.

Thus, overall gains in experience and training and entry of highly productive workers to the covered (full-time) work force tend to raise the average productivity of this group with age. But its ranks are also expanded by workers whose productivity is marginal relative to the lower bound established by the minimum wage. It appears quite possible, therefore, that the *proportion* of marginal workers in each age cell will fall by less with age than the proportionate increase of full-time covered workers. If so, a small enough increase in the productivity threshold will result in the exclusion of more older workers from these jobs than younger workers (that is, twenty- to twenty-four versus sixteen- to nineteen), even though the proportionate displacement may be less.

The second condition pertains to the availability of full-time substitutes from within a particular cohort for any workers displaced from covered jobs. These replacements must satisfy two criteria: they must be compatible in skill with those displaced, and they must have a productivity level at least as great as the threshold set by the new wage floor.

Condition 2: The number of available (and adequate) substitutes for replacing displaced covered workers falls with age.

Availability is determined by two things: the ability and willingness

---

[22] We believe these conditions hold for the young cohorts studied in this paper. There are reasons to think they are not valid for persons twenty-five and over, however, and are valid, perhaps, for only some of the sex-race cohorts aged sixteen to twenty-four. Further research is planned to verify them.

of the candidates to work full time in the covered sector. Obviously, the more people who satisfy the above criteria the more there are who could feasibly shift. But these individuals must find the incentives to covered employment sufficiently improved to warrant such a move, and this depends upon how strongly attached they are to the competing option: for example, schooling with or without part-time employment, uncovered employment, or nonparticipation in the labor force altogether.

Certainly the increased average productivity with age of persons not working full time in a covered job tends to increase availability. There are three facts, however, that work in the opposite direction and tend to reduce the availability of substitutes. First, there are simply fewer twenty- to twenty-four-year-olds *not* working in this cell than teenagers. On average, for whites the proportion in full-time covered jobs rose from 12 percent for sixteen- to nineteen-year-olds to 39 percent for twenty- to twenty-four-year-olds. Secondly, skills acquired over time in the uncovered sector cannot typically be transferred to a given covered establishment without loss of productivity. Skills acquired with a particular firm or industry are to some degree *specific* to those places of employment. Even if an individual earns a wage substantially above the minimum in an uncovered firm, his opportunity wage among covered employers would be less, thus making a move unlikely. Naturally, the cost, in terms of lost wages, of shifting from an uncovered to a covered job tends to increase with age. The same may also be true of the part-time/full-time shift within the covered sector. The most productive teenagers would appear to be more readily available as substitutes than their older counterparts whose share of nontransferable skill is larger.

The third fact is that a screening process tends to sort the more productive labor market entrants into covered jobs. The less capable end up either unemployed a greater proportion of the time or employed in uncovered establishments. The teenage group has a reservoir of nonparticipants and part-time workers who will ultimately seek full-time employment but for the time being choose to concentrate upon schooling. Some of these people could fill full-time slots in the covered sector if they desired. Because of the screening process that operates as this reservoir is dissipated with time, young adults (namely, those aged twenty to twenty-four) *not* in covered firms should be less productive, other things equal, than many of the teenagers. As mentioned before, experience will offset this difference somewhat, though it is constrained by nontransferability of skills.

It has been argued that fewer young adults are available for jobs in covered establishments than teenagers, that those who might be available may, on average, be less productive than those persons who entered the covered sector directly, and, finally, that even productivity gains are not wholly transferable (in most cases) because of firm- or industry-specific training.[23]

These facts lend support to Condition 2. If both Conditions 1 and 2 are true, moreover, then teenage full-time and nonenrolled, covered employment is likely to rise relative to young adults, as we observe in tables 3 and 4. Basically, what appears to have happened is that the full-time wage and wages of productive young people in general were bid up by higher minimum wages. The part-time wage and wages of low-productivity workers may have fallen a little but not enough to cause a substantial movement back to school or simply out of the labor force. The more productive teenagers were drawn toward full-time work and away from school and part-time work. In the case of young adults, similar incentives were created. Some people were displaced from their jobs, but because of apparent relative insensitivity of potential replacements within the cohort of these incentives, net full-time employment fell. The argument that kids go back to school because their jobs are cut off by minimum wages is not supported by our data for whites. This does not refute the argument for other cohorts or other time periods, however. We observe part-time jobs being eliminated and, in effect, full-time slots opening up earlier for capable teenagers.

Blacks. The results for black cohorts, as shown in tables 5 and 6, present a very different picture than seen in the section on whites. Each cohort will be discussed in turn.[24]

Teenage males are displaced from covered jobs, as expected, by increasing the minimum wage. In response, both uncovered employment and nonemployment grow by about the same amount in absolute terms. Unlike their white counterparts, however, black teenagers are on net displaced from full-time covered jobs. Many of these individuals appear to have extended their schooling, either taking part-time jobs in uncovered establishments or becoming disemployed (see table 7). White teenagers were found to leave school. The latter was explained in terms

---

[23] It should be noted that the case of young adult females is somewhat different. A large number of women choose not to enter the labor force upon completing school but instead typically marry (and direct home production). It seems that this choice limits the number of women who will choose to work full-time. Thus, as long as marriage is not particularly sensitive to changing incentives in covered full-time employment, the response of those women not employed to greater rewards for full-time covered employment will be limited. In fact, the responsiveness of part-time employed and nonemployed teenagers is probably larger.

[24] Estimates for blacks in general lack the robustness of the white results due to smallness of sample size. Greater caution must therefore be exercised in trying to evaluate the findings. In this section our discussion is limited to the more important highlights.

of the attraction of higher-paying full-time jobs and the probable deterioration of part-time employment opportunities among covered firms. We can only guess as to why blacks and whites differ. Two possibilities are mentioned. The wage offer for the more productive individuals (especially those choosing not to work full time) may not have risen in response to higher minimum wages. This could happen for a number of reasons. For example, if firms typically hiring black youth also experience the greatest cost increases, their efforts to reduce output (or labor usage in general) could swamp any moves to replace less productive workers.

A second possibility is that the pool of capable individuals hypothesized to exist for teenagers may not be sufficiently large in the black cohort. Recall that individuals in this pool are typically pursuing an education instead of working full time. If a young person comes from a low-income family and is a capable worker, then there is greater pressure on the person to find employment at an early age. To the extent to which black youth come from lower-income families as compared with white youth, more of the higher-quality black teenagers would be drawn into the labor force at an early age than would be true among whites. Obviously, further research must be done to resolve this puzzle.

Why do we not observe displacement of covered part-time workers? Part of the answer is that there are very few people in this cell to begin with—6 percent for black teenagers as opposed to 17 percent (of cohort) for whites. This, together with considerable sampling error, may simply mean that the expected relationship cannot be observed with our data. It may also be true that black youths hold very different types of covered jobs as compared with white youths and that among the former the expected relationship between full-time and part-time productivity does not hold. Recall, for example, the counterargument made earlier involving the collapse of work shifts and increased demand for part-time labor.

The older males also exhibit a negative response in covered employment to the minimum wage and a strong, positive uncovered response. The difference between black and white estimates is very small in this case. Similarly, no significant redistribution among employment rate categories is found (for example, full-time/part-time and not employed). As in the case of teenagers, some young male adults return to school if the wage floor is raised, though this effect is only *weakly significant*.

Black females appear radically different when compared with their white counterparts. Teenagers indicate virtually no response in any category except for a positive school enrollment effect (table 5, panel A, line 3). Evidently supply effects are offsetting the negative employment

115

effects that may occur. The positive schooling response is due almost completely to shifts within the "not employed" category. This cannot be fully explained yet and may be spurious.

Older females exhibit very strong *positive* employment responses, both with respect to covered and, to a lesser extent, uncovered employment. Nonemployment accordingly shows a large negative reaction, most of which reflects change in employment status of people already out of school. Incentives to attend school are, on balance, not affected significantly.

Why do black females, in the twenty to twenty-four age group in particular, differ so sharply from all other cohorts? Most of the earlier arguments applicable to women should apply in the case of black women. And although there are some differences in male-female comparisons between races, these should not account for the polarity observed in the female estimates.

Could it be that black women are replacing black men in covered jobs? This seems unlikely in view of the white female experience. It is true that, nationally, young-black-male labor force participation fell sharply during the 1960s while female participation jumped.[25] In order for this pattern to have any bearing upon minimum wage estimates, however, *state-specific* trends must be systematically related to the minimum wage variable *MW*.[26] Aside from direct minimum wage effects, such correlations could arise indirectly through the effect upon *MW* of changes in the average wage of white adults (by sex) that are supposed to measure movement in a cohort's productivity level. Labor force participation and schooling can be influenced by the wage structure, which in turn may be associated with this particular proxy for productivity. Although a systematic relationship may exist, it is difficult to identify one a priori. The problem may be simply that the average white female wage is not a good proxy for black productivity in the 1960s. A similar sort of answer is that we have omitted the same factor from black female estimation that influences covered employment, etc., and is systematically related to *MW* across states. Further research will investigate these possibilities. At this stage the black-female results appear anomalous in contrast to our priors and the results for the other cohorts.[27]

---

[25] White female participation also rose in this decade. Whereas older white males withdrew, teenage participation rose slightly, contrary to the case for teenage black males.

[26] Recall that adjustments were made in the data to account for national (but not state) trends in participation and school attendance.

[27] Some evidence suggests that young black females are more responsive than white females to own-wage changes with respect to labor force participation. If so, and assuming the opportunity wage of a number of the disemployed is bid up by the minimum wage, more black women would respond than white. Under appropriate circumstances, this difference could generate our results. Overall, evidence regarding participation is mixed in the literature, however, making this argument somewhat tenuous.

Conclusions

The results of this study confirm, in most respects, previous efforts. Among whites, a minimum wage reduces employment. It is with relief that we find this effect to emanate, unambiguously, from those establishments subject to minimum wage laws. As predicted, part-time work is discouraged. School attendance tends also to be reduced. This is in conjunction with lower employment of students. Overall, the evidence suggests that the part-time wage falls as compared with the full-time opportunity wage facing students.

One surprising result is that teenagers are found to be less adversely affected (in absolute terms) within the covered sector than twenty- to twenty-four-year-olds. In fact, an increase is observed in teenage employment of nonstudents and full-time workers among covered establishments in response to higher minimum wages. Young adults, however, experience decline in these categories. It is argued that this is a sound result despite being at odds with our intuition. Less productive workers from either cohort will be displaced or excluded from covered jobs. Even if more young workers are displaced, it is possible they may be replaced from among productive individuals not currently working full-time or out of school in covered jobs; for example, from part-time working students in covered firms or from nonemployed students. The older group, though more productive on average, evidently is unable to supply as many able and willing replacements.

The results for blacks are not so robust or consistent as the white results. Males experience a decline in covered employment, but only teenagers show evidence of overall decline in employment. Female results are very different. Young females exhibit virtually no net response to a minimum wage, and twenty- to twenty-four-year-olds actually appear to have experienced employment increases. Black females appear to be replacing males, but this result is difficult to justify on a priori grounds. The black results reflect weak data to some degree and may be subject to spurious correlations due to a relationship between state wage growth (a component of the minimum wage variables) and decennial change in employment and schooling decisions.

The estimation technique employed in this study treats young people in different states as being equivalent. That is, the same decisions will be made provided the options and constraints faced are identical. Significant differences do exist among states, however, and emphasis is accordingly placed upon developing a suitable means of controlling for them. The resulting approach, we believe, is a good one, but future research will attempt to refine it. In particular, the 1960s were turbulent years for young people, especially for black youth. The experience of some states may well have differed sharply from that of others, and in

117

TABLE 8

Means and Standard Deviations for White Youths
(standard deviations in parentheses)

	Males		Females	
	Age 16–19	Age 20–24	Age 16–19	Age 20–24
Outcome proportions:				
1970 (P)				
1. *EMP/COV/OUT*	.109	.449	.116	.367
	(.021)	(.060)	(.024)	(.049)
2. *EMP/COV/IN*	.214	.121	.144	.063
	(.049)	(.024)	(.050)	(.017)
3. *EMP/NCOV/OUT*	.023	.119	.022	.071
	(.012)	(.042)	(.013)	(.035)
4. *EMP/NCOV/IN*	.065	.032	.035	.009
	(.036)	(.017)	(.023)	(.004)
5. *NEMP/OUT*	.073	.121	.149	.393
	(.020)	(.024)	(.041)	(.044)
6. *NEMP/IN*	.517	.158	.534	.096
	(.039)	(.021)	(.034)	(.017)
7. *EMP/COV/FULL*	.128	.451	.112	.321
	(.021)	(.052)	(.023)	(.040)
8. *EMP/COV/PART*	.195	.120	.148	.109
	(.043)	(.019)	(.049)	(.022)
9. *EMP/NCOV/FULL*	.028	.120	.021	.061
	(.015)	(.044)	(.012)	(.030)
10. *EMP/NCOV/PART*	.059	.031	.037	.019
	(.033)	(.014)	(.023)	(.008)
Estimated ex ante out-				
come probabilities (P)				
11. *EMP/COV/OUT*	.121	.441	.126	.351
	(.023)	(.050)	(.036)	(.065)
12. *EMP/COV/IN*	.195	.103	.128	.053
	(.055)	(.029)	(.046)	(.017)
13. *EMP/NCOV/OUT*	.027	.127	.026	.082
	(.015)	(.046)	(.014)	(.038)
14. *EMP/NCOV/IN*	.062	.049	.032	.018
	(.040)	(.021)	(.022)	(.008)

TABLE 8 (continued)

	Males		Females	
	Age 16–19	Age 20–24	Age 16–19	Age 20–24
15. *NEMP/OUT*	.077	.122	.165	.402
	(.025)	(.029)	(.043)	(.047)
16. *NEMP/IN*	.521	.158	.524	.095
	(.041)	(.031)	(.036)	(.019)
17. *EMP/COV/FULL*	.142	.443	.124	.311
	(.026)	(.046)	(.035)	(.058)
18. *EMP/COV/PART*	.170	.101	.130	.093
	(.046)	(.023)	(.046)	(.023)
19. *EMP/NCOV/FULL*	.033	.132	.024	.070
	(.019)	(.049)	(.013)	(.034)
20. *EMP/NCOV/PART*	.055	.045	.034	.029
	(.036)	(.017)	(.022)	(.012)
21. *MW*	1.491	1.057	1.385	1.205
	(.470)	(.184)	(.426)	(.209)
22. *UNION*	−.126	−.126	−.124	−.123
	(.203)	(.200)	(.203)	(.201)
23. *UNEMP*	−.066	−.065	−.068	−.066
	(.178)	(.180)	(.178)	(.180)
24. *CITY*	−.088	−.086	−.087	−.086
	(.171)	(.173)	(.172)	(.174)
25. *MEDYRS*	.135	.133	.085	.085
	(.057)	(.057)	(.052)	(.052)
26. *Q*	.422	.424	.425	.426
	(.251)	(.251)	(.251)	(.252)
27. *FAMINC*	.705	.704	.705	.705
	(.067)	(.069)	(.068)	(.068)
Cell size	62,447	59,648	63,445	72,313

NOTE: For variables 1–20: *EMP* = employed, *NEMP* = not employed, *COV* = covered employment, *NCOV* = not covered, *OUT* = out of school, *IN* = in school, *FULL* = full-time employment, *PART* = part-time employment. Variables 21–27 are defined in text.
SOURCE: Author.

TABLE 9

MEANS AND STANDARD DEVIATIONS FOR BLACK YOUTHS
(standard deviations in parentheses)

	Males		Females	
	Age 16–19	Age 20–24	Age 16–19	Age 20–24
Outcome proportions: 1970 (P)				
1. *EMP/COV/OUT*	.103	.438	.071	.313
	(.032)	(.076)	(.027)	(.050)
2. *EMP/COV/IN*	.089	.047	.061	.040
	(.028)	(.026)	(.031)	(.019)
3. *EMP/NCOV/OUT*	.032	.128	.028	.106
	(.021)	(.049)	(.017)	(.046)
4. *EMP/NCOV/IN*	.036	.016	.025	.011
	(.019)	(.014)	(.014)	(.009)
5. *NEMP/OUT*	.162	.282	.230	.453
	(.035)	(.062)	(.036)	(.055)
6. *NEMP/IN*	.579	.090	.586	.077
	(.045)	(.037)	(.051)	(.027)
7. *EMP/COV/FULL*	.106	.401	.071	.275
	(.025)	(.063)	(.030)	(.052)
8. *EMP/COV/PART*	.085	.083	.061	.078
	(.024)	(.025)	(.027)	(.024)
9. *EMP/NCOV/FULL*	.033	.116	.026	.087
	(.024)	(.048)	(.015)	(.042)
10. *EMP/NCOV/PART*	.034	.027	.026	.030
	(.013)	(.013)	(.015)	(.016)
Estimated ex ante outcome probabilities (P)				
11. *EMP/COV/OUT*	.100	.402	.055	.262
	(.042)	(.078)	(.035)	(.095)
12. *EMP/COV/IN*	.069	.037	.035	.030
	(.028)	(.024)	(.033)	(.025)
13. *EMP/NCOV/OUT*	.033	.139	.038	.144
	(.021)	(.053)	(.026)	(.063)
14. *EMP/NCOV/IN*	.031	.019	.021	.019
	(.019)	(.013)	(.015)	(.014)

120

TABLE 9 (continued)

	Males		Females	
	Age 16–19	Age 20–24	Age 16–19	Age 20–24
15. *NEMP/OUT*	.184	.308	.256	.468
	(.062)	(.093)	(.053)	(.078)
16. *NEMP/IN*	.581	.092	.594	.076
	(.077)	(.038)	(.074)	(.042)
17. *EMP/COV/FULL*	.106	.375	.062	.241
	(.045)	(.072)	(.054)	(.095)
18. *EMP/COV/PART*	.062	.064	.029	.051
	(.025)	(.028)	(.025)	(.036)
19. *EMP/NCOV/FULL*	.037	.134	.035	.122
	(.022)	(.053)	(.025)	(.054)
20. *EMP/NCOV/PART*	.027	.025	.024	.042
	(.019)	(.016)	(.020)	(.034)
21. *MW*	2.089	1.392	2.125	2.054
	(.955)	(.572)	(1.482)	(1.062)
22. *UNION*	−.072	−.083	−.071	−.084
	(.203)	(.196)	(.203)	(.194)
23. *UNEMP*	−.137	−.130	−.140	−.134
	(.166)	(.173)	(.170)	(.174)
24. *CITY*	.081	.073	.080	.069
	(.173)	(.161)	(.174)	(.154)
25. *MEDYRS*	.236	.230	.177	.173
	(.077)	(.075)	(.050)	(.049)
26. *Q*	.407	.422	.413	.423
	(.308)	(.298)	(.306)	(.298)
27. *FAMINC*	.947	.928	.945	.919
	(.265)	(.257)	(.264)	(.255)
Cell size	8,924	7,224	9,324	9,360

NOTE: For variables 1–20: *EMP* = employed, *NEMP* = not employed, *COV* = covered employment, *NCOV* = not covered, *OUT* = out of school, *IN* = in school, *FULL* = full-time employment, *PART* = part-time employment. Variables 21–27 are defined in text.
SOURCE: Author.

a manner correlated with either minimum wage or average wage changes. If so, data adjustments are necessary to reduce the possibility of estimation bias.

Our findings reveal potentially important labor-supply responses. Most studies identify measured minimum wage effects with demand side phenomena or simply net changes. A complete evaluation of the minimum wage must attempt to separate supply from demand effects. It is hoped that future research will focus on this issue.

Appendix

Means and standard deviations for the data on white and black youths are given in tables 8 and 9.

Bibliography

Cunningham, James S. "The Impact of Minimum Wages on Youth Employment, Hours of Work, and School Attendance: Cross-sectional Evidence from the 1960 and 1970 Censuses." Mimeographed, October 1979.

Ehrenberg, Ronald G., and Marcus, Alan. "Minimum Wage Legislation and the Educational Decisions of Youths: Perpetuation of Income Inequality across Generations?" Manuscript, February 1979.

Freeman, Richard B. *The Over-educated American.* New York: Academic Press, 1976.

Hashimoto, Masanori, and Mincer, Jacob. "Employment and Unemployment Effects of Minimum Wages." Manuscript, National Bureau of Economic Research, April 1970.

Kosters, Marvin, and Welch, Finis. "The Effects of Minimum Wages on the Distribution of Changes in Aggregate Employment." *American Economic Review* 62 (June 1972): 323–32.

Mattila, J. Peter. "Youth Labor Markets, Enrollments, and Minimum Wages." *Proceedings of the Thirty-first Annual Meeting of the Industrial Relations Research Association, August 29–31, 1978* (1979), pp. 134–40.

Mincer, Jacob. "Unemployment Effects of Minimum Wages." *Journal of Political Economy* 84 (August 1976): S87–S104.

Parsons, Donald. "The Cost of School Time, Forgone Earnings, and Human Capital Formation." *Journal of Political Economy* 82, pt. 1 (March 1974): 251–66.

Rosen, Sherwin, and Willis, Robert. "Education and Self Selection." National Bureau of Economic Research Working Paper 249, November 1978.

Theil, Henri. "A Multinominal Extension of the Linear Logit Model." *International Economic Review* 10 (October 1969): 251–59.

U.S. Department of Labor, Bureau of Labor Statistics. *Youth Unemployment and Minimum Wages,* Bulletin 1657 (1970).

Welch, Finis. "Minimum Wage Legislation in the United States." *Economic Inquiry* 12 (September 1974): 285–318.

———. "Employment Quotas for Minorities." *Journal of Political Economy* 84 (August 1976): 105–39.

———, and Cunningham, James. "The Effects of Minimum Wages on the Level and Age Composition of Youth Employment." *Review of Economics and Statistics* 60 (February 1978): 140–45.

Some Determinants of the Level and Racial Composition of Teenage Employment

*Nabeel Al-Salam, Aline Quester,
and Finis Welch*

In 1954 when the Census Bureau's Current Population Surveys began monthly reporting of employment for black and white teenagers, a black teenage male was slightly more likely to be employed than a white. By 1956 black and white employment levels equalized, and for the next decade they followed approximately parallel trends except for a growing tendency for black employment levels to fall behind those of whites. Then the apparent congruency collapsed; white teenagers became increasingly likely to be employed—by 1978 higher fractions were working than at any time since 1954—while the experience of black teenagers was just the opposite. In 1978 only 27 percent of male teenagers classified by the census as nonwhite (of whom over 90 percent are black) were employed; the corresponding number for whites was 54 percent—exactly double the number for blacks.

The anomaly of this divergent trend, illustrated in figure 1, is that it occurred alongside convergence toward earnings equality of black and white adults and alongside convergence to equality in teenage school enrollment rates.

Because the problem is important, numerous attempts have been made to "explain" these trends, and by now the search for a single, simple explanation seems to be yielding ground to more complex attempts. This paper examines two facets, one old and one new. The old and familiar one is the minimum wage story on which this volume is based. The new wrinkle lies in an examination of the effects of the age distribution on teenage employment prospects. In particular, as is shown in figure 2, during the period of concern the teenage population grew enormously, both absolutely and relative to the adult population. How

NOTE: We are especially grateful for many helpful discussions with Robert Cotterman. Thanks are due to Bill Gould, Jim Smith, and Michael Ward for useful suggestions. Research support was provided by a grant from the Rockefeller Foundation and by the Industrial Relations Institute at the University of California, Los Angeles.

124

FIGURE 1

EMPLOYMENT OF WHITE AND BLACK MALE TEENAGERS, 1954–1978

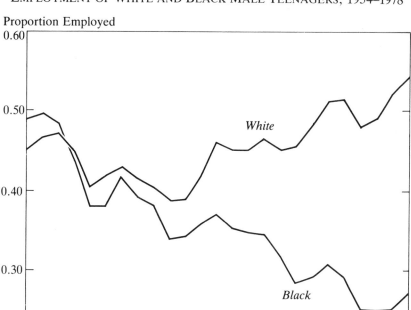

Proportion Employed

SOURCES: Civilian employment for white and black (actually, nonwhite) male teenagers is from monthly issues of U.S. Department of Labor, Bureau of Labor Statistics, *Employment and Earnings*. Total noninstitutional population for these demographic groups is from U.S. Department of Commerce, Bureau of the Census, *Population Estimates and Projections*, Current Population Reports Series P–25, nos. 311, 519, and 721.

does the sheer size of youthful cohorts affect chances for employment, and are these effects themselves dependent on minimum wages?

At the outset we should admit that our results are more suggestive than definitive. We confront the teen employment question in two steps. The first considers determinants of total male teen employment. The second confronts discrepancies in time paths of employment between black and white teens.

In an important sense our emphasis is better suited to the question of race differences in trend than to analysis of aggregate teen employment simply because the aggregate has increased for the last fifteen years and the issues we consider, minimum wages and growth in the size

125

FIGURE 2
ABSOLUTE AND RELATIVE SIZE OF THE MALE TEENAGE COHORT, 1954–1978

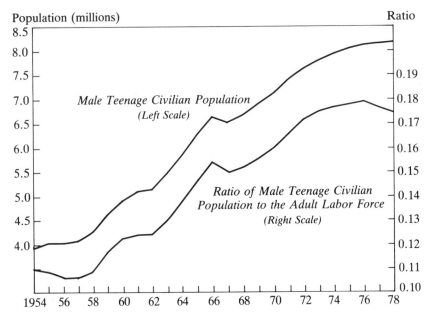

SOURCE: Monthly issues of U.S. Department of Labor, Bureau of Labor Statistics, *Employment and Earnings.*

of youthful cohorts, should not have fueled this increase. Because of this, we confine ourselves to an analysis of movements about trend, not because trend is unimportant but because we want to emphasize the role of factors that are unlikely candidates for explaining it.

In the next section, we sketch the history of minimum wage legislation and suggest a simple theoretical model of what its effects might be. After extending the model to include cohort-size effects, we present summaries of our main empirical results.

An Overview of the Federal Legislation

Our intent in this section is only to sketch some of the salient features of the federal legislation. We neither attempt a full description nor address parallel movements in state laws. The legislation specifies a basic minimum and the characteristics of firms (and within them, of employees) subject to it. Amendments raise the basic minimum, program subsequent steps, and extend coverage. Newly covered firms are initially subject to a differential minimum that is below the basic one, and the difference is itself programmed to erode the annual steps over a four- or five-year period until the differential minimum catches up with the basic one.

Table 1 summarizes this history for selected periods from 1950 to 1980. The first column is the basic minimum, and the second gives our estimate of the proportion of employed teenagers subject to it. The next two columns refer to the differential minimum (when a differential exists) and to its coverage. Notice, for example, that in February 1970 the basic minimum was $1.60 per hour (as fixed in the 1966 amendment), and 55 percent of teenagers were covered by it; yet another 20 percent

TABLE 1

THE MINIMUM WAGE AND ITS COVERAGE OF TEENAGE EMPLOYMENT

	Basic Minimum		Differential Minimum	
Date	Wage (dollars) (1)	Coverage (proportion) (2)	Wage (dollars) (3)	Coverage (proportion) (4)
February 1950	0.75	0.38	—	—
March 1956	1.00	0.39	—	—
September 1961	1.15	0.42	1.00	0.13
September 1963	1.25	0.41	1.00	0.13
September 1964	1.25	0.41	1.15	0.13
September 1965	1.25	0.54	—	—
February 1967	1.40	0.54	1.00	0.20
February 1968	1.60	0.54	1.15	0.20
February 1969	1.60	0.55	1.30	0.20
February 1970	1.60	0.55	1.45	0.20
February 1971	1.60	0.75	—	—
May 1974	2.00	0.57	1.90	0.23
January 1975	2.10	0.57	2.00	0.23
January 1976	2.30	0.57	2.20	0.24
January 1977	2.30	0.82	—	—
January 1978	2.65	0.84	—	—
January 1979	2.90	0.85	—	—
January 1980	3.10	0.85	—	—

NOTE: Coverage figures are calculated using the industry proportions of nonsupervisory personnel subject to the minimum wage provisions of the 1938 Fair Labor Standards Act and its amendments. The industry proportions are averaged using as weights the average industrial distribution of teenage employment for the years 1954–1963. The result can be interpreted as the proportion of teenage employment subject to minimum wages.
SOURCE: Authors.

were covered at a differential minimum of $1.45 per hour as a result of the expansion of the 1966 amendment. One year later, the differential caught the basic minimum, and combined coverage remained at 75 percent.

Figure 3 illustrates combined teenage coverage and the basic minimum as a fraction of the average manufacturing wage. There, the picture is one of erratic swings in the minimum when compared with other labor costs with no apparent long-run trend. In contrast, coverage is not

FIGURE 3

THE MINIMUM WAGE AND ITS COVERAGE OF TEENAGERS, 1954–1979

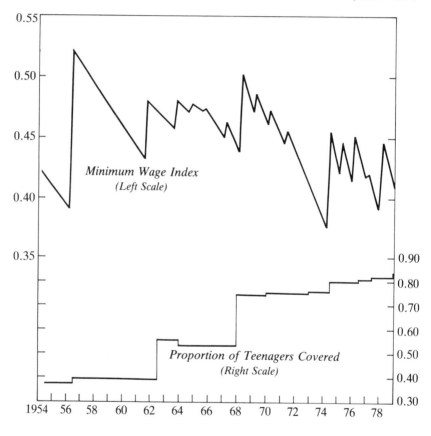

NOTE: The minimum wage index is the legislated minimum wage deflated by average hourly earnings in manufacturing. When there are two minimum wage rates in effect, the index, deflated by average hourly earnings in manufacturing, is a coverage-weighted average of the two minimums. Coverage is adjusted for the industrial distribution of teenage employment.

SOURCE: Authors.

subject to erosion by inflation or by growth in labor productivity. When the employment series that we analyzed was initially published, fewer than two in five teenage jobs were covered, and at this writing more than four in five are covered.

Minimum Wages and Employment: What Should We Expect?

There are by now numerous available empirical and theoretical studies of minimum wage effects, so we will not belabor the theory. Instead, against the historical background of what the legislation has been like, we will simply describe the measures of potential effect we construct for use in estimation.

First, we always consider the nominal minimum as a fraction of the average manufacturing wage. The idea is that whenever wages are generally higher, a proportionately higher minimum will have the same employment effect as a proportionately lower one would when wages are generally lower. For simplicity, we will henceforth refer to the ratio—the nominal minimum divided by the average manufacturing wage—as the minimum wage.

Aside from compliance, which we do not explicitly consider, coverage has two dimensions. First, there is extensive coverage of the type described in table 1 that refers to firms being liable under the law. The coverage proportions in table 1 are crude estimates of the fraction of teenagers employed in firms where legislation obtains. Second, there is intensive coverage that is more subtle. It refers to the question of whether a wage constraint is binding.

If a worker in any case would have earned more than the minimum, for example, then its imposition cannot directly affect him. Intensive coverage is an analytical problem because wages are distributed over a broad range, and, as figure 3 shows, the minimum has itself fluctuated widely over time. In a period in which the minimum is raised, it not only raises the cost of employing workers previously receiving the old minimum but spreads to cover and raise the cost of employing all those with wages between the old and new minimums. Formally, intensive coverage expansions amount to nonlinearities in measuring minimum wage effects, and subtleties of this kind are better addressed with more refined data than the aggregate series we examine. Thus, our references to coverage are only to extensive coverage.[1]

Our first construct of potential effect is the product, coverage mul-

---

[1] We did, of course, experiment in estimation with the quadratic form suggested by Finis Welch, *Minimum Wages: Issues and Evidence* (Washington, D.C.: American Enterprise Institute, 1978). However, our estimates for total effects at sample means were almost identical for the quadratic and linear specifications. Moreover, the two specifications "fit the data" equally well. Thus, under the rule that when simple and complex forms perform equally, simple is better, we opted for the simpler formulation.

tiplied by the basic minimum. In this simple form, a 1 percent increase in coverage will have the same employment effect as a 1 percent increase in the minimum. Notice that the coverage measure used in constructing this term refers to aggregate coverage and ignores the possibility that part of the coverage refers to a differential minimum.

Thus, our second construct is a correction for the first and obtains whenever a differential for newly covered sectors applies. It is the product of two numbers. The first is that part of coverage (column 4 of table 1) for which the lower of two minimums applies, and the second is the difference between the two minimums (column 1 minus column 3 of table 1, divided by the average manufacturing wage).

Finally, our third variable characterizing the federal legislation is the size of the sector not covered. It is our estimate of the proportion of teen employment in firms not subject to the legislation. The idea underlying this variable is simple. We do not have data showing employment in covered firms. Instead, we have estimates only of employment in all firms. If the minimum is increased, workers will be displaced in covered firms. The number displaced depends both on the way each covered firm responds to a wage increase and on the number of such firms. This effect is intended to be captured in our first variable characterizing the legislation. Yet workers displaced from the covered sector need not appear as reductions in aggregate employment, as opportunities persist in the uncovered sector. Because the absorptive capacity of the uncovered sector depends on its size, the third variable is designed to capture this effect.

We may now trace the probable history of minimum wage effects on three groups of employees. The first is a stereotype of workers who have low productivity and who, in the absence of legislation, would receive wages below the minimum. The second is composed of white teenage males who are heterogeneous; some would receive wages below and some above the various minimums. The third group comprises teenage males who are black; like whites, blacks are heterogeneous, but we presume that in the absence of the legislation larger proportions of blacks would receive lower wages.

For the low-productivity stereotype, the initial imposition of minimum wages (in 1938) curtailed employment in covered sectors. This displacement resulted in a shift toward jobs in uncovered sectors where increased numbers of job competitors reduced wages. As wages fell, some rejected these inferior options and total employment fell.

Until 1961, coverage remained at levels fixed in the 1938 legislation, so the only departures from the scenario just described derive from fluctuations of the minimum itself. The initial legislation fixed a nominal minimum of twenty-five cents (40.3 percent of the average manufacturing wage) in 1938 and provided for steps to thirty and forty cents in

1939 and 1945. The first step raised the minimum to 47.8 percent and the second to 39.4 percent of the manufacturing wage, although in 1945 before the jump to forty cents the thirty-cent minimum was only 29.5 percent of the manufacturing wage. From 1938 to 1961, the minimum fluctuated between 27.8 and 52.1 percent of the manufacturing average. Programmed steps and new amendments initiated sharp jumps with intervening erosion as general wage levels grew.

Then, in 1961, coverage expanded to include an extra 13 percent of teenage employment. For our homogeneous low-productivity stereotype, this expansion would have a somewhat larger employment depressant effect within newly covered firms than for those initially covered because, as a result of the initial program, these subsequently covered firms had absorbed part of the initial displacement. The first legislative variable is intended to measure the overall effect, and the third captures part of the effect of expanding coverage via shrinkage of the size of the uncovered sector. Of course, when coverage was expanded (in 1961, in 1967, and again in 1974), newly covered firms were buffered with a somewhat reduced minimum so that the initial effect was moderated. It grew as the buffer was eliminated (see table 1).

Thus, for the low-productivity group, the employment depressant effect of minimum wages fluctuates with the minimum, increases with coverage, and increases again as differentials extended to newly covered firms are withdrawn. Because the minimum itself shows no clear trend, the dominant source of growth in the effect of the minimum wage would be from expansions in coverage.

This simple picture blurs as attention shifts from the stereotype low-productivity group to white teenagers and then becomes clearer as attention shifts to black-white contrasts. The confusion for whites stems from the fact that they are heterogeneous and that some would have earned more than the minimum in any case. Although such workers are not directly affected in the sense that the legislation would not have directly changed their wages, they obviously are indirectly affected and the indirect effect may well have been beneficial. If such workers are substitutes for those who would earn less, then a minimum that raises the cost of lower-productivity workers will strengthen employment demands for them.

Need teenagers as a group be disadvantaged by minimum wage laws? It all depends. Among other things, it depends upon the proportion that would earn above the minimum in any case. It depends also on whether and, if so, on the degree to which those who would be below and those who are above the minimum are employment substitutes. Just as important, it depends on the sheer numbers of workers in other demographic groups who would receive less.

In an earlier paper, Finis Welch and James Cunningham presented a hypothetical distribution for what wages would have been in the absence of minimum wage legislation. In that paper they also reported estimates from work by Donald Parsons suggesting that the average wage of persons aged eighteen to nineteen in the absence of wage laws would have been two-thirds of the manufacturing average and that the average for those sixteen to seventeen years old would have been 52 percent of the manufacturing wage. The minimum wage itself averaged about 44 percent of the manufacturing wage, so that perhaps more than one-half of all teenagers would have received wages above this level. In fact, if we use the distribution suggested by Welch and Cunningham, 62 percent of those eighteen to nineteen years old and 50 percent of those sixteen to seventeen years old would have earned wages above a minimum that is 44 percent of the manufacturing average wage.[2]

Further work by Edward Gramlich and by Finis Welch suggests that teenagers account for only about one-third of workers in low-wage jobs whereas prime-aged adults, twenty-five to sixty-four years old, account for half of these jobs.[3] Thus, it is probably true that most teenagers would receive wages above the minimum in any case, and it is probably also true that most of those who would receive wages below the minimum are not teenagers. The question of whether higher minimums reduce teen employment is then a question, first, of the displacement of those who would have earned less than the minimum compared with the probably enhanced employment opportunities of those who would have earned more. It remains true that virtually all available empirical studies of youth employment find that higher minimums are associated with reduced employment.[4] Yet Robert Cotterman, in his contribution to this volume, finds in manufacturing that higher minimums result in increased employment for white males eighteen to nineteen years old. We are not surprised by this result and suspect that the aggregate studies, like this one and like those cited, refer to net relationships showing only that job losses outnumber gains.

By their very nature, minimum wage laws have the greatest proportionate effect on the costs of employing those who would have re-

[2] Finis Welch and James Cunningham, "Effects of Minimum Wages on the Age and Composition of Youth Employment," *Review of Economics and Statistics* 60 (February 1978):140–45; Donald O. Parsons, "The Cost of School Time, Forgone Earnings, and Human Capital Formation," *Journal of Political Economy* 82 (March 1974):251–66.

[3] Edward M. Gramlich, "Impact of Minimum Wages on Other Wages, Employment, and Family Incomes," *Activity* 2 (1976): 409–51; Welch, *Minimum Wages: Issues and Evidence*.

[4] See, for example, Gramlich, "Impact of Minimum Wages"; Jacob Mincer, "Unemployment Effects of Minimum Wages," *Journal of Political Economy* 84 (August 1976): 87–104; and James F. Ragan, "Minimum Wages and the Youth Labor Market," *Review of Economics and Statistics* 59 (May 1977): 129–36. For a review of earlier studies, see R. S. Goldfarb, "The Policy Content of Quantitative Minimum Wage Research," in *Proceedings of IRRA Winter Meetings* (San Francisco: Industrial Relations Research Institute, 1974).

ceived the lowest wage. As such, the theory of what the effects might be is much clearer for comparisons across demographic groups than it is for an isolated group, because of the heterogeneity within groups.

As for black-white contrasts, if, as we presume, it is true that blacks on average would have received lower wages than whites, then higher minimums would be expected to reduce employment of blacks relative to whites. Coverage expansions into sectors that, because of the legislation, are relatively more crowded with blacks will also take a disproportionate bite, and if coverage extensions are initially buffered with differential minimums, the black position will erode even further relative to whites as the differential is eliminated.

Effects of Cohort Size on Employment Rates

In 1954, for every teenager in the population there were more than seven adults between the ages of thirty-five and sixty-five. By 1978 the number of teenagers in the population more than doubled, and there were fewer than four adults for every teenager in the (civilian) population. The arrival of these large young cohorts crowded the labor markets and, barring perfect substitution, put downward pressure on the wages of teenagers relative to older, more skilled workers.[5] With lower relative wages, some teenagers would find employment less attractive relative to other alternatives such as full-time schooling. We would expect to find the proportion of teenagers employed to fall when they become a larger component of the labor force. Our first cohort-size variable is designed to capture this effect and is defined as the ratio of the teenage population to the adult labor force.

It is important to note that this argument makes no statements about which teenage demographic groups would experience a larger decline in their proportion employed. There are no compelling arguments to believe that low-skilled workers will be harder hit than semi-skilled workers. Workers who substitute closely for other workers whose numbers have increased will share the impact on wages of the increased supply.[6] Thus, the larger the number of closely substitutable workers there are—say, for unskilled teenagers—the smaller will be the depressant effect on wages of an increase in their population, and the smaller will be the fall in their proportion employed. An increase in the pop-

[5] See Finis Welch, "Effects of Cohort Size on Earnings: The Baby Boom Babies' Financial Bust," *Journal of Political Economy* 87 (October 1979): 565–97.

[6] Differences in the labor supply behavior of the two groups is also important to understanding the effect on the relative employment probability of black and white male teenagers. We make no assumptions about systematic differences.

ulation of teenagers may hit semiskilled teenagers harder, with the consequence of increasing the proportion of low-skilled teenagers employed relative to the same proportion for semiskilled teenagers. We do not have a prediction of the effect of our first cohort-size variable on the relative proportions of black and white male teenagers employed. To this point, however, we have ignored the way in which minimum wages modify the effects of the arrival of large teenage cohorts in the labor market.

A legislated minimum wage prevents the wage of low-skilled teenagers from falling when their numbers increase relative to more skilled workers. It was the falling wage, however, that induced employers to hire more low-skilled teenagers in relation to other workers. Firms will hire larger proportions of semiskilled teenagers whose wages are falling relative to the minimum—the wage of low-skilled teenagers. Although we do not know how the growing youthfulness of the labor force affects the relative proportions of black and white male teenagers employed, with effective minimum wages we would shift our bets toward decreases.

These arguments point to conditioning the effect of increases in the ratio of teenagers to adults on the level of the minimum wage or the extent of its coverage. We do not do this in our empirical analysis simply because highly trended aggregate time series data are not rich enough to pick up these subtleties. During the period from 1962 to 1976, however, when the proportion of teenagers in the population rose dramatically, coverage of the minimum wage was substantial, rising from 55 to 82 percent, and we believe this is important for interpreting the empirical results.

Employment rates of teenagers are also likely to be affected by the size of other cohorts—in particular, groups that compete with teenagers for their jobs. Natural candidates are young adults twenty to twenty-four years old. Another feature of this group is that what once was a large teenage cohort quickly becomes a large young-adult cohort. Does a large cohort arriving at the labor market create more room for others as they mature and leave and others replace them?

Our second cohort-size variable is the young-adult labor force divided by the adult labor force. Notice that in this specification, as the size of all groups grows proportionately, the employment rates of all groups, black male teens and white male teens in our case, remain unaffected. Employment rates are affected only by the demographic composition and not by the size of the labor force. Of course, it is not the demographic composition per se that is important; it is the composition of the labor force by types of labor that we abstractly classify as unskilled, semiskilled, and skilled.

134

Empirical Analysis

In this section we discuss the results from estimating two sets of regressions with monthly data from the Current Population Survey for the period 1954–1978. For the first regression the dependent variable is the employment of sixteen- to nineteen-year-old male teenagers divided by their total population. We frequently refer to this variable as the aggregate employment probability of male teenagers. "Aggregate" indicates that it includes both races. The dependent variable in the second regression is the ratio of the proportion of black male teenagers employed to the corresponding proportion for whites. We call this the relative employment probability of black and white teenage males. This variable is indicative of the racial composition of teenage employment. Tables 6 and 7 of the appendix report the full results from estimating these regressions.

Other than the three minimum wage variables and the two cohort-size variables, we include several "control" variables in the models we estimate. The teenage years are ones of rapid change, and even within the age span of sixteen to nineteen there are dramatic differences. Eighteen- to nineteen-year-olds are much more likely to have work experience, be out of school, and not live with their parents. As separate estimates of monthly employment rates for sixteen- to seventeen-year-olds and eighteen- to nineteen-year-olds by race and sex are not available, we add as a controlling variable the proportion of all sixteen- to nineteen-year-olds who are eighteen to nineteen years old. To capture the effects of cyclical changes in the demand for labor, we include the unemployment rate of males forty-five to fifty-four years old. To capture the large seasonal variation in the employment of teenagers, dummy variables for February through December are included.

As indicated earlier, minimum wages and the increasing relative size of the teenage population are unlikely to explain the trend since 1965 for the proportion of teenagers employed to increase. We therefore include a trend term in the regression to restrict our analysis to deviations about trend, and it is these regressions that we present in appendix table 6. We have also estimated the regressions with trend excluded. These results, presented in table 7, are broadly consistent with those including trend.

Three important determinants of teenage employment rates are the number of teenagers enrolled in school, the number in the military, and the number in federal youth programs. Unfortunately, they may themselves be influenced by minimum wage hikes or the increasing relative size of the teenage population. We experimentally exclude and include

135

these "potentially endogenous" variables. Let us postpone further discussion of them until our presentation of the empirical results.

Minimum Wage Effects

Recall that we use three minimum wage variables in our regressions. The first is the basic federal minimum (divided by average hourly earnings in manufacturing) weighted by the proportion of teenage employment subject to either the basic minimum wage or the one applied to newly covered industries, $(CB + CN)MB$. Variation in this variable is proportional to the variation in the cost of employing teenagers due to minimum wages. This assumes that the minimum wage is effective for a constant fraction of teenagers and that there is some average amount of compliance with the legislation.[7] If the fraction of teenagers for whom the minimum is effective is directly proportional to the minimum, then the cost of employing teenagers would vary with the square of the minimum wage $(CB + CN)MB^2$. We found that in our data the results were substantially the same with either specification.

The second minimum wage variable is a correction for the first because new coverage is subject to a lower minimum. It is the differential between the basic minimum and the one applied to newly covered sectors multiplied by new coverage, $CN(MB - MN)$. The third variable is the size of the uncovered sector, $(1 - CB - CN)$.

Table 2 utilizes the regression results to calculate the effects of increasing the basic minimum, increasing its coverage, extending coverage at a lower minimum, and removing the differential on the newly covered sector. Increasing the basic minimum covering one-half of teenage employment from 0.4 to 0.5 of average hourly earnings in manufacturing, which is comparable to raising the minimum from $2.50 to $3.25 when average hourly earnings are $6.50, reduces the aggregate employment probability of male teenagers by roughly one percentage point. Our point estimates indicate a positive effect on the employment probability of blacks relative to whites, but the standard errors are quite

---

[7] Orley Ashenfelter and Robert S. Smith, "Compliance with the Minimum Wage Law," *Journal of Political Economy* 87 (April 1979): 333–50, using data on straight-time hourly earnings available since 1973 from the Current Population Survey, do estimate compliance rates for fully covered white and black teenage workers in 1973 and again in 1975. Unfortunately, when they estimate compliance rates, data deficiencies compel them to assume that no workers lose their jobs in covered sectors due to minimum wage legislation. If legislated minimums cause workers to lose jobs in the covered sector, their estimates of coverage are biased downward. Because our model indicates that legislated minimums reduce employment in the covered sector for all teenagers, and more sharply for black teenagers, their estimates of compliance are not useful for our work.

TABLE 2

ESTIMATES OF EFFECTS OF INCREASES IN MINIMUM WAGES AND
COVERAGE ON THE PROPORTION OF MALE TEENAGERS EMPLOYED
AND THE RELATIVE PROPORTIONS OF BLACK TO WHITE MALE
TEENAGERS EMPLOYED
(standard errors in parentheses)

| | Potentially Endogenous Variables | | | |
| | Excluded | | Included | |
Dependent Variable	Total	Black/white	Total	Black/white
Increase basic minimum from 0.4 to 0.5 of average hourly earnings in manufacturing	−.011 (.0036)	.019 (.0185)	−.006 (.0041)	.001 (.0193)
Increase coverage of basic minimum by 10 percentage points	−.008 (.0030)	−.015 (.0150)	−.008 (.0030)	−.015 (.0141)
Extend coverage to another 10 percent of teenage employment at a new lower minimum	−.005 (.0025)	−.002 (.0121)	−.004 (.0024)	−.001 (.0113)
Eliminate the differential between the new lower minimum and the basic minimum	−.003 (.0012)	−.014 (.0060)	−.004 (.0012)	−.014 (.0058)

NOTE: The effects are calculated using the estimated regressions in appendix table 6. The derivatives are evaluated at roughly the means of the minimum wage variables—$MWB/AHE = .425$, $MWN/AHE = .375$, $CB = .5$, and $CN = .10$. For estimates of these effects evaluated at other values of the minimum wage variables, see appendix table 8.
SOURCE: Authors.

large.[8] Extending coverage of the basic minimum to another 10 percent of teenage employment reduces their employment probability by 0.8 percentage points. Again, the direction of the effect on the relative employment probability is uncertain, but the point estimates are negative. We can conclude that an increase in the basic minimum or its coverage decreases aggregate teen employment, but we cannot be certain of the effects on the racial composition of teen employment.

---

[8] When trend is omitted from the regression model, the effect of increasing the minimum wage is to reduce the employment probability of blacks relative to whites. The effect of coverage expansion of either the basic minimum or the minimum applied to newly covered sectors is to reduce the employment probability of blacks relative to whites, whether linear, quadratic, or no trend is included.

137

Increases in the coverage of the basic minimum occurred in two steps in our data: (1) Coverage is extended at a lower minimum, and (2) the differential between the basic and lower minimum is phased out in legislatively programmed increments. The third and fourth rows of table 2 decompose the effect of extending coverage of the basic minimum. Assuming the basic and lower minimums are 0.425 and 0.375, respectively, of average hourly earnings, roughly one-half of the aggregate employment losses occur when coverage is extended at the lower minimum, and the other half when the differential is withdrawn.

This decomposition shows that the effects on the relative employment probability of black and white teenage males are not balanced. There is virtually no effect of increasing coverage at the lower minimum on the relative likelihood of blacks and whites finding jobs, but as the differential is eliminated the relative employment probability falls by 0.014, which is 1.8 percent of its mean value of 0.79. Eliminating the differential is comparable to raising the minimum from $2.45 to $2.75 on 10 percent of teenage employment when average hourly earnings are $6.50. Unlike the total effect, this component is significantly different from zero.

The size of these effects is fairly small. To obtain a better grasp of their size, we break down the changes in the aggregate and relative employment probabilities attributable to each of the explanatory variables in our estimated regressions. Table 3 presents the accounting for two periods, 1965–1978 and 1954–1978. The former subperiod was chosen because beginning in 1965 the proportion of white teenage males reversed its previous trend and began increasing while the proportion of black teenage males continued to fall. Table 4 reports the same calculations using the estimated regressions that include the potentially endogenous variables.

Almost all of the changes over time in minimum wages relate to the expansion of its coverage from 39 to 85 percent of teenage employment. During the 1954–1978 period an additional 46 percent of teenage employment became subject to minimum wage legislation. Because of this, our estimated regressions "predict" that the proportion of male teens employed fell 4.0 percentage points over the entire period, of which 2.2 percentage points are attributable to changes since 1965. Although these numbers are not small, they may be surprisingly small considering the large increase in the coverage of minimum wage legislation. It is likely that a large proportion of teenagers earn more than the minimum wage and are not directly affected by it. In addition, it is likely that the minimum wage has the indirect effect of increasing the demand for semiskilled teenagers as firms substitute away from low-

TABLE 3

ACCOUNTING FOR CHANGES IN THE PROPORTION OF MALE
TEENAGERS EMPLOYED AND THE RELATIVE PROPORTIONS OF
BLACK TO WHITE MALE TEENAGERS EMPLOYED

	1965–1978		1954–1978	
Dependent Variable	Total	Black/white	Total	Black/white
Actual change	0.087	−0.356	0.046	−0.600
Estimated change attributable to:				
Minimum wages	−0.020	−0.052	−0.039	−0.072
Cohort size				
Ratio of teens to adults	−0.031	−0.019	−0.074	−0.045
Ratio of young adults to adults	0.172	−0.024	0.227	−0.032
Proportion of teens 18–19 years old	0.001	0.001	0.008	0.007
Unemployment rate of adult males 45–54	−0.004	−0.001	0.027	0.010
Unexplained change				
Trend	−0.050	−0.219	−0.110	−0.478
Residual	0.018	−0.042	0.006	0.010

NOTE: Predicted changes are calculated based on the regression specification that excludes potentially endogenous variables. See appendix table 6.
SOURCE: Authors.

skilled teenage workers as well as low-skilled workers from other demographic groups.

Cohort-Size Effects

Increases in the population of teenagers have a strong negative effect on their employment probability. A 10 percent increase in the population of teenagers relative to adults reduces the proportion employed by 0.017. The standard error of this estimate is 0.0026 in the regression excluding the potentially endogenous variables and is 0.0035 in the one including them. The same increase in the population of teenagers (in the presence of minimum wages) reduces the employment probability of black teenage males relative to white teenage males in the two regression specifications by 0.103 and 0.309, which is 13 percent and 39 percent of its

TABLE 4

ACCOUNTING FOR CHANGES IN THE PROPORTION OF MALE
TEENAGERS EMPLOYED AND THE RELATIVE PROPORTIONS OF
BLACK TO WHITE MALE TEENAGERS EMPLOYED

	1965–1978		1954–1978	
Dependent Variable	Total	Black/white	Total	Black/white
Actual change	0.087	−0.356	0.046	−0.600
Estimated change attributable to:				
Minimum wages	−0.022	−0.044	−0.040	−0.072
Cohort size				
Ratio of teens to adults	−0.032	−0.056	−0.076	−0.136
Ratio of young adults to adults	0.146	−0.122	0.193	−0.161
Proportion of teens 18–19 years old	0.001	0.000	0.007	0.002
Proportion of teens in the military	0.007	0.025	0.018	0.064
Proportion of teens enrolled in school	0.008	0.002	−0.019	−0.006
Proportion of teens in federal youth programs	0.003	0.105	0.004	0.132
Unemployment rate of adult males 45–54	−0.004	−0.001	0.030	0.010
Unexplained change				
Trend	−0.036	−0.200	−0.079	−0.435
Residual	0.016	−0.065	0.007	−0.020

NOTE: Predicted changes are calculated based on the regression specification that includes potentially endogenous variables. See appendix table 6.
SOURCE: Authors.

mean of 0.79. The standard errors of these estimates are large, but it does seem that increases in the population of teenagers hit blacks harder than whites.

The populations of teenagers, the young-adult labor force, and the adult labor force are all strongly trended. Their correlations with trend are, respectively, 0.988, 0.978, and 0.963. To investigate the importance of this, the regressions were reestimated with no trend and also with quadratic trend. In all cases the effect of increases in the population of teenagers reduces both the aggregate employment probability of teenage males and the employment probability of blacks relative to whites. The point estimates varied widely in the relative employment probability regression—from –0.71 to –3.40 with the potentially endogenous variables excluded and from –2.14 to –5.23 with them included. Considering how strongly trended these population variables are, however, the consistency of the negative relationship makes it very unlikely that it is due to a spurious correlation between the teenage population and other unknown factors not included in our model.

Whereas increases in the population of teenagers reduce their employment probability, increases in the population of young adults increase the employment probability of teenagers. This result is surprising because we view young adults as competing with teenagers, in which case an increase in the population of young adults that drives down their wages would induce firms to hire more young adults and fewer teenagers. The positive relationship indicates that other factors dominate this substitution. A 10 percent increase in the population of young adults increases the employment probability of male teenagers by 0.03. This result is a strong one and is always positive whether no trend variable is included or quadratic trend is included. The effect of increases in the population of young adults on the employment probability of blacks relative to whites is statistically insignificant and changes sign if quadratic trend is included.

Recall that the aggregate employment probability of male teenagers over time is U-shaped. It fell gradually over the 1954–1965 period and then rose through 1978. It rose by 0.087 from 1965 to 1978 and by 0.046 over the whole sample period. Effects of increasing coverage of the minimum wage and of the increasing population of teenagers relative to the adult labor force were both estimated as being negative (as we would expect on theoretical grounds) and so cannot account for the upward trend in the aggregate employment probability of teenagers. The effect of linear trend is also estimated as negative. When quadratic trend is included, it is estimated as positive but does not account for the gross trend in the employment probability of teenagers.

Table 5 reports the estimated coefficients of the young-adult to adult labor force ratio in regressions with alternative specifications of trend. These capture unknown factors that are smoothly trended. Also including trend means the relationships between our economic variables and the aggregate employment probability is estimated statistically using only residual variation of these variables about their trends. This is a severe test. Whether linear, quadratic, or no trend is included in the regression model, the estimated effect of increases in the population of young adults is strongly positive, "balancing" the negative effects of increases in the coverage of minimum wages and of increases in the relative size of the teenage population. In addition, it accounts for the

TABLE 5

ESTIMATED COEFFICIENTS OF THE RATIO OF THE YOUNG-ADULT
LABOR FORCE OR POPULATION TO ADULT LABOR FORCE VARIABLE
IN ALTERNATIVE REGRESSION SPECIFICATIONS FOR THE
PROPORTION OF MALE TEENAGERS EMPLOYED
(standard errors in parentheses)

Young Adult Trend Variables	Potentially Endogenous Variables			
	Excluded		Included	
	Labor force	Population	Labor force	Population
None	1.14	1.33	.86	1.05
	(.085)	(.098)	(.106)	(.121)
Linear	1.38	1.35	1.17	1.12
	(.094)	(.101)	(.146)	(.124)
Quadratic	.72	.55	.79	.66
	(.162)	(.160)	(.185)	(.183)

SOURCE: Authors.

gross trends in the aggregate employment probability of male teens. Adding linear trend leaves the estimated coefficients virtually unchanged. Adding quadratic trend reduces them to roughly one-half. No matter which specification is used, virtually all the increase in the employment probability of male teenagers is attributable to the increase in the relative proportion of the labor force that are young adults. We do not pretend to fully understand this empirical phenomenon, but it does minimize the importance of viewing teenagers and young adults as employment substitutes.

It is quite possible that an important factor omitted from our analysis is responsible for the increasing employment probability of male teenagers, in spite of the expanding coverage of minimum wages and the large influx of those born during the baby boom into the labor market, and is correlated with the size of the young-adult labor force. The size of the young-adult labor force clearly is not exogenous to economic factors. When employment conditions improve for teenagers, they also improve for young adults and induce young adults to enter the labor force. This, of course, is precisely the function of the control variables for business-cycle and seasonal fluctuation in the aggregate demand for labor. It is possible, however, that not all the variation is accounted for by these variables and that the young-adult labor force proxies the residual. To shed light on this possibility, the regressions were reestimated using the civilian population of young adults in lieu of young-adult labor force. Using population instead of labor force does not significantly change the estimated coefficients.

Alternatively, economic stories can be told that are consistent with the positive impact of increases in the young-adult labor force on the aggregate employment probability. First, teenagers and young adults may be complementary. Our intuition that teenagers and young adults are substitutes in production is not contradicted by this empirical observation. Teenagers and young adults tend to work "close together." That is, the industrial and occupational distribution of teenagers and young adults is more similar than it is for teenagers and other groups. So although an increase in the supply of young adults will reduce the wages of young adults relative to teenagers and will lead employers to substitute them for teenage workers, it will also reduce the relative cost of young-adult intensive goods and will lead consumers to substitute these goods for others. This increases the demand for teenagers as they work close to young adults. A second view is not fundamentally different from the first except that it puts more emphasis on the dynamic aspects of changes over time. Young adults are simply old teenagers. When a teenage cohort has a large cohort preceding it in time, its employment opportunities are improved. The large advance group will make room for the group that follows. As the wages of the advance group fall, firms will be induced to rearrange their production plans to make use of this relatively less costly factor. The reorganization creates slots and makes it more likely that the firm will continue (at least temporarily) to hire teenagers even as their cost advantage erodes.

Other Control Variables

As to the cyclic sensitivity of teenage employment, our model suggests that the effects of changes in aggregate demand would affect teenage employment probabilities, but more so for teenage blacks than for whites. M. Kosters and F. Welch examine this issue and find that minimum wages increase the cyclical sensitivity of employment of youth, blacks, and women relative to adults, whites, and men, respectively.[9] This is indirectly confirmed by the regression results: A one-percentage-point increase in the adult male unemployment rate (forty-five- to fifty-year-old males) decreases the male teenage employment probability by almost two percentage points (1.8 in one specification and 1.9 in the other). The employment probability of teenagers is cyclically sensitive. The unemployment rate of adult males is a very important variable in

[9] M. Kosters and F. Welch, "The Effects of Minimum Wages on the Distribution in Aggregate Employment," *American Economic Review* 62 (June 1972): 323–32.

the regression, explaining much of the "short-run" variation in the employment of teenagers. Equally important, a 1 percent increase in the unemployment rate reduces the employment of blacks relative to whites by 0.006. The standard error for this estimate, though, is fairly large.

There is tremendous seasonal variation in the employment of teenagers. In July, for instance, a teenage male's employment probability is almost seventeen percentage points higher than it is in January. As expected, the fraction of teenagers employed increases, as larger proportions of teenagers are in the eighteen- to nineteen-year-old age group. The point estimates in the two specifications are 0.76 and 0.67. The interpretation is that an eighteen- or nineteen-year-old has a 0.76 higher probability of being employed than a sixteen- or seventeen-year-old, and holding the proportion of all teenagers enrolled in school constant, an eighteen- or nineteen-year-old has a 0.67 higher probability of being employed than his younger counterpart. These estimates appear "too" large but do point to important differences within the teenage cohort.

The Potentially Endogenous Variables

There are three variables that are at least potentially jointly determined with the employment probability of teens: (1) the school enrollment rate, (2) the proportion "employed" in federal youth programs, and (3) the proportion in the military. Minimum wages and cohort size may be factors that influence a teenager's decision to enroll in school, join the armed forces, participate in government-sponsored employment programs, or work in the private sector. If this were the case, it would not be appropriate to include these variables as regressors and interpret their coefficients as the influence of changes in these variables on the (aggregate) employment probability of teens. In this volume both James Cunningham and Peter Mattila explicitly consider the issue of the effect of minimum wages on school enrollments.[10] We estimate two different specifications of the regression models with these variables alternately excluded and included. The results of the specifications are similar.

We derive the monthly proportion of male teenagers in the military by subtracting the civilian teenage labor force (employed and unemployed) from the total teenage labor force (employed, unemployed, and military). We then assume that all teenagers in the military are male to calculate the proportion of teenage males in the military. As the proportion of women (of all ages) in the military has been increasing, the

[10] Also see Terence F. Kelly, "Youth Employment Opportunities and the Minimum Wage: An Econometric Model of Occupational Choice," Urban Institute Work Paper 3608–1, 1975.

error of our assumption is growing over time but is of little empirical importance. Patterns of military participation over the period are quite interesting: Male teenage participation in the military increased up to 1958 when over 12 percent of the male teenage population were in the military, declined until mid-1965 to about 5 percent, and then increased during the Vietnam period to about 9 percent. Since then it has declined, and in 1978 less than 4 percent of the male teenage population were in the military.

In the aggregate employment probability regression, the coefficient of the teenage male military participation rate is –0.299. There is a 30 percent chance that each new recruit or inductee was employed before entering the military. In the relative employment probability regression, the estimated coefficient is –1.03 and has a standard error of 0.58. The negative effect is probably due to the fact that proportionately more blacks enter the military than whites.

From a base of essentially zero in the mid-1960s, federal youth employment programs have mushroomed; especially for black youth, where a larger fraction of the youth population participates, the potential effect on the employment population ratio is substantial. In the summer of 1978, for example, 994,000 youths participated in SPEDY (Summer Program for Economically Disadvantaged Youths). Of these youths, 51.6 percent were male, 57.7 percent were black, and 56.1 percent were between the ages of sixteen and nineteen.[11] Assuming these character-

---

[11] There are no data available either for average yearly enrollment in all federal government manpower programs (by age, race, and sex) or for actual monthly enrollment (by age, race, and sex). We utilized yearly Manpower Reports of the President (Employment and Training Reports of the President in later years) and relied heavily upon the work of Charles Killingsworth and Mark R. Killingsworth, "Direct Effects of Employment and Training Programs on Employment and Unemployment: New Estimates and Implications for Employment Policy," in U.S. Department of Labor, *Conference Report on Youth Employment: Its Measurement and Meaning,* Washington, D.C., 1978, pp. 249–476. The fraction of the participants in SPEDY who were sixteen- to nineteen-years-old was obtained from the Office of Youth Programs of the U.S. Department of Labor. For each year we computed two estimates of male teenage enrollments in federal youth employment programs, one for the summer months (July and August) and one for the other months of each year. These were then added together and divided by the total teenage male population to calculate an estimate of the proportion of teenage males enrolled in federal youth programs. There are substantial problems in the measurement of these variables; however, even if the numerical estimates were correct, it is not completely clear that we have the appropriate data. The Current Population Survey does not solicit information about manpower program participation from its respondents: only if the interviewee volunteers the information—and the evidence suggests that only a small proportion of enrollees do so—does the interviewer place the respondent in the category (unemployed, employed, out of the labor force) that fits the CPS estimate of the program's characteristics. Implicitly, then, we are relying upon the respondent to evaluate his labor market status as would the CPS interviewer. Though some of these classifications are understandable (Neighborhood Youth Corps work is counted as employment), some of the classifications are not (Job Corpsmen, for example, are counted as out of the labor force).

istics are independent, we calculate that 166,000 black males were employed in SPEDY in the summer of 1978. The total number of black males employed in the summer of 1978 was 519,200. Thus, 32 percent of employed black male teenagers worked in the federal government's summer manpower program. Moreover, SPEDY is not the only government manpower program that employed black male teenagers in the summer of 1978. They were also employed in fairly large numbers under Title VI of the Comprehensive Employment and Training Act (Emergency Public Service Employment), under the new programs set up as Title VIII of CETA (YIEPP, YCCIP, YEIP, and YACC), and under a variety of other, smaller programs.

Because enrollment in these programs has increasingly accounted for a large fraction of black employment, it is especially unfortunate that monthly manpower enrollment rates (by age, race, and sex) have never been compiled and that the mapping from enrollment in manpower programs to measured labor-market status is uncertain. We attempt to measure the number of enrollees who should have been counted as employed but emphasize that our measurements are crude. Caution should be exercised in the interpretation of our empirical results.

The point estimate of the coefficient of the proportion of teenagers in federal youth programs is 0.08 and has a standard error of 0.10. When trend is omitted, the point estimate jumps to 0.16 and the standard error is unchanged. The proportion of teenagers participating in federal programs does not appear to have an important effect on the aggregate proportion employed. This is not the case, however, for the employment probability of black teenage males relative to white teenage males. The estimated coefficient in this regression is 2.71. The interpretation of this coefficient is that a black youth who is not employed is much more likely to enroll in a federal youth employment program than a white youth in a similar position.

We use the October school enrollment rate for sixteen- to nineteen-year-old male teenagers of both races. As monthly enrollment rates are unavailable for the full period of our sample, the effect on teenage employment of any seasonality in the enrollment rate—that is, the monthly variation in the enrollment rate from its October value—is not captured by our variable but is attributed to the monthly dummy variables included in the regression. Its estimated coefficient in the aggregate employment probability regression is –0.20 (–0.30 with trend omitted) and has a standard error of 0.06. This indicates that students are 20 percent less likely to be employed than nonstudents. This is as would be expected. Students are less likely to find full-time work consistent with their school schedules. In addition, students who work part-time are likely to receive lower wages as part-time work is less productive.

Parsons estimated that students received roughly 25 percent lower wages than nonstudents of the same age and schooling.[12]

In 1958, 70 percent of white teenage males were enrolled in school. After 1958 their enrollment rate grew slowly, peaking in 1968 at 78 percent, and has declined somewhat since then. It was 69 percent in 1978. For black teenage males, however, the enrollment rate has increased throughout the period of our study. It was 60 percent in 1958, well below that of their white counterparts, and in 1978 it was 73 percent, actually higher than for whites. To what extent can these differences account for the divergence after 1964 in the trends of the proportions of black and white teenagers employed? The enrollment rate of white teenage males has decreased almost six percentage points since 1964, whereas for blacks it rose by almost seven. Using our estimate that students are 20 percent less likely to be employed than nonstudents, we can attribute a 0.012 rise in the proportion of whites employed and a 0.013 fall in the proportion of blacks employed to differences in trends of their enrollment rates. Much more of the employment trends remain to be explained.

Summary and Conclusions

The secular trends in the employment population ratios of teenage demographic groups have presented economists with a puzzle. Although the proportions of both black and white teenage males declined gradually from 1954 to 1965, since 1965 the trends have diverged, rising for whites and continuing to fall for blacks. What can account for this divergence?

Two important phenomena of the last twenty-five years have had important effects on teenagers' experiences in the labor market. First, the coverage of minimum wage legislation has more than doubled from 39 to 84 percent of teenage employment. Second, the post–World War II baby boom has brought a large shift in the age structure of the labor force. To understand how these factors would have an effect on the demographic composition of teenage employment, we must abandon a view of teenagers as a single, homogeneous group of workers. There is evidence of considerable dispersion in the wages of teenagers.[13] In fact, there is evidence to suggest that more than one-half of all teenagers would earn greater than the minimum in its absence. If some teenage demographic groups comprise higher proportions of low-skilled workers, increases in the minimum wage further reduce their employment. This is corroborated empirically. We estimate that the large expansion of the coverage of minimum wages has reduced the proportion of male teen-

[12] Parsons, "Cost."
[13] See, for example, Welch, *Minimum Wages: Issues and Evidence*

TABLE 6

REGRESSION ESTIMATES OF EFFECTS OF MINIMUM WAGES AND COHORT SIZE ON THE PROPORTION OF MALE TEENAGERS EMPLOYED AND THE RELATIVE PROPORTIONS OF BLACK TO WHITE MALE TEENAGERS EMPLOYED
(standard errors in parentheses)

Dependent Variable	Total[a]	Black/White[b]	Total	Black/White
Minimum wage				
Basic	−.300	−.131	−.221	−.454
	(.072)	(.354)	(.075)	(.355)
Differential	.688	2.741	.767	2.862
	(.242)	(1.193)	(.246)	(1.163)
Size of uncovered sector	−.046	.099	−.011	−.043
	(.045)	(.220)	(.045)	(.215)
Cohort size				
Ratio of civilian male teenage population to adult (35–65) labor force	−1.166 (.182)	−.712 (.894)	−1.193 (.236)	−2.137 (1.120)
Ratio of young adult (20–24) to adult (35–65) labor force	1.377 (.094)	−.192 (.465)	1.172 (.146)	−.980 (.694)
Proportion of total male teenage population 18–19 years old	.758 (.067)	.615 (.330)	.672 (.074)	.156 (.348)
Proportion of male teenagers enrolled in school	—	—	−.198 (.062)	−.059 (.296)
Proportion of male teenagers in the military	—	—	−.299 (.122)	−1.034 (.578)
Proportion of male teenagers in federal youth programs	—	—	.079 (.101)	2.707 (.480)
Unemployment rate of adult males 45–54	−.0180 (.0010)	−.0063 (.0051)	−0198 (.0011)	−.0069 (.0053)
Trend	−.0046	−.0199	−.0033	−.0181
	(.0009)	(.0045)	(.0011)	(.0051)
February	.007	.017	.006	.018
	(.004)	(.021)	(.004)	(.020)
March	.011	.014	.010	.015
	(.004)	(.021)	(.004)	(.020)
April	.025	.015	.023	.014
	(.004)	(.021)	(.004)	(.020)

TABLE 6 (continued)

Dependent Variable	Total[a]	Black/White[b]	Total	Black/White
May	.033	.010	.030	.010
	(.004)	(.022)	(.004)	(.021)
June	.111	.003	.110	.014
	(.005)	(.023)	(.005)	(.023)
July	.166	.002	.165	− .031
	(.005)	(.024)	(.005)	(.023)
August	.145	.009	.144	− .025
	(.005)	(.024)	(.005)	(.023)
September	.017	.027	.015	.030
	(.005)	(.022)	(.005)	(.022)
October	.016	.062	.014	.065
	(.005)	(.023)	(.005)	(.022)
November	.007	.035	.006	.038
	(.004)	(.022)	(.004)	(.021)
December	.007	.007	.007	.011
	(.004)	(.021)	(.004)	(.020)
Constant	.140	1.007	.335	1.786
	(.057)	(.280)	(.080)	(.379)
R^2	.9645	.8762	.9663	.8911
Standard error of estimate	.015	.074	.015	.070

NOTE: The F-statistics for the joint test that the three minimum wage variables are zero are 10.6, 2.6, 6.0, and 2.2. The corresponding probability values for these statistics are .0001, .0519, .0007, and .0927.
[a]The ratio employment to total population of males 16–19 years old.
[b]The ratio of the proportions of black and white male teenagers employed.
SOURCE: Authors.

agers employed by 0.04 and has created a gap between the proportion of black male and white male teenagers employed of roughly 0.04 as well.

Increases in the population of teenagers reduce the proportion employed as the relative supply increase depresses their wages. We estimate that a 10 percent increase in the population of teenagers reduces the proportion (of males) employed by 0.017. In addition, it is likely to reduce the proportion of black males employed more than it is the proportion of white males. An unexpected result is the strong, robust, positive relationship between the population of young adults twenty to twenty-four years old and teenage employment. Making inferences from highly correlated, smoothly trended times series for population is difficult, but we offer some speculation.

The population of teenagers and the labor force of young adults

149

TABLE 7

REGRESSION ESTIMATES OF EFFECTS OF MINIMUM WAGES AND
COHORT SIZE ON THE PROPORTION OF MALE TEENAGERS
EMPLOYED AND THE RELATIVE PROPORTIONS OF BLACK TO WHITE
MALE TEENAGERS EMPLOYED

(standard errors in parentheses)

Dependent Variable	Total[a]	Black/White[b]	Total	Black/White
Minimum wage				
Basic	−.428	−.690	−.265	−.695
	(.070)	(.342)	(.075)	(.355)
Differential	.848	3.437	.778	2.924
	(.250)	(1.222)	(.249)	(1.187)
Size of uncovered sector	−.072	−.015	−.019	−.084
	(.046)	(.226)	(.046)	(.219)
Cohort size				
Ratio of civilian male	−1.78	−3.40	−1.28	−2.64
teenage population to	(.140)	(.682)	(.237)	(1.133)
adult (35–65) labor				
force				
Ratio of young adult	1.14	−1.24	.862	−2.69
(20–24) to adult	(.085)	(.415)	(.106)	(.507)
(35–65) labor force				
Proportion of total male	.829	.927	.654	.058
teenage population	(.068)	(.333)	(.074)	(.354)
18–19 years old				
Proportion of male	—	—	−.926	−.601
teenagers enrolled in			(.054)	(.258)
school				
Proportion of male	—	—	−.242	−.721
teenagers in the military			(.122)	(.583)
Proportion of male	—	—	.159	3.147
teenagers in federal			(.099)	(.473)
youth programs				
Unemployment rate of	−.0188	−.0096	−.0206	−.0113
adult males 45–54	(.0011)	(.0053)	(.0011)	(.0053)
February	.007	.018	.006	.018
	(.004)	(.022)	(.004)	(.020)
March	.011	.015	.010	.015
	(.004)	(.022)	(.004)	(.020)
April	.024	.011	.022	.010
	(.004)	(.022)	(.004)	(.021)
May	.032	.005	.029	.004
	(.005)	(.022)	(.004)	(.021)

150

TABLE 7 (continued)

Dependent Variable	Total[a]	Black/White[b]	Total	Black/White
June	.113	.012	.113	.029
	(.005)	(.024)	(.005)	(.023)
July	.170	.017	.168	−.017
	(.005)	(.024)	(.005)	(.023)
August	.148	.022	.146	−.013
	(.005)	(.024)	(.005)	(.024)
September	.016	.022	.014	.027
	(.005)	(.023)	(.005)	(.022)
October	.014	.053	.013	.060
	(.005)	(.023)	(.005)	(.022)
November	.005	.026	.005	.034
	(.005)	(.023)	(.004)	(.021)
December	.005	−.002	.007	.008
	(.005)	(.022)	(.004)	(.021)
Constant	.205	1.290	.441	2.371
	(.058)	(.282)	(.073)	(.348)
R^2	.9613	.8674	.9651	.8862
Standard error of estimate	.016	.076	.016	.071
Autocorrelation of residuals				
First	.617	.425	.581	.428
Second	.398	−.105	.332	−.089
Third	.260	−.146	.186	−.119

NOTE: The F-statistics for the joint test that the three minimum wage variables are zero are 29.3, 3.0, 9.0, and 2.4. The corresponding probability values for these statistics are .0001, .0292, .0001, and .0642.
[a]The ratio employment to total population of males 16–19 years old.
[b]The ratio of the proportions of black and white male teenagers employed.
SOURCE: Authors.

have increased substantially during the past twenty-five years, both absolutely and relative to the adult labor force. These trends have already begun to reverse and will continue to do so for the coming decade. By 1985 the population of teenagers will fall by 17 percent from its 1978 value; relative to the adult labor force it will fall by 27 percent as the latter continues to expand. By 1990 the population of teenagers will have fallen by 23 percent and by 39 percent relative to the adult labor force, which has expanded 26 percent with the aging of the baby-boom babies. Using our estimated regression results, we find that the proportion of teenagers employed will rise by 0.05 by the mid-1980s but will then fall back below 1978 levels by 1990. On the other hand, the employment probability of blacks relative to whites will continue to improve throughout the 1980s, rising by 0.15 in 1985 and by 0.27 in

TABLE 8

ESTIMATES OF EFFECTS OF INCREASES IN MINIMUM WAGES AND
COVERAGE ON THE PROPORTION OF MALE TEENAGERS EMPLOYED
AND THE RELATIVE PROPORTIONS OF BLACK TO WHITE MALE
TEENAGERS EMPLOYED
(standard errors in parentheses)

| Dependent Variable | Potentially Endogenous Variables | | | |
| | Excluded | | Included | |
	Total	Black/white	Total	Black/white
Increase basic minimum from 0.4 to 0.5 of average hourly earnings in manufacturing	−.012 (.0048)	.031 (.0235)	−.005 (.0052)	.009 (.0298)
Increase coverage of basic minimum by 10 percentage points	−.010 (.0030)	−.016 (.0149)	−.009 (.0163)	−.017 (.0115)
Extend coverage to another 10 percent of teenage employment at a new lower minimum	−.008 (.0026)	−.009 (.0130)	−.007 (.0026)	−.010 (.0123)
Eliminate the differential between the new lower minimum and the basic minimum	−.003 (.0011)	−.020 (.0085)	−.004 (.0013)	−.018 (.0073)

SOURCE: Authors.

1990. Black teenage males, however, will still be less likely to be employed than their white counterparts.

Appendix

Tables 6 and 7 show regression estimates of the effects on minimum wages and cohort size on the proportion of male teenagers employed and the relative proportions of black to white male teenagers employed. Table 8 shows estimates of effects of increases in minimum wages and coverage on the proportion of male teenagers employed and the relative proportions of black to white male teenagers employed.

Bibliography

Ashenfelter, Orley, and Smith, Robert S. "Compliance with the Minimum Wage Law." *Journal of Political Economy* 87 (April 1979): 333–50.

Cotterman, Robert. "The Industrial Distribution of Teenage Employment." Paper presented at Labor Economic Workshop, University of California, Los Angeles, 1979.

Goldfarb, R. S. "The Policy Content of Quantitative Minimum Wage Research." In *Proceedings of IRRA Winter Meetings*. San Francisco: Industrial Relations Research Institute, 1974.

Gramlich, Edward M. "Impact of Minimum Wages on Other Wages, Employment, and Family Incomes." *Activity* 2 (1976): 409–51.

Hashimoto, M., and Mincer, Jacob. "Employment and Unemployment Effects of Minimum Wages." Paper presented at the Econometric Society meeting, New Orleans, 1971. Also in *National Bureau of Economic Research Report on Research in Labor Markets for USDL*. New York: National Bureau of Economic Research, 1972.

Kaitz, H. B. "Experience of the Past: The National Minimum." *Youth Employment and Minimum Wages*, Bulletin 1657. U.S. Department of Labor, Bureau of Labor Statistics, 1970.

Kelly, Terence F. "Youth Employment Opportunities and the Minimum Wage: An Econometric Model of Occupational Choice." Urban Institute Work Paper 3608–1, 1975.

Killingsworth, Charles, and Killingsworth, Mark R. "Direct Effects of Employment and Training Programs on Employment and Unemployment: New Estimates and Implications for Employment Policy." In U.S. Department of Labor, Office of the Assistant Secretary for Policy, Evaluation, and Research, *Conference Report on Youth Employment: Its Measurement and Meaning*, pp. 249–476. Washington, D.C., 1978.

Kosters, M., and Welch, F. "The Effects of Minimum Wages on the Distribution in Aggregate Employment." *American Economic Review* 62 (June 1972): 323–32.

Mincer, Jacob. "Unemployment Effects of Minimum Wages." *Journal of Political Economy* 84 (August 1976): 87–104.

Parsons, Donald O. "The Cost of School Time, Forgone Earnings, and Human Capital Formation." *Journal of Political Economy* 82 (March 1974): 251–66.

Ragan, James F. "Minimum Wages and the Youth Labor Market." *Review of Economics and Statistics* 59 (May 1977).

Wachter, Michael L., and Kim, Choongsoo. "Time Series Changes in Youth Joblessness." National Bureau of Economic Research Working Paper no. 384, August 1979.

Welch, Finis. "Effects of Cohort Size on Earnings: The Baby Boom Babies' Financial Bust." *Journal of Political Economy* 87 (October 1979): 565–97.

———. "Minimum Wage Legislation in the United States." *Economic Inquiry* 12 (September 1974): 285–318.

Welch, Finis. *Minimum Wages: Issues and Evidence.* Washington, D.C.: American Enterprise Institute, 1978.

————, and Cunningham, James. "Effects of Minimum Wages on the Age Composition of Youth Employment." *Review of Economics and Statistics* 60 (February 1978):140–45.

The Effects of Minimum Wages on Human Capital Formation

Linda Leighton and Jacob Mincer

The two major avenues of human capital formation are schooling and job training. But the effects of minimum wages on human capital can be quite different in the two cases. Theoretically, the effects of imposition, extension, or hikes of the minimums and of their coverage on training on the job are unambiguous: job training is discouraged. But schooling may be discouraged or encouraged. Thanks to recent research, especially that of Peter Mattila,[1] it would appear that schooling is encouraged by the minimum wage, an effect opposite to the expected job-training consequences.

As things stand, it seems that we do not, as yet, have any evidence on the theoretically predictable case of job training,[2] although we do have an empirical answer to the theoretically ambiguous prediction about effects on schooling. In this paper we try to fill two gaps: We explore the theoretical considerations regarding effects of minimum wages on schooling and bring together evidence on the job-training effects.

Effects on Schooling: Theoretical Considerations and Research

The basic question here is whether minimum wages increase or decrease the rate of return to further schooling for youngsters at the relevant levels of earning capacity (further schooling at this level is likely to mean completion of high school and more, up to perhaps junior college).

The same question was put forward in a more general form in 1976

NOTE: We are grateful to the National Science Foundation and to the Sloan Foundation for their support. We wish to thank Margaret Lennon and Frank Nothaft for their competent research assistance.

[1] J. Peter Mattila, "Youth Labor Markets, Enrollments, and Minimum Wages," *Proceedings of the Thirty-first Annual Meeting of the Industrial Relations Research Association,* August 1978; idem, "The Impact of Minimum Wages on School Enrollment and Labor Force Status of Youths," Report to U.S. Employment and Training Administration, June 1979.

[2] Work in progress by Masanori Hashimoto, "Minimum Wage and Earnings Growth of Young Males," came to our attention after completion of our research.

by one of the present authors[3] in terms of labor mobility: Since the increased wage in the covered sector is an attraction but the reduced probability of employment a deterrent, will labor on balance move to or from the covered sector when minimum wages are imposed or raised? The answer depends on whether the minimum wage hike raises or lowers wage prospects in the covered sector. Let us define "wage prospects" as $\hat{w} = p_m \cdot w_m$, where p_m is the perceived[4] probability of employment in the covered sector. If $\hat{w}$ falls (because p_m falls by more than the increase in w_m), labor moves out of the covered sector to the not-covered, reducing its wage (w_n). With unchanged prospects in the non-market, labor moves out of the market as well. The flows continue, until in equilibrium $\hat{w} = w_n = \bar{w}$ (where $\bar{w}$ is the nonmarket shadow wage). It is not easy to measure p_m, even if a definition of it could be agreed upon. Nor is $\bar{w}$ more than an abstraction. W_n might be observed, but no one has tried to do so.

The evidence observed in the 1976 study and in a 1978 Canadian study[5] was the direction of movement: from market to nonmarket. This direction of movement is implied by a drop in market wage prospects and rejects the hypothesis of their improvement via the minimum wage.

Now, if the evidence is correct, it follows that the profitability of schooling is increased by the minimum wage hike. Let s_0 be the maximal schooling attainment of youngsters facing wages near the minimum, so their wage prospects are $\hat{w}$. Let s_1 be the minimal schooling attainment at which wages w are safely above minimum wages. In the simplest model, the return to schooling is measured by $w_1 - \hat{w}$, and its (opportunity) cost by $\hat{w}$. A drop in $\hat{w}$ raises returns and lowers costs and so improves the profitability of schooling above s_0 (though not above s_1). Had $\hat{w}$ increased as a consequence of minimum wages, profitability of schooling in the $s_0 - s_1$ interval would have fallen. In that case we would have observed a decrease in school enrollment and at the same time an increase in the labor force, as well as an increase in unemployment exceeding that of disemployment resulting from the minimum wage! This scenario is rejected by the empirical observations.

Whether or not $\hat{w}$ falls, w_1 is likely to increase as a result of substitution of more educated workers for those initially employed below

---

[3] Jacob Mincer, "Unemployment Effects of Minimum Wages," National Bureau of Economic Research Working Paper no. 357, pt. 2, August 1976.

[4] $\hat{w}$ is the "expected wage" in the covered sector, in the sense of a mathematical expectation, if we assume risk neutrality. "Wage prospects" are less than "expected wages" with risk aversion.

[5] Ronald Swidinsky, "Minimum Wages and Teenage Unemployment in Canada," paper prepared for a meeting of CIRRI, London, May 1978.

the minimum. If so, school enrollment could rise or fall depending on whether w_1 rises more or less rapidly than $\hat{w}$.

Thus, the increase in school enrollment is predictable, given the observed effects of minimum wages on labor force participation. The link is economic, via changes in rates of return, not merely tautological in the sense that schooling is part of the nonmarket.

It is worth noting that the question of effects of minimum wages on the volume of welfare payments is analogous, indeed identical, to the question about effects on school enrollment. A priori, one could argue either way. Indeed, according to a survey by E. G. West and M. McKee, inducement to work has become a major argument in favor of minimum wages:

> A final purpose of the minimum wage, articulated only since the advent of widespread social security programmes, has been that of providing incentive to work for employees who are tempted to rely instead on pensions, unemployment, or welfare benefits. Most governments recognise (at least informally) the intimate relationship between social assistance and low-wage employment (since individuals may switch back and forth frequently) by attempting to set minimum wages somewhat above that which a single person can expect to earn from such schemes. A latter-day purpose of minimum wage legislation, therefore, is to induce workers to search for jobs.[6]

It is clear now, given the evidence on labor force participation and on enrollment effects of minimum wages, that the inducement argument is not valid. Indeed, the logical conclusion is to the contrary: minimum wages induce welfare, not work. However, without more direct empirical evidence, this conclusion still remains in the realm of speculation.

To return to the effects on schooling, it has been argued that these effects are asymmetrical:[7] school enrollment is likely to increase for the nonpoor and decrease for the poor. By extension, a similar difference might be observed between whites and blacks. But the theoretical basis for this prediction is weak. We would expect that the profitability of longer schooling would increase for all groups. Indeed, the lower the preminimum wage, the greater is the (percent) reduction in $\hat{w}$ if it falls, according to the Mincer model. Consequently, the rate of return to

[6] Edwin G. West and Michael McKee, "The Economics of Minimum Wages with Special Reference to Canada: A Review," Carleton University, February 1979.

[7] See Finis Welch, "Minimum Wage Legislation in the United States," *Economic Inquiry* 12 (September 1974): 285–318; and Ronald G. Ehrenberg and Alan Marcus, "Minimum Wage Legislation and the Educational Decisions of Youths," *Research in Labor Economics,* August 1979.

schooling increases *more* for the lower subminimum wage workers than for others, and the inducement into longer schooling could be strong or stronger among the poor. Mattila's empirical finding that school enrollment increased for both blacks and whites is consistent with the negative effect of minimum wages on labor force participation in both groups.[8] Mattila actually finds that black response coefficients are somewhat stronger than those of the whites, which need not be surprising.

Mattila finds also that work of black students has decreased or not increased in contrast to the growth of participation among white students. These findings are supported by aggregate (Current Population Survey) data[9] and suggest possible effects of the welfare system. Because school enrollment of children who are eighteen or younger is a condition of receipt of welfare payments in eligible families, we would conclude that increases in welfare enrollment induce reported school enrollments in such families.[10] At the same time, their reported work activities are likely to be reduced.

It is true, of course, that both the financing and the motivational (ability) factors produce a shorter schooling career of the poor compared with the nonpoor. This is true both before and after minimum wage hikes, and levels should not be confused with change. The nonstudent proportion of the relatively poorer population remains larger. This group must rely on the labor market for personal economic advancement. It, therefore, bears the brunt of the adverse minimum wage effects on job training.

Effects on Job Training

Although minimum wages may be expected to prolong the length of schooling, they create obvious barriers to job training. Job training must be financed, at least in part, by the worker or apprentice, usually in the form of a reduced initial wage. This means that even if current productivity of some of the employed youngsters warrants paying the minimum wage, job training is precluded for them because its provision would require paying initially a subminimum.[11]

---

[8] Mincer, "Unemployment Effects."

[9] Mattila, "Impact of Minimum Wage"; Richard Freeman and James L. Medoff, "The Youth Labor Market Problem in the U.S.," paper prepared for National Bureau of Economic Research Conference, May 1979.

[10] Michael Wachter and Sung Kim, "Time Series Changes in Youth Joblessness," NBER Working Paper no. 384, August 1979, found also that enrollment rates for all young (aged sixteen to twenty-four) blacks were lower than those of young whites in 1965, but the situation was reversed in 1978.

[11] This conclusion was stated earlier by Sherwin Rosen, "Learning by Experience in the Labor Market," *Journal of Human Resources*, Summer 1972; and by Martin Feldstein,

This effect is another source of an increased demand for more schooling: young persons with the ability and motivation to invest in their human capital are led to substitute longer schooling for job training.[12] Moreover, the additional schooling enables them to enter higher (than minimum) wage jobs and reopens the possibility of subsequent job training as well.

Thus, the labor market difficulties generated by the minimum wage for low-wage young workers are twofold: loss of jobs for some where wages are initially below the minimum and loss of opportunities for training and careers even for those whose initial productivity is worth as much or somewhat more than the minimum wage.

We may note, at this point, that minimum wages will tend to discourage the formation of both "general," that is, transferable, skills and firm-specific capital, although the effects on the latter may be weaker to the extent that the firm is willing to bear the costs of training the worker.

Several types of supply responses may be expected as a result of minimum wages. Those who are intellectually and financially able to prolong schooling will do so, even if their interests are primarily vocational and they would have preferred job training to staying in school. One may speculate that the growth of junior colleges and of private vocational schools, as well as the growing demand for vocationalism in college curriculums, is partly a reflection of this response, as is the growing tendency of students to combine school with market work.[13] Student work is also partly encouraged by provision of the Fair Labor Standards Act, which creates differentials and exceptions for students. The transition to full-time work at wages above the minimum wage hurdle is made easier by part-period and part-time work while at school. Although jobs of students are usually low-skilled and casual, they provide some experience and some measure of financial independence. The dead-end nature of many of these casual jobs creates no particular anxiety, as they will be left behind as soon as the student has graduated and acquired more rewarding capacities.

"Lowering the Permanent Rate of Unemployment," Report to the Joint Economic Committee of Congress, September 1973. The discouragement of training could be avoided by separating payments (of employers to workers) for work from payments (of trainees/ workers to employers) for training. It is the netting out of the two transactions that creates problems even for workers whose initial value productivity is not subminimum.

[12] Even if employers are indifferent between wage "packages" with and without training as long as labor costs per hour are the same, workers who opt for job training are worse off when the higher minimum wage without training replaces the lower wage with training. For an elaboration of the wage package analysis, see Walter Wessels, "The Effects of Minimum Wages on Firm Expenditures," in progress.

[13] This is shown to be the case in Mattila's work. There are, of course, additional reasons for this trend that need not concern us here.

The early labor market difficulties produced by the minimum wage are not easily surmounted by youths who are either unwilling or unable to prolong their schooling. Because opportunities for job training leading to advancement on the job are blocked by the minimum wage for some of them, the young school dropouts must choose jobs with little promise for advancement or become labor market dropouts as well. Nonparticipation in the labor market, which is induced by the minimum wage, may be financed by the family, by unreported market or illegal activities, or by the welfare system.

The nonstudents who do not drop out of the labor market despite their low productivity must contend with several obstacles: greater difficulties (longer unemployment) in finding jobs in the covered sector and lesser growth on the job because of the reduced availability of training on the job. Although it may seem strange to assert that higher wages increase turnover, this can happen in the longer run when minimum wages are raised, because the reduction of firm-specific training in jobs that contain it reduces the cost of turnover for the worker and for the employer. More generally, employers can be expected to adjust to the raised minimum wage in several ways: (1) by reducing employment of the relevant workers and substituting capital and a somewhat higher quality of labor for them, and (2) by reducing those components of the wage package (such as training) that are not included in (netted out of) paid-out wages. The implications for changes in turnover in the long run are ambiguous, because an upgrading of labor may well reduce it, whereas a downgrading of the wage package (in terms of reduced training opportunities) is likely to increase turnover. The workers initially exposed to the minimum wage hike, however, some of whom may be later replaced, will experience an increase in turnover because of the curtailment of job-training opportunities. In the short run, prior to full adjustment, the effects on turnover are also ambiguous, because quits will be reduced[14] and layoffs increased in the sector covered by the minimum wage.

We may summarize the relevant implications of minimum wages as follows: (1) induced prolongation of schooling coupled with increased part-time work of students (except for those on welfare); (2) reduced pace of job advancement; and (3), eventually, increased turnover for those nonstudents whose jobs contained specific training opportunities.

---

[14] Indeed, in the only study that came to our attention, J. Wilson Mixon, Jr. ("The Minimum Wage and Voluntary Labor Mobility," *Industrial and Labor Relations Review,* Summer 1972) found that minimum wages reduce quits in manufacturing industries. The estimated coefficients of the Koyck distributed lag on his quarterly data imply that this effect vanishes almost totally within a year.

Empirical Analysis of Effects on Job Training

Our empirical work is designed to explore the effects of minimum wages on job training. This task is difficult to carry out in any direct sense: We have no time series on changes in the provision of training that could be matched up with changes in minimum wage levels and in coverage. Even if such data on training were available, it may not be reasonable to expect a clear correlation between the short-run variation in minimum wages and the longer-term policies of firms regarding training of their employees. Indeed, the oscillation of minimum wages around a relatively fixed ratio to average wages and the past updrift in coverage should have convinced employers to view the minimum wage as permanent and to respond in terms of long-run adjustments.

The less direct implications about wage growth and turnover can neither be observed nor correlated with minimum wages in aggregate time series. Our approach is to analyze longitudinal microdata in which wage growth, turnover, and some responses to questions about training are available. Following Ehrenberg and Marcus, we differentiate our sample of workers by state of residence.[15] First, we estimate differences in wage levels across states for the "same worker." These differentials serve as inverse indicators of the differing potential importance of the minimum wage across states; that is, the lower the (standardized) state wage, the higher the ratio of minimum to state wages, since the minimum wage is basically uniform across states.[16] The other state variable is the ratio of covered employment to total nonagricultural employment, available in published data.[17] Following the usual formulation,[18] we combined the two variables into one: $COV/(1 + SW)$, where COV is state coverage and SW is the percent wage differential. Here coverage is multiplied by $1/(1 + SW)$, which is proportional to the ratio of the minimum to the standardized state wage.

[15] We are grateful to Ehrenberg and Marcus, "Minimum Wage Legislation," for providing the identification of states in the NLS, which they obtained laboriously. Identification of states in MID data is simpler and more accurate.

[16] There are two sources of variation: differential proportion of coverage by state laws and differences in levels of state minimum wages. On average, about 10 percent of coverage is state coverage. The variation so introduced in the minimum wage level is of minor magnitude, and we ignore it.

[17] The coverage ratio includes, in the numerator, the total number of private- and public-sector employees covered by the Fair Labor Standards Act as of February 1, 1970 (c_f) (note that the last change of coverage prior to 1970 was 1966), plus the number covered by state minimum wages only (c_s). The denominator is the total number of private and public nonsupervisory employees in the state in 1969.

[18] The multiplicative formulation is theoretically superior to the linear, though it need not be the best (cf. Welch, "Minimum Wage Legislation").

The effects of minimum wage variables are then explored in regressions where wage growth, job tenure, and training dummies alternate as dependent variables. These effects are estimated net of a set of factors that we selected as determinants of the dependent variables. In what follows, we describe the analysis of data from the 1973 and 1975 Michigan Panel of Income Dynamics (MID) for a panel of white men,[19] and for white and black young men in the National Longitudinal Survey (NLS) panels for the two periods from 1967 to 1971. We restrict both samples to nonstudents. In 1967 substantial increases in the minimum wage and its coverage went into effect. The main reason for choosing the earlier period in NLS was the availability of state identifications. The later period in MID was preferable because an appropriate question on training first became available in 1976. Although the data sets are not exactly comparable, the later MID sample is more likely to represent the long-run effects than the NLS sample.

Table 1 presents a list of dependent and independent variables used in each of the four regression analyses of wage functions, wage growth, job tenure, and training.

Wage Functions. Our first step is to estimate the relevant state differences in wages. Crude differences in wages will not do, because we want to know the effects of imposed changes in the price of labor and not whether labor of higher "quality" receives more or less training. Consequently, we estimate wages facing the "same worker" in various states by running wage functions across all individuals in the sample and using a standard set of wage determinants such as schooling, experience, and length of tenure, as well as a number of other personal and job characteristics listed in table 1. State dummies were added to the set of independent variables. Their coefficients represent estimates of wage differences (for an average worker with the same characteristics) between each of the states and an arbitrarily chosen base state. In some degree these differentials reflect cost-of-living differences, but whether or not they represent differences in real wages, the impact of the minimum wage, itself nominal, depends on its relation to the nominal wage level. We excluded states with fewer than ten observations in the sample, leaving thirty-five states in the MID and NLS regressions.

We ran both the semilog and arithmetical wage functions. The former produce percent wage differentials among states, and the latter yield dollar differentials. The two sets of estimates rank identically. We used both sets in the subsequent analyses as alternatives and noticed no clear differences in results. The semilog wage functions showed a some-

---

[19] The sample of black men was much too small in MID. The empirical analysis was not extended to women.

TABLE 1

LIST OF REGRESSION VARIABLES

	Definition
Independent Variables	
EDUC	Years of schooling
EXPER	Years of experience = *AGE-EDUC*–6 (in MID) years since first job after completion of schooling (in NLS)
EXPER2	Experience squared
JOB	Years at present job; tenure in firm
JOB2	Tenure squared
ST_i	0–1 state dummies; ST_i = 1 if individual lives in *i*th state
MAR	Marital status = 1 if individual is married
HLTH	Health = 1 if individual is in poor health
UNION	= 1 if individual is a member of a labor union
GOVT	= 1 if individual is a public employee
SW	Shift variable; coefficients of ST_i from wage function
COV	Percentage of workers on nonagricultural payrolls covered by minimum wage in a state
WG_t	Individual wage in year *t*
Dependent Variables	
WG_t	Individual wage at time *t*
Δ*WG*	Wage change over observation period
JOB	See above
TRAIN	= 1 if individual is being trained or is learning on the job

NOTE: The set of independent variables is the same in all regressions, except that (1) the wage function contains state dummies but not *SW* and *COV*, (2) the wage growth equation has a lagged wage on the right, and (3) the job tenure equation omits job tenure on the right.
SOURCE: Authors.

what higher R^2 and a larger contribution of state dummies to R^2. To save space, our tables show only the partial effects of the combined minimum wage variable: the coverage ratio (*COV*) divided by the index of the standardized state wage (1 + *SW*). Separate effects of (*SW*) and of (*COV*) are shown in the appendix.

Aside from the coefficients on the state dummies, the estimated parameters for the wage functions are similar to those found in many previous studies and are not of primary interest in the present one. The major purpose of the wage regressions here is to estimate the interstate wage differentials. Incidentally, the inclusion of state dummies has little effect on the estimated parameters of the other variables, and it raises the multiple R^2 about 25 percent (from .34 to .42) in the semilog function. Not surprisingly, personal and job characteristics account for most of the "explained" differences in observed (unstandardized) wages among states.

Wage Growth. The pace at which workers accumulate skills in their work careers is an important factor in producing the upward slope of the typical wage profile. We argue that the rate of skill acquisition, hence wage growth, will be impeded by the level and coverage of minimum wages. Of course, individual skill and wage growth are affected by a number of other factors, such as growth of the economy, the business cycle, level of education and experience, migration and job changes, changes in health and family status, and so on. We eliminate the economy-wide factors by studying wage changes of different persons over the same calendar time interval. And we standardize for the other factors listed in table 1.

Because the return on investment in human capital is measured in dollars (not in percentages), we used dollar wages to measure absolute growth rather than logarithms to measure percentage growth.[20] Indeed, if the volume of training (measured in dollars) were unaffected after an increase of the minimum wage, with a higher base wage, percentage growth would be diminished. Hence, dollar growth provides a more convincing test than percentage growth.[21]

We analyzed differences in wage growth across individuals in two alternative sets of regressions. For the findings shown in table 2 (upper panel), we used wages in 1975 as the dependent variable and wages in 1973 as one of the independent variables. Hence, wage growth is shown by differences in 1975 wages, given the wage in 1973. We also ran alternative regressions where our dependent variable is the actual change in wages between 1973 and 1975. The results were quite similar, insofar as our research questions and findings are concerned.

Our hypothesis is that lesser wage growth should be observed in states where standardized wages are lower or the coverage larger.[22]

The regression estimates in table 2 indicate the net effects of the minimum wage variable[23] on wage growth of men with the same edu-

---

[20] The slope of semilog wage functions reflects the *ratio* of investment (in job training or learning) to earning capacity. Return on the *volume* of investment is obtained in the arithmetical function; hence, the dollar volume of job training is reflected in the slope (growth) of the dollar wage function (cf. Mincer, "Unemployment Effects").

[21] We replicated our wage growth regressions in log form and found the same qualitative results as in our table 2. Hashimoto, "Minimum Wage and Earnings Growth," uses percentage growth as a test in his empirical model and observes qualitatively similar results.

[22] Although the correlation is weak, coverage is actually larger in higher-wage states.

[23] The complete equations are available on request in an appendix.

TABLE 2

EFFECTS OF MINIMUM WAGE VARIABLE ON WAGE GROWTH

	β	F	n
(1) *MID Panel, 1973–75*			
All	− 1.547	8.50	1,352
≤HS	− 1.936	11.77	814
<HS	− 2.456	8.45	318
>HS	− .819	0.60	538
(2) *NLS Panel*			
Whites			
1967–69			
All	− .577	3.45	802
≤HS	− .561	2.80	637
<HS	− .612	1.70	275
>HS	− .684	0.75	165
1969–71			
All	− 2.21	17.50	990
≤HS	− 1.44	6.56	729
<HS	− 2.58	9.84	267
>HS	− 4.60	13.35	261
Blacks			
1967–69			
All	− .410	0.882	288
≤HS	− .647	1.97	269
<HS	− .423	0.490	175
1969–71			
All	− .456	0.489	357
≤HS	− .282	0.205	332
<HS	− .899	1.50	201

NOTE: $β$ = regression coefficients of the minimum wage variable $COV/(1 + SW)$
$F = t^2$
n = number of observations
SOURCE: Authors.

cation, experience, job tenure, marital status, health status, and union membership.

In the upper panel, which refers to 1973–1975 wage growth in the MID, the effects of minimum wages are negative and significant as predicted.

The two lower panels of table 2 show results of wage growth regressions based on NLS data. These are samples of young men, nonstudents who were at most twenty-five years old in 1967. We observe their wage growth in 1967–1969 and again in 1969–1971. The sample of black youth is large enough in NLS for separate regression analyses. We ran regressions of wages in 1969 and 1971 on the various determinants as of 1967 and 1969, respectively, including the lagged wage and the minimum wage variables.

Minimum wage effects are negative and significant for whites in both time periods. They are negative and mainly not significant for blacks. A possible reason for lesser significance of black coefficients is that the components of the minimum wage variable, state wage differentials (SW) and coverage (COV), could not be estimated separately for blacks.

We would expect the minimum wage to have a stronger impact in lower-wage groups within the states. We ran our regressions on progressively smaller subgroups of people with at most a high school education (HS) and with less than a high school education ($<HS$). Although the samples became smaller, and may therefore lose statistical significance, we find that the coefficients increase in size, the lower the level of education in the MID panel. The pattern is less clear in NLS.

As an additional check we singled out the highest education group (more than thirteen years) in the MID and in the white NLS sample. This group is least likely to be affected by minimum wages in any state. We find that wage growth is not affected by minimum wages in this group in the 1973–1975 period in MID or in the 1967–1969 phase among NLS whites. The exception is a reduction in wage growth in the 1969–1971 period in NLS.

Job Tenure. Although on-the-job acquisition of transferable skills has no obvious implications for job turnover, elements of firm specificity in training are likely to strengthen the degree of firm attachment. To the extent that firm-specific training is reduced by minimum wages, turnover should increase and job tenure decrease. This implication about minimum wage effects is weaker than the wage-growth hypothesis because most acquired skills are largely transferable.

In MID data, which are not restricted to the very young, we find that the length of job tenure is indeed *shorter* when state wages are lower and coverage larger (table 3). However, the effect of minimum wage variables on job mobility of white young men in NLS (table 3, β) is to *lengthen* job tenure. For NLS blacks, minimum wages also appear to *reduce* tenure, though the coefficients only border on significance.

The difference between NLS and MID in the time periods may represent a distinction between shorter-run (NLS) and longer-run (MID) effects of the major 1967 changes in minimum wage legislation. In the short run wages rise, but the nature of the job does not change. In that period minimum wages increase layoffs and reduce quits in the

TABLE 3

Effects of Minimum Wage Variable on Job Tenure

	β	F	n
(1) *MID Panel, 1973–75*			
All	−4.478	8.36	1,538
≤HS	−5.325	5.94	913
<HS	−4.218	1.20	344
>HS	−2.899	2.00	625
(2) *NLS Panel*			
Whites			
1967–69			
All	1.09	2.01	831
≤*HS*	1.12	1.69	650
<*HS*	0.322	0.08	275
>*HS*	1.70	0.96	181
1969–71			
All	1.94	2.45	1,019
≤*HS*	1.76	1.48	749
<*HS*	2.10	0.73	265
>*HS*	2.10	2.86	270
Blacks			
1967–69			
All	−1.61	1.70	291
≤*HS*	−1.35	1.02	272
<*HS*	−1.52	0.65	181
1969–71			
All	−1.85	1.32	360
≤*HS*	−2.14	1.50	335
<*HS*	−3.32	1.76	207

NOTE: See note to table 2.
SOURCE: Authors.

covered sector. Two-thirds of the separation of young NLS whites are quits, but only half of black separations are quits. Consequently, minimum wages may reduce the turnover of young whites, but not of young blacks. In the longer run, the reduction of training produces an increase in turnover, as in the MID data. The patterns by education are not clear, which leaves the turnover hypothesis uncertain pending further evidence.

Reported Job Training. Our final test is perhaps the most direct, although the reported data may be a bit more subjective. In the MID we

TABLE 4
Effects of Minimum Wage Variable on Job Training

	β	F	n
(1) *MID Panel, 1973–75*			
1976			
All	−.125	1.37	1,454
≤HS	−.220	2.34	853
<HS	−.391	2.81	310
>HS	+.014	0.01	601
1975 HS	−.443	10.23	1,011
(2) *NLS Panel*			
Whites			
1967–69			
All	−.128	2.25	1,089
≤HS	−.140	2.60	861
<HS	−.058	0.408	371
>HS	+.026	0.009	228
1969–71			
All	−.180	2.75	1,183
≤HS	−.196	2.68	882
<HS	−.245	2.60	319
>HS	−.128	0.270	301
Blacks			
1967–69			
All	−.148	4.01	431
≤HS	−.139	3.64	408
<HS	.011	0.045	268
1969–71			
All	.064	0.857	488
≤HS	−.114	4.20	448
<HS	.011	0.000	270

NOTE: See note to table 2.
SOURCE: Authors.

examine answers to a question first posed in 1976: "Do you feel you are learning things on your job that could lead to a better job or to a promotion?" We used a dummy dependent variable with value 1 if the answer was affirmative and 0 if negative. Prior to 1976 a narrower question was asked only of those with education not exceeding high school. The question was whether during the past year they received any kind of training other than schooling. We ran the 1975 answer as

TABLE 5

Effects of State Wage Differentials and Coverage on Wage Growth

A. 1973–1975 (white men in MID)

	Lagged Wage				Change in Wage				
	SW		COV		SW		COV		
	β	F	β	F	β	F	β	F	n
All	1.36	10.0	−.48	.23	.94	5.1	−.52	.26	1,352
HS	1.75	14.4	−.69	.40	1.48	11.1	−.70	.41	814
<HS	2.33	11.0	−.61	.13	1.77	6.9	−.61	.13	318

B. 1967–1969 and 1969–1971 (young men in NLS; lagged wage specification)

	Whites					Blacks				
	SW		COV			SW		COV		
	β	F	β	F	n	β	F	β	F	n
1967–69										
All	.67	5.9	−.37	.39	802	1.16	6.7	1.30	3.5	288
HS	.74	4.4	−.59	.76	637	1.42	9.1	1.08	2.2	269
<HS	.77	2.3	−.87	.77	275	1.21	4.0	1.74	3.1	175
1969–71										
All	.66	15.3	−1.11	11.0	990	1.10	3.8	.45	.33	357
HS	1.20	7.4	−1.03	2.1	729	1.06	3.9	.66	.77	332
<HS	2.31	12.6	−1.96	3.6	267	1.78	8.2	.44	.25	201

NOTE: SW indicates state wage differentials; COV indicates minimum wage coverage.
SOURCE: Authors.

a dummy. The 1976 answers were regressed on the 1975 levels and the 1975 answers on the 1973 levels of independent variables. The results are shown in table 4.

The coefficients of the minimum wage variable are negative, as expected, and increase in size and significance as we move to the lower education groups in the MID panel.

In the NLS sample of young men, we coded answers of those who received training on the current job. The concept of training is narrower than in MID, as it appears to refer to formal rather than all training. The minimum wage reduces training in both racial groups and time periods. The coefficients are significant in most cases. No effects are

169

TABLE 6

EFFECTS OF STATE WAGE DIFFERENTIALS AND COVERAGE ON LENGTH OF JOB TENURE

A. MID, 1975

	SW		COV		
	β	F	β	F	n
1975					
All	3.30	7.1	−8.12	7.2	1,538
HS	4.05	5.3	−9.86	5.2	913
<HS	2.66	0.70	−14.67	3.4	344

B. NLS, 1969, 1971

	Whites					*Blacks*				
	SW		COV			SW		COV		
	β	F	β	F	n	β	F	β	F	n
1969										
All	−1.15	2.1	.69	0.21	831	.64	.29	−5.20	6.4	291
HS	−1.22	1.8	.57	0.10	650	.46	.13	−4.90	4.8	272
<HS	−.68	0.30	2.79	1.5	275	.44	.06	−5.47	2.8	181
1971										
All	−1.05	1.2	2.28	2.0	1,019	.42	.10	−2.47	1.6	360
HS	−1.49	1.1	1.69	1.8	749	.64	.19	−2.88	1.8	335
<HS	−1.81	0.65	2.23	0.48	265	1.26	.38	−4.15	1.8	207

NOTE: *SW* indicates state wage differentials; *COV* indicates minimum wage coverage.
SOURCE: Authors.

observed in the more educated (thirteen or more years) subsample in MID and in NLS.

The NLS data contain some information on job training off the firm, excluding school. We might expect the minimum wage to encourage such training as an alternative to in-firm training, though not (publicly subsidized) schooling. In regressions not shown here, the coefficients were generally not statistically significant, but most of the signs were in the predicted direction, that is, positive.

On the whole, the findings in the NLS regressions tend to be favorable to our hypothesis, although they are not as strong as the findings in MID.

TABLE 7

EFFECTS OF STATE WAGE DIFFERENTIALS AND COVERAGE ON IN-FIRM TRAINING ON CURRENT JOB

A. MID 1976, 1975

	SW		COV		
	β	F	β	F	n
1976					
All	.08	0.95	− .40	3.8	1,454
HS	.12	1.1	− .69	5.3	853
<HS	.30	2.5	− .50	1.1	310
1975					
HS	.40	13.3	− .05	.13	1,011

B. NLS, 1969, 1971

	Whites					Blacks				
	SW		COV			SW		COV		
	β	F	β	F	n	β	F	β	F	n
1969										
All	.15	2.7	− .06	.14	1,089	.17	5.2	− .088	0.54	431
HS	.18	3.8	− .06	.12	861	.16	4.9	− .09	0.64	408
<HS	.07	0.49	− .16	.68	371	.03	0.25	.10	1.56	268
1971										
All	.16	3.3	− .06	.23	1,183	.04	0.51	− .07	0.64	488
HS	.19	4.2	− .12	.007	882	.07	2.1	− .14	4.4	448
<HS	.21	3.3	− .20	1.00	319	− .00	0.20	− .01	0.02	270

NOTE: *SW* indicates state wage differentials; *COV* indicates minimum wage coverage.
SOURCE: Authors.

Conclusions. The hypothesis that minimum wages tend to discourage on-the-job training is largely supported by our empirical analysis. Direct effects on job training and the corollary effects on wage growth as estimated (in tables 4 and 2, respectively) are consistently negative and stronger at lower education levels. Indeed, apart from a single exception, no effects are observable among the higher-wage group whose education exceeds high school.

The effects on job turnover are a decrease in turnover among young NLS whites but an increase among young NLS blacks and MID whites. Whether these apparently conflicting findings on turnover reflect a distinction between short- and long-run adjustments in jobs is a question that requires further testing.

Appendix

Appendix tables 5–7 show the separate effects of state wage differentials (*SW*) and of coverage (*COV*) on wage growth, length of job tenure, and training.

Bibliography

Ehrenberg, Ronald G., and Marcus, Alan. "Minimum Wage Legislation and the Educational Decisions of Youths." *Research in Labor Economics,* August 1979.

Feldstein, Martin. "Lowering the Permanent Rate of Unemployment." Report to the Joint Economic Committee of Congress, September 1973.

Freeman, Richard, and Medoff, James L. "The Youth Labor Market Problem in the U.S." Paper prepared for National Bureau of Economic Research Conference, May 1979.

Hashimoto, Masanori. "Minimum Wage and Earnings Growth of Young Males." Meeting of Econometric Society, December 1979.

Mattila, J. Peter. "Youth Labor Markets, Enrollments, and Minimum Wages." *Proceedings of the Thirty-first Annual Meeting of the Industrial Relations Research Association,* August 1978.

———. "The Impact of Minimum Wages on School Enrollment and Labor Force Status of Youths." Report to U.S. Employment and Training Administration, June 1979.

Mincer, Jacob. "Unemployment Effects of Minimum Wages." National Bureau of Economic Research Working Paper no. 357, pt. 2, August 1976.

———, and Jovanovic, Boyan. "Labor Mobility and Wages." National Bureau of Economic Research Working Paper no. 357, June 1979.

Mixon, J. Wilson, Jr. "The Minimum Wage and Voluntary Labor Mobility." *Industrial and Labor Relations Review,* October 1978.

Rosen, Sherwin. "Learning by Experience in the Labor Market." *Journal of Human Resources,* Summer 1972.

Swidinsky, Ronald. "Minimum Wages and Teenage Unemployment in Canada." Paper presented at a meeting of CIRRI, London, May 1978.

U.S. Department of Labor, Wage and Hour Division. *Minimum Wages and Maximum Hours Standards under FLSA.* Washington, D.C., 1970.

Wachter, Michael, and Kim, Sung. "Time Series Changes in Youth Joblessness." National Bureau of Economic Research Working Paper no. 384, August 1979.

Welch, Finis. "Minimum Wage Legislation in the United States." *Economic Inquiry* 12 (September 1974): 285–318.

Wessels, Walter. "The Effects of Minimum Wages on Firm Expenditures." Mimeographed, North Carolina State University, 1979.

West, Edwin G., and McKee, Michael. "The Economics of Minimum Wages with Special Reference to Canada: A Review." Carleton University, February 1979.

Some Aspects of the Social Pathological Behavioral Effects of Unemployment among Young People

Llad Phillips

Introduction

The preponderance of the evidence indicates that minimum wage legislation in the United States has caused disemployment, withdrawal from the labor force, and unemployment. The population groups whose labor force opportunities have suffered the most have been young males in their teens and early twenties, both black and white, with the blacks being affected the most.

It is natural to expect that this deprivation of legitimate economic opportunity for our youth should have had adverse social consequences extending beyond the wasteful labor mobility and unemployment created by the minimum wage. During the last three decades there has been a large increase in the per capita incidence of serious felony crime. Felony arrest rates are especially high for young males and are highest for blacks. Furthermore, the most rapid rates of increase in felony arrest rates have been for teenagers.

The dislocations in the lives of young people who have been adversely affected by minimum wage legislation have likely exacerbated many aspects of pathological behavior among our youth. Certainly one of the most pervasive and serious of these has been felony crime. During the past three decades, it has been a serious problem that greatly concerns the citizens of this nation. Crime has played a part in our national politics and has engendered remedial legislation. Nonetheless, in the latter seventies we find that arrest rates for serious felonies were continuing to rise, and they were rising more rapidly for black youths than for whites.

Can minimum wage legislation and the pathological behavior of youth be linked? A plausible path of causality is that minimum wage legislation increases unemployment and lowers labor force participation for youths. As a consequence, teenagers and youths in their early twenties, faced with worsening legitimate economic opportunities, find criminal activities increasingly attractive. In this essay, we examine the evi-

FIGURE 1
Unemployment Rates for Males Age 18 and 19, by Race 1952–1978

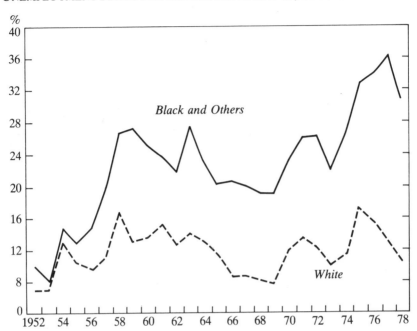

dence that the minimum wage is linked to labor force participation and unemployment and that in turn these variables are linked to crime.

Labor Force Activity

Deteriorating labor force opportunities have been part of the experience of youths in this country for several decades. Their unemployment rates started rising rapidly in the 1950s and for the most part have stayed high ever since, with a brief and partial recovery during the years of the Vietnam war, a period when many young people were in the armed services. Unemployment rates for teenagers have increased relative to those for older workers, and they have been particularly high for blacks. During the 1960s, some economists attributed the rising teenage unemployment rates to their rapidly increasing numbers in the population and discounted the negative effects of minimum wage legislation. The percentage increase in the population aged sixteen to nineteen generated by the baby boom peaked in the early 1960s, however, and the unemployment rates for teenagers have not recovered and today remain close to their post–World War II highs. This is illustrated in figure 1.

During the 1950s and 1960s, as the likelihood that youths would

175

FIGURE 2
SCHOOL ENROLLMENT FOR MALES 18 AND 19, BY RACE, 1953–1978

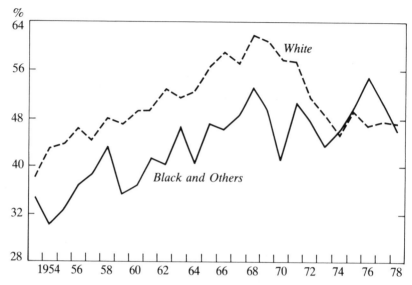

find a job declined, so did their participation in the labor force. Some young people were postponing the age of entry and remaining in school. From 1952 to 1968, the proportion of male youths aged eighteen to nineteen who were enrolled in school increased for both blacks and whites. Evidently, during the middle 1960s, some of these teenagers were motivated to stay in school to avoid the draft, since 1968 was the peak year for the proportion enrolled in school. Subsequent to 1968, school enrollment proportions declined for white males of this age, but for blacks the proportion enrolled in school has remained high, and in 1976 it surpassed both the previous peak in 1968 and the proportion enrolled for whites. (See figure 2.)

The comparison of the behavior of labor force participation of blacks (and others) and white males aged eighteen to nineteen since the early 1950s is particularly telling. In 1952, the participation rate for black males of this age was 79.1 percent, considerably above the rate for their white counterparts. But labor force participation for black youths has fallen markedly in the intervening years, reaching a low of 55.6 percent in 1976. Evidently there is a strong element of discouragement for black youths because of the high unemployment rates they face. In contrast, the participation rate for whites declined from 72.7 percent in 1952 to a low of 65.4 percent in 1966 but has since recovered to a high of 74.9 percent in 1977. (See figure 3.)

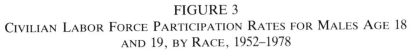

FIGURE 3

CIVILIAN LABOR FORCE PARTICIPATION RATES FOR MALES AGE 18
AND 19, BY RACE, 1952–1978

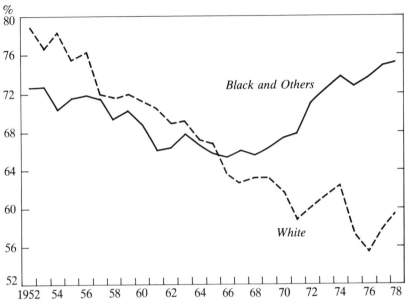

White youths are more oriented toward labor force activity than blacks and have higher rates of labor force participation whether they are enrolled in school or not. This is to be expected, given the much higher unemployment rates faced by blacks. Of every 100 black males aged eighteen and nineteen, only 37 are employed. This compares with 64 employed white males out of every 100 for these ages. (See figure 4.) At ages twenty and twenty-one, 47 of every 100 black males are employed compared with 72 of every 100 white males.

The contrast in these magnitudes for the two races underscores the importance of examining the net result of behavior in terms of employment, as well as comparing unemployment and participation rates.

Differential Impact of the Minimum Wage on Young Black Males

Jacob Mincer has provided an analysis of the minimum wage that distinguishes its impact on employment and unemployment.[1] The disemployment effects will be larger, the more elastic the demand for labor

[1] Jacob Mincer, "Unemployment Effects of Minimum Wages," *Journal of Political Economy* 84 (August 1976): S87–S104.

FIGURE 4
School Enrollment and Labor Force Status, Males Age 18 and 19, by Race, 1977

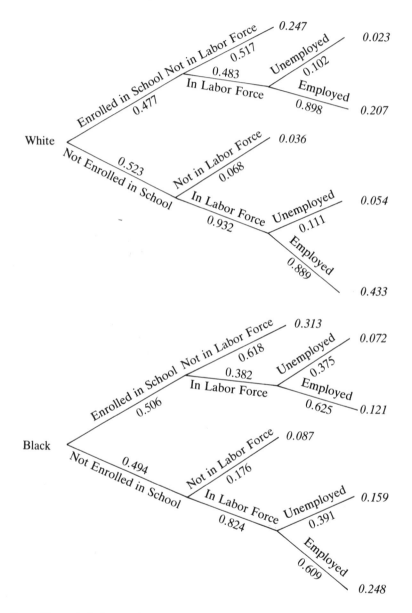

NOTE: Figures in italics are the proportion of the racial group accounted for by each labor force category.

in the sector of the economy covered by the minimum wage. If the elasticity of demand for labor in the covered sector exceeds the vacancy rate from labor turnover, there will be an outflow of labor to the uncovered sector and withdrawals from the labor force. This appears to have been the case in the United States. The greater the vacancy rate in the covered sector, the greater the impact of a minimum wage increase on unemployment. Unemployment will also be larger, the greater the proportion of workers in the uncovered sector.

Mincer mentions that the availability of alternatives, such as school enrollment, increases the incentive to drop out of the labor force when minimum wage increases create disemployment. Two alternatives not explicitly mentioned by Mincer should also be considered: the armed services and illegal activities.

Estimation of a labor market model using data for fourteen- to nineteen-year-olds in sixty-six standard metropolitan statistical areas (SMSAs) in 1960, as conducted by Arnold Katz,[2] showed that demand for nonwhite youths was quite elastic, whereas the demand elasticities for white youths were below unity. Consequently, we should expect the minimum wage to have a much greater disemployment effect for blacks than for whites. This result has been substantiated, using different data sets by both Jacob Mincer and James Ragan.[3] Mincer found that the disemployment effects of the minimum wage were greater for teenagers (sixteen to nineteen) than for young workers (twenty to twenty-four) and greater for nonwhites than for whites. Ragan estimated the disemployment effects of the minimum wage for two age groups, sixteen to seventeen and eighteen to nineteen, for males and females and for whites and nonwhites. He concluded that minimum wage legislation reduces youth employment, with nonwhite males being especially hard hit. A study by Finis Welch and James Cunningham corroborates Mincer's finding that the percentage disemployed by the minimum wage decreases with age.[4]

Statistical analysis by Finis Welch has demonstrated that the minimum wage shifted the distribution of teenage employment toward the uncovered sectors during the period 1954 to 1968.[5] This has the effect of increasing the amount of unemployment caused by further increases

[2] Arnold Katz, "Teenage Employment Effects of State Minimum Wages," *Journal of Human Resources* 8 (Spring 1973): 250–56.

[3] Mincer, "Unemployment Effects"; and James F. Ragan, Jr., "Minimum Wages and the Youth Labor Market," *Review of Economics and Statistics* 59 (May 1977): 129–36.

[4] Finis Welch and James Cunningham, "The Effects of Minimum Wages on the Level and Age Composition of Youth Employment," *Review of Economics and Statistics* 60 (February 1978): 140–45.

[5] Finis Welch, "Minimum Wage Legislation in the United States," *Economic Inquiry* 12 (September 1974): 285–318.

in the minimum wage. Data presented by Garth Mangum and Stephen Seninger indicate that, as of 1976, 64.3 percent of teenage employment was located in wholesale and retail trade and services, two industries with historically low minimum wage coverage.[6]

Mincer found that the minimum wage significantly decreased the labor force participation of teenagers and young males aged twenty to twenty-four with a larger impact on the former and a larger impact on nonwhites. In Ragan's study, the negative impact was statistically noteworthy only for black teenage males. Both Mincer and Ragan concluded that the minimum wage raises unemployment rates for male youths.[7]

Writing in the later 1960s, Edward Kalachek attributed higher teenage unemployment to the substantial increases in the supply of teenage labor. Based on the evidence in studies available at that time, he rejected the minimum wage as a significant cause of youth unemployment. Ragan found that the ratio of a group's population to total population aged sixteen and older did not affect white employment but did have a negative impact on black employment.[8] Evidently the minimum wage has affected both white and black youth while labor supply has had some adverse effect, as well, on young blacks.

The minimum wage affects both employment, or the demand for labor, and labor force participation, or the supply of labor. A strength of both the Mincer and Ragan studies is that they estimate separate employment and labor force equations as well as controlling for the effects of other variables, in addition to the minimum wage, on demand and supply. These two recent analyses have removed a great deal of the ambiguity found in the evidence from previous studies of the minimum wage, as reviewed by Robert Goldfarb.[9]

In view of the consistency of the evidence with the theory, as developed by Mincer, and mindful of the differential impact of the minimum wage on young black males, it would appear fruitful to pursue Mincer's suggestion of examining youthful activities alternative to labor force participation.

Alternatives to the Labor Force

The employment opportunities of young black males have been hit the hardest by the minimum wage, and consequently it is reasonable to

[6] Garth L. Mangum and Stephen F. Seninger, *Coming of Age in the Ghetto* (Baltimore: Johns Hopkins University Press, 1978).

[7] Mincer, "Unemployment Effects"; Ragan, "Minimum Wages and Youth."

[8] Edward Kalachek, *The Youth Labor Market* (Ann Arbor, Mich.: Institute of Labor and Industrial Relations, 1969); Ragan, "Minimum Wages and Youth."

[9] Robert S. Goldfarb, "The Policy Content of Quantitative Minimum Wage Research," *Proceedings of the Industrial Relations Research Association*, December 1974, pp. 261–68.

expect that these would be the youths most attracted by other alternatives. This is borne out by both the evidence on school enrollments and service in the armed forces. Recall figure 2. The fraction of males eighteen and nineteen years of age enrolled in school increased for both whites and nonwhites from 1953 until 1968. Since that date, the proportion enrolled in school has fallen to less than 50 percent for whites, comparable with the levels in the latter 1950s. In contrast, for blacks the proportion enrolled in school has remained high, averaging more than 50 percent for the past four years.

Of course, enrollment in school need not exclude participation in the labor force. But of eighteen- and nineteen-year-old males enrolled, labor force participation for whites averaged 46.3 percent from 1974 to 1978 while for blacks the average was 35 percent. For both races at these ages, the majority enrolled in school are not in the labor force.[10]

There is also an interesting contrast between the number of black and white youths serving in the armed forces in recent years (see figure 5). As the demands of the Vietnam war began to taper off, the number of whites and blacks in the armed services declined. This was the pattern from 1969 to 1972. With the ending of the draft and the beginning of the volunteer army, the number of white youths in the services continued to decline. Quite the opposite was true for blacks, whose numbers approached the previous peak in 1969. This behavior is consistent with a choice of the service as an alternative to the civilian labor force because of the differential impact of the minimum wage, but I am not aware of a study relating service in the armed forces to the minimum wage.

Young people choose whether to participate in the labor force, enroll in school, or join the volunteer armed forces. In the past ten years, the choices of black and white youths have been markedly different, consistent with the premise that black youths are hurt most by the minimum wage. It seems likely that the impact of the minimum wage would be reflected in the pathological behavior of youth as well.

Patterns in Crime Rates

Arrest rates for felony crimes against property, crimes such as burglary, larceny, and auto theft, are one or two orders of magnitude higher for males between the ages of fourteen and twenty-four than for males a generation older. Although arrest data undoubtedly include reporting

[10] Evidence of the effect of the minimum wage on school enrollment is not extensive. A study by Terrence Kelly ("Youth Employment Opportunities and the Minimum Wage," Working Paper no. 3608, Urban Institute, March 1975) reports that increases in the minimum wage do increase enrollments. See also J. Peter Mattila, "Youth Labor Markets, Enrollments, and Minimum Wages," *Proceedings of the Thirty-first Annual Meeting of the Industrial Relations Research Association*, August 1978, pp. 134–40.

FIGURE 5

ACTIVE DUTY IN THE ARMED FORCES FOR YOUTHS AGE 17 TO 24, BY
RACE, 1966–1976

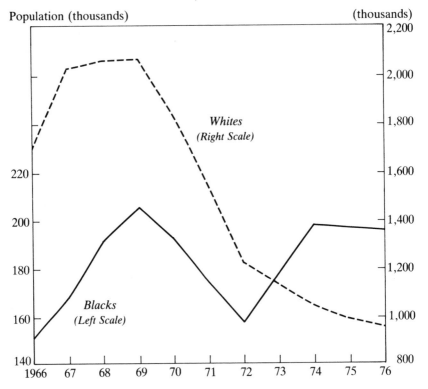

errors and possibly other biases as well, Phillips has shown that the
pattern of arrests, which decline with age starting at age fourteen, is
similar for larceny, burglary, and auto theft and that this was the pattern
in the 1960s as well as the 1950s.[11] Figures from the Uniform Crime
Report for 1978 show that for whites arrested, youths below eighteen
years of age accounted for 54 percent of the arrests for burglary, 45
percent of the arrests for larceny, and 57 percent of the arrests for auto
theft. The corresponding figures for blacks youths as a percentage of
blacks arrested, are 46, 39, and 43.

Arrest rates tend to show some variability over the business cycle,
particularly for youths and blacks. This is illustrated in figure 6. Arrest
rates showed a marked increase for young and old and black and white

[11] Llad Phillips, "The War on Crime: Prevention or Control?" in *Economic Analysis of
Pressing Social Problems*, ed. Llad Phillips and Harold L. Votey, Jr. (Chicago: Rand
McNally, 1977).

FIGURE 6
PROPERTY-CRIME ARREST RATES BY AGE AND RACE, 1964–1977

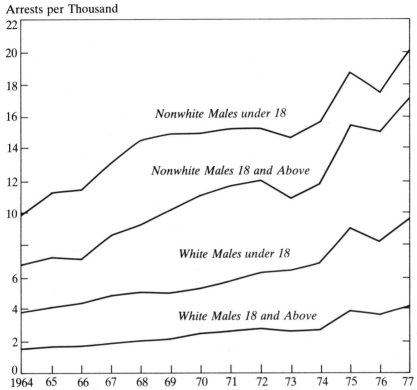

in 1975. Arrest rates for property crimes for youths did not show much increase in 1971, particularly for blacks. The record is mixed, and the relationship between economic conditions and felony crimes is not immediately obvious. It is clear, however, that arrest rates per capita are continuing to rise for whites as well as for blacks and for older males as well as for teenagers.

Labor Market Opportunities and Crime

At this date the evidence linking unemployment to crime is probably less convincing than that linking the minimum wage to unemployment. There are a number of reasons for this. Crime rates have trended upward, but the labor market experience of youths has not been uniform. During the past ten years, participation rates for young black males have been falling, while for their white counterparts participation rates have been rising. If we consider unemployment rates and labor force participation together, the fraction of the civilian labor force not working has been falling for white teenage males whereas the opposite is true for black youths. In view of their increasing crime rates, there must be factors common to whites and blacks, young and old, that cause crime to increase. Therefore, to discern the effect of changing labor market conditions on crime rates, it is necessary to standardize for this dominating trend in crime.

The literature reports conflicting evidence of the linkage between labor market variables and arrest rates, and controversy has arisen recently concerning the statistical analysis of the supply of offenses. This argument has focused on whether enough is known about crime causality and control to identify properly the deterrent effects of uncertain punishment.[12]

With regard to the theory of crime causation, Michael Block and Robert Lind have shown that an increase in wealth or future earnings will decrease the propensity to commit crime. In their analysis, and in a study by Block and John Heineke, income from illegal activity is treated as uncertain but legal income is considered certain. Treating both as uncertain, Isaac Ehrlich has shown that an increase in the unemployment rate, *ceteris paribus*, should increase illegal activity.[13]

Using both time series and cross-section data, Belton Fleisher developed evidence that arrests rates for property crimes for males aged less than twenty-five was positively related to unemployment rates.[14] Fleisher did not control for the deterrent effect of sanctions.

David Sjoquist estimated the variation of reported aggregated robbery, burglary, and larceny offenses per capita with deterrent variables such as the probability of arrest and conviction, the unemployment rate,

---

[12] For example, see Franklin M. Fisher and David Nagin, "On the Feasibility of Identifying the Crime Function in a Simultaneous Model of Crime Rates and Sanction Levels," in *Deterrence and Incapacitation: Estimating the Effects of Criminal Sanctions on Crime Rates*, ed. Alfred Blumstein, Jacqueline Cohen, and Daniel Nagin (Washington, D.C.: National Academy of Sciences, 1978). Although this critique focuses on deterrence, it is germane to the effect of other causal variables on the crime rate as well.

[13] Michael K. Block and Robert C. Lind, "An Economic Analysis of Crimes Punishable by Imprisonment," *Journal of Legal Studies* 4 (June 1975): 479–92; Michael K. Block and John M. Heineke, "A Labor Theoretic Analysis of the Criminal Choice," *American Economic Review* 65 (June 1975): 314–25; Isaac Ehrlich, "Participation in Illegitimate Activities: A Theoretical and Empirical Investigation," *Journal of Political Economy* 81 (May/June 1973): 521–65.

[14] Belton M. Fleisher, "The Effect of Income on Delinquency," *American Economic Review* 56 (March 1966): 118–37; idem, *The Economics of Delinquency* (Chicago: Quadrangle, 1966).

and other socioeconomic variables. He found the unemployment rate had a positive and significant impact on offenses per capita.[15]

Phillips, Harold Votey, and Darold Maxwell considered not only unemployment rates but labor force participation. Using age specific arrest rates for eighteen- and nineteen-year-old males, they showed that increases in the fraction of these males not working—that is, unemployed or not in the labor force—increased arrest rates. The estimations were conducted separately for four crimes: larceny, burglary, robbery, and auto theft.[16] However, deterrence variables were not included as causal variables.

Using census tract data for Los Angeles and Chicago, Burley Bechdolt found that the unemployment rate consistently had a significant positive impact on both the property crime rate and the violent crime rate.[17]

One study relates juvenile delinquency to the minimum wage. In a time series study of juvenile delinquency referrals in Utah for the period 1941–1975, Douglas Aird Macdonald found that the unemployment rate was not significant but that the minimum wage was.[18] However, the delinquency variable was highly trended and significantly and positively related to real per capita income, which suggests possible spurious correlations due to trend.

In a simultaneous equation model using data for the counties of California, Phillips and Votey found that felony offenses per capita varied inversely with the likelihood of conviction and positively with an index of labor market variables reflecting positive dependence on the unemployment rate but also positive dependence on the labor force participation rate for males aged eighteen to twenty-four.[19] Jeffrey Chapman has estimated a similar simultaneous equation model using data for cities in California. He found that property crimes per capita were inversely related to the likelihood of arrest and positively related to the fraction of men neither in the labor force nor in school.[20]

[15] David L. Sjoquist, "Property Crime and Economic Behavior: Some Empirical Results," *American Economic Review* 63 (June 1973): 439–46.

[16] Llad Phillips, Harold L. Votey, Jr., and Darold Maxwell, "Crime, Youth, and the Labor Market," *Journal of Political Economy* 80 (May/June 1972): 491–504.

[17] Burley V. Bechdolt, Jr., "Cross-sectional Analyses of Socioeconomic Determinants of Urban Crime," *Review of Social Economy* 33 (October 1975): 132–40.

[18] Douglas Aird Macdonald, "Forecasting Juvenile Delinquency Trends in the State of Utah," *Intermountain Economic Review* 8 (Fall 1977): 66–71.

[19] Llad Phillips and Harold L. Votey, Jr., "Crime Control in California," *Journal of Legal Studies* 4 (June 1975): 327–49.

[20] Jeffrey I. Chapman, "An Economic Model of Crime and Police: Some Empirical Results," *Journal of Research in Crime and Delinquency* 13 (January 1976): 48–63.

Contradicting the findings of the last two studies are the results from Ehrlich's estimation of a simultaneous equation model. Ehrlich related reported offenses per capita in the various states to deterrent and socioeconomic variables. He estimated equations for each of the major seven felonies as well as for the property crimes and violent crimes as groups. He did not find a significant relationship between the unemployment rate for urban males aged fourteen to twenty-four and these offense rates. He did find that increases in the participation rate for urban males in this age group decreased reported offenses for the crimes against persons.[21] This variable did not appear to have a significant impact on the crimes against property, however.

In sum, most of the empirical studies find that the unemployment rate has a positive impact on the crime rate. An exception is the study by Ehrlich.

Joblessness and Crime: An Update

The study by Phillips, Votey, and Maxwell related age-specific arrest rates for eighteen- and nineteen-year-old males to the fraction of this group unemployed or not in the labor force. The study spanned the years 1952 to 1967.[22] Arrest rate data disaggregated by both age and race became available only in the early 1960s and only for the broad age categories of below eighteen and eighteen and above. It is now feasible to study arrest rate behavior for males below eighteen for both whites and nonwhites.

As illustrated in figure 6, arrest rates aggregated for larceny, burglary, and auto theft have been trending upward from 1964 to 1977 for young males of both races. The fraction not working has also been highly trended. The age group selected for monitoring labor force activity is sixteen to seventeen, but their experience has been similar to that for eighteen- and nineteen-year-olds. Since 1964, the fraction not working has been falling for whites but rising for blacks (and others). Consequently, correlation of the fraction not working with arrest rates shows opposite results for whites and blacks; for example, the correlation coefficient for whites is -0.59, and for blacks it is 0.83.

There may be some causal variables common to both blacks and whites that cause their crime rates to increase. During the time period spanning this data, for example, the deterrence variables have tended to fall, which would cause crime rates to rise. There may be other trended causal variables as well. A simple model is to relate the property

---

[21] Ehrlich, "Illegitimate Activities."

[22] Phillips, Votey, and Maxwell, "Crime, Youth, and Labor."

crime arrest rate for males less than eighteen, $A(t)$, to a trend variable, t, proxying for these causal variables common to both blacks and whites. The variable specific to both races is the fraction of sixteen- and seventeen-year-old males not working, $NW(t)$. The latter is defined in terms of the civilian labor force participation rate, $p(t)$, and the unemployment rate, $u(t)$.

$$NW(t) \equiv 1 - p(t) + u(t)p(t)$$

Thus, the model for whites, variables subscripted with w, is

$$A_w(t) = a_w + b_w t + c_w NW_w(t)$$

and the model for blacks (and others), variables subscripted with B, is

$$A_B(t) = a_B + b_B t + c_B NW_B(t)$$

The a's, b's, and c's are parameters. Note that trend is the variable common to both blacks and whites in the analysis. The not-working variables are also trended, however. To eliminate correlation between the not-working variable and the trend variable, year-to-year changes in the variables are used.

$$\Delta A_w(t) = A_w(t) - A_w(t-1)$$

Using these year-to-year changes, the model for whites becomes

$$\Delta A_w(t) = b_w + c_w \Delta NW_w(t)$$

and the parameters estimated using least squares are

$$\Delta A_w(t) = \underset{(.208)}{.508} + \underset{(.116)}{.103} \Delta NW_w(t)$$

with the standard deviations of the parameters indicated in parentheses. The results for blacks are

$$\Delta A_B(t) = \underset{(.365)}{.666} + \underset{(.181)}{.165} \Delta NW_B(t)$$

Increases in the fraction of sixteen- and seventeen-year-olds not working increase the arrest rates for property crimes for males less than eighteen for both blacks and whites. The results are not statistically significant, but there are only fourteen observations for each group. Because the parameter estimates were similar for blacks and whites, the observations were pooled, yielding the following estimates.

$$\Delta A(t) = \underset{(.190)}{.606} + \underset{(.099)}{.151} \ \Delta NW(t)$$

The positive impact of the fraction not working on arrest rates is significantly different from zero at the 10 percent level. Changes in the fraction not working explain only about 9 percent of the variance in changes in arrest rates. As we saw above, however, the trend in arrest rates accounts for much of the year-to-year changes.

Only one of the time series studies of the relationship between unemployment and arrest rates substantiated its results by examining the correlations in differences, notwithstanding the possibility that correlations in levels could be spurious due to trend or autocorrelation. This was Fleisher.[23]

Summary

The preponderance of evidence indicates that the minimum wage has a heavy impact on young males, displacing them from jobs, raising unemployment, and driving them from the labor force. Young blacks have been particularly hard hit; as a consequence their participation in the labor force has continued to fall, and they have sought alternatives such as continued enrollment in school or entry into the armed services. Although young whites have also been affected by the minimum wage, they evidently have been less hard hit, as evidenced by their rising labor force participation rates in recent years, a falling proportion enrolled in school, and declining numbers in the armed services in spite of rising unemployment rates.

The preponderance of the evidence also indicates that unemployed and discouraged young males seek illegitimate alternatives to employment. Increases in the proportion not working increase property arrest rates for both black and white young males. The differential impact on blacks is probably reflected in the fact that their arrest rates are growing more rapidly than those for whites.

Of course, crime does not exhaust the list of youthful pathological behavior likely enlarged by unattractive labor market prospects. Consider girls and young women and prostitution and illegitimacy. Illegitimacy rates are much higher for young blacks than for young whites. But there is much less evidence linking illegitimacy to labor market

[23] Fleisher, "The Effect of Income"; idem, *The Economics of Delinquency.*

experience than is the case for crime, simply because there have not been the studies.

Bibliography

Bechdolt, Burley V., Jr. "Cross-sectional Analyses of Socioeconomic Determinants of Urban Crime." *Review of Social Economy* 33 (October 1975): 132–40.

Block, Michael K., and Heineke, John M. "A Labor Theoretic Analysis of the Criminal Choice." *American Economic Review* 65 (June 1975):314–25.

———, and Lind, Robert C. "An Economic Analysis of Crimes Punishable by Imprisonment." *Journal of Legal Studies* 4 (June 1975): 479–92.

Chapman, Jeffrey I. "An Economic Model of Crime and Police: Some Empirical Results." *Journal of Research in Crime and Delinquency* 13 (January 1976): 48–63.

Ehrlich, Isaac. "Participation in Illegitimate Activities: A Theoretical and Empirical Investigation." *Journal of Political Economy* 81 (May/June 1973): 521–65.

Fisher, Franklin M., and Nagin, David. "On the Feasibility of Identifying the Crime Function in a Simultaneous Model of Crime Rates and Sanction Levels." In *Deterrence and Incapacitation: Estimating the Effects of Criminal Sanctions on Crime Rates,* edited by Alfred Blumstein, Jacqueline Cohen, and Daniel Nagin. Washington, D.C.: National Academy of Sciences, 1978.

Fleisher, Belton M. *The Economics of Delinquency.* Chicago: Quadrangle, 1966.

———. "The Effect of Income on Delinquency." *American Economic Review* 56 (March 1966): 118–37.

Goldfarb, Robert S. "The Policy Content of Quantitative Minimum Wage Research." *Proceedings of the Industrial Relations Research Association,* December 1974, pp. 261–68.

Kalachek, Edward. *The Youth Labor Market.* Ann Arbor, Mich.: Institute of Labor and Industrial Relations, 1969.

Katz, Arnold. "Teenage Employment Effects of State Minimum Wages." *Journal of Human Resources* 8 (Spring 1973): 250–56.

Macdonald, Douglas Aird. "Forecasting Juvenile Delinquency Trends in the State of Utah." *Intermountain Economic Review* 8 (Fall 1977):66–71.

Mangum, Garth L., and Seninger, Stephen F. *Coming of Age in the Ghetto.* Baltimore: Johns Hopkins University Press, 1978.

Mattila, J. Peter. "Youth Labor Markets, Enrollments, and Minimum Wages." *Proceedings of the Thirty-first Annual Meeting of the Industrial Relations Research Association, August 29–31, 1978* (1979), pp. 134–40.

Mincer, Jacob. "Unemployment Effects of Minimum Wage." *Journal of Political Economy* 84 (August 1976): S87–S104.

Phillips, Llad. "The War on Crime: Prevention or Control?" In *Economic Analysis of Pressing Social Problems,* edited by Llad Phillips and Harold L. Votey, Jr. Chicago: Rand McNally, 1977.

———, and Votey, Harold L., Jr. "Crime Control in California." *Journal of Legal Studies* 4 (June 1975): 327–49.

————, Votey, Harold L., Jr., and Maxwell, Darold. "Crime, Youth, and the Labor Market." *Journal of Political Economy* 80 (May/June 1972): 491–504.

Ragan, James F., Jr. "Minimum Wages and the Youth Labor Market." *Review of Economics and Statistics* 59 (May 1977): 129–36.

Sjoquist, David L. "Property Crime and Economic Behavior: Some Empirical Results." *American Economic Review* 63 (June 1973): 439–46.

Twentieth Century Fund, *The Job Youth Crises*. New York: Praeger, 1971.

U.S. Department of Commerce, Bureau of the Census. *Current Population Reports*, ser. P–20. Washington, D.C., various issues.

U.S. Department of Justice, Federal Bureau of Investigation. *Uniform Crime Reports*. Washington, D.C., various annual issues.

U.S. Department of Labor, Bureau of Labor Statistics, *Handbook of Labor Statistics, 1978*. Washington, D.C., 1978.

Welch, Finis. "Minimum Wage Legislation in the United States." *Economic Inquiry* 12 (September 1974): 285–318.

————, and Cunningham, James. "The Effects of Minimum Wages on the Level and Age Composition of Youth Employment." *Review of Economics and Statistics* 60 (February 1978): 140–45.

The Impact of Minimum Wages on Private Household Workers

Kenneth Gordon

The 1974 amendments to the Fair Labor Standards Act extended coverage to one of the last large, uncovered occupational groups: private household workers. Approximately 1 million people were made subject to the minimum wage provisions of the act. Although some had been subject to state laws, the vast majority were covered for the first time. The legislative history of the 1974 amendments makes it clear that this extension was made neither casually nor inadvertently.

After reviewing the low wages and household incomes, short hours, and other alleged deficiencies of private household employment, the General Subcommittee on Labor argued:

> The committee expects that extending minimum wage and overtime protection to domestic workers will not only raise the wages of these workers but will improve the sorry image of household employment. The committee is convinced that the sharp decline in household employment over the past decade reflects not only the prevalence of low wages and long hours (*sic*), but the widespread conviction that these are dead end jobs. Including domestic workers under the protection of the act should help to raise the status and dignity of this work.[1]

The mechanism by which this transformation might occur is not explained. Throughout the hearings on the 1974 amendments, there are references to the low estate of household employment, laments over its decline and the difficulty of finding help, and assertions that the imposition of higher wages would raise the status of the occupation. The thought that higher wages would attract more workers to the occupation is reasonable by itself, but no attention is given to the demand side of the market. Economists' predictions that an effectively enforced minimum wage could hasten the already rapid decline of employment in this occupation are ignored.

---

[1] Rept. 93–913, cited in *United States Code Congressional and Administrative News*, 93rd Cong., 2nd sess., vol. 2 (1974), p. 2843.

FIGURE 1
Disemployment Effect of a Minimum Wage

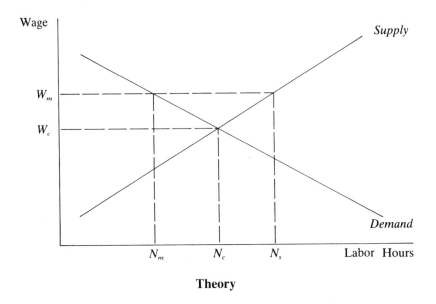

Theory

There are many thousands of employers and employees in the domestic service market, none of whom possesses any significant market power. Consequently, the competitive market model can be used to predict the effect of an effective minimum wage.

In figure 1, imposing a minimum wage of W_m greater than the current competitively determined wage W_c will lead to a drop in employment from N_c to N_m. This disemployment effect could take the form of fewer workers employed, an increase in the proportion of workers employed part-time or in domestic employment as a second occupation, or shorter hours. Because cutbacks in the hiring of domestic workers will affect the lowest-productivity workers most severely, the greatest effects should be on the employment of teenagers and others with little experience or training.

The minimum wage also creates an unemployment gap of $N_m N_s$, but the effect on the observed unemployment rate is not clear. To the extent that those who lose household jobs can find work in other occupations, the measured unemployment rate for private household workers will not rise. Some of those attracted to the occupation by the higher wages, and unable to find work, will become unemployed. They will not show up as unemployed, however, because the occupational unemployment statistics apply only to experienced workers. Therefore, the effect of minimum wages on the unemployment rates of domestics cannot be predicted with any confidence.

Demand

For any wage at or above the equilibrium rate W_c, employment will depend on the demand for household workers. A number of studies suggest that the disemployment effects could be quite large if a substantial fraction of employees earn considerably less than the minimum wage *and if* employers comply with that minimum.

George Stigler's classic study of domestic servants in the United States estimated the elasticity of demand at about -2.3.[2] Thus, a 10 percent increase in the wage rate (quite possible for many domestics with current minimums) could lead to a 23 percent decline in employment. The reasons for this relatively high elasticity are fairly clear. There is a wide range of substitutes available for household help, and in addition, the income elasticity of demand is rather high. Stigler estimated its value at about 2. Recent cross-section studies by Peter Mattila, based on data from the 1960 and 1970 censuses of population confirm these very high demand elasticities; indeed, they suggest that values as high as -2.5 to -3.5 are possible. High-income elasticities are also found.[3]

If these estimates are even roughly correct, extensive compliance with newly imposed minimum wage standards can be expected to result in even sharper drops in the employment of private household workers than would otherwise have taken place. The purpose of this paper is to examine the rather limited data that are available for this occupation in an attempt to see what impact, if any, the 1974 legislation has had.

Private Household Workers

Occupations. Domestic service employment includes a large number of detailed occupations such as cooks, waiters, butlers, maids, housekeepers, governesses, gardeners, chauffeurs, baby-sitters, and "companions." The distinguishing characteristic of these occupations is that the work is performed in or about the home of *their* employer. Hence, the employees of firms that provide similar services in homes are not included in the occupation. The two largest categories are maids and baby-sitters. Companions (to the elderly and infirm) are becoming important.

[2] George J. Stigler, *Domestic Servants in the United States, 1900–1940* (New York: National Bureau of Economic Research, 1946).

[3] J. Peter Mattila, "The Labor Supply for Lower Level Occupations: Appendix A. Supplementary Reports," National Planning Association, June 1975.

Trends in Employment. The number of private household workers in the United States has declined fairly steadily since 1940. A slight rise in 1960 is the only interruption of the dominant downward pattern. Although the broad trend is relatively clear, presenting estimates of the absolute numbers of people in the occupation is fraught with difficulty. A variety of sources must be used, and there are substantial definitional differences among them. Nevertheless, table 1 provides a reasonable overview of trends in employment in this occupation in recent years. Table 2 presents the same trends on a per household basis and highlights the relative growth in the importance of baby-sitters.

If we exclude baby-sitters (who, in the main, represent a type of worker very different from other domestics), the decline in employment per household continues unabated. Average hours per week have been maintained throughout the 1970s at twenty-four per week for all workers. For those on full-time schedules, average hours are forty-three to forty-four.

The explanations of this decline lie on both sides of the market. On the demand side, a wide range of substitutes for domestic servants has become increasingly available, and throughout the postwar period their prices have been declining relative to the costs of employing private household workers. This has stimulated a shift to providing these services outside the home and to an increased use of appliances and other labor-saving methods inside the home.

Some influences point in the opposite direction. Rising labor force participation of women should increase the demand for household help generally and, where children are present, for baby-sitters in particular. Recent changes in the tax code that permit the deduction of certain child-care expenses may provide an additional boost in this direction. Although there is a good deal of anecdotal evidence on the attempts of working couples to obtain household help, very little of a precise nature is known. Rising levels of real income also point in the direction of increased demand. The 1972–1973 Consumer Expenditure Survey shows the average family spending about $130 per year on domestic and other household services. The figure is $56 for those with incomes under $3,000, rising slowly to $95 at $12,000, and increasing to $439 for families with incomes of more than $25,000 per year. The increase in demand is particularly apparent as we move into the higher income ranges.

The very rapid increase in the wages of private household workers relative to the prices of substitutes for them suggests that factors on the supply side are also important. Mattila's 1975 study supports this view. Employment (in his supply equations) was found to be related positively to the ratio of maid's wages to wages in alternative occupations.[4] The

---

[4] Ibid.

TABLE 1

PRIVATE HOUSEHOLD WORKERS IN THE UNITED STATES
(all figures in thousands)

Year	Census (excluding sitters)	Current Population Survey			Special Surveys		
		Total	Excluding sitters	Sitters	Total	Excluding sitters	Sitters
1940	2,412						
1950	1,462						
1960	1,557	2,216					
1970	981	1,558	1,031	527			
1971		1,486	953	533	2,332	1,771	561
1972		1,437	894	543			
1973		1,353	812	541			
1974		1,228	732	496	1,633	864	762
1975		1,171	736	435			
1976		1,125	696	429			
1977		1,158	715	443			
1978		1,162	676	486			

SOURCES: Decennial censuses; U.S. Department of Labor, Bureau of Labor Statistics, *Employment and Earnings*, various issues, and unpublished data provided by the department; and two special surveys of private household workers conducted by the Current Population Survey for the Department of Labor in 1971 and 1974. No special survey has been conducted since 1974.

TABLE 2

RATIOS OF PRIVATE HOUSEHOLD WORKERS TO PRIVATE
HOUSEHOLDS AND PERCENTAGE OF BABY-SITTERS AMONG TOTAL
EMPLOYMENT IN PRIVATE HOUSEHOLDS

Year	Including Sitters		Excluding Sitters		Sitters as % of All Workers	
	CPS	Special survey	CPS	Special survey	CPS	Special survey
1960	.0420					
1970	.0246		.0163		33.8	
1971	.0231	.0362	.0148	.0275	35.9	24.1
1972	.0216		.0134		37.8	
1973	.0198		.0119		40.0	
1974	.0176	.0234	.0105	.0124	40.4	46.6
1975	.0165		.0103		37.1	
1976	.0154		.0095		38.1	
1977	.0155		.0096		38.2	
1978	.0152		.0088		41.8	

SOURCES: Table 1, and U.S. Department of Commerce, Bureau of the Census, *Statistical Abstract of the United States.*

assertion of the proponents of minimum wages that workers could be attracted to this occupation by higher wages is thus reasonable by itself—but no attention is given the fact that there may be little demand for maids and other domestic workers at high wages. It is still true that those who complain most about "the servant problem" and bemoan the fact that so many potential workers seem less than anxious to engage in honest work fail to mention that the wage they had in mind is well below the going rate.

Other factors that adversely affect the supply of domestics include the reduced availability of immigrants and black women. In the case of immigrants (legal, at least), there are simply fewer of them, and many arrive with skills that make household employment an unattractive alternative. Higher levels of education and improved employment opportunities for black women have a similar effect. Two other factors deserve mention. Mattila found a negative relationship between the level of payments of Aid to Families with Dependent Children and employment.[5] Finally, a reasonably prosperous economy offers increased opportunities for nonhousehold work or, for some women, the option of withdrawing entirely from the labor force.

[5] Ibid.

196

Wages. There are three principal sources of information on the wages of private household workers: decennial censuses, unpublished tabulations from the May Current Population Survey (CPS), and the two special surveys of private household workers mentioned earlier (table 1). In addition, the household-service component of the consumer price index provides a useful link to earlier periods, although recent changes in its method of computation have reduced its current and future usefulness. These data (along with the CPS data used earlier) include information only on those workers for whom household employment is the primary occupation. The 1971 and 1974 special surveys include all private household workers. Thus, the data for the two surveys are not strictly comparable. Table 3 presents information on wage trends for domestic service.

Wages have continued to rise more rapidly in domestic service (10 percent per annum) than the wages of production workers in manufacturing (about 8 percent per annum) throughout the 1970s. With the exception of 1976 the pace was slower than in earlier years—indeed, 1978 shows a slight decline for all wage and salary workers. Wages of full-time workers, however, rose even in that year.

It should be carefully noted that the wage statistics in the central section of table 3 are a very mixed bag. They are from the May Current Population Survey (CPS) and include baby-sitters as well as other domestic household workers. From 1974 on they include both workers who are covered under the Fair Labor Standards Act (FLSA) and those who are not, and no distinction between the two categories is made. Because the exact composition of the domestic-worker labor force with respect to these factors is unknown, these statistics are less than ideal for determining the impact of the minimum wage. Finally, the special survey for 1974 was done in November, well after the extension of FLSA coverage to domestic household workers.

Table 4 presents information computed from unpublished Current Population Survey tabulations. Minimum wage levels are presented for comparative purposes. The trend to higher wages is apparent throughout the table, whether we look at full-time employees or at the much larger number of part-time workers. The most striking feature of these data is their bimodal character. Although there is undoubtedly some crossover, it is probably true that the lower mode is comprised mainly of baby-sitters and the higher one of all other household workers. It is also likely that there is a tendency for the two groups to correlate with the covered and uncovered categories of workers, but again, the correspondence is far from perfect. Separate wage distributions from the 1974 special survey are not yet available, nor can CPS data be used for this determination without going to the original tapes. Some information on

197

TABLE 3

WAGES OF PRIVATE HOUSEHOLD WORKERS, 1939–1978

Year	Index of Wages from CPI	Median Actual Hourly Earnings, Including Sitters (dollars)			Average Hourly Earnings, Special Surveys (dollars)	
		All wage & salary	Full-time	Part-time	Private household, excluding sitters	Sitters
1939	26.2					
1948	74.1					
1958	99.3					
1964	123.5					
1970	187.4				1.34	0.72
1971		1.32	1.44	1.31		
1973		1.55	1.66	1.53		
1974		1.57	2.02	1.55	2.07[a] 1.64[b]	0.85[a] 0.72[b]
1975		2.05	2.13	2.03		
1976		2.16	2.46	2.12		
1977		2.07	2.56	2.04		
1978						

[a] Covered under FLSA.
[b] Not covered.

SOURCES: J. Peter Mattila, "The Effect of Extending Minimum Wages to Cover Household Maids," *Journal of Human Resources* 8 (1972): table 2, p. 2843; unpublished tabulations of CPS data provided by the Bureau of Labor Statistics; special surveys of private household workers by CPS for the Bureau of Employment Security, 1971 and 1974.

TABLE 4: PERCENTAGE DISTRIBUTION OF WAGES, PRIVATE HOUSEHOLD WORKERS, 1973–1978

Year	Status	Under 1.00	1.00 to 1.59	1.60 to 1.79	1.80 to 1.99	2.00 to 2.24	2.25 to 2.49	2.50 to 2.99	3.00 to 3.49	3.50 to 3.99	4.00 to 4.99	5.00 and over	Minimum Wage Domestics	Minimum Wage Other
1973	Total wage & salary	29.33	39.03	5.77	1.15	17.55	1.38	3.69	1.62	0.23	—	—	n.a.	1.60
1974		25.53	26.59	6.59	10.42	20.64	1.28	5.96	2.34	0.42	—	—	1.90	2.00
1975		21.89	29.72	0.46	1.84	37.56	1.38	4.15	2.76	—	—	0.23	2.00a	2.10a
1976		12.06	30.16	1.39	0.93	29.47	9.74	8.35	4.87	1.16	0.70	1.16	2.20	2.30
1977		7.76	28.99	2.51	—	17.12	15.98	11.87	11.19	2.74	1.14	0.91	2.30	2.30
1978		12.28	34.15	0.67	—	9.82	2.23	22.10	12.05	1.56	1.56	2.68	2.65	2.65
1973	Full-time only	25.71	31.43	11.43	—	17.14	8.57	2.86	—	—	—	—	same as above	
1974		18.75	29.17	6.25	10.42	20.83	2.08	8.33	4.17	—	—	—		
1975		14.28	25.71	5.71	31.43	5.71	14.28	2.86	—	—	—	—		
1976		2.70	10.81	—	8.11	51.35	5.40	5.40	2.70	5.40	8.11	—		
1977		3.70	24.07	—	—	5.55	18.52	24.07	7.41	7.41	5.55	1.85		
1978		2.04	36.73	—	—	4.08	4.08	26.53	20.41	2.04	2.04	—		
1973	Part-time only	29.90	39.45	5.28	1.26	17.59	0.75	3.77	1.76	0.25	—	—	same as above	
1974		26.36	26.36	6.65	10.45	20.66	1.19	5.70	2.37	0.47	—	—		
1975		22.61	30.15	—	1.51	38.44	1.26	3.27	2.51	—	—	—		
1976		12.66	31.90	1.52	0.51	27.59	10.38	8.86	4.81	0.76	—	—		
1977		8.33	29.69	2.86	—	18.49	15.62	10.16	11.72	2.08	0.52	0.78		
1978		13.28	33.83	0.75	—	10.53	2.00	21.55	11.03	1.50	1.50	3.01		

a Effective May 1, the survey month.
SOURCE: Calculated from unpublished tabulation from various May Current Population Surveys provided by the Bureau of Labor Statistics.

the distribution of wages from the 1974 special survey is discussed in the section on compliance.

Other Characteristics. According to the November 1974 special survey, there were 1.6 million persons employed in domestic service (either as the primary or a secondary job), a drop of 31 percent from the 2.4 million employed at the time of the previous survey in May 1971. There were 864,000 domestics (90 percent covered under FLSA) and 762,000 baby-sitters (25 percent covered). Whites comprised about half the domestics but around 90 percent of the baby-sitters.

The covered domestics occupations (excludes baby-sitters) were heavily female (80 percent); 40 percent were heads of households, and one in seven was over sixty-five years of age or under twenty. Thirty percent had a family income of under $3,000, and 20 percent were in the $10,000-and-over group. The average hours worked per week by covered domestics was sixteen. Finally, 70 percent received some perquisites in addition to cash wages, including free meals, transportation, employee's share of social security, lodging, and uniforms. Fewer than 5 percent lived in.

Of the 57,000 uncovered domestics, 89 percent were companions. They averaged forty-four hours per week. There were 204,000 baby-sitters covered by FLSA, of which 90 percent were white and better than 50 percent were twenty years of age or older. About three-fourths (558,000) of the baby-sitters were not covered. Almost all were young and white. Their average work week was nine hours.

The Fair Labor Standards Act Amendments

Wage Requirements. Before the 1974 FLSA amendments, private household workers were not subject to federal minimum wage requirements. The minimum wage portion of the amendments to the act imposed the requirements shown in table 5. The four-year period during which a differential minimum was set for private household workers was the only sign that adverse effects on employment might result from the new law. In January 1978 the distinction disappeared.

Coverage. Any private household employee who earns at least $50 per calendar quarter, or who works more than eight hours per week, in the aggregate, in one or more households, must be paid the minimum wage. This criterion seems quite inclusive, but there are two major exceptions. Those "employed on a casual basis in domestic service employment to provide babysitting services or employed in domestic service employment to provide companionship services" (for the elderly or infirm) are

TABLE 5

MINIMUM WAGES AND PRIVATE HOUSEHOLD WORKERS

Effective Date of Minimum	Economywide Minimum	Minimum Wage for Private Household Workers	Median Actual Hourly Earnings in Private Households[a]
February 1968	1.60	not covered	1.32[b]
May 1974	2.00	1.90	1.55
January 1975	2.10	2.00	1.57
January 1976	2.30	2.20	2 05
January 1977	no change	2.30	2.16
January 1978	2.65	2.65	2.07
January 1979	2.90	2.90	—
January 1980[c]	3.10	3.10	—
January 1981[c]	3.35	3.35	—

[a] CPS data.
[b] May 1973; succeeding figures are for May of year shown.
[c] Presently scheduled rates
SOURCE: U.S. Department of Labor, Employment Standards Administration, *Domestic Service Employees* (Washington, D.C., 1979), p. 110.

exempt from these provisions. There are also exceptions to the exemptions, which provide that if over 20 percent of a baby-sitter's or companion's time is spent on general housework, he or she is again subject to the minimum wage provisions. Trained child-care personnel are not considered baby-sitters under the law. Table 6 presents information on the coverage status of private household employees shortly after they came under FLSA.

It should be noted that covered status is neither easily nor precisely determined by knowing an employee's precise occupational classification. This is a particular problem in the case of baby-sitters, who represent an increasing proportion of private household workers. Because employment counts are not available by coverage status, the determination of minimum wage effects is quite problematic.

Possible Impact. It is clear from both theory and empirical evidence that a minimum wage for private household workers has the potential for a substantial impact on employment. The demand curve is highly elastic, and the minimum wages that have been imposed in the past and that are proposed for the future appear to be above the wage levels of substantial numbers of workers.

Under these conditions, barring changes in other circumstances, the imposition of a minimum wage will have as its primary effect a

TABLE 6

COVERAGE STATUS OF PRIVATE HOUSEHOLD WORKERS

	Total		Household Workers		Companions		Sitters	
	No.	%	No.	%	No.	%	No.	%
Covered								
U.S.	1,011	61.9	776	99.2	31	37.8	204	26.8
South	466	28.5	408	52.2	8	9.8	51	6.7
Non-South	545	33.4	369	47.2	23	28.0	153	20.1
Noncovered								
U.S.	615	37.7	6	0.8	51	62.2	558	73.2
South	145	8.9	—	—	28	34.2	116	15.2
Non-South	471	28.9	6	0.8	22	26.8	442	58.0
Total	1,633	100.0	782	100.0	82	100.0	762	100.0

NOTE: Numbers in thousands.
SOURCE: Department of Labor, *Domestic Service Employees*, table 1, p. 58.

reduction of employment in the occupation to a level below what it would otherwise have been. This effect could take several forms: fewer employees, shorter hours, or an increased reliance on part-time work. The effects need not be distributed uniformly across all workers, and this may lead to additional clues about the law's effects. There should be a larger impact where wages are especially low, as, for example, in the South. Racial groups, teenagers, or other low-productivity groups should show the greatest employment declines. Finally, although theory is not entirely clear on this point, it would be reasonable to expect at least a temporary rise in unemployment rates following the imposition of a (higher) minimum wage.

The average of all wages should also be affected. As the less productive low-wage workers lose their jobs, the median wage for the occupation as a whole will rise, and the proportion of employees earning less than the minimum wage will fall.

Other influences on the demand for and supply of household workers may have changed along with the imposition of a wage minimum, and any changes observed will be the result of these factors as well. Theory suggests that some of the important factors on the demand side are consumer income, region (the number of maids per household is much higher in the South), the labor force participation of married women, and the prices of substitutes for household workers. The latter include appliances of various sorts and the services of commercial firms that specialize in performing the more onerous household tasks.

On the supply side, there are a number of factors that could have affected wages and employment. Wage increases in related occupations or increased availability of jobs outside the household sector, reduced numbers of immigrants—a traditional source of household workers—generally higher levels of education for black women, and a higher level of Aid to Families with Dependent Children payments would all point to a smaller supply of household workers and to higher wage levels as well.

The Impact of Minimum Wages

Because the minimum wage has been in effect only four years (for which data are available), a simultaneous examination of all these effects is not feasible. Nevertheless, it is possible to examine the gross changes in employment and wages since minimum wages were imposed and to see if changes in any of the other factors mentioned earlier appear to have obscured or offset the predicted effects.

Employment Effects. An examination of tables 1 and 2 indicates that since 1974 the absolute decline in the number of private household workers has slowed or perhaps even been reversed. Even when we exclude baby-sitters, whose numbers are almost surely determined by factors different from those affecting other private household workers, there is only a modest tendency for numbers to decline. Over the four years prior to 1974, employment (excluding baby-sitters) declined at a rate of more than 7 percent, whereas after 1974 the rate of decline actually slowed to under 2 percent. On a per household basis, the same periods showed declines of 10 percent and less than 5 percent, respectively. This is precisely the opposite of what one would expect to observe if the minimum wage were having a serious adverse effect on employment. Although other factors could have been at work, and undoubtedly were, the finding remains striking. An attempt to test the significance of this alteration of trend more formally was inconclusive.

A look at the figures for women only, by age group, confirms the previous result. In no age group is there any significant decline in numbers. The one exception to this conclusion appears to be for black women. Between 1974 and 1978 (CPS May wage survey data) the total number of black private household workers dropped between 15 percent and 18 percent. Although it is tempting to attribute this drop to the minimum wage, on the argument that the productivity of black workers is relatively low, the hourly wage data contradict this interpretation. Wages for blacks are considerably higher than the wages for whites (as much as double), and blacks in this occupation are less likely than whites

203

to be affected directly by minimum wages. In addition, the downward trend in numbers is very long-standing.

A decline in employment could show up in other ways. Data on persons with work experience during a given year (classified by longest job) show a sharp drop in the percentage of persons in private household jobs who worked full-time, year-round. This figure rose in the late 1960s and early 1970s to about 17 percent, but since 1974 it has been in the 10 percent to 12 percent range. Although there is a problem of comparability with earlier years because of technical adjustments to the data, it is unlikely that the entire drop is a statistical artifact.

In the CPS data the changes are somewhat less dramatic. From 1971 to 1974 the proportion of workers on part-time for economic reasons was 12.1 percent, whereas from 1975 to 1978 it averaged 14.5 percent. The number on full-time schedules fell from about 34 percent to 30 percent. The fall in average hours per week at work (all workers) was more modest still: 24.5 to 23.

Thus, the data suggest that if the minimum wage had any effect it was to reduce hours of work slightly and to increase the amount of part-time employment. Needless to say, this could also have been the result of higher wages brought on by other factors.

The unemployment rate for all age groups of females rose slightly (less than one percentage point) after 1974. The major jump, however, took place in 1973, a year before the extension of minimum wages to household workers. In addition, the rise in unemployment was considerably less than it was for most other service workers in the economy. It is not clear whether minimum wages had any connection with this rise.

Wage Effects. Wage distributions for private household workers are available from the Bureau of Labor Statistics (unpublished tabulations from the May CPS), but they include baby-sitters and do not distinguish between workers who are covered by the minimum wage law and those who are not. Given the large fraction of baby-sitters represented, it is hard to draw any firm conclusions from the data.

If we are willing to assume that the lower modes of the wage distributions represent uncovered workers (from 1974 on) and the upper modes covered workers, it is possible to convince oneself that the higher portions of the distributions tend to follow the minimum wage upward. Although such an association may be present, it is important not to attribute too much significance to it. Minimum wage levels have changed relatively frequently in recent years, maintaining a fairly steady relationship to wages in the economy as a whole, and wages in household employment have risen more rapidly than the average. It is quite possible that wages would have increased in this fashion in any case.

Finally, even when we confine our attention to the upper portion of the distributions, there are fairly substantial numbers of workers earning less than the minimum wage.

A final warning is needed. Employers are permitted to count the value of noncash perquisites toward meeting minimum wage requirements. According to the 1974 special survey, these could amount to as much as 20 percent of the cash wage. To the (unknown) extent to which these additions are present, the figures shown in tables 3 and 4 should be revised upward.

The trend in wages has continued upward since 1974 at about a 9 percent annual rate, which is slightly higher than the rate of increase in private, nonagricultural wages. But this is not a new feature—wage growth in domestic service has been above the economywide averages for some time.

Other Factors. It is possible that changes in one or more of the variables underlying the supply and demand for private household workers has caused us to overestimate or underestimate the effect of the minimum wage. There are a number of possibilities.

Per capita disposable personal income (1972 dollars) rose at a 2.7 percent per year rate from 1974 to 1978, a drop from the 3.5 percent rate of the previous five-year period. Hence, it seems quite unlikely to have been responsible for the flattening of the decline in employment or the rise in wages.

The labor force participation of married women continued to rise throughout this period and presumably increased the demand for private household workers. Mattila's studies suggest this effect will be small,[6] but it could have had some impact—though not any greater than in earlier periods. The tax changes with respect to child-care expenses, mentioned earlier, could also have played a role.

Prices of appliances began to rise more rapidly after 1974, in line with overall price trends. This meant that their decline in price *relative* to private household wages ended. This could have slowed the shift away from private household workers and made demand higher than it would otherwise have been.

On the supply side, two factors should be noted. Current dollar payments in the Aid to Families with Dependent Children program rose at a 6.8 percent annual rate compared with 6.6 percent for the previous

[6] Ibid.

five-year period. In real terms, however, payments have declined. Mattila found a reliable negative relationship between constant dollar payments and the supply of labor to domestic service,[7] and this may help explain some of the reduction in the rate of employment decline. A factor pointing in the opposite direction is that educational levels of black women have continued to rise, making possible a shift to higher-paying sectors of the economy.

Conclusion. The evidence seems to indicate that previous trends in the private household worker economy have more or less continued and that where they have not, as in the case of employment, the change is in the opposite direction from what we would have expected from the imposition of a minimum wage. Only in the cases of hours worked and the proportion of workers involuntarily employed part-time is there any sign of an impact. The extension of minimum wages to private household workers has had almost no effect on the occupation except, perhaps, to reduce hours worked somewhat.

Although reduced hours and/or increased reliance on part-time work are not trivial matters for the people involved, the question remains: Why do the effects seem so small when a large number of *covered* workers were earning rates below the minimum when the law was passed? The 1974 special survey reported that 46 percent of covered workers were earning less than the minimum wage in November of that year, six months after the law was passed. More recent coverage statistics are not available, but wage distributions that are available provide a strong hint that many nominally covered workers continue to earn less than the minimum.

The Matter of Compliance

It seems fairly likely that the principal reason for the modest effects observed lies in the even more modest level of enforcement of, and compliance with, the law. Policing the minimum wage is an extraordinarily difficult task in as decentralized an industry as this one. When this is coupled with the fact that some employees may not wish to report income for tax purposes (payments in currency are reputed to be common), it is not hard to imagine a low degree of compliance. Nevertheless, it would be desirable to have more direct evidence.

Orley Ashenfelter and Robert Smith have suggested measuring compliance by looking at the proportion of workers earning below the

---

[7] Ibid.

TABLE 7

COMPLAINTS, 1975–1977

Fiscal Year	No. of Complaints
1975	467
1976	398
June 21, 1976–September 20, 1976[a]	119
1977	357

[a] A transition quarter.
SOURCE: Department of Labor, *Domestic Service Employees*, p. 15.

TABLE 8

COMPLIANCE ACTIONS, 1974–1977

Fiscal Year	No. of Actions	Domestics Underpaid		
		Total	Min. wage	Overtime
1974	28	28	27	2
1975	356	367	343	76
1976	359	349	332	87
1977	351	430	390	100

SOURCE: Department of Labor, *Domestic Service Employees*, p. 16.

specified minimum.[8] For this method to be accurate, however, all workers in the wage distribution must be covered by the law, and this requirement is not even approached by the data for this occupation.

Another method is to examine enforcement directly. The Employment Standards Administration, which is responsible for enforcing FLSA, acts only when presented with complaints, at least in the private household sector. Complaints received are shown in table 7. Statistics on compliance actions are shown in table 8.

The numbers presented in tables 7 and 8 are quite small relative to the number of workers earning less than the minimum and are even less impressive than similar actions brought in other industries. Typically, only one worker and one employer are affected by an enforcement action. As a result, the productivity of enforcement effort is very low and the cost high. The Employment Standards Administration has apparently decided it can use its enforcement resources more wisely elsewhere. Another factor ensuring relatively low productivity in enforce-

[8] Orley Ashenfelter and Robert S. Smith, "Compliance with the Minimum Wage Law," *Journal of Political Economy* 87 (April 1979): 333–50.

ment is the lack of any strong tendency of enforcement to spread. Workplaces are relatively isolated from one another.

Given the small probability of detection and the rather small penalties (mostly back wages), there is little reason to fear running afoul of the law. A far more common reason for paying wages at or above the minimum (which is not the same thing as complying when one would prefer not to) is the inability to find help at lower wages.

Final Comments

Although the extension of the minimum wage to private household workers has not had a dramatic effect on the industry, several comments are in order.

First, there is a suggestion in the data that hours may have been somewhat reduced and the amount of involuntary part-time work increased. If this occurred as a result of the minimum wage, some workers are worse off than they would otherwise be. The increased average wages appear likely to have been brought about by market forces; thus, it is hard to see any offsetting positive effects of the minimum. On these grounds, continuation of coverage is probably (slightly) undesirable.

A second point concerns compliance. Presumably, a large expenditure on enforcement activities could increase the number of workers receiving at least the minimum wage—but at the cost of reduced employment and shorter hours. Thus, it is tempting to be satisfied with the current level of enforcement. As Stigler has pointed out, this may be the only politically possible way of repealing a law that is so widely supported, at least in principle.[9]

This is not a completely benign solution, however. Complaints are now brought by disgruntled employees—indeed, most likely by former employees. A policy of enforcement by complaint converts the minimum wage law from an instrument of public policy to a tool of private disputes. This is an unhappy consequence, which can be avoided only by removing this group from coverage or changing the enforcement policy. Neither outcome seems likely, and the latter would probably do more harm than good.

Bibliography

Ashenfelter, Orley, and Smith, Robert S. "Compliance with the Minimum Wage Law." *Journal of Political Economy* 87 (April 1979): 333–50.

[9] Stigler, *Domestic Servants*.

Mattila, J. Peter. "The Effect of Extending Minimum Wages to Cover Household Maids." *Journal of Human Resources* 8 (1972): 30.

———. "The Impact of Extending Minimum Wages to Private Household Workers." Columbus, Ohio, 1971.

———. "The Labor Supply for Lower Level Occupations: Appendix A. Supplementary Reports." National Planning Association, June 1975.

Stigler, George J. *Domestic Servants in the United States, 1900–1940.* New York: National Bureau of Economic Research, 1946.

U.S. Congress, *United States Code Congressional and Administrative News*, 93rd Congress, 2nd Session, vol. 2 (1974).

U.S. Department of Labor, Bureau of Labor Statistics. *Employment and Earnings*. Washington, D.C., various issues.

———. Employment Standards Administration, *Domestic Service Employees*. Washington, D.C., 1979.

———. *Handbook of Labor Statistics, 1978.* Washington, D.C., 1978.

———. *Private Household Workers, 1971.* Washington, D.C., 1971.

———. "Survey of Domestic Service Employees, 1974." Mimeographed, 1979.

———. Unpublished tabulations from Current Population surveys.

What Have Minimum Wages Done in Agriculture?

Bruce Gardner

The Nature of the Farm Labor Market

In order to make sense of events in the farm labor market, it is necessary first to recognize the extreme heterogeneity of the labor force employed in agriculture. It encompasses the lowest-skilled manual workers and highly skilled managerial talent, from child workers to retired part-time workers. Moreover, the relative importance of different types of workers in the mix has changed substantially over time. Many of these changes have occurred in the past ten years and are still occurring. The effects of legal minimum wages are likely to be even more important in changing the composition and mix of characteristics in the farm labor force than in affecting the summary statistics of wage rates and employment in agriculture as a whole.

The most important dichotomy for present purposes in the farm labor force is between self-employed and hired labor. The former category includes farm operators and their families and numbered 2.7 million in 1978. The hired labor force averaged 1.3 million[1] in the U.S. Department of Agriculture quarterly surveys in 1978. A considerably larger number did some farm work for pay at some time during the year. The total hired farm work force in this sense was estimated at 2.7 million in 1977, suggesting that the self-employed and hired segments are of roughly equal size.[2] The ratio of hired workers to family workers has increased over the post–World War II period, rising from 0.53 in 1949 to 0.96 in 1976 (using the Bureau of Census hired labor count) or

---

[1] The 1.3 million figure is an average of four quarterly surveys, each covering one week, conducted by the U.S. Department of Agriculture. Unpaid family members are included if they work fifteen or more hours in the survey week.

[2] The hired farm working force data in this more comprehensive sense are derived from an annual survey conducted by the Bureau of the Census as a supplement to the December Current Population Survey. Of the 54,000 households interviewed in December 1976, some 1,740 contained persons who had done hired farm work at some time during 1976.

from 0.29 in 1949 to 0.47 in 1978 (using the Department of Agriculture hired labor count).

The demarcation line between hired and self-employed workers is in some cases difficult to draw. Sharecroppers, for example, are counted as self-employed, but many of them also work for wages at times. The Department of Agriculture (USDA) counts sharecroppers as hired farm workers if they worked for wages in the survey week. A sharecropper who worked at all for wages would be counted as a hired farm worker by the Current Population Survey (CPS). In addition, many farm owner-operators work for wages on other farms, as manual laborers but also as providers of custom services on other farms. Indeed, U.S. farm operators receive more income from off-farm sources than from farming—61 percent of total income in 1977, according to USDA estimates—and about half of total income resulted from off-farm work for wages, a good deal of it from work on other farms.

The distinction between self-employed and hired work effort is important in assessing the impact of legal minimum wages, of course, because such constraints on the labor market would be expected to increase the intrafirm, nonmarket utilization of labor. There are two other aspects of the farm labor market that are important in a minimum wage study, the first having to do with characteristics of workers and the second with characteristics of employers.

Characteristics of Farm Workers. Traditionally it has seemed appropriate to classify farm workers as one of two types. Some farm workers could be characterized as full-time hired farm or ranch hands. Typically they would live on the farm or ranch and receive part of their pay in the form of meals and lodging, "perquisites" in the USDA terminology. In dairying, for example, they would live and work on the farm all year and, even in more seasonal farming, would reside on the farm half or more of the year. The other main category of workers comprises seasonal workers who are employed on the farm for only peak-season activities such as chopping weeds in growing crops or harvesting fruits and vegetables. These workers may be migrants, moving from farm to farm as the peak-season activities change latitude, or they may be local residents who live permanently in rural areas or small towns but take seasonal employment on farms. Workers in both categories are typically low-skilled, manual laborers. They are often single young men, perhaps school dropouts. Their job turnover, even for full-time hired hands, is high.

During the post–World War II period there has been a marked change in the residential pattern of hired farm workers. In 1947/1949,

TABLE 1

Distribution of Hired Farm Workers, by Duration of Farm Work, 1946–1976

Year	Total Workers (thousands)	Days Worked at Farm Employment (percentage)			
		Less than 25	25–74	75–250	More than 250
1946	2,770	29.5	27.0	23.5	19.9
1951	3,274	34.1	28.3	20.8	16.8
1956	3,575	41.9	25.7	20.0	12.4
1961	3,488	45.9	24.3	18.2	12.2
1966	2,763	40.9	26.0	19.9	13.3
1971	2,488	46.7	25.4	16.7	11.2
1976	2,767	41.4	23.6	23.0	12.0

Source: Smith and Rowe, "Hired Farm Working Force."

65 percent were farm residents. By 1975/1977 the percentage had dropped to 21 percent, the remaining 78 percent not living on a farm. At the same time, the fraction of the farm labor force working on farms twenty-five days or less per year increased, while the fraction who worked on farms essentially full-time, 250 days or more, decreased (table 1).

As of 1976, 54 percent of those who did farm work (about 1½ million workers) were not in the labor force most of the year.[3] Of these, 1.1 million were students. Only 676,000 workers, 24 percent of the CPS total hired workers, had farm work as their principal activity.

Hired farm workers as a group tend to be low-skilled, young, and low-paid. As of 1978, 30 percent were under twenty-five years of age and 53 percent had four years or less of farm work experience. Other demographic characteristics include: 74 percent white, 14 percent black, and 11 percent Hispanic; 75 percent male; 41 percent in the South and 23 percent in the West. Migratory status is less common in the CPS survey than might be expected, 7 percent of the total. The survey probably undersampled this group, but even so the farm labor force is *not* predominantly composed of migrant workers.

In 1978, the average farm wage rate was $3.07 per hour, 50 percent of the average nonfarm wage rate in manufacturing, 66 percent of the average wage rate in wholesale and retail trade, and 36 percent of the

[3] The CPS question was: "What was————doing most of 1976—working, going to school, keeping house, or something else?"

wage rate in construction. Generally, farm wage rates have run at about half the average nonfarm wage rate in the postwar period. In part, the low average farm wage rates stem from the relative youth and part-time status of the group. Even those in the prime age groups, however, had low wages and earnings. In 1976, males aged twenty-five to forty-four who did hired farm work earned an average of only $23.50 per day; and with an average of 210 days worked, their mean annual earnings were $4,935. Even workers who did both farm and nonfarm work in 1978 received substantially lower wages for their farm work. Males aged twenty-five to thirty-four earned $20.35 per day in farm work, whereas these same individuals reported average earnings of $30.37 per day in their nonfarm work. This suggests that low hired farm wages are not entirely a matter of worker skills.[4]

At the same time, there have always been farm hands highly skilled with machinery, farm-worker families who have lived for many years with the same farm operator, and other exceptions to these generalizations. There have always been professional farm managers who may be thought of as part of the farm working force, although not counted as such by the Bureau of the Census.

In recent years there has been a change toward a higher-skilled segment of the farm labor force. The managerial component of many farm jobs has increased. Where a worker once chopped weeds with a hoe, he now mixes chemicals for machine application (a task that the Environmental Protection Agency is increasingly insisting not be done at all without prior formal training). Still, most jobs remain much as they have always been, and others (for example, those involving the use of tractor power where animal power was once used, or improved specialized machinery instead of older do-it-yourself machinery) require less skill today then they did years ago. Nonetheless, there is a trend toward a better-educated, more experienced, more specialized hired farm labor force, both absolutely and relative to the nonfarm labor force. One of the issues concerning legal minimum wages is the effect upon these and related developments.

Characteristics of Employers. The basic distinction to be made here is between the small or moderate-sized family farm and large commercial operating units. The distinction is important because of the clear intent

---

[4] The data cited in the preceding paragraphs are mostly from L. W. Smith and G. Rowe, "The Hired Farm Working Force of 1976," Economics, Statistics, and Cooperatives Service, U.S. Department of Agriculture, Ag. Econ. Rpt. no. 405, July 1978; and Gene Rowe, "The Hired Farm Working Force of 1977," Economics, Statistics, and Cooperatives Service, U.S. Department of Agriculture, Ag. Econ. Rpt. no. 437, October 1979.

of Congress to exempt the former category from the necessity of paying legal minimum wages. The demarcation line must of course be arbitrary. The main criterion is that, if a farmer employed 500 or more workdays of labor in his peak calendar quarter of labor use, then all his employees, unless specifically exempt, are covered by the Fair Labor Standards Act. Other farms are exempt. Department of Labor estimates during the 1970s indicate that 40 to 50 percent of hired farm workers are covered. However, only about 3 percent of *farms* are covered, and only about a third of all farmers employ any hired labor at all.

Many agricultural operations are classified as farms but have neglible commercial significance. Of the 2.7 million farms in 1978, 500,000 accounted for three-fourths of U.S. production. More than half of all farms had sales of less than $10,000. This is the market value of the product of about seven dairy cows, or fifty acres of corn, or forty acres of cotton—impossibly small enterprises to be commercially viable today. Indeed, operators of these "farms" earned an average of about $16,000 from off-farm sources, mostly nonfarm jobs, in 1977. This is ten times their estimated mean net returns from farming.[5]

Many of the larger commercial farms, especially those that specialize in crop production in the Corn Belt and Great Plains, have remained essentially family farms relying on family labor, even while increasing the size of their operations considerably. Thus, in Illinois the average amount of cropland per farm increased from 163 acres in the mid-1960s to 209 in the mid-1970s, while the number of hired workers was 35,000 in both 1965 and 1978. The reason is that technical change has taken the labor-saving form of larger tractors and other equipment, so that output per worker has increased. This machinery does not increase output per acre so much and in some instances actually reduces it by increasing harvesting losses. Of course, technical change did not take this form by accident—large equipment was developed to economize on labor use. Indeed, mechanization is one of the major ways that producers can adjust to higher wage rates as caused by increases in the legal minimum wage. (The question of the direction of causality between labor-saving technical innovation and farm employment is an issue in a case in which California farm labor representatives are suing the University of California, attempting to stop agricultural research there. One theory is that mechanization is an independently caused phenomenon that displaces labor, so stopping research will end it. The alternative theory is that mechanization is induced by rising real wage rates.)

---

[5] As of 1979, the Department of Agriculture changed its definition of a farm to require $1,000 or more in annual sales of farm products. This change eliminates 300,000 or about 11 percent of farms counted in 1978 under the former definition, but many noncommercial operations are still included.

Legal Minimum Wages in the Farm Sector

The Fair Labor Standards Act, in its application to agriculture,[6] has always been subject to two sets of special pressures. One is a tendency to treat agricultural employment as an exception, exempting farm laborers from the act's protection. The other is a set of counter-pressures to treat farm workers like other workers by ending agricultural exemptions. Recent years have seen a trend toward political dominance of the second set of pressures, so that the treatment of farm labor under the act is coming closer to the treatment of the nonfarm labor force in general.

There are both economic and political reasons for this trend. Farm workers in fact are more similar to nonfarm workers, and the farm and nonfarm labor markets are in fact more closely integrated than has been the case in the past. The main purpose of this paper, however, is not to explain the trend of policy but to investigate the consequences of minimum wages as applied to U.S. agriculture.

Legal minimum wages at the federal level were first applied to agriculture in the 1966 amendments to the Fair Labor Standards Act. Agriculture remained exempt, as it does to the present day, from over-time-pay provisions. The exemptions from minimum wages for employers who hired less than 500 days of labor was introduced at this time.

The employment of one worker for six days per week in a thirteen-week peak quarter amounts to 78 days. It would take seven workers to get to the 500-day cutoff point. About 55 percent of workers are employed on farms having seven or more workers. Actual coverage is less than 55 percent because some of the farmers having seven or more employees used part-time workers, all workers in the range production of livestock (cowboys and shepherds) are exempt, and temporary seasonal workers who commute from their homes to the farm where they work are exempt (this exempts most tobacco labor), as are field workers seventeen years of age or younger working on the same farm as their parents. Most migrant labor is covered. The employer, however, often is not the farm but a "crew leader" who supplies labor-management services to farmers (usually growers of fruit or vegetable crops). In 1978, 8,000 crew leaders with 500,000 crew workers were registered with the U.S. Department of Labor under the Farm Labor Contractor Registration Act. (It is not clear how the 500,000 figure here fits in with the

---

[6] "Agriculture" is used in this paper in its narrow sense as applying to primary production activities for farm products. Other elements of the food system—processing, retailing, and so forth—have not received special treatment under the Fair Labor Standards Act.

190,000 total migratory workers estimated by the CPS. Apparently some crew workers are registered with more than one crew.)

The legal minimum wage in agriculture was placed at a lower rate than for nonfarm workers, $1.00 per hour compared with $1.40 for the general minimum in 1967. The amendments of 1974, however, brought the agricultural minimum up to the general minimum in a series of steps completed in January 1978, when the legal minimum wage became $2.65 per hour for all covered workers.

Some states had agricultural minimum wage legislation prior to 1966 and have kept state legal minimums above the federal level. California's has often been above the federal minimum by 20 percent or so, and the state had a slightly less liberal exemption—any employer of fewer than five workers in the peak calendar quarter. Connecticut, Massachusetts, New York, New Jersey, Michigan, Minnesota, and Wisconsin have all had legal minimums for farm workers slightly above the federal level at one time or another. It does not seem likely that the effects of these could have been great.

The effects of the agricultural minimum wage are made difficult to predict by the heterogeneity of the farm labor force and the exempt status of many employees and employers. Questions have also been raised about the enforcement, even the knowledge of the legal requirements, among farmers and farm workers. For example, immediate family members of a farm operator are exempt, but often cousins or nephews engage in farm work on their relatives' farms. They are technically covered by the Fair Labor Standards Act, but there must be a great temptation to forgo the formalities in such cases. Similar impediments to enforcement are likely to exist in other cases where there are long-standing relationships between farmers and neighborhood workers from nearby towns or crop-share tenant farms.

Analysis of Labor Market Effects

Basic data on U.S. farm wage rates, the legal minimum wage applicable to covered farm workers, and the size of the hired farm labor force are shown in table 2. The wage data are deflated by the gross national product (GNP) deflator (1972 = 100). Thus, the increase in wage rates shown over time is an increase in real wages. The overall historical pattern is that the real farm wage rate was essentially constant during the postwar period until 1957/1958, after which it rose at a fairly constant annual rate of about 1.9 percent. This period of stagnant real growth in wage rates between the war's end and the late 1950s did not of course occur in the nonfarm economy. The farm wage rate's stagnation reflects the general excess supply of labor resources that underlay the "farm

TABLE 2

Data on the U.S. Farm Labor Market, 1946–1978

Year	Hourly Wage Rate (1972 $)	Legal Minimum Wage (1972 $)	Hired Farm Workers (thousands)	Family Farm Workers (thousands)
1978	2.02	1.74	1,256	2,681
1977	2.03	1.55	1,296	2,859
1976	1.99	1.50	1,377	2,999
1975	1.91	1.42	1,317	3,026
1974	1.94	1.38	1,314	3,075
1973	1.89	1.23	1,163	3,232
1972	1.84	1.30	1,152	3,240
1971	1.80	1.35	1,165	3,281
1970	1.79	1.42	1,175	3,348
1969	1.82	1.50	1,176	3,419
1968	1.73	1.39	1,195	3,550
1967	1.68	1.27	1,256	3,679
1966	1.60		1,360	3,854
1965	1.53		1,482	4,128
1964	1.48		1,604	4,506
1963	1.46		1,780	4,738
1962	1.43		1,827	4,873
1961	1.43		1,890	5,029
1960	1.41		1,869	5,249
1959	1.41		1,925	5,459
1958	1.39		1,955	5,570
1957	1.35		1,895	5,682
1956	1.37		1,921	5,899
1955	1.34		2,017	6,347
1954	1.36		2,060	6,579
1953	1.39		1,935	6,645
1952	1.40		1,921	6,748
1951	1.34		2,223	7,799
1950	1.29		2,308	8,043
1949	1.31			
1948	1.34			
1947	1.37			
1946	1.46			

Source: U.S. Department of Agriculture, Crop Reporting Board, *Farm Labor*, various quarterly issues.

problem" so much discussed at the time. (The acceleration of the rate of growth of farm wage rates in the late 1960s and 1970s to rates exceeding the rate of growth of nonfarm wages is a sign that the farm problem had ended by that time even though policies ostensibly intended to curve it via production controls continue to the present day.)

The hired farm labor force declined at an average annual rate of 2.3 percent during the 1950s and 4.6 percent during the 1960s. During the 1970s, the number of hired farm workers has actually increased a little. The imposition of the legal minimum wage in agriculture occurred at about the end of the trend decline in the labor force. Even so, the raw data suggest that the minimum wage reduced farm employment below the level that would have been observed in its absence. The period during which farm employment stabilized was one in which the minimum wage actually fell in real terms. The ratio of the legal minimum to the mean market wage rate for farm workers reached a low of 0.65 in 1973, down from 0.82 in 1969, and 1973 was the year in which the trend of farm-worker decline was reversed. In 1977 and 1978 the legal minimum took a substantial jump, the result of the 1974 amendments to the Fair Labor Standards Act, which ended the differential between the agricultural and nonagricultural minimum wage rates in a series of steps completed in 1978. The hired farm labor force resumed its decline in 1977 and 1978. The quarterly survey for April 1979 shows a 4 percent decline from a year earlier, a sharper rate of decrease in farm workers than had occurred since 1968.

These suggestions from the raw data are consistent with informal statements by participants in the farm labor market but are analytically unsatisfactory. As earlier discussion indicates, there has been much more going on in agriculture than the minimum wage, which is in fact probably a relatively minor mover of events in the farm economy. Among the other exogenous events that should be considered are the export-demand shift dating from 1973 that has increased the demand for U.S. farm products and hence the labor used in producing them. There have also been continuing changes in U.S. farm commodity policy, in technical progress, and in the prices of nonlabor inputs (energy, chemicals, machinery). Finally, there have been exogenous labor market disturbances other than minimum wages, notably fluctuations in nonfarm unemployment and wage rates, unionization of some field workers, the end of the "bracero" program in 1964, and the extension of unemployment insurance and Occupational Safety and Health Administration (OSHA) protections to some farm workers.

In view of these complications, an econometric model incorporating the main exogenous determinants of farm employment and wage rates is necessary to draw meaningful conclusions about the effects of the

218

agricultural minimum wage. Attempts at such models are contained in studies by H. F. Gallasch and B. L. Gardner, building upon earlier econometric studies of G. Edward Schuh; E. W. Tyrchniewicz and Schuh; T. D. Wallace and D. H. Hoover; and M. Gisser.[7] The approach used in this paper is basically the same, but there are now more than twice as many annual observations of the farm labor markets under minimum wage constraints than were available to Gallasch or Gardner, whose data ended in 1971 and 1970, respectively.

The econometric model is based on the standard theory of demand for and supply of labor in a competitive industry. The demand for farm labor is derived from the demand for farm products. It is shifted by: (1) events that shift U.S. farm product demand—for example, real income, population, foreign agricultural output; (2) shifts in the supply of cooperating inputs—for example, machinery or land; and (3) technical change, adjustments to past disequilibriums, and institutional changes such as OSHA or social security requirements. The supply of farm labor is shifted by changes in wage-earning opportunities in the nonfarm sector, nonpecuniary aspects of work, and perhaps the income or wealth of workers.

These factors cannot in general be incorporated into the model simply by incorporating prices—for example, farm product prices, substitute-input prices, or land prices. The reason is that these prices are not independent causes of changes in farm wage rates and employment but are mutually determined with them. Thus, a complete behavioral or structural model would need an explicit specification of many supply and demand functions besides the ones for farm labor. And the relevant reduced-form equations would have as exogenous variables only those factors not significantly influenced by any events in the farm sector. Experience with modeling farm labor markets, however, suggests that a number of reasonable simplifications are possible to construct a tractable econometric model that captures the main determinants of farm wage rates and employment.

On the supply-of-labor side, the nonfarm opportunities for employment are so little influenced by farm-labor movements that nonfarm

[7] H. F. Gallasch, Jr., "Minimum Wages and the Farm Labor Market," *Southern Economic Journal* 41 (January 1975): 480–91; B. L. Gardner, "Minimum Wages and the Farm Labor Market," *American Journal of Agricultural Economics* 54 (August 1972): 473–76; G. Edward Schuh, "An Econometric Investigation of the Market for Hired Labor in Agriculture," *Journal of Farm Economics* 44 (May 1962): 307–21; E. W. Tyrchniewicz and G. E. Schuh, "Econometric Analysis of the Agricultural Labor Market," *American Journal of Agricultural Economics* 51 (November 1969): 770–87; T. D. Wallace and D. H. Hoover, "Income Effects of Innovation: The Case of Labor in Agriculture," *Journal of Farm Economics* 49 (May 1966): 325–36; M. Gisser, "Schooling and the Farm Problem," *Econometrica* 33 (July 1965): 582–92.

wage rates and unemployment rates, for the United States as a whole or its principal regions, are essentially exogenous variables. The studies cited earlier consider several variables to measure the relevant nonfarm wage. They all turn out to be important explanatory variables, with no single proxy outperforming the others noticeably. The regressions to follow use average hourly earnings in total private nonagricultural employment (including manufacturing, construction, and wholesale and retail trade). This wage rate is multiplied by one minus the unemployment rate to make a crude cyclical adjustment for the likelihood of a farm worker not being able to find work at the measured opportunity wage.

On the labor-demand side, the effects of product demand can plausibly be captured by lagged prices. Current-year product prices in agriculture are to a large extent determined by random output deviations from intended production plans undertaken early in the year or in the previous year. Crop production in 1980 is a function not of observed prices of crops harvested toward the end of 1980 but of prices expected at the beginning of 1980. These expectations are often modeled as being formed on the basis of prices observed in 1979 and earlier in a distributed-lag process. This approach is helpful econometrically because past prices are exogenous determinants of current-year events.

The specification of nonlabor-input effects can also be plausibly simplified for present purposes. First, many purchased inputs—chemicals, machinery, building materials—may be reasonably represented as perfectly elastic in supply to the farm sector. Within the relevant range of variation, they are available at given prices. Therefore, a USDA index of prices paid by farmers for production items is used as an independent variable. Second, for natural-resource inputs, land and water, the quantities available are relatively fixed, or at least not significantly affected by annual changes in farm labor markets, so that the USDA quantity index of land (including irrigation facilities) is used as an independent variable.

The preceding discussion suggests that the farm labor market can be handled empirically with variables specified as follows:

Endogenous variables	*Exogenous variables*
hired farm wage rate	nonfarm opportunity wage rate
hired farm employment	unemployment rate
	lagged product prices
	purchased input prices
	land quantity
	legal minimum wage

There remain two analytical problems: first, how to handle substitution between hired and self-employed or contracted farm labor and, second, how to aggregate when there exist exempt employers and non-covered workers.

One of the best substitutes for labor whose price has increased due to an increase in the minimum wage is labor whose price has not been increased by the minimum wage. Thus, the demand for self-employed workers is increased. However, self-employment, even in crop-sharing arrangements, always involves a good deal of managerial effort and risk bearing. So the substitutability may not be large. The possibilities appear greater for contracting labor. The essence of contracting is to pay a fee for getting a task done rather than to pay a worker by the hour or day or month to do it—for example, a farmer can hire services of firms, often farm-service cooperatives, to apply fertilizer or preemergence pesticides. Contracting for grain harvesting has long been important. When the contractor is self-employed, the minimum wage does not apply. When he hires labor, he would have been covered before the agricultural minimum wage existed (or, since 1967, was increased) so that the relative demand for contracted services would be increased by the agricultural minimum wage. Piecework methods of payment are essentially a form of labor contracting, as defined above, with a single worker. Piecework rates on an hourly basis must equal the minimum wage. Employers have traditionally found, however, that the productivity of farm workers is higher under piecework payments, and so hourly wages by this method of contracting typically have been higher than when hiring time instead of a task. The USDA farm labor survey in April 1979, for example, found the U.S. average hourly wage rate for piecework to be $4.26 per hour compared with $3.33 per hour for straight-time employment. Thus, if the minimum wage were to push some workers' wage rates over the straight-time rate, the employer could possibly gain enough added net productivity to meet the higher wage by switching to piece-rate payment. Many kinds of farm work do not lend themselves to this kind of contracting, however. The supply of contracted services as a substitute for hired farm labor is represented in the econometric model by the price index for purchased inputs. The supply function of self-employed farm labor is more difficult. There is no market price to observe, and the quantity is obviously an endogenous variable. Therefore, family labor as a substitute for hired labor is simply left out of the model. Its effects show up as an increase in the effect of the minimum wage on hired farm employment; that is, the existence of the self-employed alternative makes the demand for hired labor more elastic.

The problem of aggregation arises because workers have differing inherent characteristics, which will be summarized under the label "skills," and because certain categories of workers and farms have differing legal standing under the Fair Labor Standards Act, summarized as "covered" or "noncovered." Let skills be dichotomized into those

FIGURE 1
AGGREGATION OF FARM LABOR SUBMARKETS

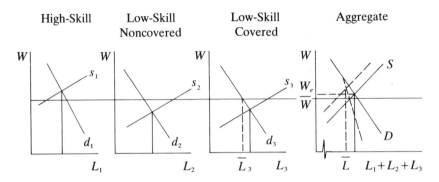

that, under supply-demand conditions in the absence of a legal minimum wage, would earn greater than ("high wage") and less than ("low wage") the legal minimum being studied. The two skill levels may be considered as two different but highly substitutable inputs in the production process.

There are four relevant submarkets for hired farm labor: high-skill, noncovered labor; high-skill, covered labor; low-skill, noncovered labor; low-skill, covered labor. Only the last category is prima facie affected by a legal minimum wage. The first two categories involve the same wage rate—coverage is a slack variable. Figure 1 illustrates the aggregation of the three differing categories. Although the horizontal axis is the sum of the three labor categories, the aggregate demand and supply curves are *not* a horizontal summation of the categorical demand and supply curves. The equilibrium mean wage where S and D intersect, W_e, is obtained by weighting the individual wages rates by the fraction of the labor force in each category. The "aggregate demand curve" D shows how the mean wage changes when s_1, s_2, and s_3 shift, but it depends on how they shift. Let D be derived by proportional shifts in s_1, s_2, and s_3. Similarly, let S be traced out as the result of mean wage rates observed as d_1, d_2, and let d_3 shift proportionally; for example, demand for each increases 10 percent at all prices.

When a legal minimum wage is imposed at $\overline{W}$, L_1 and L_2 are unaffected, but L_3 declines to $\overline{L}_3$. This shows up as a decline to $\overline{L}$ at the aggregate level. The constrained aggregate demand curve shows what happens to employment as s_1, s_2, and s_3 shift proportionally given that L_3 employment is constrained at $\overline{L}_3$. At the aggregate level, the minimum wage is equivalent to a reduction in the aggregate demand for hired labor. This result does not mean, however, that the mean wage will fall, because W_3 is constrained to be higher and the weight of the low-wage category falls. Thus, the "aggregate supply curve" S shifts to the left. In sum, even though the legal minimum wage is below the mean wage in its absence (as in fact has been the case), hired farm employment is reduced and the average market wage rate is increased.

The figure as drawn does not tell the whole story, however, because there can be movement among the categories. Low-skill workers can acquire skills. More important in the short run, noncovered employment can substitute for covered employment. Thus, d_1 and especially d_2 will increase when the legal minimum is imposed, so that noncovered farm wage rates increase with the minimum wage. For example, students are exempt, so that the demand for their services in summer employment in agriculture will be increased by the minimum wage. Still, it must be the case that aggregate hired farm employment is decreased, even though the effect may be substantially reduced by this substitution.

The data are not available to estimate wage rates and employment for the submarkets; yet the aggregate labor demand and supply curves are no longer specifiable as a function of the mean wage, at least not in any straightforward way, in the presence of a legal minimum wage. For this reason one must be careful in assuming that the whole labor market can be represented as in the L_3 market in figure 1, so that the wage rate becomes an exogenous policy variable and one can regress employment on the wage rate to identify the demand curve under the minimum wage constraint.[8] Instead, we will limit ourselves to estimation of reduced-form equations that explain farm employment and the mean farm wage rate as functions of the legal minimum wage and other exogenous variables.

The preceding discussion suggests two additional endogenous variables. The substitutability of self-employed labor suggests testing whether family labor is influenced by the minimum wage. The discussion of submarket wages suggests that the minimum wage should narrow the dispersion of wages paid. We do not have data on wages by skill categories of workers, nor is there available an annual time series of the size distribution of farm wage rates. There is, however, a strong regional component to these submarkets. In 1971 the Department of Labor estimated more than twice as great a fraction of farm workers earning less than the minimum wage in the South as in the rest of the country (although the incidence of noncovered employers was higher, too).[9] A

[8] This approach is taken by T. P. Lianos, "Impact of Minimum Wages upon the Level and Composition of Agricultural Employment," *American Journal of Agricultural Economics* 54 (August 1972): 477–84.

[9] U.S. Department of Labor, Employment Standards Administration, *Hired Farm Workers*, Washington, D.C., 1972, p. 22.

FIGURE 2
FARM EMPLOYMENT, ACTUAL AND FITTED (I), 1946–1978

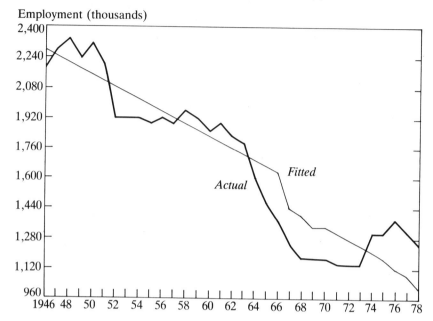

tendency would therefore be expected for the extension of the Fair Labor Standards Act to agriculture to have reduced the regional dispersion of wage rates.

Regression Results

Consider first the simple regressions of hired workers and the farm wage rate on time and the minimum wage (figures 2 and 3). The least-squares regression line shows a strong downward trend in employment and an increasing trend in the real farm wage rate. The minimum wage coefficients indicate that its average effect during the years it applied to agriculture (1967–1978) was to increase the average wage rate by twenty-eight cents per hour (15 percent) and to reduce hired farm employment by 160,000 (12 percent). A couple of features of the data suggest caution in interpreting these coefficients as minimum wage effects, however. First, the employment data take a sharp drop in 1952, preceded and followed by relative stability. This suggests some sort of structural shift, but time series analysis of the post-1952 data still tells essentially the same story about minimum wage effects. A second and more important fact is that the growth in the real-wage time series accelerates in 1965,

224

FIGURE 3
FARM WAGE RATE, ACTUAL AND FITTED (I), 1946–1978

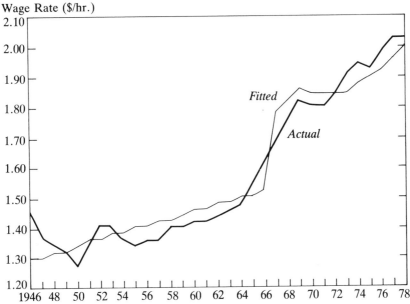

Wage Rate ($/hr.)

two years before the Fair Labor Standards Act was extended to farm workers. Two factors are prima facie plausible as explanations. The first is the elimination of the "bracero" program in 1964, a program dating from World War II in which Mexican workers were used to supply temporary labor in U.S. agriculture. It was ended because of labor union pressure on the grounds that imported workers were displacing U.S. workers and reducing U.S. wages. The second factor is that rapid general economic growth was raising real wages generally in the mid-1960s. The bracero program seems at first thought the more plausible explanation, but consideration of the time series of farm employment dispels this idea, for farm employment *declined* sharply after 1964. A third possible explanation is that after 1963 the federal government essentially gave up its attempts to hold the prices of farm products at the politically preferred levels, and average real prices received by farmers dropped substantially. This could possibly explain the employment decline but is inconsistent with the simultaneous increase in real farm wages. In short, the data are inconsistent with any sort of demand-for-labor shift as the main cause of events in the mid-1960s. The simultaneous advantage in real farm wage rates and decline in farm employment is consistent with the economic-growth idea, however, following the economic modeling of the supply side of the farm labor market as discussed in the preceding section.

The general point that this discussion reinforces is that a proper analysis of the agricultural minimum wage should be undertaken in the context of a complete model, or as nearly complete as the data allow, of the market for hired farm labor. Regression results using the independent variables listed in table 3 are shown in tables 4 and 5. They show that the nonfarm wage rate is in fact an important determinant of farm wage rates and employment. The plots of actual observations and the predictions of the regressions (figures 4 and 5) indicate that the more complete model provides a more satisfactory explanation of the transition period just before and after the imposition of the agricultural minimum wage.

The regression results do not allow detailed conclusions about the adjustment process by which inputs substitute for hired labor when the minimum wage increases. The fact that a quantitatively significant response exists for total hired farm labor indicates that substitution of noncovered employment (or noncompliance with the legal minimum) does *not* render the minimum wage ineffective. Separate regressions on self-employed (family) farm labor suggest that there has been no significant effect of the minimum wage in increasing self-employment. Thus, it appears that adjustment to the minimum wage has occurred through substitution of nonlabor for labor inputs in production processes rather than, or at least in addition to, adjustments within a farm labor force of fixed total size.

There are two additional kinds of regression experiments that may illuminate this historical episode. The first uses an alternative data source for hired farm labor; the second makes use of regional data.

The data on the hired farm work force are simple annual averages of total workers in the quarterly USDA surveys. The universe sampled is farms that are potential employers of hired labor. Every person reported to have been hired for one hour or more during the survey week is counted in the hired farm labor force. It could be that a time series for total hours worked or full-time workers would behave differently over time than the USDA measure of hired farm employment. The only alternative estimate is the Census Bureau's CPS sample mentioned earlier. This is an annual survey of employees, whereas the USDA surveys employers. The farm labor force measured by the CPS includes anyone who reported any farm work at any time during the year. Thus, it should include every worker counted in the peak week surveyed by the Department of Agriculture (in July) plus those working at other times missed by that survey. The CPS survey results give a less complete time

TABLE 3

EXOGENOUS VARIABLES IN FARM LABOR MARKET, 1946–1978

Year	Nonfarm Hourly Wage (1972 $)	Real Product Price (index)[a]	Real Purchased Input Price (index)	Land Quantity Index
1978	3.51	1.10	1.17	97
1977	3.44	1.03	1.17	97
1976	3.35	1.11	1.19	97
1975	3.26	1.16	1.18	96
1974	3.45	1.32	1.18	95
1973	3.54	1.35	1.14	97
1972	3.49	1.00	1.00	98
1971	3.38	0.94	0.97	99
1970	3.36	0.96	0.98	101
1969	3.38	0.98	0.99	98
1968	3.33	0.99	1.00	99
1967	3.25	1.01	1.04	100
1966	3.21	1.10	1.08	99
1965	3.16	1.05	1.06	99
1964	3.08	1.04	1.06	100
1963	3.00	1.08	1.09	100
1962	2.97	1.11	1.10	100
1961	2.88	1.11	1.11	100
1960	2.87	1.11	1.10	100
1959	2.82	1.14	1.14	101
1958	2.75	1.21	1.15	100
1957	2.78	1.16	1.14	102
1956	2.74	1.17	1.14	102
1955	2.68	1.22	1.18	105
1954	2.61	1.31	1.23	105
1953	2.65	1.38	1.25	105
1952	2.54	1.58	1.35	105
1951	2.45	1.69	1.37	105
1950	2.36	1.54	1.32	105
1949	2.29	1.52	1.30	104
1948	2.20	1.73	1.35	103
1947	2.18	1.77	1.30	103
1946	2.16	1.71	1.26	102

[a] Current-year values shown. The exogenous variables are lagged prices.
SOURCE: U.S. Council of Economic Advisers, *Economic Report of the President.*

TABLE 4

REGRESSION COEFFICIENTS EXPLAINING HIRED FARM WAGE RATES

(t-values in parentheses)

Equa-tion	Minimum wage effect	Nonfarm wage	Purchased input price	Land index	Lagged Output Price	Time[a]	R^2
			Independent Variables				
1.	.203					0.11	.950
	(7.6)					(5.7)	
2.	.185	.264	.270	−.022	.164		.972
	(7.9)	(3.6)	(1.7)	(4.3)	(1.6)		
3.	.139	.419	−.106	−.031	.277[b]		.982
	(5.9)	(5.5)	(0.6)	(6.2)	(2.6)		
4.	.128	.256	−.243	−.024	.359[b]	.009	.983
	(5.2)	(2.0)	(1.3)	(3.6)	(3.1)	(1.6)	
Means	$1.42[c]	$2.95	1.16	100.6	1.27		

Dependent variable mean: $1.57

[a] Measured as year minus 1900.
[b] Coefficient is of price lagged one year. Prices lagged two and three years were also included in the regression. The coefficients (and t-values) are: two-year lag, −.010 (0.1) in equation 3 and −.086 (0.8) in equation 4; three-year lag, 0.297 (3.0) in equation 3 and 0.310 (3.2) in equation 4.
[c] During 1966–1978; value in 1972 dollars.

series, however, with data available only from 1945 to 1977, except for 1953 and 1955, when no survey was conducted. In addition, the CPS survey has a breakdown by duration of employment throughout this period (except 1950 and 1958), so that full-time employment in agriculture can be looked at separately.

Regional data help in eliminating factors such as unionization or the bracero program, which have regionally concentrated effects. Thus, the same model was fit to data for all of the United States except the Pacific Coast states. Unfortunately, the data for some of the independent variables are not available by region, and when they are—for example, for land—their quality is suspect. Moreover, the USDA land series is constructed for different regions than the USDA farm labor series, and the regionalization of the farm labor series was changed in 1974.

Regressions on both the regional USDA and the national CPS data resulted in coefficients with the same signs as in tables 4 and 5 but with lower t values. Regional data were used to test crudely the hypothesis that the agricultural minimum wage has equalized farm wage rates across regions. Although the standard deviation of the mean wage across ten regions of the United States fell from thirty-three cents in 1951 to eleven

FIGURE 4
Farm Employment, Actual and Fitted (II), 1946–1978

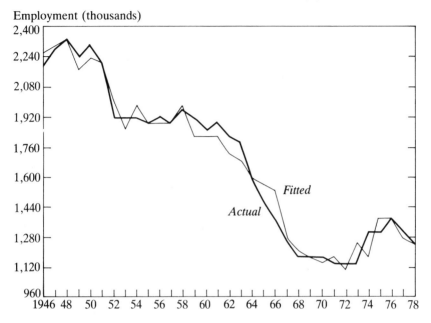

Employment (thousands)

TABLE 5

Regression Coefficients explaining Farm Employment
(*t*-values in parentheses)

Equa-tion	Minimum wage effect	Nonfarm wage	Purchased input price	Land index	Lagged Output Price	Time	R^2
	Independent Variables						
1.	−114					−32	.880
	(1.7)					(6.5)	
2.	−83	−970	1212	−17	−614		.974
	(2.2)	(8.8)	(4.9)	(2.1)	(3.8)		
3.	−67	−1025	1336	−14	−638[a]		.975
	(1.5)	(7.1)	(4.1)	(1.4)	(3.1)		
4.	−82	−1229	1163	−5	−541[a]	11	.976
	(1.7)	(4.9)	(3.1)	(0.4)	(2.4)	(1.0)	

Dependent variable mean: 1,685 (thousand workers)

[a] See notes to table 4. The coefficients for two- and three-year lags are: equation 3, −24 (0.1) and −88 (0.5); and equation 4, −120 (0.5) and −72 (0.4).

229

FIGURE 5
FARM WAGE RATE, ACTUAL AND FITTED (II), 1946–1978

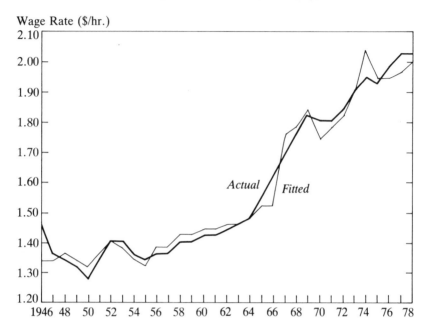

Wage Rate ($/hr.)

cents in 1977, the data evidence does not allow a rejection of the null hypothesis that this reduction was simply a postwar trend rather than a minimum wage effect. Even if a regional effect could be demonstrated, one would like to be able to tie this effect to characteristics of the workers in the region. Some evidence is presented by Gallasch and Gardner that the schooling of workers affects the impact of the minimum wage.[10]

Conclusions

The results of the regressions confirm previous findings that the extension of the Fair Labor Standards Act to hired farm workers increased the average farm wage rate, but the price paid has been a reduction in hired farm employment. The best estimate of the effect on the mean hourly wage is that it has been increased about ten cents (1972 dollars), or 5 percent of its 1979 value. The best estimate of the employment

[10] H. F. Gallasch, Jr., and B. L. Gardner, "Schooling and the Agricultural Minimum Wage," *American Journal of Agricultural Economics* 60 (May 1978): 264–68.

effect is that the minimum wage reduced the number of hired farm workers by about 60,000, also about 5 percent of its 1979 value. (Because of partial coverage, one cannot draw the structural inferences that the elasticity of demand for either covered or all hired farm labor is approximately unity, as discussed earlier with reference to figure 1.) These effects are smaller than those estimated previously by Gallasch, Gardner, or Lianos.[11]

The effects on those workers actually covered by the minimum wage must be substantially greater than the aggregate effects. Because some workers are unaffected (those who are exempt because they work on small farms or commute from an off-farm residence or are students or cowboys or who would have earned wages above the minimum even without the legislation), the wage and employment effects will be magnified for those who are affected. About 45 percent of workers currently are covered. Suppose two-thirds of these would earn less than the minimum wage in its absence. Then 30 percent of all workers have their wage increased. If the mean wage for all workers goes up ten cents, then the wage rate for these workers might have gone up about thirty-three cents. This is an oversimplification because exempt farm workers would find the demand for their services increasing and so may also have experienced wage increases as a result of the minimum wage. This could be a reason for the shift toward more short-term farm employment and more commuting to farms from nonfarm residences by farm workers. The seasonality of farm employment has been complicated, however, by other factors not considered in this paper, such as the extension of unemployment benefits to some farm workers.[12] The CPS data could not reject the null hypothesis that trend, as opposed to the minimum wage, accounts for the shift toward part-time employment shown in table 1.

The employment effects on covered workers are understated by the regression results. The reason is that, to the extent that exempt farm workers substitute for covered workers, there is no change in total measured hired farm employment. If 30 percent of farm workers were originally affected, it could be that the 5 percent reduction was obtained by replacing *all* the affected workers by fewer exempt workers. This is an extreme illustration. The point is that the 5 percent figure is a *minimum* estimate of the labor-displacement effect of the Farm Labor Standards Act.

[11] Gallasch, "Minimum Wages and Farm Labor"; Gardner, "Minimum Wages and Farm Labor"; Lianos, "Impact of Minimum Wages."

[12] See Barry R. Chiswick, "The Effect of Unemployment Compensation on a Seasonal Industry: Agriculture," *Journal of Political Economy* 84 (June 1976): 591–602.

Bibliography

Chiswick, Barry R. "The Effect of Unemployment Compensation on a Seasonal Industry: Agriculture." *Journal of Political Economy* 84 (June 1976): 591–602.

Fuller, Varden, and Mason, Bert. "Farm Labor." *Annals of the American Academy* 429 (January 1977): 63–80.

Gallasch, H. F., Jr. "Minimum Wages and the Farm Labor Market." *Southern Economic Journal* 41 (January 1975): 480–91.

————, and Gardner, B.L. "Schooling and the Agricultural Minimum Wage." *American Journal of Agricultural Economics* 60 (May 1978): 264–68.

Gardner, B. L. "Minimum Wages and the Farm Labor Market." *American Journal of Agricultural Economics.* 54 (August 1972): 473–76.

Gisser, Micha. "Schooling and the Farm Problem." *Econometrica* 33 (July 1965): 582–92.

Lianos, T. P. "Impact of Minimum Wages upon the Level and Composition of Agricultural Employment." *American Journal of Agricultural Economics* 54 (August 1972): 477–84.

Rowe, Gene. "The Hired Farm Working Force of 1977." Economics, Statistics, and Cooperatives Service, U.S. Department of Agriculture, Ag. Econ. Rpt. no. 437, October 1979.

Schuh, G. Edward. "An Econometric Investigation of the Market for Hired Labor in Agriculture." *Journal of Farm Economics* 44 (May 1962): 307–21.

Smith, L. W., and Rowe, G. "The Hired Farm Working Force of 1976." Economics, Statistics, and Cooperatives Service. U.S. Department of Agriculture, Ag. Econ. Rpt. no. 405, July 1978.

Tyrchniewicz, E. W., and Schuh, G. E. "Econometric Analysis of the Agricultural Labor Market." *American Journal of Agricultural Economics* 51 (November 1969): 770–87.

U.S. Council of Economic Advisers. *Economic Report of the President.* Washington, D.C., January 1979.

U.S. Department of Agriculture, Crop Reporting Board. *Farm Labor.* Washington, D.C., various quarterly issues.

U.S. Department of Labor, Employment Standards Administration, *Hired Farm Workers.* Washington, D.C., 1972.

————. *State Minimum Wage Laws.* Labor Law Series, various issues.

————, Employment Standards Administration. *Minimum Wage and Maximum Hour Standards under the Fair Labor Standards Act,* January 1974.

Wallace, T. D., and Hoover, D. M. "Income Innovation: The Case of Agriculture." *Journal of Farm Economics* 49 (May 1966): 325–36.

The Impact of Federal Minimum Wage Laws on Employment of Seasonal Cotton Farm Workers

John M. Trapani and J. R. Moroney

Introduction

In 1966 the Fair Labor Standards Act was amended to extend federal minimum wage coverage to certain agricultural workers. The statutory minimum wage for covered farm workers was $1.00 per hour beginning February 1, 1967, $1.15 on February 1, 1968, and $1.30 on February 1, 1969. The amendment included all workers on farms that employed at least 500 man-days of labor during any quarter of the preceding calendar year.[1] In spite of the limited coverage, the legislated wage floor appears to have had a significant impact on employment in agriculture. Studies by B. L. Gardner, T. P. Lianos, and H. F. Gallasch all provide statistical evidence that the 1966 amendment was effective in raising the average farm wage and reducing employment in this sector.[2] Indeed, the great mobility of seasonal farm workers and the competitive nature of this labor market would force most employers who were not legally bound by the amendment nonetheless to pay the statutory minimum wage.

Within the agricultural sector, the legislation is predicted to have differential effects upon the various farm crop activities and their related occupations; for example, the impact of higher wages on unit costs would be greater for those activities that are more labor-intensive and that afford fewer options for substituting other inputs for labor. The impact on employment would be more pronounced among occupations in which market-determined wage rates were relatively low and in which technical

[1] The provisions of the 1966 amendment to the Fair Labor Standards Act are given in U.S. Department of Labor, Wage and Hour and Public Contracts Division, *Farmer's Guide to the Agricultural Provisions of the Fair Labor Standards Act*, WHPC Publication no. 1888, Washington, D.C., 1970; and idem, Workplace Standards Administration, *Fair Labor Standards Act of 1938 as Amended*, Publication no. 1318, Washington, D.C., 1971.

[2] B. L. Gardner, "Minimum Wages and the Farm Labor Market," *American Journal of Agricultural Economics* 54 (August 1972): 474–76; T. P. Lianos, "Impact of Minimum Wages upon the Level and Composition of Agricultural Employment," *American Journal of Agricultural Economics* 54 (August 1972): 477–84; H. F. Gallasch, Jr., "Minimum Wages and the Farm Labor Market," *Southern Economic Journal* 41 (January 1975): 480–91.

substitutes for labor are readily available. For labor-intensive farm activities, higher labor costs lead to lower profits, at least until less labor-intensive techniques can be adopted. And within the unskilled, low-wage occupations, higher wages may reduce employment levels significantly, producing involuntary unemployment. One group notably affected by the 1966 amendment are seasonal workers employed in producing cotton.

Total employment in this occupation fell from a peak-month level of 279.9 thousand in 1965 to peaks of 120.3 thousand in 1967 and 68.2 thousand in 1969 (see appendix, table 3).[3] Although this retrenchment is not wholly ascribable to the minimum wage legislation of 1966, a significant portion almost certainly appears to be. In the first place, the average farm wage rate was less than $1.00 per hour in eight of the fourteen major cotton-growing states in 1966, and in some states it was substantially below the legislated minimum.[4] Second, herbicides and mechanical harvesters were by 1966 well-established (and widely used) technical substitutes for labor employed in weeding and harvesting cotton. The minimum wage schedule embodied in the 1966 amendment seems to have quickened the process of mechanization that was already under way.

The independent influence of the 1966 amendment on employment in this occupation is clouded to some extent by the trends toward increasing farm size and mechanization initiated after World War II,[5] for as shown in the appendix, table 3, employment of seasonal workers declined during the period 1960–1965 even though aggregate cotton production remained remarkably stable.

The object of this paper is to identify the importance of the 1966 amendment in contributing to the dramatic decrease in the employment of seasonal cotton workers after 1965. In particular, we show how the artificial wage floors in the south-central and southeastern states accelerated the substitution of mechanical processes for labor, thereby inducing involuntary unemployment.

[3] These figures are taken from U.S. Department of Labor, Bureau of Employment Security, "Estimated Number of Seasonal Hired Farm Workers in Cotton." The employment figures used here (see table 3) are for the peak month of season in fourteen cotton-producing states. These states accounted for 99.7 percent of all cotton produced in the United States during the 1960s.

[4] The fourteen cotton-growing states considered here are Alabama, Arizona, Arkansas, California, Georgia, Louisiana, Mississippi, Missouri, New Mexico, North Carolina, Oklahoma, South Carolina, Tennessee, and Texas. Average farm wage rates are reported in U.S. Department of Agriculture, Statistical Reporting Service, *Farm Labor*.

[5] See Robert G. Ainsworth, "Causes and Effects of Declining Cotton Employment," in U.S. Department of Labor, Bureau of Employment Security, *Farm Labor Developments*, Washington, D.C., 1976, for a discussion of the extent of mechanization in cotton farming and its impact on employment.

To do so, we specify a model of supply and demand for seasonal workers in the fourteen major cotton-producing states. The parameters of this model are then estimated using data for the period 1960 through 1966, prior to the extension of the minimum wage coverage. The estimated parameters are then used to predict the equilibrium wage and employment levels for the period 1967 through 1969. The predicted wages and employment levels are estimates of what would have occurred in the absence of the 1966 amendment. These projections are compared with the actual employment levels to assess the impact of the extended federal minimum wage coverage.

The Labor Market Model

The model consists of a demand and a supply equation for seasonal cotton workers, with states as units of observation. The demand equation is therefore an aggregate of individual cotton producers' demands for labor within the state. We assume that the producer minimizes the cost of harvesting any given quantity of cotton. We are not concerned with explaining the volume of cotton harvested and treat this quantity as a predetermined variable. The cotton producers' equilibrium level of employment nonetheless depends on the quantity harvested, as well as on the wage rate of farm workers and the cost of competing inputs. The major competing input for labor in this sector is farm equipment in chemical weeding and machine harvesting. The ability of producers to employ mechanical processes profitably depends partially on farm size and the development of custom work (machine rental) markets. Therefore, we specify the aggregate state demand for labor in cotton production as

$$LD = f(WF, PE, SZE, TECH, QCH) \qquad (1)$$

where WF is the average farm wage rate,[6] PE is a price index for agricultural equipment and machinery,[7] SZE is the average number of

---

[6] The appropriate wage rate is that for cotton choppers and pickers. Unfortunately, continuous time series on that wage rate are not available, so the average farm wage rate, by state, is used instead. The average wage of cotton pickers and choppers is somewhat less than the average farm wage rate, but the difference is not prohibitively large.

[7] The rental price of capital (r_e) may be expressed as $r_e = PE [r + (P_e/P_e) + d - (PE/PE)]$, where PE is the price index of equipment and machinery, r is the real rate of return, (P_e/P_e) is the expected rate of general inflation, and d is the depreciation rate. During the period 1960–1966, (P_e/P_e) and (PE/PE) were very nearly equal: with 1967 as the base year, the general price index ranged from .887 in 1960 to .972 in 1966; the price index of agricultural machinery and equipment increased from .861 in 1960 to .968 in 1966. Since r and d were essentially constant throughout this period, the bracketed expression can be treated as constant, and PE is a precise scalar surrogate for r_e.

235

acres per cotton farm, *TECH* is an index of technology (represented by a linear time trend) included to capture refinements in farm equipment and the development of custom work markets, and *QCH* is the quantity of cotton harvested.

Following World War II there was a nationwide trend toward larger farm size. In the western states this trend issued from increased irrigation, which became economically feasible only when applied to larger-scale farms. In the southeastern and south-central states the larger farms facilitated the adoption of mechanical weeders and pickers. Hence we view the trend toward larger farm units as a process enabling capital-using (labor-saving) technological change: larger producing units will employ less labor-intensive techniques, other things being equal. Similarly, a higher wage rate reduces employment, other things being equal. On the other hand, higher prices of farm equipment and larger quantities of cotton harvested each induce greater farm employment, *ceteris paribus*. Accordingly, we hypothesize negative coefficients for the variables *WF*, *SZE*, and *TECH*; and positive coefficients for the variables *PE* and *QCH*. Measurement of each variable is discussed in the appendix.

To develop the supply of labor we follow the traditional utility maximization model for the individual worker, then aggregate over workers for each state. This implies that labor supply available for cotton production depends on the real farm wage rate, the real income opportunities elsewhere, and the number of potential cotton workers available in the state. In accounting for the size of the potential cotton worker force, we recognize that most seasonal farm workers are migratory and that the supply available for harvesting cotton may be temporarily larger than the permanent farm labor force of the state. According to G. K. Bowles, there are three migratory farm labor groups: one from Florida that works along the east coast; one from southern Texas that migrates within the south-central and southeastern states; and a smaller group from Arizona and New Mexico working within these states and along the West Coast.[8] Therefore, we include in the supply equation a dummy variable to indicate from which migratory group the individual state draws its work force. In addition to these demographic variables, we wish to account for general occupational shifts away from agriculture[9] and the potential influence of public assistance within the state on the farm labor supply. The resulting supply function for each state is

$$LS = g(WF/CPI, WM/CPI, AID/CPI, TREND, DMYE, DMYW) \quad (2)$$

[8] G. K. Bowles, "The Current Situation of the Hired Farm Labor Force," in *Farm Labor in the United States*, ed. C. E. Bishop (New York: Columbia University Press, 1967).

[9] See ibid. for a discussion of trends in the number of hired farm workers.

where *CPI* is the consumer price index, *WM* is the manufacturing wage rate in the state, *AID* is the average household payment for aid to dependent children within the state, *TREND* is trend for occupational shift, and *DMYE* and *DMYW* are migratory labor group dummy variables. We hypothesize a positive coefficient for the variable *WF/CPI* and negative coefficients for *WM/CPI*, *AID/CPI*, and *TREND*. The last three variables shift the cotton worker supply schedule in response to alternaive sources of income and trend-related demographic variables.

Equations (1) and (2) simultaneously determine the level of employment and the wage rate. For purposes of estimation, we consider the current farm wage rate and current level of employment as endogenous variables and all other variables as predetermined. We recognize the shortcomings of this specification, in particular the absence of any expectational variables, but more elaborate specifications do not seem warranted, given the data currently available.[10]

Estimation of the Model

The supply and demand equations are specified as linear with additive disturbance terms. Each equation is overidentified; so the structural parameters are estimated by two-stage least-squares. The sample is a cross section of fourteen cotton-producing states with observations for each state taken for the years 1960 through 1966. The two-stage least-squares estimates are given below, with *t*-values under the null hypothesis that the coefficient is zero listed in parentheses.

$$
\begin{aligned}
LD = {} & - 502254.66 - 28711.25 \; WF \\
& \;\;(1.2559) \qquad (2.3189) \\[6pt]
& - 15.98 \; SZE + 22.48 \; QCH \\
& \;\;(1.8687) \qquad (12.9924) \\[6pt]
& - 14516.37 \; TECH + 6566.82 \; PE \\
& \;\;(1.8008) \qquad\qquad (1.3817) \\[6pt]
& \bar{R}^2 = .6851
\end{aligned}
\tag{3}
$$

---

[10] Various specifications to incorporate expectations and lags in adjustment to equilibrium were estimated. These regressions, which included lagged values of either the dependent variable or the regressors, produced a high degree of multicollinearity and imprecise estimates. Because the data base required for this study is strictly limited, we could not correct this problem and abandoned attempts to estimate more sophisticated forms of the model.

237

$$LS = 56215.90 \, DMYW + 39504.09 \, DMYE$$
$$(3.3346) \qquad\qquad (2.8354)$$

$$+ \, 637590.16 \, WF/CPI - 148478.44 \, WM/CPI$$
$$(7.0883) \qquad\qquad\qquad (6.5232)$$
$$\tag{4}$$

$$- \, 2467.47 \, AID/CPI - 10332.39 \, TECH$$
$$(8.4209) \qquad\qquad\quad (7.5289)$$

$$\bar{R}^2 = .5810$$

All of the estimates are significant at the 95 percent confidence level, except the constant and the coefficient of *PE* in the demand equation, and each has the predicted sign. (In one-tail tests with ninety-two degrees of freedom, the critical *t* statistics at the 95 percent and 90 percent confidence levels are 1.67 and 1.29.) From the demand equation the coefficient of *WF* yields an estimated elasticity of demand for labor (at sample mean values) of − .83. This estimate is slightly below that found in other studies of hired farm workers by T. D. Wallace and D. H. Hoover and by L. L. Bauer but greater than that found by E. W. Tyrchniewicz and G. E. Schuh in their study of total agricultural employment.[11] The negative coefficient of *SZE* indicates that larger farms use less labor, after standardizing for output and other variables in the demand equation. Similarly, the negative trend coefficient shows an independent time-related reduction in employment; and, as expected, a larger volume of cotton harvested increases the demand for seasonal cotton workers. Finally, we note that the positive coefficient of the farm equipment price index confirms that machinery and labor are substitutes.

In estimating the supply equation, we permitted the constant term to vary with the migratory labor groups discussed above. In doing so, we combined the Florida and Texas groups into one eastern group, as the two werre not statistically distinguishable.

The coefficient on *WF/CPI* yields an elasticity of supply (evaluated at the sample means) of 20.1. This highly elastic supply of cotton workers with respect to the real wage rate is broadly consistent with the findings of D. E. Wise in his study of seasonal farm workers in California and

[11] T. D. Wallace and D. H. Hoover, "Income Effects of Innovation: The Case of Labor in Agriculture," *Journal of Farm Economics* 49 (May 1966): 325–36; L. L. Bauer, "The Effect of Technology on the Farm Labor Market," *American Journal of Agricultural Economics* 51 (August 1969): 505–18; E. W. Tyrchniewicz and G. E. Schuh, "Econometric Analysis of the Agricultural Labor Market," *American Journal of Agricultural Economics* 51 (November 1969): 770–87.

the long-run regional elasticities found by Tyrchniewicz and Schuh.[12] The fact that our estimated elasticity (at the sample means) is larger than these other estimates is not surprising, since we are analyzing a comparatively much smaller labor pool within the states. The significant negative coefficients on the real manufacturing wage rate and aid to dependent children suggest that the seasonal farm workers are sensitive to both market and nonmarket alternative sources of income. Similarly, the negative trend coefficient indicates a decreasing labor supply, over time, attributable to long-term occupational shifts away from the grueling manual work in the cotton fields.

Assessment of Employment Effects

In this section we use the estimated parameters of the model to predict equilibrium wages and employment levels that would have prevailed in the absence of the 1966 amendment. Because the states in the sample vary so widely in their characteristics—both with respect to wage levels and production technologies—we divide them into three groups: western states (Arizona, California, New Mexico, Texas, and Oklahoma); south-central states (Alabama, Arkansas, Louisiana, Mississippi, Missouri, and Tennessee); and southeastern states (Georgia, South Carolina, and North Carolina). These three groups differ in several important ways associated with their geographic location, as may be seen in table 1. The western states are characterized by relatively larger farms, substantially greater production (and production per farm), higher manufacturing wages, and higher payments for aid to dependent children than the south-central or southeastern states. The latter two groups differ less dramatically when compared with each other, but some differences are nonetheless apparent: the south-central states display slightly larger average farm size, considerably greater output, higher manufacturing wages, but slightly lower payments for aid to families with dependent children than the southeastern states. This geographic division gives us three distinct groups for which the impact of the minimum wage may be assessed. The required projections and related data for each group are given in table 2. The estimated market wage and estimated employment in the absence of the minimum wage are obtained by solving the estimated supply and demand equations using sample mean values of the variables, within each group, for each of the years listed in table 2.

[12] D. E. Wise, "The Effect of the Bracero on Agricultural Production in California," *Economic Inquiry* 12 (December 1974): 547–58; and Tyrchniewicz and Schuh, "Econometric Analysis."

239

TABLE 1

MEAN VALUES OF SELECTED VARIABLES FOR STATE GROUPS,
1966–1969

Group	Average Farm Size (acres per farm)	Cotton Production (1,000 bales per state)	Aid to Dependent Children (dollars per month)	Manufacturing Wage Rate (dollars per hour)
Western states				
1966	642	1,063	132	2.66
1967	642	921	131	2.78
1968	642	1,253	128	2.93
1969	642	1,048	138	3.01
South-central states				
1966	255	589	82	2.25
1967	292	396	82	2.38
1968	326	667	82	2.56
1969	361	691	86	2.71
Southeastern states				
1966	230	230	86	1.99
1967	261	149	92	2.10
1968	291	212	93	2.27
1969	322	195	99	2.42

NOTE: The figures reported here are averages for the states in each regional group.
SOURCE: Columns 1–2: U.S. Department of Agriculture, *Agricultural Statistics*, various issues; Columns 3–4: U.S. Department of Commerce, Bureau of Census, *Statistical Abstract of the United States*, various issues.

For the western states, the predicted wage and employment levels indicate that the extended minimum wage coverage exerted no effect.[13] This conclusion follows inasmuch as the projected market-determined wages are above the legal minimum wage for the years 1967–1969. This finding also accords with the fact that the actual average farm wage in these western states was above the minimum in all three years considered. The projections for the south-central states, however, suggest a significant reduction in employment following the imposition of the minimum wage. The projected market-determined wages are below the minimum wage in each year, resulting in a reduction of approximately 8,200 and 9,700 peak-month workers demanded in the typical south-

[13] Actual employment figures for 1968 were not available from the Bureau of Employment Security, and therefore the reduction in employment for 1968 was not computed. The projected values for 1968 were in all cases greater than the projected levels for 1967 because of an increase in cotton production in 1968.

TABLE 2

EMPLOYMENT EFFECTS OF MINIMUM WAGE ON SEASONAL WORKERS IN COTTON, 1965–1969

Region	Actual Peak-Month Employment (L_A)[a]	Estimated Market Wage	Estimated Peak-Month Employment $(\hat{L})$	Reduced Employment Attributable to Minimum Wage
Western states				
1965	19,571			
1966	14,192	1.17	13,028	
1967	12,498	1.22	13,791	no effect
1968	—[b]	1.27	18,426	no effect
1969	7,209	1.33	10,528	no effect
South-central states				
1965	22,153			
1966	12,779	.91	16,038	
1967	6,619	.97	14,828	8,209
1968	—	1.03	17,193	—
1969	4,130[c]	1.10	13,817	9,687
Southeastern states				
1965	16,379			
1966	9,994	.86	9,910	
1967	6,020	.93	10,762	4,742
1968	—	.99	8,575	—
1969	3,840	1.07	7,328	3,488

[a] Actual peak-month employment levels are mean values for the states in the region.
[b] Actual employment figures for 1968 are not reported.
[c] This figure does not include Mississippi, since the data for 1969 were not reported.
SOURCE: Column 1: U.S. Department of Labor, Bureau of Employment Security, "Estimated Number of Seasonal Hired Farm Workers in Cotton," mimeographed.

central state in 1967 and 1969. A notable impact occurred in the southeastern states as well. We estimate that a typical southeastern state experienced a reduction in peak-month employment of about 4,700 workers in 1967 and roughly 3,500 workers in 1969 because of the minimum wage.

To approximate the total impact on the employment in cotton farming due to the federal minimum wage schedule, we assume that the reduction estimated for the typical state is the same for all states in the region. Using this assumption, the total reduction in employment is estimated to be approximately 63,000 peak-month workers in 1967 and roughly 69,000 peak-month workers in 1969. The fact that our estimate of the impact does not differ significantly between 1967 and 1969 suggests that the greater part of the wage-induced reduction in employment had occurred by the end of 1967. Cotton producers were presumably able to make adjustments by 1967 in anticipation of the statutory minimum of $1.30 per hour that was to prevail as of February 1, 1969. Finally, our estimates of wage-induced reduction may be compared with the total decline in employment of seasonal workers in cotton production during this period. Reported peak-month employment plummeted from 177,619 in 1966 to 68,264 in 1969 (see appendix, table 3). Our estimates indicate that about 69,000 of these workers were displaced by minimum wage legislation while approximately 40,000 peak-month cotton-farming jobs were eliminated by other economic and demographic forces. Put somewhat differently, of the total reduction of 109,000 peak-month jobs that occurred between 1966 and 1969, our model ascribes roughly 63 percent (69,000 ÷ 109,000) to the extended minimum wage coverage, and the remaining 37 percent to other variables in the demand equation.[14] The reduction in employment attributable to the 1966 amendments was concentrated in the south-central and southeastern states. The burden of public relief would be correspondingly centered.

Conclusion

This paper presents a method for estimating the impact of minimum wage legislation on employment of seasonal cotton workers. Specifically, we attempt to separate the effects of minimum wages from the nonwage forces that were already evolving after World War II and were independently reducing employment. We estimate a simple market model of supply and demand for workers during the years preceding minimum wage coverage, then project the hypothetical market-determined values of wages and employment in the postsample period. An estimate of the minimum wage impact is obtained by comparing the projected peak-month employment that would have occurred in an unfettered market, with actual employment following the minimum wage coverage.

This methodology is straightforward. Indeed, it would seem to be applicable to a wide range of markets in which observations are available both before and after minimum wage coverage. Nonetheless, our conclusions must be interpreted with several qualifications. First, the data are less than ideal. Hourly wage rates for seasonal cotton workers, by state and year, are not available. Accordingly, we must use the average

[14] This figure may underestimate the full impact of minimum wages: total employment declined from 279,910 in 1965 to 177,619 in 1966, and certainly some portion of this drop in demand was in anticipation of a higher wage.

hourly wage rate for all farm workers, by state and year, as a proxy. Because it is surely closer to the mark in some states than in others, our estimates are based on data subject to moderate, but apparently tolerable, measurement error.

Second, the estimates are conditional on a linear approximation to some true, but unknown, model. We have not experimented with nonlinear demand and supply equations, although nonlinear equations could be implemented within our framework. Our partition of wage and non-wage impacts may be either sensitive or reasonably robust with respect to model specification. Some clustering of regression residuals, by state, suggests there are state-specific influences (on both the demand and the supply sides) not adequately represented in the model. These caveats notwithstanding, the evidence from our model convincingly indicates that minimum wage legislation hastened the extinction of seasonal cotton worker employment in the south-central and southeastern states.

Appendix

Description and source for each variable used in the study:

LD, LS: Estimated number of seasonal hired farm workers in cotton, by state, during the peak month of the season. This series was developed by U.S. Department of Labor, Bureau of Employment Security.

WF: Average hourly farm wage rate (without room or board) by state. This series is developed by the Agricultural Marketing Service based on farmers' reports of average farm wage rates paid in their localities. The series is taken from U.S. Department of Agriculture, Statistical Reporting Service, *Farm Labor,* various issues.

SZE: Average size of commercial cotton farms by state. This series is available for 1959, 1964, and 1969 in U.S. Department of Commerce, Bureau of the Census, *Census of Agriculture,* 1959, 1964, and 1969 issues. The remaining years were estimated by simple linear methods.

PE: Wholesale price index for Agricultural Machinery and Equipment. This series is taken from U.S. Department of Commerce, *Business Statistics,* 1973.

TECH, TREND: This variable is a simple time trend.

QCH: Cotton production by state is reported each year in U.S. Department of Agriculture, *Agricultural Statistics.* The series is the number of 500-pound gross weight bales.

WM: Average hourly wage rate of production workers on manufacturing payrolls by state is reported in U.S. Department

TABLE 3

SELECTED STATISTICS CONCERNING NATIONAL COTTON PRODUCTION, 1960–1969

Year	Acreage Harvested (1,000 acres)	Production of 500-lb. Bales (1,000 bales)	Season Average Price Received by Farmers (¢/lb.)	Estimated Number of Seasonal Workers (peak month)	Mechanical Cotton Pickers Manufactured in U.S.
1960	15,309	14,272	30.19	653,053	6,257
1961	15,634	14,318	32.92	578,797	6,201
1962	15,569	14,867	31.90	475,817	5,056
1963	14,212	15,334	32.23	395,826	5,012
1964	14,055	15,182	29.76	352,680	3,984
1965	13,615	14,973	28.14	279,910	4,586
1966	9,552	9,575	20.84	177,619	1,159
1967	7,997	7,458	25.59	120,264	497
1968	10,160	10,948	22.15	n.a.	n.a.
1969	11,058	10,009	21.09	68,264	n.a.

SOURCES: Columns 1–3: U.S. Department of Agriculture, *Agricultural Statistics 1971*, table 84, p. 59. Column 4: U.S. Department of Labor, Bureau of Employment Security (provided by Cotton Council). Column 5: Department of Agriculture, *Agricultural Statistics 1971*, table 646, p. 451.

of Commerce, Bureau of the Census, *Statistical Abstract of the United States*, various issues.

AID: Aid to dependent children, by state. This series is the average monthly payment in December for aid to dependent children per family in the state. It is taken from U.S. Department of Commerce, Bureau of the Census, *Statistical Abstract of the United States*, various issues.

DMYC: A binary variable defined as equal to one if the state is Alabama, Arkansas, Georgia, Louisiana, Mississippi, Missouri, Tennessee, North Carolina, South Carolina, Texas, or Oklahoma, and as equal to zero otherwise.

DMYW: A binary variable defined as equal to one if the state is California, New Mexico, or Arizona, and as equal to zero otherwise.

Table 3 gives some statistics relevant to understanding the general trends in cotton production and employment during the time period of this study.

Bibliography

Ainsworth, R. G. "Causes and Effects of Declining Cotton Employment." In U.S. Department of Labor, Bureau of Employment Security, *Farm Labor Development.* Washington, D.C., 1967.

Bauer, L. L. "The Effect of Technology on the Farm Labor Market." *American Journal of Agricultural Economics* 51 (August 1969): 505–18.

Bowles, G. K. "The Current Situation of the Hired Farm Labor Force." In *Farm Labor in the United States,* edited by C. E. Bishop. New York: Columbia University Press, 1967.

Gallasch, H. F., Jr. "Minimum Wages and the Farm Labor Market." *Southern Economic Journal* 41 (January 1975): 480–91.

Gardner, B. L. "Minimum Wages and the Farm Labor Market." *American Journal of Agricultural Economics* 54 (August 1972): 474–76.

Lianos, T. P. "Impact of Minimum Wages upon the Level and Composition of Agricultural Employment." *American Journal of Agricultural Economics* 54 (August 1972): 477–84.

Tyrchniewicz, E. W., and Schuh, G. E. "Econometric Analysis of the Agricultural Labor Market." *American Journal of Agricultural Economics* 51 (November 1969): 770–87.

———. "Regional Supply of Hired Labor to Agriculture." *American Journal of Agricultural Economics* 48 (August 1966): 537–56.

U.S. Department of Labor, Wage and Hour and Public Contracts Division. *Farmer's Guide to the Agricultural Provisions of the Fair Labor Standards Act,* WHPC Publication no. 1888. Washington, D.C.: Government Printing Office, 1970.

———, Workplace Standards Administration. *Fair Labor Standards Act of 1938 as Amended,* Publication no. 1318. Washington, D.C., 1971.

Wallace, T. D., and Hoover, D. H. "Income Effects of Innovation: The Case of Labor in Agriculture." *Journal of Farm Economics* 49 (May 1966): 325–36.

Wise, D. E. "The Effect of the Bracero on Agricultural Production in California." *Economic Inquiry* 12 (December 1974): 547–58.

Minimum Wages and the Distribution of Economic Activity

Marshall R. Colberg

The regional conflict inherent in federal minimum wage legislation was well stated by Henry Simons of the University of Chicago over thirty years ago. He wrote:

> Southern workers may be intrigued by the wage expectations held out by organizers from northern unions and by the Fair Labor Standards Act. They may in a few cases get such wages, but if they get much employment at such wages, it will be only in spite of the intentions of the northern unions and the Massachusetts senators.[1]

Simons considered the Fair Labor Standards Act to be similar in purpose to tariffs except that protection to northern manufacturers was from competition from the South rather than from foreigners.

Interestingly, Senator John F. Kennedy, just a few years later, published an article in the *Atlantic Monthly* detailing the struggle for industry between New England and the South. Although Kennedy claimed in the article that he did not oppose migration of industry from New England to the South based on "normal competition and competitive advantages," he wrote:

> But the final reason for migration, with which I am particularly concerned, is the cost differential resulting from practices or conditions permitted or provided by Federal Law which are unfair or substandard by any criterion. Massachusetts manufacturing industries in May of 1953 paid an average hourly wage of $1.64; but because the Federal minimum wage is only an outdated 75 cents an hour, many industries migrating to the rural communities of Mississippi pay workers only that less-than-subsistence wage, and those employees under "learners permits" even less.[2]

The clear implication is that the federal government should pass laws

[1] Henry C. Simons, "Some Reflections on Syndicalism," *Economic Policy for a Free Society* (Chicago: University of Chicago Press, 1948), chap. 6, p. 135.

[2] John F. Kennedy, "New England and the South: The Struggle for Industry," *Atlantic Monthly,* January 1954, p. 33.

to raise production costs in the South in order to protect New England industry. Raising and extending coverage of the minimum wage is one way to do so. Another would be repeal of section 14(b) of the Taft-Hartley Act, which permits states to have right-to-work laws.[3] Consistent with his article, Senator Kennedy was cosponsor of a bill to raise the minimum wage from seventy-five cents to one dollar per hour, which he was able to sign as president.

A "Yankee Trick"

Although proponents of higher minimum wages use many arguments, I believe that interregional competition, especially in manufacturing, agriculture, and wholesaling, is usually the main force at work. My view is that the minimum wage is basically a "Yankee trick" (or, perhaps better, a "union trick") played on the South. Many southern workers are skeptical of receiving net benefits, especially in the longer run, by joining unions. From the viewpoint of the labor unions, a uniform federal minimum wage is a partial substitute for universal unionization, although the level at which the minimum is set is obviously of vital importance. In some ways, raising the legal minimum is even more useful to unions than negotiating a wage increase, because higher production costs and any unemployment that is generated will be felt by other companies and by nonunion workers.

Employers may have ambivalent feelings about supporting higher federal minimum wages. If their own plants are already paying all workers well above the legal minimum, they probably welcome any opportunity to raise the production costs of competitors. The same firms, however, may now or in the future own plants in lower-wage areas. Support of higher minimum wages and support of repeal of right-to-work laws tend to close their escape hatches from union power.

An interesting recent example is the establishment by Firestone Tire and Rubber Company of a large nonunion plant in Wilson, North Carolina. This plant employs about 1,200 production workers and produces about 5.5 million tires per year.[4] This tends to reduce the bargaining power of the United Rubber Workers in northern plants, especially since additional tire plants could be built in the South. In addition, it helps Firestone in the competitive race with imported tires (about 17 million tires were imported in 1978). In addition, Michelin

---

[3] See, for example, M. R. Colberg, *The Consumer Impact of Repeal of 14(b)* (Washington, D.C.: Heritage Foundation, 1978).

[4] Ralph E. Winter, "Nonunion Rubber Plants Help Lift Hopes of Averting Strike in Current Labor Talks," *Wall Street Journal*, March 16, 1979, p. 42.

has established three tire plants in South Carolina—a right-to-work state where only about 8 percent of nonagricultural workers belong to unions.[5]

Since February 1, 1967, when federal minimum wage coverage of agricultural workers was initiated, regional competition in farming has also influenced voting in this field. Public Law 89–601, effective on that date, was the first to incorporate the new technique of legislating a whole series of future yearly increments to the minimum wage. Although a lower minimum wage was applied to covered farm workers, there was clearly a move toward putting all workers on the same basis, and this trend has continued.

The desired use of an agricultural minimum wage to reduce regional competition was brought out clearly in 1966 by a representative from New York:

> Mr. Resnick: Mr. Chairman, I would like to point out to all the members from the Northeast and from the city what this legislation means to them.
>
> For one thing, Mr. Chairman, it means that that the farmers of the Northeast can compete fairly with the farmers from the rest of the country.
>
> Now, Mr. Chairman, we have poultry farmers in our part of the country. Our farmers pay anywhere from $1.25 to $1.75 an hour for help. I ask you how can they compete with the poultry farmers in Mississippi who pay $3.00 a day for a 10-hour day?[6]

The economic interest of California in raising the cost of agricultural production in other states to promote "equity" is brought out well in the remarks of a Republican congressman from that state:

> We in California are paying the highest agricultural wage rates, with the exception of Hawaii, in the entire Nation. Yet our State is the target today of those who say we are not paying enough. We feel that if we are a target when we are exceeding the minimum wage and leading other areas, it is wrong to exempt 600,000 workers who work for our competitors across the Nation and not force our competitors at least part of the way up to the level of wages which we in California are paying and will continue to pay.[7]

Congressman Charles Gubser was speaking in opposition to a proposed

---

[5] Paul S. Dempsey, "Legal and Economic Incentives for Foreign Direct Investment in the Southeastern United States," *Vanderbilt Journal of Transnational Law* 9 (Spring 1976):247–93, emphasizes the large package of tax incentives offered by South Carolina—as well as state right-to-work legislation—as attractions to direct foreign investment.

[6] *Congressional Record*, May 25, 1966, p. 11383.

[7] Ibid., p. 11394.

amendment that would exempt farms with less than 500 man-days per quarter of labor input. The amendment was, however, included in Public Law 89–601.

Key Votes

Although statements of the sort just quoted give valuable insights into the true feelings of legislators, statistical investigation of actual voting on minimum wage bills should provide more comprehensive information on the politics of such legislation. Compilation of votes must be done with caution if true feelings are to be disclosed. A legislator who is really against any increase may vote for a twenty-five-cent-per-hour increase, for example, if he feels that a thirty-five-cent increase might otherwise occur—or, in the words of the *Congressional Quarterly Almanac, 1966,* "Sometimes Congressmen approve final passage of bills after vigorously supporting amendments which, if adopted, would have scuttled the legislation."[8] This is why votes on important amendments are often a better barometer of actual preferences than final votes.

A good example occurred in 1974, when Richard Nixon signed into law Public Law 93–259, a bill raising the minimum wage for most non-farm workers from $1.60 to $2.30 per hour in three steps. The bill was very similar to one he had vetoed in 1973, when the veto was nearly overridden by the House. Worsening inflation apparently contributed to a political climate in 1974 in which Nixon did not expect another veto to be sustained. Representatives from southern states voted 81 percent in favor of adopting the conference report on S. 2747, which sharply raised the legal minimum wage and extended its coverage. It would be a serious mistake to interpret this vote as a sincere joining of minds by the North Carolina and Massachusetts delegations, both of which voted unanimously for the bill. Instead, most congressmen voted for the bill when it was clear that it would be passed and not vetoed. The 1973 House vote in which President Nixon's veto was sustained by a rather small margin is also a poor test of regional sentiment on the minimum wage increase because the vote was so heavily along party lines. Seventy-three percent of the Republicans voted to support the presidential veto, and almost all of the northern Democrats voted to override. The twenty-eight votes of southern Democrats in favor of the veto can, however, be considered to have swung the balance against override.

The statistical portion of this paper consequently is based on analysis of congressional votes by state on key amendments. The analysis is

[8] *Congressional Quarterly Almanac, 1966* (Washington, D.C.: Congressional Quarterly, 1966), p. 13.

restricted to the period since 1961, when the minimum was raised and for the first time the categories of coverage were extended. As a preliminary step, some key amendments since 1961 will be described briefly to indicate why they have been chosen for special consideration. For each of these amendments the South versus non-South vote will be shown as an indication of the regional nature of the minimum wage battle. The vote on amendments with little or no implications for the location of economic activity will also be included as key tests in order to see whether South–non-South voting is different in these cases. Later, additional variables will be considered in a multiple correlation analysis of congressional voting.

1961: The Monroney Amendment

The "Monroney amendment" in the Senate in 1961 qualifies as a key test of actual sentiment for the minimum wage because it would have limited coverage of retail, gasoline-station, laundry, and construction workers to firms that had establishments in more than one state. It was therefore in part a test of the legal meaning of interstate commerce. Defeat of the Monroney amendment by a 39-to-56 Senate vote contributed to the present definition of almost all economic activity as interstate commerce subject to federal regulation. On this amendment, senators from southern states (as defined in the census) voted 75 percent for the amendment, and those from the non-South voted 75 percent against. (Sixty-two percent of the Republicans supported the amendment, and 70 percent of the Democrats opposed it.)[9]

1966 Legislation

The minimum wage law (P.L. 89–601) passed in 1966 was considered by the AFL-CIO to be "the most important and best ever passed."[10] It was signed into law by Lyndon Johnson, who, however, was not a strong advocate of the minimum wage idea. He opposed any increase above $1.40 per hour becoming effective before late 1968, whereas George Meany publicly insisted on an increase to that figure by September 1, 1966. Moreover, President Johnson did not push for minimum wage legislation in 1964 or 1965. Probably his true feeling was brought out best in 1949 when, as a senator from Texas, his votes on minimum

---

[9] In this paper, congressmen who "pair for" an amendment are added to the yea votes, and those who "pair against" are added to the nay votes. The Senate vote on the Monroney amendment was not analyzed by multiple regression analysis. Two 1966 votes and two in 1977 were so analyzed, with results as shown in the following sections.

[10] *Congressional Quarterly Almanac, 1966*, p. 821.

wage amendments closely followed those of Senator Spessard Holland of Florida—a consistent opponent of the minimum wage—rather than those of Senator Claude Pepper of Florida, a long-time supporter of this type of regulation.

A key vote was taken in 1966 on the proposal of Republican Congressman David Martin of Nebraska to recommit H.R. 13712 to the Education and Labor Committee with instructions to delete agricultural coverage and to provide broader exemptions for canneries. Seventy-two percent of the representatives from the South voted in favor of the Martin proposal, and 28 percent of the nonsouthern representatives voted for the proposal. Some farm states such as Nebraska and South Dakota supported the proposal, but, as indicated by the vote, the regional aspect was important.

Youth Differential

An interesting and extremely close House vote took place in 1977 on the "Cornell amendment" to H.R. 3744, which would have permitted employers to pay 85 percent of the minimum wage to workers under eighteen years of age during their first six months on the job. The amendment was rejected 210 to 211. Although this can be viewed as weakening the minimum wage, southern support was less clear than usual with a 60 percent yea vote. Nonsouthern representatives were 45 percent in favor.

One interpretation may be that the regional economic implications are not clear. Teenage unemployment among blacks is especially obvious in the large northern and western cities, and some southern congressmen may have felt that the youth differential would especially aid nonsouthern firms. It is interesting that all of the black representatives voted against the Cornell amendment. They have not been impressed with the idea that black teenage unemployment in large cities is due in substantial measure to the minimum wage; they feel that any employment gains by this group would be at the expense of older workers. They are also unimpressed with the idea that a job usually provides important training that will be of future value to the occupant. Parren Mitchell, chairman of the Congressional Black Caucus, argued that teenagers get jobs as "stock clerks, elevator operators, and amusement park workers," jobs that can be learned quickly.[11]

---

[11] *Congressional Quarterly Almanac, 1977*, p. 141. Finis Welch, *Minimum Wages: Issues and Evidence* (Washington, D.C.: American Enterprise Institute, 1978), p. 44, raises the question: "Why not have a differential for all who would earn less than the minimum? In other words, why have a minimum wage at all?"

It should be noted that most of the white congressmen from New York and New Jersey, where teenage unemployment is especially serious, also voted against the youth differential. There is widespread belief that the total number of jobs available in the short run is virtually fixed, so that employment of one person displaces the opportunity of someone else to work. This thinking also underlies the retirement test under the social security law, since added work by older persons has been assumed by legislators to be at the expense of younger workers.[12] In part, the blame for this attitude may be traceable to the popularity of measurements of the large amount of capital needed "to create a new job." George Stigler, however, has emphasized the variability of proportions of labor and capital in most fields of production.[13] The opposite, more common view, is due in part to the work of econometricians who find fixed proportions to be more manageable in their equations.

District of Columbia Coverage

Another vote on a matter with little significance for the location of economic activity, and consequently useful in testing the hypothesis, concerned the extension of minimum wage and overtime provisions to a much large number of workers in the District of Columbia. This was approved in 1966 by a large margin, with most of the northern and western senators and 63 percent of the southern senators voting in favor. Even such strong opponents of the federal minimum wage as Holland of Florida, Everett Dirksen of Illinois, and Sam Ervin of North Carolina voted yea. Evidently, voting on the minimum wage is not strictly a matter of principle.

Indexing

An important aspect of the legislative struggle preceding enactment of 1977 legislation signed by President Carter dealt with automatic indexing of the minimum wage. Indexing was strongly supported by the labor unions as an effective device in preventing the less unionized regions

---

[12] This "lump of labor fallacy" appeared to dominate congressional thinking even during World War II when it was at its most fallacious. See M. R. Colberg, *The Social Security Retirement Test: Right or Wrong?* (Washington, D.C.: American Enterprise Institute, 1978), p. 3.

[13] For example, George Stigler, *The Theory of Price* (New York: Macmillan Company, 1966), p. 144, shows that most of the variation of output in cotton spinning over time did not require a change in the number of active spindles.

from increasing any competititve advantage in labor costs, regardless of the size of wage increases received by union members and the rate of inflation. The main indexing proposal would keep the minimum wage at 53 percent of the average wage in manufacturing in the United States.

Some congressmen were repelled by the complexity of the calculation of the "average wage." A major difficulty is presented by the evaluation of fringe benefits, which loom large in many labor contracts; also, if fringe benefits are included in the average wage, they should be evaluated in checking on minimum wage compliance. The difficulties Congress has experienced with the "tip credit" for waitresses and other service employees would be multiplied. Even if the handling of fringe benefits could be defined legislatively, the compliance problem would still be especially formidable.[14]

The difficulties inherent in indexing, along with the feeling that inflation would be promoted, probably account for the substantial (40 percent) vote of nonsouthern members of the House to delete indexing provisions. Eighty-three percent of the southern vote was in favor of deletion, probably because of the unfavorable regional competitive implications. In all, indexing was defeated by a 193–223 vote.[15]

Independent Variables

In addition to region, some variables that may influence congressional voting on key minimum wage issues are: (1) whether the state has a right-to-work law; (2) average hourly wage in manufacturing; (3) percentage of population living in urban areas; (4) percentage of nonagricultural workers belonging to labor unions; and (5) percentage of Democratic congressmen. In theory, the right-to-work states should be unfavorable to minimum wage increases because of general antiunion sentiment; states with higher manufacturing wage rates should favor stronger minimum wage legislation in order to raise costs of competitors in lower-wage states; more urbanized states should favor the minimum wage because nominal wage rates are higher in urban areas; more highly unionized states should favor higher minimum wages because of strong union support for such legislation; and states with more Democratic

---

[14] Useful information on the early problems connected with minimum wage enforcement is given by George Macesich and Charles T. Stewart, Jr., "Recent Department of Labor Studies of Minimum Wage Effects," *Southern Economic Journal* 26 (April 1960):281–90. They point out that "an increase in the minimum wage is equivalent to a reduction in the price of evasion and avoidance" (p. 288).

[15] This vote was on the Erlenborn (Republican, Illinois) amendment to H.R. 3744 to delete procedures in the bill for automatic adjustment of the minimum wage and substitution of specified annual increases. *Congressional Quarterly Almanac, 1977*, p. 148-H.

congressmen should be more favorable to higher minimum wages and broader coverage.

The effect of these variables on congressional votes will be determined by multiple regression analysis for the four votes, already mentioned, taken in 1966 and 1977. As a preliminary step, the voting in 1961 on the Monroney amendment (Senate) is shown in the appendix, tables 1 and 2, by state along with data on the independent variables mentioned above. Table 1 is for southern and table 2 for nonsouthern states.

As already mentioned, 75 percent of the southern vote favored the Monroney amendment, compared with 25 percent of the nonsouthern vote. Among right-to-work states, in the South 85 percent of the votes favored the amendment, and in the non-South 56 percent were favorable. There appears to be positive correlation between both percentage of urban population and unionization and pro–minimum wage (anti–Monroney amendment) voting. The effect of party is not obvious, probably because of the well-known affiliation of some southern Democrats and northern Republicans.

Multiple Regressions, 1966

For the 1966 House vote on the Martin amendment to delete coverage of agriculture by the minimum wage and to provide broader exemptions for canneries, the most important variables by far turned out to be southern or nonsouthern representation and right-to-work or non–right-to-work status of the represented state. Regression coefficients of –32.3 and –30.9 show strong anti–minimum wage (prodeletion) votes. The percentage of Democrats in a state's representation also was significant. The percentage of urban population, union membership, and average wage rate in manufacturing did not show up as significant in the t test.[16]

The other 1966 vote (Senate) was chosen to test whether voting on the minimum wage is strictly a matter of principle or is quite different when there is little or no probable effect on production costs in a congressman's own state. The issue was the broadening of minimum wage coverage of workers in the District of Columbia. The "South" variable

[16] Regression coefficients and their t-values were:
South, -32.3 (-3.5)
right-to-work law, -30.9 (-3.6)
percentage of urbanization, -0.37 (-0.78)
percentage Democrats, $+0.59$ (4.08)
average manufacturing wage, -9.04 (-0.78)
percentage union, $+0.68$ (1.25)
$R^2 = .66$

255

no longer showed up as significant (it had a low *t*-value). Right-to-work status was still important, reducing the yea vote substantially.[17]

Multiple Regressions, 1977

The Erlenborn amendment to H.R. 3744 to delete automatic indexing of the minimum wage was passed by the House. The "South" variable was the only clearly significant factor in the antiindexing vote. Right-to-work status and percentage of union membership within a state had the expected signs but had rather low *t*-values.[18]

The final vote investigated by multiple correlation analysis was the extremely close vote in 1977 on the Cornell amendment to H.R. 3744, which would have permitted a youth differential in the minimum wage as described earlier. This vote is included because its regional economic implications are not very clear. It was intended to increase teenage employment in general.

The South in this case is slightly more favorable to the minimum wage than the non-South (interpreting a youth differential as a cut in the minimum wage), but the *t*-value is low. Higher percentages of Democratic congressmen and union membership were significant positive factors in the vote, but regression coefficients were low.[19]

---

[17] Regression coefficients and their *t*-values were:
South, −8.0 (−0.6)
right-to-work law, −27.1 (−2.2)
percentage of urbanization, 0.03 (0.09)
percentage Democrats, −0.17 (−0.81)
average manufacturing wage, 8.34 (0.49)
percentage union, −0.03 (0.04)
$R^2 = .49$

[18] Regression coefficients and their *t*-values were:
South, −29.2 (−3.0)
right-to-work law, −7.8 (−0.7)
percentage of urbanization, −0.01 (0.35)
percentage Democrats, 0.09 (0.63)
average manufacturing wage, −0.02 (−0.06)
percentage union, 1.05 (1.53)
$R^2 = .43$

[19] Regression coefficients and their *t*-values were:
South, 5.6 (0.6)
right-to-work law, −5.1 (0.5)
percentage urbanization, −0.004 (−0.172)
percentage Democrat, +0.51 (3.89)
average manufacturing wage, 0.45 (0.37)
percentage union, 1.28 (2.02)
$R^2 = .46$

Summary

The belief of Henry Simons that the national minimum wage is basically a device to reduce the competitive advantages to the South that can flow from lower nominal wage rates seems to be well founded. Empirical investigation of congressional votes on three key amendments to minimum wage bills in 1961, 1966, and 1977 shows opposition to higher and broader legal minimum wages to come heavily from the South and support to come from nonsouthern states. This is undoubtedly due to perceived unfavorable economic effects on the South and relative advantages to the other states.

Right-to-work states (currently eleven in the South and nine outside the region) vote strongly against measures that strengthen the minimum wage, whereas other states tend to favor the same measures. No other variables have the strong significance of southern location and existence of a state right-to-work law. The latter reflects antiunion political sentiment, which promotes opposition to union-supported attempts to strengthen the minimum wage. It is probable that right-to-work states are seeking to promote their own economic development by providing a favorable labor environment, and this is consistent with their opposition to higher and broader legal minimum wages. Such states as South Carolina appear to be especially attractive to new investment, including foreign investment, because of a low level of union organization and a right-to-work law.

Votes on three important issues were investigated in this paper: the 1961 Monroney amendment to limit minimum wage coverage of some types of business to firms with multistate locations; the 1966 Martin amendment to delete agricultural coverage; and the 1977 Erlenborn amendment to delete indexing of the minimum wage. These issues provide a better gauge of the true feelings of congressmen than do many votes on final bills, where congressmen tend to jump on the bandwagon when passage is certain. In all three cases, southern location and right-to-work status brought heavy anti–minimum wage votes.

A vote on the extension of coverage of workers in the District of Columbia was included as a measure with little significance for regional competition and hence useful in checking the basic hypothesis of the paper. Here the southern congressmen were quite supportive of the legislation, being happy to raise some other firms' costs for a change.

The amendment to provide a youth differential was also investigated because it does not have clear implications for regional competition. In this case, there was little difference between South and non-South voting. Although economists tend to support a youth differential in the minimum wage, congressmen from such states as New York and New Jersey, where teenage unemployment is especially high, voted strongly against a youth differential. Black congressmen voted unanimously against the differential. Evidently they do not believe that the minimum wage is an important cause of black teenage unemployment.[20]

Appendix

Tables 1 and 2 show the voting patterns of Senate delegations from southern and nonsouthern states on the Monroney amendment in 1961, as well as other relevant data. Tables 3 and 4 show voting patterns of congressional delegations from southern and nonsouthern states for a variety of issues related to minimum wages between 1966 and 1977.

[20] Legislation in 1973 pertaining to the minimum wage was analyzed by Jonathan I. Silberman and Garey C. Durden, "Determining Legislative Preferences on the Minimum Wage: An Economic Approach," *Journal of Political Economy* 84 (April 1978): 317–29. They used n-chotomous multivariate probit analysis and determined the important variables to be: (1) campaign contributions of organized labor; (2) campaign contributions of small businesses; (3) region; and (4) teenage workers. Their method of analysis is probably superior to the multiple regression analysis used in the present paper, but it is believed that the present choice of voting issues better reveals true preferences of legislators.

TABLE 1

SOUTHERN STATES' SENATE VOTE ON MONRONEY AMENDMENT AND OTHER STATE DATA, 1961

State	Average Wage in Manufacturing	% Urban	% Senators Democrats	% Unionized	% Vote Pro–Minimum Wage
Alabama[a]	$2.00	43.8	100	19.2	0
Arkansas[a]	1.61	33.0	100	17.0	0
Delaware	2.32	62.6	0	21.8	50
Florida[a]	1.93	65.5	100	13.6	0
Georgia[a]	1.69	45.3	100	14.2	0
Kentucky	2.21	36.8	0	27.1	50
Louisiana	2.22	54.8	100	18.3	50
Maryland	2.34	69.0	0	22.8	0
Mississippi[a]	1.56	27.9	100	12.3	0
North Carolina[a]	1.58	33.7	100	6.9	0
Oklahoma	2.14	51.0	100	15.0	0
South Carolina[a]	1.61	36.7	100	6.7	50
Tennessee[a]	1.88	44.1	100	18.9	50
Texas[a]	2.25	62.7	100	13.7	50
Virginia[a]	1.85	47.0	100	15.5	0
West Virginia	2.48	34.6	100	44.1	100
Average	1.98	46.8	81.3	17.9	25

[a] Had right-to-work law in 1961.

SOURCE: Average wage in manufacturing—U.S. Department of Commerce, Bureau of the Census, *Statistical Abstract of the United States, 1967*, p. 424, for 1966; percentage urban—U.S. Department of Commerce, Bureau of the Census, *Census of Population, 1970*, vol. 1; percentage Democrat—*Congressional Quarterly Almanac, 1961*; percentage unionized—Bureau of the Census, *Statistical Abstract, 1967*, for 1966; percentage of vote—*Congressional Quarterly Almanac, 1961*.

TABLE 2

Nonsouthern States' Senate Vote on Monroney Amendment and Other State Data, 1961

State	Average Wage in Manufacturing	% Urban	% Senators Democrats	% Unionized	% Vote Pro–Minimum Wage
Alaska	$3.50	26.6	100	30.2	100
Arizona[a]	2.52	55.5	50	17.9	50
California	2.72	80.7	50	32.0	100
Colorado	2.53	62.7	50	22.2	50
Connecticut	2.39	77.6	100	26.1	100
Hawaii	2.15	69.0	50	26.6	100
Idaho	2.28	42.9	50	18.4	100
Illinois	2.52	77.6	50	36.0	50
Indiana[a]	2.56	59.9	50	36.5	50
Iowa[a]	2.45	47.7	0	21.4	50
Kansas[a]	2.43	52.1	0	17.5	0
Maine	1.83	51.7	50	19.9	100
Massachusetts	2.17	84.4	50	26.2	50
Michigan	2.80	70.7	100	40.5	100
Minnesota	2.45	54.5	100	32.8	100
Missouri	2.30	61.5	100	35.6	100
Montana	2.55	43.7	100	34.0	100
Nebraska[a]	2.15	46.9	0	18.8	0
Nevada[a]	2.89	57.2	100	29.8	100
New Hampshire	1.82	57.5	0	19.0	50

New Jersey	2.44	86.6	50	31.3	100
New Mexico	2.13	50.2	100	15.8	100
New York	2.38	85.5	0	37.3	100
North Dakota[a]	2.09	26.6	50	14.2	100
Ohio	2.68	70.2	100	35.5	50
Oregon	2.60	53.9	100	32.7	100
Pennsylvania	2.35	70.5	50	37.7	100
Rhode Island	1.94	84.3	100	26.8	100
South Dakota[a]	2.09	33.2	0	10.4	0
Utah[a]	2.59	65.3	50	16.6	50
Vermont	1.89	36.4	0	17.1	100
Washington	2.72	63.2	100	40.3	100
Wisconsin	2.41	57.9	50	32.1	100
Wyoming	2.56	49.8	100	20.4	100
Average	2.41	59.2	58.8	26.8	77.9

[a] Had right-to-work law in 1961.
SOURCES: See table 1.

TABLE 3

SOUTHERN STATES' CONGRESSIONAL VOTES ON SELECTED ISSUES,
1966 AND 1977
(% voting yea)

State	1966—House,[a] to Delete Agricultural Coverage	1966—Senate,[b] to Increase D.C. Coverage	1977—House,[a] to Delete Indexing	1977—House,[a] to Provide Youth Differential
Alabama[c]	100	0	67	71
Arkansas[c]	67	100	75	50
Delaware	0	100	100	100
Florida[c]	67	100	80	67
Georgia[c]	70	100	100	70
Kentucky	71	100	86	43
Louisiana[d]	86	0	75	75
Maryland	25	100	63	37
Mississippi[c]	100	0	100	100
North Carolina[c]	100	100	100	55
Oklahoma	67	100	100	50
South Carolina[c]	100	100	100	33
Tennessee[c]	56	100	75	37
Texas[c]	73	50	67	33
Virginia[c]	100	0	90	90
West Virginia	0	100	50	0
Average (un-weighted)	67.6	71.9	83.0	56.9

[a] A yea vote is anti–minimum wage.
[b] A yea vote is pro–minimum wage.
[c] Had right-to-work law in both years.
[d] Had right-to-work law in 1977 but not in 1966.
SOURCES: *Congressional Quarterly Almanac, 1966* and *1977*.

TABLE 4

NONSOUTHERN STATES' CONGRESSIONAL VOTES ON SELECTED
ISSUES, 1966 AND 1977

(% voting yea)

State	1966—House,[a] to Delete Agricultural Coverage	1966—Senate,[b] to Increase D.C. Coverage	1977—House,[a] to Delete Indexing	1977—House,[a] to Provide Youth Differential
Alaska	0	100	0	0
Arizona[c]	33	100	75	75
California	16	100	39	38
Colorado	0	100	40	75
Connecticut	0	100	17	17
Hawaii	0	100	0	0
Idaho	50	100	100	100
Illinois	38	100	50	54
Indiana	45	100	55	73
Iowa[c]	17	100	33	40
Kansas[c]	80	100	100	80
Maine	0	100	100	100
Massachusetts	0	100	0	17
Michigan	28	100	50	42
Minnesota	29	100	29	50
Missouri	30	100	50	30
Montana	100	100	50	100
Nebraska[c]	67	0	67	67
Nevada[c]	100	100	100	100
New Hampshire	50	100	50	100
New Jersey	7	100	15	31
New Mexico	0	100	100	100
New York	20	100	35	23
North Dakota[c]	50	100	0	100
Ohio	52	100	51	68
Oregon	25	100	50	25
Pennsylvania	28	100	33	37
Rhode Island	0	100	0	0
South Dakota[c]	100	100	100	100
Utah[c]	100	50	100	100
Vermont	100	100	0	100
Washington	14	100	29	43
Wisconsin	40	100	22	67
Wyoming[c]	50	0	0	0
Average (unweighted)	37.3	92.6	45.3	57.4

[a] A yea vote is anti–minimum wage.
[b] A yea vote is pro–minimum wage.
[c] Had right-to-work law in both years.
SOURCES: *Congressional Quarterly Almanac, 1966* and *1977.*

The Overtime Pay Provisions of the
Fair Labor Standards Act

Ronald G. Ehrenberg and Paul L. Schumann

It has long been recognized in the United States that excessive use of overtime hours may be partially responsible for continued high rates of unemployment. For although a large proportion of overtime hours is due to disequilibrium phenomena, such as rush orders, seasonal demand, mechanical failures, and absenteeism, a substantial amount of overtime appears to be regularly scheduled. If even a fraction of this overtime were converted to new full-time jobs, the effect on the unemployment rate might be substantial. In 1977, for example, average weekly overtime in manufacturing was 3.4 hours/employee. If one-fifth of this had been eliminated *and* converted into new full-time jobs, employment levels for production workers would have risen by 1.7 percentage points. As a consequence, proposals for amending the overtime provisions of the Fair Labor Standards Act (FLSA) to restrict the use of overtime, including those that would increase the overtime premium to double time, have been periodically introduced in Congress.

Our paper is a contribution to the debate over the efficacy of such proposals. We begin by providing a brief history of hours-of-work legislation in the United States and discussing a conceptual framework within which the evolution of the legislation can be explained and/or understood. We then trace the growth of the share of nonwage items in total labor cost and of employers' use of overtime hours, and discuss the possible connection between these two trends. We then critically evaluate the available empirical evidence on the relationship between the overtime premium, hours of work, and employment. This section results in an agenda for future research needs, rather than a set of definitive conclusions. Finally, our concluding section discusses the policy implications of our study. Although we believe additional research, some of which we are currently starting to undertake for the Minimum Wage Study Commission, is required before one can fully

NOTE: We are grateful to numerous colleagues at Cornell, and to Solomon Polachek, Gregg Lewis, Finis Welch, and Steven Welch for their comments on an earlier version.

evaluate the wisdom of amending the overtime provisions of the FLSA, a number of general conclusions are presented in this section.

History of Hours-of-Work Legislation in the United States

The earliest forms of hours-of-work legislation in the United States were initiated at the state level, applied to women and children, and had the aim of reducing fatigue and exhaustion.[1] For example, maximum-hours-of-work legislation was introduced in Massachusetts in 1879, where its supporters claimed that long workweeks were exhausting and caused women to grow prematurely old.[2] The first hours laws covering men in the private sector were also at the state level and covered occupations in which long workweeks adversely affected third parties or employees themselves. An 1890 Ohio law limited hours of workers who operated trains in the hope that this would reduce railroad accident rates and protect the traveling public. This law was quickly followed by state laws limiting workweeks in mining to protect miners who were subject to unhealthy and unsafe working conditions.[3]

One may argue that in each of these cases the rationale for the protective labor legislation is that the marginal social cost of longer workweeks exceeded the marginal private cost to employers. In the absence of government intervention these divergencies persisted because low family incomes did not permit many women and children the luxury of turning down jobs with low wages and long hours, because no good alternatives to the railroads existed for long-range travel and railroad passengers were not always accurately informed about railroad employees' workweeks, and because the limited alternative employment opportunities in mining communities (the "company town") often restricted the occupational choice of individuals in those areas. In each case, then, markets failed, in the sense that compensating wage (or price) differentials did not arise to compensate employees (or railroad passengers) for the full risks they incurred because of long hours of work. The case for government intervention was strong; the only real issue was why the legislation took the form of outright restrictions on hours rather than the use of tax or penalty schemes to increase em-

---

[1] John R. Commons and John B. Andrews, *Principles of Labor Legislation* (New York: Harper and Bros., 1920), pp. 242–63; George E. Paulsen, "The Legislative History of the Fair Labor Standards Act" (Ph.D. dissertation, Ohio State University, 1959), pp. 1–10; Orme Phelps, *The Legislative Background of the Fair Labor Standards Act* (Chicago: Chicago University Studies in Business Administration, 1939), p. 4; and U.S. Department of Labor, *Premium Payments for Overtime under the Fair Labor Standards Act* (Washington, D.C., 1967).

[2] Marion Cahill, *Shorter Hours* (New York: Columbia University Press, 1932), pp. 106–7.

[3] Paulsen, "History of FLSA," pp. 14–15.

265

ployers' marginal private cost of longer hours. The well-known preference of Congress and state legislatures for standards rather than tax-subsidy schemes may reflect only the fact that the majority of their members are lawyers who are comfortable with the standards approach.[4]

Although the average workweek in manufacturing had fallen from 51.0 hours in 1909 to 44.2 in 1929, throughout the early 1930s bills were repeatedly introduced into Congress to limit the length of the workweek. While the goal of protecting existing employees from the ills associated with excessive fatigue remained, a second explicit purpose of such legislation was to increase employment by distributing the available work. Ultimately, on June 25, 1938, the Fair Labor Standards Act (FLSA) was enacted. Its overtime provisions established a minimum rate of time-and-a-half of the regular hourly rate for hours worked in excess of 44 per week by covered employees, with the penalty rate beginning after 42 hours in the next year, and 40 hours per week thereafter. (Initial drafts of the legislation established outright prohibitions of long hours. The idea of instituting a penalty for overtime instead apparently was instituted only as a compromise during the late stages of the debate.)[5] In its final form, the act covered less than one-fifth of all employees. Since then, coverage under the overtime provisions of the act has been expanded until now approximately 58 percent of all employees are covered (table 1). The major noncovered categories are supervisory employees, outside salespersons, employees in seasonal industries (including agriculture), state and local government employees, employees in small retail trade establishments, and some household workers.

Once again, the provisions of the act can be rationalized in terms of the divergence between private and social costs. Even if employers and their employees in the 1930s were satisfied with long workweeks, their private calculations ignored the social costs borne by the unemployed. The time-and-a-half rate for overtime can be thought of as a tax to make employers bear the full marginal social cost of their hours decisions; it should serve to reduce the use of overtime hours and, to the extent that the increased costs do not *substantially* reduce total man-hours demanded, stimulate employment.[6] Furthermore, if employees

[4] Allen Kneese and Charles Schultze, *Pollution, Prices, and Public Policy* (Washington, D.C.: Brookings Institution, 1975). A discussion of the standards-versus-tax-subsidy issue is included in Russell F. Settle and Burton Weisbrod, "Governmentally Imposed Standards: Some Normative Aspects," in Ronald G. Ehrenberg, editor, *Research in Labor Economics*, vol. 2 (Greenwich, Conn.: JAI Press, 1978), pp. 159–91.

[5] Paulsen, "History of FLSA," pp. 240–44; Phelps, *Legislative Background*, pp. 4–6; and Jonathan Grossman, "Fair Labor Standards Act of 1938: Maximum Struggle for a Minimum Wage," *Monthly Labor Review* 101 (June 1979): 22–30.

[6] As with any other tax designed to correct an externality, such as an effluent tax designed to reduce the emission of pollutants, the time-and-a-half rate for overtime should lead to

were not satisfied with long workweeks during the 1930s but, because of market imperfections, did *not* have the freedom to choose employment with employers who offered shorter workweeks, the direct payment of the tax to employees who worked longer workweeks can be understood as an attempt to remedy this imperfection. We shall discuss this point in more detail when we evaluate proposals to modify the overtime provisions of the FLSA.[7]

The Employment-Hours Trade-off: The Growth of Fringe Benefits and Overtime Hours

Although coverage under the overtime pay provisions of the FLSA has increased substantially over the last forty years, the premium itself has remained constant at time and a half. Periodically proposals have been introduced in Congress to raise the premium to double time.[8] Supporters of the increase argue that even though unemployment remains a pressing national problem, the use of overtime hours has increased in recent years. Moreover, the deterrent effect of the overtime premium has been weakened since enactment of the FLSA because of the growing share of hiring and training costs, fringe benefits, and government-mandated insurance premiums in total compensation. Many of these costs (such as vacation pay, holiday pay, sick leave, hiring costs) are "quasi-fixed" or employee-related, rather than hours-related; that is, they do not vary with overtime hours of work. An increase in these costs reduces employers' marginal costs of working their existing work forces overtime relative to their costs of hiring new employees.[9] It is claimed that the

---

a reduction in output and *some* decline in total man-hours demanded. One cannot, however, evaluate the tax as being "bad" simply because output is lower, as Sol Polachek suggested in his conference comments; that is a necessary consequence of the attempt to correct the externality.

[7] Literally hundreds of court decisions handed down since the FLSA was enacted confirm that Congress had the dual intent of (a) inducing employers to reduce hours of work *and* increase employment, and (b) compensating employees for the "burden" of long workweeks. See, for example, Walling v. Youngerman-Reynolds Hardwood Co., Ala. 1945, 65 S.Ct. 1242, 1250, 325 U.S. 419, 89 L. Ed. 1705, rehearing denied 66 S.Ct. 12, 326 U.S. 804, 90 L. Ed. 489.

[8] The most recent attempt was made by Congressman John Conyers in H.R. 1784, introduced into Congress on February 1, 1979.

[9] The formal theory of how these quasi-fixed costs influence employers' employment and hours decisions is detailed in a number of studies. See, for example, Ronald G. Ehrenberg, *Fringe Benefits and Overtime Behavior* (Lexington, Mass.: D.C. Heath, 1971), pp. 5–47; idem, "Heterogeneous Labor, the Internal Labor Market, and the Employment-Hours Decision," *Journal of Economic Theory* 3 (March 1971): 85–104; Walter Oi, "Labor as a Quasi-Fixed Factor of Production," *Journal of Political Economy* 70 (October 1962): 535–55; Sherwin Rosen, "Short-Run Employment Variations in Class I Railroads," *Econometrica* 36 (July/October 1968): 511–29; and idem, "The Supply of Work Schedules and Employment," in National Commission for Employment Policy, *Work Time and Employment*, Special Report no. 28 (Washington, D.C., 1978), pp. 145–74.

TABLE 1

WAGE AND SALARY WORKERS AND THEIR OVERTIME COVERAGE, SEPTEMBER 1977

(in thousands of workers)

Industry	Total	Executive, Administrative, and Professional[a]	Outside Sales[a]	Non-supervisory[b]	Non-supervisory Subject to Overtime	Percentage of Non-supervisory Subject to Overtime[c]	Percentage of Total Subject to Overtime[d]
All	87,164	16,363	2,111	68,690	50,586	74	58
Private sector	71,647	10,137	2,111	59,399	48,085	81	67
Agriculture	1,505	74	0	1,431	0	0	0
Mining	862	99	0	763	751	98	87
Contract construction	4,157	417	3	3,737	3,682	99	89
Manufacturing	19,941	2,323	403	17,215	16,913	98	85
Transportation and public utilities	4,653	529	6	4,118	2,454	60	53
Wholesale trade	4,428	629	750	3,049	2,930	96	66
Retail trade	14,035	1,390	127	12,518	8,885	71	63
Finance, insurance, and real estate	4,554	658	791	3,105	2,968	96	65
Service industries	15,618	4,018	31	11,569	8,412	73	54
Private household	1,894	0	0	1,894	1,090	58	58

Public sector	15,517	6,226	0	9,291	2,501	27	16
Federal	2,717	509	0	2,208	2,156	98	79
State and local government	12,800	5,717	0	7,083	345	5	3

a Section 13(a)(1) of the FLSA includes among exempt covered employees "any employee employed in a bona fide executive, administrative, or professional capacity (including any employee employed in the capacity of academic administrative personnel or teacher in elementary or secondary schools) or in the capacity of outside salesmen."

b Excluding outside sales workers.

c Provisions of FLSA (5)/(4)·100.

d Provisions of FLSA (5)/(1)·100.

SOURCE: U.S. Department of Labor, Employment Standards Administration, *Minimum Wage and Maximum Hours Standards under the Fair Labor Standards Act* (Washington, D.C., October 1978), table 11.

269

growth of these items has been at least partially responsible for the increase in overtime and that an increase in the overtime premium is required to offset this adverse effect.

Data on average weekly overtime hours for manufacturing industries have been collected and published by the Bureau of Labor Statistics (BLS) since 1956. Using annual data for all manufacturing, durable manufacturing, and nondurable manufacturing industries, we have estimated equations in which weekly overtime hours were specified to be a function of a time trend and the growth in real gross national product (GNP), the latter to control for cyclical factors (table 2). These equations indicate that after controlling for cyclical factors and autocorrelation in the residuals, average weekly overtime hours have increased by 0.028 to 0.029 hours each year.[10] This implies that average weekly overtime hours have increased by 0.616 hours over the twenty-two-year period covered by our sample. *If all* of this increase in overtime had been converted to full-time (forty hours/week) jobs, employment in manufacturing would have been 1.5 percent higher in 1977.[11]

Could this increase in the use of overtime have been due to the increase in quasi-fixed nonwage costs, which increased the marginal cost of new employees relative to that of overtime hours? The answer depends upon both the magnitude of the increase in quasi-fixed costs and the empirical relationship existing among these costs, employment, and overtime hours. Empirical evidence on the increase in fringe benefits is quite abundant. For example, Department of Commerce data for the nation as a whole (table 3) show that forms of compensation other than wages and salaries (supplements) rose from 6.2 percent of total compensation in 1956 to 14.7 percent in 1977. These data understate the importance of nonwage items in total compensation because they include holiday, vacation, and sick pay as wages. A more comprehensive measure, although for a more limited sample, comes from the biennial U.S. Chamber of Commerce Survey of Manufacturing Establishments. These data show that total fringe benefits as a percentage of payroll rose from 20.3 percent to 37.3 percent during the 1957–1977 period (table 4). Both

---

[10] Only for the nondurable manufacturing equation, however, is the estimated annual increase statistically significantly different from zero. Moreover, as Sol Polachek noted in his conference comments, when a quadratic trend term is added to the equation, one observes that the upward drift in overtime hours appeared to cease sometime between 1971 and 1973. This evidence should therefore be considered only suggestive. We should stress, however, that in any case evidence on the trend in overtime hours is *not* central to our concern in the next section: whether an increase in the overtime premium would lead to a reduction in overtime hours *and* an increase in employment.

[11] The percentage change in employment is (0.616/40)(100). We should caution, of course, that while our evidence does provide some tentative support for the view that the use of overtime has been increasing, the potential employment increase if overtime had not increased is a hypothetical maximum figure.

TABLE 2

DETERMINANTS OF AVERAGE WEEKLY OVERTIME HOURS, ANNUAL DATA, 1956–1977

Statistical Determinant	All Manufacturing		Durable Manufacturing		Nondurable Manufacturing	
Ordinary least squares						
Time trend	.045*	.036*	.048*	.037*	.040*	.034*
	(.014)	(.012)	(.019)	(.017)	(.009)	(.008)
Change in real GNP		.010*		.012*		.006*
		(.003)		(.004)		(.002)
R^2	.317	.532	.236	.456	.472	.626
Durbin-Watson	.940	.721	.985	.830	.803	.520
Corrected for auto-correlation						
Time trend	.041**	.028	.044	.028	.038*	.029*
	(.023)	(.020)	(.029)	(.026)	(.015)	(.014)
Change in real GNP		.009*		.011*		.005*
		(.002)		(.003)		(.001)
Average weekly overtime hours						
1956	2.8		3.0		2.4	
1957	2.3		2.4		2.2	
1958	2.0		1.9		2.2	
1959	2.7		2.7		2.7	
1960	2.4		2.4		2.5	
1961	2.4		2.3		2.5	
1962	2.8		2.8		2.7	
1963	2.8		2.9		2.7	
1964	3.1		3.3		2.9	
1965	3.6		3.9		3.2	
1966	3.9		4.3		3.4	
1967	3.4		3.5		3.1	
1968	3.6		3.8		3.3	
1969	3.6		3.8		3.4	
1970	3.0		3.0		3.0	
1971	2.9		2.8		3.0	
1972	3.5		3.6		3.3	
1973	3.8		4.1		3.4	
1974	3.2		3.4		3.0	
1975	2.6		2.5		2.7	
1976	3.1		3.1		3.0	
1977	3.4		3.6		3.1	

NOTES: Asterisk (double asterisk) indicates coefficient statistically different from zero at the .05 (.10) level of significance, two-tail test. Time trend equals 1 in 1956. Standard errors are in parentheses.
SOURCE: U.S. Department of Labor, *1979 Employment and Training Report of the President* (Washington, D.C., 1979).

TABLE 3

COMPENSATION OF EMPLOYEES, 1956–1977
(in millions of constant 1972 dollars)

Year	Total	Wages and Salaries	Supplements	Ratio of Supplements to Total (percent)
1956	243.5	228.3	15.2	6.2
1957	256.5	239.3	17.2	6.7
1958	258.2	240.5	17.7	6.9
1959	279.6	258.9	20.6	7.4
1960	294.9	271.9	23.0	7.8
1961	303.6	279.5	24.1	7.9
1962	325.1	298.0	27.1	8.3
1963	342.9	313.4	29.5	8.6
1964	368.0	336.1	31.8	8.6
1965	396.5	362.0	34.5	8.7
1966	439.3	398.4	40.9	9.3
1967	471.9	427.5	44.4	9.4
1968	519.8	469.5	50.3	9.7
1969	571.4	514.6	56.8	9.9
1970	609.2	546.5	62.7	10.3
1971	650.3	580.0	70.3	10.8
1972	715.1	633.8	81.4	11.4
1973	797.7	700.9	96.8	12.1
1974	873.0	763.1	110.0	12.6
1975	931.1	805.9	125.2	13.4
1976	1,036.8	890.1	146.7	14.1
1977	1,153.4	983.6	169.8	14.7

NOTE: "Compensation of employees" is the income accruing to employees as remuneration for their work. "Wages and salaries" consist of the monetary remuneration of employees, including the compensation of corporate officers, commissions, tips, and bonuses, and of payments in kind, which represent income to the recipients. "Supplements" to wages and salaries are employer contributions for social insurance and other labor income. Employer contributions for social insurance comprise employer payments under old-age, survivors, disability, and hospital insurance, state unemployment insurance, railroad retirement and unemployment insurance, government retirement, and a few other minor social insurance programs. Other labor income includes employer contributions to private pension, health, unemployment, and welfare and privately administered workers' compensation funds; compensation for injuries; and directors' fees.

SOURCES: U.S. Department of Commerce, Bureau of Economic Analysis, *Business Statistics, 1975*, p. 6; and U.S. Department of Commerce, Bureau of Economic Analysis, *Survey of Current Business*, January 1979, p. S–2.

TABLE 4

FRINGE BENEFITS AS A PERCENTAGE OF PAYROLL IN
MANUFACTURING, 1957–1977

Year	Legally Required Payments (employer's share)	Pensions, Insurance	Paid Rest	Pay for Time Not Worked	Other Items	Total Fringe Benefits
1957	4.1	5.8	2.4	6.5	1.5	20.3
1959	4.5	6.1	2.7	6.7	1.6	21.6
1961	5.5	6.8	2.8	7.2	1.3	23.6
1963	5.9	6.7	2.9	7.3	1.4	24.2
1965	5.3	6.7	2.7	7.2	1.7	23.6
1967	6.4	7.0	3.0	7.3	1.9	25.6
1969	6.8	7.6	3.1	7.8	1.7	27.0
1971	6.9	9.9	3.5	8.6	1.7	30.6
1973	8.3	10.2	3.5	8.5	1.5	32.0
1975	8.8	11.6	3.7	10.1	1.9	36.1
1977	9.3	12.9	3.6	9.2	2.3	37.3

SOURCE: U.S. Chamber of Commerce, *Fringe Benefits and Employee Benefits* (various issues).

data sets indicate, then, an approximate doubling of the share of fringe benefits in total compensation. The increase is due both to an increase in employers' legally required insurance payments (social security, unemployment insurance, workers' compensation, etc.) and to the favorable tax treatment of many fringe benefits under the personal income and payroll tax provisions, which encourage employers to provide benefits rather than higher wages.

(The BLS also collects data on employers' expenditure for employee compensation, but their data span a shorter number of years. They tell a similar story, however. For example, between 1959 and 1974, straight-time and premium pay in manufacturing fell from 85.4 to 76.9 percent of total compensation.)[12]

We should caution, however, that not all nonwage forms of compensation are independent of employees' hours of work; those that vary with hours do *not* encourage the substitution of hours for employment. Over time, some forms have become "more" related to hours. For example, between 1960 and 1978 the Old-Age, Survivors, Disability,

[12] U.S. Department of Labor, Bureau of Labor Statistics, *1977 Handbook of Labor Statistics* (Washington, D.C., 1977), table 108.; and idem, *1973 Handbook of Labor Statistics* (Washington, D.C., 1973), table 118.

and Health Insurance (OASDHI) maximum taxable earnings rose from $4,800 to $17,700. This increase caused the fraction of total covered employees with earnings at or above the maximum taxable earnings level to fall from 0.28 at the start of the period to 0.10 in 1977. The fraction of employees for whom the OASDHI tax could be considered not to be related to hours declined by over 50 percent. Focusing on the growth of nonwage compensation costs may well overstate the increasing incentives employers have to substitute overtime hours for additional employment.

The Overtime Pay Premium, Hours of Work, and Employment: Empirical Evidence

Attempts to estimate the effects of raising the overtime premium from time and a half to double time have exploited the fact that although the overtime premium is fixed (legislatively) at a point in time, its value relative to weekly "quasi-fixed" costs per employee varies substantially among establishments because the level of nonwage benefits varies among establishments. One of us published the first major published study on the subject; this was followed by replications and extensions by Nussbaum and Wise, and Solnick and Swimmer.[13] These studies used individual establishment data from the 1966, 1968, 1970, 1972, and 1974 BLS "Employer Expenditure for Employee Compensation" surveys and estimated variants of equations of the form

$$OT = a_0 + a_1R + a_2X \qquad (1)$$

where OT is annual overtime hours per employee, R is the ratio of *measured* weekly quasi-fixed nonwage labor costs per employee to the overtime wage rate, and X is a vector of other variables expected to influence establishments' use of overtime.

All of these studies confirm that, across establishments, a strong positive relationship exists between the use of overtime hours and the ratio of weekly nonwage labor costs per employee to the overtime wage rate (table 5). From these studies one can simulate what the effect of

---

[13] Ehrenberg, *Fringe Benefits*; idem, "The Impact of the Overtime Premium on Employment and Hours in U.S. Industry," *Western Economic Journal* 9 (June 1971); Joyce Nussbaum and Donald Wise, "The Employment Impact of the Overtime Provisions of the F.L.S.A." (Final Report, U.S. Department of Labor, Contract J–9–E–6–0105, 1977); idem, "The Overtime Pay Premium and Unemployment," in *Work Time and Employment*; Loren Solnick and Gene Swimmer, "Overtime and Fringe Benefits—a Simultaneous Equations Approach" (mimeographed, 1978); and Susan Van Atta, "An Analysis of Overtime Hours for Production Workers in Manufacturing Industries, 1957–1965" (Ph.D. diss., University of California, Berkeley, 1967).

TABLE 5

ESTIMATED COEFFICIENTS OF THE WEEKLY NONWAGE LABOR COST
DIVIDED BY THE OVERTIME WAGE RATE VARIABLE, VARIOUS
STUDIES

Industry	Ehrenberg (1971)	Solnick & Swimmer I (1978)	Solnick & Swimmer II (1978)	Nussbaum & Wise (1977)
Manufacturing		6.73*	17.33*	
Ordnance				
Food	26.398*			15.68*
Tobacco				
Textile	29.898*			14.03*
Apparel	5.137*			19.63*
Lumber	9.836			35.53*
Furniture	21.390			13.98
Paper	85.758*			42.62*
Printing	25.793*			7.59
Chemicals	25.805*			16.43*
Petroleum				
Rubber	40.429*			9.84
Leather				
Stone-clay-glass	11.029			30.08*
Primary metals	19.727*			29.53*
Fabricated metals	26.392*	23.53*		
Machinery	33.695*		19.71*	
Electric equipment	32.481*		13.16*	
Transportation equipment	4.121			19.00*
Instruments				−2.69
Miscellaneous manufacturing	63.146*			
Mining	0.343	0.00	47.62*	
Construction	30.959*	4.23	5.08*	
Transportation	42.888*	−2.50	8.59	
Utilities	7.899			
Wholesale trade	39.093*	11.05*	59.41*	
Retail trade	35.101*			
Finance, insurance and real estate	14.673	3.41	−10.05	
Services	40.370*	5.91*	41.18*	

NOTE: Asterisk indicates coefficient statistically different from zero at the .05 level of significance.
SOURCES: Ehrenberg, *Fringe Benefits*, table 3; Solnick and Swimmer, "Overtime and Fringe Benefits," table 2 (for estimate I) and table 3 (for estimate II); Nussbaum and Wise, "Employment Impact," table 4.3.

increasing the overtime premium would be on overtime hours if one assumes that employers fully comply with the legislation and that the change in the premium affects neither straight-time wage rates nor the levels of weekly quasi-fixed nonwage labor costs. Moreover, if one also assumes that all of the reduction in overtime would be converted to new full-time positions, one can simulate what the effect on the employment level would be. We have tabulated the implied results from such simulations in table 6; they suggest maximum employment increases in the range of 0.3 to 4.0 percent.[14]

These estimates clearly *overstate* the increase in the number of full-time employment positions that would go initially to *nonemployed* individuals. They assume wage elasticities of demand to be zero; they ignore the possibility of increased moonlighting by existing employees; they ignore problems relating to skill mismatches and indivisibilities; they assume full compliance with the legislation; and they ignore the possibility that the levels or rates of growth of straight-time wages and fringe benefits might be adjusted downward. Each of these factors will reduce the employment creation effects of an increase in the overtime premium; let us examine current knowledge of each factor.

---

[14] These estimates are derived as follows: The decrease in annual overtime hours per employee is given from (1) by $\Delta OT = a_1 \Delta R$ where ΔR is the change in R caused by the increase in the premium. If total man-hours demanded remained constant *and* new full-time positions averaging 2,000 hours a year were created, the total number of new jobs created in an industry would be $\Delta E = (-\Delta OT/2,000)E$, where E is the initial industry employment level. In percentage terms, $\%\Delta E = (\Delta E/E)100 = (-\Delta OT)/20$. So, for example, since $\Delta OT = -32$ in Ehrenberg (*Fringe Benefits*), the resulting simulated $\%\Delta E$ was 1.6 percent.

We must caution, however, that a number of statistical problems associated with the studies cause us to conclude that their results should be considered extremely tentative. First, none took account of the fact that reported overtime hours could not be negative and that some establishments use zero overtime. Use of ordinary least squares leads to biased estimates under these circumstances; an estimation method such as Tobit analysis is required.

Second, it may be argued that to the extent that overtime hours are perceived as being unavoidable by employers, they can try to reduce their overtime costs, and total labor costs, by offering their employees compensation packages which substitute fringes for higher straight-time wages. If this occurs, a positive correlation would be induced between R and OT; however, the direction of causation would run from OT to R. To estimate the effect of R on OT accurately requires a simultaneous equations approach. Only Solnick and Swimmer have attempted to do this; however, their specification of the nonwage labor cost/overtime wage rate (R) equation was seriously incomplete.

As a final note, Nussbaum and Wise did estimate employment effects directly using mean values of industry variables as the units of observation. (Nussbaum and Wise, "Employment Impact.") We have serious doubts both about the validity of such inter-industry equations and their particular specification. Furthermore, the underlying regression coefficients upon which their estimates were based were all statistically insignificant. Thus, very little confidence should be placed in the precision of their 2.0 percent estimate (table 6).

TABLE 6

UPPER-BOUND ESTIMATES OF THE CHANGES IN FULL-TIME
EMPLOYMENT FROM INCREASING THE OVERTIME PREMIUM FROM
TIME AND A HALF TO DOUBLE TIME, VARIOUS STUDIES

Study	Group	Maximum Absolute Change	Maximum Percentage Change
Ehrenberg (1971)	1966 manufacturing production workers	218,500	1.6
Nussbaum and Wise (1977)	1968 manufacturing production workers	491,400	3.7
	1970 manufacturing production workers	487,700	3.7
	1972 manufacturing production workers	361,900	2.8
	1974 manufacturing production workers	549,700	4.0
	1968–1974 pooled manufacturing inter-industry data employment equation estimated directly	320,000	2.0
Solnick and Swimmer (1978)	1972 private nonfarm nonsupervisory workers (OLS[a] analysis)	159,264	0.3
	1972 private nonfarm nonsupervisory workers (3SLS[b] analysis)	1,521,664	3.1

[a] Ordinary least squares.
[b] Three-stage least squares.
SOURCES: Ehrenberg, "Impact of Overtime Premium," table 3; Nussbaum and Wise, "Employment Impact," tables 4.11A, 4.11B, 4.11C, and 4.11; and Solnick and Swimmer, "Overtime and Fringe Benefits," table 5.

Nonzero Wage Elasticities. The estimates in table 6 assume that the demand for *man-hours* is completely inelastic. That is, they ignore the fact that an increase in the overtime premium raises the average cost per man-hour of labor; this may induce a shift to more capital-intensive methods of production and, to the extent that the cost increase is passed on to consumers in the form of higher prices, a reduction in the quantity of output demanded. Both the substitution and the scale effect should

277

lead to a decline in the number of man-hours employed by employers.

We can roughly estimate the magnitude of these effects. Daniel Hamermesh has surveyed time-series estimates of the wage elasticity of demand for labor and has concluded that a reasonable estimate for the long-run (four-quarters) elasticity is –0.3.[15] Suppose that before an increase in overtime premium the standard workweek was forty hours and employees averaged three hours of overtime per week. Suppose also that the increase in the overtime premium induced a reduction of 1.2 hours of overtime per week; the latter figure would lead to a 3 percent increase in full-time employment *if* total man-hours remained constant. The reduction in overtime, coupled with the increase in the premium to double time, would cause the average hourly (including overtime) wage rate to rise by about 0.8 percent.[16] This would imply a 0.24 percent decline in total man-hours and, since hours had declined by 2.8 percent, an increase in employment of roughly 2.56 percent. Thus, the estimated maximum number of new jobs created falls by about 0.5 percentage points if one accounts for nonzero wage elasticities of demand.[17] Of course, if a larger wage elasticity is more appropriate, the estimate of employment gain would be reduced accordingly.

Moonlighting. The employment gain estimates cited in table 6 also neglect supply-side responses of currently employed workers, who would simultaneously face an increase in the overtime premium and a reduction in their hours of work. One possible response is increased moonlighting at part-time jobs; this would further reduce the creation of new jobs for the unemployed.

Previous investigators have discounted the possibility that increased moonlighting would be a serious problem.[18] Among the evidence relevant to this point is that there is currently very little moonlighting in the economy (less than 5 percent of all employed workers had second jobs in 1978), many moonlighters are individuals whose primary jobs

---

[15] Daniel Hamermesh, "Econometric Studies of Labor Demand and Their Implications for Policy," *Journal of Human Resources* (Fall 1976): 507–25. It should be noted that virtually all of the studies he cites use man-hours as the measure of labor and fail to include nonwage labor costs in their analyses.

[16] The percentage wage gain is given by $\{[40W + (2.0)(1.8)W]/41.8\}/\{[40W + (1.5)(3.0)W]/43\}$.

[17] As Solomon Polachek notes in his conference comments, there is a certain inconsistency in the procedure we have used here. It clearly would be preferable to estimate hours/man *and* employment level equations together as part of a simultaneous system and then to derive the estimated employment effects directly from this system. Unfortunately, there exists no individual establishment data set which permits this, and as we noted in footnote 14, we are highly suspicious of the validity of the one interindustry study that attempted to do so.

[18] See Department of Labor, *Premium Payments for Overtime.*

are in agriculture, and moonlighters tend to be employed in lower skill-level positions than their primary jobs; the latter reduces the attractiveness of moonlighting as a substitute for overtime.[19]

We would caution, however, that the small number of individuals currently holding second jobs is not indicative of the potential expansion in moonlighting that might occur if overtime hours were severely restricted. Between 1973 and 1978, roughly 27 percent of all wage and salary workers with only one job regularly worked more than forty hours a week.[20] If overtime were restricted, *many* of them might seek second jobs. Clearly, evidence on the overtime-moonlighting relationship is required.

Two recent studies have dealt with the effect of weekly hours of work on the moonlighting decision.[21] Using their data, we can simulate the effects of a simultaneous reduction in overtime hours *and* increase in the overtime premium on both the probability of an individual's moonlighting and his or her average hours on the second job if moonlighting does occur. We have conducted such a simulation using Shishko and Rostker's estimates, and our analyses suggest that a simultaneous reduction in overtime hours of two hours per week and increase in the overtime premium to double time would lead to an increase of approximately 6 percent in moonlighting hours.[22] Given that moonlighting is

---

[19] See Carl Rosenfeld, "Multiple Jobholding Holds Steady in 1978," *Monthly Labor Review* 102 (February 1979): 59–61; and Scott Brown, "Moonlighting Increases Sharply in 1977," *Monthly Labor Review* 101 (January 1978): 27–30, for data on multiple job holding. See Jeffrey Perloff and Michael Wachter, "Work Sharing, Unemployment, and the Rate of Economic Growth," in *Work Time and Employment,* for analyses of the likely effects of moonlighting on work-sharing arrangements.

[20] George D. Stamas, "Long Hours and Premium Pay, May 1978," *Monthly Labor Review* 102 (May 1979): 41–45.

[21] Robert Shishko and Bernard Rostker, "The Economics of Multiple Job Holding," *American Economic Review* 66 (June 1976): 298–308; and John F. Connell, "Multiple Job Holding and Marginal Tax Rates," *National Tax Journal* 32 (March 1979).

[22] Details of our calculations are found in the appendix. We should note that neither of the published studies cited above is completely satisfactory in our view. They both assume that overtime hours of work on individuals' primary jobs are solely employer determined and that individuals do not have the right to refuse overtime. In fact, data from the *1977 Quality of Employment Survey,* conducted by the Michigan Survey Research Center for the U.S. Department of Labor, indicate that for 44 percent of the workers in the sample who regularly worked overtime, it was "mostly up to the worker whether he or she works overtime" and for another 29 percent it was "mostly up to the employer, but the worker can refuse without penalty." Indeed, only for 16 percent was the decision solely up to the employer and could the worker not refuse overtime without a penalty (Robert Quinn and Graham Staines, *The 1977 Quality of Employment Survey: Descriptive Statistics* [Ann Arbor, Mich., 1977], pp. 90–91).

While these data may overstate the freedom that individual workers actually have in choosing overtime hours, they do suggest that the relationship between overtime hours and moonlighting is much more complicated than the models used in previous research suggest. Therefore, our estimate of the likely increase in moonlighting that would result from an increase in the overtime premium should be considered extremely tentative.

in any case infrequent, our crude calculation suggests that increased moonlighting is unlikely to be a substantial deterrent to the employment creation effects of an increase in the overtime premium.

The Skill Distributions of the Unemployed and Those Who Work Overtime. The estimates of maximum employment gain cited in table 6 assume that the skill distributions of the unemployed and those who work overtime are sufficiently similar to permit all of the reduction in overtime to be converted into new full-time employment. That is, they assume that the skill mix of the unemployed does *not* constrain employers' employment-hours decisions.

Data are available on the occupational distributions of both the experienced unemployed and those working overtime for premium pay. We have tabulated these data for 1978 in table 7. At first glance, these data do not suggest that at the aggregate *one-digit* occupational level skill mismatches are likely to limit employment/hours substitution. Only for craftsmen and kindred workers and transportation operatives are the number of experienced unemployed in an occupation as low as 30 percent of the number working overtime (column 5). Since even the most optimistic estimates in table 6 suggests a maximum employment effect of 4 percent, one is tempted to conclude that the "skill-mix" problem is not a serious constraint.

Although these data are suggestive, one should not place too much faith in this conclusion. The use of aggregate one-digit occupational data may obscure more than it reveals. The range of narrow occupational categories within each broad category is enormous; for example, the craftsmen category includes bakers, carpenters, tailors, and stationary engineers. To draw any meaningful conclusions about potential "skill-mix" bottlenecks requires that analyses be performed at a more detailed occupational level. Moreover, the relevant question is how these narrowly defined skill distributions contrast at the local labor market level. Until such analyses are undertaken, one must remain agnostic about the likely biases due to the "mismatch" problem.

Indivisibilities. The maximum employment gain estimates ignore two types of indivisibilities. On the one hand, there are indivisibilities associated with an integrated team production process. Specialization and division of labor within an enterprise may give rise to time complementarities among workers and between workers and capital that prevent the substitution of additional employment for hours.[23] For example, a firm in a continuous process industry may regularly work its existing work force an average of two hours a week overtime by scheduling three

[23] Rosen, "Supply of Work Schedules," pp. 145–75.

TABLE 7

OVERTIME HOURS AND UNEMPLOYMENT, BY OCCUPATION, 1978

	Total Overtime Workers[a] (in thousands)	Total Unem-ployed	Share of Overtime Workers	Share of Unem-ployed	Ratio of Unem-ployed to Overtime Workers[b]
All occupations	8,141	6,047	—	—	0.74
White collar	2,412	1,717	0.30	0.28	0.72
Professional and techni-cal	676	381	0.08	0.06	0.56
Managers and administra-tors	449	214	0.06	0.04	0.48
Sales	201	256	0.03	0.04	1.27
Clerical	1,087	866	0.13	0.14	0.80
Blue collar	5,152	2,323	0.63	0.38	0.45
Craft and kindred	2,099	603	0.26	0.10	0.29
Operatives	1,908	960	0.23	0.16	0.50
Transpor-tation oper-atives	617	195	0.08	0.03	0.32
Nonfarm la-borers	527	566	0.06	0.09	1.07
Service workers	540	1,029	0.07	0.17	1.91
Farm workers	33	110	0.00	0.02	3.33
No previous expe-rience (new en-trants)	—	868	—	0.14	—

[a] Number of full-time wage and salary workers who worked forty-one hours or more and received premium pay in May 1978.
[b] Total unemployed divided by number working overtime in the occupation (column 2/ column 1).
SOURCES: Stamas, "Long Hours and Premium Pay," table 3, p. 43; and U.S. Bureau of Labor Statistics, *Employment and Earnings*, January 1979, table 11.

shifts of forty hours and one of forty-eight (24 × 7 = 168 hours). If men/machine ratios are relatively fixed, at least in the short run, it would be difficult to substitute new *full-time* employment for hours in such an industry.

On the other hand, the employment estimates also ignore indivisibilities associated with establishment size. While a large establishment *may* have the option of substituting one new full-time employee for twenty employees who each work two hours/week overtime, small establishments with only a few employees working overtime may not face such options. Following this line of reasoning, an increase in the overtime premium might induce a substitution of additional employment for overtime hours in large establishments; however, indivisibilities might prevent such substitutions in smaller establishments and result in those establishments' being placed at a relative cost disadvantage. *If* this were the likely outcome, one might consider making any increase in the overtime premium applicable only to establishments above a minimum size; historically there have been size class exemptions under various provisions of the FLSA for similar reasons.[24]

One of us has, in fact, attempted to ascertain if the relationship between the use of overtime hours and the ratio of quasi-fixed nonwage costs to the overtime wage rate does vary across size classes of establishments.[25] For the *nonmanufacturing* industries, the relationship *was* fairly stable across all size classes of establishments within each major nonmanufacturing industry; small establishments appeared to face the same employment-hours trade-off as did large establishments.[26] The results for the manufacturing sector were quite different, however. For these industries, the marginal effect of an increase in the overtime premium on hours *did* vary across size classes of establishments within each two-digit industry. Moreover, there was no consistent pattern across industries in the way the magnitude and the statistical significance of the effect varied with establishment size. Indeed, in several cases, it was the *smallest* size classes of establishments for which the largest marginal effects were observed. Since the magnitude and statistical significance of the relationship between the use of overtime hours and the ratio of quasi-fixed nonwage costs to the overtime wage rate does not appear to vary across size classes of establishments in any systematic way across manufacturing industries, it would *not* appear reasonable to institute a set of size class exemptions for any increase in the overtime premium.[27]

Compliance with the Overtime Pay Provisions. An additional reason why

---

[24] Exemptions for reason of size have declined over time.

[25] See Ehrenberg, *Fringe Benefits*, chaps. 5 and 6.

[26] In that study, establishments were grouped into eight size classes: fewer than 20 employees; 20–49; 50–99; 100–249; 250–499; 500–999; 1,000–2,499; and 2,500 or more employees.

[27] It is possible that the sample sizes used in the manufacturing industry analyses reported in Ehrenberg, *Fringe Benefits*, were too small (an average of 60 establishments per two-digit industry as compared to an average of 150 in each nonmanufacturing industry) to estimate precisely how the effects varied with establishment size. This is another area in which more research is needed.

the estimates presented in table 6 may *overstate* the magnitude of the increase in employment that would result from an increase in the overtime premium to double time relates to the issue of compliance with the overtime provisions of the FLSA. Although analyses of the effects of labor market legislation typically assume that legislation is fully complied with, noncompliance is always a potential problem.[28] Since an increase in the overtime premium would increase the amount employers save by *not* complying with the legislation, such an increase may well lead to a reduced compliance rate. This would moderate the actual decline in overtime hours and further reduce the positive employment effects of the legislation.

A number of data sources provide some information on compliance with overtime legislation. A U.S. Department of Labor compliance survey conducted in 1965 indicated that 30 percent of establishments in which overtime was worked were in violation of the overtime provisions of the FLSA and 5.9 percent of the employees working overtime were not paid in accordance with the overtime provisions (see table 8). More recently, Labor Department investigations in FY 1977 of complaints of violations under the FLSA found a greater dollar volume of violations of the overtime pay provisions than they did of the minimum wage provisions.[29] Finally, data from the annual May supplements to the *Current Population Surveys* indicate that between 1973 and 1978 less than 43 percent of full-time wage and salary workers who worked forty-one or more hours a week at one job reported receiving premium pay.[30] While many of these individuals may work in noncovered employment, these data do suggest that noncompliance with the overtime premium provisions may be a serious problem.[31]

Knowledge of the correlates of noncompliance is important for policy makers. Such information can serve as a guide to the allocation of the limited resources the government has to ensure compliance. Moreover, if noncompliance is found to be widespread, policy makers may decide to push for an increase in the resources devoted to compliance investigations and also for an increase in the penalties for noncompliance. Finally, information on the relationship between compliance and individuals' wage rates may shed some light on the question whether

---

[28] Orley Ashenfelter and Robert S. Smith, "Compliance with the Minimum Wage Law," *Journal of Political Economy* 87 (April 1979): 333–50.

[29] Department of Labor, *Premium Payments for Overtime*. These data refer to fiscal year 1967.

[30] Stamas, "Long Hours and Premium Pay," p. 41.

[31] Of course, as table 1 indicates, only 58 percent of all wage and salary workers are covered by the overtime provisions of the FLSA. Since one may reasonably conjecture that noncovered workers are more likely to work overtime, these data should be considered only suggestive.

TABLE 8
VIOLATION OF OVERTIME PROVISIONS OF THE FLSA, 1965
(percent)

Category	Establishments in Violation[a]	Workers Not Paid in Accordance with Provisions for Overtime Hours[b]
All industries	30	5.9
Manufacturing	26	3.6
Food and tobacco	37	8.1
Textiles, apparel, and leather	24	3.3
Lumber and furniture	30	3.6
Paper, printing, and publishing	25	3.6
Chemicals, petroleum, rubber	27	9.6
Stone, clay, and glass	27	4.4
Metals and metal products	22	1.7
Miscellaneous manufacturing	19	3.1
Nonmanufacturing	32	9.8
Mining	26	7.0
Construction	29	8.2
Transportation, communications, and utilities	17	4.5
Wholesale trade, food and farm products	37	11.7
Wholesale trade, all other	40	15.2
Retail trade	47	10.8
Finance and insurance	27	11.7
Real estate	37	39.2
Business service	29	8.9
Other industries	46	10.7
All regions	30	5.9
Northeast	22	3.3
South	37	9.5
Middle West	29	4.3
West	30	7.6
All sizes of establishments	30	5.9
Fewer than 10 employees	31	24.9
10–19 employees	38	10.9
20–49 employees	33	11.1
50–99 employees	28	4.7
100 or more employees	25	2.6

[a] As a percentage of all establishments in which overtime was worked.
[b] As a percentage of all employees working overtime.
SOURCE: Author's calculations, based on data from U.S. Department of Labor, Wage and Hour and Public Contracts Division, *1965 Compliance Survey* (Washington, D.C., 1966), tables 9, 10, 11, 17, and 18.

284

increasing the overtime premium will lead to a reduction in the compliance rate.

Orley Ashenfelter and Robert S. Smith have recently presented and estimated a model of compliance with the minimum wage.[32] We are now building and estimating a similar model for the overtime pay provisions of the FLSA. Although we have not yet developed a complete formal model, several of the factors likely to influence compliance seem obvious. For example, compliance is probably greater in unionized establishments, in situations where workers have permanent attachment to a firm, in noncompetitive industries where employers can pass cost increases on to consumers in the form of higher prices, in situations where workers have better knowledge of their rights (perhaps higher education levels), and in areas where labor markets are tight (low unemployment) and employers are trying to retain employees. The estimates we ultimately obtain should provide some information on whether noncompliance would seriously reduce the employment-creation effects of an increase in the overtime premium.

Compensating Wage and Fringe Benefit Adjustments. The final problem with the employment gain simulations reported in table 6 is that they ignore the possibility that an increase in the overtime premium may lead to compensating adjustments in straight-time wages or fringe benefits.[33] For example, suppose that firms and their employees are initially in an equilibrium situation in which overtime hours are regularly scheduled. Now from employers' perspectives, one plausible response to a legislated increase in the overtime premium is for them to attempt to reduce the level (or rate of growth) of straight-time wages and fringe benefits. If they are successful and the total compensation of workers for the initial equilibrium level of hours (including overtime) remains the same as it would have been in the absence of the legislated change, one may argue that employers would have no incentive to reduce their use of overtime hours.

This argument is simplistic. From the employer's perspective what is relevant in the determination of overtime hours is not the overall level of labor costs but rather the ratio (R) of quasi-fixed weekly labor costs per employee (F) to the overtime wage rate (WP), the product of the straight-time wage (W) and the overtime premium (P):

$$R = F/WP \qquad (2)$$

---

[32] Ashenfelter and Smith, "Compliance with the Minimum Wage Law."

[33] This section was "provoked" by stimulating comments from Gregg Lewis and Finis Welch. Our conclusions here are strictly our own, however, and do not reflect their views.

The simulations reported in table 6 *assume* that an increase in *P* induces no change in either *W* or *F*. What is certainly true is that if a compensating decline in straight-time wages occurs, the decline in *R* will be *smaller* and the resulting decrease in hours and increase in employment *smaller* in absolute value than the simulations reported in table 6. However, as equation (2) indicates, a compensating decline in the quasi-fixed costs, *F,* would cause the actual decline in *R* to be *larger,* and the resulting decrease in hours and increase in employment would be *larger* in absolute value than the simulations indicate, *ceteris paribus.* Thus, one cannot predict a priori what the direction of the bias is here; it depends upon the extent, if any, to which compensating adjustments occur in both straight-time wages and fringe benefits.

Evidence on the magnitudes, if any, of these compensating adjustments is required before one can conclude that their omission substantially biases the estimated employment gains that would result from increasing the overtime premium. As part of our research, we will attempt to use the *Employer Expenditure for Employee Compensation* data to test whether an inverse relationship exists across establishments between straight-time wage and fringe benefit and the magnitude of the overtime premium, *ceteris paribus.* Unfortunately, cross-section variations in the overtime premium are due both to collective bargaining agreements and to differences in coverage under the FLSA; this may make it difficult to distinguish the effects of legislated and collectively bargained differences in the premium.[34]

Should the Overtime Provisions of the FLSA Be Amended?

Previous studies have demonstrated that, across establishments, a strong positive relationship exists between the use of overtime hours and the ratio of weekly nonwage labor costs per employee to the overtime wage rate. They suggest that an increase in the overtime premium to double time would substantially reduce the use of overtime hours if compliance with the legislation did not change and if straight-time wage rates were not affected. Moreover, to the extent that the reduction in hours could be converted into new full-time employment, such a change in the leg-

---

[34] It seems somewhat ironic that for years researchers have analyzed the employment effects of minimum wage changes without considering the possibility that there might be *none* because firms may respond to an increase in the minimum wage by reducing nonwage forms of compensation for low-wage workers. Of course, one might argue that there is no room for an increase in the minimum wage to reduce other forms of compensation that low-skill workers receive, because such compensation is already close to zero. Nevertheless, we believe that this too remains an empirical issue. For a more detailed discussion of this point, see Walter Wessels, "The Effects of Minimum Wages in the Presence of Fringe Benefits: An Expanded Model," *Economic Inquiry* (forthcoming).

islation has the potential to increase employment by several percentage points. However, whether this increase in employment would actually occur and whether the new jobs would go to currently nonemployed individuals are another matter. We have discussed a number of factors that might reduce the job creation aspects of the proposal; they include nonzero wage elasticities of demand for labor, the possibility of increased moonlighting, the similarity or lack of similarity between the skill distributions of the unemployed and of those who work overtime, indivisibilities associated with integrated team production processes and with establishment size, the possibility of increased noncompliance with the legislation, and the possibility that compensating variations in straight-time wages might occur. We have documented the available evidence on these points wherever possible. In a number of cases the evidence is simply nonexistent or too incomplete to make reasoned judgments, however. We plan to undertake empirical research on several of the areas during the next year and will reserve our final judgments about the wisdom of increasing the overtime premium until our research is completed. Nevertheless, we can offer a number of general conclusions at this time.

First, we would emphasize that even if one ultimately can show that increasing the overtime premium would lead to a substantial increase in employment of individuals who were initially not employed, it does *not* necessarily follow that the policy should be implemented. Presumably other policies, such as the use of marginal employee tax credits, could accomplish the same goal.[35] However, the distribution of costs associated with the two types of legislation would be different. In the former case, the costs would be borne by consumers of products produced in industries where overtime was worked (higher prices), owners of these industries (lower profits), and employees (less overtime, but at higher pay). In the latter case, the costs would be borne primarily by taxpayers and consumers in general, in the form of higher taxes to fund the deficit induced by the tax credit and/or higher rates of inflation. In general, we need benefit/cost analyses of the alternative policies designed to accomplish a given objective (such as these two), not merely evidence that a single policy option will have a postulated impact.

Second, as discussed earlier, an overtime pay premium may be thought of as a tax to make employers bear the full marginal social cost of their hours decisions. In the premium's absence their calculations ignore the costs borne by society because of unemployment. It does *not* necessarily follow, however, that the revenue that would accrue from

---

[35] See Robert Eisner, "Employment Taxes and Subsidies," in *Work Time and Employment*.

any increase in the "tax" should be distributed to employees in the form of higher premium pay for overtime. Indeed, over the years several proposals have suggested that the revenue from any increase in the "tax" on overtime go directly to the unemployed, in the form of contributions either to the unemployment insurance fund and/or to employment and training program budgets.[36] Such proposals make a good deal of sense to us. Unless it can be demonstrated both that market imperfections prevent existing employed workers from freely choosing the length of their workweeks *and* that the existing overtime premium does not fully compensate these workers for the disutility associated with long workweeks, then no increase in the premium paid to employees is justified. One can thus logically be in favor of raising the "tax" paid by employers when they use overtime hours but *not* in favor of raising the overtime premium paid to employees.

Finally, one may more generally ask why the FLSA regulates only two dimensions of the hours relationship, the number of hours after which the premium goes into effect and its level, and whether the legislation should be extended to other dimensions? In their legislation, several European countries require either prior governmental approval for overtime and/or that employees give their consent to working overtime.[37] The bill to amend the FLSA (H.R. 1784), introduced into Congress on February 1, 1979, by Congressman Conyers, contained a similar provision that would prohibit mandatory assignment of overtime.

As noted earlier, a common rationale for many forms of protective labor legislation is that they are attempts to correct for failures of private markets. These failures may occur for a variety of reasons, including market imperfections that limit workers' choices and cause a divergence between private and social costs. Legislation regulating overtime hours can easily be analyzed in this framework, for even if both employers *and* their employees were satisfied with long workweeks and no premium pay for overtime, their private calculations ignore the social costs of unemployment. An overtime premium can be thought of as a tax that attempts to make employers bear the full marginal social cost of their decisions about work hours. Its intent (as with all marginal taxes) is to reduce the use of overtime hours and stimulate employment growth.

---

[36] See Department of Labor, *Premium Payments for Overtime,* Washington, D.C., 1967. More recently Kenneth Morris, representing the United Auto Workers, argued in favor of paying part or all of the additional premium into the unemployment insurance fund. See U.S. Congress, House of Representatives, Subcommittee on Labor Standards of the Committee on Education and Labor, *Hearings on H.R. 1784,* 96th Congress, 2d sess., 1980, pp. 41–49.

[37] See National Board for Prices and Incomes, *Hours of Work, Overtime and Shiftwork,* report no. 161 (London, 1970), pp. 42–49 and supplements, pp. 92–116. Employee consent to overtime is required in both Belgium and the Netherlands.

The payment of the premium directly to *employed* workers is justified in this framework if market imperfections prevent workers from freely choosing their desired workweeks and force them to work "excessively" long hours. The payment is then seen as an attempt to reduce their disutility from long workweeks.

Proposals to legislate prohibitions against mandatory overtime, such as Congressman Conyers's, can be viewed in this context as being based upon the belief that market imperfections persist in the labor market and that the overtime premium does *not* fully compensate employees for mandatory overtime. One may, however, question if markets have failed here. As noted earlier, for only 16 percent of the individuals who worked overtime in the *1977 Quality of Employment Survey* was the overtime hours decision made unilaterally by their employer and was overtime mandatory (in the sense that employees who refused it suffered a penalty).[38] Moreover, roughly 20 percent of employees covered by major collective bargaining agreements in 1976 had explicit provisions in their contracts that gave them the right to refuse overtime (table 9). (Over 50 percent of the workers covered by this provision were in the transportation equipment industry, however.)

To the extent that labor markets are competitive and establishments offer a variety of overtime hours provisions (that is, employer determines, employee determines, penalty for refusal, etc.), an unabashed neoclassical economist would argue that compensating wage differentials should arise. That is, establishments which offered "distasteful" mandatory overtime provisions would have to pay higher *straight-time* wages to attract labor than establishments in which such provisions did not occur. If fully compensating wage differentials exist, no case for legislated prohibitions against mandatory overtime is present.

As with most problems in economics, the case for or against such prohibitions can *not* be decided at the theoretical level. Rather, empirical evidence is needed on the extent to which employees are or are not compensated, in the form of higher straight-time wage rates, for being required to work overtime. Once this evidence is available, policy makers can debate whether the estimated wage premiums are sufficient or a legislated prohibition on mandatory overtime is required. In future research we plan to use data from the *1977 Quality of Employment Survey* to estimate the extent to which the various overtime assignment provisions (employee choice, employer assignment, penalty for refusal, etc.) are currently associated with market wage differentials. We intend to estimate wage equations from these survey data, including the various assignment provisions as explanatory variables. Our analyses will at-

---

[38] See footnote 22 above.

TABLE 9

OVERTIME PROVISIONS IN MAJOR COLLECTIVE BARGAINING
AGREEMENTS, JULY 1, 1976

	Number of Agreements	Workers Covered
Total number of agreements	1,570	6,741,750
Daily overtime provisions	1,393	6,069,750
Time and one-half	1,243	5,552,000
Double time	105	350,800
After 8 hours/day	1,268	5,266,650
Weekly overtime provisions	997	4,393,750
Time and one-half	942	4,222,300
Double time	33	106,450
After less than 40 hours/week	54	209,350
Overtime outside regularly scheduled hours	570	2,153,300
Graduated overtime rates	370	1,518,350
Equal distribution of overtime	661	2,832,700
Right to refuse overtime[a]	280	1,346,650
Premium pay for weekends	1,430	6,070,400
Saturday not part of regular workweek	880	3,741,400
At more than time and one-half	171	533,400
Sunday not part of regular workweek	1,211	5,136,200
At more than time and one-half	871	3,461,550
Saturday part of regular workweek	39	104,400
Sunday part of regular workweek	193	1,545,850

[a] Over 50 percent of the workers covered by this provision are in the transportation equipment industry.
SOURCE: U.S. Bureau of Labor Statistics, Bulletin 201, *Characteristics of Major Collective Bargaining Agreements, July 1, 1976* (Washington, D.C., February 1979).

tempt to "correct" for the possibility that individuals with preferences for long hours of work are attracted to firms which offer "mandatory overtime provisions" by using techniques described by Heckman.[39] The problem here is to correct for sample selection bias; wage premiums may not be reflected in the "uncorrected" data if workers with preferences for longer hours of work systematically seek out firms which expect their employees to work overtime and thus have "mandatory" overtime provisions.

We hope such analyses will provide policy makers with useful information on this issue. Our discussion has neglected the whole issue of what should determine whether a particular condition of employment

[39] James Heckman, "Sample Bias as a Specification Error," *Econometrica* 47 (January 1979): 153–61.

is determined through collective bargaining and/or through government intervention. Given the incomplete collective bargaining coverage in the United States, if market imperfections *do* occur, a case for potential government intervention is usually present. In the absence of such information, we would be extremely reluctant to support legislated prohibitions against mandatory overtime.

Appendix: Simulations on the Effect of a Simultaneous Increase in the Overtime Premium and Reduction in Overtime Hours

Robert Shishko and Bernard Rostker specify a model of the form:

$$h_m = a_0 + a_1 W_m + a_2 W_p + a_3 h_p + a_4 I + \bar{a}_5 \overline{X} + \varepsilon \quad \text{(A1)}$$

where:

h_m = weekly hours on second job
W_m = hourly wage rate on the second job
W_p = hourly wage rate on the primary job
h_p = weekly hours on the primary job
$I = (W_m - W_p)h_p$ for Specification A
$I = W_p h_p + Z$ for Specification B
Z = labor income earned by members of the family other than the head of the household
$\overline{X}$ = a vector of descriptive variables including age and family size
ε = an error term

Since the distribution of moonlighting hours is truncated at zero hours, Shishko and Rostker utilize Tobit analyses. If, for expositional convenience, we place all of the explanatory variables in a vector X, the mode may be written:

$$h_m = \bar{a}'X + \varepsilon$$

Now in the Tobit model, a change in any of the predetermined variables, say X_k, is given by:

$$\frac{\delta h_m}{\delta X_k} = a_k \, \Phi\left(\frac{\bar{a}'\overline{X}}{\sigma}\right) \quad \text{(A2)}$$

where a_k is the coefficient of X_k and $\Phi\,(\cdot)$ is the cumulative normal density function.[40] Similarly, the elasticity is given by:

$$\frac{\delta h_m}{\delta X_k} \cdot \frac{X_k}{h_m} = \frac{a_k X_k \Phi(\bar{a}'\overline{X}/\sigma)}{h_m} \quad \text{(A3)}$$

---

[40] More precisely, $[\delta E(h_m|X)]/\delta X_k = a_k \, \Phi(a'X)/\sigma$. This is *not* conditional on h_m. It represents the behavioral response of the "average individuals" being greater than zero.

Shishko and Rostker report in their table 3 elasticity estimates for all of their variables. For our purposes, the important elasticities $[(\delta h_m / \delta X_k)(X_k / h_m)]$ are:

Predetermined Variable	Specification A	Specification B
W_p	-0.126	-0.862
h_p	-1.406	-1.255
I	0.074	-0.175

Clearly, the percentage change in moonlighting hours for any specified percentage change in each of these predetermined variables can be approximated by:

$$\%\Delta h_m = \frac{\Delta h_m}{h_m} = \left(\frac{\delta h_m}{\delta W_p} \cdot \frac{W_p}{h_m}\right) \cdot \frac{\Delta W_p}{W_p}$$

$$+ \left(\frac{\delta h_m}{\delta h_p} \cdot \frac{h_p}{h_m}\right) \cdot \frac{\Delta h_p}{h_p} + \left(\frac{\delta h_m}{\delta I} \cdot \frac{I}{h_m}\right) \cdot \frac{\Delta I}{I} \quad \text{(A4)}$$

Since the terms in parentheses are the elasticities tabulated above, all that remains to be indicated is the percentage changes in W_p, h_p, and I induced by a change in the overtime premium.

Now suppose that weekly hours on an individual's primary job fall from forty-four hours per week to forty-two when the overtime premium increases from time and one-half to double time. Define the mean wage on the primary job as:

$\overline{W}_p = [$(regular hours)(regular wages)

$\qquad + $ (overtime hours)(overtime premium)(regular wage)$]$ (A5)

$\qquad \div [$(regular hours) + (overtime hours)$]$

If the overtime premium goes into effect after forty hours per week, then since the mean value of the straight-time primary wage in Shishko and Rostker's sample is \$3.77, we have:

$$\overline{W}_p^0 = \frac{(40)(3.77) + (4)(1.5)(3.77)}{44} = \frac{173.42}{44} = \$3.9414$$

$$\overline{W}_p^1 = \frac{(40)(3.77) + (2)(2)(3.77)}{42} = \frac{165.88}{42} = \$3.9495$$

Next consider the interaction terms. Under specification A, we have (making use of the fact that the mean value of the moonlighting wage is \$3.40):

$$I_A^0 = (W_m^0 - W_p^0)h_p^0$$
$$= (3.40 - 3.9495)(44) = -24.18 \tag{A6}$$
$$I_A^1 = (3.40 - 3.9495)(42) = -23.08$$

Under the assumption that labor income earned by others in the household does not change, the analogous values of the interaction term under specification B are:

$$I_B^0 = W_p h_p + Z$$
$$= (3.9414)(44) + Z = 173.42 + Z \tag{A7}$$
$$I_B^1 = (3.9495)(42) + Z = 165.88 + Z$$

Thus, the relevant percentage changes[41] to be used are:

$$\frac{\Delta h_p}{h_p} = \frac{42 - 44}{44} = -4.545\%$$

$$\frac{\Delta W_p}{W_p} = \frac{3.9495 - 3.9414}{3.9414} = 0.206\%$$

$$\tag{A8}$$

$$\frac{\Delta I_A}{I_A} = \frac{(-23.08) - (-24.18)}{-24.18} = -4.549\%$$

$$\frac{\Delta I_B}{I_B} = \frac{165.88 - 173.42}{173.42} = -4.348\%$$

Substituting (A8) and the parameters for specification A and B into (A4), the percentage change in moonlighting hours under specification A is given by:

$$\%\Delta h_m = (-0.126)(0.206) + (-1.406)(-4.545) \tag{A9}$$
$$+ (0.074)(-4.549) = 6.03\%$$

and that under specification B:

$$\%\Delta h_m = (-0.862)(0.206) + (-1.255)(-4.545) \tag{A10}$$
$$+ (-0.175)(-4.549) = 6.32\%$$

---

[41] Note that this is an approximation since the exact term for $\Delta I_B/I_B$ is given by:

$$\frac{\Delta I_B}{I_B} = \frac{(165.88 + Z) - (173.42 + Z)}{173.42 + Z} = \frac{165.88 - 173.42}{173.42 + Z}$$

Unfortunately, the mean value of Z in the sample was not reported. The approximation used above assumed that $Z = 0$. Thus, $\Delta I_B/I_B = -4.348$ percent represents an upper bound. To obtain a lower bound, let Z approach infinity. This implies that $\Delta I_B/I_B$ is close to zero, and that a lower bound for the percentage change in moonlighting hours under specification B is:

$$\%\Delta h_m = (-0.862)(0.206) + (-1.255)(-4.545) = 5.53\%$$

Taken together, they suggest that our best estimate is that the simultaneous increase in the overtime premium and the reduction in overtime hours would increase moonlighting hours by approximately 6 percent.

Bibliography

Ashenfelter, Orley, and Smith, Robert S. "Compliance with the Minimum Wage Law." *Journal of Political Economy* 87 (April 1979).

Brown, Scott. "Moonlighting Increases Sharply in 1977." *Monthly Labor Review* 101 (January 1978).

Cahill, Marion. *Shorter Hours.* New York: Columbia University Press, 1932.

Commons, John R., and Andrews, John B. *Principles of Labor Legislation.* New York: Harper and Brothers, 1920.

Connell, John F. "Multiple Job Holding and Marginal Tax Rates." *National Tax Journal* 32 (March 1979).

Ehrenberg, Ronald G. *Fringe Benefits and Overtime Behavior.* Lexington, Mass.: D.C. Heath, 1971.

———. "Heterogeneous Labor, the Internal Labor Market and the Employment-Hours Decision." *Journal of Economic Theory* 3 (March 1971).

———. "The Impact of the Overtime Premium on Employment and Hours in U.S. Industry." *Western Economic Journal* 9 (June 1971).

Eisner, Robert. "Employment Taxes and Subsidies." In National Commission for Employment Policy, *Work Time and Employment,* Special Report no. 28. Washington, D.C., October 1978.

Grossman, Jonathan. "Fair Labor Standards Act of 1938: Maximum Struggle for a Minimum Wage." *Monthly Labor Review* 101 (June 1978).

Hamermesh, Daniel. "Econometric Studies of Labor Demand and Their Application to Policy Analysis." *Journal of Human Resources* 11 (Fall 1976).

Hamermesh, Daniel, and Grant, James. "Econometric Studies of Labor-Labor Substitution and Their Implications for Policy." *Journal of Human Resources* 14 (Fall 1979).

Heckman, James. "Sample Bias as a Specification Error." *Econometrica* 47 (January 1979).

Kneese, Alan, and Schultze, Charles. *Pollution, Prices and Public Policy.* Washington, D.C.: Brookings Institution, 1975.

National Board for Prices and Incomes. *Hours of Work, Overtime and Shiftwork,* Report no. 161: 42–49; supplements: 92–116. London, 1970.

Nussbaum, Joyce, and Wise, Donald. "The Employment Impact of the Overtime Provisions of the F.L.S.A." Final Report, U.S. Department of Labor Contract J–9–E–6–0105, 1977.

———. "The Overtime Pay Premium and Employment." In National Commission for Employment Policy, *Work Time and Employment,* Special Report no. 28. Washington, D.C., October 1978.

Oi, Walter. "Labor as a Quasi-Fixed Factor of Production." *Journal of Political Economy* 70 (October 1962): 535–50.

Paulsen, George E. "The Legislative History of the Fair Labor Standards Act." Ph.D. dissertation, Ohio State University, 1959.

Perloff, Jeffrey, and Wachter, Michael. "Work Sharing, Unemployment, and the Rate of Economic Growth." In National Commission for Employment Policy, *Work Time and Employment,* Special Report no. 28. Washington, D.C., October 1978.

Phelps, Orme. *Introduction to Labor Economics.* New York, 1950.

———. *The Legislative Background of the Fair Labor Standards Act.* Chicago University Studies in Business Administration. Chicago, 1939.

Quinn, Robert, and Staines, Graham. *The 1977 Quality of Employment Survey: Descriptive Statistics.* Ann Arbor, Mich., 1979.

Rosen, Sherwin. "Short-Run Employment Variations in Class I Railroads." *Econometrica* 36 (July/October 1968): 511–29.

———. "The Supply of Work Schedules and Employment." In National Commission for Employment Policy, *Work Time and Employment,* Special Report no. 28. Washington, D.C., October 1978.

Rosenfeld, Carl. "Multiple Jobholding Holds Steady in 1978." *Monthly Labor Review* 102 (February 1979).

Settle, Russell F., and Weisbrod, Burton. "Governmentally Imposed Standards: Some Normative Aspects." In *Research in Labor Economics,* vol. 2, edited by Ronald G. Ehrenberg. Greenwich, Conn.: JAI Press, 1978.

Shishko, Robert, and Rostker, Bernard. "The Economics of Multiple Job Holding." *American Economic Review* 66 (June 1976): 298–308.

Solnick, Loren, and Swimmer, Gene. "Overtime and Fringe Benefits—A Simultaneous Equations Approach." Mimeograph, 1978.

Stamas, George D. "Long Hours and Premium Pay, May 1978." *Monthly Labor Review* 102 (May 1979): 41–45.

U.S. Bureau of Labor Statistics. *1973 Handbook of Labor Statistics.* Washington, D.C., 1973.

———. *1977 Handbook of Labor Statistics.* Washington, D.C., 1977.

U.S. Congress, House of Representatives. *Hearings before the Subcommittee on Labor Standards of the Committee on Education and Labor on H.R. 1784. 96th Congress, 2d session, 1980.*

U.S. Department of Labor. *Growth of Labor Laws in the United States.* Washington, D.C., 1967.

Premium Payments for Overtime under the Fair Labor Standards Act. Washington, D.C., 1967.

U.S. Department of Labor, Employment Standards Administration. *Minimum Wage and Maximum Hours Standards under the Fair Labor Standards Act, 1978.* Washington, D.C., 1978.

U.S. Department of Labor, Wages and Public Contracts Division. *Compliance Survey, 1965.* Washington, D.C., 1966.

Van Atta, Susan. "An Analysis of Overtime Hours for Production Workers in Manufacturing Industries 1957–1965." Ph.D. dissertation, University of California at Berkeley, 1967.

Wessels, Walter. "The Effects of Minimum Wages in the Presence of Fringe Benefits: An Expanded Model." *Economic Inquiry* (forthcoming).

Differential Legal Minimum Wages

Philip Cotterill

Differential legal minimum wages are a means of moderating the negative employment impact of a uniform minimum wage by selectively applying different minimum wage rates to different groups of workers. In principle, differentials could be based on industrial, geographical, and/or demographic distinctions. Explicit differentials of this type have not been a significant part of the Fair Labor Standards Act (FLSA), the federal minimum wage law passed in 1938.

However, implicit differentials have existed in U.S. minimum wage policy. The most important source of differentials has been the incomplete coverage of the FLSA. Before 1961, important low-wage sectors, such as retail trade and the services, were largely exempt from FLSA coverage. A trend to extend coverage to these sectors began in 1961. Coverage was based on the annual sales of the establishment and firm to which it belonged. At first only the largest enterprises were covered, but the sales size criterion has gradually been lowered to include businesses with gross annual sales of at least $250,000. Newly covered workers have also been subject to differential minimum wages when wage levels have been raised to the standard minimum in a series of step increases.

State minimum wage laws have also been a source of differentials, both explicit and implicit. For example, there is a tendency for state laws to cover workers not covered by federal legislation and to establish a lower legal minimum than that set by the FLSA, thus creating different legal minimum wages for workers covered by federal and state laws. In addition, some geographical differentials between states with and without minimum wage laws have existed for workers not subject to the FLSA. In general, the trend toward more comprehensive federal coverage has tended to diminish the significance of these differentials. Various state laws also contain explicit demographic differentials for minors, students, and/or learners.

Recent interest in legal differentials at the federal level has focused on a teenage or youth differential. In 1972, a youth differential was included in FLSA amendments which failed to achieve final congressional approval. In 1974, while not directly approving a youth differential, Congress expanded the provisions which since 1961 have permitted employers to pay full-time students subminimum rates. Again in 1977, Congress defeated across-the-board proposals for a youth differential, but made further changes in the full-time student provisions. The 1977 amendments also increased from four to six the number of full-time students who may be hired by retailers or farmers at eighty-five percent of the minimum wage without prior authorization by the Department of Labor.[1]

The number of authorized job slots under the full-time student certificate program increased from 153,000 in fiscal 1974 to 513,600 in fiscal 1975. Since fiscal 1975, there have been significant year-to-year fluctuations. The number of authorized job slots in fiscal 1973 was 512,174. Over one-half the job slots are in institutions of higher education. The number of job slots in retail trade went from 56,000 in fiscal 1974 to 237,275 in fiscal 1978.[2]

Currently two bills that would create a youth differential are pending in Congress. Senator Stevenson of Illinois has introduced a bill that would permit the hiring of persons under age twenty at 85 percent of the minimum wage. Senator Hatch of Utah also introduced a similar bill that would establish a 75 percent differential for persons under age twenty. Under the Hatch bill, the subminimum rate could be paid for no more than six months at the same job unless the person is a full-time student. (This provision creates an incentive for employers to turn over youth employment every six months. It is not known whether this would be a problem in practice.) The Stevenson bill contains no time limitation, but stipulates that no worker can be paid the subminimum rate if that person is earning at least the minimum wage at the time the subminimum provision is enacted. Both bills contain penalties for employers who displace higher wage workers in order to take advantage of the differential minimum.[3] (Penalties might discourage displacement, but they would not prevent the substitution of youth for adults in the case of new jobs or replacements for voluntary quits.)

High youth unemployment rates, combined with evidence that federal minimum wage policy has adversely affected youth employment, lend support for a youth differential. However, there are reasons for adopting a cautious approach to the youth differential. Although un-

[1] P. Elder, "The 1977 Amendments to the Federal Minimum Wage Law," *Monthly Labor Review* 101 (January 1978): 9–11.

[2] U.S. Department of Labor, Employment Standards Administration, Wage and Hour Division, personal communication, August 1979.

[3] National Institute of Public Management, "Pending Sub-minimum Wage Action Controversy," *Income Security Newsletter* 4 (July 1979): 5–6.

employment statistics call attention to the youth employment problem, with a few exceptions, adults with employment problems are not identified in the aggregate statistics. Since they represent a small proportion of all adults, their problems are easily overlooked. In fact, among the low-wage workers most subject to the impact of the minimum wage, adults far outnumber youth. Gramlich[4] reported that in 1975 teenagers constituted only 30 percent of all workers earning less than $2.25 per hour. Adult males made up 20 percent, and adult females 50 percent, of the total.

In addition, empirical research has concentrated on the impact of the minimum wage on youth employment, for reasons related to the available data. To quote Welch:

> The empirical literature is largely restricted to effects on youth employment, not because older workers, especially the aged, or lower wage workers of intermediate age are less affected, but because the data are less complete for these workers.[5]

Assuming that wage rates are highly correlated with productivity, the fact that adults account for roughly 70 percent of low-wage workers suggests that a simple youth differential would place adults at a disadvantage in competing for many low-wage jobs. Welch also notes the possibility that the adult minimum might be raised if a youth differential were established.[6] Policy dynamics of this variety are not discussed in this paper. The differentials considered are assumed to be "equilibrium" differentials.

Whether the youth unemployment problem requires a differential minimum wage, regardless of its effects on other groups, is also debatable. On the one hand, youths are better able to cope with unemployment than are low-wage adults whose nonmarket alternatives (notably school) are probably inferior to those of youths. In addition, data for 1972 indicate that low-wage adults tend to have significantly lower family incomes than do low-wage youths. A representative comparison among workers earning less than $2.00 an hour in 1973 reveals median 1972 family incomes of $13,131 for teenagers, $6,752 for adult males, and $7,400 for adult females.[7] On the other hand, concern has been expressed that today's unemployed youths will become the working poor

---

[4] E.M. Gramlich, "Impact of Minimum Wages on Other Wages, Employment, and Family Incomes," *Brookings Papers on Economic Activity* 2 (1976): 409–51.

[5] F. Welch, "Minimum Wage Legislation in the United States," *Economic Inquiry* 12 (September 1974): 288.

[6] Ibid., pp. 316–17.

[7] Gramlich, "Impact of Minimum Wages," p. 488.

FIGURE 1
DISTRIBUTION OF WORKERS BY VALUE OF PRODUCTIVITY

Relative Frequency

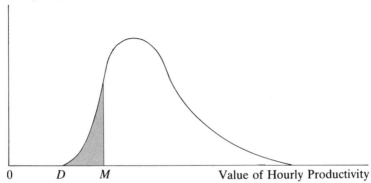

0   D   M   Value of Hourly Productivity

of the future. Becker and Hills report evidence which supports this concern for black, but not for white, youths.[8]

This paper assumes that the objective of differential minimum wage policy is to moderate the negative employment effects of minimum wage policy for all low-wage workers, and not to just redistribute the negative impact from one group to another. The next section of this paper describes the problems encountered in attempting to design a general policy of differential minimum wages. Because it is currently the object of policy interest in differentials, however, the youth differential receives special attention. The following section reviews existing research relevant to the evaluation of a youth differential and describes additional research needs. The final section of the paper presents a brief review of the policy issues and alternatives related to differential minimum wages.

Differential Minimum Wages: Objectives and Problems

Let us assume: first, that policy makers were given the task of designing a differential minimum wage policy which would counteract the negative employment effects of the standard minimum wage; second, that policy makers know how productive capacities are distributed among the work force and that the distribution depicted in figure 1 represents the distribution of the value to employers of workers' productivity; and, third,

[8] B. E. Becker and S. M. Hills, "Today's Teenage Unemployment—Tomorrow's Working Poor?" *Monthly Labor Review* 102 (January 1979): 69–71.

that employers are willing to hire a person as long as the value of the person's hourly marginal productivity is at least as great as the hourly wage rate the employer must pay. (It is also assumed throughout the paper that the minimum wage is ineffective in achieving its intended legislative purpose of raising the wage rates of individual low-wage workers.) Given these assumptions, the minimum wage has the effect of making unemployed those workers whose productivity is valued less than the minimum wage (the shaded area of figure 1). The objective of the differential minimum wage is to improve the employment opportunities of these persons.

It is readily apparent that the simplest solution to the employment problem would be to eliminate the minimum wage altogether, a solution assumed to be politically infeasible. Alternatively, if everyone's productivity has a positive value, the minimum wage could be set so low as to be ineffective (point D in figure 1). This solution is also assumed to be infeasible. These examples illustrate the fact that a differential minimum wage is a "second best" approach to alleviating the employment problems created by a minimum wage, and that the preferred solution is to remove the minimum wage.

If the minimum wage law cannot be repealed or left to become ineffective with time and inflation, the task is to design a differential minimum wage which will most efficiently offset the negative employment impact of the minimum wage. Again, there is a simple, but infeasible solution: Make the differential apply to everyone who in the absence of legislation would earn less than the minimum wage. In figure 1, the employment effect of the minimum wage would be eliminated if the differential minimum wage were set at D. (It would reduce, but not totally eliminate, the employment impact if it were set somewhere between D and the standard minimum wage.) Defining a differential in terms of the wage rate a person earns, while most efficient in identifying the target group, is assumed to be infeasible because it directly contradicts the legislative intent of the minimum wage law.

The problem for a realistic program of differential minimum wage rates is to identify characteristics which are very highly correlated with the value of productive capacities and which can be used to define differential minimums. For example, if teenagers make up about 30 percent of those who in the absence of legislation would earn less than the minimum wage, then a teenage differential would exclude a large proportion of the target group.

This problem can be illustrated graphically. Figure 2 depicts the value of productivity distributions of two groups of workers: Group 1 is assumed to be subject to a differential minimum (D) and Group 2 to

FIGURE 2
DISTRIBUTION OF TWO GROUPS OF WORKERS,
BY VALUE OF PRODUCTIVITY

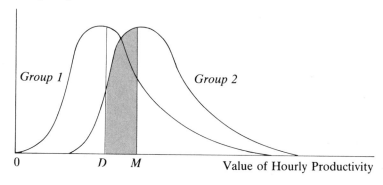

the standard minimum (M). The workers who benefit from the differential are those Group 1 workers whose productivity has a value of at least D, but less than M. Under our simple assumptions, these workers (represented by the area under the Group 1 curve between D and M) will now be employed because they can now be paid the value of their productivity. However, Group 2 workers whose productivity is valued between D and M will not gain because they must be paid at least M, which exceeds the value of their productivity. These are the workers most directly harmed by the differential. They are as productive as the Group 1 beneficiaries of the differential; yet they are placed at a wage disadvantage because they must be paid at least M, whereas Group 1 can be paid less than M. If M is already the minimum wage, they are not harmed by being displaced. However, they are harmed in that they are at a disadvantage in competing for jobs created by the differential. Roger Reynolds[9] has pointed out that the size of this group depends on the value of M, as well as on the size of the differential, D/M.

The jobs created for the beneficiaries of the differential may come from two sources. New jobs may be created because the differential reduces the cost of labor relative to nonlabor inputs. Also, additional jobs may result from the change in the relative cost of different types of labor brought about by the differential. In either case, Group 2 workers between D and M will be at a disadvantage in competing for these jobs. The relative wage effect may adversely affect members of both groups who earn more than M. For example, production methods

[9] Roger Reynolds, personal communication, October 1979.

which use a smaller proportion of higher productivity labor may now become economically efficient.

This analysis breaks down the potential effects of a differential minimum wage into two parts. First, and most direct, is the exclusion effect. The magnitude of this effect could be evaluated if we knew the value of productivity distributions for different groups of workers. Since productivity is not directly measurable, wage rate distributions would be the best alternative. But as a result of minimum wages and other possible constraints on low wages, the wage rate distribution will be truncated as compared with the productivity distribution. That is, wage rate distributions of the employed will be truncated relative to productivity distributions of the labor force. The greater the degree of overlap between the distributions, the more serious the exclusion problem. In figure 2, for example, if the Group 2 distribution is shifted to the left, the area under the Group 2 curve between D and M increases. Second, and more difficult to evaluate, is what we shall call the relative wage effect. Its evaluation requires the estimation of production functions, which means that competing groups of labor and other inputs must be correctly defined and the prices of the inputs must be accurately measured.

At one extreme, the solution to the exclusion problem might lead to a complicated set of differentials based on a large number of categories defined to include as many as possible of the target group. In principle, any combination of demographic, industrial, and/or geographical characteristics might be employed. As the complexity of the system of differentials increased, administrative and compliance costs would rise, leading to a policy trade-off between employment benefits to the target group and higher costs of administering the minimum wage program.[10]

In practice, however, there are factors other than rising administrative costs which would probably restrict the proliferation of multiple differentials. For example, the number of demographic characteristics which could be used is limited. Differentials based on race and sex are clearly impossible. Given the trend of the FLSA toward expanded coverage of industries with significant proportions of low-wage workers, industry differentials seem unlikely to attract sufficient political support for passage. It should be apparent that exempting an industry from coverage has the same effect as making that industry subject to an ineffective differential minimum. Despite the support for a youth differential, the political trend in federal legislation has generally been toward a more comprehensive uniform minimum wage law.

---

[10] For evidence on the completeness of compliance under existing legislation, see Gramlich, "Impact of Minimum Wages," pp. 424–26.

Youth Differentials: Evidence from Existing Research

Considerable research has been conducted to evaluate the impact of the minimum wage on youth employment. Several reviews of this research have been published,[11] and it is sufficient here to note that very little of the research is directly relevant for evaluating the impact of a youth differential. Though the findings are not wholly consistent, they do suggest that the minimum wage has adversely affected youth employment. On the surface, this result suggests that a youth differential would increase youth employment. However, as indicated earlier, it is necessary to take account of the consequences of a youth differential for low-wage adult workers. These studies may have masked the effect of the minimum wage on low-wage adults because they generally have investigated the minimum wage impact on national unemployment rates or employment ratios for specific demographic groups. Since low-wage adults constitute a small proportion of all adult workers, the proportion of adults who are employed is not very sensitive to changes in the minimum wage. Using this approach, it is much more likely that the impact of the minimum wage will be detected for youths because a large proportion of youths earn low wage rates.

A few studies have avoided this problem. Welch[12] investigated the extent of substitution between teenage and adult labor, both in the aggregate and for four industry categories. Welch and Cunningham[13] examined substitutability among three teenage subgroups (ages fourteen to fifteen, sixteen to seventeen, and eighteen to nineteen). These studies attempted to estimate elasticities of substitution derived from production functions. Using different empirical methods, Cotterill and Wadycki[14] attempted to determine whether or not the minimum wage had altered the teenage-adult employment mix in retail trade. For the purpose of analyzing a youth differential, these studies are more useful than the general youth employment literature.

[11] M. C. Lovell, "The Minimum Wage, Teenage Unemployment and the Business Cycle," *Western Economic Journal* 10 (December 1972): 414–27; A. A. Fisher, "The Minimum Wage and Teenage Unemployment: A Comment on the Literature," *Western Economic Journal* 11 (December 1973): 514–24; R. S. Goldfarb, "The Policy Content of Quantitative Minimum Wage Research," in Industrial Relations Research Association, *Proceedings of the Twenty-seventh Annual Meeting*, Madison, Wis., 1974, p. 261; Welch, "Minimum Wage Legislation"; and Gramlich, "Impact of Minimum Wages."

[12] Welch, "Minimum Wage Legislation," and "Minimum Wage Legislation in the United States: Reply," *Economic Inquiry* 15 (January 1977): 139–42.

[13] F. Welch and J. Cunningham, "Effects of Minimum Wages on the Level and Age Composition of Youth Employment," *Review of Economics and Statistics* 60 (February 1978): 140–45.

[14] P. Cotterill and W. Wadycki, "Teenagers and the Minimum Wage in Retail Trade," *Journal of Human Resources* 11 (Winter 1976): 69–85.

In the previous section, the impact of a differential minimum wage on groups not subject to the differential was divided into two parts: the exclusion effect and the relative wage effect. The exclusion effect describes the impact of the differential on workers of equal productive capacity and affects only workers who earn wage rates in the range from the differential to the standard minimum. The relative wage effect includes the impact of the differential on workers of differing productive capacities and may affect workers who earn more than the standard minimum as well as those in the range from the differential to the standard minimum. By design, the Welch and the Welch and Cunningham studies are limited to addressing the relative wage effect. However, it is possible that, by incorrectly defining labor inputs, they fail to obtain accurate estimates of the relative wage effect. The study by Cotterill and Wadycki is less ambitious theoretically than the other studies, because the empirical work is not rigorously derived from a specific production model. However, the approach of Cotterill and Wadycki is more directly interpretable in terms of the exclusion effect.

The Production Function Studies. Implicitly, if not explicitly, all production function studies must define the inputs and outputs involved in the production process. In economics textbooks, the output is frequently widgets, and the inputs are men (or man-hours) and machines (or machine-hours). In most empirical research, however, defining the output and the inputs is more difficult than in textbook examples. The problems of defining output and capital have attracted attention because it is usually necessary to combine several different products and types of capital equipment in estimating production functions. However, while the problem may be more obvious in the case of output and capital inputs, it may be just as serious in the case of labor. Human capital research has made some impact in recognizing differences in labor inputs. However, data problems seriously hinder empirical efforts to define labor inputs accurately. The studies discussed here reflect the type of compromise which must usually be made in attempting to take into account differences in labor inputs and, at the same time, to obtain measurable inputs using the available data.

The production function model implies that labor inputs should consist of groups, each of which is homogeneous in terms of the productive capacity or human capital of its members. That is, labor inputs should be defined so that within-group variation in human capital is minimized and between-group variation is maximized. In practice, the assumption must typically be made that productive capacity is sufficiently highly correlated with demographic characteristics, particularly age, to justify treating different age groups of workers as separate labor

FIGURE 3
OVERLAPPING PRODUCTIVITY DISTRIBUTIONS

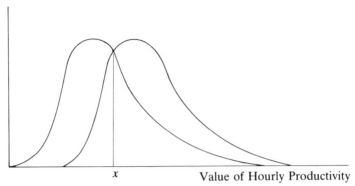

Relative Frequency

x

Value of Hourly Productivity

inputs. Accordingly, Welch disaggregated labor inputs into two groups, teenagers (persons fourteen to nineteen years old) and adults (persons twenty years and older).[15] Welch and Cunningham disaggregated teen-age labor into three groups: ages fourteen to fifteen, sixteen to seventeen, and eighteen to nineteen.[16]

Empirically, the issue can be stated in terms of the productivity distributions discussed earlier: The greater the overlap between the productivity distributions of two groups of workers, the less appropriate it is to define the two groups as distinct labor inputs. The reason is simple: workers of equal productivity are equally capable of performing a particular job and hence, in a production sense, are the same input. The greater the overlap in productivity distributions, the more the two groups are equivalent inputs. If we knew the shapes of the productivity distributions, it would be more appropriate to define the inputs in terms of the value of their productivity or potential wage rates. For example, in figure 3, two labor inputs could be defined as those persons with a potential wage rate greater than and less than x dollars per hour. (This approach implies that any two workers with different amounts of human capital are different labor inputs. In the extreme, this leads to treating each worker as a separate input. For empirical research, it would be necessary to aggregate workers into productivity classes.) Another way of stating the point is that if there is substantial overlap, it would be more appropriate to define labor inputs in terms of "low" and "high"

---

[15] Welch, "Minimum Wage Legislation."
[16] Welch and Cunningham, "Effects of Minimum Wages."

productivity groups which have different roles in production than in terms of demographic groups of persons, many of whom have similar production roles.

It may be thought that the only consequence of overlapping productivity distributions is that estimation of elasticities of substitution would reveal that the two groups are more highly substitutable than if less overlap occurs. This is not the case. Inputs should be defined in terms of their production roles if production function parameters are to be meaningful. If similar jobs are performed by persons of heterogeneous demographic characteristics, labor inputs should not be defined in terms of demographic characteristics.

Welch attempted to determine the sensitivity of the youth-adult employment ratio to changes in wage rates brought about by the minimum wage. He used time series data on youth and adult employment for the period 1954–1968 both for the aggregate of all industries and for four industry groups: manufacturing, retail trade, services, and an "other" category. Under certain assumptions, his estimates can be interpreted as elasticities of substitution, or the percent change in the youth-adult employment ratio which results from a 1 percent change in the relative wage rate of youth and adults.[17]

I am unwilling to draw any conclusions about the aggregate estimate, since quite different results are obtained when the data are disaggregated by industry group. The statistical significance of the aggregate estimate did not differ from zero.[18] Of more interest is the fact that the youth-adult employment ratio was more sensitive to changes in wage rates in manufacturing than in retail trade or the services. The results imply that a 10 percent increase in minimum wage impact on wage rates is associated with a reduction of approximately 4 percent in the youth-adult employment ratio in manufacturing, a reduction of 0.8 percent in retail trade, and a reduction of 0.04 percent in services. Statistical significance tests imply that the services estimate is not different from zero. (The estimate for the "other" category was statistically significant, but of the wrong sign. I ignore this result because of the extreme heterogeneity of the category. Mining and finance are two of its components, for example.)

Welch notes that productivity distinctions between youths and adults are less pronounced in retail trade and the services than in manufacturing. This fact might appear to imply a larger change in the youth-adult employment ratio for a given wage rate change in retail trade and

---

[17] Welch, "Minimum Wage Legislation" and "Reply."

[18] F. B. Siskind, "Minimum Wage Legislation in the United States: Comment," *Economic Inquiry* 15 (January 1977): 135–38; and Welch, "Reply."

the services because adults are more easily substitutable for youths in these sectors. What is the explanation of the observed finding? Welch argues that the retail trade and services coefficients are biased downward because of measurement error. He asserts that his minimum wage variable overstates changes in the youth-adult relative wage rate in retail trade and the services as a result of overlap in the productivity distributions of youths and adults in those sectors. In addition, he cites the possibility that uneven industrial coverage produced counteracting changes in the youth-adult employment ratios in retail trade and the services before and after 1961, when those sectors were first covered to any significant extent.[19]

However, these results can be explained solely in terms of the differences among industries in overlap of the productivity distributions of youths and adults. Neither downward bias nor relative wage effects are necessary to explain the observed results. Assume, for example, that there were no productivity distinctions at all between youths and adults; that is, that their productivity or wage rate distributions were identical (complete overlap). In this case, an increase in the minimum wage would result in equal percentage reductions in employment for youths and adults. As a result, there would be no change in the youth-adult employment ratio occasioned by the minimum wage increase. Both groups would suffer equal proportionate employment losses. As the degree of overlap in the productivity distribution decreases, the youth-adult employment ratio becomes more sensitive to the wage rate increase because teenagers suffer a larger proportionate employment loss than adults.

Welch's results may not tell us anything about relative wage effects of the minimum wage in sectors like retail trade and services. Instead, his results may just reflect the fact that larger proportions of both youths and adults are subject to the direct employment effects of minimum wage policy in retail trade and the services than in manufacturing. The only way to distinguish these effects from relative wage effects is to define labor inputs in terms of their relative productivity as suggested in the section "Differential Minimum Wages: Objectives and Problems." If my interpretation is correct, Welch's results also suggest that a youth differential would produce a significant exclusion effect in retail trade and the services.

Whereas the work of Welch discussed here was not directly applied to the issue of a youth differential, Welch and Cunningham[20] explicitly investigated the impact of a differential. However, they did not examine the effects of a youth differential on adult workers, but rather on three

[19] Welch, "Minimum Wage Legislation," pp. 312–13.
[20] Welch and Cunningham, "Effects of Minimum Wages."

subgroups of youths. The authors were very adept at devising ways around data and estimation problems. However, even evaluated on its own terms, the paper is only partially successful in estimating demand and substitution elasticities for the three groups of teenagers. The study utilizes cross-section data on youth employment by state.

The same issues raised with regard to Welch's earlier work apply to this study by Welch and Cunningham: the greater the overlap among the productivity distributions of the three groups of teenagers, the less meaningful are production function parameters because they are based on incorrectly defined labor inputs.

Welch and Cunningham did not have actual wage data for these teenage groups. Rather they assumed, based on some work by Parsons,[21] that the average wage rates were related to one another (and to the average manufacturing wage) in a particular way. Further, they assumed that within each group, wage rates were distributed in accordance with a particular probability density function which, they assert, reasonably describes observed empirical wage distributions of low-wage workers.

The density function chosen is a gamma distribution, a two-parameter family of distributions:

$$f(t; \alpha, \beta) = \frac{1}{\alpha! \, \beta^{\alpha+1}} \, t^\alpha e^{-t/\beta} \qquad 0 < t < \infty \qquad (1)$$

Welch and Cunningham set $\alpha = 1$ and $1/\beta = p$, which yields $f(t) = p^2 t e^{-pt}$. The result is that there is a fixed relationship between the mean $(2/p)$ and the variance $(2/p^2)$. They had information about mean wage rates, but not about the variance.

It seemed logical, therefore, to evaluate the degree of overlap implied by their use of this particular distribution. Integrating the gamma for a specific group of teenagers from zero up to the relevant wage rate yields the proportion of the group earning less than the particular wage rate. The expression is $1 - (pt+1)e^{-pt}$, where t is the relevant wage rate. This exercise yielded the following results: 59 percent of the fourteen- to fifteen-year-olds would have earned less than their implied 1970 mean wage rate of $1.19. In addition, 43 percent of the sixteen- to seventeen-year-olds and 31 percent of the eighteen- to nineteen-year-olds also would have earned less than $1.19 per hour. While 59 percent of the sixteen- to seventeen-year-olds would have been below their implied 1970 mean wage rate of $1.64, 46 percent of the eighteen- to nineteen-year-olds also would have fallen below $1.64 per hour. The implied mean wage rate of the eighteen- to nineteen-year-olds was $2.13 per hour. This high degree of overlap among the three wage rate dis-

[21] D. Parsons, "The Cost of School Time, Forgone Earnings, and Human Capital Formation," unpublished manuscript, Ohio State University, February 1973.

tributions is a consequence of the particular distribution function assumed by Welch and Cunningham.

In particular, it is a consequence of the large variance implied by the gamma distribution they used. Since the gamma is very difficult to evaluate unless $\alpha = 1$, I experimented with a lognormal distribution, a distribution which can be justified on human capital grounds. The results are highly sensitive to the assumptions made about the variance. Since I had no information about the variance for wages of youth, the results were inconclusive. They ranged from minimal overlap when I assumed that the mean was 1 percent greater than the median, to substantial overlap when I assumed the mean was 10 percent greater than the median (still less overlap than using the gamma, however).

Since they do not present any evidence to support its applicability, we should not necessarily conclude that their work supports the view expressed elsewhere in this paper that the exclusion effect of a youth differential may be a significant problem. The chief conclusion to be drawn from their study is that better information is needed on the shapes of youth wage rate distributions. Data on mean wage rates are not sufficient for analyses of youth differentials.

Welch and Cunningham's selection of a distribution with a large variance has several consequences for their results. First, they probably have overstated the increases in the cost of hiring teenagers brought about by the minimum wage: 15 percent for eighteen- to nineteen-year-olds, 27 percent for sixteen- to seventeen-year-olds, and 46 percent for fourteen- to fifteen-year-olds (the mean of all states as of 1970). Second, given their assumption of significant overlap in the wage rate distributions of the three groups, their treatment of them as separate inputs misrepresents the demand and substitution elasticities which they attempt to estimate. Finally, little confidence can be placed in their estimates of teenage employment gains which would result from a 20 percent youth differential, because these estimates are based on demand and substitution elasticities which are probably incorrectly specified.

An Alternative Approach. Cotterill and Wadycki[22] attempted to determine whether the expansion of minimum wage coverage in retail trade between 1961 and 1967 had produced differential changes in the youth-adult employment mix between covered and noncovered retail jobs. The justification given here for their empirical tests is simpler and more correct than that given in their paper. The explanation there relies on relative wage changes for youths and adults and is subject to the same criticism made in this paper of the production function studies.

[22] Cotterill and Wadycki, "Teenagers."

Assume that initially the same wage rate distribution existed for covered and noncovered retail jobs. Assume also that coverage has the effect of truncating the wage distribution for covered jobs by eliminating all jobs which paid less than the legal minimum. One consequence of coverage will be to raise the average wage rate for covered jobs relative to that for noncovered jobs, assuming that noncovered wage rates either remain constant or fall.

An attempt to determine whether covered retail establishments pay higher wage rates because of the minimum wage or because of their larger size was reported by Cotterill and Wadycki.[23] While there is no good theoretical reason why larger establishments per se should pay more, they are frequently observed to do so. Size effects on wages in retail trade appear to be associated only with the largest enterprises (annual sales of more than $1 million), but it is not really possible to separate size and coverage effects.[24]

However, if employers eliminate the subminimum wage jobs in the covered sector, the youth-adult employment mix may also be altered. (Some estimates of the negative impact of the minimum wage on retail employment are reported by Cotterill.[25]) Suppose that youths hold a disproportionate share of the affected jobs. Then the youth-adult employment ratio in covered jobs should fall. To the extent that youths are absorbed in the noncovered sector, the youth-adult employment ratio there should rise. This example illustrates the simplest case in which differential changes in the age mix of employment would occur between covered and noncovered jobs. The greater the degree of overlap between the productivity distribution of youths and other low-wage workers, however, the smaller will be the youths' share of the affected jobs, and the less the youth-adult employment ratio would be expected to fall as a result of minimum wage coverage. In turn, the difference between the age mixes of employment in covered and noncovered jobs would also be smaller.[26]

Cotterill and Wadycki selected a sample of 353 male and 391 female retail trade employees from the 1967 *Survey of Economic Opportunity*.

[23] P. Cotterill and W. Wadycki, "Minimum Wage Coverage and Relative Wage Rates in Retail Trade," *Proceedings of the Business and Economic Statistics Section of the American Statistical Association,* Washington, D.C., 1973, pp. 319–24.

[24] P. Cotterill, "The Minimum Wage and Employment Growth in Retail Trade," *Proceedings of the Business and Economic Statistics Section of the American Statistics Section of the American Statistical Association,* Washington, D.C., 1974, pp. 345–50.

[25] P. Cotterill, "The Development and Evaluation of Minimum Wage Policy towards Youth: Some Research Guidelines," prepared for the U.S. Department of Labor, Office of the Assistant Secretary of Planning, Evaluation, and Research, December 1974.

[26] Gramlich, "Impact of Minimum Wages," pp. 412–13, summarizes Welch's and Mincer's theoretical results on possible changes in noncovered wage rates.

Wage rates (last week's earnings divided by last week's hours worked) and personal characteristics (age, education, race, etc.) were known. Some 23 percent of the men and 14 percent of the women were aged fourteen to nineteen years. Thirty-one standard metropolitan statistical areas (SMSAs) and eight subindustries within retail trade were represented in the sample. It was not possible to determine whether or not an individual in the sample worked in an establishment covered by the minimum wage. However, using data from the 1967 *Census of Business,* it was possible to estimate the degree of minimum wage coverage for each subindustry and SMSA represented in the sample. Each individual was matched with the degree of minimum wage coverage in the subindustry and SMSA in which he/she worked. This minimum wage coverage variable can be thought of as the probability that the worker was covered, since the greater the degree of coverage in an area, the more likely that a person included in the sample was, in fact, covered.

The effects of the minimum wage on wage rates and the age mix of employment should have been greater where minimum wage coverage was greater. Assuming that, for a given subindustry, the SMSAs with high minimum wage coverage in 1967 were the same as in 1961 and during the intervening years, the hypothesized impacts should have been detectable in the 1967 sample.

Cotterill and Wadycki found that persons with a higher probability of minimum wage coverage received higher wage rates. This finding is consistent with the view that minimum wage coverage truncates the wage rate distribution and tends to raise the average wage rate in covered jobs relative to those in noncovered jobs. Typical differentials ranged from highs of 15 percent for men and 11 percent for women in drug stores to a low of about 2 percent for both sexes in general merchandise stores. For food stores, the differential ranged from 4 to 6 percent. For other subindustries (apparel, furniture, gas stations, lumber and building materials, and miscellaneous stores) the range was between 3 and 11 percent.[27]

However, Cotterill and Wadycki did not find evidence that the higher wage rates in SMSAs where coverage was greater were associated with a reduced proportion of teenage employees in those SMSAs. Cotterill and Wadycki's empirical tests are similar to those Weiss[28] used to determine why workers in more concentrated industries had higher earnings than workers in less concentrated industries. Put another way, a

---

[27] These differentials were computed by multiplying the regression coefficient of the minimum wage variable by its standard deviation for the relevant group. For a more detailed description, see Cotterill and Wadycki, "Teenagers," p. 78.

[28] L. W. Weiss, "Concentration and Labor Earnings," *American Economic Review* 57 (March 1966): 96–117.

teenager's probability of obtaining covered employment was not lower than an adult's. In general, a person's probability of obtaining covered employment did not depend on age.[29] This result is consistent with the view that considerable overlap exists in the productivity distribution of the different age groups employed in retail trade. Like Welch's results for retail trade, Cotterill and Wadycki's results suggest that a youth differential would produce a significant exclusion effect for adult workers in retail trade.

Some further comparison of the results obtained by Welch and by Cotterill and Wadycki is warranted. For example, while Welch found a small but significant reduction in the youth-adult employment ratio in retail trade over the period 1954–1968, Cotterill and Wadycki, using an indirect test, found no relationship between the age mix of retail employment and minimum wage impact among retail trade workers in SMSAs in 1967. Welch's explanation for the small size of impact he found was that, before 1961, youths were shifted to retail trade (a non-covered sector before 1961) and away from manufacturing (a covered sector) but, since 1961, expanded coverage in retail trade had resulted in a counteracting shift of youths away from retail trade. Cotterill and Wadycki's results do not support this interpretation of minimum wage impact since 1961.

However, the period 1961–1967 was one of economic expansion and *falling* teenage unemployment rates. This fact in itself need not have affected Cotterill and Wadycki's cross-section study except that minimum wage coverage and the rate of economic expansion in an SMSA were positively correlated.[30] Thus, the employment effects of economic expansion may have offset the minimum wage impact in high-coverage SMSAs. This interpretation is consistent with the finding of Kosters and Welch[31] that minimum wage policy has increased the youth share of "transitory" employment and that, given sufficient slack in the labor market, proportionately more adults would have been hired instead of youths. Employment rates for youths vary more than the overall employment rate.

Alternatively, Cotterill and Wadycki's results may reflect long-run factors that are reducing the productivity distinction between youths and adults in retail trade. Under the FLSA, minimum wage coverage was first applied to the largest retail establishments. The sales size criterion was then gradually lowered to include establishments with annual

---

[29] Results of regressions of the minimum wage variable on age and other variables are reported in Cotterill and Wadycki, "Minimum Wage Coverage."

[30] Cotterill and Wadycki, "Teenagers," p. 82.

[31] M. Kosters and F. Welch, "The Effects of Minimum Wages on the Distribution of Changes in Aggregate Employment," *American Economic Review* 62 (June 1972): 323–32.

sales of at least $250,000. At the same time, there has been a trend toward larger retail establishments, a decrease in the service component of retail output, and an increase in the real value of the average transaction.[32] These trends, along with other changes (such as cash registers, which require fewer mathematical skills), may have made youths better substitutes for adults in retail jobs.

A related possibility is that minimum wage policy itself has given impetus to this trend. Minimum wage policy may have induced greater use of labor-saving techniques which are embodied in larger establishments. If, at the same time, these techniques have reduced the productivity differences between youths and adults, the negative effect of minimum wage policy on the total number of retail jobs may have become more equally distributed between youths and adults.

Summary. Differential legal minimum wages, such as a youth differential, may, in the course of expanding employment for the group or groups to which the differential applies, create an exclusion effect for workers not subject to the differential, as well as a relative wage effect for higher-wage workers. These two effects may have negative employment consequences for workers not subject to the differential and should be taken into account in evaluating proposed differential legal minimum wage policy.

The exclusion effect is more serious, the larger the number of low-wage workers excluded from the differential. Gramlich[33] presented evidence that suggests that a youth differential would exclude a majority of the low-wage group. Results obtained by Welch and by Cotterill and Wadycki are also consistent with the view that a youth differential would produce a significant exclusion effect among retail trade and service workers, a large segment of the low-wage population. More research on the importance of the exclusion effect is needed. The analysis presented here suggests that the issue can be investigated by examining the extent of overlap in the wage rate distributions of different groups of workers. The absence of appropriate wage rate data for demographic groups has hindered such research in the past.

Existing research has attempted to draw inferences about the relative wage effect of a youth differential by analyzing the relative wage effect of existing minimum wage policy. Unfortunately, since this research has defined labor inputs in terms of demographic groups, it mis-

---

[32] D. Schwartzman, "The Growth of Sales Per Manhour in Retail Trade, 1919–1963," in V. R. Fuchs, editor, *Production and Productivity in the Service Industries* (New York: National Bureau of Economic Research, 1969).

[33] Gramlich, "Impact of Minimum Wages."

represents substitution possibilities among workers of various productivity levels when significant overlap occurs in the productivity distributions of demographic groups. Hence, the same evidence which suggests that the exclusion effect may be significant also implies that existing evidence on the relative wage effect may be highly unreliable. An important consequence of defining labor inputs in terms of demographic groups is that it is impossible to separate substitution effects of relative wage changes from employment effects due to differences in the proportions of the demographic groups which are directly affected by minimum wage changes. Research on the relative wage effects of minimum wage policy, using appropriately defined labor inputs, is needed. This endeavor requires greater knowledge of production processes and better data than are usually available. However, this paper suggests, as a starting point, consideration of attempts to define labor inputs in terms of workers' potential productivity.

In more general terms, we need a clearer picture of the nature of low-wage work. The analysis presented in this paper is based on the view of low-wage jobs as jobs requiring general, low-level skills which can be satisfactorily performed by persons of varying ages and backgrounds. This situation would produce a set of jobs which are relatively homogeneous with respect to their required skills, but a work force very heterogeneous in its demographic characteristics. This view may be applicable to most retail trade and service sector jobs. Its applicability to other parts of the low-wage sector needs to be investigated.

Conclusion

This paper has described the problems encountered in using differential minimum wages to lessen the employment impact of the standard minimum wage on low-wage workers. Caution should be exercised in singling out a single demographic group such as youth in creating a differential, especially since, as Welch indicated, there is no reason to believe that low-wage workers of other ages are less affected.

Industry differentials or exemptions from coverage are alternatives to demographic differentials. It might be easier to identify low-wage workers by occupation or industry than by demographic characteristics. It at least seems worthwhile to investigate whether or not the exclusion effect would be less with industry than with demographic differentials.

The biggest obstacle to industry differentials may be political. The trend of federal minimum wage legislation since 1961 has been toward more complete coverage by industry. In addition, a youth differential appears on the surface to be a logical way of attacking a significant youth employment problem. Industry differentials, however, can easily be labeled subsidies to sweatshop employers.

Finally, geographical differentials deserve some consideration in federal minimum wage policy. Even in terms of its expressed legislative intent—to provide workers a "living wage"—a uniform nominal minimum wage is not appropriate. A higher real minimum wage is imposed in low-cost-of-living areas than in high-cost areas. In turn, a larger employment effect is imposed on lower-wage areas. There is no justification for the federal law to create unequal geographical effects on employment, unemployment, migration, etc. These minimum wage effects could be reduced by defining an area's minimum wage in terms of either the area's general wage level or its cost of living. While geographical differentials would not solve all the employment problems created by the minimum wage, they would, in contrast to demographic differentials, treat even-handedly all low-wage workers within the same area.

Objections can be raised about each type of differential minimum wage. As indicated early in this paper, differentials represent a second-best policy. They are an attempt to alleviate problems caused by the standard minimum wage without removing the basic cause of the problem. However, if differentials are to be taken seriously, they require much more careful study than they have received to date. Otherwise, differential minimum wage policy is likely to be just another example of government regulation chasing its own tail.

Bibliography

Becker, B. E., and Hills, S. M. "Today's Teenage Unemployment—Tomorrow's Working Poor?" *Monthly Labor Review* 102 (January 1979): 69–71.

Cotterill, P. "The Development and Evaluation of Minimum Wage Policy towards Youth: Some Research Guidelines." Prepared for the U.S. Department of Labor, Office of the Assistant Secretary of Planning, Evaluation, and Research, December 1974.

———. "The Minimum Wage and Employment Growth in Retail Trade." *Proceedings of the Business and Economic Statistics Section of the American Statistical Association,* 1974: 319–24.

Cotterill, P., and Wadycki, W. "Minimum Wage Coverage and Relative Wage Rates in Retail Trade." *Proceedings of the Business and Economic Statistics Section of the American Statistical Association,* 1973: 345–50.

———. "Teenagers and the Minimum Wage in Retail Trade." *Journal of Human Resources* 11 (Winter 1976): 69–85.

Elder, P. "The 1977 Amendments to the Federal Minimum Wage Law." *Monthly Labor Review* 101 (January 1978): 9–11.

Fisher, A. A. "The Minimum Wage and Teenage Unemployment: A Comment on the Literature." *Western Economic Journal* 11 (December 1973): 514–24.

Goldfarb, R. S. "The Policy Content of Quantitative Minimum Wage Research." Industrial Relations Research Association, *Proceedings of the Twenty-seventh Annual Meeting,* 1974: 261–68.

Gramlich, E. M. "Impact of Minimum Wages on Other Wages, Employment, and Family Incomes." *Brookings Papers on Economic Activity 2* (1976): 409–51.

Kosters, M., and Welch, F. "The Effects of Minimum Wages on the Distribution of Changes in Aggregate Employment." *American Economic Review* 62 (June 1972): 323–32.

Lovell, M. C. "The Minimum Wage, Teenage Unemployment and the Business Cycle." *Western Economic Journal* 10 (December 1972): 414–27.

National Institute of Public Management. *Income Security Newsletter* 4 (July 1979).

Parsons, D. "The Cost of School Time, Forgone Earnings, and Human Capital Formation." Unpublished manuscript, Ohio State University, February 1973.

Schwartzman, D. "The Growth of Sales Per Manhour in Retail Trade, 1919–1963." In *Production and Productivity in the Service Industries,* V. R. Fuchs, editor. New York: National Bureau of Economic Research, 1969.

Siskind, F. B. "Minimum Wage Legislation in the United States: Comment." *Economic Inquiry* 15 (January 1977): 135–38.

U.S. Department of Commerce. *Survey of Economic Opportunity.* Washington: U.S. Government Printing Office, 1967.

U.S. Department of Commerce, Bureau of the Census. *Census of Business,* vol. 1. Washington: U.S. Government Printing Office, 1967.

Weiss, L. W. "Concentration and Labor Earnings." *American Economic Review* 57 (March 1966): 96–117.

Welch, F. "Minimum Wage Legislation in the United States." *Economic Inquiry* 12 (September 1974): 285–318.

———. "Minimum Wage Legislation in the United States: Reply." *Economic Inquiry* 15 (January 1977): 139–42.

Welch, F., and Cunningham, J. "Effects of Minimum Wages on the Level and Age Composition of Youth Employment." *Review of Economics and Statistics* 60 (February 1978): 140–45.

Macroeconomic Implications the Minimum Wage

J. Huston McCulloch

In this paper we examine the impact of a legally mandated minimum wage on several aspects of the economy, which we call macroeconomic for want of a better name. The direct, microeconomic effect of the minimum wage on unemployment is discussed at great length elsewhere in this volume. It concerns us here, but only indirectly.

We first consider the effect of the minimum wage on the price level and the inflation rate: Is indexation of the minimum wage to a price or wage index particularly inflationary? We then examine the implications of the minimum wage for monetary policy, in particular its effect on the so-called natural unemployment rate, and the political difficulties this implies for counterinflationary monetary policy. Finally, we discuss the effects of the minimum wage on the rate of capital formation, the long-run demand for labor, and income equality.

The Minimum Wage and Inflation

A common misconception regarding minimum wage legislation holds that the minimum wage rate is inflationary.

Rayburn M. Williams, for example, recently argued that the January 1, 1978, increase in the minimum hourly wage from $2.30 to $2.65 "alone contributed about .45 of a percentage point to the rate of inflation in 1978" and that the increase to $2.90 an hour on January 1, 1979, "added about one third of a percentage point to the 1979 inflation rate."[1]

This argument is attractive. If costs to any particular firm or industry rise, they will be passed along to consumers in the form of higher prices. Labor, even labor on the margin of being affected by the minimum wage, is an important component of those costs. If the wages of workers who are most directly affected by the minimum wage are x percent of

NOTE: The author is indebted to Michael Darby, Belton Fleisher, Laurence McCulloch, and Simon Rottenberg for helpful comments and suggestions.

[1] Rayburn M. Williams, *Inflation: Money, Jobs and Politicians* (Arlington Heights, Ill.: AHM Publishing Corporation, 1980), p. 90.

total costs, it seems obvious that a *y* percent increase in the minimum wage will increase the price level by *xy* percent.

In addition to this "cost-push" effect described by Williams, we may also expect a "demand-pull" effect on inflation. Workers whose wages are increased by the minimum wage will (assuming they remain employed) have that much more to spend. Their increased demand for goods and services would drive prices even higher than cost considerations alone might predict.

Finally, it may be argued that the disemployment effect of a minimum wage increase could also affect prices. Unemployment implies reduced output of goods and services. It would seem that for any given level of demand, reducing output would cause shortages and price increases.

Why the Minimum Wage Is Not Inflationary

However plausible these intuitive arguments are, we believe they are erroneous, because the cost-push, demand-pull, and disemployment effects are each directly offset elsewhere in the economy.

Higher costs of production may drive up the prices of some goods. However, the consumers who must pay higher prices for these goods will have less to spend on other goods. Since demand for these other goods will be reduced, their prices will tend to *fall*. The net effect of the minimum wage increase from the cost side will be to raise the price of goods requiring much low-skill labor to produce relative to the price of goods requiring little low-skill labor. Thus, changing costs may induce a change in *relative* prices, but not a general increase in prices.

As for the demand-pull argument, higher wages mean higher earnings for employed workers, but at the same time they also mean lower profits for employers. The workers may spend more, driving up the prices of the goods they buy. But at the same time, dividends and/or retained earnings must be smaller. Expenditures by shareholders or by the firm on new investment must be lower. This reduction in purchasing power will have a depressing effect on the prices of goods that would have been bought by the shareholders or the firm. To the extent that employers and employees have different spending habits, there will be changes in relative prices, but not a general increase in prices.

Even the disemployment effect does not clearly influence the price level, at least immediately. As workers are laid off because of a minimum wage increase, output will fall somewhat, but this output has approximately the same value as the earnings lost by the displaced workers. Aggregate supply decreases, but so does aggregate demand. Once again, there is no reason to expect the net effect to be inflationary.

318

What Does Determine Inflation?

According to what is known as the quantity theory of money, the price level that the economy settles on is the one that equalizes the demand and supply for money. The real demand for money is determined by the total volume of real transactions that money must be used to execute and the average period of time each dollar is held in the process. The money supply, on the other hand, is set in nominal (current dollar) terms by the policies of the Federal Reserve System and the operations of the banking system. There is only one value of the price that will give the nominal money supply the same real value as the demand for real cash balances.

Changes in the minimum wage rate are therefore not useful in explaining inflation. We have had rapid inflation since 1965 because the monetary base (to which other monetary aggregates are roughly proportional) has been growing at an annual rate of over 8 percent. Real income (and therefore the demand for real cash balances) usually grows by only about 3 percent per year. The difference has been made up by inflation. The rapid acceleration in inflation during 1979 was the delayed effect of a sustained increase in the monetary growth rate to over 9 percent per year early in 1977, not the result of the recent substantial raises in the minimum wage rate.

Accidental Imbalance

Even though the cost-push, demand-pull, and disemployment effects each have an inflationary aspect offset by a comparable deflationary aspect, the two aspects may not affect prices simultaneously. Furthermore, different prices do not respond with equal speed to imbalances of supply and demand. It is true, therefore, that there may be an accidental net effect in one direction (or the other) on the price level. Such an accidental net effect would be evident in the short-run inflation rate. However, it could not become permanent unless it were deliberately "ratified" by an appropriate adjustment of the money supply.

If the accidental net effect were a rise in prices, the real value of the number of dollars in the economy would be reduced to an inconveniently low level. Individuals and firms would try to reduce their demand for goods and services a little (relative to the amount they were supplying) in order to replenish their real cash balances. This shortfall of demand relative to supply would eventually depress prices, negating the accidental inflationary effect of the increase in the minimum wage.

The accidental net effect could just as easily be deflationary as inflationary, increasing the real value of the money supply. Individuals would feel free to spend or invest their surplus cash balances, causing an excess of demand over supply of goods. This excess demand for goods would tend to raise prices, cancelling out the accidental net effect. Whatever the accidental net effect, the price level would eventually return to the value dictated by money supply and demand.

The Minimum Wage and Money Demand

The minimum wage *could* raise prices, but only indirectly through the demand for money. The demand for money depends on the level of real output, which we have thus far tacitly assumed to be constant. In fact, a minimum wage will tend to cause less employment of low-skilled workers, reducing output and consequently the demand for real cash balances. For any given money supply, a somewhat higher price level will therefore be necessary to equalize money supply and demand than would have been the case without a minimum wage. While this effect is undeniable, it is also quite small and could easily go unnoticed. It is not what Williams and others have in mind when they claim that the minimum wage rate is inflationary.

Furthermore, this effect cannot cause sustained inflation. With a minimum wage, the equilibrium price level would be slightly higher than without. Introducing a minimum wage or raising the minimum wage relative to average wages will cause a small one-time-only shift in the price level, but then will have no further effect on the inflation rate. Sustained inflation must have other causes.

Indexation of the Minimum Wage

Since World War II, the minimum wage rate has been steadily eroded by inflation. As prices rise, the real purchasing power value of any given dollars-and-cents value of the minimum wage is reduced, so that the minimum wage is essentially repealed by the inflation. The response of Congress has been to restore the real value of the minimum wage by periodically mandating a new nominal level for it. In this way, it has been between about 40 and 50 percent of the average wage in manufacturing.[2] Since 1961, Congress has actually tried to anticipate future inflation by writing several increases over a period of time into a single bill. This practice has one disadvantage, however: if inflation is less than

---

[2] This ratchet effect is illustrated in *Minimum Wage Legislation,* AEI Legislative Analysis no. 7, 95th Congress (Washington, D.C.: American Enterprise Institute for Public Policy Research, 1977), p. 2.

Congress anticipated, the real value of the minimum wage will be greater than Congress intended.

To avoid this erratic behavior of the minimum wage, some economists have proposed indexing it to a price or wage index. Such indexing has been proposed since 1947 at least and has received increased attention in the past few years.[3] A perennial concern with such indexation is the fear that it would fuel inflation. It would seem that with indexation, a little inflation somewhere in the economy will be translated immediately into an increase in the minimum wage, raising costs and prices, spurring a further increase in the dollar value of the indexed minimum wage, and so on.

In fact, an indexed minimum wage would be no more inflationary than an unindexed one. The indexed adjustment does immediately raise costs and earnings of employed workers and simultaneously reduce output of disemployed workers. But these factors are immediately offset by the reduced purchasing power of those buying products requiring relatively much unskilled labor, the reduced profits of employers, and the reduced income of the disemployed workers. The mechanism by which the minimum wage rate is set does not alter its effects on the price level.

Indexation would force Congress to confront the basic issues involved: Should there even be a minimum wage? And if so, at what level relative to average wages should it be fixed? In the past, the damage done by any fixed dollar minimum wage has largely been undone by inflation. Even the mandated increases built into the dollar value of the minimum wage since 1961 have been effectively repealed by accelerating inflation that has proceeded faster than Congress had anticipated. If the minimum wage were indexed at a high fraction of average wages, however, Congress would finally have to examine the full implications for unemployment of its intended policy.

The Minimum Wage and Monetary Policy

Macroeconomists speak of the "natural unemployment rate" as that rate that would prevail if inflation were fully anticipated. According to the natural unemployment rate hypothesis, this rate is the same no matter what the actual inflation rate is. Thus, if people expect 10 percent inflation and there actually is 10 percent inflation, there will be the same unemployment rate, other things held constant, as if people expected zero inflation and prices turned out to be constant.

The use of monetary policy to control inflation is hampered by the

[3] Ibid., pp. 19–20.

effects of inflation on the natural unemployment rate. If inflation is less than anticipated, unemployment tends to rise above the natural rate of unemployment, along what is called the short-run Phillips curve. On the other hand, a monetary policy that allows inflation to accelerate will move the economy in the opposite direction along the short-run Phillips curve, reducing unemployment below the natural rate to the extent that the inflation is underanticipated.

One important factor that macroeconomists do not ordinarily dwell upon when they discuss the natural rate hypothesis is that the "other things constant" that determine the size of the natural rate do not in fact remain constant. "Frictional unemployment," due to the prohibitive cost of matching unemployed persons to jobs instantly, is one ever-present component of the natural rate and probably always will be. In the 1920s the natural rate of unemployment was about 3 or 4 percent, and most of this was probably frictional unemployment.

Since the 1930s, however, a number of factors may have operated to increase the natural rate. The Wagner Act of 1936 gave a majority of workers at any covered work place the power to impose union bargaining on all other workers at that work place, as well as on all potential workers there. This greatly reduced competition in the covered sectors of the labor market. The Fair Labor Standards Act of 1938 introduced the minimum wage itself, which tends to reduce the employment rate of unskilled workers, especially of teenagers, blacks, and women. If even a fraction of these disemployed persons shows up in the unemployment statistics, the measured natural unemployment rate will have been increased. Finally, many transfer programs (some of which were already present before the Vietnam war, but which have increased dramatically since the war) are conditional on the recipient's being unemployed. This encourages people who are between jobs not to look as hard for new employment as they otherwise would.

All these factors have increased the natural rate of unemployment that monetary policy must start from. By the early 1960s, the natural rate was probably 5 or 6 percent. Today it is surely at least 7 percent, and possibly 8 percent or even higher. The unemployment rate was below 6 percent throughout 1979, but that was only because the 13.3 percent inflation rate for 1979 was far greater than anyone had anticipated.

Although the minimum wage is not directly inflationary, it may have an indirect influence on monetary policy and therefore on inflation through its effect on the natural rate of unemployment. Without the minimum wage, the natural rate would probably be lower, and the monetary authorities would feel themselves under less political pressure to accelerate the inflation rate through more rapid monetary expansion.

The acceleration of the monetary expansion rate in 1964 and again in 1977 was, at least in part, a response to an unemployment rate considered to be unacceptably high.

On the other hand, deceleration of the inflation rate through monetary restraint would increase the unemployment rate to a level above the natural rate. Recent polls indicate Americans would very much like to see inflation reduced or even eliminated. Reducing or removing the minimum wage would make it much easier politically for the government to accomplish this.

The Minimum Wage and Capital Formation

The wage that labor can command in a competitive market depends upon its marginal product, the additional output that could be obtained by employing one additional worker. The marginal product of labor declines as the ratio of labor to other factors of production increases and ordinarily rises as the ratio of any of these factors to labor increases.

If a fixed quantity of land were the only factor of production besides labor and the population were growing, the real marginal product of labor would fall over time. Full employment would require real wages to fall, and a fixed real minimum wage would imply ever-growing unemployment. The importance to the economy of exhaustible resources, such as coal, oil, and other extractable minerals, would imply a declining marginal product of labor even with zero population growth.

Historically, real wages have risen without growing unemployment in spite of population growth, constant land surface of the earth, and exhaustion of natural resources. This increase has been made possible by the rapid accumulation of capital. Capital has increased not just in proportion to labor, but considerably more; and this increase has more than offset the declining ratios of land to labor and of resources to labor. The "increasing productivity of labor" that we have come to take for granted is partly due to the improved training that labor receives. But to a large extent it is due not to labor at all, but rather to the increasing amount of capital that labor has to work with.

For any given level of the capital stock, a mandatory minimum wage will increase the real wages of at least some workers, namely, those who compete most directly with the submarginal workers who become unemployed or who are forced to work for lower wages in uncovered industries. Political support for a minimum wage comes primarily from this group that stands to gain. If we take into account the effects of the minimum wage on capital formation, however, it is not clear that even this group gains in the long run.

Capital does not spring into existence of its own accord. It becomes

323

available only because investors believe it will be profitable. A minimum wage reduces the profitability of investment, on the average, and thus reduces the incentive to invest. It may actually increase the profitability of investing in uncovered industries, but this will be more than offset by decreased profitability in covered industries. The long-run effect of a minimum wage will therefore be to reduce the capital stock, and thus the marginal product of labor, below what it would otherwise have been.

A minimum wage set at a certain fraction of the average wage of employed workers may therefore ultimately reduce the real earnings even of those who receive a short-run benefit from the minimum wage. Attempts to offset this tendency by increasing the minimum wage relative to average wages would be futile, since they would simply increase the probability that the workers who would otherwise benefit in the short run would themselves end up unemployed.

Michael Darby of UCLA has argued that the capital stock will in fact ultimately decrease so far that the quality-adjusted marginal product of employed workers will end up just where it would have been without the minimum wage. In this case, employed workers would eventually entirely lose their short-run gain from the minimum wage before taxes. After taxes, they would actually lose if they were liable for additional taxes to provide welfare and unemployment benefits to the disemployed workers.[4]

We must conclude that even those workers who stand to gain from the minimum wage in the short run will probably lose in the long run. Conversely, those workers who might lose in the short run from removing or reducing the minimum wage may well end up gaining before long.

The Minimum Wage and Income Equality

A minimum wage is sometimes advocated in spite of its negative effects on employment, economic efficiency, and investment incentives, in the belief that it will nevertheless increase income equality. Proponents of this argument value equality for its own sake and believe that, at least up to a point, equalizing the portions would justify a reduction in the size of the total pie divided.

To examine this problem, the present author has modeled the economy as consisting of three interest groups, each of which is affected differently by the minimum wage: unskilled workers who either become unemployed or must seek lower-paying work in the uncovered sector

---

[4] Michael Darby, "A Long-Run Analysis of Minimum Wage Laws," University of California at Los Angeles Economics Department Discussion Paper no. 68, November 1979.

of the economy, unskilled workers who remain employed and who receive higher wages, and a third group including both skilled workers and owners of nonlabor factors such as land, natural resources, and capital.[5]

The model showed that a minimum wage would increase the second group's share in total income at the expense of the shares of the first and third groups. Since the first group has the lowest income and the third group has the highest income, the minimum wage has an ambiguous effect on equality; it brings the second group more nearly into equality with the third at the same time it creates inequality between the first and second groups.

In order to combine the two effects, we investigated the behavior of the well-known Gini index of equality.[6]

Depending on the choice of simplifying assumptions about the production technology, a minimum wage could either raise or lower the Gini index. For the most plausible values of the parameters reflecting production technology, however, the net effect on equality would be negative. That is, the deteriorated position of the first group relative to the second would most likely more than offset the improved position of the second relative to the third. Therefore, the minimum wage is probably not the way to achieve the goal of greater equality.

If the minimum wage is universally applicable, so that the displaced workers are unemployed rather than employed in the uncovered sector, and if unemployment compensation is sufficiently generous (approaching the full earnings of employed counterparts), a minimum wage would increase equality. After taxes to pay for the transfers to the unemployed, however, both the first and second groups might well be worse off in absolute terms.

Conclusion

We have shown that the direct effect of the minimum wage on inflation is negligible, even if the minimum wage is indexed to the price level or to a wage level. It may, however, indirectly make an inflationary monetary policy more attractive politically, through its effect on the natural rate of unemployment. A far more serious direct macroeconomic implication of the minimum wage is its effect on long-run capital formation

[5] J. Huston McCulloch, "The Effect of Minimum Wage Legislation on Income Equality: A Theoretical Analysis," National Bureau of Economic Research (West), Discussion Paper no. 171, March 1977.

[6] The Lorenz curve is a graph showing the fraction of total income earned by the lowest-income x percent of the population. The Gini index is the area under this curve as a fraction of its maximum possible value.

and the future earnings and employment prospects of the economy. Finally, we have pointed out that a minimum wage is more likely to reduce than to increase the equality of income distribution in the economy.

Minimum Wages in Puerto Rico

Simon Rottenberg

The experience of Puerto Rico reveals in striking form the adverse effects that legal minimum wages can have upon the standard of life of the working population and some of the hidden purposes sought by those who promote the enforcement of minimum wages by law.

The Fair Labor Standards Act was enacted by Congress in 1938 and has been amended some twenty times. The act defines the segments of the labor market to which it applies and specifies the minimum hourly wage that may be legally paid to covered workers. With minor exceptions, there is a single, uniform minimum wage for all covered workers in the fifty states.

The minimum hourly wage under the law was $0.25 in 1938. It has been ratcheted up by amendment to $3.10 in 1980 and will become $3.35 in 1981.

The $0.25 minimum of 1938 also applied to Puerto Rico, where it produced massive disemployment. As a result, the law was amended in 1940 to provide an arrangement for that island different from that applied to the continental United States. The arrangement has been modified from time to time, but fundamentally it provided for industry committees, convened by the U.S. Department of Labor, which would recommend to the department minimum wages for the industries or industry parts defined by the committees' terms of reference.[1] The committees, which held hearings before making their recommendations, were tripartite, with representatives of the public, organized labor, and employers, all named by the Department of Labor.

The committees were instructed by Congress to recommend "the highest minimum wage rate (not in excess of the minimum wage rate then applying uniformly for covered employees in the continental United States) which (1) will not substantially curtail employment (in the in-

---

[1] For a good, succinct review of the changes in minimum-wage-making procedures in Puerto Rico under the Fair Labor Standards Act, see Josephine C. Stein, "The Fair Labor Standards Act and Its Relation to the Economic Development Process in Puerto Rico" (Paper prepared for presentation at a Conference of the Society of Government Economists, San Juan, P.R., April 1976), duplicated.

327

dustry classification for which the recommendation is being made) and (2) will not give a competitive advantage to any group in the industry." In the administration of the law, the words "will not give a competitive advantage to any group in the industry" were interpreted to mean "will not give firms in Puerto Rico a competitive advantage over firms in the continental United States that produce the same or similar products."

By 1980 several hundred industry committees had met and made recommendations to the Department of Labor. At the end of 1977, minimum wage rates had been specified for 140 industry classifications, from certain machine operators on sugar farms, through workers manufacturing rubber products, to employees in motion picture theaters.

In 1978 the industry committee procedure was abandoned by the secretary of labor, and certain clauses of the amended statute that provided for automatic increases took over. In 1981 the continental U.S. minimum wage of $3.35 per hour will be effective in Puerto Rico for all but 29 of the 140 classifications for which separate minimums were specified in 1977. Most of those 29 are in agriculture or agricultural processing, and even most of them are to be close to $3.35 per hour.[2]

The Fair Labor Standards Act is comprehensive in its coverage in Puerto Rico. Of 513,000 employed, nonsupervisory wage and salary workers in March 1976, 473,000 were subject to the minimum wage provisions of the act. Coverage has been extended over the years by amendments to the act. Of the 473,000 workers covered in 1976, 213,000 would have been covered before 1966, 101,000 were covered as a result of amendments of 1966, and an additional 159,000 were covered by amendments of 1974.[3]

The imposition of minimum wages has had much more significant effects in Puerto Rico than in the continental United States. Except in a few industries and occupations, only a very small fraction of mainland workers are paid wages at, or close to, the legal minimum. In Puerto Rico, on the other hand, the wage rates paid to most workers in a large number of economic activities are at, or close to, the legal minimum. In 1975 through 1977, for example, some 90 percent of workers in agriculture were paid exactly the minimum wage or not over twenty cents per hour more. The corresponding percentages in some other industries were filler tobacco processing, 99 percent; belt manufacturing, 81 percent; women's hosiery manufacture, 63 percent; children's dress manufacture, 79 percent; milk processing and distribution, 62 percent;

[2] U.S. Department of Labor, Wage and Hour Division, *Minimum Wage Rates for Puerto Rico,* WH Publication 1348, duplicated (Washington, D.C., April 1978).

[3] U.S. Department of Labor, *Wage Structure and Fringe Benefits in Puerto Rico* (Prepared for the Puerto Rico Economic Study Commission, May 1979 update), duplicated (Washington, D.C., 1979), p. 187.

candy and gum products manufacture, 62 percent; and vitreous china manufacture, 69 percent.[4]

Since the minimum wage greatly affects the actual wages paid, it substantially determines the market price of labor in Puerto Rico. Legal minimum wages are thus more powerful and less superfluous in Puerto Rico than on the mainland. If they have perverse, distorting, and mal-allocational effects, those effects will be stronger and their adverse consequences correspondingly larger. In fact, the distortions generated by the systematic overpricing of labor, by federal law, in the Puerto Rican labor market are evident.

Puerto Rico is a labor-abundant community. Its population is now about 3.5 million, and its area is about 3,500 square miles. The density of population is thus about 1,000 per square mile; the population density in the mainland United States is about 61 per square mile.

The relative abundance of human resources in the island would be reflected in the price of labor services if the terms of transactions for such services were unconstrained by law or by the exercise of labor market monopoly power. It would be a price that would instruct and guide market behavior. Those offering services would find buyers for them. Resources complementary to labor in the production of commodities and services would be combined with labor in their proper proportions. Economic activities that are labor-intensive would tend to locate in the island. Efficient price sets, expressing the relative scarcities of different resources, would generate behavior that maximized the island's economic output.

The minimum wage law, however, distorted the relative prices of resources. It produced a set of signals, to which economic behavior adjusted, that had perverse effects. It caused labor services to carry a price higher than that which expressed their true relative scarcity value and therefore caused the services of resources complementary to labor to carry prices lower than those appropriate to their relative scarcity values.

In these circumstances, economic theory teaches, the minimum wage law would forestall labor service transactions that both some workers and some employers would find attractive and advantageous. Some aspirant workers would be pushed into unemployment; the quantity of capital formed in Puerto Rico, either by insular domestic saving or by importation, would be diminished; the structure of economic activity would be less labor-intensive than was appropriate to the true social value of labor and other resources; techniques of production would be put in place that used too little labor and too much of other resources;

[4] Ibid., p. 137.

some owners of capital assets making locational decisions would search out other places to lodge their investments; and there would be less on-the-job training of workers, especially in general skills that are usefully transferable to employment in firms other than that in which the training occurs.

The aggregate effect of all of these distortions was that Puerto Rico could be expected to produce fewer goods and services than would otherwise have been produced and that the rate at which insular per capita income rose toward mainland United States income standards could be expected to be dampened. In sum, the minimum wage law could be expected to reduce the rate of improvement in the standard of life of the Puerto Rican people and to intensify poverty in the island.

Some of these consequences of overpricing labor are difficult to observe. Unemployment of labor, however, is an effect that is clearly seen. Perloff's study of the Puerto Rican economy, published in 1950, says that "the application of the federal wage-and-hour regulation [in 1938] almost killed the entire needle-work industry and threatened the existence of other industries as well."[5] A report by Robert R. Nathan Associates states:

> When the Congress established a minimum wage of 25 cents per hour in 1938, the average hourly wage in the United States was 62.7 cents. . . . It resulted in a mandatory wage increase for only some 300,000 workers out of a labor force of more than 54 million. In Puerto Rico, in contrast, . . . the new Federal minimum far exceeded the prevailing average hourly wage of the major portion of Puerto Rican workers. If a continuing serious attempt at enforcement . . . had been made, it would have meant literal economic chaos for the island's economy. In fact, a later congressional committee said, in referring to the 1938 act, "The effect was disastrous to the economy of the island."[6]

The unemployed are reported to have been 16.0 percent of the labor force in 1940. The rate declined to 10.3 percent in 1970, but it was 20.0 percent in 1977, 18.8 percent in 1978, and 17.5 percent in 1979.[7] Another source shows the 1977 unemployment rate as an even higher 23.0 percent and the 1980 rate as 20.0 percent. In 1980 the rate for sixteen- to nine-

[5] Harvey S. Perloff, *Puerto Rico's Economic Future: A Study in Planned Development* (Chicago: University of Chicago Press, 1950), p. 152.

[6] Robert R. Nathan Associates, Inc., *Minimum Wage Issue in Puerto Rico, 1973,* duplicated (Washington, D.C., May 1973), p. 3.

[7] Puerto Rico, Junta de Planificacion, *Informe Económico al Governador, 1979,* duplicated (San Juan, 1980), p. 301.

teen-year-olds was 48.0 percent and for twenty- to twenty-four-year-olds 33.0 percent.[8]

Unemployment is exacerbated by short workweeks; the number of hours in any time period for which the services of labor will be hired is also partially a function of the price of labor. An effective minimum wage will tend to cause part-time employment to be substituted for full-time employment.[9] The rate of unemployment in 1976 was 19.5 percent of the labor force, but an additional 11.7 percent of the labor force were reported as underemployed. A large fraction of the underemployed are persons who work less than thirty-five hours per week for a salary or a wage and are reported to want to work more hours.[10] Between a fifth and a quarter of all people at work in Puerto Rico work less than thirty-five hours per week.[11]

The underemployed are also defined to include "self-employed persons who wanted to work more hours" and subsistence farmers. These persons are engaged in economic activities not covered by the minimum wage law. Since the enforcement of that law will decrease the number employed in industries and occupations to which it applies, those who are disemployed in those industries and occupations will make their way either to unemployment or to employment in the interstices of the economy where the minimum wage law does not apply. Much of the underemployment in self-employed activities and in subsistence farming is thus attributable to the enforcement of legal minimum wages in the wage-and-salary segments of the economy.

Even the large quantity of unemployment and of underemployment in Puerto Rico does not tell the whole story of the perverse effects of minimum wages on the insular economy. Workers who learn from their own job search experience or from that of kinfolk, friends, and neighbors that the search for work, at prices specified by law, will be fruitless withdraw from the labor market. If they are not actively seeking work, they are counted as "out of the labor force," rather than as "unemployed."

Labor force participation rates are much lower in Puerto Rico than in the mainland United States. In 1978, 44 percent of the adult popu-

[8] U.S. Department of Commerce, *Economic Study of Puerto Rico*, vol. 1, 1980, p. 70.

[9] Edward M. Gramlich, "Impact of Minimum Wages on Other Wages, Employment, and Family Incomes," *Brookings Papers on Economic Activity 2* (1976): 442.

[10] Commonwealth of Puerto Rico, Office of the Governor, *An Agenda for a Socio-economic Study of Puerto Rico,* Part Two, *Problems Affecting Development of Puerto Rican Society,* duplicated (June 1977), p. 157 and table III–A–10.

[11] U.S. Department of Commerce, Bureau of the Census, *Statistical Abstract of the United States,* 100th ed., 1979, table 1529, p. 877.

lation of the island were in the labor force;[12] the corresponding percentage in the continental United States was 62. The participation rate for sixteen- to nineteen-year-olds in Puerto Rico was only half the rate on the mainland. Low participation rates in the island are said to reflect "the lack of job prospects."[13] They mask unemployment, and the reported unemployment rates are thus underestimates.

The disemployment effects of minimum wages were graphically presented at congressional committee hearings in the mid-1950s by a needlework industry employer who had had, at that time, almost forty years of experience in the industry. Her testimony is especially interesting in revealing the substitution possibilities for the location of needlework manufacturing activity that put employment opportunities for workers in Puerto Rico in jeopardy when their services are overpriced by the law.

She testified (in condensed form):

> The needlework industry of Puerto Rico is considered its second in importance for the many thousands of workers it employs. It started in a small way by producing items like handkerchiefs, collar and cuff sets, and table linens, all embroidered and drawn-worked by hand, for sale in small linen gift shops.
>
> During the First World War, European and Asiatic articles of embroidery and drawn work were not available to United States importers and factories were opened in Puerto Rico.
>
> After the War, needlework contractors in Puerto Rico copied the stitches made in France and Ireland and taught the workers how to make French hand rolling and bullion stitches, colored passed threads imitating the Swiss cords, and many other fancy stitches which were used in the embellishment of handkerchiefs, cotton underwear, and household linens.
>
> In 1934, the NRA was approved by the Congress and a code was drafted for the needlework industry. This was applicable to Puerto Rico. With the enforcement of the NRA code, which imposed higher wages and shorter hours of work, a number of manufacturers and contractors vanished from the island. Manufacturers who were operating here opened new factories in the Philippines and others made connections in China and the industry had a collapse. The NRA was in effect for only one year and the industry continued in existence.
>
> In 1938, the Fair Labor Standards Act was passed by the Congress and Puerto Rico was included in the provisions of the law.

[12] Puerto Rico, Bureau of Labor Statistics, *Informe Estadístico* 1, no. 11 (November 1979): table 1.

[13] U.S. Department of Commerce, *Economic Study of Puerto Rico,* vol. 1, pp. 70–71.

The conditions and problems of the island were not considered. We were compelled to pay the same minimum wages as applied in the mainland.

Seven or eight factories manufacturing children's dresses in Puerto Rico practically disappeared. When the minimum wage rates were increased, the manufacturers who were sending work to Puerto Rico for hand embroidery substituted making them by machine because it was cheaper, and some of the stitches that were done by hand, such as smocking, fagoting, and even embroidery, were done by machine and no longer is it necessary to send the work to Puerto Rico. Furthermore, for combined machine sewing and hand embellishing, Madeira and the Philippine Islands entered into competition with us.

After two long years of difficulties, uncertainty, and disruption of the industry the Act was amended to provide for special industry committees. The committees set wage rates that were higher than the industry could afford to pay to compete with foreign countries.

In 1944 the handkerchief industry was revived, and 18,000 workers were employed. In 1947, the handkerchief industry started to move to China and the Philippines. The handkerchief industry disappeared and by the mid 1950s no hand-embroidered handkerchiefs are being made in Puerto Rico. As to hand-rolled edge, this also has gone to the Philippine Islands where the prices for labor do not admit competition.

Table or household linens that constituted the second most important line of work in the needlework industry were affected considerably by the wage rates promulgated in 1945. The minimum wage rates established in 1949 made it prohibitive to use the various stitches used in the embroidery and appliqué work on towels, bridge sets, scarves, doilies and pillowcases. Similar goods produced in the Azores, Madeira, China and Japan are imported into the United States, duty paid, at prices much lower than what we have to pay here for labor only.

At present household linens all done by hand have practically disappeared from the island. Should labor wages go still higher it would be cheaper to get the table linen work we still do from Ireland and have it shipped by airfreight and even paying duty it would be possible to land these items in New York at a lower figure than they could be made in Puerto Rico.[14]

The opportunities to locate economic activity in other places than Puerto

[14] U.S. Congress, House, Committee on Education and Labor, *Hearings on Amending the Minimum Wage Law as Applied to Puerto Rico and the Virgin Islands,* testimony of Maria Luisa Arcelay, 84th Congress, 1st session, December 1, 2, and 5, 1955, pp. 50–75.

Rico and the jeopardy in which employment opportunities for Puerto Rican workers in particular industries are put by minimum wage laws are strikingly exhibited by comparing average hourly earnings and legal minimum wages in Puerto Rico with average hourly earnings in other countries where the price of labor is permitted to express more correctly the relative abundance of human resources.

In the early 1970s, average hourly wages in all manufacturing industries in India were 8 percent of average manufacturing wages in Puerto Rico, in Taiwan they were 10 percent of Puerto Rican wages, in Korea 13 percent, in Singapore 12 percent, in the Dominican Republic 20 percent, in Columbia 16 percent, in El Salvador 19 percent, and in Mexico 38 percent.[15] Average hourly earnings in the textile industries in Puerto Rico were $2.36 in 1976, and the minimum wage rates were from $2.00 to $2.30 in different sectors of the textile industry in late 1977. Average hourly earnings in textiles in 1976 were $0.42 in Taiwan, $0.44 in Korea, $0.78 in Hong Kong, and $1.29 in Mexico.[16]

Apparel manufacture is an important industry in Puerto Rico; in 1978 about 35,000 workers were employed in it. In the mid-1970s, average hourly earnings in apparel manufacture in Puerto Rico were $2.14, and the legal minimum wage rates in the industry were close to that number. At that time average hourly earnings in apparel manufacture were $0.37 in Bangladesh, $0.07 to $0.16 in Sri Lanka, $0.25 in India, $0.24 in Malaysia, $0.20 to $0.25 in Pakistan, $0.14 in the Philippines, and $0.29 in Singapore.[17]

The apparel manufacturing industry seems to survive in Puerto Rico because of explicit and implicit duties on foreign apparel imports into the United States; most of the output of the industry is marketed in the United States and, of course, there are no import duties on goods moving from Puerto Rico to the United States. Clearly, pushing the price of labor in Puerto Rico by law above the level at which it would be found by the market imperils the industry's survival in the island. Each artificially induced rise in the price of labor produces an incremental incentive to locate and relocate the industry in other places and thus compels workers in Puerto Rico to confront a dispreferred condition.

In 1965, 30 percent of all U.S. imports of clothing originated in Puerto Rico, 14 percent in Hong Kong, 1 percent in Korea, and 2 percent in Taiwan. In 1976 Puerto Rico's share had fallen to 9 percent, and the share of Hong Kong had risen to 32 percent, of Korea to 17

---

[15] Nathan Associates, *Minimum Wage in Puerto Rico,* p. 16.

[16] U.S. Department of Commerce, *Economic Study of Puerto Rico,* vol. 1, p. 109.

[17] U.S. Department of Labor, Wage and Hour Division, *The Apparel Industry in Puerto Rico,* October 1977 update, duplicated (1977), p. 27.

334

percent, and of Taiwan to 16 percent.[18] The minimum wage makers had signaled to apparel producers that they should search out other loci of production; the producers had responded.

The legal minimum wage can be expected to have depressed the level of skill of the Puerto Rican working population and to have reduced the rate at which the earnings of workers rise over the course of their working lives.

Training on the job is much more important in Puerto Rico than in the mainland United States from the point of view of the formation of a stock of skills embedded in the human resources of the working population. On the mainland the manufacturing tradition is older, and there has been a longer period in which skills have passed from parents to children. The network of institutions for vocational training is much larger and much more diverse in relation to population. The average number of years of formal schooling completed is also much higher. On-the-job training is important in Puerto Rico to compensate for its relatively disadvantaged position in the command of a stock of skills useful in the production and distribution of commodities and services.

On-the-job training is, however, costly. It consumes the time of skilled and experienced workers engaged in the instruction of neophytes; it physically depreciates machines and equipment; it wastes materials and spoils goods. If firms are to bear the costs of on-the-job training to communicate skills that can be "transported" to other firms as workers move among employers, the system must compensate them for it, or it will not be done.[19]

Where minimum wages do not intervene, on-the-job training does occur, and employers engaged in it are compensated. Their compensation is the payment of a lower wage to workers who are learning on the job than to others employed in the same occupations who already command the relevant skills. Workers earn less in the years in which they are learning on the job and, when they come to command the skill, they earn more. When they offer their skilled work, they are paid a wage that compensates them for their lower earnings when they were learners. Their real earnings are higher in the later years of their working lives than in the beginning years.

The enforcement of minimum wages in Puerto Rico, by raising the price of the services of employed young workers, can thus be expected to deprive employers of remuneration for training costs. Therefore, less training will be done on the job, with the result that the lifetime earning

---

[18] U.S. Department of Commerce, *Economic Study of Puerto Rico,* vol. 1, p. 108.

[19] Sherwin Rosen, "Learning and Experience in the Labor Market," *Journal of Human Resources* 7, no. 3 (Summer 1972):326–42.

pattern of Puerto Rican workers will be flatter than it would have been and the stock of skill they command will be less. A less skilled labor force will produce a smaller output of goods and services. The real income of the people will be smaller.

In on-the-job training, workers "buy" the training services of employers by implicitly "paying" in the form of lower earnings in the years when skills are being acquired. If minimum wage laws force wage rates up in those early working years, firms will do less training on the job because they are less adequately compensated for their training costs.

In those circumstances, workers might substitute other training strategies, at their own explicit cost, for the forestalled training activities of employers. If they are to trouble to acquire incremental skills in those ways, however, they must be reimbursed for the cost of training by payoffs in the form of higher earnings in later years when they perform more skilled services. Anything that compresses wage differentials for workers of different levels of skill will diminish the payoff for investment in the acquisition of skill. The smaller the differences between the wages of unskilled workers and those of skilled workers, the smaller is the incentive to individual workers to add to the stock of skill that they command.

A much higher percentage of employed workers in Puerto Rico are employed at the legal minimum wage or at a wage just above the minimum than in the mainland United States. It appears that the minimum wage compresses the wage structure by pushing up the wage rates of less skilled workers and thus diminishes the incentive for workers to invest in acquiring skills at their own explicit cost. As a result, the check on the growth of the aggregate stock of skill in the island is compounded; not only is less training done on the job, but less is also done through other arrangements for forming human capital. To repeat, less skill means less output in the economy, and less output means more deprivation and poverty for the island's people.

If the enforcement in Puerto Rico of minimum wages higher than those that would prevail in a competitive market economy has the adverse effects previously noted, why has such a law been enacted?

In part, it has been enacted because of a genuinely beneficent intention to improve the conditions of life of the Puerto Rican worker by people who do not understand its full consequences. They observe that the costs of some commodities are higher in Puerto Rico than on the mainland because the density of population raises land rents and because exchanged goods must be transported longer distances. They define a comfort-and-decency standard of life, calculate the cost of its acquisition and the hourly wage that would be necessary to acquire it, and believe that the legal enforcement of such a wage will tend to make that standard of life available to the island's workers. They do not understand the infinite variety of adjustment in the economy that changes in relative prices can generate; they do not understand that the conquest of poverty requires the enlargement of the community's output of commodities and services; they do not understand that well-intentioned policies can be perverse in their effects and can produce consequences exactly the opposite of those that are intended.

The enactment by Congress of minimum wage statutes that apply in Puerto Rico results also, however, from pressure on Congress that is not essentially intended to advantage Puerto Rican workers, but rather to do them damage. The pressures exerted on Congress by trade unions of mainland American workers are a case in point.

Trade unions of workers who live and work on the mainland adopt policies that serve the interests of those workers. One such policy is to enlarge the demand for the services of those workers by diminishing the demand for substitutes, such as the services of Puerto Rican workers. The quantity of insular workers' services that is wanted in the market is a partial function of its price. The higher the wage rate in Puerto Rico, the more Puerto Rican workers become imperfect substitutes for mainland workers.

Mainland trade unions know this. They have been the most aggressive promoters of minimum wage policies to raise the price of Puerto Rican labor. They sometimes employ a generous rhetoric ("we want a higher standard of life for the Puerto Rican worker"), but, fundamentally, they push the principle of insular "unfair competition" with U.S. mainland production as the ground for increasing wage rates in Puerto Rico.

It is clear that their intention is not to improve the conditions of Puerto Rican workers so much as to deprive those workers of employment opportunities by compelling them to offer their services at a high, legally defined price. Their interest lies in influencing the spatial distribution of particular kinds of economic activity so that more of the kinds of goods produced by their members will be made on the mainland and less in Puerto Rico. They want to affect the distribution of wealth and income to the advantage of particular sets of mainland workers at the expense of competitive Puerto Rican workers. The minimum wage law is an instrumental tactic employed by the unions to achieve that purpose. To the degree that they are successful, the effects are regressive, since Puerto Rican workers are poorer than mainland workers. The record is replete with evidence that U.S. trade unions pursue such a strategy. Testimony before a Senate subcommittee illustrates the point:

As long as the wage levels in Puerto Rico are held back, the insular industry gains an increasing unfair competitive advantage. . . . The growing unfair competitive advantage of Puerto Rico as against the mainland is evident . . . for all industries combined. . . . Let me illustrate how unfair competitive advantage offered by the low minimum wage standard in Puerto Rico spurs on industrial growth to the detriment of the mainland. . . . The nature of the expansion in Puerto Rico of this brassiere manufacturing industry illustrates the effect of unfair competition. . . . The story of the brassiere industry is about to be duplicated by the knitting mills producing sweaters and similar garments. . . . The unfair competitive advantage brought about by wage differentials is a distinct threat to mainland employers. . . . Runaways come to the island. . . . Let me give you one case. . . . It closed its doors, left its workers jobless, and moved to Puerto Rico. . . . The firm's owner walked out on his mainland obligations and on his 80 employees.[20]

The Fair Labor Standards Act is thus used by the trade unions to prevent the allocation of activity in space that would be appropriate to differences among regions in resource endowments, especially to differences in the endowment of human resources. The law becomes a machine that distorts the structure of the relative prices of labor in different places and slows the improvement of the material conditions of life of the people of Puerto Rico.

Thirty-five years ago, George J. Stigler published a paper on the economics of minimum wage legislation[21] in which he said that such legislation would not diminish poverty, would reduce aggregate output and decrease the earnings of workers who had previously been receiving materially less than the minimum, and would lead to the discharge of workers. The manipulation of individual prices (of labor), he maintained, is neither an efficient nor an equitable device for changing the distribution of personal income. The Puerto Rican experience confirms Professor Stigler's expectations. Those who believe otherwise have failed to keep in mind what actually determines the standard of material well-being of the people.

A minimum wage law cannot increase the income or wealth of a country. National income per capita cannot be increased by a statutory

---

[20] U.S. Congress, Senate, Subcommittee on Labor, Committee on Labor and Public Welfare, *Hearings on Amending the Fair Labor Standards Act of 1938*, testimony of David Dubinsky, president, International Ladies' Garment Workers' Union, AFL, accompanied by Arthur Goldberg, counsel, and Lazar Teper, research director of ILGWU, 84th Congress, 1st session, April 20, 1955, pp. 221–56.

[21] George J. Stigler, "The Economics of Minimum Wage Legislation," *American Economic Review* 36 (1946):358–65.

provision for the payment of higher wages. The income of a country is determined by the quantity of goods and services it produces, and the average standard of life is that quantity divided by the number in the country's population. Income per capita is affected by the size of the population, the percentage of the population engaged in production, the fraction of each time period devoted to work, and the average productivity of hours spent at work. Productivity depends on the assiduousness with which work is done, the skill of workers, the quantity of mechanical energy with which each worker is combined, and the level of technology embedded in the processes of work. Minimum wage laws do not produce favorable changes in any of these components that fundamentally determine a people's material standard of welfare.

With a given community output, it is possible to transfer income from one class to another. This is a risky business, however it is done, because transfers create disincentives that may diminish output, but surely a manipulation of relative resource prices that masks their true social values is an inept instrument for achieving income redistribution.

The Fair Labor Standards Act as applied to Puerto Rico is a failed and flawed public policy.

The Impact of Minimum Wages on Industrial Employment in Chile

Vittorio Corbo

Before 1973, Chilean politicians and economists generally believed that a minimum wage would serve as a direct way of providing a "decent" income to low-wage workers. Lately, although effective and legal minimum wage legislation has not been abolished, its enforcement has been modified, and the long-run distortions and disemployment effects of minimum wages are thought to outweigh any possible short-run benefits.

Minimum wage legislation in Chile has a long history. In 1937 a minimum salary for employees of the private sector (*sueldo vital*) was legislated. In 1953 a minimum wage for agricultural workers was established, and in 1956 a minimum wage for the industrial and commercial sectors was created. Thus, in Chile a minimum agricultural wage (MAW) existed before a minimum industrial wage (MIW). The minimum industrial wage is uniform across the country.

In table 1, the evolution of the *sueldo vital* (SV), minimum agricultural wage, and minimum industrial wage are presented.

From this table it is seen that the MAW increased substantially in 1959 and in 1965, so that by 1967 the MAW and the MIW were the same. In the early 1970s the gap between the SV and the MIW started to close rapidly, and by 1973 the two were about the same.

Starting in 1974, the SV, MAW, and MIW were increased yearly at a rate lower than inflation and thus became less relevant as a means of guaranteeing a "decent income." Furthermore, any wage distortion started to vanish after 1974.

Minimum wage legislation was introduced in Chile in an attempt to alter the distribution of income. It has been argued, however, that minimum wages distort relative factor prices and hence affect overall economic efficiency. The most important element in determining the income distribution effect of minimum wages is the creation of unem-

---

NOTE: I am grateful to Luis Riveros and M. Stelcner for their comments on an earlier version of this paper.

TABLE 1

EVOLUTION OF MINIMUM WAGES, 1956–1973

(in Chilean escudos)

	Sueldo Vital (SV)	Minimum Agricultural Wage (MAW)	Minimum Industrial Wage (MIW)
1956	323.5	81.4	146.0
1957	421.0	109.6	189.8
1958	505.3	135.5	233.6
1959	690.6	203.8	321.2
1960	690.6	247.5	321.2
1961	860.0	293.8	411.7
1962	1,001.3	339.5	478.9
1963	1,239.8	444.9	592.8
1964	1,802.8	662.5	861.4
1965	2,495.0	1,043.2	1,191.4
1966	3,143.2	1,421.3	1,498.0
1967	3,675.2	1,752.0	1,752.0
1968	4,480.2	2,135.6	2,135.6
1969	5,730.0	2,731.3	2,731.3
1970	7,408.9	4,380.0	4,380.0
1971	9,960.0	7,220.0	7,220.0
1972	15,240.0	13,800.0	13,800.0
1973	54,240.0	53,160.0	53,160.0

SOURCE: 1956–1970: R. Ffrench-Davis, *Políticas Económicas en Chile: 1952–1970* (Universidad Católica, 1973); 1970–1973: *Monthly Bulletin Central Bank*, different issues. The SV and MAW were established at the provincial level. Those included in this table refer to the Province of Santiago.

ployment.[1] In the case of Chile no measure which accounts for the employment losses resulting from minimum wage legislation has ever been provided.[2] If employment losses are minor, then minimum wage legislation could be a desirable instrument for redistributing income toward low-wage workers. If employment losses are substantial, however, these losses weaken considerably the case for minimum wages as a basis for redistributing income.

The objective of this paper is to evaluate the employment losses

[1] See J. Mincer, "Unemployment Effects of Minimum Wages," *Journal of Political Economy* 84, pt. 2 (August 1976): S87–S104; and E. M. Gramlich, "Impact of Minimum Wages on Other Wages, Employment, and Family Income," *Brookings Papers on Economic Activity* 2 (1976): 409–51.

[2] Estimates for other countries are given by R. S. Goldfarb, "The Policy Content of Quantitative Minimum Wage Research," in Industrial Relations Research Association, *Proceedings of the Twenty-seventh Annual Meeting* (Madison, Wis.: University of Wisconsin, Madison, 1974), pp. 261–68.

FIGURE 1
FACTOR PRICE DISTORTION AND ITS EFFECT ON INPUT MIX

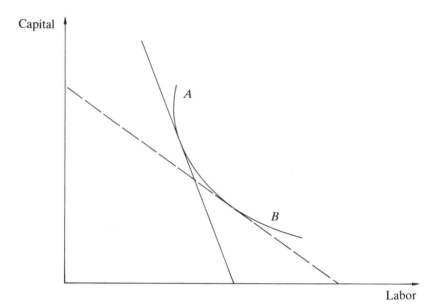

in Chilean manufacturing stemming from minimum wages in 1967, the year of the last census of manufacturing. First the methodology is developed, and then the employment losses are estimated empirically.

Technology and Factor Requirements in Chilean Manufacturing

The employment effect of minimum wages in the industrial sector is measured using labor demand equations obtained from sectoral production functions. Production functions were estimated for forty-four sectors in manufacturing.

For each sector, we estimate the technology of production, and then ask, How much more employment could have been generated if the MIW had been 10 percent below the observed one?[3]

Figure 1 presents for the case of two inputs, labor and capital, the

[3] It is difficult to measure the distortion brought about by the minimum wage. In theory one would need to solve a general equilibrium model with and without the minimum wage and compare both solutions. Short of this method, what is usually done is to compute the supply price for unskilled worker from direct interviews. Thus, using this method Schenone estimated the monthly supply price of unskilled labor to be between 21,000 and 30,000 escudos in July 1974. The 30,000 is around 10 percent below the minimum industrial wage, and this is the measure of distortion used in our calculations. O. Schenone, "El Precio Sombra del Trabajo en Chile," *Cuadernos de Economía* 34 (December 1974): 124–33.

input choice for a given output level ($Q = \overline{Q}$) and factor price ratio. Point A corresponds to the input mix with minimum wage above the equilibrium wage. Point B corresponds to the input mix when minimum wage is reduced to eliminate the distortion. As long as there is factor substitution (that is, elasticity of substitution greater than zero), the reduction in minimum wage will reduce capital requirements and increase labor requirements. We estimate the increase in labor requirements for a given level of output for forty-four industrial sectors. Hence, the total employment measure is the sum of these individual effects.

The study of the technology in Chilean manufacturing is based on work by Corbo and Meller.[4] A summary of the main findings of these studies concerning factor requirements functions follows.

The employment response to wage changes depends upon the substitution properties of the technology. Thus, it is important to estimate substitution possibilities starting with a general technology which does not restrict a priori the value of the elasticity of substitution. Starting with a general translogarithmic function, an empirical investigation is made to see if this function can be reduced to a more restricted functional form.

A function consisting of three inputs is used: raw labor (LM), skill (LS), and capital (K). Then the employment implications of minimum wage legislation are examined by analyzing the impact on raw labor of a reduction in minimum wages.

The translog function for these three inputs can be written as:

$$
\begin{aligned}
\ln Y_{ij} = {} & \alpha_0^i + \alpha_1^i \ln LM_{ij} + \alpha_2^i \ln LS_{ij} + \alpha_3^i \ln K_{ij} \\
& + \frac{1}{2} \gamma_{11}^i (\ln LM_{ij})^2 + \gamma_{12}^i (\ln LM_{ij})(\ln LS_{ij}) \\
& + \gamma_{13}^i (\ln LM_{ij})(\ln K_{ij}) + \frac{1}{2} \gamma_{22}^i \ln (LS_{ij})^2 \\
& + \gamma_{23}^i (\ln LS_{ij})(\ln K_{ij}) + \frac{1}{2} \gamma_{33}^i (\ln K_{ij})^2
\end{aligned}
\tag{1}
$$

where Y is value added, the factor inputs were defined above, i is an index of a four-digit ISIC (international standard industrial classification) industry, and j is an index of a firm within the ith industry.

The definitions of the input variables used in the estimations are as follows:

[4] Vittorio Corbo and P. Meller, "The Translog Production Function: Some Evidence from Establishment Data," *Journal of Econometrics* 10 (June 1979): 193–99; idem, "The Substitution of Labor, Skill, and Capital in Chilean Manufacturing," *Estudios de Economía* 14 (second semester, 1979): 15–43; and idem, "The Translog Function and the Substitution of Labor, Skill and Capital: Its Implications for Trade and Employment," in J. Behrman, J. M. Henderson et al., *Alternative Trade Strategies and Employment in Developing Countries: Supply Responses and Factor Market Links* (Chicago: University of Chicago Press for National Bureau of Economic Research, forthcoming).

LM = Average annual number of man-days, measured as the sum of production workers, blue-collar workers in auxiliary activities, white-collar workers, and entrepreneurs times the number of days worked by the establishment. The units of LM are defined in such a way that, for a given industry i, the mean of LM equals one.

LS = Skill days units, measured as the average annual number of equivalent blue-collar days minus LM. The average annual number of equivalent blue-collar days is measured as the ratio of the total wage payments, plus an imputation for entrepreneurs, to the minimum wage rate of the whole industrial sector. The wage rate of entrepreneurs is assumed to be twice the average wage rate of white-collar workers within a given firm. The minimum wage rate of the whole industrial sector is computed as the simple average of the ten lowest wage rates of blue-collar workers observed in the census. The units of LS are defined in such a way that for a given industry i, the mean of LS equals one.

K = Book value of machinery at 1967 prices less accumulated depreciation. The units of K are defined in such a way that for a given industry i, the mean of K equals one.[5]

Translog functions for four-digit ISIC sectors were estimated by Corbo and Meller using data from individual industrial establishments. There are 11,468 establishments, grouped into eighty-five industries according to the four-digit ISIC. From these eighty-five industries a subset of forty-four was selected in order to allow for at least ten degrees of freedom for the estimation of equation (1).[6] A general translog func-

---

[5] Meller previously used a measure of capital services instead of the value of the stock. The capital service variable was defined as $K = .10K_M + .03K_B + .020K_V + .10(K_M + K_B + K_V + K_I)$, where K_M, K_B, K_V, and K_I are the book values of machinery, buildings, vehicles and inventory goods. Geometric depreciation rates of 0.10, 0.03 and 0.020 were used for machinery, buildings, and vehicles, and a 10 percent real interest rate is used as the cost of capital. The simple correlation between the capital service measure and the book value of machine measure was above 0.95 in sixteen of the twenty-one industrial sectors considered in that study, the smallest correlation coefficient being 0.823. P. Meller, "Production Functions for Industrial Establishments of Different Sizes: The Chilean Case," *Annals of Economics and Social Measurement*, vol. 4, no. 4 (Fall 1975), p. 600.

[6] Within each industry we selected a subset of establishments that passed each one of the following restrictions: number of days worked by the establishment > 50; wage bill of blue-collar workers > 0; book value of machinery > 0; cross value added > 0; nonwage gross value added > 0; number of persons employed > 10; number of white-collar workers > 0; number of blue-collar workers > 0; (book value of machinery/gross value)$_{ij}$ > $\frac{1}{10}$ (book value of machinery/gross value)$_i$. All these restrictions are self-explanatory with the exception of the last restriction, which was used to eliminate establishments which satisfied the restriction on book value of machinery but had a very small book value of machinery, which was judged to be due to an error of measurement. Corbo and Meller, "Substitution in Chilean Manufacturing."

tion was estimated for the forty-four industrial sectors. Then a test was performed to see if the general translog function could be reduced to a constant-return-to-scale (CRTS) one and then if it could be reduced to a Cobb-Douglas function.

When tested for constant returns to scale, in forty-one of the forty-four sectors studied, the CRTS hypothesis could not be rejected. For these forty-one CRTS sectors, another test for a Cobb-Douglas technology was performed. For thirty-five of the forty-one sectors, the Cobb-Douglas technology could not be rejected. For the three sectors for which the CRTS hypothesis was rejected, a test for complete global separability was undertaken. In the three cases the null hypothesis could not be rejected. For these three sectors the authors tested for a Cobb-Douglas technology. In two cases the null hypothesis could not be rejected.

The study of technology in the Chilean manufacturing sector was undertaken with the idea of working with less restrictive functional forms. In evaluating the results, one must reach the conclusion that a Cobb-Douglas technology cannot be rejected from the data for thirty-seven of forty-four four-digit Chilean industries. In thirty-five cases the function is a CRTS Cobb-Douglas and in two cases a non-CRTS Cobb-Douglas.

The results for the estimated Cobb-Douglas functions under CRTS are presented in table 2, and the results of the non-CRTS Cobb-Douglas functions appear in table 3.

Employment Effects of Minimum Wages

In this section, a simulation of factor intensities is performed using the estimated production function of the previous section and a measure of wage distortion.

In the simulations under CRTS for the thirty-five sectors for which a Cobb-Douglas technology was not rejected, the estimated Cobb-Douglas function (table 2) is used. For the six CRTS sectors for which the Cobb-Douglas technology was rejected (ISICs 3211, 3311, 3420, 3812, 3824, and 3829), the technology is approximated by the estimated Cobb-Douglas function. This was done to avoid the need of finding solutions for a nonlinear system of equations on the factor intensities.

For the simulations of the three non-CRTS sectors, a non-CRTS Cobb-Douglas function was used. Based on the testing results, for only two of these sectors was the Cobb-Douglas non-CRTS technology appropriate to use; for the third case (sector 3117) a non-CRTS Cobb-Douglas function was used as an approximation to avoid the nonlinearities involved. (For the results, see table 3.)

Before proceeding to the simulation results, two complications re-

TABLE 2

COBB-DOUGLAS FUNCTIONS WITH CONSTANT RETURNS TO SCALE

(from $\ln Y = \alpha_0 + \alpha_1 \ln LM + \alpha_2 \ln LS + \alpha_3 \ln K$; subject to $\alpha_1 + \alpha_2 + \alpha_3 = 1.0$)

ISIC Code	Number of Observations	α_0	α_1	α_2	α_3	R^2	SSR	F
3111	100	-.168 (-2.126)	.396 (5.577)	.357 (5.666)	.247 (4.333)	.758	42.766	1.49133
3112	46	-.163 (-1.347)	.506 (4.865)	.118 (2.000)	.377 (3.307)	.828	21.733	2.04007
3113	32	.072 (.507)	.429 (3.516)	.237 (4.740)	.334 (3.408)	.820	8.886	.29551
3114	37	.335 (2.681)	.648 (8.307)	.094 (2.350)	.258 (3.440)	.808	8.550	2.5984
3115	34	.033 (.251)	.556 (4.672)	.316 (1.745)	.128 (.969)	.670	13.624	4.1110
3119	26	.015 (.151)	.213 (2.505)	.372 (4.428)	.416 (6.933)	.958	3.082	1.490
3121	39	-.912 (-6.561)	.389 (3.087)	.261 (3.222)	.351 (3.375)	.817	15.490	2.1778
3131	25	.003 (.018)	.263 (1.574)	.463 (2.967)	.274 (1.764)	.705	11.496	4.740
3132	70	-.111 (-1.219)	.692 (6.989)	.018 (.666)	.289 (3.010)	.591	31.249	.3074
3211	232	.096 (2.181)	.584 (16.680)	.208 (8.320)	.207 (6.088)	.874	53.764	8.1024

3212	22	.045 (.542)	.438 (4.132)	.163 (1.273)	.399 (3.764)	.847	2.384	2.583
3213	145	−.177 (−3.933)	.578 (11.115)	.172 (5.058)	.250 (5.681)	.890	25.509	.5030
3231	57	−.127 (−1.628)	.527 (5.377)	.365 (3.842)	.109 (1.379)	.835	13.799	.7164
3233	30	.076 (.783)	.329 (2.350)	.450 (4.639)	.221 (2.511)	.797	4.976	1.2404
3240	138	−.122 (−2.541)	.397 (8.446)	.338 (8.243)	.264 (6.285)	.908	24.680	3.646
3311	252	.116 (2.829)	.646 (18.450)	.088 (5.866)	.266 (7.600)	.751	80.192	15.267*
3312	27	.172 (1.653)	.710 (8.160)	.083 (3.458)	.208 (2.337)	.638	4.922	3.855
3320	132	−.111 (−2.055)	.672 (14.933)	.073 (3.041)	.255 (5.666)	.800	29.685	3.640
3411	19	.105 (1.019)	.406 (3.123)	.333 (1.947)	.262 (4.158)	.979	1.629	.7124
3420	149	.073 (1.520)	.411 (10.024)	.233 (9.708)	.357 (9.394)	.870	32.850	19.710*
3511	32	.083 (.439)	.352 (2.378)	.547 (3.022)	.101 (.782)	.574	18.059	3.131
3521	25	−.148 (−1.510)	.221 (.884)	.291 (1.841)	.487 (2.459)	.851	4.757	1.268
3522	45	.044 (.666)	.210 (2.121)	.369 (3.690)	.421 (5.134)	.905	6.645	2.841
3523	52	.011 (.098)	.146 (1.315)	.562 (4.973)	.292 (3.792)	.883	14.498	.4071

(table continues on next page)

TABLE 2 (continued)

ISIC Code	Number of Observations	α_0	α_1	α_2	α_3	R^2	SSR	F
3529	37	.123 (1.230)	.386 (3.446)	.322 (2.576)	.292 (2.862)	.815	10.538	.8753
3559	24	.022 (.266)	.554 (3.668)	.481 (4.219)	−.035 (−.284)	.919	3.322	.5717
3560	77	−.083 (−1.238)	.417 (5.712)	.289 (5.160)	.295 (4.538)	.827	20.101	3.905
3620	32	.048 (.475)	.506 (4.147)	.231 (1.560)	.262 (2.977)	.914	6.355	2.313
3710	42	.062 (.738)	.219 (2.281)	.464 (4.000)	.317 (4.594)	.892	9.787	.1741
3811	26	−.123 (−1.149)	.608 (5.477)	.264 (1.639)	.128 (1.040)	.873	5.064	.9661
3812	47	−.190 (−2.043)	.498 (6.225)	.390 (5.416)	.112 (1.349)	.849	11.050	6.851*
3813	76	−.137 (−1.851)	.489 (8.890)	.200 (4.444)	.311 (5.759)	.833	20.837	2.790
3814	56	.086 (1.303)	.418 (8.360)	.140 (3.888)	.441 (8.480)	.898	10.292	3.563
3815	31	−.063 (−.583)	.434 (3.312)	.194 (1.437)	.372 (2.676)	.843	7.016	.8249
3819	86	−.098 (−1.606)	.657 (14.600)	.109 (4.360)	.235 (5.875)	.842	15.140	1.689

3822	30	.023 (.244)	.561 (7.480)	.230 (5.111)	.209 (3.370)	.821	5.235	4.842
3824	19	.011 (.082)	.544 (4.000)	.036 (.642)	.419 (3.103)	.560	4.972	8.027*
3829	89	−.139 (−2.074)	.574 (10.830)	.131 (4.517)	.296 (5.285)	.874	23.965	5.909*
3839	19	.102 (.980)	.072 (.452)	.612 (3.517)	.316 (4.051)	.856	2.803	.8199
3841	19	.007 (.058)	.446 (3.185)	.375 (2.884)	.179 (2.486)	.956	1.707	4.493
3843	73	−.455 (−5.617)	.292 (2.891)	.507 (5.761)	.202 (2.589)	.819	25.237	.7746

NOTE: Figures in parentheses are t-values for the null hypothesis that the respective coefficient is zero. SSR is the sum of squares of the residuals, and F is the computed F-statistic for the null hypothesis that the CRTS translog function is Cobb-Douglas. An asterisk next to the computed value of the F-statistic indicates that the null hypothesis is rejected at a 1% significance level.

TABLE 3

COBB-DOUGLAS FUNCTIONS WITHOUT CONSTANT RETURNS TO SCALE

$$(\ln Y = \alpha_0 + \alpha_1 \ln LM + \alpha_2 \ln LS + \alpha_3 \ln K)$$

ISIC Code	Number of Observations	α_0	α_1	α_2	α_3	R^2	SSR	F
3117	293	-.2215	.8507	.0548	.2293	.7404	66.7679	20.45*
		(-5.270)	(16.158)	(5.663)	(8.132)			
3220	239	-.1548	.8504	.1398	.1943	.8575	50.5693	2.909
		(-4.091)	(14.175)	(5.326)	(5.297)			
3693	39	.0076	.8463	.1243	.2315	.8639	6.31686	2.1209
		(.086)	(6.262)	(4.238)	(3.715)			

NOTE: Figures in parentheses are t-values for the null hypothesis that the respective coefficient is zero. SSR is the sum of squares of the residuals, and F is the computed F-statistic for the null hypothesis that the nonconstant returns translog function is Cobb-Douglas. An asterisk next to the computed value of the F-statistic indicates that the null hypothesis is rejected at a 1 percent significance level.

main to be solved: the Cobb-Douglas function could not be estimated for all eighty-two four-digit sectors because of insufficient observations, and the Cobb-Douglas function for sector 3559 was not well behaved. In particular, it was not monotonic on the capital inputs. As a solution for these two problems, the technology was approximated for the missing sectors and for sector 3559, by using the simple average of the value-added elasticities of the four-digit Cobb-Douglas functions belonging to the same three-digit industry. The values of the elasticities used in the simulations are presented in table 4.

In studying the effect of factor market distortion on factor requirements, first an expression to relate factor intensity to the price of factors is developed.[7] Then, in the case of CRTS, the expressions developed are independent of the level of output, that is, they are globally valid. On the other hand, for the non-CRTS case, the expressions are valid only for a given level of output, that is, they are only locally valid.

The CRTS Cobb-Douglas Case. In this case the starting point is an aggregate production function at the industry level given by:

$$Y_i = A_i \, LM_i^{\alpha_1} \cdot LS_i^{\alpha_2} \cdot K_i^{\alpha_3} \tag{2}$$

where $\alpha_1 + \alpha_2 + \alpha_3 = 1.0$. Then we introduce the following side conditions for cost minimization:

$$\frac{\dfrac{\partial Y_i}{\partial LM_i}}{\dfrac{\partial Y_i}{\partial LS_i}} = \frac{w}{P_{s,i}} \tag{3}$$

$$\frac{\dfrac{\partial Y_i}{\partial LM_i}}{\dfrac{\partial Y_i}{\partial K_i}} = \frac{w}{P_{k,i}} \tag{4}$$

where w is the minimum wage rate, $P_{s,i}$ is the price of a unit of skill, and $P_{k,i}$ is the price of capital services.[8] Using the CRTS condition, equations (3) and (4) are solved for K_i/LM_i and LS_i/LM_i as a function of $P_{s,i}/w$ and $P_{k,i}/w$. Then they are substituted into the production function to obtain Y_i/LM_i. Finally, the terms K_i/Y_i, LM_i/Y_i and LS_i/Y_i are

---

[7] In this section factor inputs and value added are expressed in terms of their original units; in the case of a Cobb-Douglas function only the constant of the regressions depends on the units of measurement. The expressions developed below for the study of the impact of factor price distortion do not involve the constant term of regression.

[8] Skill is expressed in units of unskilled labor. Therefore, its price is also equal to the minimum wage rate.

TABLE 4
VALUE-ADDED ELASTICITIES

ISIC Code	Labor	Skill	Capital
3111	.396	.357	.247
3112	.506	.118	.377
3113	.429	.237	.334
3114	.648	.094	.258
3115	.556	.316	.128
3116	.448	.251	.302
3117*	.851	.055	.229
3118	.448	.251	.302
3119	.213	.372	.416
3121	.389	.261	.351
3122	.448	.251	.302
3131	.263	.463	.274
3132	.692	.018	.289
3133	.478	.241	.282
3134	.478	.241	.282
3140	.430	.302	.268
3211	.584	.208	.207
3212	.438	.163	.399
3213	.578	.172	.250
3214	.533	.181	.285
3215	.533	.181	.285
3219	.533	.181	.285
3220*	.850	.140	.194
3231	.527	.365	.109
3233	.329	.450	.221
3240	.397	.338	.264
3311	.646	.088	.266
3312	.710	.083	.208
3319	.678	.086	.237
3320	.672	.073	.255
3411	.406	.333	.262
3412	.406	.333	.262
3419	.406	.333	.262
3420	.411	.233	.357
3511	.352	.547	.101
3512	.352	.547	.101
3513	.352	.547	.101
3514	.352	.547	.101
3521	.221	.291	.487

TABLE 4 (continued)

ISIC Code	Labor	Skill	Capital
3522	.210	.369	.421
3523	.146	.562	.291
3529	.386	.322	.292
3530	.430	.302	.268
3540	.430	.302	.268
3551	.430	.302	.268
3559	.430	.302	.268
3560	.430	.302	.268
3610	.417	.289	.295
3620	.506	.231	.262
3691*	.846	.124	.232
3692*	.846	.124	.232
3695*	.846	.124	.232
3699*	.846	.124	.232
3710	.219	.464	.317
3721	.430	.302	.268
3729	.430	.302	.268
3811	.608	.264	.128
3812	.498	.390	.112
3813	.489	.200	.311
3814	.418	.140	.441
3815	.430	.194	.372
3819	.657	.109	.235
3822	.561	.230	.209
3823	.560	.132	.308
3824	.544	.036	.419
3825	.560	.132	.308
3829	.574	.131	.296
3831	.072	.612	.316
3832	.072	.612	.316
3833	.072	.612	.316
3839	.072	.612	.316
3841	.446	.375	.179
3842	.369	.441	.191
3843	.292	.507	.202
3844	.369	.441	.191
3845	.369	.441	.191
3849	.369	.441	.191
3851	.430	.302	.268
3852	.430	.302	.268
3901	.430	.302	.268

(table continues on next page)

TABLE 4 (continued)

ISIC Code	Labor	Skill	Capital
3902	.430	.302	.268
3903	.430	.302	.268
3909	.430	.302	.268

NOTE: An asterisk indicates non-CRTS sectors. For the four-digit industries for which, because of insufficient observations, a production function could not be estimated, the average elasticities of all the other CRTS functions of other sectors in the same three-digit category were used.

solved as a function of relative factor prices. These factor intensities are the conditional factor demand equations.

Totally differentiating the factor demands, yields:

$$d\frac{LM_i}{Y_i} = \frac{LM_i}{Y_i}\left[\alpha_3\, d\ln P_{k,i} + \alpha_2\, d\ln P_{s,i} - (1-\alpha_1)\, d\ln w\right] \quad (5)$$

$$d\frac{LS_i}{Y_i} = \frac{LS_i}{Y_i}\left[\alpha_3\, d\ln P_{k,i} - (1-\alpha_2)\, d\ln P_{s,i} + \alpha_1\, d\ln w\right] \quad (6)$$

$$d\frac{K_i}{Y_i} = \frac{K_i}{Y_i}\left[-(1-\alpha_3)\, d\ln P_{k,i} + \alpha_2\, d\ln P_{s,i} + \alpha_1\, d\ln w\right] \quad (7)$$

The Non-CRTS Cobb-Douglas Case. In this case, the production function is given by (2) without the CRTS restriction on the parameters. The side conditions for cost minimization are still given by equations (3) and (4). The only difference from the CRTS case is that now the solution for the factor intensities K_i/Y_i, LM_i/Y_i and LS_i/Y_i will depend not only on relative factor prices but also on the level of value added.

In this case totally differentiating the factor intensities, for a given level of value added, yields:

$$d\frac{LM_i}{Y_i} = \frac{LM_i}{Y_i}\left[-\left(\frac{\alpha_2 + \alpha_3}{\alpha_1 + \alpha_2 + \alpha_3}\right) d\ln w_i\right.$$
$$\left. + \left(\frac{\alpha_2}{\alpha_1 + \alpha_2 + \alpha_3}\right) d\ln P_{s,i} + \left(\frac{\alpha_3}{\alpha_1 + \alpha_2 + \alpha_3}\right) d\ln P_{k,i}\right] \quad (8)$$

$$d\frac{LS_i}{Y_i} = \frac{LS_i}{Y_i}\left[\left(\frac{\alpha_1}{\alpha_1 + \alpha_2 + \alpha_3}\right) d\ln w_i\right.$$
$$\left. - \left(\frac{\alpha_1 + \alpha_3}{\alpha_1 + \alpha_2 + \alpha_3}\right) d\ln P_{s,i} + \left(\frac{\alpha_3}{\alpha_1 + \alpha_2 + \alpha_3}\right) d\ln P_{k,i}\right] \quad (9)$$

354

$$d\frac{K_i}{Y_i} = \frac{K_i}{Y_i}\left[\left(\frac{\alpha_1}{\alpha_1 + \alpha_2 + \alpha_3}\right) d\ln w_i\right.$$

$$\left.+ \left(\frac{\alpha_2}{\alpha_1 + \alpha_2 + \alpha_3}\right) d\ln P_{s,i} - \left(\frac{\alpha_1 + \alpha_2}{\alpha_1 + \alpha_2 + \alpha_3}\right) d\ln P_{k,i}\right] \quad (10)$$

With these results, it is possible to study the employment effect of an across-the-board reduction in the MIW. The average of the ten lowest daily wages per establishment in the industrial sector was 7.06 escudos in 1967; this number is very close to the MIW of the year. Thus, it is assumed that a 10 percent reduction in the MIW will also reduce by 10 percent the wage of unskilled labor in manufacturing.

Employment, measured by the number of persons employed per million escudos of value added, was 42.2 in 1967. A reduction of the MIW by 10 percent will increase employment to 43.3 persons. Hence, the employment growth is about 2.6 percent, and the wage elasticity of demand for labor in manufacturing is -0.26. This elasticity is a long-run elasticity after skill and capital have been optimally adjusted to minimize production costs.

The employment effect that has been measured thus refers to the change in total number of persons employed. For income distribution purposes, a measure of the employment effect of MIW just on low-wage workers is needed. Then the estimates above need modification. If the demand for workers at greater than the MIW is fairly insensitive to a change in the MIW, then to obtain the wage elasticity of the demand for low-wage workers, it is necessary to weight upward the elasticity given above by the inverse of the proportion of low-wage workers in the total number of persons employed.

In the case of Chile, for the year here analyzed, the proportion of low-wage workers in the total number of manufacturing employees was 25.4 percent.[9] This result implies a wage elasticity of -1.02 for low-wage workers. Thus, manufacturing employment losses from MIW are certainly not negligible. These employment losses are an important parameter to consider in the overall evaluation of the distributional effects of minimum wages.[10]

---

[9] Programa Regional del Empleo para América Latina y el Caribe. *Asalariados de Bajos Ingresos y Salarios Mínimos en América Latina* (Santiago, Chile: PREALC, 1979).

[10] Here, it is assumed that the relative wage structure in the manufacturing sector is not affected by a change in the MIW. If it is affected, with wages higher than the MIW adjusting slowly, then labor substitution away from MIW workers will take place, and the elasticity given above will underestimate the true one.

Bibliography

Corbo, Vittorio, and Meller, P. "The Substitution of Labor, Skill, and Capital in Chilean Manufacturing." *Estudios de Economía* 14 (second semester, 1979): 15–43.

———. "The Translog Function and the Substitution of Labor, Skill and Capital: Its Implications for Trade and Employment." In J. Behrman, J. M. Henderson, et al., *Alternative Trade Strategies and Employment in Developing Countries: Supply Responses and Factor Market Links.* Chicago: University of Chicago Press for National Bureau of Economic Research, forthcoming.

———. "The Translog Production Function: Some Evidence from Establishment Data." *Journal of Econometrics* 10 (June 1979): 193–99.

Goldfarb, R. S. "The Policy Content of Quantitative Minimum Wage Research." In Industrial Relations Research Association. *Proceedings of the Twenty-seventh Annual Meeting.* Madison: University of Wisconsin, 1974.

Gramlich, E. M. "Impact of Minimum Wages on Other Wages, Employment, and Family Incomes." *Brookings Papers on Economic Activity* 2 (1976): 409–51.

Krueger, A., et al., eds. *Trade and Employment in Developing Countries: Strategies and Results in Ten Countries.* Chicago: University of Chicago Press for National Bureau of Economic Research, forthcoming.

Meller, P. "Production Functions for Industrial Establishments of Different Sizes: The Chilean Case." *Annals of Economics and Social Measurement* 4 (Fall 1975): 595–634.

Mincer, J. "Unemployment Effects of Minimum Wages." *Journal of Political Economy* 84, pt. 2 (August 1976): S87–S104.

Programa Regional del Empleo para América Latina y el Caribe. *Asalariados de Bajos Ingresos y Salarios Mínimos en América Latina.* Santiago, Chile: PREALC, 1979.

Schenone, O. "El Precio Sombra del Trabajo en Chile." *Cuadernos de Economía* 34 (December 1974): 124–33.

The Effects of Minimum Wage Regulation in France

Jean-Jacques Rosa

Minimum Wage Regulation: An Overview

Minimum wage regulation in France dates from 1936. It has been amended in 1945, in 1950, and most recently in 1970.[1] These regulations continue an older tradition of state intervention in wage determination. In 1848 a decree fixed a minimum wage for manpower subcontractors, that is, firms that temporarily place employees at other firms but continue to manage and pay them. In 1915 a minimum wage law for domestic workers was established. In neither of these cases, however, were the categories of covered workers numerous.

The 1936 general minimum wage law mandates collective bargaining between employers and wage earners once firms are covered by the law and requires that bargaining agreements provide minimum hourly wages by occupation and region. The minister of labor can order these agreements extended to all branches of an industry. In this case, privately bargained wages become minimum wage rate regulations imposed on employers.

After the wage freeze of World War II, a new administrative stance was adopted in 1945: commissions were set up composed of representatives of workers, employers, and government. They had the task of fixing not only a minimum wage but also a wage hierarchy for all wage earners of industry, commerce, and the professions. The minister of labor could modify these wages at his discretion without, however, modifying the hierarchy established by the commissions.

NOTE: I wish to thank Laurence Forteville and Jacques Généreux for excellent research assistance and Bernard Lentz for comments and generous help in translation. Any shortcomings remain my own responsibility.

[1] The Law of June 24, 1936, completing the Matignon agreements of June 7–8, 1936, permits the imposition on a whole industry of signed collective bargaining agreements between employer associations and union representatives. The legal character of bargaining agreements had been recognized by the Law of March 25, 1919. On the demand of either a worker or an employer organization, the minister of labor calls together the representatives of the two parties at either a local or a national level. The accord reached at this time must specify minimum wages by category of wage earners. The agreement is then made mandatory for the whole industry.

The Law of February 11, 1950, returned to a more flexible system of collective bargaining matched by the introduction of an interoccupational guaranteed minimum wage (SMIG) fixed by government order. While this minimum covers all sectors of economic activity, it allows for geographic differences in the cost of living. The SMIG does not cover agriculture, where there is an agricultural guaranteed minimum wage (SMAG), usually lower than SMIG. SMIG is tied to the consumer price index whenever the index has an increase of 2 percent or more sustained for two months.

This system has evolved into a single minimum wage for all regions and professions, which came about for all practical purposes in 1968.

Current Legislation. The Law of January 2, 1970, replaces SMIG by SMIC, interoccupational minimum wage growth, the system currently in force. SMIC is in part indexed on the cost of living and in part fixed at the discretion of the government. All price increases of 2 percent or more lead to a readjustment of SMIC by the same percentage on the first day of the month after the publication of the price index. The government further revises SMIC at its discretion. Finally, the 1970 law provides that "in no case may the annual purchasing power growth of SMIC be less than half the growth in the purchasing power of the mean hourly earnings recorded in the quarterly survey of the Ministry of Labor."

Because of the diversity of terms and conditions of employment embodied in total compensation, it is useful to state the forms of remuneration affected by the regulation.[2] The law provides that the hourly wage to be considered "is that which corresponds to an effective hour of work taking account of the working conditions and of the diverse benefits which have the character of complementing wages, but excluding reimbursed employee expenses, benefits and wage premiums provided by law, and for the Paris region the transportation premiums."

The SMIC covers all wage earners eighteen or older in the entire country with the exception of overseas departments.[3] Apprentices and

[2] Various premiums and fringe benefits come to be added to the base wage. Their diversity makes it difficult to evaluate the effective hourly wage. In general, premiums intended to compensate for particular kinds of work are not considered fringe benefits. On the other hand, seniority premiums, piecework premiums, and the thirteenth and fourteenth months of salary that some firms pay their workers constitute fringe benefits in those cases where they are permanent or constitute an "important" part of total compensation. Regulation sets the amount beyond which pleasant working conditions or fringes are considered wages.

[3] In the overseas departments, the minimum wage is set each year by a decree "with account taken of the local economic situation." Nevertheless, when the metropolitan SMIC is increased, the overseas minimum wage must be increased in the same proportion.

physically handicapped workers are excluded from coverage, as are prisoners, about whom the regulations are imprecise, and draftees, who receive only a nominal daily allowance.[4]

While SMIC affects hourly wages, an additional regulation establishing a minimum legal monthly earning was introduced in 1972.[5] This monthly minimum is calculated by multiplying the SMIC by the monthly hours of work. In practice, the legal workweek is fixed at forty hours; in calculating the monthly hours of work, account is taken of holidays.[6] If a firm reduces the workweek below forty hours, it is considered to have paid the worker an additional allowance while still assuring him of the monthly SMIC. The state reimburses the firm for one-half his allowance up to a certain ceiling.

Finally, it must be remarked that the fixing of SMIC is in principle independent of the determination of other salaries. Collective negotiations settle the structure or hierarchy of wages for the various grades of labor. They may establish a base wage below SMIC, but this wage will be "fictitious" because no pay actually received may be below SMIC. This system does allow the establishment of the wage structure, however, without reference to SMIC.

Furthermore, the SMIC may not in principle be used as a basis for

---

[4] With respect to apprentices, the 1972 decree of application and the Law of July 1971 on occupational training and apprenticeship provide for a minimum wage reduced to a certain proportion of SMIC. This proportion varies with the length of time the apprentice has been working, from 15 percent for the first six months to 45 percent for months in the fourth semester of employment. These rates are increased by 10 percent when the apprentice reaches age eighteen.

Concerning wage earners under age eighteen, the decree of February 1, 1971, in general fixes the abatement of SMIC at the following rates: 20 percent for those under seventeen and 10 percent for those between seventeen and eighteen. Those reductions must be ended after six months of occupational experience in the same branch of activity. However, the abatements apply only to young hourly wage earners. For those who are paid on a piecework basis, the floors for compensation are the same as those for adults. Wage earners with a reduced physical capacity can be paid as much as 10 percent below SMIC to the extent that their output is below the mean output. In these three cases, the abatements define wage floors, and employer-union agreements can provide higher compensation.

[5] Law of December 23, 1972.

[6] The Law of December 23, 1972, guarantees to full-time workers a minimum monthly compensation obtained by multiplying the hourly SMIC rate by the legal work month. The legislature introduced the idea of a legal workweek equal to forty hours. Beyond this, hours worked must be paid at the higher rate for overtime hours. In no case may the total workweek exceed the legal weekly maximum of forty-eight hours (Labor Code L 2/2–1, L 2/2–2; Decree of May 19, 1939, on the methods of application of the forty-hour week). However, bargaining agreements can establish a maximum workweek below forty-eight hours. These particular arrangements may also be imposed by decree on certain industries or regions. These are, however, exceptions to these rules, which may be granted by the Ministry of Labor to some occupations, for example, the restoration industry. For calculating the monthly SMIC, the legal duration of work is 174 hours per month for those businesses that pay monthly rather than weekly salaries.

indexing other wages, except when the law expressly authorizes such indexation: "It is prohibited that collective bargaining agreements contain clauses indexing on SMIC or references to it with regard to the fixing or revision of wages."[7] Since SMIC itself is indexed on the cost of living, this arrangement is intended to avoid the general indexation of wages on the price index.

Evolution of the Minimum Wage. The evolution of the minimum wage in the period before 1967 differed from that after that date. Whereas in the former period SMIC grew more slowly than other wages on the whole, a rapid catching up began with the 1968 increase of more than 35 percent. In the 1970s the minimum wage grew more rapidly than other wages or the gross domestic product, as shown in figures 1 and 2 and table 1.

Who Is Affected by SMIC? The data on how many workers earn the SMIC are not numerous. They come from two sources. First, the quarterly survey conducted by the Ministry of Labor at the time of a SMIC increase permits an estimate of the number of beneficiaries of these readjustments. The question asked employers is, "How many wage earners benefited from the last SMIC increase, that is, those whose wage rate was below the new SMIC rate before the increase?"

These surveys are limited to commercial and industrial establishments of ten or more wage earners, however. Further, the proportion of wage earners at the SMIC level is much more important as the size of the establishment becomes smaller, as shown in table 2. These surveys thus underestimate the number of "smicards" (those who earn SMIC) by neglecting small establishments.

The annual declarations of wages (DAS), legally required of all employers by the treasury department, provide information on the annual income of wage earners. One can estimate the number of smicards by calculating the annual income of a person who works the average annual hours at the hourly SMIC rate. Nevertheless, those who earn this amount could have received an hourly wage higher than SMIC and have worked fewer hours than the mean. There are also individuals who receive less than the hourly SMIC but work a larger number of hours in a year, such as apprentices.

As shown in table 3, the ratio of smicards to all wage earners fluctuates wildly with the rate of increase of SMIC; there were peaks in 1954–1955 and 1968 and troughs in 1965–1967 and 1972.

[7] Law of January 2, 1970.

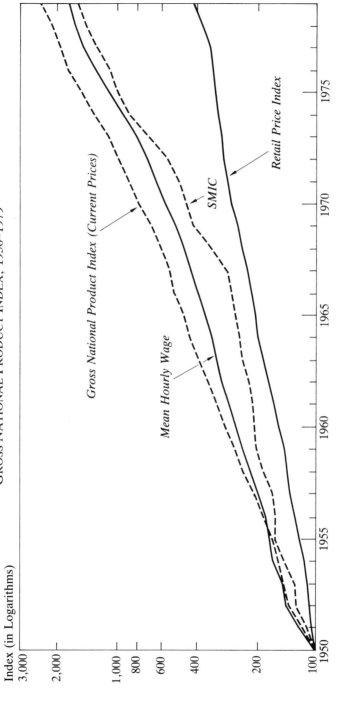

FIGURE 1

MEAN HOURLY WAGE, MINIMUM WAGE, RETAIL PRICE INDEX, AND GROSS NATIONAL PRODUCT INDEX, 1950–1979

Index (in Logarithms)

SOURCES: *Bulletins Mensuels du Ministère du Travail* (note that the SMIG used here [until 1968] is the unabated one); *Bulletins Mensuels de Statistiques*, INSEE; and *Comptes de la Nation*, INSEE.

361

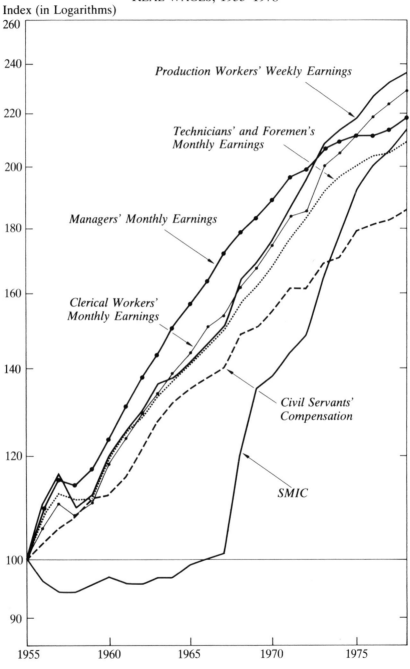

FIGURE 2
REAL WAGES, 1955–1978

Index (in Logarithms)

Production Workers' Weekly Earnings

Technicians' and Foremen's Monthly Earnings

Managers' Monthly Earnings

Clerical Workers' Monthly Earnings

Civil Servants' Compensation

SMIC

TABLE 1

CHANGES IN AVERAGE WAGE, MINIMUM WAGE, CONSUMER PRICE
INDEX, AND GROSS DOMESTIC PRODUCT INDEX, 1950–1979

	SMIC Index	Nominal GDP Index	Average Wage Index	Consumer Price Index
1950	100	100	100	100
1951	112.8	121	122	106
1952	128.2	142.3	142.3	108
1953	128.2	148.1	145.5	111.3
1954	145.6	155.8	165.4	116.8
1955	159.6	167.4	167.3	123.8
1956	161	183.8	181.3	129.9
1957	165.5	207	195.8	137.7
1958	187.8	237	219.3	141.4
1959	200.1	258.2	233.3	145.6
1960	206.4	286.2	248.8	155.7
1961	210.3	312.3	267.6	163.4
1962	220.3	349	290.8	174.8
1963	235.9	391.5	317	183.5
1964	242.3	434	340.2	194.5
1965	252.6	466.8	360.7	204.2
1966	264.1	505.4	382.1	214.4
1967	273.1	545.9	404.2	222.9
1968	343.5	593.2	452.4	231.8
1969	405.1	677.2	500.6	248
1970	438.5	755.4	551.2	262
1971	482.1	842.3	611.3	275.1
1972	531.3	947.6	679.3	291.6
1973	634.6	1,076	774.3	306.1
1974	820.5	1,234	928.4	315.2
1975	968	1,400	1,089	318.3
1976	1,049	1,611.4	1,250	334.2
1977	1,195	1,805.4	1,408	344.2
1978	1,388	2,045.3	1,681	375.4
1979	1,554	2,305.5	1,731	415.8

Consequences of Minimum Wage Legislation

In his recent study *Minimum Wages: Issues and Evidence*, Finis Welch
recapitulates various analyses of the economic effects of minimum wage
regulations.[8] He shows that these theories are fairly straightforward and

[8] Finis Welch, *Minimum Wages: Issues and Evidence* (Washington, D.C.: American Enterprise Institute, 1978).

TABLE 2

PERCENTAGE OF WAGE EARNERS AT SMIC BY SIZE OF ESTABLISHMENT

Number of Employees	Oct. 1964	Mar. 1965	Mar. 1966	Jan. 1968	June 1968	Dec. 1968	Apr. 1969	Oct. 1969	Mar. 1970	July 1970	July 1971	May 1972
Old data series												
10 to 20	3.5	3.1	2.4	2.5	16.2	6.1	6.9	7.4	5.4	5.3	5.1	3.5
21 to 50	3.2	2.4	1.7	2.0	16.4	5.4	6.4	6.5	5.3	4.6	4.0	2.8
51 to 100	2.1	2.1	1.4	1.9	17.5	4.8	5.9	6.1	4.1	4.1	3.6	2.1
More than 100	0.6	0.6	0.4	0.6	7.2	1.8	2.1	1.8	1.2	2.0	0.9	0.6
	June 1974	July 1975	June 1976	June 1977	June 1977							
Revised data series												
10 to 49	9.2	8	8.7	6.6	6.3							
50 to 199	7.8	7.1	6.2	5.2	4.8							
200 to 499	5.2	4.3	4.4	4.1	3							
More than 500	2.5	2.3	1.4	1.1	1.5							

SOURCE: *Suppléments aux Bulletins Mensuels du Ministère du Travail.*

TABLE 3

Employees Affected by SMIC Increases

Date	Workers Earning SMIC (percent)	SMIC Increase (percent)
October 1954	16	5.7
April 1955	17	3.7
August 1957	6.9	5.9
March 1958	8.1	4
June 1958	7.7	3.1
June 1959	7.6	4.5
November 1959	7.3	2.7
December 1961	3.5	2.9
November 1962	3.7	4.5
October 1964	2	2.5
March 1965	1.6	2
March 1966	1.2	2.1
June 1967	1.4	3.3
June 1968	12.5	35.1
December 1968	3.5	2.7
April 1968	4.4	2.3
October 1969	4.3	3.8
March 1970	3.2	2.8
July 1970	3.6	4.2
July 1971	2.6	4.6
May 1972	1.7	4.1
November 1972	2.7	5.8
July 1974	5.8	7.6
July 1975	5.4	6
July 1976	5.1	6.2
July 1977	4.1	2.6
July 1978	3.8	3.8

SOURCE: *Suppléments aux Bulletins Mensuels du Ministère du Travail.*

that a wide agreement on them has developed among economists. Let us repeat his principal conclusions.

When the minimum wage is fixed by regulation above the equilibrium level of the labor market, the quantity of labor supplied exceeds the quantity demanded, and employment is reduced. Those workers who keep their jobs at the regulation wage rate are subsidized by those whose jobs have been ended because of the increase in that wage.[9]

[9] G. J. Stigler, "The Economics of Minimum Wage Legislation," *American Economic Review*, June 1946.

The regulation, however, affects just the money wage, which constitutes only one aspect of the remuneration for work. When we take account of the other terms and conditions of employment, we can expect employers to maintain a constant total compensation by reducing non-wage benefits to offset the increased money wage. This adjustment may equally affect on-the-job training in the firm.

Moreover, the location of employment has various advantages and disadvantages for wage earners. Certain work environments constitute pleasant working conditions and lead to compensating wage reductions. Thus in France there exists a negative wage premium for workers of equal qualification in the Midi relative to the north. In addition, a firm has an interest in locating in those regions where wage premiums are negative. A uniform increase in money wages moves firms toward choosing a location independently of the preferences of its workers and closer to places preferred by consumers. Instead of firms moving toward workers, it is workers who must move toward firms. The 1968 termination of the regional differences in SMIC must have had such an effect.

Welch also restates the minimum wage consequences for part-time workers. To the extent that the cost of part-time work is increased more than that of full-time work, a firm will substitute full-time for part-time workers. This effect will be clearer when the minimum wage is regulated on a monthly, rather than an hourly, basis. Finally, increases in SMIC discourage businesses from taking on apprentices; however, the French minimum wage is lower for youths under eighteen for the first six months of a job.

The effect of SMIC on unemployment is ambiguous in theory. A simple analysis of the problem shows that it reduces employment, but the diminution of job offers by business does not create an equivalent number of unemployed. The smicards lucky enough to keep their jobs have an incentive to reduce their mobility. Those who do not find employment may be discouraged and drop out of the labor force. On the other hand, a higher minimum wage encourages new entrants to try their luck at looking for work. Paradoxically, those who have the most to gain, that is, those who have the lowest productivity, are encouraged to search the longest. If the productivity of applicants is identical, employers have a margin of discretion for choosing among applicants: SMIC promotes discrimination on criteria other than economic efficiency. When jobs are not homogeneous, SMIC reduces the relative demand for less productive labor and increases that for more productive labor.

Concerning the effects on other wages—ripple effects—Welch emphasizes that an increase in the minimum wage does not necessarily lead to an increase of all wages, which would maintain the hierarchy, or structure, of wages unchanged; nor does it necessarily have a stronger effect on the wages closest to the minimum. It drives firms to demand more of the qualifications that are most easily substitutable for those of the smicards. It drives consumers to switch from products with a large unskilled labor content toward products with a large skilled labor or capital content. The ripple effect of SMIC on other wages points to the beginning of these substitutions. If they did not take place, there would be no ripple effect, and cost of products would be higher.

The analysis of incomplete minimum wage coverage hardly applies to France's SMIC. What comes closest is the difference between SMAG in agriculture and SMIG in the other industries. We will not deal with this aspect of the problem, except to point out that SMIC exerts differential effects according to industry since the employment of youths and of less qualified workers varies considerably from one industry to another.

Let us now briefly review some scholarly work done since Welch. Welch reminds us that "Pure theory is clean and neat, and abstraction is at a premium. The theory can be developed as though there is an initial equilibrium that is shocked by imposing a minimum, and nothing else in the initial situation has changed."[10] But he does not cite the arguments of institutional economists in favor of the shock: when the employer possesses monopsony power, it is possible that a minimum wage increases employment rather than reducing it. Second, a minimum wage might have a positive effect on productivity and compensate for the predicted reduction of employment in a competitive labor market. E. G. West and M. McKee reexamine these arguments and conclude that all the empirical evidence available in 1979 shows that the minimum wage significantly decreases employment, which leads to the conclusion that employer monopsony power is exceedingly rare.[11] The reduction of employment also shows that all wage earners do not benefit from SMIC and that even if there is a positive effect on productivity, it is not sufficient to compensate for the negative effect on employment.

Keith Leffler maintains that the minimum wage does not reduce the well-being of low-wage workers, especially young workers, if there is unemployment insurance.[12] Instead, it creates a transfer from the unemployment insurance contributors to the low-wage workers. It further accelerates turnover in the labor market. An analysis by J. Huston McCulloch shows that the minimum wage may increase the equality of

[10] Welch, *Minimum Wages*, p. 21.

[11] E. G. West and M. McKee, "Monopsony and 'Shock' Arguments for Minimum Wages," *Southern Economic Journal*, January 1980.

[12] Keith B. Leffler, "Minimum Wages, Welfare, and Wealth Transfers to the Poor," *Journal of Law and Economics*, October 1978.

the distribution of income, as measured by the Gini coefficient, if there is unemployment insurance.[13] On the other hand, the minimum wage increases inequality if there is no such insurance. These new analyses cast doubt on the interpretation of the minimum wage as a tax from the poor to the poor.

In another connection Robert E. Hall asserts that the minimum wage does not create an excess supply of young workers on the labor market.[14] According to Hall, the principal effect of the minimum wage is to increase turnover rather than to make it more difficult to be hired. He does not consider the compensating impact on the welfare of the young implicit in their receiving unemployment insurance, but he emphasizes the loss of efficiency in the allocation of resources resulting from excessive turnover and from the instability of young workers, a well-known characteristic of the contemporary American labor market.

Another hypothesis was recently examined by J. Mincer and L. Leighton: the minimum wage increase discourages human capital formation in the firm. The authors conclude that this hypothesis is largely confirmed by empirical analysis.[15]

Finally, a recent dissertation by David M. Luskin reexamines the effects of the minimum wage on working conditions, fringe benefits, and part-time work and concludes that there is no convincing evidence of the first point but there is confirmation that a minimum wage reduces firms' demand for part-time workers.[16]

Recent works give a more complex and subtle theoretical analysis of the economic effects of the minimum wage: it seems possible that the combined system of SMIC and unemployment insurance increases money transfers to the young and less qualified, but at the price of increased employment instability, a reduction in occupational training, and a detriment to wage earners seeking part-time work.

From the perspective of these works, it is interesting to report that various French public sector interventions have sought to stimulate firms to train young wage earners better, to hire more young workers, and to promote part-time work in a period when SMIC was catching up to the mean wage and unemployment insurance was spreading.

Unfortunately, it is difficult to test these effects empirically in the

[13] J. Huston McCulloch, *The Effect of Minimum Wage Legislation on Income Equality: A Theoretical Analysis*, National Bureau of Economic Research Working Paper no. 171 (New York, 1977).

[14] Robert E. Hall, "The Minimum Wage and Job Turnover in Markets for Young Workers," mimeographed, April 1979.

[15] J. Mincer and L. Leighton, *Effects of Minimum Wages on Human Capital Formation*, National Bureau of Economic Research Working Paper no. 441 (New York, 1980).

[16] David M. Luskin, "The Economics of Minimum Wage Laws" (Ph.D. diss., University of Rochester, 1979).

French economy because of the paucity of statistical data on terms and conditions of employment, the duration of employment, the turnover of young workers, and on-the-job training. The descriptive data we have seem to show that this segment of the market exhibits a trend toward reduced on-the-job training even though various legislation provides subsidies to firms that provide such training. But no rigorous test can yet be performed.

Thus we will content ourselves, in the empirical part of this paper, with testing the most classic effects of SMIC on the employment of young workers, on their rate of participation, and on the ripple effects on other wages.

Empirical Results

There are practically no empirical studies of the effects of SMIC in France.[17] A recent article by Jean Bégué is devoted to the assessment of ripple effects of SMIC on other wages.[18] The author is exclusively interested in "immediate" effects and excludes "deferred" effects, whether they are subsequent wage movements reestablishing the preexisting hierarchy or effects induced by extrawage variables that react immediately to the wage increase. Because of the growth of manpower costs, for example, prices can rise and lead to new increases in wages. Finally, the author works exclusively with the wage bill at constant total employment, that is, with the mean wage.

The author's method consists of a graphic presentation of an arbitrary relation between the level of SMIC after increases and the distribution of wages as it was before the change in SMIC. This comes from assuming that wages at the upper end of the hierarchy remain unchanged while wages near SMIC are raised by a proportion chosen by the author. Similarly, the choice of the wages that are affected by the SMIC increase is not explained. That is, the conclusion reached by the article that "we estimate 6.7% as the percentage increase in the wage bill which, under certain hypotheses, would have directly resulted from fixing SMIC at 2,400 Frs gross per month, based on 40 hours per week" is worth no more than the hypothesis in question. It is purely arbitrary.

In what follows, we present some classic estimates of the effects of

---

[17] In his monograph *Le salaire minimum* (Paris: Presses Universitaires de France, Que sais-je?, 1978), Jean-Paul Courthéoux is satisfied with describing the administrative structure of SMIC and analyzes none of its effects. His bibliography cites no studies of these effects.

[18] Jean Bégué, "Hausse du SMIC et effets sur la masse salariale," *Economie et Statistique*, no. 100, May 1978.

SMIC, such as those found in the literature previously cited. They tend to shed light on the consequences of variation in SMIC relative to the mean level of wages on the employment and participation of young workers in the labor market as well as on the possible ripple effects on the mean level of wages.

The Effect on Youth Employment. Two equations are tested. One of these has as its dependent variable the employment of youths relative to that of adults, which conforms to the tests of Welch.[19] The variable is defined as the ratio of the number of young persons fifteen to twenty-four who have a job to the number of employed persons twenty-five to sixty years old.

Theory predicts that the higher SMIC is raised relative to the mean wage, the more the employment of youths will be reduced relative to that of adults, thus giving rise to discrimination against the young. The SMIC is not the only variable to influence the rate of youth unemployment, and we can measure the degree of stability of this employment by introducing a business cycle variable, such as the unemployment rate of adult males.

The results in table 4 show that increases in SMIC relative to the mean salary significantly reduce the employment of fifteen- to twenty-four-year-olds relative to that of twenty-five- to sixty-year-olds. Using the logarithmic specification of all variables, we report that a 1 percent increase in the SMIC/mean wage ratio reduces by 0.46 percent the relative employment of the young. In addition, a 1 percent increase in the unemployment rate of adult males reduces by 0.12 percent the relative employment of young persons.

These effects are much stronger and more significant for young men than for young women. For the latter the effect of SMIC is insignificant, and the ratio of the employment of young women to adult women appears to be insensitive to the business cycle. This does not mean, however, that female employment might be insensitive to the cycle, as we will soon see.

Indeed, another method of studying the impact of SMIC on youth employment is to take as our dependent variable the rate of employment of the young, that is, the ratio of employed persons fifteen to twenty-four to the total population of fifteen- to twenty-four-year-olds.

Table 4 shows that the rate of youth employment is very significantly affected by the level of SMIC relative to the mean salary. This is equally true of the rate of employment of young women. On the other hand, the rate of employment is not strongly cyclic, but it is more so for young

[19] Welch, *Minimum Wages*.

TABLE 4

THE IMPACT OF SMIC ON RELATIVE EMPLOYMENT, EMPLOYMENT RATE, AND PARTICIPATION OF THE YOUNG

(annual data, 1963–1979)

Equation Number	Dependent Variable	Constant	LSMIC	LMIL	LPJ	LUA	R^2	DW
1	LERJ	-4.12 (-3.82)	-0.46 (-1.65)	—	—	-0.12 (-2.68)	0.76	0.41
2	LERJM	-5.85 (-6.12)	-0.68 (-2.77)	—	—	-0.15 (-3.65)	0.87	0.76
3	LERJF	-3.48 (-2.45)	-0.17 (-0.48)	—	—	-0.95 E-01 (-1.51)	0.41	1.00
4	LTEJ	-2.57 (-3.63)	-0.41 (-3.84)	0.11 (2.33)	-0.22 (-1.19)	-0.85 E-01 (-4.04)	0.96	1.15
5	LTEJM	-3.14 (-2.95)	-0.61 (-3.73)	0.91 E-01 (1.22)	-0.57 (-2.02)	-0.10 (-3.35)	0.95	1.00
6	LTEJF	-3.44 (-5.24)	-0.17 (-1.74)	0.14 (3.21)	0.22 (1.31)	-0.59 E-01 (-3.03)	0.93	0.96
7	LTPJ	-1.42 (-2.04)	-0.41 (-3.85)	0.58 E-01 (1.18)	-0.50 (-2.73)	-0.40 E-01 (-1.97)	0.95	1.00
8	LTPJM	-2.36 (-2.25)	-0.61 (-3.80)	0.50 E-01 (0.68)	-0.96 (-2.76)	-0.72 E-01 (-2.93)	0.95	1.07
9	LTPJF	-1.89 (-2.87)	-0.16 (-1.61)	0.70 E-01 (1.51)	-0.15 (-0.19)	-0.39 E-01 (-0.19)	0.82	0.91

NOTE: Number of observations, 17; t-statistics in parentheses; significance levels are $t_{01} = 2.76$, $t_{05} = 2.05$, and $t_{10} = 1.70$. For definitions of variables, see appendix.

males than for young females. The demographic variables (JP) and the number of draftees called (MIL) exert only a small influence. We still note a positive influence of the number of draftees on the rate of employment of young women as well as of young men.

The Effect on the Participation Rate of the Young. While the effect of SMIC on the employment of the young is well determined in theory, the effect on participation is ambiguous because there is a negative effect on employment and a possibly positive effect on unemployment. The explanation for the latter is either that the higher SMIC attracts a larger number of youths into the labor market to search for employment or that the increase in SMIC accelerates the turnover of young employed workers, which increases the unemployment rate.[20]

In view of the results of table 4, it appears that an increase in SMIC reduces the participation rate of the young, that is, that the effect on employment is stronger than the effect on unemployment. This is true for the group of young workers as a whole and for young men, but the effect is less strong and less significant for young women. This result is consistent with what we know about the strong rise in the unemployment rate of the young in the 1970s when SMIC grew faster than the mean wage and the decrease in participation of young men and increase in participation of young women.

Summary of Table 4. The results of table 4 strongly support the classic predictions of economic theory concerning the effect of SMIC on young people's employment. Equations 1 through 3 show a clear effect of SMIC increases relative to the mean wage on the relative employment of young men, the very cyclical character of their employment (coefficient on LUA, male unemployment), and no clear effect of SMIC on the relative employment of young women. Equations 4 through 6 show that the same results as those for relative employment are obtained when the employment rate is used as the dependent variable. Again, the effect on young men is clear and more important than that on young

---

[20] Equations (4) and (7) jointly give an implicit estimate of the impact on youths' unemployment rate of a variation in the SMIC/mean wage ratio. The elasticity of unemployment to the variation of this ratio can be expressed as:

$$E_U \frac{SMIC}{W} = (\beta_{TPJ} - \beta_{TEJ}) \frac{E/PA}{U/PA}$$

where β_{TEJ} is the regression coefficient of $LSMIC$ in the employment equation (4) and β_{TPJ} is the regression coefficient of $SMIC$ in the participation equation (7). E/PA is the employment rate, and U/PA is the unemployment rate. It can be seen that $\beta_{TPJ} = \beta_{TEJ} = -0.41$ in both equations. Thus an increase of SMIC relative to the mean salary does not affect the unemployment rate of the young.

TABLE 5

The Ripple Effects of SMIC on Wages: Tentative Results

(quarterly data, 1962–1979)

Equation Number	Dependent Variable	Constant	DP	DP_{t-1}	DSP	DSP_{t-1}	UA	UA_{t-1}	UA_{t-2}	UA_{t-3}	DPIB	$DPIB_{t-1}$	R^2	DW
1	DW	0.84 E–02 (3.52)	−0.33 (−2.53)	0.21 (1.69)	0.22 (7.71)	0.60 E–01 (2.05)	—	—	—	—	0.11 (2.99)	−0.98 E–01 (−2.49)	0.69	2.33
2	DW	−0.46 E–02 (−0.47)	−0.24	—	0.27 (7.58)	—	0.45 (0.30)	0.64 (0.30)	−0.55 (−0.26)	0.22 (0.17)	0.48 E–01 (1.42)	—	0.57	2.45

NOTE: Number of observations, 17; t-statistics in parentheses; significance levels are $t_{01} = 2.76$, $t_{05} = 2.05$, and $t_{10} = 1.70$. For definitions of variables, see appendix.

women. Finally, equations 7 through 9 demonstrate that the participation rate of young men, more than that of young women, is reduced by increases in SMIC relative to the mean wage and that there are weak cyclical effects on participation.

Ripple Effects. Despite the legal prohibition against wages being indexed on SMIC, can we observe an effect of SMIC increases on the mean salary? Table 5 shows that SMIC exerts a positive and very significant effect on the rate of increase of the mean salary. This effect occurs for the most part during the quarter of the SMIC increase. There is thus a de facto indexation, at least partially, which reflects the resistance of the hierarchy of wages to being squeezed from below.

Conclusion

The SMIC significantly reduces the employment and participation of the young, especially of young men more than of young women. On the other hand, it is possible that it gives rise to a strong increase in the unemployment rate of young women. These results are strongly in agreement with what has been found for other countries.

Concerning young men, for whom the unemployment effect is more doubtful, there appears to be less confirmation of Leffler's finding—that SMIC can increase the income of the young and less qualified when there is an unemployment system—since participation of young men in the labor market has been steadily decreasing in the last few years. It could, however, affect young women, whose participation has been increasing.

In sum, the social character of SMIC appears at least dubious.

Appendix: Definition of Variables

SMIC: Nominal hourly SMIC divided by the general index of hourly wages (W)

SP: Real hourly SMIC, that is, SMIC divided by the price index

UA: Rate of unemployment of adults (twenty-five- to sixty-year-olds)

PIB: Gross domestic product at 1970 prices

W: General index of nominal hourly wages

P: Consumer price index

MIL: Ratio of draftees to total number of young people (fifteen- to twenty-four-year-olds)

JP: Ratio of fifteen- to twenty-four-year-olds to total population
EJ: Number of fifteen- to twenty-four-year-olds employed
EJM: Number of fifteen- to twenty-four-year-old males employed
EJF: Number of fifteen- to twenty-four-year-old females employed
ERJ: Relative employment of the young, that is, *EJ* divided by total number of twenty-five- to sixty-year-olds employed
ERJM: Relative employment of young males, that is, *EJM* divided by total number of twenty-five- to sixty-year-old males employed
ERJF: Relative employment of young females, that is, *EJF* divided by total number of twenty-five- to sixty-year-old females employed
TEJ: Employment rate of the young, that is, *EJ* divided by total population of fifteen- to twenty-four-year-olds
TEJM: Employment rate of young males
TEJF: Employment rate of young females
TPJ: Participation rate of the young, that is, unemployed and employed fifteen- to twenty-four-year-olds divided by total population of fifteen- to twenty-four-year-olds
TPJM: Participation rate of young males
TPJF: Participation rate of young females
L means the logarithm of the concerned variable.
D means the rate of growth of the concerned variable.

Bibliography

Bégué, Jean. "Hausse du SMIC et effets sur la masse salariale." *Economie et Statistique*, no. 100, May 1978.

Courthéoux, Jean-Paul. *Le salaire minimum.* Paris: Presses Universitaires de France, Que sais-je?, 1978.

Gramlich, E. M. "The Impact of Minimum Wages on Other Wages, Employment and Family Incomes." *Brookings Papers on Economic Activity*, no. 2. Washington, D.C., 1976.

Hall, Robert E. "The Minimum Wage and Job Turnover in Markets for Young Workers," mimeo, April 1979.

Leffler, Keith B. "Minimum Wages, Welfare, and Wealth Transfers to the Poor." *Journal of Law and Economics*, October 1978.

Luskin, David M. "The Economics of Minimum Wage Laws." Ph.D. dissertation, University of Rochester, 1979.

McCulloch, J. Huston. *The Effect of Minimum Wage Legislation on Income Equality: A Theoretical Analysis.* National Bureau of Economic Research, Working Paper no. 171, 1977.

Mincer, J., and Leighton, L. *Effects of Minimum Wages on Human Capital Formation.* National Bureau of Economic Research, Working Paper no. 441, 1980.

Stigler, G. J. "The Economics of Minimum Wage Legislation." *American Economic Review*, June 1946.

Welch, Finis. "Minimum Wage Legislation in the United States." In *Evaluating the Labor-Market Effects of Social Programs*, edited by O. Ashenfelter and J. Blum. Princeton: Princeton University Press, 1976.

————. *Minimum Wages: Issues and Evidence*. Washington, D.C.: American Enterprise Institute, 1978.

West, E. G., and McKee, M. "Monopsony and 'Shock' Arguments for Minimum Wages." *Southern Economic Journal*, January 1980.

Legal Minimum Wages as an Instrument of Social Policy in Less Developed Countries, with Special Reference to Costa Rica

Peter Gregory

Along with a proliferation of independent countries in the third world since World War II has come a proliferation of minimum wage regimes. Following the example of the industrialized countries and the encouragement of the International Labor Organization, the less developed countries have created machinery for defining and administering legal minimums. The justifications offered for such intervention in the wage determination process are the familiar ones advanced in the more developed countries.[1] In the presence of great poverty, minimum wages are proposed as an ameliorative measure which can protect wage earners from the depressive influences of competitive or, even worse, monopsonistic labor market forces on wage levels. Implicit is a belief that the labor market cannot be relied upon to yield secularly increasing wage levels because of the existence either of perfectly elastic labor supply schedules or of unspecified "market imperfections."[2] That a shift in demand could maximize another professed goal, that of employment, in the presence of an elastic supply and wage stability seems to be overlooked. Therefore, aggressively administered minimum wages have been advocated as a means of raising the real incomes of the laboring poor, sharing widely the fruits of economic growth, and effecting a more

---

NOTE: This paper is based on a study undertaken by the author as a consultant to the International Labor Office's Programa Regional del Empleo para America Latina y el Caribe (Regional Employment Program for Latin America and the Caribbean). Some of the findings of that study appear in *Salarios, Precios y Empleo en Coyunturas de Crisis Externa. Costa Rica 1973–75,* Investigaciones Sobre Empleo No. 16 (Santiago: PREALC, 1979), chap. 2. The views expressed in this essay are the sole responsibility of the author and do not necessarily represent those of PREALC.

[1] International Labor Office, *Minimum Wage Fixing and Economic Development* (Geneva, 1968), pp. 5–9.

[2] This view overlooks the theoretical implications of monopsony. If the employer is a monopsonist and faces the entire upward-sloping labor supply schedule (increases in demand for labor supply schedule), increases in demand for labor must be followed by increases in wages, though, of course, the wage will lie below the marginal revenue product of labor. On the other hand, if the supply of labor schedule facing the monopsonist is perfectly elastic in the relevant range, the employer will have no effective monopsony power over the wage.

egalitarian income distribution. In the eyes of many, the existence of legal minimum wage regimes and an active administration of these have become an important test of a government's concern for the welfare of its people, of its commitment to "social justice."

The intended scope of coverage of minimum wage regulations varies, as does the degree of detailed administration.[3] Initially, many of the regimes were limited to employment in larger establishments and only gradually extended to other urban and rural groups. Some countries, including Costa Rica, have adopted very complicated systems which discriminate among industries, occupational groups, and regions. The frequency of review and adjustment of minimums is often specified by law though adjustment by executive decree is not uncommon in the face of unusual circumstances such as accelerating inflation.

The stated objectives with respect to coverage are ambitious, and the results almost universally fall short of their achievement. In fact, it is generally agreed that the legal minimums are effective primarily in the larger establishments in urban areas and in the modern large-scale commercial agricultural sector where workers are also frequently organized in trade unions. The degree of evasion increases as one moves toward smaller enterprises and less urbanized areas. Indeed, most governments make no serious effort to enforce the minimums in such employments, since the administrative agencies usually do not have sufficient personnel for such an undertaking. Furthermore, the authorities often concede privately that the legal minimums may lie beyond the "ability to pay" of small employers, so that enforcement could result in their elimination.

There seems to be little disposition in the less developed countries to question the desirability or efficacy of legal minimum wages, presumably because they are viewed as "a good thing" and as a proper instrument of policy for pursuing laudable objectives. This essay represents an attempt to examine these premises within a single small developing country, Costa Rica. The study of the evolution of the labor market and the role of minimum wages in determining effective wages was undertaken for a decade, from the mid-1960s to the mid-1970s. During this period, it is possible to distinguish three policy objectives which minimum wage administration was intended to pursue. The first was the general objective of promoting the economic welfare of wage and salary earners by periodic adjustments in the legal minimums. The second objective, evident particularly toward the end of the studied period, was the alteration of the distribution of income within the covered labor force by acting on interindustry and occupational minimum

[3] International Labor Office, *Minimum Wage Fixing*, pp. 77–122.

378

TABLE 1

INDEX OF NOMINAL AND REAL WAGES AND OF EMPLOYMENT IN THE
INDUSTRIAL SECTOR, 1966–1975

(1968 = 100)

Year	Nominal Wages	Percent Change	Real Wages	Percent Change	Employ- ment	Percent Change
1966	84.76	—	89.22	—	83.63	—
1967	91.24	7.65	94.94	6.41	90.85	8.63
1968	100.00	9.60	100.00	5.33	100.00	10.07
1969	108.68	8.68	105.82	5.82	111.35	11.35
1970	117.98	8.56	108.95	2.96	126.14	13.28
1971	126.81	7.48	114.44	5.04	138.31	9.65
1972	136.92	7.97	118.14	3.23	147.54	6.67
1973	154.09	12.54	119.01	0.74	159.49	8.10
1974	189.26	22.82	115.72	−2.76	171.80	7.72
1975[a]	225.70	19.25	111.46	−3.68	167.84	−2.31

[a] January–November only.

SOURCE: Banco Central de Costa Rica. The indexes are derived from data supplied by the Caja Costarricense de Seguro Social, the national social security agency. The data are from a sample of 562 industrial firms.

wage differentials. Finally, minimum wages were viewed as an appropriate instrument for addressing the problem of poverty, as a means of altering the income distribution generally in favor of the poor.[4] The efficacy of minimum wages as a policy instrument for achieving these three objectives will be examined in order in the following sections.

Minimum Wages and the General Wage Level

The decade 1966–1975 is characterized by two sharply contrasting subperiods. From 1966 through 1972, both money and real wages rose steadily in the industrial sector (see table 1). Real wages rose at an annual compound rate of 4.8 percent. Since this rate of increase exceeds that in the economywide average productivity, which I have estimated to have been about 3.2 percent, industrial workers would appear to have improved their economic position relative to other economic groups.[5]

---

[4] These objectives were consistent with those defined by the Constitution, the elevation of the standard of living and the redistribution of income.

[5] The increase in national productivity was estimated by calculating the rate of change in real output per member of the labor force. Output was defined as the gross internal product adjusted by the implicit national income deflator.

379

Unfortunately, however, the eruption of worldwide inflationary forces did not pass Costa Rica by. Wholesale prices began to rise rapidly in late 1973 and continued to do so through the first half of 1974. Consumer prices lagged behind the increases in wholesale prices but still rose 16.3 percent in 1974 and another 24.6 percent in 1975. The crisis was reflected in a sharp decline in the rate of economic growth. In per capita terms, GNP increased on the order of only 1 percent in each of these two years. While money wages advanced substantially during this inflationary outburst, they fell behind the rate of increase in prices. Real wages in the industrial sector, derived from a sample of 562 firms, declined about 3 percent in each of the two years so that, by 1975, average real wages had fallen back almost to the level prevailing in 1970. In that part of the private sector covered by the social security system, average real remunerations declined even faster, by 5.8 and 5.3 percent in 1974 and 1975, respectively.[6]

To what extent can the observed course of average earnings be attributed to the intervention of public policy measures? In Costa Rica, the principal instrument of wage policy is the system of minimum wages, which extends to the private sector as a whole.[7] In addition, the wage policies pursued by the central government and the various quasi-autonomous public agencies may have "spillover effects" to the extent that remunerations they offer lead those in the private sector. (In fact, remuneration levels in the central government lagged behind those in the private sector between 1971 and 1975 while those in the autonomous agencies led. During my fieldwork in Costa Rica in 1976, various government authorities expressed concern over the central government's inability to establish control over the wage policies pursued by the autonomous agencies. The latter were viewed as having potential (undesirable) spillover effects and as upsetting established wage structure relationships vis-à-vis both the rest of the public sector and the private sector.) Before 1974, minimum wages were reviewed and revised every

[6] Wage changes for the private sector were calculated from an unpublished index of the Caja Costarricense de Seguro Social, the national social security agency.

[7] Minimum wages are determined by the tripartite Consejo Nacional de Salarios, a largely autonomous body. Minimums are set on an industry-by-industry basis as well as by occupational groups within industries. The criteria according to which minimums were determined are generally considered to have been rather vague. Beginning in 1974, however, the central government has intervened in a more direct fashion to influence the consejo's decisions in line with its views on the size and form of minimum wage adjustments. For a review of the minimum wage determination machinery and practice, see Q. F. Delgado and O. L. C. Mora, *Fijación de Salarios Mínimos en Costa Rica, Análisis y Recomendaciones* (San José: Banco Central, 1976); Helen I. Lom, *Salarios Mínimos en Costa Rica* (San José: Universidad de Costa Rica, 1975); Ministerio de Trabajo y Seguridad Social, "Antecedentes para una Política Nacional de Salarios en Costa Rica," mimeo. (San José: 1974).

other year. Since then, with the onset of severe inflation, annual revisions have become the rule.

I do not wish to minimize the difficulty of distinguishing the various forces that may act on wage levels. In the absence of rigorous testing, one is well advised to be cautious in making strong statements about causation. In the case of Costa Rica, an analysis of the available wage data provides strong support for a hypothesis that revisions in minimum wages have not been the only, and probably not the principal, determinant of wages in important sectors of the economy. To be sure, in the case of some low-wage employment, particularly in agriculture, minimum wages may have caused effective wages to rise faster than they would otherwise have risen, or at least affected the timing if not the rate of change of such wages. With respect to wage levels in the nonagricultural sectors, however, the available annual and monthly data suggest that wage levels have been subject to the influence of forces that have operated independently of changes in legal minimums. For example, during each of the years in which *no* adjustment was made in legal minimum wages, average earnings in the industrial sector nevertheless advanced (see table 2). Indeed, the rate of change in earnings in the off-years (that is, the years of no minimum wage adjustment) was not much different than that in the on-years and in some cases exceeded

TABLE 2

RATE OF CHANGE IN AVERAGE MONTHLY EARNINGS IN THE
INDUSTRIAL SECTOR AND IN MINIMUM WAGES, 1967–1976

Year	Average Monthly Earnings— Rate of Change over Previous Year	Date and Size of Adjustment in Legal Minimum Wages
1967	7.65	No adjustment made
1968	9.60	October 1—10% or less
1969	8.68	No adjustment
1970	8.56	October 1—10% or less
1971	7.48	No adjustment
1972	7.97	October 1— 7.5-15%
1973	12.54	No adjustment
1974	22.82	April 1—10-41%
1975[a]	20.68	January 1—9.5-11%
1976	—	January 1—8-18%

[a] Average January–November only.
SOURCES: Banco Central, "Indice de Salarios del Sector Industrial"; and Ministerio de Trabajo, Consejo Nacional de Salarios, "Informe sobre el Estado Actual del Sistema de Salarios Mínimos en Costa Rica."

the increases of the latter. It is quite clear that the increases in earnings substantially exceeded the changes in the minimums even in the years in which the minimums changed, with the possible single exception of 1974. Even though in 1968, for example, the rate of change in the average earnings appears as 9.60 percent and the change in the minimum appears as 10 percent or less, it should be kept in mind that the increased minimum was effective for only the final three months of the year. Thus, if there had been no wage changes independent of the minimum wage in that year, the rate of change in average earnings would have been in the neighborhood of only 2.5 percent for the year as a whole.

This same tendency for earnings to outrun changes in the minimum wage can also be observed in sectors other than the industrial. Consider, for example, the rates of change in earnings and minimum wages during a period in which a change in minimum wages was effected. For this purpose we compare the rate of increase in average earnings over the interval June 1972 to December 1973; a change in the minimum became effective October 1, 1972. In the mining sector, the various minimum wages were adjusted upward by 10 to 15 percent. Nevertheless, average earnings during this period increased by 32.6 percent, a rate more than double that of the minimum wage increase. In agriculture, minimum wages were increased by 7.5 to 15 percent; yet average earnings increased by 23.8 percent. In construction, for which an interim increase had been effected in June 1971, the 1972 determination increased wages for most occupations by 5 percent; average earnings increased by 9.2 percent. In commerce, the margin of increase in actual over minimum wage increases was much narrower, 15.2 to 12 or 13 percent.

Differences in the rates of adjustment in these two wage variables carry over into the inflationary years 1974 and 1975. For example, the construction industry, which was enjoying a boom, saw wages rising faster than average minimum wages applied to the sector. In April 1974, increases in minimum wages applied to the sector ranged between 20 and 30 percent. Average earnings in December 1974 stood 27.4 percent above the level of the previous December. In 1975, the increase in the legal minimum amounted to 10 percent; however, average earnings advanced by 22.2 percent. Apparently, the strength of market forces sufficed to give a substantial upward impetus to wages in that industry. In 1975, the agricultural sector also recorded a larger increase in average earnings than that effected in the minimum wage. Whereas the minimum increased by only 11 percent, actual earnings increased by 22.3 percent. We have no explanation for this large difference, though we note that during the previous year, actual wages increased by 20.7 percent, a rate considerably less than the adjustments in agricultural minimum wages, which ranged from 25 to 41 percent. It is possible that the sector lagged in adjusting to the large increases of 1974, with some part of these "spilling over" into 1975.

Unpublished monthly data for the whole private sector based on wages reported to the Caja Costarricense de Seguro Social are available and permit us to observe the immediate impact of changes in minimum wages as well as the course of wages on a month-to-month basis. It is quite clear that, between 1973 and 1976, the introduction of a change in the minimum wage has had only a minor immediate or direct impact on wage levels in the private sector (see table 3). For example, in 1975, the new minimum wage went into effect on January 1, with increases ranging from 9.5 to 11 percent. Yet in January, average earnings in the private sector increased by only 1.83 percent. However, they continued to increase steadily during the year, so that by the end of December they had risen an *additional* 16.3 percent over the January level. In January 1976, minimum wage increases of 8 to 18 percent were promulgated. Yet in that month, reported average earnings actually declined slightly from December levels. Thereafter, average earnings can be observed rising again. In April they stood 6.8 percent above the January level.

Indeed, in all of the years for which we have monthly data, it can be observed that average earnings consistently tended upward over the

TABLE 3

INDEX OF MONTHLY EARNINGS IN THE PRIVATE SECTOR, 1973–1976
(July 1971 = 100)

Month	1973	1974	1975	1976
January	124.05	134.41	*168.82*	*193.95*
February	121.58	130.23	166.16	193.19
March	126.13	133.27	162.90	198.51
April	124.61	*146.77*	175.10	207.06
May	126.32	151.90	175.10	
June	124.24	149.81	171.48	
July	123.10	153.04	181.18	
August	126.13	154.94	177.42	
September	129.36	158.17	184.07	
October	128.22	163.12	186.73	
November	129.93	162.55	183.69	
December	133.35	165.78	196.42	
Annual average	126.42	150.33	177.42	

NOTE: Numbers in italics indicate months in which a change in the minimum wage became effective.
SOURCE: Caja Costarricense de Seguro Social, unpublished data.

year both before and after the introduction of a new minimum wage. The course of earnings recorded here thus suggests that minimum wages probably have played a minor role in propelling wages upward. A stronger case can be made for the proposition that labor market forces dominated. Note, for example, the impressive rate of growth in industrial employment recorded in table 1. Between 1966 and 1973, employment expanded at an annual rate of 9.7 percent. During this same period GNP grew at an impressively high rate of 6.75 percent per annum, which supported a high rate of absorption of the growing labor force. In spite of levels of unemployment which might appear high by some subjective standard, some classes of labor were clearly in short supply during the expansive years of the 1960s and 1970s.[8] Employers reported that pirating of experienced labor was a common practice during this period, lending support to the conclusion that market forces were actively bidding up the price of labor.

It is noteworthy that government officials with whom I spoke attributed to minimum wage administration a more important influence on earnings than the data would seem to indicate. However, my assignment of a lesser role to minimum wage administration is supported by other research on the course of minimum wages in Costa Rica. One study traced the course of minimum wages from 1954 to the mid-1970s.[9] From the data presented it appeared that minimum wages in most categories were adjusted upward at a rate only slightly greater than the rate of inflation and well below the rates of increase in national productivity and actual average earnings. What the Costa Rican experience suggests is that, under conditions of steady and rapid growth, market forces do assert themselves and can exert upward pressure on the general wage level, at least in the urban sectors of employment.

In judging the impact of legal minimums on agricultural wages, one is on less solid ground, for extensive wage data over time are lacking. Nevertheless, it seems probable that the minimums do play a greater

---

[8] The national unemployment rate as reported in the censuses of 1963 and 1973 was 6.9 and 7.3 respectively. It is of interest to note that despite a significant rural-urban shift in population in the intercensal period it did not appear to have brought with it aggravated problems of unemployment in urban areas. For example, the unemployment rate in the country's capital and largest city, San José, was lower than the national rate in the 1973 census year, 6.6 percent as compared to 7.3 percent. Furthermore, a household labor force survey inaugurated in 1976 reported that open unemployment in that year had declined since the census year to 5.1 percent in May and 6 percent in July. Ministerio de Trabajo y Seguridad Social, Dirección General de Planificación del Trabajo y el Empleo, "Encuesta de Hogares en el Area Metropolitana de San José: Empleo y Desempleo, Adelanto de las Informaciones mas Importantes" (May 1976), and *Encuesta Nacional de Hogares: Empleo y Desempleo, Julio 1976.*

[9] Delgado and Mora, *Fijación de Salarios Mínimos.* For a sample of rates of change in minimum wages since 1954, see pp. 12–16.

role in determining these than wages in other sectors. For example, it was commonly believed that, except for the organized banana-producing sector, the legal minimums represented the maximum rates paid to the bulk of the agricultural labor force. In addition, evasion of the legal minimums was believed to be fairly widespread in agriculture, lending support to the view that the minimums lay above the market price of labor. Minimum wage administration during the decade 1963–1973 treated the various agricultural subsectors in a discriminatory fashion. While the real value of the minimums in coffee and cocoa was either unchanged or actually declined, in the other branches of the sector except bananas, the annual rates of increase were positive and on the order of 1.3 to 2 percent. To the extent that the minimums represented actual wage levels of agricultural workers, this would imply that urban-rural earnings differentials widened over the decade.[10]

Minimum Wages as a Redistributive Mechanism within the Covered Labor Force

We noted above that one of the stated objectives of minimum wage administration in Costa Rica was the narrowing of income inequality. To this end, differential rates of increase in minimums could be applied to high- and low-wage occupational or industrial classes. According to Delgado and Mora, minimum wages were administered in a way intended to narrow interindustry and interoccupational differentials from 1954 on.[11] Lower minimums tended to be adjusted upwards at a slightly faster rate than high minimums. Whether these intentions were realized with respect to occupational earnings cannot be determined, for earnings data by occupation are not available over time. However, such a policy could hope to effect a narrowing only if the legal minimums for high-wage skilled classes of labor (or applicable to high-wage industries) are already above the opportunity cost of workers so employed. If the market for such employments exceeds the legal minimums, as appeared to be the case in parts of the industrial sector, there is no reason to expect

[10] This statement assumes that the degree of evasion of legal minimums remained constant over time. If the degree of evasion declined, the actual differential would be narrower than that implied by a comparison of urban earnings and agricultural minimums. One of the difficulties in assessing the relation of legal minimums to the market price of labor in agriculture arises out of the variation in the latter over the various seasons of the year. While the minimum may lie above the market wage during some parts of the year, at others, such as the harvest, wages may be bid up above the minimum levels. For example, during the coffee harvest of 1976 when coffee prices were at very high levels, shortages of labor were said to be commonplace and wages were being offered which exceeded the legal minimums.

[11] Delgado and Mora, *Fijación de Salarios Mínimos,* pp. 16–23.

that actual earnings differentials would conform to the structure of minimum wages.

In 1974, following the onset of inflation, the degree of discrimination applied in the adjustment of minimums increased sharply. Rather than promulgating increases for all covered employments in approximately the same proportion in accordance with past practice, administrators applied a wide range of rates of change, with the size of the adjustment inversely related to the level of the minimum in effect during the preceding period. Furthermore, the government urged firms whose employees were not directly affected by the legal minimums to adhere to a similar discriminatory policy of wage adjustment. The disparity in the proposed rates of adjustment was very large indeed, ranging from 41 percent for the lowest rates to 10 percent for the highest. Two justifications were offered for the policy of graduated increases. First, while wage restraint was considered desirable as an anti-inflationary measure, it was felt that the lowest-income groups had been hardest hit by the sharp rise in prices of basic consumption items and should not be asked to sacrifice their already low living standard. Thus a heavier burden of restraint would have to be applied to higher-income groups. Second, a narrowing of wage differentials was viewed as a desirable step toward the realization of the government's objective of reduced income inequality in the society.

While the principle of larger increases for the lowest-wage workers was said to have been widely supported, even among the high-wage earners who were discriminated against by the policy, it is likely that such support will tend to erode in the face of continuing inflation. In the case of Costa Rica, employers reported that the continued deterioration in the real income position of the higher-wage workers led to increased pressure from them to adjust their wages upward. If employers generally responded to these pressures, this might explain the large excess in the rate of advance in average earnings over the change in minimum wages during 1975. In that year, legal minimum wages were increased by 9.5 to 11 percent. Yet average earnings in the private sector increased during the year by 18 percent. A lagged adjustment to the sharply graduated wage adjustments of the previous year may provide at least a partial explanation for this large divergence in the two rates of change.

There are surely limits to the effectiveness of graduated minimum wage changes as a tool for narrowing wage differentials. Indeed, had the graduated differentials introduced since 1972 really been effective in determining wage differentials, these would have been narrowed substantially and would have inflicted a very sharp reduction in the real wage of the higher-wage worker. Table 4 illustrates what would have

TABLE 4

EXTREME RATES OF CHANGE IN LEGAL MINIMUM WAGES AND
THEIR HYPOTHETICAL EFFECTS ON OCCUPATIONAL DIFFERENTIALS

	Sept. 1972	1972– 1974	1974	1975	1976
Extreme rates of change in minimum wages (in percent)	—	7.5–15	10–41	9.5–11	8–18
Value of lowest minimum wage (in colones)	13.04	15.00	21.15	23.48	27.71
Value of highest minimum wage (in colones)	32.60	35.05	38.56	42.22	45.60
Ratio of highest to lowest	2.50	2.34	1.82	1.80	1.65

SOURCE: Calculations based on information contained in each year's *Decreto de Salarios Mínimos* (San José: Consejo Nacional de Salarios).

happened to the relationship between the wages of two occupational groups which stood in the ratio of 2.5:1 prior to the promulgation of the 1972 wage adjustment. The two wages chosen for this exercise were the highest minimum wage to which the 41 percent increase was applied and the lowest minimum to which the 10 percent increase was applied in 1974. The table assumes that the larger percentage change in each year applied to the low-wage job and the smaller change to the high-wage occupation. The table then chronicles the wage paid in each year. The accumulated effect of the graduated increases on the size of the occupational wage differential is impressive even within the scope of four short years. From a ratio of 2.5:1 in 1972, the differential shrinks by a third to 1.65. The change in the real value of the two wages is strikingly different in the two cases. While the value of the lowest minimum wage rose by approximately 6.2 percent, that of the highest actually fell by 30.5 percent.

(The changes in the real minimum wage were computed as follows: The average real value of the minimum wage during the base period during which that wage was in force was computed, for October 1970 through September 1972. Then the real value in February 1976 was computed, that is, for the month after the latest adjustment in minimum wages became effective.)

The assumptions under which this calculation was made were of course rather extreme, and it does not seem that, in practice, the extreme permissible rates of change were actually consistently applied. However, there were many industries in which a significant compression of minimum wage differentials was effected. A number of industries in which

387

narrowing occurred are listed in table 5 along with the ratio of the highest to the lowest minimum wage for the industry in each of two years, 1972 and 1976. The lowest rate was that assigned to a production or related worker (for example, a "peon"), thus omitting the minimum wage applying to custodial personnel. As can be seen, in some of the included cases, the shrinkage of the differentials was substantial.

The impact of this discriminatory policy on the real value of occupational minimum wages can be appreciated better by reference to the summary data for ninety-six occupational titles which appeared in both the 1970–1972 and the 1976 revisions. These were classified into unskilled, skilled, and other occupational groups, though I emphasize that the classification is only a rough one, one suggested by the occupational titles appearing in the decrees. The "other" category applies principally to "other production operations workers" (*otros trabajadores de proceso*), which suggests a range of production operations usually characterized by low- or semi-skilled occupations. Table 6 shows the

TABLE 5

RATIO OF THE HIGHEST TO THE LOWEST LEGAL MINIMUM WAGE IN VARIOUS INDUSTRIES, JULY 1972 AND JANUARY 1976

Industry	July 1972	January 1976
Fine cookies and crackers	1.66	1.35
Bread	1.80	1.55
Macaroni products	1.50	1.33
Breweries	1.43	1.25
Shoes (machine-made)	1.27	1.16
Tailors	2.31	1.69
Sawmills	1.44	1.27
Furniture and woodworking	1.65	1.39
Printing	3.40	2.30
Rubber	1.95	1.54
Machinery	1.76	1.45
Sugar mills and refineries	1.39	1.24
Candy	1.35	1.22
Textiles	1.21	1.15
Soap and detergents	1.21	1.13
Tanneries	1.18	1.15
Electrical products	1.42	1.28
Construction	1.63	1.36
Railroads	2.30	1.75

SOURCE: Calculations based on information contained in each year's *Decreto de Salarios Mínimos*.

TABLE 6

NUMBER OF OCCUPATIONAL CATEGORIES WITH INCREASES OR
DECLINES IN THE REAL VALUE OF THEIR MINIMUM WAGE,
1972–1976

			Decreases[a]	
Occupations	Total	Increases	Small	Large
Unskilled	38	33	2	3
Skilled	30	2	4	24
Other	30	22	2	6

[a]A decrease was classified as small if it did not exceed 5 percent, large if it did.
SOURCE: Ministerio de Trabajo y Seguridad Social, Consejo Nacional de Salarios, *Salarios Mínimos*, various years.

number of occupations in each skilled classification reporting increases or declines in their real minimum wage. As can be seen, few of the skilled occupational titles escaped a reduction in their real value, while the reverse was true for the unskilled and semiskilled titles. Of the thirty skilled occupations, twenty suffered declines in excess of 10 percent.

One may question the wisdom of an explicit policy aimed at narrowing occupational wage differentials further. After all, such differentials are generally believed to perform an economic function, that of providing a return on the cost of acquiring a higher level of skill or of attracting into skilled employments persons with the personal and educational qualifications deemed desirable for skilled workers but who qualify for a broader range of employment opportunities, including some outside the manual category. To the extent that high-quality workers are desired in skilled occupations, it will be necessary to offer wages that are comparable to those paid in other manual or nonmanual fields requiring a similar quality of labor. The arbitrary definition of narrower minimum wage differentials than those which would be consistent with this objective would seem to be misguided. Indeed, as suggested above, market forces will tend to maintain the wider differentials as long as the existing legal minimums applicable to the higher-wage employments do not exceed the opportunity cost of the workers occupying them. If it is an objective of national wage policy to effect a narrowing of differentials because high-wage workers are believed to receive large economic rents, a more effective response would be to encourage an increase in the supply of persons possessing the requisite skills. This would involve the identification of the occupations or employments yielding economic rents and a concerted effort to facilitate access to training. In addition, it would imply a measure of restraint on any other institutional forces, like collective bargaining, which might, by administrative means, try to preserve the wider rent-yielding differentials.

One final test of the redistributive effects of the government's policy of graduated adjustments in minimum wages is possible. I have compared the interindustry wage structure within the manufacturing sector at two times, December 1971 and November 1975 (see table 7). If the graduated wage policy had actually achieved the objective of narrowing

TABLE 7

MONTHLY AVERAGE EARNINGS BY INDUSTRY, DECEMBER 1971 AND NOVEMBER 1975

| Industry | Monthly Earnings (colones) | | Percentage Change |
	Dec. 1971	Nov. 1975	
Food products	698.4	1,136.5	62.7
Beverages	1,170.2	1,430.6	22.3
Tobacco	1,298.0	2,140.4	64.9
Textiles	615.4	966.0	57.0
Clothing except footwear	562.2	868.3	54.4
Leather, footwear, & other accessories	491.2	781.3	59.1
Footwear except rubber & plastic	532.8	829.5	55.7
Wood products except furniture	542.8	857.3	57.9
Furniture & accessories except metal	611.6	859.1	40.5
Paper & paper products	768.7	1,461.5	90.1
Printing & publishing	850.5	1,315.2	54.6
Industrial chemicals	1,069.9	1,640.2	53.3
Petroleum refining	1,269.9	1,664.6	31.1
Petroleum & coal products	628.3	877.4	39.6
Rubber products	903.9	1,340.7	48.3
Plastic products not elsewhere classified	684.5	1,177.7	72.1
Porcelain wares & tiles	724.4	1,504.8	107.7
Glass & glass products	800.5	1,141.1	42.5
Other nonmetallic mineral products	650.7	1,109.4	70.5
Basic metals	704.7	1,515.2	115.0
Metal products except machinery	764.8	1,153.6	50.8
Machinery except electrical	874.6	1,257.1	43.7
Electrical machinery & apparatus	784.8	1,528.4	94.8
Transportation equipment	853.3	1,421.4	66.6
Other manufacturers	617.0	1,038.4	68.3
Average	734.8	1,156.1	57.3

SOURCE: Data provided by Banco Central de Costa Rica. The original source is the Caja Costarricense de Seguro Social.

wage differentials, we would expect to find a negative correlation between the rate of wage change over the two points in time and the original level of average earnings by industry. While the data do yield a negative correlation coefficient of -0.276, it is statistically significant only at the 10 percent level. In fact, the extremes of the interindustry wage structure actually widened over the period. The ratio of the highest-wage to the lowest-wage industry increased slightly, from 2.64 to 2.74. However, the variance among the twenty-five industry groups as measured by the coefficient of variation (the ratio of the standard deviation to the mean) declined slightly, from 27.8 to 26.1 percent. Thus, overall, it cannot be said that the policy objectives had been realized to any appreciable extent by the end of 1975.

Wages, Poverty, and the Distribution of Income

One of the objectives of wage policy that had been enunciated in Costa Rica was a reduction in poverty and in the inequality in the distribution of income among social classes. Before we discuss the efficacy of a wage policy for this purpose, it would be advisable to consider the interrelationships among wages, poverty, and income distribution in order to assess the possible contribution of wage policy measures to the realization of the stated objectives.

It is tempting to assume that a close relationship exists between the wage level accruing to an individual and the level of economic well-being of that person and his family. That is, it is frequently assumed that a low level of wages is necessarily indicative of poverty or, conversely, that poverty is a function of the wage earned. A moment's reflection, however, should make clear that the relationship between a wage and a state of poverty is not so simple. Poverty is a function of more than just the wage accruing to an individual. While a wage or a rate of earnings is associated with an individual, the concept of poverty is associated with the well-being of a household or family. Therefore, the presence or absence of poverty is dependent not solely on the earnings of any particular member of the household but on the number of wage earners and their earnings, other nonwage sources of income, either in cash or in kind, and the number of persons in the household unit. Thus, given the existence of differences among households in the number of income recipients per household, one would expect differences to exist between the distribution of individual earnings and that of household incomes. Let us then consider what can be known about the conditions associated with the distribution of income in Costa Rica.

Unfortunately, the data that are available and also relevant for our purposes are limited in quantity. Nevertheless, I believe that enough useful observations can be derived from the available data to permit us to comment on the efficacy of wage policy as an instrument for dealing with poverty and for redistributing income.

Perhaps the most extensive study of income distribution is that of Victor Hugo Cespedes S., which is based on a special survey of households, national in scope, undertaken in 1971.[12] While it does not undertake an analysis of the relationship between individual incomes and family incomes, it does provide some information relevant to our inquiry. First of all, average family incomes of urban residents are 2.1 times as great as those of rural residents (1,703 to 796 colones per month).[13] Within the rural sector there appears to be no difference between the average family incomes of those families with heads engaged in agriculture and those with heads engaged in nonagricultural employment. Unfortunately, the distribution of families over the various income categories is not presented on a rural-urban basis but rather on the basis of the sector of employment of the head of family. However, some notion of the differences in the pattern of distribution as between the rural and urban sectors can be gained from the data presented by sector of employment in table 8.

As can be seen, low family incomes are more frequently found among families headed by persons employed in agriculture than by persons employed in any other sector. Nearly 40 percent of the families headed by a person employed in agriculture enjoyed a monthly family income of less than ¢500, or about U.S. $75, in 1971. In no other sector of employment of a head of household did more than 17.5 percent of the families fall into this lowest income category. Since this latter percentage includes rural nonagricultural families, it cannot be taken as a guide to the proportion of urban families in this income category. We can derive a crude estimate of the proportion of urban families in this income category if we assume that the distribution of family incomes of the rural nonagricultural families is identical to that of agricultural families.[14] Following this procedure, we derive an approximate proportion of urban families with incomes of less than ¢500 of only 6.5 percent.

Returning to the data in table 8 once again, we note that almost as poorly off as families in agriculture were those households headed

[12] Victor Hugo Cespedes S., *Costa Rica: La Distribución del Ingreso y el Consumo de Algunos Alimentos.* (San José: Universidad de Costa Rica, 1973).

[13] Cespedes, *La Distribución del Ingreso,* table 9, p. 51. The official exchange rate in 1971 was ¢6.64 to U.S. $1.

[14] Recall that the average income of these two sets of rural families is virtually identical. The reader is cautioned to keep in mind that when I speak of "agricultural" or "nonagricultural" families, I am referring to families headed by a person employed in the agricultural or nonagricultural sector. The less precise expression is used to simplify the textual presentation.

TABLE 8
Family Monthly Income Level by Sector of Employment of Family Head

	Total	Agriculture	Services	Manufac- turing	Commerce	Construc- tion	Transport and Com- munications	Misc.[a]	Others[b]
Number of families	2,965	1,010	494	341	277	165	144	44	490
Monthly income (colones)									
Less than 499	25.9%	39.8%	15.8%	17.5%	11.6%	7.9%	9.7%	13.6%	33.5%
500–799	24.0	26.8	17.2	26.4	20.2	32.7	23.5	29.5	22.0
800–999	10.7	9.5	9.3	14.7	10.1	15.8	14.6	2.3	10.2
1,000–1,299	11.9	10.3	15.0	13.8	12.6	13.3	15.3	18.2	8.4
1,300–1,499	5.9	5.1	5.7	5.9	8.7	10.3	4.2	9.1	4.9
1,500–1,999	8.2	4.5	10.5	8.2	13.4	9.1	17.4	11.4	7.8
2,000–2,499	4.5	1.2	8.1	5.0	7.2	4.9	4.1	6.8	5.5
2,500–2,999	2.6	0.8	5.1	3.2	5.8	2.4	1.4	—	2.1
3,000–3,499	2.0	0.9	2.6	1.2	3.6	0.6	4.9	6.8	2.2
3,500–3,999	1.1	0.5	1.6	0.9	2.8	—	2.1	—	1.2
4,000–4,499	0.9	0.3	3.4	0.9	0.4	1.2	—	—	0.2
4,500 or more	2.3	0.3	5.7	2.3	3.6	1.8	2.8	2.3	2.0
Average family income (colones)	1,175	773	1,624	1,213	1,539	1,203	1,401	1,372	1,056

[a]Mines and quarries, electricity, water, and activities not adequately specified.
[b]Includes female household heads and others who are not in the labor force.
Source: Víctor Hugo Céspedes S., *Costa Rica: La Distribución del Ingreso y el Consumo de Algunos Alimentos,* appendix, table 4, p. 114.

by a woman or with no active labor force members—the category iden-tified in the table as "others." Such households reported incomes about 35 percent greater than the average for agricultural households but below those reported by families employed in all other sectors. As in the agricultural sector, families in this category were disproportionately represented in the lowest income group. Indeed, of all the families with incomes of less than ¢500 per month, those in agriculture and with an inactive head of household accounted for three-fourths, while all of the families in these two categories represented barely half of the total sample of the study. This concentration of poverty among households headed by a person classified as "other" or by one employed in agri-culture, or more generally among rural households, should be kept in mind in any policy initiatives intended to reduce poverty or reduce income inequality among households.

Among the interesting findings of this study is that self-employed workers reported a family income distribution virtually identical to that of salaried workers. This is contrary to a commonly prevailing belief that the self-employed sector represents a repository of low-productivity, low-income workers who form a disproportionate part of the population in poverty.[15]

A more precise indicator of poverty is one that takes income per household member rather than income per household unit as a measure of well-being. Given the findings that family size is larger in rural than in urban areas and that family size seems to be inversely related to level of family income, it should not surprise us to find that the gap in per capita income between the rural and urban areas is even greater than that in family incomes.[16] Whereas urban family incomes are 2.1 times the rural, income per capita is 2.3 times as great. Fully 77 percent of rural families reported per capita incomes below ¢200 per month; only 3 percent of the urban families did so.[17]

Finally, the study by Cespedes provides some insight into the re-lationship between family incomes and the level of education of the head of household. For our purposes, it would have been preferable to

[15] Cespedes, *La Distribución del Ingreso*, appendix table 2, p. 112. The reader is cautioned, however, that even an identical pattern in the distribution of family income in these two employment categories could mask substantial differences in the earnings of the heads of families so employed. A similar family income distribution could result even if earnings in self-employment were much lower than in wage employment as long as there was a systematic tendency for secondary earners in the families of the self-employed to earn more than secondary income recipients in families headed by wage earners. However, this would seem to be an unreasonable event to assume.

[16] The inverse relationship between family income and family size was inferred from data on per capita income and family size presented in table 16 (p. 64) of Cespedes's study.

[17] Cespedes, *La Distribución del Ingreso*, table 9, p. 51.

relate the level of education to the individual wage earner or income recipient. Unfortunately, such a tabulation is not provided by this study. However, to the extent that it can be reasonably assumed that the head of household is the principal wage earner of the family and that the level of education of other employed members of the family is significantly correlated with that of the head, the information provided may be useful. As expected, within both the urban and the rural areas, there is a clear and direct relationship between the level of education of the head of household and the level of family income. As can be seen from table 9, incomes of the low-education families are higher in urban than in rural areas, but relative to the average income in each sector, the poorly educated urban families are worse off. The significance of the relationship between income and education is as follows. If it can also be assumed that the same relationship exists between the earnings of an individual wage earner and his education, then there may be limits to the extent to which wage policy can improve the income position of the poor possessing little formal education. To the extent that the wage received is an accurate reflection of the productivity of the poorly educated person, an attempt to raise his wage may have the effect of rendering him unemployable. Unskilled labor is a class of service which is easily replaceable by machines in industrial as well as in many types of agricultural employment.

The 1973 *Census of Population* provides a basis for verifying and confirming the assumption made above for purposes of relating individuals' remuneration to their education. As expected, the incidence of low income is clearly related to low levels of schooling completed. For

TABLE 9

AVERAGE FAMILY MONTHLY INCOME BY RESIDENCE AND
EDUCATIONAL LEVEL OF FAMILY HEAD
(in colones)

Educational Level	Total	Metropolitan	Urban[a]	Rural
All family heads	1,175	1,846	1,463	796
None	637	772	920	603
Primary	971	1,315	1,248	784
Secondary	1,695	1,860	1,728	1,322
University (incomplete)	2,823	2,920	2,653	2,710
University (completed)	5,255	5,458	4,282	7,777
Other and vocational	2,378	2,874	1,872	1,704
Not known	1,701	2,455	1,422	631

[a]Excludes the metropolitan San José area.
SOURCE: Cespedes, S., *La Distribución del Ingreso,* table 4, p. 41.

TABLE 10

WAGES AND HOURS OF AGRICULTURAL WORKERS IN COSTA RICA, 1974

Region	Hourly Wage Rate	Daily Hours Worked	Daily Wage Income
Vertiente Atlántico	2.75	7.6	20.85
Pacífico Sur	2.30	7.3	16.80
Pacífico Norte	2.40	6.1	14.60

SOURCE: IFAM, *Análisis Comparativo*, p. 39.

example, 69 percent of those with no schooling and 54 percent of those with uncompleted primary schooling earned incomes of less than ¢400 per month. Of those with incomplete secondary schooling, only 23 percent earned less than that amount.[18]

The greater incidence of low wages in rural than in urban areas implied by Cespedes's report is confirmed by other sources as well. The population census of 1973 clearly found the incidence of low remunerations (less than ¢400 a month) to be greater in rural employments. For example, of all men employed in Costa Rica who received less than that amount, 81 percent are rural residents, while the rural male labor force represents less than 60 percent of the total. While wages in agriculture are generally low in comparison to urban wages, nevertheless there appear to exist some significant differences in wage rates and income among the various regions of the country. One study of three regions, Vertiente Atlántico, Pacífico Sur, and Pacífico Norte, found a significant difference in daily earnings of agricultural workers due more to differences in the number of hours worked than in hourly earnings (see table 10). Indeed, the latter appears to have a very close relationship to the lowest minimum wage for the dominant agricultural activities of the respective regions.[19] One implication of these observations is that a change in the wage rate may be of less importance for lifting poor agricultural workers out of poverty than an increase in hours of work. (This assumes that short hours are not a result of the worker's personal choice.)

I also explored more generally the extent to which low levels of earnings were a function of short hours of work. The *Census of Population* provides us with some insight into this question. Clearly the problem of short hours is considerably more important for men than for

[18] Dirección General de Estadística y Censos, *Censo de Población 1973*, vol. 2, table 69, p. 520.
[19] Instituto de Fomento y Asesoria Municipal (IFAM), *Análisis Comparativo de Tres Regiones Periféricas sobre Producción Agropecuaria, Empleo, Ingresos y Migración, 1975*.

TABLE 11

WAGE EARNERS RECEIVING LESS THAN ¢400 PER MONTH FOR
FORTY OR FEWER HOURS PER WEEK

	Number of Workers	Less than 25 Hours	25–32 Hours	33–40 Hours	Total ≤ 40 Hours
All workers					
Total	172,359	3.2	4.1	15.9	23.2
Men	121,167	2.9	5.0	20.6	28.5
Women	51,192	4.1	2.0	4.8	10.9
Rural workers					
Total	115,756	2.9	5.0	21.1	29.0
Men	97,725	2.6	5.5	23.8	31.9
Women	18,030	4.5	2.3	6.8	13.6

SOURCE: *Censo de Población 1973*, vol. 2, table 65, p. 482.

women and in rural areas than in urban. Table 11 provides a measure of the incidence of short hours among men and women earning less than ¢400 per month. Short hours prove to be a contributing cause of low earnings for a significant minority of the wage-earning male population in rural areas. Almost a third of those with incomes below ¢400 worked for wages fewer than forty-one hours per week. Obviously to raise the income of such workers over some threshold would require more than just an increase in wage rates. It should be pointed out, however, that in the case of rural workers, wage employment may not be the only source of family income. To the extent that they also engage in subsistence farming with different frequencies in these three regions, the differences in wage earnings reported here would not provide a reliable guide to the total income accruing to any particular worker.

Finally, a few additional insights can be gained from tabulations based on the results of a household survey of income and expenditures made in 1974.[20] This survey was undertaken among urban families only. As indicated earlier, total family income provides an initial basis for indentifying foci of poverty. Table 12 provides a summary of some of the information extracted from the survey. One of the more notable observations is the small number of families in the lowest income stratum, that of under ¢500 per month. The proportion of all urban families in this income group, 5.8 percent, is comparable in its general order of magnitude with our estimated 6.5 percent of Cespedes's urban sample

[20] Unpublished data, Ministerio de Economía, Industria y Comercio, Dirección General de Estadística y Censos.

TABLE 12

Income of Urban Families in Costa Rica, 1974

Monthly Income (in colones)	Number of Families	Number of Persons per Family	Number of Employed Persons per Family	Average Monthly Income (in colones)		
				Per family	Per capita	Per employed person
500 or less	186	4.1	0.81	314	77	379
501–1,000	640	4.5	1.2	766	169	655
1,001–1,250	304	5.5	1.5	1,136	206	743
1,251–1,500	289	5.3	1.6	1,373	260	837
1,501–1,750	252	5.8	1.9	1,626	282	847
1,751–2,000	237	5.5	1.7	1,885	340	1,129
2,000–2,500	307	5.7	1.9	2,245	392	1,194
2,501–3,000	246	5.8	2.1	2,740	471	1,337
3,001–3,500	157	5.8	2.0	3,251	564	1,659
3,501–4,000	135	5.8	2.0	3,756	652	1,841
4,001–4,500	87	5.6	2.2	4,231	757	1,906
4,501–5,000	66	5.9	1.8	4,774	910	2,713
5,001–5,500	40	7.2	2.2	5,230	732	2,345
5,501 or more	273	5.3	1.8	9,620	1,815	5,404
Total	3,219					
All families (averages)		5.3	1.6	2,500	470	1,527

SOURCE: Unpublished data, Ministerio de Economía, Industria y Comercio.

for 1971. It also reaffirms our earlier statement that extreme poverty is more a rural than an urban phenomenon.

Perhaps the most striking observation about the family income distribution is its close relationship to the number of persons per household who are employed. Thus, family income increases steadily with the number of workers up to a level of approximately ¢2,500 and over. Thereafter, the number of workers per household varies only within a narrow range around 2. In the poorest households there is fewer than 1 or 0.8 employed person per household. Some of the households with no employed members may represent households of retired persons. However, there were also twenty-six unemployed persons present among the 186 households in this income class, though we have no way of knowing how many of these were parts of households without any other employed member. The next lowest income stratum, ¢500–1,000, also reported a small number of employed persons per household, barely 1.2, as well as seventy-nine unemployed members in the 640 households. The incidence of unemployment is clearly greater in these two lowest-income categories than in the higher-income families. While the families in these categories account for 25.7 percent of the total, they account for 33.1 percent of the unemployed.

In contrast with the findings reported by Cespedes, this urban survey indicates that income per family tends to overstate the degree of poverty in the lower-income families in relation to families in other income strata. The reason for this is the existence of a positive relationship between the level of family income and the number of family members. The lowest-income group reported an average of only 4.1 members. Thereafter, family size increases along with family income, leveling off at about 5.8 members per household at an income level of ¢2,001–2,500 per month.[21] Thus, per capita differences in income are narrower than those in family incomes. Furthermore, the differences in the remunerations per employed individual are narrower still. To illustrate, consider two income classes, that with income under ¢500 and that with ¢2,001–2,500. Average income per family in the latter is 7.15 times that in the former, income per capita is 5.09 times, while income per employed person is 3.15 times greater. The number of employed persons per household is 2.35 times greater. On the other hand, the number of unemployed persons per household is 1.56 times greater in the lower-income category.

---

[21] The inverse relationship between family income and number of household members which Cespedes reported must be due to a very strong tendency in this direction among rural households that overcomes the urban pattern we have observed here. Unfortunately, Cespedes does not provide an urban-rural breakdown so that this presumption might be tested.

Conclusion

On the basis of the observations made in the sections above, several conclusions follow regarding the efficacy of minimum wages as an instrument for influencing the general wage level and the distribution of income.

1. During a period in Costa Rica characterized by high and steady rates of economic growth and generally favorable labor supply conditions, wage levels also rose steadily. The evidence suggests that the wage policies pursued by government, as expressed through minimum wage administration, had only a marginal impact on the advance in wage levels. Labor market forces appear to have been the dominant source of pressure on wages.[22] Furthermore, the gains of economic growth appear to have been distributed quite widely, at least over the non-agricultural sectors for which wage data are available.

2. In the Costa Rican environment, minimum wages would appear to represent an indiscriminate instrument for effecting a reduction in the degree of inequality in the distribution of income. The limited relevant information at my disposal suggests that an aggressive administration of minimum wages would be likely to have a much greater impact on the incomes of the nonpoor than on the poorest groups in society. There are three reasons for expecting this to be the case:

First, poor households have fewer members employed than do the nonpoor, because of either unemployment among household members or an inactive labor force status. Furthermore, those with the lowest incomes tend to have a larger proportion of part-time workers, that is, those working fewer than forty hours per week. Therefore, an attempt to raise the poor out of poverty through general increases in minimum wages is less likely to achieve this objective than it is to increase the incomes of nonpoor families with multiple or fully employed wage earners.

Second, the lowest-income households are disproportionately distributed in rural areas where the enforcement of minimum wages is weakest. Since minimum wages are most easily evaded in rural employments, the incomes of the rural poor are less likely to be affected by an increase in the minimums than are those of urban workers who

---

[22] This paper has implicitly assumed throughout that the only significant institutional source of influence on wages lies in the government's administration of minimum wages. It has thus ignored other possible nonmarket forces such as collective bargaining which might have intervened effectively. The omission of trade unions from consideration as a significant force stems from the wide consensus I found in Costa Rica that they are not particularly powerful and do not represent a significant independent influence on wage levels except perhaps in some of the semiautonomous public corporations.

already occupy a more favorable position in the distribution of incomes by households.

Third, because the lowest-income households, and particularly the rural poor, are characterized by low levels of formal education, they may be perceived as unqualified for employment at wages significantly above their market-determined wage. Thus, the establishment of high minimum wages may serve only to block the access of the poor to covered employments and thus contribute little to the achievement of a more egalitarian distribution of income.

3. The attempt of public policy to effect a redistribution of income within the wage-earning group by the application of graduated rates of minimum wage change cannot be dismissed unequivocally as unsuccessful. It seems likely to me that this policy had at most only a temporary effect on the distribution of income, however. To the extent that occupational differentials tended to be reestablished, though with a lag, the redistributive effects of the initial graduated changes could be expected to be largely dissipated. This is likely to be a reasonable expectation, particularly in a case such as this, since the minimum wages applicable to the higher-wage occupations lie below the opportunity cost of those occupying them.

4. This paper has not considered an additional way in which an aggressive minimum wage policy might have perverse effects on the incomes distribution. To the extent that such a policy were to result in a substantial increase in the price of labor relative to the price of capital goods which may be substitutable for labor in production, the displacement of labor might be expected to follow, with negative consequences for employment. In particular, low-skilled labor is likely to be subject to easy substitution both in agricultural and in nonagricultural employments. Widespread displacement of labor in rural areas would pose particularly difficult problems of absorption in the absence of rural alternative sources of employment. And to the extent that the workers displaced possess very limited amounts of human capital, their chances of obtaining urban employment at the legal minimum wage would be reduced.

Indeed, one is tempted to speculate that the favorable evolution of employment conditions in Costa Rica over the decade studied might be related to the observation that minimum wage administration did not appear to have created significant distortions in the price of labor, at least in the nonagricultural sectors of the economy. While the price of capital does appear to have been maintained below its social opportunity cost, at least this source of distortion in the relative prices of labor and capital was not further magnified by effectively raising wages above their market-determined levels. Unfortunately, I am in no position to render an informed judgment on wage-employment relationships in Costa Rica. The favorable evolution of the labor market there does pose an interesting question about the possible contribution made by the restrained policy followed in the administration of minimum wages over most of the studied period, however.

I believe that the evidence presented here supports the conclusion that minimum wages are not likely to prove an effective instrument of income redistribution in favor of the poorest groups in Costa Rican society. Since alternative instruments are available to the government which are also potentially more efficient, I would suggest that the burden of effecting changes in the distribution of income be shifted to these.[23]

---

[23] A prime example of an instrument with a significant redistributive potential that could also be efficient in discriminating among different degrees of poverty and addressing its benefits only to those deemed worthy of increases in income is the Programa de Asignaciones Familiares (Program of Family Allowances). The program provides a very substantial fund, amounting to approximately 2 percent of national income, to be used to redress the distribution of income. Were the whole fund to reach the poorest quintile of the income distribution, this could imply an increase in average incomes within that quintile of from 33 to 40 percent. Whether the funds will actually reach the poorest elements of the society depends on the way in which they are distributed. At the time of my visit, the government was contemplating the assignment of these funds to fourteen government institutions for twenty-two different classes of activities intended to provide disbursements in kind and services to poor communities rather than cash to poor households. The one exception was the provision of old-age pensions to those who could not qualify for them under the social security system. I have not yet seen an evaluation of the program's redistributional effects.

The Determinants of Minimum Wage Levels and Coverage in State Minimum Wage Laws

James C. Cox and Ronald L. Oaxaca

Traditionally, the focus of economic inquiry concerning legislated minimum wages has been in attempting to estimate the impacts of such laws. There have been numerous studies which examine the effects of minimum wages on unemployment, relative employment, and earnings of various subsets of the labor force, especially youthful workers. There have also been studies of compliance under minimum wage laws. The modal response of professional economists, when asked their opinion of the merits of legal minimum wages, is that they are undesirable on efficiency grounds. That is to say, most geographical labor markets are workably competitive so that an effective legal minimum wage would be expected to lead to resource misallocation. The economic inefficiency implied by this misallocation means, simply, that the total income gained by the beneficiaries of the policy is less than the total income lost by others.

The major concern of the present paper is not the traditional questions about the effects of legal minimum wage rates but, rather, an attempt to understand why we have them. In other words, why have many federal congresses and many state legislatures repeatedly voted for minimum wage legislation? Ignorance on the part of the legislators is one possible answer. However, we do not find ignorance to be a compelling explanation. After all, the first state minimum wage law was passed (by Massachusetts) in 1912 and the first federal minimum wage legislation was implemented in 1938. There would thus seem to have been ample time for dispelling ignorance as to the effects of legal minimum wages. In addition, recent debates in the U.S. Congress on pending minimum wage legislation show that legislators are aware of such effects of the policy as increased inflation and increased unemployment, especially of young workers, and more especially of minority teenagers. We think that an answer to the question why we have legal minimum wages can be found by identifying those groups that gain from the policy

NOTE: The authors wish to thank Ted James for his research assistance and Dan Dolk for computer programming.

and are also organized to influence legislators to vote for it. In the following pages we attempt such an identification.

We begin with an analysis of the direct and indirect effects of a legal minimum wage on nominal wage rates and product prices. We then examine the effects of the policy on equilibrium real wages and the real rate of return to capital. Next comes a brief introduction to the political economics of minimum wage legislation. We then conclude with a presentation of our empirical findings. The econometric testing of our hypothesis is based on cross-section data from 1970 that relates state legal minimum wage rates and coverage to a set of hypothesized determinants.

Direct Effects of a Minimum Wage

Consider the market for low-skilled (or low-wage) labor and assume that the supply curve for low-skilled labor is upward-sloping and the demand curve for low-skilled labor is downward-sloping. By the supply curve being upward-sloping we mean simply that the higher the money wage rate, the larger will be the quantity supplied, given that other variables that affect supply do not change. By the demand curve being downward-sloping we mean that the lower the money wage, the larger the quantity demanded, given that other variables that affect demand do not change. Supply and demand curves that have these slopes are drawn in figure 1. The wage rate that would equate the quantity of low-skilled labor demanded with the quantity supplied is labeled w_c in figure 1. The market-clearing number of hours of employment is labeled l_c. Now suppose that a legal minimum wage is implemented. Let the minimum wage be w_m in figure 1. At the wage rate w_m, with demand and supply curves D and S, the number of hours of employment demanded is l_d and the number of hours supplied is l_s. Thus there is an unemployment gap of $(l_s - l_d)$; in addition, there is a disemployment $(l_c - l_d)$. Thus, given the supply and demand curves S and D, imposition of the minimum wage would increase the money wage rate of low-skilled workers who kept their jobs; however, the decrease in hours of employment from l_c to l_d would be manifested in loss of employment for some low-skilled workers and reduced hours for others.

It is important to bear in mind that an economy is an interdependent system. Therefore, the preceding analysis of the single labor market directly affected by the minimum wage is only the beginning of an analysis of the effects of implementing a legal minimum wage. Consider another labor market, for example, the market in medium-skilled labor. There will be some jobs at some firms that could be filled by either low-skilled or medium-skilled workers. The medium-skilled workers would

404

FIGURE 1
PARTIAL EQUILIBRIUM EFFECTS OF A MINIMUM WAGE

Money Wage Rate of Low-Skilled Workers

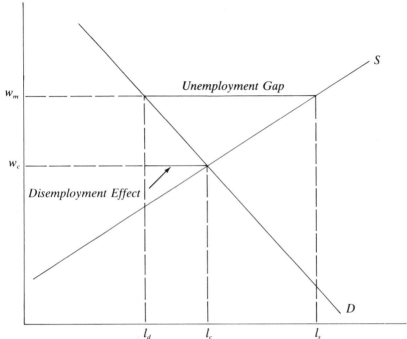

Hours of Employment of Low-Skilled Workers

be more productive in these jobs than the low-skilled workers, but an employer would have to pay a higher wage rate to medium-skilled workers than to low-skilled workers. Therefore, in deciding whether to fill a job vacancy with a medium-skilled or a low-skilled worker, an employer would need to compare the effect on the firm's revenue of the greater productivity of the medium-skilled worker with the effect on the firm's cost of the higher wage rate such a worker would have to be paid. So long as the wage rate of medium-skilled workers exceeded the wage rate of low-skilled workers, some of these jobs would be filled by workers from one category and some would be filled by workers from the other category. Only when the wage differential was of such a magnitude that no employer wanted to replace one type of worker with the other could the labor markets for low- and medium-skilled workers be in equilibrium.

Let us return now to the effects of a minimum wage on both the

405

FIGURE 2
Minimum Wage Effects on the Demand for Higher-Wage Labor

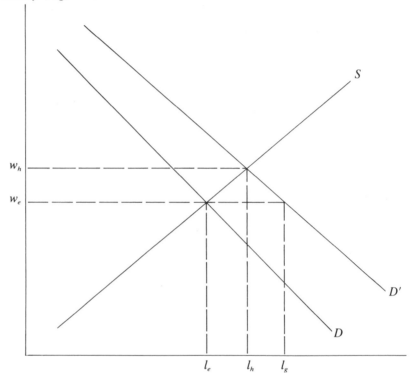

Money Wage Rate of Medium-Skilled Workers

Hours of Employment of Medium-Skilled Workers

low-skilled labor market and the medium-skilled labor market. Consider figures 1 and 2. Before the legal minimum wage is introduced, the market-clearing wage rate for low-skilled labor is w_c and the market-clearing wage rate for medium-skilled labor is w_e. Now suppose that the minimum wage w_m is imposed. As we saw before, given demand and supply curves D and S in figure 1, the minimum wage w_m causes a decrease in hours of employment for low-skilled workers from l_c to l_d. But the story does not end here, because some of these hours of employment lost by low-skilled workers will be gained by medium-skilled workers. At the now higher wage of low-skilled workers, w_m, some employers will reach a different conclusion than before, with respect to some jobs, in comparing wage rates and productivity differences for the

406

two types of workers. That is, some jobs that would have been made available to low-skilled workers at the wage rate w_c will now be offered to medium-skilled workers. This would occur at all relevant wage rates for medium-skilled labor and is introduced in figure 2 by the shift in the demand curve from D to D'. After the minimum wage is imposed, demand exceeds supply at the wage rate w_e in the medium-skilled labor market by the amount $l_g - l_e$. This puts upward pressure on the wage rate in this market; it would only clear with demand and supply curves D' and S if the wage rate rose to w_h. But at the higher wage rate w_h in the medium-skilled labor market the same logic that led us to conclude that the demand curve for medium-skilled labor will shift when the wage rate for low-skilled labor increases from w_c to w_m now leads us to conclude that the increase in the medium-skilled wage rate from w_e to w_h will feed back on the low-skilled labor market and cause the demand curve there to shift.

Let us now consider figure 3 and ignore the supply curve S'. Figure 3 presents the same supply and demand curves S and D, the wage rates w_c and w_m, and the hours of employment l_c that are contained in figure 1, and also the shifted demand curve D'. An outward shift of the demand curve in figure 3 might be caused, among other things, by the feedback effects of the increased wage in the medium-skilled labor market on demand for low-skilled labor, as we have discussed. Let us once again recall that an economy is an interdependent system. We have by now already discussed the direct effects of the legal minimum wage on the low-skilled labor market, the effects of the minimum wage on the medium-skilled labor market from direct substitutions by employers of medium-skilled for low-skilled workers, and the feedback effects of minimum-wage-induced wage increases in the medium-skilled labor market on the demand for low-skilled labor. But we are still only at the beginning of a complete analysis of the effects of implementing a minimum wage. Introduction of the minimum wage will affect other factor markets in addition to the medium-skilled labor market. For example, a higher wage for unskilled labor will accelerate the rate at which capital is substituted for low-skilled labor through mechanization and automation. This accelerated substitution process involves an increase in demand for capital which is analogous to the increase in demand for medium-skilled labor that we explained above. It will increase the price of capital which will then have a feedback effect on the demand for low-skilled labor.

We could continue this discussion of the effects in other factor markets of imposition of the minimum wage brought about through direct substitution of one factor for another in production processes. Instead, let us now turn our attention to product market effects of a

FIGURE 3
Minimum Wage Feedback Effects from Other Markets

Money Wage Rate of Low-Skilled Workers

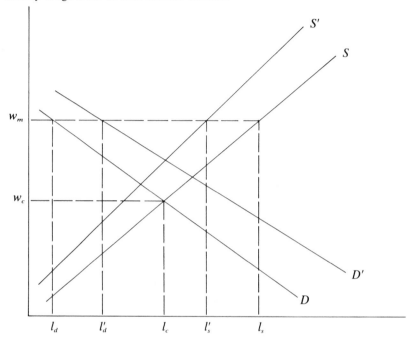

Hours of Employment of Low-Skilled Workers

minimum wage. This part of our discussion will focus on minimum wage effects on product prices and the feedback effects of higher product prices on factor markets. The factor price increases caused by imposition of the minimum wage are cost increases to the firms that employ the factors. These cost increases will lead to increases in the prices of the products and the product price increases will have feedback effects on the factor markets. The feedback effects on factor markets of the product price increases resulting from the minimum wage are an important component of the adjustment process to which we now turn our attention.

Indirect Effects of a Minimum Wage

Factor supplies generally depend on product prices as well as on factor prices. This is hardly surprising, since any given nominal factor price only has meaning for the command over economic goods that the factor owner obtains from selling the services of the factor when that price is related to the prices of the goods purchased by the factor owner. For example, a $2.50 minimum wage has far different implications for a minimum wage worker at 1979 consumer goods prices than it would at the level of those prices that prevailed in 1967. The product price increases that are part of the inflationary process of adjustment to imposition of the minimum wage will affect labor supply in two opposing ways. On the one hand, higher product prices, with any given wage rate, reduce the amounts of consumer goods that any number of hours of employment will provide the income to purchase. This tends to make leisure more attractive and reduces the supply of labor hours at any given wage rate. Such a reduction in labor supply would be represented by a leftward shift of the labor supply curve such as the shift from S to S' in figure 3. On the other hand, higher product prices reduce the real incomes of wage earners. Such a reduction leads to decreases in demand for most goods, including leisure. A reduction in demand for leisure implies an increase in the supply of labor, such as the shift from S' to S in figure 3. Which of these two opposing effects of an increase in product prices on labor supply predominates in any specific case cannot be predicted on the basis of theoretical arguments.

The product price effects of a minimum wage are important for further analysis in that they lead to indirect factor substitutions. To illustrate their interrelationship, let us consider the simple example of two industries, A and B. We assume that industry A uses low-skilled labor but does not use medium-skilled labor, and we assume that industry B uses medium-skilled labor but does not use low-skilled labor. We assume, as before, an initial equilibrium allocation of factors and products with associated equilibrium factor and product prices. If a legal minimum wage is imposed at a level that is greater than the previous equilibrium value of the wage rate for low-skilled labor but less than the previous equilibrium wage rate for medium-skilled labor, and if industry A continues to employ only low-skilled labor and industry B continues to employ only medium-skilled labor, imposition of the minimum wage will not cause a direct substitution of medium-skilled workers for low-skilled workers in either industry.

Imposition of the minimum wage will still affect the demand for medium-skilled workers, however. The minimum wage increases the cost of producing every quantity of output in industry A. Thus industry A will now require a higher price than before in order to cover the costs of producing any given quantity of output. So the supply curve for industry A output is shifted upwards, which increases the market price of the output of industry A. But the higher price for industry A's product will cause buyers to decrease their purchases of industry A's product and increase their purchases of the now relatively cheaper product of industry B, increasing demand for industry B's product. But this increase in demand leads to increases in both price and quantity sold in the market for the product of industry B. The increased price and quantity for industry B's product implies increases in the derived demands for the factors of production used in industry B. One of these factors is medium-skilled labor. Thus, imposition of a minimum wage would cause an increase in demand for medium-skilled labor, like that portrayed in figure 2, even if employers did not directly substitute medium-skilled workers for low-skilled workers, so long as an increase in the price of industry A's product caused an increase in demand for industry B's product.

Equilibrium Effects of a Minimum Wage

The preceding discussion based on supply and demand curves illustrates the complicated set of adjustments in interrelated markets that is initiated by introduction of a wage floor. This approach cannot be used to answer all of the questions of interest concerning the equilibrium effects of a legal minimum wage, however. In order to understand this point, one only has to attempt to answer the following questions using the supply and demand curve approach:

- Where does the shifting of all of these supply and demand curves end?
- Is the *real* wage of low-skilled workers higher or lower in equilibrium?
- Are the other *real* factor prices higher or lower in equilibrium?
- Is there an equilibrium disemployment effect for low-skilled workers?

The last question is of considerable interest in analyzing the effects of a wage floor. In addition, it makes abundantly clear the need to use a general equilibrium model to begin to understand the effects of a legal minimum wage. To illustrate this point, suppose that we had ended the preceding discussion after formulating and discussing only figure 1. This would constitute a partial equilibrium model of the effects of a wage floor. We would then be tempted to conclude that the equilibrium disemployment effect of a wage floor was $(l_c - l_d)$ in figure 1. But, as we saw above, since an economy consists of many interrelated markets, the general adjustment process will cause the supply and demand curves in figure 1 to shift. When they finally stop shifting, we will have attained an equilibrium. But is there a disemployment effect? One cannot answer this question with the preceding qualitative supply and demand curve approach. This point is illustrated in figure 4. S and D are the supply

FIGURE 4
ZERO EQUILIBRIUM DISEMPLOYMENT EFFECTS OF A MINIMUM WAGE

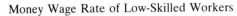

Money Wage Rate of Low-Skilled Workers

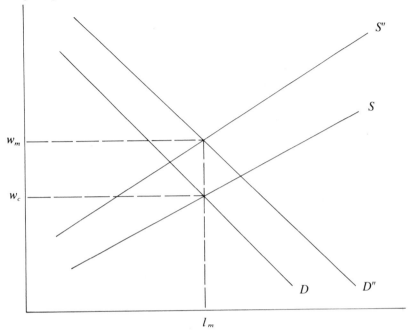

l_m

Hours of Employment of Low-Skilled Workers

and demand curves for low-skilled labor before introduction of the minimum wage, w_m. These are the same S and D curves that appear in figure 1. S'' and D'' are possible supply and demand curves after imposition of the wage floor and the establishment of a new equilibrium in all markets. In this case, the new equilibrium quantity of employment of low-skilled labor, l_m, also happens to be that quantity where S and D intersect. In other words, in this case l_m in figure 4 and l_c in figure 1 are the same quantity and the disemployment effect is zero. A zero equilibrium disemployment effect of a wage floor cannot be ruled out by the qualitative supply and demand curve approach. The partial equilibrium model consisting solely of figure 1 only seems to provide an answer to the question of the disemployment effect of a wage floor by begging the question.

In order to gain more insight into the effects of a legal minimum wage, we have constructed general equilibrium models that include si-

411

multaneous determinations of equilibria in factor and product markets.[1] We identify possible equilibria in these models, both in the absence and in the presence of a wage floor. We then compare the equilibria to get predictions of the effects on all markets of an effective legal minimum wage. One useful model includes two production sectors, a household sector and a monetary sector. One of the production sectors is unionized and uses high-skilled labor and capital as inputs in the production process. The other production sector is nonunionized and uses high-skilled labor, low-skilled labor, and capital as inputs. In addition, the union sector is assumed to be more high-skilled labor (relative to capital) intensive than is the nonunion sector. The household sector is included simply by assuming that the products of the two production sectors are "gross substitutes," which means that an increase in the relative price of the product of one sector causes an increase in demand for the product of the other sector. The monetary sector is included by alternative assumptions about the disemployment effect of a given increase in the minimum wage.

This general equilibrium model illustrates how the economic self-interest of high-skilled workers and capitalists can be involved in a minimum wage policy. In addition, the two cases that we examine highlight some trade-offs that are inherent in the policy. One trade-off is that between a possible increase in the real wage rate of low-skilled workers and the equilibrium level of employment of such workers. Given some familiar simplifying assumptions, we find that an increase in the equilibrium real wage rate of low-skilled workers can only be obtained at the cost of a decrease in their employment.

This minimum wage policy trade-off leads us to examine two cases. The first case is one where introduction of the legal minimum wage is accompanied by an accommodating monetary policy that stabilizes employment of low-skilled workers. The second case is one where introduction of the wage floor does cause disemployment of low-skilled labor but the accompanying monetary policy stabilizes real output. We will next discuss the implications of the model in each of these cases.

First consider the case where there is a zero disemployment effect in the new general equilibrium that is attained after the legal minimum wage is introduced. The model tells us that in this case the equilibrium *real* wage rate of low-skilled (minimum wage) workers cannot be increased by the wage floor although their nominal wage rate will, of course, be increased. What are the other possible equilibrium effects

---

[1] James C. Cox and Ronald L. Oaxaca, "The Political Economy of Minimum Wage Legislation," unpublished paper, University of Arizona, 1980.

of the minimum wage in this case? One possibility is that the equilibrium factor allocation does not change and equiproportional inflation is the only effect. This would imply that all real factor prices would be invariant. Alternatively, if the equilibrium factor allocation is changed by the wage floor, then the real wage rates of unionized and nonunionized high-skilled workers are increased and the real rental rate of capital is decreased. This means that union labor gains, and owners of capital lose, from the minimum wage in both absolute and relative terms. The real wage rate of unionized high-skilled labor increases, as do its wages relative to the rental rate of capital and its factor share in the value of output. In the same vein, capitalists lose in both absolute and relative terms in the present case of a zero disemployment effect for minimum wage workers.

Next, consider the case where the real wage of low-skilled workers is increased and there is a decrease in their employment following introduction of a legal minimum wage. If we assume that the accompanying monetary policy keeps real output from falling, then the equilibrium effects of the minimum wage are as follows. The real rental rate of capital falls and the wage rate of unionized high-skilled labor increases relative to the rental rate of capital and to the price of the product of the union sector. Therefore, owners of capital lose in both absolute and relative terms. Union labor gains in various ways from the minimum wage. There is an increase in employment of union labor, which may be perceived as a benefit by unions. In addition, the union wage rate relative to the price of capital increases, as does the factor share of union labor in the value of the product of the union sector. The real wage rate of union labor does not necessarily increase in this case, however, because it does not necessarily increase relative to the price of the product of the nonunion sector.

Elements of the Political Economics of Minimum Wage Legislation

Up to now we have focused on the effects of a legal minimum wage on equilibrium allocations of factors and equilibrium real factor prices. The purpose of this discussion was to illustrate the nature of the complex adjustment process that is initiated by imposition of a wage floor and to identify some classes of economic agents whose economic self-interest is affected by it. We have explained how high-wage workers can gain from the indirect effects of imposition of a minimum wage and how capitalists can lose from those effects. Thus we have explained why high-wage workers might favor minimum wage legislation and why owners of capital might oppose it. There is an important difference between favoring such legislation and effectively promoting it, and there is an analogous distinction between being opposed to the legislation and effectively resisting it, however. We will now point out the implications of this distinction.

Obviously, if there is to be a legal minimum wage, it must be contained in legislation passed by a legislature. Therefore, if higher-skilled workers are to effectively promote the legislation, they must find a way to influence legislators to vote for it. Similarly, owners of capital must be able to promote votes against the legislation. Effectiveness of an interest group in influencing legislative voting often depends on that interest group being organized. The costs of organization are usually substantial, sometimes so high that it is not in the interest of an affected group to bear the organizational costs in order to more effectively promote their desired legislation. If an interest group is already organized to promote its interests in related areas, however, then the incremental costs of promoting the legislation will be relatively low. Thus we would predict that organized labor unions of higher-skilled workers would promote minimum wage legislation, but that nonunionized higher-skilled workers might not find it in their interest to bear organizational costs just to promote legislation of this type. Analogously, capitalists may not find it in their interest to organize just to promote votes against minimum wage legislation, but if they are already organized then they might well find it in their interest to bear the incremental costs of campaigns against minimum wage legislation.

This discussion leads us to hypothesize that labor unions will promote minimum wage legislation and that organizations of capitalists will campaign against such legislation. Thus we would expect there to be a higher probability of observing a legal minimum wage where unions are stronger and capitalists' organizations are weaker. Analogously, given the existence of a legal minimum wage, we would expect the level of the minimum to be higher, and its coverage of the labor force broader, where unions are stronger and capitalists' organizations are weaker.

The source of unionized labor's interest in promoting legal minimum wages that we have identified is the implied increase in the derived demand for union labor which follows from the increased demand for the products of unionized firms. This same reasoning would lead to the prediction that unions would also support restrictive tariffs and other barriers to the importation of goods produced domestically by unionized firms. It is our impression that unions generally do support restrictive trade legislation which applies to manufactured goods. However, we have not attempted to provide empirical support for this view.

Finally, we may note that the interests of corporation executives are not necessarily identical to the interests of owners of capital. This

414

possible divergence of interests has been studied at length in various contexts and we do not claim to have any important new insights on the question. However, one possible source of divergence may be important for understanding an additional source of support for minimum wage legislation. To the extent that corporation executives possess some human capital that is specific to particular firms or industries, their interests may diverge from the interests of capitalists. For example, minimum wage legislation that increases the labor costs of nonunionized southern textile firms would increase the demand for the products of unionized textile firms in New England. This will in turn increase the derived demand for the factors of production employed by the unionized firms, including corporation executives that have human capital which is specific to those firms. Therefore, we would not be surprised to find New England textile executives supporting federal minimum wage legislation that covered southern textile workers. More important, this example suggests a more general problem of identifying organizations that represent the interests of capitalists. Does, say, the National Association of Manufacturers mainly represent the interests of capitalists or the interests of corporation executives? To what extent are the interests of these two groups divergent? What about the U.S. Chamber of Commerce? Does it mainly represent the interests of capitalist-entrepreneurs or corporation executives?

Characteristics of States with and without Minimum Wage Laws

In 1970 there were twelve states that did not have minimum wage laws. Among the remaining thirty-eight states there was considerable variation in coverage provisions and to a lesser extent in the level of the wage itself.[2] Twelve states explicitly had coverage exclusions designed to minimize overlap between federal and state coverage. There were thirty-five states where the minimum wage was less than or equal to the federal minimum of $1.60 per hour. For these states any overlap between federal and state coverage would render the state law inoperative insofar as workers covered under both federal and state statutes are concerned. This is because the Fair Labor Standards Act (FLSA) takes precedence over state law in such instances. Only for the three remaining states that had minimum wages above the federal level could the state law have any effect on workers covered under both federal and state law.

The only consistent data available that pertain to state minimum

---

[2] Ten states in 1970 had differential minimum wage rates in effect. For purposes of the present study we assigned to these states their highest respective minimum wage rates in effect at the time.

wage coverage concern the number of workers covered under state law only. With the possible exception of the three states with legislated minima exceeding the federal minimum in 1970, the number of workers covered only under state law is a reasonable measure of effective state discretion in desired coverage. Accordingly, our state coverage rate variable is defined as the number of workers covered only by state law as a proportion of the total number of workers not covered by the minimum wage provisions of the FLSA.

In 1970, thirty-six states had either no minimum wage or minimum wages below the federal level, and eleven states had minimum wages equal to the federal level. Table 1 presents the distribution of state minimum wages as of 1970. The three states with minimum wages above the federal level were California ($1.65 per hour), New York ($1.85 per hour), and Alaska ($2.10 per hour). Arizona and Kentucky technically had state minimum wages set by wage orders in the amounts of $0.60 per hour and $0.75 per hour, respectively, in 1970. However, Arizona had not changed its wage order since 1954, and Kentucky had not changed its wage order since 1961.

In the foregoing discussion we concluded that two important determinants of the level of the minimum wage and its coverage are prob-

TABLE 1

DISTRIBUTION OF STATE MINIMUM WAGES, 1970

Minimum Wage (dollars per hour)	Percentage of States
0	24
0.60	2
0.75	2
1.00	8
1.10	2
1.25	18
1.30	4
1.45	10
1.50	2
1.60 (federal minimum)	22
1.65	2
1.85	2
2.10	2

NOTE: Those states with differential minimum wages were assigned the highest minimum wage applied under state law.
SOURCE: U.S. Department of Labor, Employment Standards Administration, *Wages and Hours of Work of Nonsupervisory Employees in All Private Nonfarm Industries by Coverage Status under the Fair Labor Standards Act* (Washington, D.C., 1972), table 5.

ably (1) the influence of organized labor and (2) the influence of that segment of the business community which stands to absorb the windfall profit loss from the imposition of or an increase in state minimum wages. Our empirical proxy for the potential influence of organized labor in a state is the proportion of total employment comprising union members and members of employee associations. Obtaining a good proxy for the influence of that segment of the business community that has a strong vested interest in the level and extent of minimum wages is more difficult because of the possible divergence of interests of owners of capital and some corporation executives that was discussed in the preceding section. For example, unionized employers would experience little or no direct effect of legislated minimum wages that are well below the union scale. In fact, union employers can benefit from legislated minimum wages to the extent that the wages reduce the cost advantage of nonunion direct competitors, and to the extent that the products of the union firms are substituted by consumers for nonunion products in general whose prices have risen. Thus a variable such as membership in state chambers of commerce could be an ambiguous measure of the interests of the business community on the subject of minimum wages. In any event such membership data are not easy to come by. The proxy we have selected is proprietor income as a proportion of total personal income. This variable measures the importance of proprietorship in a state—a business constituency that would largely feel adversely affected by minimum wage laws.

In table 2 we present the mean values of selected variables for minimum wage states and non–minimum wage states. The average state minimum wage coverage among the minimum wage states was just under half of the employment not covered by the FLSA. A number of observations can be made in distinguishing minimum wage states from non–minimum wage states. Minimum wage states are unionized more heavily than non–minimum wage states—an average of 26.1 percent of the total employment compared with 20.7 percent for non–minimum wage states. Proprietary income constitutes a smaller average share of personal income in minimum wage states (12.4 percent) than in non–minimum wage states (14.5 percent). The average proportion of workers covered by the minimum wage provisions of the FLSA was equal to 60 percent for both minimum wage and non–minimum wage states. Interestingly, the extent of poverty was noticeably smaller in minimum wage states. The average proportion of families below the 1969 poverty level was 10.7 percent for minimum wage states and 15.7 percent for non–minimum wage states. (We will return to a discussion of this association later.) Finally, it is not surprising that proportionately fewer minimum wage states are right-to-work states as compared with

417

TABLE 2

MEAN VALUES OF SELECTED VARIABLES, 1970

Variable	All States	Minimum Wage States	Non–Minimum Wage States
MW	1.045	1.375	0
CRATIO	0.362	0.476	0
URATIO	0.248	0.261	0.207
PR	0.129	0.124	0.145
FCOV	0.600	0.600	0.600
FP	0.119	0.107	0.157
RTW	0.380	0.289	0.667

NOTES: MW is the state hourly minimum wage.

CRATIO is the number of workers covered by state minimum wage laws only, as a proportion of total employment.

URATIO is the number of union members plus members of employee associations as a proportion of total employment.

PR is total proprietor income as a proportion of total personal income

FCOV is the number of workers covered under the minimum wage provisions of the Fair Labor Standards Act as a proportion of total employment.

FP is the proportion of families whose incomes are below the 1969 official poverty level.

RTW is a dummy variable that takes on the value of 1 if the state has a right-to-work law, otherwise it takes on the value of 0.

SOURCES: U.S. Department of Labor, Employment Standards Administration, *Wages and Hours of Work of Nonsupervisory Employees in All Private Nonfarm Industries by Coverage Status under the Fair Labor Standards Act* (Washington, D.C., 1972).

U.S. Department of Labor, Bureau of Labor Statistics, *Directory of National Unions and Employee Associations*, Bulletin 1750 (Washington, D.C., 1971).

U.S. Department of Commerce, Bureau of the Census, *1970 Census of Population*, vol. 1: *Characteristics of the Population* (Washington, D.C., 1973).

U.S. Department of Commerce, Bureau of Economic Analysis, *Local Area Personal Income 1970–1975* (Washington, D.C., 1977).

U.S. Department of Labor, Bureau of Labor Statistics, *Employment and Earnings, States and Areas 1939–1975*, Bulletin 1370–12 (Washington, D.C., 1977).

U.S. Department of Labor, Employment Standards Administration, *Minimum Wage and Maximum Hours Standards under the Fair Labor Standards Act* (Washington, D.C., 1972).

non–minimum wage states. In 1970 there were nineteen right-to-work states. Eleven of these were minimum wage states and constituted just under 30 percent of the total number of minimum wage states. Eight of the twelve or two-thirds of the non–minimum wage states were right-to-work states.

Table 3 presents the actual values of selected variables of interest for the twelve states without minimum wages in 1970. As is evident from the table, Illinois is not a typical non–minimum wage state. It is highly unionized, proprietory income is a relatively small proportion of state personal income, a very small proportion of families were below the

TABLE 3

CHARACTERISTICS OF STATES WITHOUT MINIMUM WAGE LAWS, 1970

State	URATIO	PR	FCOV	FP	RTW
Alabama	0.191	0.111	0.608	0.269	1
Florida	0.143	0.109	0.613	0.127	1
Illinois	0.365	0.086	0.652	0.077	0
Iowa	0.198	0.258	0.580	0.089	1
Kansas	0.168	0.210	0.568	0.097	1
Louisiana	0.175	0.114	0.598	0.215	0
Mississippi	0.120	0.185	0.578	0.289	1
Missouri	0.353	0.116	0.628	0.115	0
Montana	0.282	0.243	0.500	0.104	0
South Carolina	0.103	0.099	0.641	0.190	1
Tennessee	0.214	0.113	0.639	0.182	1
Virginia	0.162	0.084	0.609	0.123	1

NOTE: Variable definitions are given in notes to table 2.
SOURCE: See table 2.

poverty line, and it is not a right-to-work state. The probability that a state with Illinois's characteristics would have a minimum wage law is very high. As it turns out Illinois had a minimum wage law prior to 1970, but it had become officially inoperative. In 1972 a new minimum wage law took effect in Illinois. The minimum wage was set at $1.40 per hour, and workers covered under the FLSA were excluded. This is in contrast with Arizona and Kentucky, which had minimum wage laws still on the books even though their minimums were probably below the free market clearing wage of the lowest class of unskilled labor. Thus even though Arizona's and Kentucky's laws probably had no economic significance by 1970, the political decision to officially render them null and void had not been taken. Since our purpose is to examine the political determinants of minimum wage laws and not estimate their economic impacts, we choose not to relegate Arizona and Kentucky to the list of states without minimum wage laws.

Empirical Results

The preceding theoretical discussion, buttressed by some general observations on the characteristics of minimum wage and non–minimum wage states, suggests several variables of primary interest for empirical work on the determinants of minimum wage legislation. The primary endogenous variables that characterize state minimum wage legislation are the nominal minimum wage and the extent of minimum wage cov-

419

erage. For reasons given earlier, the latter is measured as the proportion of workers not covered by the minimum wage provisions of the FLSA who are covered by state law (*CRATIO*). The primary determinants of state minimum wage legislation are the importance of organized labor in the state (*URATIO*) and the proportion of personal income in a state that accrues to proprietors (*PR*). These variables are expected to have positive and negative effects, respectively, on state minimum wages and coverage.

It is recognized that the effectiveness of state minimum wage laws depends on both the wage rate and the extent of coverage. It may be that legislators and their constituents have separable preferences over the level of the nominal minimum wage and the extent of coverage of the minimum wage. Alternatively, they may only be concerned with some measure of the effectiveness of the legislation that can be represented by a simple index of the wage rate and the extent of coverage. Because we cannot decide *a priori* whether these preferences are separable, we include both possibilities in the empirical work by using as dependent variables the (nominal) minimum wage, the coverage rate (*CRATIO*), and an index defined as the product of the minimum wage and the coverage rate.

Our study is confined to the determinants of state minimum wage laws in 1970. As we have already observed, at this time there were twelve states without minimum wage laws. This presents some complications for consistent estimation of the parameters of a statistical model of the minimum-wage–determining process. For those states without minimum wage laws, the state minimum wage variables (nominal wage, coverage, and nominal wage times coverage) take on the value zero. It can be shown that with a concentration of values at the lower limit (zero) of the dependent variables, the ordinary least squares estimator is inconsistent.[3] The problem of inconsistency in the ordinary least squares estimator cannot be avoided by restricting the sample to those observations with nonzero dependent variables. In this case the omission of non–minimum wage states yields a censored sample.[4] Therefore, in order to obtain consistent estimates of the parameters of the minimum wage and coverage relationships, the Tobit estimator is used.[5]

[3] James Tobin, "Estimation of Relationships for Limited Dependent Variables," *Econometrica* 26 (January 1958): 24–36.

[4] James J. Heckman, "The Common Structure of Statistical Models of Truncation, Sample Selection and Limited Dependent Variables and a Simple Estimator for Such Models," *Annals of Economic and Social Measurement* 5 (October 1976): 475–92.

[5] The algorithm we use to obtain the Tobit estimator may be found in Ray C. Fair, "A Note on the Computation of the Tobit Estimator," *Econometrica* 45 (October 1977): 1723–27.

The best results are obtained with the Tobit model when the constant term is omitted and the basic explanatory variables are specified as regressors in negative exponential form, that is, e^{-x}, where x is the basic variable. Our empirical findings are reported in table 4 for the case where the nominal minimum wage and the coverage rate are the dependent variables. Table 5 presents the results for the case where the dependent variable is the product of the nominal minimum wage and the coverage rate. The empirical findings are consistent with the predictions that labor unions have a positive effect and proprietary business interests have a negative effect on nominal state minimum wages and state minimum wage coverage. The estimated coefficients are jointly significant at the 5 percent level. Of course, our interest is not in these coefficients per se, but rather in the marginal effects of the explanatory variables on the (dependent) policy variables. These marginal effects, evaluated at the mean, are estimated for both a minimum wage state and a randomly selected state. The estimated effects for the latter incorporate the probability that a state selected at random would be a minimum wage state.

It is evident from table 4 that the level of the nominal minimum wage is more responsive to organized labor and proprietary business interests than is the extent of coverage. The implications of these estimates can, perhaps, be most easily appreciated when they are presented in terms of elasticities evaluated at the mean. Thus for a minimum wage state with the mean extent of unionism and proprietary personal income ratio, a 10 percent rise in the extent of unionism would be associated with an average increase of 3.2 percent in the minimum wage and an increase in the extent of coverage of nearly 2 percent. On the other hand, a 10 percent rise in the proportion of state personal income accruing to proprietors is associated on average with a 2.3 percent reduction in the minimum wage and a 1.5 percent reduction in coverage. To take an example, consider a state with a minimum wage of $1.15 per hour, a coverage rate of 43 percent of the employment not covered by the FLSA, 26 percent of its employment in unions or employee associations, and 12 percent of its personal income accruing to proprietors.[6] A state with a 20 percent higher extent of unionism (31.2 percent) and the same proprietor income ratio would have on average a state minimum wage of $1.22 per hour and a state coverage rate of about 44.6 percent. Or let us consider a state with a 20 percent higher proprietor

---

[6] Because of the statistical estimation technique employed, the estimated mean values of the minimum wage and the coverage rate conditional on the actual mean values of the unionism and proprietary income variables are not in general the same as the actual sample mean values of the minimum wage and the coverage rate. See Cox and Oaxaca, "Political Economy."

TABLE 4

Tobit Regression Results for State Minimum Wages and Coverage, 1970

Regressors	Estimated Coefficients	Estimated Marginal Effects (at the mean)		Estimated Elasticities (at the mean)	
		All states	Minimum wage states	All states	Minimum wage states
State Minimum Wages					
$e^{-URATIO}$	−2.541	1.775	1.407	0.445	0.323
	(−2.33)				
e^{-PR}	3.341	−2.630	−2.122	−0.343	−0.231
	(3.45)				
N	50				
$\hat{\sigma}$	0.76				
ln L	−56.58				
−2 ln λ	37.18				
$\chi_2^{2,\ 0.95}$	5.99				
State Minimum Wage Coverage					
$e^{-URATIO}$	−0.662	0.428	0.320	0.305	0.197
	(−1.38)				
e^{-PR}	0.950	−0.693	−0.526	−0.257	−0.153
	(2.23)				
N	50				
$\hat{\sigma}$	0.33				
ln L	−24.23				
−2 ln λ	25.86				
$\chi_2^{2,\ 0.95}$	5.99				

NOTES: Ratio of estimated coefficients to estimated standard errors are given in parentheses.

URATIO is the number of union members and members of employee associations as a proportion of total employment.

PR is the total proprietor income as a proportion of total personal income.

$\hat{\sigma}$ is the estimated standard deviation of the disturbance term.

L is the value of the likelihood function.

λ is the likelihood ratio under the null hypothesis that all of the coefficients are jointly zero.

$\chi_2^{2,\ 0.95}$ is the critical value of the chi square variate at the 95% confidence level with two degrees of freedom.

income ratio (14.4 percent) but the same extent of unionization (26 percent); then this state's expected minimum wage would be about $1.10 per hour and its coverage rate would be 41.6 percent of the employment not covered under the FLSA.

The effective minimum wage index results reported in table 5 are

TABLE 5

Tobit Regression Results for the Index of Effective State
Minimum Wages, 1970

Regressors	Estimated Coefficients	Estimated Marginal Effects (at the mean)		Estimated Elasticities (at the mean)	
		All states	Minimum wage states	All states	Minimum wage states
$e^{-URATIO}$	−1.476	0.947	0.706	0.462	0.302
	(−2.11)				
e^{-PR}	1.816	−1.313	−0.996	−0.333	−0.202
	(2.93)				
N	50				
$\hat{\sigma}$	0.48				
$\ln L$	−37.83				
$-2 \ln \lambda$	26.41				
$\chi_2^{2, \, 0.95}$	5.99				

NOTES: Ratio of estimated coefficients to estimated standard errors are given in parentheses. The index of effective state minimum wages is the product of the state minimum wage times the state minimum wage coverage rate (*CRATIO*). Variable definitions are given in notes to table 4.

qualitatively the same as those corresponding to the nominal minimum wage and coverage reported separately in table 4. In fact, the estimated effective minimum index elasticities are very close in magnitude to those estimated for the nominal minimum wage. Of course the estimated wage rate and coverage elasticities do not sum to those elasticities estimated for the index since the estimating equation for the index is not obtained as the product of the separate equations corresponding to the minimum wage and the coverage rate.

In preliminary experimentation with the data, we tried using as additional explanatory variables the federal coverage rate and the proportion of families with incomes below the official poverty levels in 1969. The coverage rate under the FLSA was never a significant factor in determining the level of state minimum wages and coverage under state laws. A hint that this might well be the case is found in table 2, where the average extent of federal coverage is identical for minimum and non–minimum wage states. One could argue that the federal coverage rate might have been expected to have a positive effect at least on coverage under state law. This is because the marginal costs in economic and political terms would be rather modest, but the political advantages to state legislators from the gesture of more coverage of a shrinking noncovered sector could be attractive.

The extent of poverty was found to be negatively associated with the level of the minimum wage and the extent of state coverage. Its intercorrelation with the extent of unionism in a state always rendered the latter insignificant, however. It may be that the extent of poverty actually affects only the probability that a state will have a minimum wage law rather than the actual level of the minimum wage and extent of coverage conditional upon having the law. This possibility will be explored in further research. For the present, we speculate that in states where poverty is relatively high, legislators are less inclined to support a minimum wage law or perhaps are inclined to support only a modest effort. Legislators may genuinely fear that the minimum wage will have deleterious effects on the poor. Or perhaps they would rather not appear to support a law which essentially prohibits the employment of relatively unproductive workers in a state with large numbers of such workers.

One might argue that the causation runs in both directions because the level and extent of state minimum wage coverage can influence the poverty rate. It might appear from the data that high minimum wages and/or extensive coverage may alleviate poverty because of the negative association between the two. Considering the relatively modest coverage under state laws, however, it is difficult to see how the typical state law could have much effect on poverty. A state with 60 percent coverage under the FLSA and 50 percent state coverage of those not covered by the FLSA would cover only 20 percent more of the state's employment. If the poverty rate were 15 percent and uniformly distributed between the FLSA sector and the state-coverage-only sector, the state law would cover additionally only 20 percent of the poor, or 3 percent of total employment.

Concluding Remarks

The present paper is concerned with the political economics of minimum wage legislation. Our primary objective is to explain why minimum wage laws exist rather than to investigate their economic effects. Some examination of these economic effects is necessary, however, in order to identify the economic groups that receive the benefits and those that bear the costs of legal minimum wages. Having identified the gainers and losers, we hypothesize that the subsets of these two groups that are organized to pursue their economic interests will have significant (opposing) effects on the legislation. Our predictions about the determinants of minimum wage levels and coverage are tested on cross-section data for states in 1970.

We first use a simple supply and demand curve approach in discussing the effects of a legal minimum wage on nominal wage rates and product prices. This yields some insight into the complex adjustment

424

process that is initiated by imposition of a minimum wage. In particular, it allows us to identify some possible beneficiaries of a legal minimum wage policy other than the supposed ones, who are low-skilled minimum wage workers. The supply and demand curve analysis suggests that higher-skilled workers can gain from the policy through its effects on the derived demand for their services. This can occur through direct substitution by some employers of higher-skilled workers for low-skilled workers whose wage rates have been increased by the legal minimum wage. The possibilities for this type of labor substitution may be quite limited for many employers, however. Thus we are led to examine the indirect effects of a minimum wage on the derived demands for the services of higher-skilled workers and other factors of production.

The indirect effects of a minimum wage policy are transmitted through product markets. Imposition of a legal minimum wage increases the costs of all employers of minimum wage workers, and it increases the relative costs of those firms that are relatively low skilled labor intensive. This tends to increase the relative price of the product of firms that are low skilled labor intensive and can cause consumers to substitute the products of other firms for the products of those that are low skilled labor intensive. Such product market substitutions can imply an increase in the derived demands for the services of other factors such as higher-skilled labor. It is not possible to analyze such indirect effects of a minimum wage using only supply and demand curves. Thus we were led to construct some general equilibrium models. Although these models are too technical to include in the present paper, we do report their implications.[7]

Within the framework of a multisector general equilibrium model, we find that minimum wage legislation cannot raise the *equilibrium real* wage rate of low-wage workers unless it decreases their employment. Furthermore, we are able to identify other classes of economic agents whose economic self-interest is affected by a wage floor. Specifically, we find that high-wage workers can gain and owners of capital can lose from imposition of a legal minimum wage.

The implications of the general equilibrium model are that organized labor would find it in its interest to promote minimum wage legislation to the extent that it reduces competition from the nonunion sector. Similarly, the largely nonunion, proprietary business community would be opposed to minimum wages. These propositions are examined empirically in the context of a study of the determinants of state minimum wage legislation as of 1970. Through Tobit estimation techniques, it is seen that the extent of unionization in a state has positive effects

---

[7] The general equilibrium models are discussed in Cox and Oaxaca, "Political Economy."

on: (1) the probability that a state will have a minimum wage law; and (2) the nominal wage and coverage rate, conditional on the existence of the law. At the same time, we find that the larger the proportion of state personal income accruing to proprietors, the lower the probability the state will have a minimum wage law and, conditional upon having such a law, the smaller will be the legislated wage and coverage.

An important observation that should be made concerns the appropriate specification of the dependent variable in a study of the determinants of minimum wage legislation. We argue that the appropriate dependent variable should be the *nominal* minimum wage (or minimum wage index). It should be fairly obvious that the *real* minimum wage cannot be controlled by minimum wage legislation. The real minimum wage can only be constructed by deflating the nominal minimum wage set by legislation with a price index (or average wage in manufacturing) that is *not* determined by law.[8] Even with minimum wage indexing, there would be practical limits on the frequency with which adjustments could be made in a nominal minimum wage.[9] In studies of the economic effects of a minimum wage, however, the *real* minimum wage may be the appropriate choice for inclusion as an explanatory variable.

This is not to say that the general level of prices and wages has no role in the minimum-wage–determining process. In a monetary economy the nominal wage must be set with reference to the given level of prices or wages. This argues for treating the price level or average wage as an explanatory variable in the determination of the nominal minimum wage. If one believes that prices do not vary cross-sectionally, then the effect of the price level is subsumed in the estimated parameters of a cross-section relationship. For example, this is the usual assumption underlying the estimation of cross-section labor supply functions. Since general price indexes are not constructed for states, one has to rely on something like average hourly earnings in manufacturing, which do vary across states, in order to include a variable that represents the price level. Our preliminary empirical work using this variable did *not* find it significant.

[8] A case can also be made that the minimum wage coverage rate cannot be set by politicians because resources are mobile between the covered and noncovered sectors. However, depending on the ubiquity of coverage and the specific type of economic activity covered under the law, the incentives to shift production to avoid the law may be weak. Consequently, the divergence between the desired coverage rate and the actual coverage rate may turn out to be quite small.

[9] Increases in nominal minimum wages tend to seem irreversible. Thus, if the real minimum wage were to rise above some legislated target value, then the law might not be amended to lower the nominal minimum wage by the appropriate amount. Of course, in an inflationary environment this issue never has to be confronted. Nevertheless, the possible asymmetry between increases and decreases in the nominal minimum wage merits further research.

Our use of the proprietors' share in income as a measure of the size of the effective opposition to minimum wage legislation is certainly not ideal. The most serious shortcoming of this measure is that it does not refer to the size of an *organization* that pursues its economic interests. This measure of the size of the opposition is therefore not completely comparable with our measure of the size of the interest group promoting the legislation, which is the percentage of the labor force belonging to unions and employee associations. Our first choice for a variable to measure the size of the opposition to minimum wage legislation was membership in state chambers of commerce, but we were not able to obtain these data.

Another possible problem with the proprietors' share in income variable was raised at the conference. This variable can be viewed as $N\bar{y} / Y$, where N is the number of proprietors, $\bar{y}$ is average income per proprietor, and Y is total personal income. Thus our measure does not distinguish between the number of proprietors and their average size. We do not think this is an important problem. One would expect that both the number of proprietors and their average income would be important in determining their ability to affect the political process. Thus a simple index that includes both variables would appear adequate to capture the importance of this interest group.

It was also pointed out at the conference that very small firms are typically excluded from coverage by minimum wage laws, and that proprietorships tend to be small firms. We agree with this observation. However, it does not follow that this will bias the results in favor of our hypothesis. The construction of the state minimum wage coverage variable makes the direction of any potential spurious correlation bias indeterminant. Our dependent variable is incremental state coverage, that is, the proportion of those workers who are not covered under federal law but who are covered under state law. In the absence of our hypothesized effect of proprietary business interests on incremental state coverage, it is not clear that there is any association between incremental state coverage and our proprietary income share variable.

A final point concerns the use of current values of the minimum-wage–determining variables to explain the values of the minimum wage and coverage rate in effect in 1970. An alternative approach, suggested by Ronald Ehrenberg, would be to use the values of the explanatory variables at the time the state's minimum wage laws were amended to incorporate those provisions that were effective in 1970. This approach is consistent with the notion of substantial transaction costs that impede changes in minimum wage laws so that such changes are made only when a threshold is reached in response to changed political/economic conditions. On the other hand, the approach taken in this paper is consistent with the absence of transactions costs in amending the law. Thus at any time, the observed provisions of the minimum wage laws are regarded as the ones appropriate to the current political/economic scene. The alternative approach will be examined in future work.

Minimum Wages and
Personal Income

Carolyn Shaw Bell

Most of the economic literature on the minimum wage has dealt with the impact of such legislation on output and employment. But wages also provide income to the persons earning wages, an aspect which has not received as much analysis. This paper will briefly explore the relationships between wages and income, and between income and employment. It presents special tabulations from the May 1978 Current Population Survey (CPS), showing the implication of these relationships for workers earning wages at or below the legal minimum, and casting considerable doubt on the efficiency of a policy of raising minimum wages in alleviating poverty.

The Living Wage and the Poverty-Level Income

Even before Congress passed the first minimum wage legislation in the thirties, a floor under wage payments had been advocated in the argument that every worker should receive "a living wage." This phrase, like other normative terms associated with the legislation, clearly refers to the concept of wages as a kind of income, not as a payment for service rendered, or for output. Most changes in legislation since the thirties, whether to extend the number of covered workers or to raise the dollar level of the minimum, have been strongly supported by similar references to income. "An honest day's work deserves an honest day's living," or "every workingman should be paid enough to support him and his family," or "a fair wage is a living wage." Confronted with such appeals, few have opposed minimum wages by raising the question of output or amount of service rendered by the worker.

Early work by the Massachusetts Commission on Labor, the National Industrial Conference Board, and a host of charitable organizations ranging from New York settlement houses to the Chicago Associated Charities attempted to express the normative abstraction, "a

NOTE: The research was partially funded by Wellesley College. I am grateful to Eleanor Lonske and Lorraine Keating for technical assistance with the data.

living wage," in concrete terms. Their analysts used actual spending records of workers and their families or else they produced lists of necessary or suitable items by consulting nutritionists, family health personnel, and other experts. In every case, subjective evaluation or "judgment" was required, either to select an item or quantity for the approved list or to approve the records kept by particular households as typical or representative.[1]

Although they may not have been recognized, these judgments were in fact normative; similar value judgments lay at the basis of *all* quantitative substitutes for the phrase, "a living wage," whether measured in dollars or physical terms.

Today, we speak of poverty rather than a living wage, but all contemporary attempts to *define* poverty rely on value judgments, like those used in an earlier period. The Orshansky method, which has been so generally accepted, apparently obviates such normative judgments by using actual expenditure data in an ingenious fashion. But it is worth quoting the originator herself on this point:

> Counting the poor is an exercise in the art of the possible. For deciding who is poor, prayers are more relevant than calculation because poverty, like beauty, lies in the eye of the beholder. Poverty is a value judgement; it is not something one can display or demonstrate, except by inference and suggestion, even with a measure of error. To say one is poor is to use all sorts of value judgements.[2]

Neither "a living wage" nor a poverty level can be expressed without normative judgments.[3] Nevertheless, without much reference to this problem, both concepts have been used to justify, first, a minimum wage and, second, a rise in the minimum wage *amount*.[4]

Before exploring the issues raised by this argument, another issue

[1] See, among other sources, John Ryan, *A Living Wage* (New York: Macmillan, 1920); Jessica Blanche Peixotto, *How Workers Spend a Living Wage* (Berkeley: University of California, 1920); Louis Bosworth, "The Living Wage of Women Workers," *Annals* (May 1911); Robert Coit Chapin, *The Standard of Living among Workingmen's Families in New York City* (New York: Charities Publication Committee, 1909); the successive Research Reports of the National Industrial Conference Board, variously entitled, dealing with family budgets and the cost of living, published from 1911 to the mid-1920s; and the Massachusetts Commission on the Cost of Living, *The Cost of Living* (Boston: Wright J. Potter, 1910).

[2] Mollie Orshansky, "How Poverty Is Measured," *Monthly Labor Review* (February 1969): 37.

[3] See also U.S. Department of Health, Education and Welfare, *The Measure of Poverty* (Washington, D.C., April 1976), especially Technical Papers II, III, X, XII, and XIV.

[4] The use of the poverty income concept replaced that of the living wage, or the wage sufficient to provide health and decency, once the poverty income concept had become sufficiently established and its use was widespread. For example, a 1977 article in the AFL–CIO *American Federationist* was entitled "Minimum Wage—Still Fighting the War on Poverty" and a special report from the AFL–CIO on H.R. 3744 and S. 1871 (undated,

needs clarification. What relationship exists between the wages paid to a worker and the income accruing to that worker or the worker's household? This question arises not only for the minimum wage but for wages at any level, paid for any amount of services or output.

The early writers on standards of living and decent wages recognized that, for the great bulk of the population, income equaled wages.[5] The other sources of earned income—rents, interest, or profits from the use of property—were restricted to a very few owners.[6] Transfer income existed only in the private sector, where charitable donations allowed emergency relief in what was taken to be a purely temporary situation. Charity rarely provided a continuing flow of income payments. Consequently, since for most people wages equaled income, calculating a living wage was equivalent to calculating a decent income. Those who constructed lists of "necessities" knew that different concepts of "decency" existed, but they attempted to designate broad areas of agreement. Thus they created separate "budgets" for workingmen, factory operatives, university faculty, women workers, farmhands, and so on. For each of these distinguishable groups, not only spending patterns but the subjective standard of decency varied, probably in unconscious response to class bias. Once the budgets were established, it was fairly safe to say that if payments to workers conformed with such standards of a living wage, then a decent income for all could pretty well be assured.

In today's economy, those who equate wages and income explicitly in this fashion or implicitly in any way deliberately ignore critical facts about the labor force, the distribution of income, and the way people live.

It is still true that most people receive most of their income from wages. However, property ownership is far more widespread than formerly, and transfer payments constitute a major part of the total income stream. As a result, the identity of wages and income holds true for only a minority.

In 1977, for example, only 6 million individuals and 14 million

but circulated in 1977) stated "What should the minimum wage be? It should be high enough so a worker who works 40 hours a week, year round, will earn enough to keep his or her family out of poverty."

[5] See, in addition to sources quoted in footnote 1 above, Frank Streightoff, *The Distribution of Incomes in the United States* (New York: Columbia University, 1912). For example: "The number of families deriving any considerable income from the direct ownership of tangible wealth is exceedingly small" (p. 145).

[6] Farmers, whose income combined wages and property income, became a minority of the employed population early in the nineteenth century. Farm *workers* were outnumbered by nonfarm workers in 1880. In 1900, of a total civilian labor force of 29 million, 6 million were classified as farmers and farm managers. The number of working farm *owners* would of course be considerably smaller. [U.S. Bureau of the Census, *Historical Statistics of the United States*, Series D 182–232 (Washington, D.C., 1976), p. 139.]

families depended solely on earnings from employment for their total incomes. They represent only about one-quarter of all income recipient units. (Note that for *families,* total dependence on labor income does not necessarily mean that total income consists of *one* worker's wages.)

These people do not lie at the low end of the income distribution: those reporting only earnings as a source of income occur in roughly the same proportion at every level of income. For individuals, both mean and median incomes of those receiving nothing but employment earnings exceed those of all individuals. Families whose income derives solely from earnings show a slightly lower mean and median income than those with other sources of income.[7] As for other sources of income, 54 percent of families and 43 percent of unrelated individuals report property income, excluding interest. Transfer payments, including both private and public and both means-tested and non-means-tested programs, accrue to 46 percent of families and 51 percent of unrelated individuals. These data and others from the Current Population Survey deserve far more detailed analysis than they ever received. It is hoped that data from the new Survey of Income and Program Participation will receive more attention.

That income other than earnings is so broadly distributed in today's economy vitiates the effectiveness of any policy attempting to change *income* levels by changing the level of wages. Just as we cannot equalize the distribution of income by defining maximum allowable earnings, so we cannot alleviate poverty by setting a minimum for wages. People do not live on labor income any more.[8]

In analyzing the relationship between wages and income, changes in the sources of payment available require less attention than changes in the number of earners and the composition of the income unit.

The accepted mode of analyzing income distribution considers figures for *family* income, and the number of earners per family has been

---

[7] U.S. Bureau of the Census, *Monthly Income in 1977 of Families and Persons in the United States,* Current Population Reports, Series P–60, No. 118 (March 1979), pp. 124–27.

[8] This problem has been discussed at length by objectors to the current measure of poverty. In fact, before determining what types of income should be considered in setting a "poverty level" the question of income concepts should be faced squarely. Presumably, if no accepted measure of that income exists (especially for groups of people or over time), other definitions of income must be accepted. To the extent that for some persons in a given group, real (nonmonetary) income substitutes for the money income used by others in the group, it is clearly improper to measure only money income for all persons in the group. Unfortunately, this leads directly to controversies over how to evaluate the nonmonetary income, especially when it is available to some but not all persons, and especially when one confronts the question of distinguishing between income sources available and income received. In this paper I merely draw attention to the reduced role played by money *wages* in any person's total money income, and by extension its reduced role in total real income.

steadily rising. Obviously this prevents a link between wages and income unless data exist to sort workers and their wages into the appropriate family units and family income classes. The steady growth of multi-earner families has never been illuminated with such data.

As early as 1951 the Bureau of the Census observed that:

the number of families having more than one earner has increased substantially since the late thirties. It is very likely because of the greater employment opportunities which exist today, many families who were formerly at low income levels were able to improve greatly their economic status as a result of the employment of other family members in addition to the head. This fact may be an important part of the explanation of the diminution of inequality in the distribution of income in the United States today.[9]

In 1950, 39 percent of all families contained more than one worker; in 1978, 53 percent of all families received earnings from more than one person. Since the percentage of families lacking *any* earned income has also risen, multiearner families should be counted not as a fraction of *all* families, but as a proportion of those with earnings. The increase is more dramatic: 42 percent of all families with earnings in 1950 contained two or more paid workers, but in 1978 almost two-thirds, or 61 percent, of these families received income from two or more wage earners. In fact, most workers live with other workers and share their earnings with other wage earners. It follows that a steady decline has occurred in the number of families dependent for their total income on the wages of one worker.

A separate phenomenon, of equal significance, consists of the steady decrease in the number of *people* in such worker-dependent families. Three different changes explain the decrease in size of family: more older people live in separate households from their children, more young people live separately from their parents, and more adults live apart because of divorce or separation. The impact of these changes has been obscured by the decline in the birth rate since 1950, but average household size declined from 3.3 persons in 1960 to 2.81 in 1978. All these separate households, of course, receive separate incomes, and very few, if any, exist solely on private transfers from a single wage earner. Again, the relationship between wages and income has become less clear.

Using wage policy to influence income levels, therefore, requires confronting extremely difficult situational barriers. These consist of

---

[9] Bureau of the Census, Current Population Reports, Series P–60, No. 9 (Washington, D.C., 1952), p. 6.

widespread availability of nonwage income, a preponderance of multi-earner families in the total population, and even where only one family member is employed, a small number of people supported by the wages of that worker.

Curiously the argument still persists that minimum wages protect families against poverty and that raising the minimum wage level would alleviate poverty. A recent example of this argument states:

> For millions of Americans the rewards from work are too meager to eradicate poverty. Welfare, training, and other remedial government programs do little for the working poor. To date, the minimum wage has been the most direct and comprehensive policy tool designed to help improve their lot . . . A major goal of minimum wage legislation has been to provide a basic level of income or a minimum standard of living for working Americans. For a 25-percent increase in the minimum wage, the income gains appear to be larger than the social costs.[10]

Why Work for the Minimum Wage? What facts exist about how wages earned by real people relate to the income of those people? For some years the Census Bureau has collected data that would allow some answers to be given. Because of a variety of statistical cautions, the Bureau of Labor Statistics has not published any findings dealing with minimum wage workers. Tapes of the data have been available to the public; this article analyzes one survey, that for May 1978. Before turning to the data, however, we should review some basic concepts.

For any individual, the supply of labor is some kind of function of the wages of labor. To define the precise nature of the function requires knowledge of (or assumptions about) the individual worker's marginal rate of substitution between the real income provided by wages (what the wages will buy, including rights to future income) and the real income provided by "leisure" or not working. It will be argued that this ratio itself is a function of the other sources of income available to the worker or potential worker and that it is not possible to define, a priori, the shape of this function. Furthermore, the supply of labor is also some kind of function of nonmonetary returns to labor; workers compare the real income or satisfaction provided by working, per se, aside from the money wages earned, to that provided by whatever activity occurs during "leisure."

For example, if people have property income with which to purchase all the goods and services which will satisfy their self-defined needs or luxuries, they may supply labor in response to nonmonetary returns. In

---

[10] Sar Levitan and Richard S. Belous, *More than Subsistence* (Baltimore: Johns Hopkins University Press, 1979), pp. vii, 109, 161.

such cases viewing labor supply as a function of wages will be misleading. Nor is it sufficient to state that labor supply is a function of real wages, because this allows for no distinction between two different types of real wages provided by employment. One consists of the consumption level assured by the receipt of money wages, which will vary with prices and can be identical across many types of occupations. The other consists of the rewards to the individual (satisfaction, utility) assured by the activity involved in the work, which does not vary with prices and will not necessarily be identical across occupations.

To understand fully the supply of labor, therefore, requires specifying the income available to workers besides wages. The data already quoted about multiearner families and alternative sources of income suggest that the majority of earners do not equate wages received with total income available. Table 1 lists the possible sources of income (or disposable funds) available to people, including all persons legally entitled to seek or hold employment. With these money sources, people can purchase goods and services to obtain a given consumption level or amount of real income.

The table indicates that to determine the impact of any wages on the money or real income of any worker depends on the details of

---

TABLE 1

SOURCES OF FUNDS PROVIDING REAL INCOME (CONSUMPTION)

Earnings from employment
Property earnings
    Business profits
    Rent
    Interest
    Dividends
Transfer income, public
    Social security benefits
    Pensions
    Unemployment benefits
    Means-tested transfers
        Supplemental Security Income
        Aid to Families with Dependent Children
        Other
Transfer income, private
    Gifts and allowances
    Alimony and child support
Other (including criminal and illegal income:
        larceny and theft, blackmail, ransom, etc.)
Dissaving

TABLE 2

Sources of Activity Providing Real Income in Direct Satisfaction

Employment
  Paid
  Nonpaid
    Personal (at-home production)
    Social ("volunteer work")
Human capital investment
  In self
    Formal education
    Other education and training
    Health care, therapy, exercise
  In others
    Maintaining health or providing therapy
    Care of children
    Rehabilitating disabled
Recreation, legal
Illegal recreation and crime
    Stealing, kidnaping, extortion
    Violence against people
    Violence against property

sources and uses of funds by that worker. Such detail, by income recipient, would throw more light on the total distribution of income and incidence of poverty in this country than much of the analysis of existing data can provide. To be completely accurate the table must be enlarged to show nonmonetary receipts as well as money sources. The work done at the Michigan Institute for Social Research provides the best discussion of these issues to date.[11]

To understand fully the supply of labor also requires specifying the activities available to people besides working. Table 2 lists such possible uses of time. Depending on the alternatives available from the list, the individual may choose to spend time employed in a paid job or in some other activity. The real income from such time use has been labeled "direct satisfaction" on the table to distinguish it from the indirect satisfaction obtained by earning money wages with which to purchase consumer goods, whose use will yield satisfaction, on table 1. Nonmonetary

[11] James N. Morgan, Martin David, Wilbur Cohen, and Harvey Brazer, *Income and Welfare in the United States*, (New York: McGraw-Hill, 1962); Nancy Baerwaldt and James Morgan, "Trends in Intra-family Transfers," in Lewis Mandell et al., eds., *Survey of Consumers 1971–1972* (Ann Arbor: Institute for Social Research, 1973); and James N. Morgan, "Intra-family Transfers Revisited," in *Five Thousand American Families*, vol. 6 (Ann Arbor: Institute for Social Research, 1978).

rewards from work, the first item listed, have, of course, a long and respected history in economic theory, but the table poses these as the opportunity cost of some other nonmonetary rewards, from other forms of activity.

The two tables describe two separate determinants of the supply of labor. The quantity of labor offered by any individual varies in response to the desire to earn money wages in order to attain some level of real income or consumption, and also according to the satisfaction or utility yielded by the activity involved. If the individual lacks other sources of funds, the desire to earn money wages becomes paramount: it is a need, since without obtaining real income or consumption the individual cannot survive and cannot perform work. But where other sources of income exist, the opportunity cost of the individual's time determines the quantity of labor offered. The potential sources of real income, the potential activities available, and the utility to be produced by both can be estimated only by the individual concerned.

For any individual, the two tables may contain related items beyond the obvious paid employment (table 2) leading to earnings from employment (table 1). At-home production may yield private transfer income, investment in oneself by health care or exercise may yield higher pension benefits, caring for children may provide both direct satisfaction and also the means-tested public transfer income of the Aid to Families with Dependent Children program. But the tables also suggest a significant relationship between earnings and income for any individual: Do earnings provide income solely to the individual earner? Or to a larger family or household group of which he is a part? Or to both, as is frequently the case with private transfers? Thus, an individual whose *primary* source of funds consists of paid earnings (table 1) may share some of these with others via private transfers to nonpaid workers (table 2). The workers within a household will also share earnings via the public transfer system: for example, financing social security benefits (table 1) for those who care for the disabled (table 2). And any or all of the individuals may also receive income directly (table 1) as the result, say, of business profits or unemployment benefits. Consequently, the link between money earnings and real income for any individual must be extremely fragile.

It is against this conceptual background that the analysis of data for wages and earnings proceeds. It is hypothesized that some workers at or below the minimum wage level have been freed from the need to earn money wages because they have access to other sources of funds: the earnings from their minimum wage job are secondary earnings.

This term has nothing to do with the meaningless term "secondary worker." A worker, as an individual, is a primary unit of labor supply and a primary unit among income recipients. *Secondary earnings,* on the other hand, can be identified by the worker as those earnings from an occupation or activity which *that worker* does not regard as primary. Thus, to a retired worker pension income may be primary because he works at a low-wage part-time job to "keep busy," or pension income may be secondary income to a person totally occupied as a highly paid consultant.

It is hypothesized also that some workers at or below the minimum wage level receive real income in terms of direct satisfaction (table 2) which exceeds that available from other activities or from other uses of the time spent on the job. Of course, no data have been collected with these hypotheses in mind, nor can they be adequately tested by the data presented in the following pages, but they form the framework of analysis.

The poverty question can be posed with the following hypotheses. To the extent that minimum wages represent secondary earnings to the worker, they cannot be responsible for poverty: It is total income, not earnings or any one source of income, that is measured against the poverty-level standard. To the extent that workers choose employment and the wages paid by considering the direct satisfaction involved, they must either receive income above the poverty level or choose to exist below the poverty level. The data can be analyzed for their evidence about these hypotheses.

The Data and Their Preliminary Analysis

The Current Population Survey conducted by the Bureau of the Census each month is designed to provide information about the labor force and its employment and unemployment; at various intervals other information is picked up by a supplementary schedule added to the basic survey.[12] The May supplement collects details of wages, hours worked, and weekly earnings for those employed; and details of employment history, job preference, and job search for those not working. This paper presents special tabulations of the survey designed to shed light on those employed persons reporting hourly wages at or below the legal minimum. Aside from the usual cautions of interpreting sample data, some particular warnings must be given.

First, the survey unit consists of a household; information is obtained about every member of that household over fourteen years old. The person who provides information may or may not be the person

---

[12] U.S. Bureau of the Census, *The Current Population Survey: Design and Methodology,* Technical Paper 40 (Washington, D.C., January 1978).

for whom data are collected: thus, the wage rates, hours worked, and weekly earnings reported may differ from those actually existing, because of ignorance. Second, if the person answering questions does know the facts, they may not be accurately reported; response rates to inquiries about earnings (or any form of income) are lower than to inquiries about other information.[13]

In an attempt to gauge the usefulness of earnings data, the Bureau of Labor Statistics conducted a special survey in January 1977 matching the earnings reported for particular workers with the earnings for those workers reported by their employers. Although the difference in the calculated *median* was relatively small, about 3 percent, it is not safe to assume that the error for all earnings data is equally small. The bureau notes that

> There were. . .relatively larger differences between the two sets of data in terms of the proportions of workers in specific earnings intervals, particularly at the lowest end of the earnings distribution. Also, the differences between the two sets of data were greater where the household information was obtained from proxy respondents than where it was obtained from the workers.[14]

It also notes that nonresponse to the questions about hourly earnings occurs less frequently than to questions about weekly earnings. For the analysis presented here, nonrespondents were excluded, and the other warnings about reliability apply only insofar as the number of people reporting wages at or below the minimum wage level may be either overstated or understated. But no attempt will be made to quantify such wage earners; the analysis consists only of comparing subsets *within* the sample of low-wage earners and of identifying various characteristics of the group. The findings are so strong, and so mutually consistent, that even if data were available on the actual group of people receiving wages at or below the minimum they would be unlikely to overturn the conclusions reached.

The month during which the data were collected, May 1978, set a new record for the U.S. employment situation, with the highest labor force participation rate ever calculated. On a seasonally adjusted basis, over 100 million people were in the labor force. Other data for that month appear in table 3. The table presents statistics reported by the Bureau of Labor Statistics from the same sample data that were used for the special tabulations in this paper.

---

[13] U.S. Department of Labor, Bureau of Labor Statistics, *Weekly and Hourly Earnings Data from the Current Population Survey,* Special Labor Force Report 195, 1977.

[14] Janice N. Hedges and E. F. Mellor, "Weekly and Hourly Earnings of U.S. Workers, 1967–78," *Monthly Labor Review* 102 (August 1979): 41.

TABLE 3

Employment Situation, May 1978

	Number of Workers (in thousands)		
	Total seasonally adjusted	Males	Females
Total noninstitutional population	160,713	77,000	83,714
Armed forces	2,113	1,992	121
Civilian labor force	100,261	58,447	41,814
Participation rate (percent)	63.2	78.5	50.1
Persons at work, nonagricultural industries	90,877	52,808	38,069
Full-time	76,000	49,014	26,986
Part-time for economic reasons	3,212	1,485	1,727
Voluntary part-time	14,638	4,812	9,827
Unemployed (looking for full-time work)	4,411	2,330	2,081
Unemployed (looking for part-time work)	1,047	367	680

	Number of Workers Receiving Hourly Wages (in thousands)
White males	21,175
White females	16,765
Black males	2,706
Black females	2,227

Source: U.S. Department of Labor, Bureau of Labor Statistics, *Employment and Earnings* (Washington, D.C., June 1978), tables A–1, A–8; and Janice N. Hedges and Earl F. Mellor, "Weekly and Hourly Earnings of U.S. Workers, 1967–78," *Monthly Labor Review* 102 (August 1979): 8.

Those workers in the sample for whom hourly wages were reported were selected for analysis. First, three groups were identified: those receiving $2.30 or less, those with hourly wages between $2.30 and $2.65, and those receiving over $2.65 hourly. In 1977 the legal minimum wage was $2.30; it rose to $2.65 in 1978. The general characteristics of these workers were tabulated, and detailed analysis of the low-wage workers (those receiving hourly wages at or below $2.65) followed.

Potential Income Sources and Activities of Wage Earners

The first special tabulation of the data (table 4) suggested that workers at or below the $2.65 minimum are likely to share several characteristics.

TABLE 4

HOURLY WORKERS, BY AMOUNT OF EARNINGS AND SELECTED
CHARACTERISTICS
(percentage distribution)

	Total	Under $2.30	Between $2.30 and $2.65	Over $2.65
Employment status				
Full-time	100	1.8	7.8	90.4
Part-time for economic reasons	100	9.1	27.5	63.5
Part-time for noneconomic reasons	100	17.6	31.2	51.2
Race and sex				
White male	100	3	9	88
Other male	100	3	12	85
White female	100	10	19	71
Other female	100	7	22	71
Family status				
Household heads, male	100	.8	2.8	96.4
Household heads, female	100	6.7	17.0	76.3
Wives of head	100	4.5	15.4	80.1
Relatives of head, male	100	8.4	27.5	64.1
Relatives of head, female	100	21.8	31.7	46.5
Single males	100	1.5	6.7	91.7
Single females	100	7.6	15.1	77.3
Age				
14 through 17	100	32	42	25
18 through 21	100	6	23	71
22 through 24	100	3	11	86
25 through 44	100	3	8	89
45 through 59	100	3	9	89
60 through 64	100	4	12	85
65 through 69	100	10	22	68
70 and over	100	17	39	44
Marital status, activity:				
Young workers under 21				
School, single	100	22	43	35
School, married, widowed, divorced	100	25	29	46
Other, single	100	6	25	69
Other, married, widowed, divorced	100	4	16	81
Total (all hourly workers)	100	6	14	80

SOURCE: Current Population Survey, May 1978 tabulations.

Only a tiny fraction of household heads of either sex fell into the group, and the percentages of those between ages twenty-five and sixty were small. Low-wage employment was more common for females than for males, but there was no significant racial difference. Significantly, a high proportion of part-time workers appeared in the low-wage group, compared with only one in ten full-time workers receiving less than $2.65. Among young workers, those who combined a job with school tended to work at or below the minimum rather than above. The second tabulation (table 5) refers to all workers receiving $2.65 or less and clarifies the characteristics noted.

Both tables provide supporting evidence for the two hypotheses concerning income sources and activity opportunities. The multiearner family appears common: almost four out of five low-wage workers live in families with at least one other relative. Consumption levels for these low-paid workers could be maintained by the other family members' income. The existence of other sources of income is also strongly suggested by the data on usual weekly earnings: 30 percent received less than forty dollars and another 30 percent between forty dollars and eighty dollars weekly. On the other hand, that alternatives to employment may prove attractive seems likely from the data on part-time work: 57 percent of all low-wage workers do not work full time.

Since most persons working at or below the minimum wage appear to be young, does their employment tend to support either or both of the hypotheses?

When age is combined with household relationship, most young workers appear to be teenagers living at home. About 89 percent of all the low-wage "relatives," that is, workers who lived with their families but were not family heads, were younger than twenty-one years. Young people predominated at *very* low wages; one out of three between fourteen and eighteen years of age was reported to be earning $2.30 or less, and 60 percent of the workers in this lowest-paid group were relatives of the head, living in a family. Figures on full-time or voluntary part-time status by age round out the picture: three out of four low-wage workers under twenty-one were employed part-time for noneconomic reasons.

The last section of table 5 combines data on age with information on the marital status and activity of those under twenty-one. The survey question reads, "What was this person doing most of LAST WEEK—Working, Keeping House, Going to School, or something else?" Tables 4 and 5 use two activity categories: school and "other." Among all young workers at low wages, 91 percent were single and the number reported with keeping house as the major activity was insignificant. A

TABLE 5
HOURLY WAGE WORKERS RECEIVING $2.65 or LESS, by SELECTED CHARACTERISTICS

	Percentage
Labor force status	100
Employed full time	34.5
Part-time, economic reasons	8.7
Part-time, noneconomic reasons	56.8
Race and sex	100
White males	28.0
Other males	4.5
White females	59.1
Other females	8.4
Household relationship	100
Household heads, male	5.9
Household heads, female	6.3
Wives of head	24.1
Relatives of head, male	23.4
Relatives of head, female	29.5
Single males	2.2
Single females	5.3
Age	100
14 through 17	30.7
18 through 21	22.2
22 through 24	7.2
25 through 44	21.5
45 through 59	13.8
60 through 64	3.2
65 through 69	2.1
70 and over	2.3
Marital status, age, activity	100
Workers 16 to 21	44.5
School, single	24.3
School, married, widowed, divorced	16.4
Other, single	3.5
Other, married, widowed, divorced	0.3
Not 16 to 21	55.5
Usual weekly earnings	100
Under $40	30.4
$40 through $79	30.6
$80 through $99	11.8
$100 through $124	21.1
$125 and over	6.1

SOURCE: Current Population Survey, May 1978 tabulations.

different tabulation of *all* hourly workers at any wage level found one out of five to be under twenty-one; 35 percent of them were in school.

Most young people who work while attending school full time must work part time, and their opportunities for employment are limited by their daily schedules. Their availability for work at hourly wages above $2.65 is also constricted.[15] (The further argument that their on-the-job skills may be less than workers who have left school to join the labor force need not be dealt with; it may be noted but not analyzed that among the hourly workers under twenty-one *not* in school, 47 percent reported earnings above $2.65).

Where school exists as a significant alternative use of time for potential workers, two effects follow. The combination of part-time employment with full- or part-time attendance at school produces low weekly earnings. Of those reporting usual weekly earnings below sixty dollars, young people in school accounted for almost half. Customary earnings below forty dollars weekly were prevalent among younger teenagers; one out of four workers between the ages of fourteen and seventeen reported such amounts. Presumably their part-time work consisted not only of "regular" jobs after school in retailing or service enterprises, but also of "odd jobs" or "casual work," which frequently represent both services for and payment by parents or family friends.

Second, the opportunity cost calculation of the young person will reflect the differing benefits of time use in school and time use on the job. Presumably the voluntary part-time worker in school finds the opportunity cost of more time at work to be higher than that of an equivalent amount of time elsewhere. The need for time-use data appears crucial: most students use the word "work" to refer to their schooling, and the hours of "schoolwork" may exceed those attending school.[16]

The suggested relationship between school and employment for people under twenty-one also appears in data on job search. Among all persons looking for work (tabulated from the total civilian labor force), males number 40 percent of those searching for part-time employment.

[15] See the following Special Labor Force Reports: No. 158, *Young Workers in School and Out;* No. 170, *Employment of School-Age Youth;* No. 180, *Students, Graduates, and Dropouts in the Labor Market;* and No. 191, *Students, Graduates, and Dropouts in the Labor Market.*

[16] Employment decisions for many people, not merely low-wage workers, depend on similar calculations. Labor market analysis urgently needs data on people's total time use (at least by major activities) for the potential as well as the actual labor force. Cf. the author's testimony before the National Commission on Employment and Unemployment Statistics, New York, May 23, 1978; Harold Watts and Felicity Skidmore, "The Implications of Changing Family Patterns and Behavior for Labor Force and Hardship Measurement," National Commission on Employment and Unemployment Statistics, technical paper, June 1978.

Almost 80 percent of these males are less than twenty-one years old. Of the females looking for part-time work, only 62 percent were under twenty-one. Housekeeping provides another alternative to paid employment, more likely for adults than for young women.

Since the opportunity cost calculation leading to a decision to work part time at low wages requires some other source of income, the data reinforce both hypotheses. Most low-wage workers are "relatives of head" living in families; table 1 lists the potential sources of income to the teenager working part time at low wages. For this largest group of workers at or below the minimum wage, it is doubtful that the quantity of labor supplied is a simple function of money wages. Certainly the link between employment and income is fragile.

Data from the same categories—relationship, age, weekly earnings, full-time/part-time status—may similarly indicate time-use alternatives and potential income sources for other workers. The identification of employment alternatives cannot be as clear for adults as for young people. From table 4 we may hypothesize nonpaid work, investment in human capital, and recreation and leisure as potential activities.

The last two categories are correlated to some extent with age. The number of all male workers reporting part-time employment drops off sharply after the age of twenty-four; the number between twenty-five and fifty-nine amounts to only one-third of the number of younger workers. But at age sixty, and more significantly at sixty-two and sixty-four, both employment rates and the number of part-time workers or persons seeking part-time work increase. Many of these, and many older female workers, hold jobs at or below minimum wage levels: 32 percent of those between sixty-five and seventy years old.

With the rise in labor force participation among older people, congressional action voiding compulsory retirement at age sixty-five was to be expected: higher levels of health and vigor among older workers will presumably lead to an increased demand for paid work as a means of remaining active. The expanding field of industrial gerontology has produced research findings showing that performance does not correlate perfectly with age and that work-related abilities may be even less predictable from chronological age alone. The growth of occupations in the technical field, requiring less physical strength or stamina than other types of work, also supports the contention that older people can produce for more years than was previously thought to be the case. Finally, recognition is growing that enforced idleness, whether from unemployment or enforced retirement, carries significant private and social costs of mental and physical deterioration and severe psychological loss.

Because social security retirement benefits become available after age sixty-two, the growth of part-time work among older people can also be seen among those between sixty-two and sixty-five. In 1978, retirement benefits were reduced by $1.00 for each $2.00 of earnings: thus part-time work and low weekly earnings fit the demand for supplementary income and activity.

For wives, the other large group of low-wage workers, part-time employment also occurs frequently. Yet it is impossible to infer a woman's alternatives to paid employment from her marital status. Among all women classified as "married, spouse present," three out of four held full-time jobs; among the low-wage workers, 46 percent did so. For the 44 percent working part-time voluntarily at low wages (and with low weekly earnings), several potential uses of time exist. Almost 40 percent of the low-wage wives live in families with two or more children under eighteen; presumably part of their time represents human capital investment at home. Some 8 percent are over sixty years old and may find part-time work a supplementary activity to retirement interests. Finally, unpaid social production (volunteer work) exists as an attractive alternative, although it is not one of the categories used in the survey. In spite of general agreement on the value of such work in hospitals, service organizations, political campaigns, and local government, continuing data on volunteer services and the people who perform them have yet to be collected. As for the remaining low-wage workers, adults who are household heads, any discussion of potential uses of time would be purely speculative.

In regard to alternative sources of income, we must ask the extent to which low wages determine the real income or consumption level of low-wage workers. Almost 80 percent of all low-wage workers were not household heads but lived in families which, presumably, contained other members with income. Of the remaining 20 percent, one out of three reported only part-time work, on a voluntary basis. It must be concluded, therefore, that either other sources of income existed or that total earnings sufficed as total income to the individual worker.

Any analysis of the decisions about income requires two kinds of information: first, the total claims on the individual worker's wages and income, and second, the individual's choice of a satisfactory consumption level. The survey does not, of course, yield hard data on either topic. However, clues about the first exist in tabulations of family size and household relationship; a later section of the paper will discuss family income and individual wages as clues to the second.

Table 6, like table 5, uses the term "singles" in an attempt to avoid the awkward, if more accurate, census terminology, "household heads living without relatives." Colloquially, "singles" used as a substantive has come to mean people living by themselves without specific reference

TABLE 6

SINGLES, BY SEX AND SELECTED CHARACTERISTICS
(percentage distribution)

	All Single Adults		Adult Low-Wage Earner, Single	
	Male	Female	Male	Female
Employment status				
Total	100	100		
Working	70	42		
Hourly wages over $2.65	92	77		
Hourly wages under $2.65	8	23		
Looking	4	2		
Housekeeping	2	45		
At school	2	1		
Unable	2	2		
Other and retired	20	9		
Time worked[a]				
Full-time workers	52.6	30	59	44
Part-time, economic reasons	1.9	2.2	2	10
Voluntary part-time	3.4	8.2	32	46
Usual weekly earnings				
Total	100	100	100	100
Below $40	2	6	13	19
40–79	3	11	26	34
80–99	2	5	8	15
100–149	12	23	42	29
150–249	32	34	10	2
250–299	15	10	—	—
300 or over	35	12	—	—
Age				
Total	100	100	100	100
Under 21	20	24	15	13
22–24			17	8
25–44	45	44	37	19
45–64	30	28	18	31
65–69			8	12
70 and over	4	4	5	14

[a] Figures are for all adults, not singles, and for work experience in 1977. Source: *Consumer Income*, Current Population Reports, Series P–60, No. 119, pp. 59–60.
SOURCE: Current Population Survey, May 1978 tabulations.

to marital status, and thus carries the implication that such persons are householders. "Single" as an adjective refers solely to marital status and not to living arrangements. Other sources make it clear that single persons frequently share living quarters.[17]

No matter how extensive, data on marital status and household relationship do not yield certainty about claims on individual income, since persons neither in the family nor in the household may receive support from the surveyed individual. It will be useful, nevertheless, to present tabulations for householders living with and without relatives. Table 6 deals with the latter.

It contains information on singles derived first from the total population and then from the group of low-wage workers previously identified. For the total population, it shows data on employment status and, for those reporting, usual weekly earnings. For the low-wage workers (earning the minimum of $2.65 or less) it shows full-time/part-time status, usual weekly earnings, and age. Low-wage workers numbered less than 10 percent of employed single males and only 23 percent of the employed single females.

In the total population, single males amount to about 79 percent of the number of single females: women, of course, outlive men, and the customary age gap between husband and wife produces more widows than widowers among single adults, especially at older ages. Employment, however, occurs more frequently among single men than it does among women.

Among all employed "unrelated individuals, living in separate households" (hereafter called singles), women number 85 percent of the male total. Although the percentage of workers receiving hourly wages does not vary by sex, women hold a much higher percentage of jobs paying low *hourly* wages. This is generally true for all female employment; occupational segregation by sex, and the equation between women's jobs and low-paying jobs, explain most of the persistent earnings differential between men and women who work full time, year round.

Table 6 also shows that male retirees far outnumber female retirees. Although fewer elderly women have held jobs, most women (including single women) never retire. They always have the occupation of housekeeping. Although this occupation frequently provides income (as discussed previously), it does not get reported as employment, and generally no retirement, either voluntary or compulsory, is allowed. Thus,

---

[17] U.S. Bureau of the Census, *Marital Status and Living Arrangements,* Current Population Reports, Series P–20, No. 323323.

the widows among the single females whose continued income derives from former housekeeping services to husbands report themselves as still housekeeping rather than retired. For women, housekeeping, either as an occupation or as a reason for not working, is also socially acceptable behavior: the older man who is actually taking care of the house may be more apt to report his status as retired (see table 8).

Part-time work also occurs more frequently among single workers receiving low wages than among more highly paid earners. A look at the age distribution will clarify the picture. Most single workers with earnings are between twenty-five and sixty-five, but low-wage workers without relatives cluster at either end of the age distribution. Young people probably supplement their low wages with income received from gifts or allowances from family members living elsewhere, an especially likely situation for those in school. Older people may receive social security retirement benefits but take jobs at low wages to supplement this income. Such benefits (and those to unemployed workers or disabled workers) will be reduced if earned income exceeds specified amounts, so that part-time employment and low levels of earnings will be preferred to full-time work.

Neither earnings nor earnings-related transfers exhaust the sources of income to single individuals, as table 1 suggests. In 1977 the median *income* of unrelated individuals who worked part time was $4,075, and for those who worked part time for fewer than twenty-six weeks it was $2,809.

Minimum Wages and Poverty

The argument that the minimum wage does not provide a "living wage" calls for a different analysis, one which calculates the total sums which can be earned from legal minimum wages and compares these amounts with the appropriate poverty-level income. The Bureau of the Census calculates 124 different income thresholds at the poverty level; information about methodology, together with the year's dollar figures, appears in each annual issue of *Consumer Income* (Current Population Reports Series P–60), which deals with the population below the poverty level; No. 119 was issued March 1979.

In 1977, the poverty-level income for an individual living alone was $3,067. This figure is the weighted average of the poverty threshholds calculated separately for farm and nonfarm residence and for ages 65 and over. The minimum wage of $2.30, assuming an average work week of thirty-six hours (the actual average in 1977) and year-round employment of fifty weeks, yields a calculated income of $4,140, well above this average. It also exceeds the highest of the separate thresholds, which is $3,267 for a male between fourteen and sixty-four years old. If poverty exists among single individuals living by themselves, full-time employment or somewhat less in a job paying the minimum wage would enable these people to move out of poverty. The chief reasons for continued poverty among such persons do not lie in low wages but in the absence of work, if they are employable, or the absence of transfer income if they are not.

The Census Bureau reported, for the year 1977, about 243,000 unrelated individuals who worked full-time year round and also received income below the poverty level. Several explanations exist. Self-employment may result in losses or extremely low earnings for the year; such earnings need not constitute the only funds available. Farming or homesteading may provide both steady work and a satisfactory level of *real* income, although *money* income may be low. Finally, someone leaving school in June who vacations until October and starts working at $12,000 per annum will report an income *for the year* which is less than the poverty level.

It is the other group of low-wage workers, the household heads, who arouse the greatest concern for the "working poor." These adults, few in number, include both men and women with other family members living with them. The family income may depend largely on the earnings of the family head.

How many household heads can earn only a poverty-level income because they are employed at the minimum wage?

> About 2.5 million working heads of families still remained below the poverty level—nearly one of ten working family heads. Included among the working poor were about 1 million heads of families who worked at full-time, full-year jobs.[18]

The quotation leads directly into an argument for raising the minimum wage: it appears to be the latest in a long succession of pleas for a minimum that will provide "a living wage" or, in today's version, an income above the poverty level for the worker and his family.[19] The data from the May CPS provide one method of analyzing the argument:

[18] Levitan and Belous, *More than Subsistence*, p. 11.

[19] The pronoun "his" has been used in the text deliberately: Both the value judgments and the analysis expressed by those who advocate higher wages to keep people out of poverty consist almost entirely of references to workers as exclusively masculine. The worker's wage should be (for the value judgment) or is not (for the analysis) sufficient to keep "him and his family" out of poverty. Empirical data, of course, are at odds with both these phrasings. See Carolyn Shaw Bell, "Working Women's Contribution to Family Income," in *Economic Independence for Women*, ed. J. R. Chapman (Beverly Hills, Calif.: Sage Publications, 1976).

450

before turning to those findings, some other details about the 1 million full-time workers whose families are poor may be noted.

Documentation for the quotation cites the Current Population Report P–60, No. 107, published in September 1977, entitled "Money Income and Poverty Status of Families and Persons in the United States: 1976"; the number 853,000 (± 9,492) has been rounded to 1 million. A later report, P–60, No. 119, refers to 1977 income data, which correspond to those analyzed in this paper. That publication, entitled "Characteristics of the Population below the Poverty Level: 1977," makes the same point about the "working poor." The front cover displays a pie chart of the poverty population, with a healthy slice (17 percent) identified as "householder worked year-round fulltime," and the corresponding number, 912,000 (± 4,338), can be found in the summary at the beginning. Rounding this number also to 1 million confirms the data used in the quotation.

Detailed statistics in the report provide more information: 150,000 of the million workers suffered absolute business losses. Presumably some unknown number of those reporting low incomes (including the 36,000 with income of less than $500) enjoyed marginal business profits. It is doubtful that the term "working poor" should be applied to unsuccessful entrepreneurs, whose experience for the year was probably not representative of the usual family income.

Second, 115,000 of the million full-time workers whose families were in poverty had incomes above $7,000. The majority of these families contained more than seven persons, most consisting of children under eighteen years. Of the 124 income thresholds calculated to represent poverty, 58 exceeded $7,000.

It can be forcefully argued that the cause of poverty in such cases is not employment at the minimum wage but family size. The argument that wages are "too low" for the worker to support his family may be logically countered by the argument that his family is "too large." The value judgments involved will not be analyzed in this paper, but it *is* significant that little attention has been given, either by proponents or opponents of the minimum wage, to the relation between poverty and family size. For any kind of rational discussion of the policy issues involved, it is even more unfortunate that customary usage refers to "*the* poverty-level income" as if only one such income level existed. When the argument for a minimum wage referred to the concept of fair wages, or a living wage, at least the relationship was clear between wages paid and wages required. Now that the "living wage" has been replaced by the "poverty-level income" as the criterion of equity in compensation, the question of family size need never be considered. Never discussed is the simple fact that no one minimum wage, or sum

451

of money wages, can be calculated that will provide an income above poverty for every worker and his family.[20]

However, the purpose of this paper is to explore the status of low-wage workers. How many families, supported by workers at the minimum wage, live in poverty as a result? What evidence exists that the minimum wage is not a "living wage"? Do the data suggest, as the quotation does, that higher wages might alleviate poverty for those embracing the work ethic?

Table 7 provides data on some relevant characteristics of family heads, classified by sex, first for the total population and then for the group employed at the minimum wage or below.

Among all heads of families, almost 80 percent of the men and over half of the women were employed, with a further fraction (3 percent of the men, 5 percent of the women) looking for work. The proportion of family heads employed at or below the minimum wage was approximately the same for both sexes; again more female family heads than males received wages below $2.30 (see table 5).

By age, the family heads employed at these low wage rates were distributed quite differently. About 14 percent of the workers of both sexes were young (below twenty-four years old), but the sex ratio differs significantly among older workers who were family heads. Only 7 percent of the women but 26 percent of the men receiving low wages were family heads over sixty-five. The workers in their middle years, between twenty-five and sixty-four, also showed a distinct difference: 77 percent of the low-wage female heads fell into this group, while only 54 percent of the males did so. Table 7 illustrates these and other characteristics of family heads, using both published and unpublished census data.

The table shows that families headed by low-wage workers differ markedly from other families; the disadvantages of female-headed families show up clearly. Among male family heads, the percentages of those receiving low wages is much higher at either end of the age distribution than for the general population; as discussed previously, this represents chiefly the fact that working is not the chief activity for either group. It follows that the percentage of men in their middle years, or with children under eighteen, is smaller among low-wage earners than among the general population.

The same is not true for women; the percentage of women between twenty-five and sixty-four is almost the same for all female-headed families and for those receiving income from hourly earnings. However, the women working at low wages to support others tend to be concentrated in the lowest age groups, compared with all female heads. The difference

[20] Cf. Carolyn Shaw Bell, "Should Every Job Support a Family?" *The Public Interest* 40 (1975).

452

TABLE 7

FAMILY HEADS, BY SEX AND SELECTED CHARACTERISTICS
(percentage distribution)

	All Family Heads		Low-Wage Workers	
	Male	Female	Male	Female
Employment status				
Total	100	100	100	100
Working	76	52		
Hourly wages over $2.65			96	76
Hourly wages under $2.65			4	24
Looking	3	5		
Housekeeping	—	33		
At school	—	2		
Unable	2	1		
Other and retired	16	5		
Age	100	100	100	100
Under 21	6	1	6	5
22–24			8	9
25–44	43	47	28	52
45–64	36	29	32	26
65–69			10	5
70 and over	14	14	16	2
Work time			100	100
Full-time workers	78	49	62	58
Part-time, economic reasons			11	15
Voluntary part-time			28	27
Number of children under 18	100	100	100	100
None	47	31	52	23
1–2	39	51	26	53
3–4	12	15	14	21
5 or more	2	3	7	3
Usual weekly earnings				
Under $40			14	13
$40–79			23	27
$80–99			11	14
$100–149			43	39
$150–249			6	4
$250–299			1	1
$300 and over			2	—

SOURCE: *Money Income in 1977 of Families and Persons*, Current Population Reports, Series P–60, No. 18; Current Population Studies, May 1978 tabulations.

in age distribution by sex reflects two phenomena: the difference in longevity between the two sexes and the rise in female-headed families among women who are divorced or separated.

Aside from occupational segregation, women who have families to support find themselves further restricted in the employment market if they have children. Part-time work, or work conveniently close to home, or jobs with working hours that fit other family needs, may take precedence over any preference for higher wages. Data on the reasons for part-time employment and for no employment, by sex, confirm this: Table 8 refers to the total population. Although housekeeping provides the major reason for women's lack of employment, the highest percentage reporting this reason occurs among those between twenty-five and fifty-four, the age group containing most of the female family heads among low earners. The table also shows the extent to which women

TABLE 8

Main Reason for Part-Year or No Employment, 1977
(percentage distribution)

	Females, 25–54	All Males	All Females
Part-year employment			
Number in thousands	10,664	19,879	22,455
Percentage	100	100	100
Could not find work	22	37	19
Ill or disabled	9	9	7
Going to school	3	32	23
Keeping house	61	1	43
Armed forces		—	
Retired		6	1
Other	7	15	7
No employment			
Number in thousands	14,098	17,030	40,066
Percentage	100	100	100
Could not find work	3	4	2
Ill or disabled	8	20	10
Going to school	2	34	16
Keeping house	86	1	61
Armed forces	—	1	—
Retired	—	38	9
Other	1	3	2

Source: Bureau of the Census, *Consumer Income*, Current Population Reports, P–60, No. 118, tables 60, 61.

report "housekeeping" rather than "retirement" or "other" for their lack of employment: among all women over sixty-five only one in four reports retirement as a reason for not seeking employment, a fraction smaller than that expected, given the number of women with prior work experience.

The combination of part-time work and low-wage employment accounts for the large number of female heads reporting usual weekly earnings below $100. Among low-wage women with families, 54 percent reported such amounts, although only 20 percent of all family heads who were employed did so.

The question whether the head's earnings constitute the only source of family income cannot be answered from the data so far reported. Table 1 suggests, of course, a number of income sources which may exist, including private and public transfer payments. Comparing minimum wages with the poverty-level income for the families of household heads cannot be done, either. What constitutes the "poverty level" must be calculated for families of different sizes and composition: thus in 1977 the poverty threshold for a three-person nonfarm family consisting of a woman and two children was $4,849, while that for a three-person nonfarm family containing a man, wife, and one child was $4,910. A minimum wage of $2.65, assuming a thirty-six-hour week and year-round employment, would not quite provide either sum.

Turning to the facts on family income of these low-wage workers, how many represent the working poor, in poverty because minimum wages are too low? Table 9 provides summary data on total family income, for all persons earning $2.65 or less, with some categories shown for household relationship and time worked. Cross-classification does not give significant results, owing to the sample size.

Aside from the constraints of the data, the income brackets shown in table 9 were selected to illustrate hypothetical totals available from minimum wage work and also to pinpoint various poverty levels.

Thus, $3,000 roughly describes the 1977 poverty level for an individual: at a $2.30 minimum wage this income could be earned with thirty-six weeks of employment. At the $2.65 wage the income could be exceeded by only thirty-one weeks' work.

The 1977 poverty level for three-person families is approximately $5,000. This slightly exceeds what could be earned at the $2.65 wage with year-round employment.

The 1977 median income for all families with female heads was approximately $7,400. This exceeds the poverty income for most types of five-person families.

The poverty-level income for families with seven or more persons was approximately $10,000. This is also close to the 1977 median incomes

TABLE 9

LOW-WAGE EARNERS BY FAMILY INCOME, TIME WORKED, AND SELECTED HOUSEHOLD RELATIONSHIPS
(percentage distribution)

Income Class	% of All Income Classes	Selected Household Relationship			Time Worked		
		Relations	Wives	Heads	Full-time	Part-time, economic reasons	Part-time, voluntary
Under $3,000	6	1.2	0.7	2.1	2.5	1.2	2.7
3,000– 4,999	8	1.8	1	2.7	4.1	1.2	3.7
5,000– 7,499	12	3.6	2.7	2.9	6.1	1.4	4.0
7,500– 9,999	8.7	3.4	3.1	1.5	3.7	0.9	7.7
10,000–11,999	7.8	3.3	3.1	1.0	3.4	0.7	3.7
12,000–14,999	11.4	6.0	4.2	0.8	3.9	0.9	6.7
15,000–19,999	14.9	9.1	4.9	0.6	4.5	1.1	9.3
20,000–24,999	11.2	8.4	2.3	—	2.6	0.7	7.8
25,000–49,999	13.9	12.1	1.5	—	2.2	—	11.2
50,000 and over	1.6	1.5	—	—	—	—	1.3
Not answered	3.7						
Total	100	52.8	24.1	12.2	34.5	8.7	56.8

SOURCE: Current Population Survey, May 1978 tabulations.

calculated for families headed by young people, by black people, and by those with an elementary education.

Because of the wide variation in the amounts of income defined as "poverty-level," which depend on family size and composition, inference from the data becomes virtually impossible at all income classes above the poverty level for an individual. For example, $5,000 exceeds the poverty level for a two-person family, but cross-tabulations of family size and income for the low-wage group cannot reveal, with any degrees of significance, how many people in the families (which include one-person families) below this income depend totally upon the minimum wages earned by one worker. Although some types of families with incomes of $10,000 were defined as poor, it cannot be correct to conclude of the 34 percent of all families of low-wage workers with incomes below this sum, that they all live in poverty.

Turning to the potential population of working poor, it is immediately apparent that the table yields little information about such people. About 6 percent of the low-wage workers live in families with incomes below $3,000, which falls below the poverty income for an individual. We do not know, however, whether income consists entirely of wages, nor do we know the earnings of these workers, which may be low because of part-time work.

The sample is too small to permit of significant cross-tabulations. The same is true for full-time workers with low incomes; we do not know how many of them live with other people who have claims on their earnings. Among all low-wage workers, 54 percent of those employed live in families with at least one person under eighteen, but we do not know the total incomes of these families, and the full-time low-wage worker may be identical with the person under eighteen. Quite aside from these constraints of a small sample lie the deficiencies of income data at these low levels, including inaccurate reporting, insufficient knowledge, nonmonetary sources of income, temporary fluctuations of income where household consumption can be maintained by dissaving, and misleading results from the time period used for reporting.

What becomes strikingly clear from the table, however, is the concentration of low-wage workers in families with incomes above *any* published poverty level. Nearly two-thirds of all low-wage workers lived in families with incomes above $10,000; over 40 percent in families with incomes above $15,000. The 1978 median income for *all* families was $16,000. The distribution of persons by time worked confirms this fact; 40 percent of all low-wage workers lived in families with incomes above $10,000 (30 percent above $15,000) *and* worked part time.

The analysis of opportunity cost and alternative uses of time explains this phenomenon for many young workers, and those below twenty-one constitute the majority of low-wage earners. The analysis of income sources available to individuals helps explain the high incidence of part-time work among low-wage earners in a variety of situations. Previous analysts have noted the presence of low-wage earners from high income families, correctly attributing this to teenage employment.[21] This paper shows that not only teenagers but also elderly adults and working wives may be included in the group of low-wage earners with family incomes well above poverty.

The analysis also suggests that the labor supply approach to employment may be lacking in its failure to consider other motives for work besides the income from wages. For many workers, as has been shown, employment represents useful activity rather than a primary source of income; for young people and wives, employment may produce some human capital investment. Where this is true, both job search and work experience will respond to other incentives than wage levels. Among such incentives may be time of day, week, or year worked; job location; training; practice provided for existing skills; work surroundings; etc. It may be more useful to see the labor market's conditions of supply and demand unconventionally: people with a demand for jobs, employers with a supply of jobs.

Finally, it remains to reiterate the impossibility of establishing any link between the money wages earned by an individual and the real income of welfare enjoyed by that individual, whether a family member or an individual. Total income may or may not be provided by employment efforts alone: certainly such "independent workers," living solely on their earnings and sharing their earnings with no one else, are in the minority in this country. Since that is so, to establish the adequacy of any wage requires knowing the total claims on the sum earned and the fraction of total income made up by that sum. Obviously, table 9 reinforces the significance of the multiearner family, showing that low-wage "relatives" and "wives" contribute to families with incomes below the median. And since only the people involved can define whether or not a given family income is adequate, it may very well be that minimum wage workers do, in fact, keep millions of families from "poverty"—in this case defined by the wants and needs of those families. But raising the minimum wage would not, in fact, assist many families with incomes below the *official* poverty levels, and would provide sizable additional income to families with incomes well above those levels.

[21] Edward M. Gramlich, "Impact of Minimum Wages on Other Wages, Employment and Family Incomes," *Brookings Papers on Economic Activity* 2 (1976): 409–51; and Terence Kelly, "Two Policy Questions Regarding the Minimum Wage" (mimeographed, The Urban Institute, February 1976), are the only published works known to the author.

The Low-Wage Workers: Who Are They?

Thomas J. Kniesner

> *The Congress hereby finds that the existence . . . of labor con-*
> *ditions detrimental to the maintenance of the minimum standard*
> *of living necessary for health, efficiency, and general well-being*
> *of workers causes commerce and the channels and instrumen-*
> *talities of commerce to be used to spread and perpetuate such*
> *labor conditions among the workers of the several states . . . It*
> *is hereby declared to be the policy of this Act . . . to correct and*
> *as rapidly as practicable to eliminate the conditions above re-*
> *ferred to . . . without substantially curtailing employment or*
> *earning power.*

Fair Labor Standards Act of 1938

Because a major goal of the Fair Labor Standards Act (FLSA) is to help
workers achieve a minimum standard of living, it should be evaluated
as other antipoverty programs, by comparing its social costs and benefits.
Probably the most controversial provision of FLSA is section 6, which
establishes a minimum wage. Whenever Congress considers increasing
the federal wage floor, proponents argue that such a policy is a straightforward, effective way to raise the incomes of the poor and that the
economic costs imposed on the "losers" (disemployed workers and owners of small firms) are relatively small. Opponents of a minimum wage
contend that it violates section 2 of FLSA because it *does* "substantially
curtail employment" for certain important population subgroups (teenagers). Moreover, critics cite a potentially loose linkage between low
wages and poverty. Somewhat surprisingly, economists have devoted
most of their attention to the relatively subtle issue of quantifying the
costs imposed on the losers from a federal minimum wage. Almost

NOTE: I would like to thank the American Enterprise Institute for Public Policy Research
for its financial support and Belton M. Fleisher, Deborah A. Freund, Solomon W.
Polachek, Simon Rottenberg, George Tauchen, and Finis Welch for their helpful comments.

nothing is known about the more basic questions of who the potential winners are and whether they are also society's poor.[1]

My research is an attempt to produce the most comprehensive empirical description of low-wage workers available to date, using the simplest of statistical techniques. Such an exercise seems crucially important if future proposals to increase the minimum wage are to receive meaningful debate. If my results fail to show, for example, that individuals with low wages are also poor, then it would seem unreasonable to continue to debate the value of the minimum wage as an antipoverty device. It would make more sense to focus instead on an alternative issue, perhaps the social costs and benefits of the minimum wage as a type of tariff that reduces interregional differences in labor costs.

In the following section I discuss the data used to identify the characteristics of low-wage workers in the United States. The third section describes their labor market characteristics. In the fourth section I present a "snapshot" of the personal characteristics of low-wage workers, and in the section "Are Low-Wage Workers Also Poor?" I attempt to determine the overlap between low wages and poverty in the United States. The "Concluding Remarks" section summarizes my key empirical findings and their implications for policy and future research.

Data

The data for my research are taken from the May 1978 Current Population Survey (CPS), which encompasses 126,676 individuals from the civilian noninstitutional population at least fourteen years old. The CPS is a monthly sample of households conducted by the Bureau of the Census and for two reasons provides the best set of data with which to describe the characteristics of low-wage workers in the United States. First, it is a nationally representative sample of a size large enough to permit fairly detailed categorizations. Second, the May CPS contains hourly wage rates reported by households rather than imputed from some measures of earnings and hours of work. Of the 26,415 individuals for whom hourly wage rates were reported, 20 percent were at or below the 1978 minimum wage of $2.65 per hour.[2] In order to get a relatively complete idea of the incidence of low wages in the United States, I also calculated the fraction of workers with reported hourly wages at or below the federal minimum for 1979 ($2.90) and for 1980 ($3.10); these

---

[1] Exceptions are the research of Finis Welch, *Minimum Wages: Issues and Evidence* (Washington, D.C.: American Enterprise Institute, 1978), pp. 13–20, and Edward M. Gramlich, "Impact of Minimum Wages on Other Wages, Employment, and Family Incomes," *Brookings Papers on Economic Activity* 2 (1976): 443–49.

[2] Only 4.2 percent were *below* $2.65, however.

figures are 27 percent and 35 percent, respectively. The last group is somewhat interesting because $3.10 is approximately the hourly wage supposedly necessary to keep a family of four with one full-time worker out of poverty in May 1978.[3]

Workers not paid by the hour are nonetheless covered by the minimum wage provision of FLSA. A complaint that one is not receiving the minimum wage is evaluated by the Employment Standards Administration, Wage and Hours Division, of the Department of Labor by examining one's usual hours and earnings.[4] To include in my data set workers with low *implicit* hourly wage rates, I first selected those workers who did *not* list themselves as paid by the hour and imputed their hourly wages by taking the ratio of their usual weekly earnings to their usual weekly hours of work. This yielded 1,664 individuals with implicit hourly wages of less than or equal to $2.65; 2,035 individuals with implicit hourly wages less than or equal to $2.90; and 2,415 individuals with implicit hourly wages less than or equal to $3.10.

Reported wages may differ in accuracy from imputed wages, though. Thus, for purposes of analysis I consider six sets of low-wage workers: those with *reported* hourly wages less than or equal to $2.65, $2.90, or $3.10 in May 1978, and those with *imputed* hourly wages less than or equal to $2.65, $2.90, or $3.10 in May 1978. Finally, since one of my objectives is to evaluate the *concept* of a minimum wage as a means to alleviate poverty, I do *not* limit my analysis to only those workers actually covered by FLSA or some state minimum wage statute.

Labor Market Characteristics of Low-Wage Workers

Tables 1 and 2 indicate that low-wage workers are relatively underrepresented in large cities and in the Northeast and West census regions. Among workers with low reported wages, approximately twice as many (34 percent) live in the South as in the Northeast, for example. Although 28 percent reside in the North-Central census region, many are located in its West North-Central Division, which is largely the Great Plains.[5] These results change only slightly if we examine workers with low imputed wages. Again, only about 40 percent live in the West and the Northeast. Relatively more live in the South, however, than in the case of workers with low reported wages. Finally, only about 20 percent of

---

[3] This figure is obtained by dividing the 1977 poverty line, $6,191, by 2,000, the number of hours in a full-time work year.

[4] See the appendix for a facsimile of the forms one uses to report an FLSA violation.

[5] The West North-Central division of the North-Central census region includes Iowa, Kansas, Minnesota, Missouri, Nebraska, North Dakota, and South Dakota.

TABLE 1
DISTRIBUTION OF LOW-WAGE WORKERS BY REGION, MAY 1978
(percent)

Region[a]	Reported Wage			Imputed Wage[b]		
	Less than or equal to $2.65	Less than or equal to $2.90	Less than or equal to $3.10	Less than or equal to $2.65	Less than or equal to $2.90	Less than or equal to $3.10
Northeast	17.3	17.6	18.1	17.3	17.2	17.8
North-Central	28.7	28.1	27.9	22.7	22.9	22.6
South	33.9	34.1	33.1	39.8	40.1	40.6
West	20.0	20.3	20.9	20.1	19.7	19.0
	(N = 5,291)	(N = 7,173)	(N = 9,325)	(N = 1,664)	(N = 2,035)	(N = 2,415)

[a] Northeast ≡ Connecticut, Maine, Massachusetts, New Hampshire, Rhode Island, Vermont, New York, and Pennsylvania. North-Central ≡ Illinois, Indiana, Michigan, Ohio, Wisconsin, Iowa, Kansas, Minnesota, Missouri, Nebraska, North Dakota, and South Dakota. South ≡ Delaware, District of Columbia, Florida, Georgia, Maryland, North Carolina, South Carolina, Virginia, West Virginia, Alabama, Kentucky, Mississippi, Tennessee, Arkansas, Louisiana, Oklahoma, and Texas. West ≡ Arizona, Colorado, Idaho, Montana, Nevada, New Mexico, Utah, Wyoming, Alaska, California, Hawaii, Oregon, and Washington.
[b] Imputed wage is an estimated wage for those respondents who reported that they were *not* paid by the hour. Imputed wage ≡ usual weekly earning divided by usual hours worked per week.
SOURCE: Current Population Survey, May 1978.

TABLE 2

DISTRIBUTION OF LOW-WAGE WORKERS BY RESIDENTIAL LOCATION, MAY 1978

(percent)

Residential Location[a]	Reported Wage			Imputed Wage[b]		
	Less than or equal to $2.65	Less than or equal to $2.90	Less than or equal to $3.10	Less than or equal to $2.65	Less than or equal to $2.90	Less than or equal to $3.10
Central city of SMSA	18.7	19.5	19.8	20.0	20.8	21.4
In SMSA, but not in central city	26.8	26.6	27.5	22.2	22.3	22.7
Not in SMSA	36.5	35.9	34.4	42.5	41.4	40.2
Not identified	17.9	18.0	18.3	15.2	15.4	15.7
	(N = 5,291)	(N = 7,173)	(N = 9,325)	(N = 1,664)	(N = 2,035)	(N = 2,415)

[a] The U.S. Office of Federal Statistical Policy and Standards designates certain metropolitan areas as standard metropolitan statistical areas (SMSAs). The general concept is one of an integrated economic and social unit with a large population nucleus. An SMSA includes at least (a) one city with 50,000 or more inhabitants, or (b) a city with at least 25,000 inhabitants, which, together with contiguous places having population densities of at least 1,000 persons per square mile, has a combined population of 50,000 and constitutes for general economic and social purposes a single community, provided that the county or counties in which the city and contiguous places are located has a total population of at least 75,000. In addition, an SMSA includes the county in which the central city is located and adjacent counties that are determined to be metropolitan in character and economically and socially integrated with the county of the central city, according to specific rules. The largest city in each SMSA is designated a central city; there may be up to two additional central cities if certain criteria are met. An SMSA may include other cities of 50,000 or more besides its central cities and may encompass territory in more than one state.

[b] See note b to table 1.

SOURCE: Current Population Survey, May 1978.

463

low-wage workers live in central cities of a standard metropolitan statistical area (SMSA); 35–40 percent do not live in an SMSA at all.

The industrial/occupational distribution of low-wage workers is somewhat more difficult to discern. Tables 3 and 4 summarize results from relative frequency distributions of rather detailed industry and occupation groupings.[6] I define an industry or an occupation as "overrepresented" if it contains approximately 5 percent or more of all low-wage workers, about twice the fraction that would occur if there were a random distribution of low-wage workers across industries or occupations. Among workers with low reported hourly wages, only four industries are overrepresented. Approximately 40 percent of all workers are in two industries, retail eating and drinking establishments and other retail trade. Private household services and education are the other two "large" employers of workers with low reported wages, employing about 8–9 percent each. This is in contrast to workers with low imputed wages where private household service has the greatest concentration of low-wage workers. Moreover, seven industries are overrepresented in the imputed-wage group versus four in the reported-wage group; agricultural production, welfare and religious organizations, and personal services except private household comprise the difference. Finally, it should be noted that the lower fraction of workers in eating and drinking establishments probably results from the fact that imputed wages reflect tip income to a greater degree than do reported wages.

Given the distributions of low-wage workers by industry, the occupational distributions observed in table 4 are not unexpected. Food service workers are about 20–27 percent of workers reporting low wages, the largest occupational group. Those with low imputed wages are again relatively more dispersed. Private household workers and paid farm laborers and foremen are the largest occupational groupings, each with 10–12 percent of the total. The rather high incidence of low imputed wages for salaried managers not in manufacturing is due largely to their relatively high usual hours of work per week; this fact leads us to a related issue.

One reason to suspect that low-wage workers may not in general be part of the poverty population is that they may work relatively long hours. This does not appear to be the case, however. The multiple jobholding rate for both groups of low-wage workers is only 3 percent, approximately half that of the population at large. In addition, only 6–9 percent of workers with low reported wages work over forty hours per week, in contrast to about 28 percent for the entire labor force. The

---

[6] The detailed industry grouping of the May 1978 CPS contains fifty-two categories, and the detailed occupation grouping contains forty-five categories.

TABLE 3

DISTRIBUTION OF LOW-WAGE WORKERS BY INDUSTRY, MAY 1978
(percent)

Industry	Reported Wage			Industry	Imputed Wage[a]		
	Less than or equal to $2.65	Less than or equal to $2.90	Less than or equal to $3.10		Less than or equal to $2.65	Less than or equal to $2.90	Less than or equal to $3.10
Retail eating and drinking establishments	22.5	19.8	16.9	Private household services	17.1	14.8	13.3
Other retail trade	20.9	22.6	22.6	Agricultural production	12.0	10.9	9.8
				Other retail trade	11.3	11.6	11.8
				Education	9.4	9.9	10.4
Private household services	9.4	7.1	6.0	Welfare and religion	6.4	5.7	5.7
				Retail eating and drinking establishments	5.7	5.5	5.3
Education	8.9	8.4	8.3	Personal services except private household	5.5	5.8	5.7
All others	38.3	42.1	46.1	All others	32.6	35.8	38.0
	(N=5,291)	(N=7,173)	(N=9,325)		(N=1,664)	(N=2,035)	(N=2,415)

[a] See note b to table 1.

SOURCE: Current Population Survey, May 1978.

TABLE 4

DISTRIBUTION OF LOW-WAGE WORKERS BY OCCUPATION, MAY 1978
(percent)

Occupation	Reported Wage			Occupation	Imputed Wage[a]		
	Less than or equal to $2.65	Less than or equal to $2.90	Less than or equal to $3.10		Less than or equal to $2.65	Less than or equal to $2.90	Less than or equal to $3.10
Food service	26.6	23.9	20.5	Private household workers	12.7	11.0	9.8
Unskilled clerical workers[b]	11.5	12.5	13.1	Paid farm laborers and foremen	12.0	10.7	9.6
				Unskilled clerical workers	7.5	8.6	9.9
				Nonfarm laborers not in construction or manufacturing	7.2	6.5	6.1
				Salaried managers not in manufacturing	6.1	6.5	6.7
				Food service	5.8	5.7	5.5
				Sales workers not in retail trade	5.3	5.0	4.5
Private household workers	8.1	6.1	5.1	Personal services	5.1	5.0	4.9
Retail sales workers	7.9	8.6	8.3	All others	38.3	41.0	43.0
All others	45.9	48.9	53.0		(N=1,664)	(N=2,035)	(N=2,415)
	(N=5,291)	(N=7,173)	(N=9,325)				

a See note 1.
b Clerical workers *not* classified as bookkeepers, office machine operators, stenographers, typists, or secretaries.
SOURCE: Current Population Survey, May 1978.

incidence of long weekly hours is the same for the low-imputed-wage group as for the labor force at large. One factor underlying the relatively short work schedules of those who report low wages is that one-fourth to one-third report that going to school was their major activity during the survey week.

Finally, the results of this section shed some additional light on the issue of organized labor's political support for minimum wage legislation. Jonathan Silberman and Garey Durden find that union campaign contributions have a significant effect on favorable votes across congressional districts.[7] In fact, when the marginal impacts of their independent variables are examined in terms of standardized units, union donations to a representative's campaign proved to have the most substantial influence. Besides a genuine desire to help the poor, are there other economic reasons why unions might find it worthwhile to back federal minimum wage legislation? One (unsophisticated) explanation is that unionists wish to reduce competition from their (low-wage) nonunion counterparts. We have just seen, however, that the typical low-wage worker is a retail sales clerk, food service worker, or household maid—occupations not heavily unionized even in large cities in the Northeast or the West. Thus, more sophisticated justifications for union support of the concept of a minimum wage must be offered, such as a desire to raise the relative price of unskilled nonunion labor, which may substitute for skilled union labor.

Personal Characteristics of Low-Wage Workers

Tables 5–7 present the race, sex, and age distribution of the low-wage labor force. Although there seem to be no surprises concerning the racial distribution of low-wage workers in that it is virtually identical to the population at large, this is not the case for sex composition. In 1978, approximately 41 percent of the total labor force was female. In contrast, two-thirds of workers with low reported wages and 55 percent of workers with low imputed wages were female. There is yet another surprise, however. Given the focus of past research on the labor market impact of minimum wage legislation, one typically thinks of the low-wage worker as a teenager or someone in their early twenties. Only 50 to 60 percent of workers with low reported wages and about a third of workers with low imputed wages fall into these age categories, however. Table 7 indicates that a sizable number of the two wage groups are prime aged,

---

[7] Jonathan I. Silberman and Garey C. Durden, "Determining Legislative Preferences on the Minimum Wage: An Economic Approach," *Journal of Political Economy* 84 (April 1976): 317–29.

TABLE 5

DISTRIBUTION OF LOW-WAGE WORKERS BY RACE, MAY 1978

(percent)

Race	Reported Wage			Imputed Wage[a]		
	Less than or equal to $2.65	Less than or equal to $2.90	Less than or equal to $3.10	Less than or equal to $2.65	Less than or equal to $2.90	Less than or equal to $3.10
White	87.1	86.8	86.9	84.9	85.1	85.3
Black	10.6	10.8	10.7	14.0	13.7	13.4
Other	2.3	2.4	2.4	1.1	1.2	1.3
	(N = 5,291)	(N = 7,173)	(N = 9,325)	(N = 1,664)	(N = 2,035)	(N = 2,415)

[a] See note b to table 1.
SOURCE: Current Population Survey, May 1978.

TABLE 6

DISTRIBUTION OF LOW-WAGE WORKERS BY SEX, MAY 1978

(percent)

Sex	Reported Wage			Imputed Wage[a]		
	Less than or equal to $2.65	Less than or equal to $2.90	Less than or equal to $3.10	Less than or equal to $2.65	Less than or equal to $2.90	Less than or equal to $3.10
Male	32.5	31.8	33.0	46.5	45.4	44.7
Female	67.5	68.2	67.0	53.5	54.6	55.3
	(N = 5,291)	(N = 7,173)	(N = 9,325)	(N = 1,664)	(N = 2,035)	(N = 2,415)

[a] See note b to table 1.
SOURCE: Current Population Survey, May 1978.

469

TABLE 7

DISTRIBUTION OF LOW-WAGE WORKERS BY AGE, MAY 1978

(percent)

Age Group	Reported Wage			Imputed Wage[a]		
	Less than or equal to $2.65	Less than or equal to $2.90	Less than or equal to $3.10	Less than or equal to $2.65	Less than or equal to $2.90	Less than or equal to $3.10
14–19	45.3	40.4	35.9	21.6	20.5	19.2
20–24	14.8	16.3	18.0	13.6	15.2	16.1
25–64	35.5	39.4	42.2	55.1	55.3	56.4
65+	4.4	4.0	3.8	9.7	9.0	8.2
	(N = 5,291)	(N = 7,173)	(N = 9,325)	(N = 1,664)	(N = 2,035)	(N = 2,415)

[a] See note b to table 1.
SOURCE: Current Population Survey, May 1978.

twenty-five to sixty-four. In fact, more than half of the workers with low imputed wages are prime aged.

We have just seen that the prime aged and women make up unexpectedly large fractions of low-wage workers in the United States. To obtain a more complete picture, see table 8, which presents a cross-tabulation by age, race,[1] and sex for workers with wages less than or equal to $2.65.[8] Among the set of workers for whom hourly wage rates were reported, two groups stand out. White teenagers and prime-aged white females compose about two-thirds of the total. This two-thirds is fairly evenly split between male teenagers, female teenagers, and prime-aged white women. The story is somewhat different among workers with low imputed wages, where white male teenagers and prime-aged white females are again overrepresented but are now joined by prime-aged white males.

The picture of the low-wage worker emerging from tables 5–8 is confirmed by the results in table 9, which presents the distribution of low-wage workers by "household position." Workers with low reported wages are largely a male relative of the head of household (son), a wife of the head of household, or a female relative of the head of household (daughter). These three groups are also overrepresented among workers with low imputed wages. Moreover, approximately one-fourth of the low-imputed-wage group were male heads of households.

The results of this section yield some interesting surprises. The overwhelming majority of low-wage workers are women, with about 40 percent of them aged twenty-five to sixty-four. This differs dramatically from the stereotype of the low-wage worker as a male teenager. Instead, we observe white women, a sizable number of whom are prime aged.

Are Low-Wage Workers Also Poor?

One way to examine the overlap between low wages and poverty is to look at data for the family incomes of the low-wage-rate population accounting for family size. Table 10 exhibits data on the fraction of low-wage workers with family incomes in the categories $0–7,499, $7,500–14,999, and $15,000 + . Figures for 1977 indicate a poverty cutoff point of $6,191 for a family of four and $7,320 for a family of five.[9] Even if we use the higher figure, only about one-fourth of workers with low

---

[8] In order to conserve space, I do not present results of cross-tabulations for the groups with wages less than or equal to $2.90 and $3.10. These results differ only slightly from those in table 8.

[9] As a point of reference, about 11 percent of the low-reported-wage group and 8 percent of the low-imputed-wage group lived in families with more than three children.

TABLE 8

DISTRIBUTION OF LOW-WAGE WORKERS BY AGE, RACE, AND SEX, MAY 1978
(percent)

Age Group	Reported Wage Less than or Equal to $2.65				Imputed Wage Less than or Equal to $2.65			
	White male	White female	Nonwhite male	Nonwhite female	White male	White female	Nonwhite male	Nonwhite female
14–19	18.0	23.6	1.6	1.7	13.8	6.2	0.9	0.5
20–24	4.0	8.9	0.7	1.2	5.9	5.9	0.6	1.1
25–64	4.4	24.3	1.9	5.3	18.0	27.0	3.1	7.2
65 +	1.5	2.3	0.4	0.3	3.4	4.5	0.6	1.3

SOURCE: Current Population Survey, May 1978.

472

TABLE 9
DISTRIBUTION OF LOW-WAGE WORKERS BY HOUSEHOLD POSITION, MAY 1978 (percent)

Household Position	Reported Wage			Imputed Wage[a]		
	Less than or equal to $2.65	Less than or equal to $2.90	Less than or equal to $3.10	Less than or equal to $2.65	Less than or equal to $2.90	Less than or equal to $3.10
Male head, with relatives in household	5.9	6.6	8.3	19.8	20.3	20.8
Male head, without relatives in household	2.2	2.5	2.8	5.2	4.9	4.7
Male relative of household head	23.4	21.8	20.7	19.1	18.0	17.1
Male nonrelative of household head	0.9	1.0	1.3	2.4	2.1	2.0
Female head, with relatives in household	6.3	6.6	6.6	5.3	5.7	6.2
Female head, without relatives in household	5.3	5.3	5.4	8.1	7.8	7.7
Wife of household head	24.1	27.3	28.7	26.0	27.0	27.6
Female relative of household head	29.5	26.5	23.9	10.8	10.8	10.6
Female nonrelative of household head	2.3	2.4	2.5	3.3	3.3	3.2
	(N = 5,291)	(N = 7,173)	(N = 9,325)	(N = 1,664)	(N = 2,035)	(N = 2,415)

[a] See note b to table 1.
SOURCE: Current Population Survey, May 1978.

TABLE 10

DISTRIBUTION OF LOW-WAGE WORKERS BY FAMILY INCOME, MAY 1978

(percent)

Total Family Income	Reported Wage			Imputed Wage[a]		
	Less than or equal to $2.65	Less than or equal to $2.90	Less than or equal to $3.10	Less than or equal to $2.65	Less than or equal to $2.90	Less than or equal to $3.10
$0–7,499	26.9	26.5	26.0	35.8	34.4	33.1
$7,500–14,999	27.9	28.5	28.9	28.7	28.8	29.7
$15,000 and over	41.5	41.4	41.4	32.0	33.1	33.5
Missing values	3.7	3.6	3.7	3.5	3.7	3.7
	(N = 5,291)	(N = 7,173)	(N = 9,325)	(N = 1,664)	(N = 2,035)	(N = 2,415)

[a] See note b to table 1.

SOURCE: Current Population Survey, May 1978.

reported wages and one-third of workers with low imputed wages live in poverty.

This is not to imply, of course, that low-wage workers come from high-income families. Only 33–40 percent of low-wage workers were in the $15,000+ family income group. Moreover, there may be "pockets of poverty" within the set of low-wage workers that cannot be detected in table 10. This possibility is examined in table 11, which is a cross-tabulation of household position by income class for workers with wage rates less than or equal to $2.65.[10] We see that in the reported-wage group, approximately 75 percent of female heads of households with relatives have total incomes below $7,500, for example. However, there are only 318 such individuals. For the three groups that compose the vast majority of workers with low reported wages—male relative of household head, wife of household head, and female relative of household head—the incidence of low family income is 12 to 16 percent. In the case of those with imputed wages, the three groups just mentioned plus male heads of households compose the bulk of the total of low-wage workers. About 53 percent of male heads come from low-income families. Figures for the incidence of low family income among the three other key imputed-wage subgroups are similar to those for individuals with reputed wages.

The results of this section indicate that although low-wage workers certainly cannot be classified as wealthy, it is also difficult to call them poor. It does not seem reasonable to continue to debate the efficacy of the minimum wage as an antipoverty device when two-thirds to three-fourths of those with low wages have family incomes above the poverty line.

Concluding Remarks

Although the stereotypical low-wage worker is probably a male teenager from a poor family, my research, which attempts to create a relatively detailed empirical picture of the low-wage population, indicates otherwise. Over 60 percent of all low-wage workers are women, and less than 40 percent are teenagers. Moreover, low wages do not appear to be strongly associated with poverty as commonly defined. Less than 25 percent of low-wage workers are heads of households, and only about 30 percent live in families with incomes below the poverty line for a family of five. Not surprisingly, low-wage workers tend to live in relatively small towns in the South and in the Great Plains.

[10] Again, in order to conserve space, I do not present results of cross-tabulations for the four other wage groups. These results differ only slightly from those in table 11.

TABLE 11

DISTRIBUTION OF LOW-WAGE WORKERS BY HOUSEHOLD POSITION AND FAMILY INCOME, MAY 1978

Household Position	Reported Wage Less than or Equal to $2.65			Imputed Wage Less than or Equal to $2.65		
	$0–7,499	$7,500–14,999	$15,000+	$0–7,499	$7,500–14,999	$15,000+
Male head of	48.2	38.0	13.8	40.7	38.8	20.5
household with	10.3	7.8	1.9	21.7	25.8	12.2
relatives	2.9	2.3	0.8	8.0	7.7	4.0
Male head of	88.1	16.1	0.1	77.4	17.9	4.8
household without	6.7	0.7	1.8	10.9	3.1	0.8
relatives	1.9	0.2	0.0	4.0	0.9	0.2
Male relative	14.9	26.2	58.9	18.6	22.5	58.8
of household head	12.4	21.1	32.0	9.6	14.5	33.8
	3.5	6.1	13.8	3.6	4.3	11.2
Male nonrelative	56.3	27.1	16.9	66.7	11.1	22.2
of household head	1.9	0.9	0.4	4.0	0.8	1.5
	0.5	0.3	0.2	1.5	0.2	0.5
Female head of	75.2	70.4	4.4	75.0	19.3	5.7
household with	16.8	4.4	0.6	11.1	3.6	0.9
relatives	4.7	1.3	0.3	4.1	1.1	0.3
Female head of	94.9	4.4	0.7	82.6	15.2	2.3
household without	18.3	0.8	0.1	18.3	4.2	0.6
relatives	5.1	0.2	0.0	6.8	1.2	0.2

Wife of household head	18.5	44.2	37.3	21.7	37.9	40.3
	16.2	37.3	21.2	15.3	33.3	31.7
	4.5	10.8	9.1	5.7	9.9	10.5
Female relative of household head	11.8	24.7	63.5	15.4	34.3	50.3
	12.3	24.8	43.0	4.4	12.2	15.9
	3.4	7.2	18.5	1.6	3.6	5.3
Female nonrelative of household head	60.2	26.3	13.6	51.9	22.2	25.9
	5.0	2.1	0.7	4.7	2.5	2.6
	1.4	0.6	0.3	1.7	0.7	0.9
	(N = 1,423)	(N = 1,478)	(N = 2,194)	(N = 595)	(N = 477)	(N = 533)

NOTE: The first row of data for each household position shows the percentage distribution by row; the second row shows the percentage distribution by column; the third row shows the percentage distribution overall.

FIGURE 1

U.S. DEPARTMENT OF LABOR
EMPLOYMENT STANDARDS ADMINISTRATION
WAGE AND HOUR DIVISION

DATE:
REPLY TO
ATTN OF:

SUBJECT:

TO:

This acknowledges receipt of the information you furnished us about the firm named above. You may be assured that any information furnished the Division will be kept confidential.

The conditions you describe will be looked into as soon as possible and we will be in touch with you again. The enclosed informational material will explain the Act or Acts which may be applicable in your situation.

Meanwhile, if you care to submit additional information (such as a change in your address or directions on how to reach your home if you furnished us a post office box as an address or if you live in a rural area), please contact our Area Office listed above. In writing, please refer to this firm by the name shown in the above Subject.

Enclosure:

☆ U.S. GOVERNMENT PRINTING OFFICE: 1977—720-088/2211 3-1   **Form WH-87 (Rev. 8/71)**

FIGURE 2

<table>
<tr><td colspan="2">U.S. DEPARTMENT OF LABOR
EMPLOYMENT STANDARDS ADMINISTRATION
WAGE AND HOUR DIVISION</td><td>EMPLOYMENT INFORMATION FORM</td></tr>
</table>

This report is authorized by Section 11 of the Fair Labor Standards Act. While you are not required to respond, submission of this information is necessary for the Division to schedule any compliance action. Information received by this Office will be treated confidentially.

1. PERSON SUBMITTING INFORMATION

A. Name (Print first name, middle initial, and last name)

Mr.
Miss
Mrs.

B. Date

C. Telephone number:
(Or No. where you can be reached)

D. Address: (Number, Street, Apt. No.)

(City, County, State, ZIP Code)

E. Check one of these boxes

☐ Present employee of establishment   ☐ Former employee of establishment   ☐ Job Applicant   ☐ Other_____
(Specify: relative, union, etc.)

2. ESTABLISHMENT INFORMATION

A. Name of establishment

B. Telephone Number

C. Address of establishment: (Number, Street)

(City, County, State, ZIP Code)

D. Estimate number of employees

E. Does the firm have branches? ☐ Yes ☐ No ☐ Don't know

If "Yes", name one or two locations: _____

F. Nature of establishment's business: (For example; school, farm, hospital, hotel, restaurant, shoe store, wholesale drugs, manufactures stoves, coal mine, construction, trucking, etc.)

G. If the establishment has a Federal Government or federally assisted contract, check the appropriate box(es).

☐ Furnishes goods   ☐ Furnishes services   ☐ Performs construction

H. Does establishment ship goods to or receive goods from other States?
☐ Yes ☐ No ☐ Don't know

3. EMPLOYMENT INFORMATION
(Complete A, B, C, D, E, & F if present or former employee of establishment; otherwise complete F only)

A. Period employed (month, year)

From: _____

To: _____
(If still there, state present)

B. Date of birth if under 19 or if information concerns age discrimination

Month _____ Day _____ Year _____

C. Give your job title and describe briefly the kind of work you do

(Continue on other side)

Form WH-3 (Rev. Apr. 1977)

479

FIGURE 2 (*continued*)

1. Method of payment		E. Enter in the boxes below the hours you usually work each day and each week (less time off for meals)							
		M	T	W	T	F	S	S	TOTAL
$ _____ per _____ (Rate) (Hour, week, month, etc.)									

1. CHECK THE APPROPRIATE BOX(ES) AND EXPLAIN BRIEFLY IN THE SPACE BELOW the employment practices which you believe violate the Wage and Hour laws. (If you need more space use an additional sheet of paper and attach it to this form.)

☐ Does not pay the minimum wage

☐ Does not pay proper overtime

☐ Men and women perform equal work but do not get equal pay

☐ Discrimination against employee or applicant (40-65 years of age) because of age

Approximate date of alleged discrimination _____

☐ Does not pay prevailing wage determination for Federal Government or federally assisted contract

☐ Discharged employee because of wage garnishment (explain below)

☐ Excessive deduction from wages because of wage garnishment (explain below)

☐ Employs minors under minimum age for job

☐ Other (explain below)

_____

_____

_____

_____

_____

_____

_____

_____

_____

_____

_____

_____

_____

_____

(NOTE: If you think it would be difficult for us to locate the establishment or where you live, give directions or attach map.)

COMPLAINT TAKEN BY:

_____

_____

Two important implications emerge from my research. First, the minimum wage is currently not an antipoverty program. Second, it would seem fruitful for economists, when analyzing the winners and losers created by a minimum wage, to focus some of their attention on prime-aged married women.

Appendix

Figures 1 and 2 display the forms used to file a complaint of violation of the Fair Labor Standards Act.

Bibliography

Gramlich, Edward M. "Impact of Minimum Wages on Other Wages, Employment, and Family Incomes." *Brookings Papers on Economic Activity* 2 (1976): 409–61.

1977 Minimum Wage Law: Fair Labor Standards Act with 1977 Amendments. Washington, D.C.: Bureau of National Affairs, 1977.

Silberman, Jonathan I., and Durden, Garey C. "Determining Legislative Preferences on the Minimum Wage: An Economic Approach." *Journal of Political Economy* 84 (April 1976): 317–29.

U.S. Department of Commerce, Bureau of the Census. *Statistical Abstract of the United States, 1979.* 100th ed.

Welch, Finis. *Minimum Wages: Issues and Evidence.* Washington, D.C.: American Enterprise Institute, 1978.

Commentary

An Overview of the Effect of Minimum Wages on Employment Opportunities

Sherwin Rosen

Recent research in labor economics has concentrated in large measure on the allocation of time to various uses, and it is now generally recognized that the earlier search for unemployment-creating effects of minimum wage legislation was a somewhat misguided research strategy based on simpleminded distinctions. The uses of time are too varied and complicated to be examined so easily. Instead, the best research in this field has concentrated on the employment-reducing aspects of minimum wage legislation rather than on the more nebulous effects on unemployment. The papers presented here extend the problem further, and investigate the effects of minimum wage legislation on schooling and other investment decisions as well. On the whole, they suggest that minimum wages reduce employment opportunities, but also tend to increase school enrollment of the young and to reduce the extent of on-the-job training of young workers. Although there are some substantial differences in the conclusions of the studies that will have to be reconciled eventually, that is far too difficult a job for a mere discussant, and I shall content myself with a more piecemeal critique of several papers.

The paper by Leighton and Mincer is one of the first attempts to ascertain the effects of minimum wages on on-the-job training. It uses an ingenious and convincing method for extracting these effects from panel data, which undoubtedly will be used by others in future research. The first part of the paper summarizes a model of market equilibrium, under minimum wage legislation, that Mincer developed a few years ago. This is fine so far as it goes, but I find the argument somewhat unconvincing because it seems to depend on the assumption of homogeneous labor categories. In fact, this is a confusing aspect of the whole literature on minimum wages, especially for those who (like me) think in terms of heterogeneous workers (for example, "quality" variations) within each job or skill classification. In that case, extra schooling can improve the worker's quality or efficiency within a given category. Since the minimum wage is not an efficiency standard, but rather is expressed in absolute units, schooling can increase productivity or efficiency above the minimum wage level within groups as well as between them. This is a simple and direct effect of minimum wages on schooling decisions and may well dispose of the second possibility raised by Leighton and Mincer: that the minimum wage rises by more than the probability of employment in the covered sector. My argument suggests that the probability rises to unity if enough schooling raises the worker's productivity above the minimum wage level.

I am not convinced by the argument, propounded in the paper, that absolute wage growth rather than relative wage growth (that is, the change in logarithms) is unquestionably the correct empirical specification. I would like to see the results supplemented by estimates based on relative changes. Perhaps the fundamental issue is whether the wage profile is better described in absolute or percentage terms. Mincer's previous work shows convincingly that the latter is the appropriate specification, so why was it abandoned here? On a more abstract level, the proper specification depends on the technology of human capital investments and the extent to which the marginal costs of investment increase with the level of investment. Since investment costs are never observed, there is no point in arguing strongly in favor of one specification or another on strictly a priori grounds. Why not let the data decide?

I also was not convinced by the arguments advanced for the effects of minimum wages on job tenure to the exclusion of other readily available and indistinguishable hypotheses. Arguments based on specific training among this group of young, low-wage and low-skilled workers strike me as rather artificial. What would the content of specific investment actually be in these cases? There are two other reasons why minimum wages might tend to increase tenure, however. First, if there really is queuing in the covered sector, then those persons who were lucky enough to obtain rationed jobs there at high wages would be foolish to give them up readily because of the rents they are earning. Second, it would appear to be rational for firms to hire people with better and more stable work records to fill jobs at the minimum wage. On both counts tenure as reported in the data would tend to increase. Perhaps looking at quit rates would be a useful supplement to Leighton and Mincer's work in this connection.

Finally, Leighton and Mincer have set up a fine apparatus that should be extended to the whole range of working conditions. The economic arguments suggesting that minimum wages adversely affect on-the-job training also apply to many other aspects of employment and working conditions, including on-the-job leisure and fringe benefits, such as vacation pay, life insurance, pensions, and so forth. I hope someone will use these methods to investigate those matters in greater detail than has been done in previous research.

The paper by Mattila is a fine complement to that of Leighton and Mincer, concentrating as it does on the effects of minimum wages on formal schooling decisions (as well as employment) of youth and using aggregate time series data rather than cross-sections and panels. Mattila makes a convincing case that minimum wages have induced people to remain in school longer than they otherwise would have done, presumably because the minimum wage increases the rate of return to schooling by reducing opportunity costs, and makes it worthwhile to bring productivity above the minimum standard set by the minimum wage as discussed above. It is surprising that these effects appear to go beyond high school level. It remains to be verified, but post-high-school training might consist of trade schools and junior college enrollments, which may be good substitutes for informal on-the-job training apprenticeship programs that Leighton and Mincer show to be impeded by minimum wages.

The paper itself is a model of clarity, and it would be superfluous for me to attempt to summarize it here. So let me make a few detailed remarks instead. First, Mattila examines the effect of minimum wages on enlistment in the armed services but does not discuss the estimates. This question deserves greater study, because one might anticipate effects here to be similar to those on formal schooling decisions. Second, it would be preferable to differentiate whites and blacks in these data, since relative wage differentials apparently have changed over time and also because there have been different school enrollment patterns among these groups, especially in recent years. Since both of these changes are in large part due to influences other than the minimum wage, they might well provide some additional information.

Third (this holds for some of the other studies too), the meaning of various labor force categories among children in the fourteen to sixteen age range and how this is or should be measured leaves something to be desired and seems to raise conceptual difficulties that are almost impossible to solve. It may be noted, for example, that the very definition of the labor force has changed, successively removing fourteen- and fifteen-year-olds from the definition, and this trend will probably extend to higher age cutoffs in the future. In addition, the very definition of unemployment in the Current Population Survey data changed during the period. Among this age group, conceptual difficulties of classification are clearly related to school enrollment. This problem does not affect the findings on school enrollment patterns, the main point of the paper. However, it is important in determining what normative significance one attributes to the labor force activity results. My own opinion would be "not very much."

Finally, as I understand it, the minimum wage index refers to all covered workers and not specifically to the youth labor market per se. Since we know from Welch's work that the industrial distribution of teenage labor has changed a great deal over this period, and that it is substantially different from the adult distribution, the most important part of the index, the measure actually used is almost surely in error. I do not mean to suggest that this vitiates Mattila's results, for which the specification has been set very intelligently. But perhaps some discussion of the possible biases resulting from use of this measure is in order.

The paper by Ragan resembles that of Mattila and uses the same kind of data, but differs somewhat in specification. Ragan concentrates on employment effects, not on school enrollment effects per se. Actually I was surprised to learn that Ragan's earlier study of this data showed no systematic effects of minimum wages on enrollments, especially since I found Mattila's results rather convincing. Ragan uses data for a shorter period than Mattila, which seems unlikely to be a major cause of any differences in results. Rather than annual data Ragan uses quarterly data, which are likely to be more informative about enrollment decisions because few people quit in mid-term, but rather tend to finish out the semester or year. The most interesting differences are in the way the data are classified. Anyone who is enrolled is classified "in school" by Mattila, while Ragan only classifies persons as such if they indicate that school is their major activity, that is, occupying the bulk of their time. These differences suggest that minimum wages largely affect part-time schooling, such as night school. This idea seems plausible enough to be worth further research. It is not entirely consistent with some other parts of Mattila's research, however, so some differences still remain to be resolved.

In his study, Ragan does find the expected employment effects. He also uses a minimum wage variable based on teenage employment weights instead of total covered adult and youth employment weights, which should be better in principle than the standard measure applied to this group. He did, however, use adult wage rates and not youth wages. A selection problem that relates to the choice of categories exists for both Ragan's and Mattila's work. If, as Mattila indicates, minimum wages keep people in school longer, the people they are likely to affect in this way probably come from the upper portion of the ability and motivation distribution among those who would otherwise have quit school. If so, the not-enrolled group as well as the enrolled group would tend to change its composition over time, the former decreasing in quality and the latter increasing in quality. Thus, one might expect the relative minimum wage effects on both groups to change over time.

I have two brief comments on Ragan's indirect approach. First, it seems to me that the measures of the minimum wage and youth wage variables contain a built-in positive correlation, so that it is not surprising that the estimated effect is positive. The youth wage measure includes minimum wages and its coverage is somewhat similar to that of the minimum wage measure, so it is not clear that they are independent measures. While I have no better measure to suggest, this possible dependence should be kept in mind in interpreting the results. Second, the specification relating changes in wages to changes in minimum wages, or changes in employment to changes in wages, when the other variables such as unemployment and population are in level form, is somewhat mysterious. In terms of the theory of the minimum wage, an equation all in level form, or one in which all variables are first differenced clearly, seems more appropriate. I would not even be surprised if there were many distributed lag effects lurking in the data that have not been examined.

Cunningham's paper is the most ambitious that I read and also presents some results that are at variance with those of other authors. He first analyzes the employment effects of a minimum wage within the context of a general equilibrium model with three factors of production. This is an interesting exercise because it shows that the effects are not generally all in one direction, independent of substitution possibilities and supply parameters of the model. Cunningham also analyzes some of the circumstances under which school enrollment is encouraged or discouraged in the context of this kind of model, again showing that the effects could be either negative or positive. Finally, his empirical work is based on cross-section rather than time series data and is rendered difficult by the necessity of holding constant values for employment and school status probabilities in the absence of the minimum wage. While this is an important conceptual point, it is not clear that the data are sufficient for this difficult task, and Cunningham does not explain his methods in sufficient detail. In any case, he does find the employment effect of minimum wage legislation that most other people find. He also finds discouragement of school enrollment rather than the encouragement found by Mattila in time series data. There is some major work to be done in resolving these findings, especially since Mattila's specification includes estimates of rates of return to schooling as independent variables. These estimates in a sense begin to resolve the conceptual problem of controls that Cunningham's specification is designed to deal with.

One final and perhaps most important comment: All these papers have attempted to ascertain the direction of the minimum wage effects, more or less resting content with a negative or positive finding. Clearly this is the first order of business, especially since data deficiencies have been a major limitation. However, these papers are very sophisticated and contain some actual estimates of the empirical magnitude of the effects being studied. This is clearly the most important question of all. We are beginning to get to the position of actually ascertaining the magnitude of the welfare loss of minimum wage legislation. Do the effects reported here suggest a significant reduction in national income and product due to minimum wage legislation as a fraction of GNP? I believe that most economists of today, as distinct from the case even fifteen years ago, agree that minimum wages lead to distortions and welfare losses, without having a major useful impact on income distribution. What major disagreement exists now concerns the practical magnitude of the effects and whether these issues are important enough to fight about with so many other distortions worth attacking in the economy. The research in this session should begin to answer that important question.

Employment Aspects of the Fair Labor Standards Act: Comments on the Phillips and Ehrenberg-Schumann Essays

Solomon William Polachek

The Fair Labor Standards Act has been in existence for over forty years. As indicated by the papers in this volume, many consequences of the law are not well understood. Many aspects have not even been examined. The Phillips and Ehrenberg-Schumann papers are examples of such studies analyzing dimensions of employment that have not yet been formally modeled. The Phillips paper posits that the increased unemployment caused by higher minimum wages increased criminal ("socially pathological") behavior most particularly among black youth. The Ehrenberg-Schumann paper examines the impact of the overtime provision. I discuss both of these works, but concentrate on Ehrenberg and Schumann mainly because legislation is currently being considered to increase the overtime pay premium from time and a half to double time. Thus the topic has political significance and warrants attention.

The Phillips Essay

Many governmental programs have unanticipated side effects. In the case of minimum wage legislation, few, if any, studies analyze the impact of such programs on criminal behavior. The Phillips paper is an exception, and thus noteworthy. The story told is simple: Minimum wages increase unemployment, and thus raise the relative wage of illegitimate versus legitimate activities. Given the increased relative wages (not to mention flexible hours), those groups most affected by the disemployment effects of minimum wage have the highest propensity to move into crime. Phillips illustrates his point by a series of graphs depicting the rise in (teenage) unemployment rates, the relative increase of black-to-white school and military enrollments, and the relative increase in property crime arrest rates, especially for blacks. In addition, regression

NOTE: The author wishes to thank John Cogan for making available some of the time series data used in this comment. In addition, he has received helpful comments from John Cogan, Thomas Kniesner, and Simon Rottenberg, and most able research assistance from Nancy Kawakita.

491

analysis indicates a positive (though statistically weaker) relationship between the time derivatives of the number of blacks and whites not working and the arrest rates.

Phillips's story is plausible. One can view crime as an industry not covered by the minimum wage. As unemployment in the covered sector increases, the number of individuals entering crime should increase. Since the strongest impact is on teenagers, we would expect participation in criminal activity to increase most for this group. The statistical analysis presented relates minimum wages to unemployment, and unemployment to criminal activity; it does not deal with a direct relationship between minimum wage and arrests. With no *direct* evidence linking minimum wage to arrests, it is difficult not to be skeptical about the strength of the hypothesis. To illustrate, I present what I see as three paradoxes presented in Phillips's figure 6—the crux of the paper.

First, evidence exists that certain groups are more affected by a minimum wage than others. Teenagers, and especially black teenagers, suffer more unemployment than adults (see Phillips's figure 1 illustrating the widening of the black-white unemployment gap). If unemployment is correlated with criminal activity, then criminal activity should rise more quickly for nonwhites than whites, and least quickly for adults. Figure 6 does *not* show such data. The relative increase in arrest rates is *not* significantly greater for nonwhites than for whites (arrests for both groups nearly doubled between 1964 and 1977); and the relative increase in teenage arrests (especially for nonwhites) does *not* exceed that of adults.

Second, dollar increases in minimum wages have occurred only in selected years. In the period under study, these increases occured in 1963, 1967, 1968, 1974, 1975, 1976, and 1978. While the minimum wage rose in these years, inflationary increases in other wages necessarily caused the *real* minimum wage to *fall* in the intervening years. Such declines in the minimum wage should, according to Phillips's hypothesis, imply a decline in the growth rate of arrests. Such declines (with the exception of black arrests during the period 1968–1972) are not obvious.

Third, barring reporting problems, female crime rates are increasing more quickly than those of males or blacks (table 1). This pattern implies that the minimum wage affects females more than males, when in fact studies reveal the opposite.

Even though data and reporting problems answer some of these questions, I suspect the simultaneous influence of many socioeconomic factors. For this reason, I suggest direct tests of the hypothesis that minimum wage increases result in greater crime rates. One needs to perform statistical multivariate analysis comparable to the analyses of

Mincer and Welch on unemployment effects.[1] In addition, it is essential to include an explicit account of the coverage rate changes.

The Ehrenberg-Schumann Essay

The Overtime Provision of the Fair Labor Standards Act. The overtime provision of the Fair Labor Standards Act calls for a time-and-a-half payment to employees working over forty hours per week. The intention of this provision was partly humanitarian, to limit working hours to reasonable and healthy amounts, but for the most part, it was aimed at raising the number of people employed. The logic is obvious: high overtime payment would motivate firms to substitute *new* workers at straight time instead of increasing the hours of the existing work force.

Ehrenberg and Schumann in their tables 3 and 4 assert that fixed hiring costs as well as fringe benefits have been increasing over the last few decades. Such increases in the "fixity" of labor implies that the relative costs of firms paying time and a half for overtime versus hiring new workers is secularly declining, and should lead to increases in the amount of overtime observed throughout the economy. In order to raise employment levels and at the same time decrease unemployment, some have suggested increasing the required overtime from time and a half to double time. The Ehrenberg-Schumann study assesses the impact on employment of such a change in the overtime pay provisions of the Fair Labor Standards Act.

The analysis uses Ehrenberg's past work[2] on the relationship between the ratio of per employee nonwage labor cost to the overtime wage rate, and average annual overtime hours per employee. The procedure entails using this relationship to calculate the decrease in overtime hours associated with increased overtime wages. This estimate, divided by 2,000 hours, serves as an upper bound for the number of new employees to be hired. This amounts to between 160,000 and 1,500,000 workers, or an increase in employment from 0.3 to 4.0 percent.

The Ehrenberg-Schumann estimates are preliminary and perhaps premature. Even so, I contend that their approach is misleading. Ehrenberg and Schumann suggest that there is a positive (negative) relationship between mean average weekly overtime hours and unemployment (employment). Direct macroeconomic evidence, however, implies

---

[1] J. Mincer, "Unemployment Effects of Minimum Wages," *Journal of Political Economy* 84 (August 1976): S87–S104; and F. Welch, "Minimum Wage Legislation in the United States," *Economic Inquiry* 12 (September 1974): 285–318.

[2] R. Ehrenberg, "Fringe Benefits and Overtime Behavior" (Lexington, Mass.: D.C. Heath, 1971).

TABLE 1
PROPERTY CRIME ARREST RATE FROM FBI UNIFORM CRIME REPORTS, 1963–1977

A. BY SEX

Year	Estimated Population per 1,000 Arrests	Number of Reporting Agencies	Male		Female	
			Under 18	18 or over	Under 18	18 or over
1963	103,146	3,239	222,515	183,151	25,433	31,545
1964	110,340	3,115	277,394	216,788	35,222	40,168
1965	114,969	3,355	295,772	227,227	43,131	45,019
1966	129,384	3,678	332,778	244,890	51,002	49,762
1967	129,384	3,678	354,108	266,607	55,069	58,442
1968	128,095	3,999	372,368	269,887	58,364	59,395
1969	128,095	3,999	317,898	289,050	69,024	70,711
1970	139,239	4,483	416,284	369,875	86,777	94,859
1971	139,239	4,483	432,653	399,524	92,297	104,522
1972	148,175	5,575	402,700	369,552	93,763	106,745
1973	148,175	5,575	426,471	384,879	98,216	118,660
1974	113,918	3,948	423,539	385,240	101,062	118,443
1975	145,720	5,974	513,351	510,264	123,857	167,152
1976	188,580	9,582	576,426	629,690	136,228	204,204
1977	188,580	9,582	568,764	611,564	136,470	206,780

494

B. By Race

Year	Estimated Population per 1,000 Arrests	Number of Reporting Agencies	White		Black	
			Under 18	18 or over	Under 18	18 or over
1963	116,952	3,951	370,326		152,815	
1964	117,874	3,940	230,289	178,814	92,139	80,593
1965	125,139	4,043	241,986	187,997	105,814	90,023
1966	128,163	4,021	264,459	192,433	109,839	89,740
1967	135,203	4,508	290,236	219,039	126,987	120,020
1968	136,780	4,216	387,127	294,103	59,652	65,655
1969	133,078	4,627	298,152	243,146	146,955	134,903
1970	142,474	5,208	315,173	284,611	148,208	152,463
1971	146,564	5,610	343,051	315,489	150,260	165,785
1972	150,922	6,114	365,298	334,846	155,163	175,627
1973	144,956	5,914	371,133	327,987	150,415	164,805
1974	124,353	5,222	390,980	345,833	155,220	182,361
1975	169,455	7,993	500,599	492,827	189,691	244,604
1976	173,488	10,058	444,930	467,827	174,592	246,048
1977	197,004	10,864	515,536	548,701	199,206	286,140

NOTES: Estimated population reprents the sum of the population of each reporting agency, not total national population. Property crime is defined as offenses of burglary, larceny-theft, and motor vehicle theft.

SOURCE: Table 1 figures are obtained from two tables in the Arrest Data Section of the FBI Uniform Crime Reports (1963–1977). The two tables are labeled "Total Arrest Trends by Sex" and "Total Arrests by Race."

that a rise in the overtime wage would actually *decrease* employment, *increase* unemployment, and *lower* per capita real output. This is so because the number of workers and their hours are partially "tied goods." Increasing the cost of overtime implicitly raises the total cost of *each* worker and thereby lowers the *number* of workers demanded *as well as* their hours. While my results are preliminary, they are strong enough to warrant some concern in taking the Ehrenberg-Schumann findings at face value.

Others may even argue that overtime pay changes neither increase nor decrease hours, but instead that the overtime provision is superfluous and ineffective. Such arguments claim that if some hours of the week are paid at higher overtime wage rates and others at lower normal wages rates, then the market will adjust the lower rates downward, so that average rates for all hours worked will be what they would have been in the absence of legal constraints. Such an argument is incorrect. Hours are determined by *marginal, not average,* wage rates. Thus constraints on marginal wage rates affect hours. This effect is synonymous to the impact of alternative pay schemes (for example, piece rates versus hourly wage rates) on work hours and on allocation of agricultural resources under various share tenancy plans.[3]

Evidence. Average weekly overtime hours depend on cyclical as well as secular changes. Ehrenberg and Schumann measure time trends in overtime hours by means of regression analysis reproduced in table 2 (columns 1 and 3). (I concentrate on data on nondurable manufacturing because these data exhibited the largest time trend, according to the Ehrenberg-Schumann study.) Their linear model yields a 3–4 percent annual increase. Not having the appropriate series for real changes in GNP, I replicate their analyses using the unemployment rate to adjust for cyclical changes. As can be seen (columns 2 and 3), I obtain similar trends. However, estimation using a quadratic time term (columns 5 and 6) yields a *significant negative value.* Thus it is not obvious that overtime hours are secularly increasing. My results indicate a peak near 1970, with declining overtime hours thereafter. Direct evidence of the relationship between overtime and employment (unemployment) also does not conform to the Ehrenberg-Schumann hypothesis. Figures 1 and 2 (and table 3) illustrate a strong *positive* correlation between employment and overtime. Figures 3 and 4 (and table 4) illustrate a strong *negative* correlation between unemployment and overtime. These results

[3] R. Woodward, "Professional Work Leisure Decisions under Alternative Remuneration Methods," paper presented at the Econometric Society Meetings, Atlantic City, N.J., 1976; and S. Cheung, "Private Property Right and Share Cropping," *Journal of Political Economy* 76 (November/December 1968): 1107–22.

TABLE 2
TIME TRENDS IN OVERTIME, 1956–1977

Dependent Variable: Nondurable Manufacturing Average Weekly Overtime

	E-S linear time trend	Replication linear time trend	E-S linear time trend cyclically adjusted	Replication linear time trend cyclically adjusted	Quadratic time trend	Quadratic time trend cyclically adjusted
C	NR	2.116	NR	2.772	0.341	1.67
		(10.9)		(18.1)	(0.8)	(4.2)
T	0.040	0.039	0.034	0.047	0.224	0.153
	(4.4)	(4.2)	(4.3)	(8.4)	(5.1)	(4.2)
T^2					−0.0052	−0.003
					(4.3)	(2.9)
G			0.006			
			(3.0)			
U				−0.183		−0.141
				(6.3)		(4.9)
R^2	.47	.47	.63	.83	.73	.88

NOTE: C = constant (intercept)

T = time trend (equals 1 in 1948 for columns 2,4,5, and 6)

G = change in real GNP

U = unemployment rate (males 16 and over)

NR = not reported

t-values are given in parentheses. Ehrenberg-Schumann is abbreviated E-S.

SOURCES: U.S. Department of Labor, *1979 Employment and Training Report of the President*; U.S. Department of Labor, *Manpower Reports of the President* (prior to 1975); and Ehrenberg and Schumann, "Overtime Pay Provisions," this volume, table 2 (for overtime data).

FIGURE 1
AVERAGE WEEKLY OVERTIME HOURS IN NONDURABLE MANUFACTURING AND UNEMPLOYMENT RATE FOR MALES AGE 16 AND OVER, 1956–1977

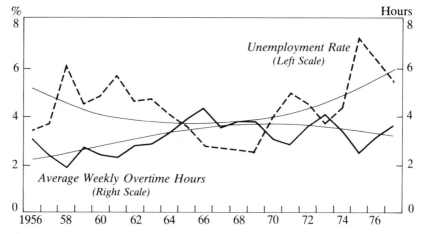

NOTE: Thin lines represent values with cyclical components removed.

SOURCES: U.S. Department of Labor, *1979 Employment and Training Report of the President;* idem, *Manpower Report of the President,* prior to 1975; and Ehrenberg and Schumann, "Overtime Pay Provisions," table 2, for overtime data.

hold even when using two- and three-stage least squares to adjust for cyclical variations in each time series (see the two-stage least-squares results of tables 3 and 4, as well as the three-stage least-squares estimates presented in table 5). These tables clearly indicate that decreasing overtime hours by increasing the overtime wage does not correspond to higher levels of employment and *lower* levels of unemployment. How does one explain the discrepancy between my findings and the assertions of Ehrenberg and Schumann?

The Resolution of a Paradox. Ehrenberg and Schumann use a microeconomic approach based on Ehrenberg's past research.[4] Essentially they solve an equation of the form

$$OT = a_0 + a_1 R + a_2 X \qquad (1)$$

using establishment data (where OT is annual overtime hours per employee, R is the ratio of measured weekly quasi-fixed nonwage labor costs per employee to the overtime wage rate, and X is a vector of exogenous predetermined standardizing variables). By appropriately

[4] Ehrenberg, "Fringe Benefits."

498

FIGURE 2
Average Weekly Overtime in Durable Manufacturing and Unemployment Rate for Males Age 16 and over, 1956–1977

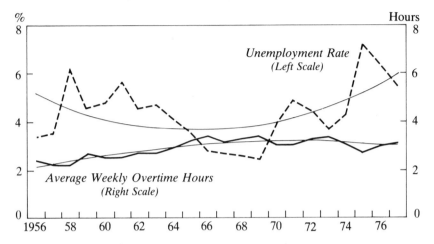

NOTE: Thin lines represent values with cyclical component removed.

SOURCES: See figure 1.

modifying R, Ehrenberg and Schumann use equation (1) to extrapolate the effect of increasing the premium on overtime hours. They find a 4 to 50 percent decline in overtime hours. If all this reduction in overtime were converted to new full-time positions, employment would increase between 0.3 and 4.0 percent. Ehrenberg and Schumann admit that this projection is an overestimate and attempt adjustment by considering five factors: (1) the possibility of nonzero wage elasticities, (2) moonlighting, (3) the skill distribution of the unemployed and those who work overtime, (4) indivisibilities, and (5) compliance with the overtime pay provisions. They claim that each factor is of relatively minor importance, however. *They make no mention of the possibility that in combination these factors could actually cause a reduction in total employment.*

I claim that the findings of the Ehrenberg-Schumann paper are inherently biased. By estimating the reduction in overtime hours with one equation, and correcting for employment changes with other independently calculated equations (such as the Hamermesh[5] total manhour demand equation), the authors neglect the fact that hours overtime *and* number of employees are *simultaneously* related.

The simultaneity is obvious when we view production in the classical

[5] D. Hamermesh, "Econometric Studies of Labor Demand and Their Application to Policy Analysis," *Journal of Human Resources* 11 (Fall 1976): 507–25.

TABLE 3

The Relationship between Employment and Overtime, 1956–1977

| | *Dependent Variable: Percent Employed (Males 25–54)* | | Two-stage least-squares |
| | Ordinary least-squares | | |
	Linear time trend	Quadratic time trend	Linear time trend
C	86.33	85.87	80.12
	(65.7)	(53.8)	(30.1)
O	4.33	4.02	4.32
	(7.5)	(4.9)	(6.0)
T	−0.31	−0.17	−0.28
	(9.3)	(0.6)	(7.2)
T^2		−0.003	
		(0.5)	
R^2	.82	.83	$F = 34.7$

NOTE: $C \equiv$ Constant (intercept)
$O \equiv$ Nondurable manufacturing average weekly overtime
$T \equiv$ Time trend (1948 = 1)
t-values are given in parentheses.
SOURCES: U.S. Department of Labor, *1979 Employment and Training Report of the President*; idem, *Manpower Reports of the President* (prior to 1975); and Ehrenberg and Schumann, "Overtime Pay Provisions," this volume, table 2 (for overtime data).

TABLE 4

The Relationship between Unemployment and Overtime

| | *Dependent Variable: Adult Male Unemployment Rate* | | Two-stage least-squares |
| | Ordinary least-squares | | |
	Linear time trend	Quadratic time trend	Linear time trend
C	11.46	10.90	15.67
	(8.5)	(6.7)	(5.3)
O	−3.71	−4.09	−3.04
	(6.3)	(4.9)	(3.8)
T	0.19	0.36	0.13
	(5.55)	(1.3)	(3.1)
T^2		−0.004	
		(0.6)	
R^2	.69	.70	$F = 8.25$

NOTE: See table 3 for definitions.

FIGURE 3

AVERAGE WEEKLY OVERTIME HOURS IN NONDURABLE MANUFAC-
TURING AND PERCENTAGE OF MALES AGE 25–54 EMPLOYED, 1956–1977

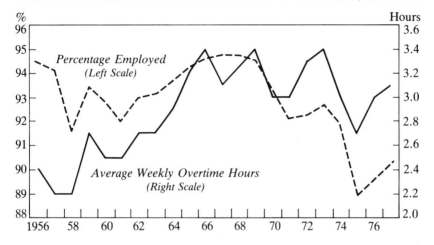

framework. Consider output (Q) determined by capital (K) and labor
(L):

$$Q = Q\,(K, L) \tag{2}$$

The quantity of labor can be augmented by increasing either hours per
worker (H) or number of workers (N). Thus labor (L) can be viewed
as a vector [L = (H,N)], and equation (2) can be rewritten as

$$Q = Q\,(K, H, N) \tag{3}$$

Capital, number of workers, and hours per worker are thus inputs. Each
can be traded for another in accordance with inherent substitutability
parameters within the production process. Holding capital constant and
assuming normal properties of the production function, one can draw
isoquants illustrating combinations of H and N that yield given output
levels (figure 5). An isocost curve (defined by ABC) changes direction
at forty hours per worker, the point where overtime wages are mandated. For a given output, optimal inputs of H and N are determined
by the tangency between the isocost curve and the relevant isoquant.

A secular decline in the overtime wage implies a rotation of the
right-hand portion of the isocost curve (for example to ABD), and
appropriate changes in hours overtime *as well as* number of workers
[from (H,H) to (H',N')]. Obviously the relationship between overtime
hours and number of workers depends on the isoquant structure. How-

501

FIGURE 4

AVERAGE WEEKLY OVERTIME HOURS IN DURABLE MANUFACTURING
AND PERCENTAGE OF MALES AGE 25–54 EMPLOYED, 1956–1977

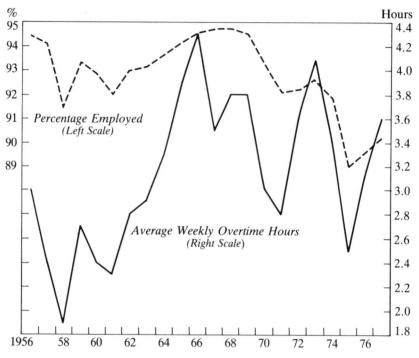

ever, when the isoquants are drawn as usually depicted, increases in the overtime wage (rotation of isocost curve from ABC to ABE) cause a decrease in overtime hours *as well as* a decrease in number of workers; that is, equilibrium point (H'',N'') compared with (H,N). This result is strengthened when scale effects are permitted.

It is essential to realize that number of workers and hours per worker are determined simultaneously. Treating each as an independent decision necessarily biases estimates of the impact of changing overtime wages. Tacitly assuming infinite substitutability (as Ehrenberg and Schumann attempt) is obviously erroneous. I therefore suggest that demand functions for hours per worker and number of workers be estimated together within a simultaneous equation approach. Only then can the true substitutability be determined and estimates be obtained for trade-offs between hours and workers. Not estimating them simultaneously leads to biases that could account for the discrepancy between the results I present and those of Ehrenberg and Schumann.

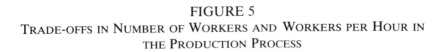

FIGURE 5

TRADE-OFFS IN NUMBER OF WORKERS AND WORKERS PER HOUR IN
THE PRODUCTION PROCESS

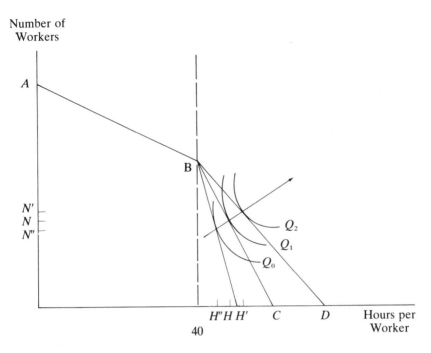

The Efficiency of Modifying the Overtime Provision: A Concluding Comment. Even if modification of the overtime provision were to lead to greater employment, it is not obvious that increasing overtime wages would be an appropriate policy. Increasing overtime wages raises production costs and necessarily leads to lower per capita output. Increasing the overtime wage premium may not be optimal even if it were to raise employment. In a welfare sense, governmental transfer policies could achieve greater per capita income levels as well as a more appropriate income distribution. Rather than dictating inefficient means of production, firms and workers receiving excess profits and wages could be taxed so that wealth could be spread throughout the population. Creating inefficiencies in the production process only creates lower output levels. As a result, less wealth remains to be distributed, and on the average all suffer.

Taken together, the Phillips and Ehrenberg-Schumann papers address important topics not as yet analyzed in the literature. Their approaches are interesting and novel. My comments are designed not to

TABLE 5
THREE-STAGE LEAST-SQUARE ESTIMATES

Unemployment Rate $= 15.67 - 3.04$ Overtime $+ 0.13\ T + X_1$
　　　　　　　　　　　(5.3)　(3.8)　　　　　　　(3.1)

Overtime $= 0.26 + 0.008$ Unemployment Rate $+ 0.24\ T - 0.005T^2 + X_2$
　　　　　(0.2)　(0.1)　　　　　　　　　　　　　(2.3)　(-1.8)

Employment Rate $= 80.12 + 4.32$ Overtime $- 0.28\ T + X_1$
　　　　　　　　　(30.1)　(6.0)　　　　　　(7.2)

Overtime $= 0.99 - 0.007$ Employment Rate $+ 0.249\ T - 0.005\ T^2 + X_2$
　　　　　(0.1)　(0.1)　　　　　　　　　　(2.0)　　(1.5)

$X_i \equiv$ exogenous identifying variables

NOTE: See table 2 for definitions; t-values are given in parentheses.

criticize, but to present alternative viewpoints and encourage the authors and others to extend this research and offer more precise answers to important policy issues.

Bibliography

Cheung, S. "Private Property Right and Share Cropping." *Journal of Political Economy* 76 (November/December 1968): 1107–22.

Ehrenberg, R. *Fringe Benefits and Overtime Behavior.* Lexington, Mass.: D.C. Heath, 1971.

Hamermesh, D. "Econometric Studies of Labor Demand and Their Application to Policy Analysis." *Journal of Human Resources* 11 (Fall 1976): 507–25.

Mincer, J. "Unemployment Effects of Minimum Wages." *Journal of Political Economy* 84 (August 1976): S87–S104.

Welch, F. "Minimum Wage Legislation in the United States." *Economic Inquiry* 12 (September 1974): 285–318.

Woodward, R. "Professional Work Leisure Decisions under Alternative Remuneration Methods." Paper presented at the Econometric Society Meetings, Atlantic City, 1976.

Comments on the Substitution Effects of Minimum Wage Legislation

William Fellner

Three interesting papers presented here are concerned with the impact of minimum wages on specific areas of activity. These include that of Professor Gordon on the household sector, that of Professor Gardner on agriculture, and that of Professors Trapani and Moroney on seasonal cotton farm work. The activities in question have on the whole been of declining relative significance, and the papers discuss the factors that need to be taken into account in an appraisal of the effect of minimum wages.

From the Gordon study, I conclude that attempts to isolate the effect of the extension of minimum wage legislation to household workers must for the time being be based on very general considerations, and that so far these do not suggest any noteworthy effect. This result may well have to do with the ease with which it is possible to get around the provisions in that sector of the labor market. The Trapani-Moroney paper presents a regression analysis as well as a general discussion of the presumptive effect of minimum wages on seasonal cotton farm workers, and the authors suggest proportionately significant negative employment effects for two of the three geographical regions examined. In the Gardner paper, too, a negative employment effect is demonstrated in part by regression analysis, here relating to agricultural workers in general.

To the extent that minimum wages raise real wage rates for specific types of workers, they reduce employment for these worker categories. This conclusion is unavoidable, given reasonable assumptions. To deny this would be to deny that, barring very eccentric assumptions, a demand function needs to have a negative partial derivative with respect to the "own price" of the commodity or service demanded. Extending this proposition concerning a negative employment effect to minimum wage legislation in general, however, assumes that the legislation does in fact raise real wage rates for the workers in question. This in turn implies that the required minimum wage is high enough to have this effect and that the requirement is not circumvented. The first of these assumptions does not seem to have been satisfied in one of the geographical regions explored by Trapani and Moroney, and the second does not seem to have been satisfied in the household-work market explored by Gordon.

But despite such exceptions, these considerations strongly suggest that, in the markets to which the minimum wage requirement applies, there will develop a negative employment effect *whenever the minimum wage requirement achieves what it intends to achieve.* This general conclusion, analogous to that asserting the negative sign of the partial derivative of demand with respect to price, is worth stressing because of the very large difficulties standing in the way of obtaining trustworthy quantitative results from regression analysis. The uncertainties attaching to the regression technique are substantially greater in all areas of research than is nowadays typically suggested. These uncertainties grow particularly large when we are considering a small segment of the labor market that is interrelated with many other markets, and when there exist no easily defensible assumptions as to the explanatory variables that should be included in models of limited size striving for quantitative precision. This, by the way, is clearly recognized by those of our authors who use regression analysis.

Two other papers—that of Professors Cox and Oaxaca and that of Professor Colberg—consider a question of great interest and direct one's thoughts to an aspect of the social-political process which is intriguing and deserves further exploration. The question which I and, I think, *they* have in mind is: *Which* groups are motivated by the desire to raise the real wage rates of some recipients of substandard wages at the expense of the employment of other substandard wage earners?

I will somewhat further elaborate on this problem by referring to the excellent 1978 study of Finis Welch.[1] The data to which I am referring are for employees paid by the hour, outside agriculture and households.

With some speculative filling in of gaps in the information which I as a nonspecialist in this area could readily find, I conclude from Welch's data that in 1973 the age classes sixteen through twenty-four and beyond sixty-four years made up the greater part (possibly about 60 percent) of those workers who in that year earned less than the wage to which the minimum was about to be raised (from $1.60 to $2.00). A high proportion of those earning less than the minimum were part-time workers, which is true not only of those low-wage workers belonging to the very young and the old age classes just mentioned but also of those belonging to other age classes. The total percentage earning less than the $2.00 minimum wage was probably about 20 percent if we limit ourselves to hourly wage workers outside agriculture and households.

[1] *Minimum Wages, Issues and Evidence* (Washington, D.C.: American Enterprise Institute, 1978), pp. 16–19.

The below-minimum percentage was presumably between 10 and 15 percent for all employees in the American economy. Given the presumption that the greater part of this 10 to 15 percent belonged to the age classes sixteen through twenty-four and (to a lesser extent) to those beyond sixty-four, the question then is: Who had such an intense interest in raising the wages of *some part* of the low-wage population by a method involving the worsening of the employment outlook for *another part* of the same 10 to 15 percent of all workers, knowing that the very young and the old are very highly represented in this 10 to 15 percent subset of all workers? After all, there *was* enough interest in doing this to achieve the adoption of raising minimum wage requirements on that occasion (1973) as well as on many earlier and later occasions, in spite of resistance that cannot have been lacking. Further, such legislation has been adopted again and again in spite of the fact that the general value judgments of the political community at large surely give precedence to employment opportunities for the young and the old and for other part-time workers over the entirely arbitrary notion that a person should be employable only if he is worth to an employer at least about 50 percent of the average factory wage. I think very few people would subscribe to this latter judgment if they were asked for their opinion directly.

Along the lines of the Cox-Oaxaca and the Colberg papers, the answer presumably is that it is possible to identify articulate and in part very well organized groups *outside* the 10–15 percent of low-wage workers whose representatives believe that their membership also benefits along with direct minimum wage beneficiaries. Colberg stresses mainly regional interests; Cox and Oaxaca call attention mainly to the interests and influence of unions. These indirect beneficiaries are likely to be among the relatively highly paid whose real wage rates are expected to be pulled up along with the minimum. Assuming that the representatives of these articulate and well-organized groups know how to serve their own interests effectively—"know what they are doing"—the question remains: *In what way* are these groups in fact benefitting?

They may benefit in one of two ways. In whichever of these two ways they benefit, it is important to realize that politically *their* benefit is at the heart of the matter. To paraphrase Finis Welch, regulating markets in order to give some of the have-nots somewhat more by depriving other have-nots of their jobs is not a program for which any influential group would be likely to develop much enthusiasm. The fact that the indirect benefit of the relatively well paid is politically at the heart of the matter should strengthen the opposition of most observers, since those members of the labor force whose employment opportunities this interference with market forces *reduces* are low-paid workers.

Nevertheless, the consequences depend very much on whether the relatively well-paid benefit by one or the other of two distinguishable processes. This is the point I would like to stress in my present comments.

To the extent that the indirect benefits accrue as a result of the substitution of relatively well paid for poorly paid workers (because some of the poorly paid workers now earn a somewhat higher wage while others become unemployed), there is at least an increase in the demand for the services of the relatively well-paid workers. However, the large proportion of the very young and of the old, and of part-time workers in general, in the low-wage population makes it exceedingly unlikely that this should be the whole story. Substitution is very unlikely to describe the whole story because the elasticity of substitution away from the very young and from the old (and away from part-time workers in general) toward groups in the prime-age full-time category is very unlikely to be high. Part of the indirect benefit seems to have accrued to the relatively well paid in a different way, not by the substitution of well-paid for low-wage workers. Part of the benefit has developed as a result of the resistance of the highly organized groups to a narrowing of wage differentials and, indeed, of their ability to increase these differentials in the bargaining process. Recently these differentials in favor of the highly organized have risen in relation to the wages of the relatively low paid, that is, not merely relative to the minimum wage population but also relative to those workers who may have done no better than to maintain their differentials over the minimum wage. The highly organized would presumably have found it more difficult to achieve their actual money-wage increases if these increases had involved an *even greater* increase of the differentials in their own favor. This is so because of the attention paid to relative positions in the bargaining process.

To the extent that rising minimum wages have led to higher money-wage increases across the board, they have given rise to a problem that needs to be distinguished from that of the substitution of relatively well-paid for low-wage workers. If an across-the-board money-wage-raising effect with unchanging or rising differentials for the relatively well-paids is accommodated by demand-management policy, it leads to inflation. If, on the other hand, demand-management does not accommodate these money-wage increases, then during a possibly lengthy adjustment period the rate of resource utilization will remain subnormal.

In other words, to the extent that minimum wage policies become essentially part of the general money-wage raising mechanism, these policies make it more difficult for the monetary authority to remain on a noninflationary course or to return to it. It remains true, of course, that within the low-wage population minimum wages raise the incomes of some and deprive others of their jobs. What needs to be added is that aside from the substitution aspect of the problem, which at present may not be its most prominent aspect, minimum wages have helped the relatively well paid to raise their wages without having to face the difficulties of creating an *even greater* increase of the differentials in their own favor than those which they have already succeeded in securing for themselves in the bargaining process. Creating even greater differentials through wage bargaining might have been difficult for the relatively well paid, quite aside from any adverse substitution effects they might have suffered. In view of the seriousness of the inflation problem with which we are faced, the role of minimum wage policies in the general wage-raising process deserves a good deal of attention—no less attention than do the microeconomic allocational consequences of these policies.

Employment Effects and Determinants of Minimum Wage Laws: An Analysis of Current Research

Barry R. Chiswick

Five of the papers presented here fall neatly into two categories. One is the traditional minimum wage research topic, the analysis of the effects on employment of the coverage and level of the minimum wage. The second is a newer and less well researched topic, the determinants of minimum wage laws. I have some comments on both sets of papers. My task has been easier because each of the papers was both interesting and stimulating.

Employment Studies

The three employment studies include two econometric analyses of agriculture, the papers by Bruce Gardner on hired farm workers and by John Trapani and J. R. Moroney on seasonal cotton farm employment. The third is Kenneth Gordon's study of private household workers.

In industry studies it is important to recognize that there are two major aspects of substitution. There is substitution within the sector of other factors of production for low-wage workers, and there is substitution among sectors in the economy. The three sectoral employment studies vary in the extent to which these differential substitutions are explicitly considered. This is a matter of substantial importance in estimating the effect of the minimum wage. For example, is the estimated employment and unemployment impact of the minimum wage in the agricultural sector a reflection solely of substitutions within the sector, or does it also include the effect on the size of the sector? Indeed, it is because of sectoral substitutions that regional interests favoring a high minimum wage seek to impose it nationwide.

On a related point, is the minimum wage outside of the sector under study assumed to be held constant, or is it assumed that the minimum wage increases by the same proportion in all sectors? The disemployment effects may differ quite sharply under the two situations.

I am troubled by the lack of consideration of mandated employer

510

financed fringe benefits in all of the minimum wage studies. As nearly all firms are competitive in the labor market, particularly for workers with few specialized skills, average factor costs are relevant in the demand for labor. Average factor costs for labor exceed the wages workers receive by various direct and indirect taxes related to social legislation. In addition to the social security tax, there is unemployment insurance, workmen's compensation, the increased labor costs of Occupational Safety and Health Administration (OSHA) regulations, in some instances private pensions (Pension Reform Act of 1974), and possibly in the near future mandated contributions for national health insurance. These taxes raise the legal minimum employment cost of labor. (Employment tax credits would tend to have the opposite effect.)

Because of various ceilings, the mandated employer fringe benefits are not proportional to the wage rate, but rather are relatively greater for unskilled than for skilled workers. The relative minimum employment cost, the minimum wage plus mandated employer expenditures relative to the average employment cost, is greater than the relative minimum wage.

Perhaps more important, the absolute and relative difference between the relative minimum employment cost and the relative minimum wage has increased in the past four decades. First, there has been a spread of coverage of other social legislation. Domestic and farm work, the two occupations considered at this session, are now generally covered by social security, unemployment insurance, workmen's compensation, and, for farm workers, OSHA. Second, there has been a rise in the relative tax rates in the social insurance programs, particularly social security.

Time series studies of the minimum wage have ignored mandated employer fringe benefits. This misspecification increases the negative magnitude of the trend variable in an analysis of the employment of farm workers and domestics. That is, the trend variable captures the effect of the interaction of the minimum wage and the trend increase in mandated fringe benefits. Controlling for the trend, exclusion of the mandated fringe benefits from the analysis increases the measurement error in the minimum wage variable, biasing toward zero the total effect of the minimum wage on employment. Explicit incorporation of mandated employer-financed fringe benefits into the analysis would permit an estimation of the direct and indirect (interaction) effects of the minimum wage.

The expanded social insurance programs also affect the supply side of the market. For example, the recent extension of unemployment compensation to agriculture has altered the seasonality of the supply of farm labor.[1] An important variable in the labor supply equation not fully exploited in Kenneth Gordon's discussion of private household employment is the magnitude of relative welfare payments. During the 1960s and up through 1974, the package of welfare benefits available for unskilled women with young children increased as a result of new programs (Medicaid, food stamps, housing subsidies), easier eligibility (Aid to Families with Dependent Children), and increased benefits within the programs. Since 1974, however, there has been no program expansion, eligibility has been tightened, and real welfare benefits have declined. These factors, combined with higher unemployment rates in alternative employment, may be responsible for ending and perhaps reversing the declining trend in household employment.

I do not share Gordon's pessimism about the fruitfulness of econometric research in the private household employment sector. Using data prior to the 1974 extension of minimum wage legislation to this sector, an econometric equation can be developed to explain statistically employment in this sector. Predicted employment after the extension of coverage could then be compared with observed employment to estimate the minimum wage effect. This technique was used successfully in the Trapani and Moroney study of the effect of the minimum wage on cotton farm employment, and in my own study of the effect of unemployment compensation on agricultural employment.

One of the assumptions of most time series econometric analyses, whether of the minimum wage or some other issue, is that the parameters are stable over time. In doctoral research recently completed, F. Terry Elder has analyzed the stability of the partial effect of the minimum wage on employment of selected demographic groups for the postwar period, replicating the equations of others (for example, Welch and Mincer), using a recursive residual procedure.[2] His preliminary findings are interesting and important. The magnitude (and in many instances even the sign) of the estimated minimum wage coefficient varies in a nonrandom pattern over the period. This may provide the means for reconciling the contradictory findings in the literature among studies covering different time periods.

Elder's findings must make us all more cautious in analyses of time series, whether of the minimum wage or other issues. And they raise two related questions: The first, obviously, is why does the effect vary in a nonrandom manner? What variables, not explicitly incorporated

[1] Barry R. Chiswick, "The Effect of Unemployment Compensation on a Seasonal Industry: Agriculture," *Journal of Political Economy* 84 (June 1976): 591–602.

[2] F. Terry Elder, "Employment and Labor Force Effects of Changes in the Federal Minimum Wage from 1966 to 1978: A Box Jenkins Approach"(Ph.D. dissertation, University of Illinois at Chicago Circle, 1980).

512

into the analysis, make the effect of the minimum wage vary over time? The second, how does one determine the relevant parameter for forecasting the effect of future increases in the relative minimum wage?

Determinants of Minimum Wage Laws

The two studies of the determinants of minimum wage laws are intriguing, but I am left with the unhappy feeling that the stories are incomplete. In his study of congressional voting patterns, Marshall Colberg finds that the primary economic variable, the state average manufacturing wage, is not significant. The existence of a state "right-to-work" law always has the "correct" sign and is often highly significant. But since right-to-work laws and minimum wage laws are very close cousins, are they not both determined by the same process? If so, the right-to-work law variable is endogenous. If it is to be included in the analysis, either a simultaneous system or an instrumental variables approach should be used.

Controlling for the effects of other variables, what is it about the South that results in stronger opposition to the spread of minimum wage coverage or higher minimum wage rates? Presumably region is a proxy for some relevant characteristic that varies geographically. In some studies it may represent climate, while in others, the level of economic development. In this instance climate is not relevant, and average wages may be a good proxy for the level of development. The opposition of the southern states is not ideological, for Colberg shows that region was not relevant for explaining voting patterns for a higher minimum wage in the District of Columbia. In addition, Florida congressmen were strong advocates in 1974 of extending the federal minimum wage at the mainland level to hotel and restaurant workers in the U.S. Virgin Islands. Without additional discussion of the interpretation of the region variable, and without further attempts to identify the underlying but unmeasured variables for which region is a proxy, the role of the region variable is a mystery.

James Cox and Ronald Oaxaca use mathematics and graphs to develop a complex four-sector model to explain attitudes toward the minimum wage. The only implications of the model are that high-wage workers benefit and the owners of firms that employ low-wage workers lose when minimum wage coverage is introduced, or the rate increased. I am reminded of Ockham's Razor—that simpler models are preferred to complex models if the result is the same. The Cox-Oaxaca implications could have been developed in a few paragraphs of prose. Or (since I do not pay for their time) they could return to their multisector model to see if there are any additional testable implications that could not be obtained from a simple two-sector structure.

The empirical counterparts of the Cox-Oaxaca theoretical variables are disturbing. Relative union membership in the state is used as a proxy for high-wage workers. The rate of union membership, however, varies systematically with industrial structure. And the rate of union membership for low-wage unskilled workers at or near the minimum wage also varies by state. Measures of the distribution of skills (for example, schooling and labor market experience) may be more useful proxies for high-wage workers than is union membership. Their only other explanatory variable is relative proprietary income, as a proxy for employers of low-wage workers. Proprietors are, however, heterogenous. The earnings of doctors and lawyers are generally reported as proprietary income, yet their employment of low-wage workers is quite different from that of small manufacturing, retail and related enterprises. In addition, from their procedure we do not know whether it is state differences in the relative number of proprietors or the relative income of the average proprietor that is responsible for the effects that emerge.

There is also an econometric problem. To the extent that the minimum wage has influenced unionization and proprietary income (and Cox and Oaxaca hypothesize that it lowers the latter), the explanatory variables are endogenous. Perhaps values of the explanatory variables in an earlier decade or a simultaneous system should have been used to guard against the endogeneity.

Because of these problems it is not surprising that the empirical results are disappointing. There are three dependent variables: the existence of a state minimum wage law, the extent of coverage if the law exists, and the state minimum wage. Unionization is significant only for the existence of a law. Relative proprietary income is negatively associated with the existence of the minimum wage and with its rate. Given the implications of their own model, however, the direction of causation for the proprietary income variable is ambiguous.

I share the thesis of the Colberg and Cox-Oaxaca papers that the enactment of minimum wage laws is not the result of ignorance. In spite of the adverse effects on many low-productivity workers, their employers, and the consumers of the goods and services they produce, minimum wage laws do benefit others. The beneficiaries include workers earning above the minimum wage, who are substitutes in production for low-wage labor, and employers (and their workers) in high-wage industries, producing goods and services that are substitutes in consumption for the goods and services produced by low-wage workers. For one reason or another, the latter are more effective in the political process. More research on the determinants of minimum wage laws will increase our understanding of both the political and the economic systems.

Comments on Differential Minimum Wages and Minimum Wage Policies

Isaac Ehrlich

Cotterill's and Gregory's papers share one specific theme: both deal, at least to some extent, with the desirability or effectiveness of differential minimum wages. The purposes of the differential wage policies they discuss are very different, however, and so is the general focus of the two papers. I shall therefore discuss them separately.

Cotterill: Differential Legal Minimum Wages

Phillip Cotterill's analysis is prompted by legislation pending in the U.S. Congress to create a youth minimum wage differential that would permit the hiring of persons under the age of twenty at a specific "discount" rate below the standard minimum wage for adults. This proposed legislation may, of course, share the fate of previous unsuccessful attempts at supplementary minimum wage legislation in Congress, but the fact that similar programs have already been adopted in other countries (Costa Rica is one such example) suggests that the topic will remain alive. Cotterill is concerned with the possible adverse consequences of a youth differential (and, in general, of any other group differential) on the employment opportunities for neighboring groups. His thesis, which he bases partly on his own work with Wadycki, is that such adverse consequences are likely to be dramatic in specific industries such as retail trade and services.

In the first section of his paper the author argues that since a differential minimum wage policy based on a distinction between teenagers and adults is still likely to be highly distortive, an alternative differentiating policy might be more desirable. He then sets out to explore criteria for devising a superior, yet realistic program for wage differentials. He identifies neither the political constraints nor the specific social welfare function that must be considered for devising a second-best program that would be superior in some sense to the proposed youth differential, and yet fall short of a de facto abolition of minimum wages for all workers. In any case, the more immediate policy issue now seems to be not whether to institute alternative minimum wage schemes,

515

but whether the proposed two-tier policy for youth and adults is more desirable by some reasonable criteria than the *present* system in which a uniform minimum wage standard is applied to all workers. While Cotterill does not confront this issue directly, he does evaluate the potential effects of a youth differential on adult and youth employment in particular industries.

The effect of a wage differential favoring any one group on the employment opportunities of that and other groups is conventionally analyzed in economic and econometric studies in terms of the relevant own and cross elasticities of the derived demand functions for the various groups. Cotterill finds fault with this standard analysis as applied to different age groups because he believes that youth and adult workers who are employed in specific low-wage occupations are not entirely distinct factors of production. He argues that in reality the distribution of productive capacities among individual members of neighboring age groups are largely overlapping. If so, he expects a reduction in the minimum wage for youths to produce a particularly harmful effect on the employment opportunities of adults whose productivities lie below the standard minimum wage for adults but above the differentiated wage for the youth—a consequence he identifies as the "exclusion effect." He concludes that this exclusion effect must be added on to the expected conventional relative wage effect of a youth differential in calculating the total adverse effects of the differential on adult employment.

The point is not without merit, but its significance is greatly overstated in the context of this paper. After all, the group of adults with productivity below the standard minimum wage may already be largely excluded from full-time jobs in the covered industries. The basic problem of this group stems from its real productivity level falling short of the improved minimum wage for adults, not from its wage's being higher than the proposed minimum wage for the youth. The creation of a youth differential need not have much of an additional adverse impact on the employment opportunities of this group of workers even under dynamic conditions. It is true, however, that those marginal adult workers whose productivity just qualifies them for employment at the standard minimum wage would be particularly hard hit by the youth differential compared to adult employees of higher productivity levels. But this is in agreement with the conventional analysis.

In the main body of his paper Cotterill evaluates the evidence on the potential empirical implications of youth differentials that can be inferred from existing research. While the existing research does not provide any direct evidence on this issue, a number of studies provide at least indirect evidence about the effects of relative wages on the relative employment of different age groups. Cotterill criticizes these studies, particularly the ones by Welch and by Welch and Cunningham, mainly on the following grounds: The existing research defines labor inputs in terms of demographic groups which, according to Cotterill's argument, are not entirely distinct factors of production. Since inputs are not defined in terms of their genuine production role, the parameters of the production functions that have been estimated empirically are not very meaningful and at best are highly unreliable.

The issue that Cotterill raises, while valid, is certainly not unique to studies identifying different age groups as distinct factors. It applies to all studies that assign to measured "labor" and "capital" inputs their presumed theoretical role. Clearly, measured labor may reflect many of the characteristics of capital inputs and vice versa. While the specification and estimation of theoretical production functions defined in terms of genuine characteristics of production is certainly desirable, one cannot dismiss estimates of production functions defined in terms of observable inputs as not useful so long as these inputs have stable links to the bundles of production characteristics they represent. We believe, for example, that cars and trains have overlapping consumption characteristics that are the true arguments in the utility function. This does not, however, invalidate estimates of "derived demand functions" for cars and trains or estimates of the elasticity of substitution between them. The basic issue is not whether different age groups constitute genuine factors of production, but whether the statistical production functions defined over these factors, and the corresponding demand functions, are well behaved and stable. Since this is an empirical issue it can be explored through repeated or robust estimation of the relevant partial elasticities of substitution or derived demand elasticities using independent samples. The evidence on the nature of the interdependencies between adult and teenage labor that Cotterill has developed in his own work with Wadycki does not have direct bearing on the stability of the derived demand relations estimated by Welch and others, because it is based on a very different methodology and may be subject to different specification errors.

I wish at this point to return to the more basic issue I raised earlier: If we are to choose between the existing policy of uniform minimum wages applied to an expanding universe of covered sectors, and a policy that relaxes the minimum wage constraint for the youth, would we be more inclined to accept or reject the proposed differential on the basis of some generally accepted criterion?

At present, most of the published work in labor economics bearing on this issue, at least indirectly, has focused on the measurement of the *employment effects* of (minimum) wages in specific industries, evaluated through the specification of partial equilibrium settings. That this approach is not adequate for addressing the broader policy issue of relevance should be clear from the following illustration. When a uniform minimum wage is imposed on workers in a competitive economy, we expect an unambiguous decrease in social income (NNP) because of the distorting effect of the artificial minimum on the allocation of productive resources (the equilibrium bundle of goods produced moves inside the economy's efficient production frontier). The minimum wage may generate, however, conflicting employment effects on different groups of workers in the labor force: While the total employment of low-wage workers falls, that of higher-wage (skilled) workers whose real productivity exceeds the imposed minimum wage level is likely to increase as firms substitute skill-intensive for less skill-intensive production methods. Clearly, then, even accurate estimation of the relative employment effects of changes in (minimum) wages in different industries, studied separately, would be insufficient for determining the true net effect of economy-wide changes in minimum wages on the value of total output. In general, the latter issue must be addressed through the relevant general equilibrium analysis.

A relaxation of the legal minimum wage for teenage workers would unambiguously increase the national product if the new minimum wage level for the group is set below the real productivity level of workers in this group. For then the minimum wage constraint would remain effective only for adult workers. By a simple application of Le Châtelier's principle, one can easily show that the removal of the wage constraint for any *one* group of workers would unambiguously increase the real value of total output.[1] This would be true, of course, regardless of the conflicting employment effects on the youth and adult employment levels! If there is only a marginal reduction in the legal minimum wage for teenagers, however, the analysis becomes more complicated and requires additional assumptions. Taking other factors to be fixed, one

[1] The fundamental hypothesis of general equilibrium analysis is that in a competitive economy the owners of factors will contract with each other in such a way as to maximize the value of private, and indirectly social, income. The exhaustion of gains from trade implies that the value of final output is maximized subject to the relevant resource constraints, as well as any other constraints imposed through public intervention. Under a general specification of the model, say an economy with two sectors, and three factors of fixed supplies: unskilled adults (A), teenagers (T), and capital (K), the equilibrium total output (*NNP*) is given by $V^* = P_1X_1^* + P_2X_2^*$, where P_i denotes the endogenous output prices. The equilibrium output levels, in turn, are determined by the functions

$$X_i^* = X_i^* (A,T,K,W_A^o, W_T^o), \ i = 1,2$$

where W_A^o and W_T^o denote the imposed minimum wage rates for adult and teenage workers, which need not be identical. Le Châtelier's principle implies that if W_T^o (or W_A^o) is relaxed so as to become ineffective, then the value of total output V^* would necessarily increase.

would expect that if the ratio of the uniform minimum wage to the competitive wage for teenage workers is higher than that for adults, as is plausible to assume given the greater labor market experience of adults, then a marginal reduction in the minimum wage for teenagers, again, is likely to increase national income, regardless of the opposing employment effects it generates.

Of course, the conflicting employment effects of a removal of the wage constraint for teenagers also generates changes in the relative wage *bills* of the two groups. To the extent that there is social concern for the *distributional* consequences of changes in minimum wages, in addition to their impact on the national product, the desirability of a differential minimum wage policy would have to be assessed more generally in light of a well-specified social welfare function. My basic argument is only this: If we are willing to use maximization of social income, or another well-specified criterion, as a guide for social policy in connection with a youth wage differential, then economic theory can at least help us trace the relevant repercussions of such policy that should be assessed in order to arrive at a rational choice. Relative employment effects do not tell the whole story.

One final comment on this issue: It is possible that the tendency toward establishing a youth differential can be explained not just in terms of its expected beneficial effects on aggregate (legitimate) income, but also in terms of its potential impact on the aggregate volume of crime. The general impression that one gets from examining arrest statistics is that teenagers' contribution to criminal activities—especially of the felonious type—is higher than that of any other age bracket. An improvement in the legitimate opportunities of teenagers may therefore alleviate the crime problem in addition to its potential positive effect on national legitimate income, even if it comes at the expense of an incremental unemployment of low-wage adults. If this expectation is valid, it may indeed explain why relaxation of the minimum wage for the young may seem socially more attractive than a similar program for an alternative age bracket. My argument is only conjectural, however, since I am not now aware of any systematic research into the effect of the minimum wage laws on the relative participation in crime of different age groups.

Gregory: Minimum Wages as an Instrument of Social Policy

The essay by Peter Gregory attempts to study the role of minimum wages and a differential minimum wage policy in Costa Rica. It distinguishes three basic objectives of the general policy:

1. Promoting the wage level and the wage bill of wage and salary earners by periodic adjustments in the legal minima.
2. Changing the distribution of income within the covered labor force by enacting interindustry and occupational minimum wage differentials.
3. Altering the personal distribution of income in favor of the poor.

The author then sets out to explore the extent to which each of the three objectives has been achieved over the period 1966–1975.

1. With respect to the first objective the author cleverly notes that real wages in Costa Rica rose at an annual rate which clearly exceeds the economy-wide average increase in productivity over the period in question. Thus, it appears that workers have improved their relative position in the income distribution. As the author recognizes from the outset, he really is in no position to perform rigorous testing of the possible role that minimum wages have played in effecting these changes, because of the serious limitations of his data. He does, however, make the following observations on the basis of the raw data at his disposal:

   a. Annual changes in real wages usually ran ahead of changes in minimum wages.
   b. The rate of change in actual earnings in years of no minimum wage changes was not much different from that in years of minimum wage changes.
   c. Generally, the contemporaneous rates of change in the minimum and average wages were quite different in magnitude.

From this evidence, and similar reports by researchers who traced the course of minimum and average wages in different periods, the author concludes that minimum wages have played a minor role in propelling wages and the wage bill upward in Costa Rica. Now, while the author's conclusion in this regard seems reasonable, the statistics he examines are not sufficiently compelling to support this or an alternative inference, the main reasons being:

   a. There is in all probability some lag structure underlying the relationship between changes in minimum wages and actual wages. Thus, whether minimum wages have in fact led, or lagged behind, average wage levels cannot be determined from a simple inspection of the raw data.
   b. The potential existence of a lag structure may also explain why the simple monthly or yearly correlation between contemporaneous values of the two variables is not pronounced.

c. The fact that the annual rate of change in real wages typically exceeded the rate of change in the minimum wages does not invalidate the proposition that changes in minimum wages still have exerted a significant, albeit *partial*, influence on the movement in wage levels.

Whether the minimum wage policy has had an important impact on the growth in wage levels might best be determined, in theory, by studying the actual changes in employment in the covered sectors. Clearly, a minimum wage policy could be effective in promoting wages only if it reduces the rate of growth of employment below the level that would have been anticipated as a result of general labor market forces. I do not know, however, whether the relevant statistics with which to test such employment effects are presently available to the author.

2. As for the second presumed target of minimum wage policy—that of narrowing actual wage differentials by narrowing the range of imposed minimum wages—the author questions the effectiveness of the graduated wage adjustment policy in view of his general impression that the minimum wage levels have been set below the effective wage levels in most industries. At the same time, his statistics show that, especially since 1974, the significant compression in minimum wages has been at least weakly associated with the narrowing of actual wage differentials within manufacturing. If this association is also indicative of a causal relationship of minimum and actual wages, then this policy of graduated minimum wage adjustments might have introduced significant distortions in the manufacturing industries and the economy as a whole, as my previous theoretical analysis indicates. Indeed, the distortions resulting from an effective imposition of more uniformity in minimum wage levels would have the potential of seriously undermining economic growth in a small country like Costa Rica.

3. Finally, as for the goal of making the family or per capita distribution of income more equitable in Costa Rica, the author's raw data are at least not inconsistent with the hypothesis that the general minimum wage policy may have had little effect in practice. But, again, the statistics do not allow for rigorous testing of the hypothesis.

Despite the reservations I have raised in connection with the data presented by Professor Gregory, I tend to agree with his basic premise that even in a less developed country like Costa Rica, a minimum wage policy is not likely to prove an effective instrument for either economic growth or income distribution. It is possible that specific labor markets in underdeveloped countries are more segmented and oligopsonistic than those in developed countries, so that a prudent minimum wage policy might improve economic efficiency and promote a more equitable

521

distribution of income. But there are also important reasons to expect the opposite effects. A minimum wage policy aimed at an artificial equalization of wage levels might be particularly distorting in less developed countries because of the relatively large concentration of employment in agriculture, and because of the potentially detrimental effects of minimum wages on the incentive to provide on-the-job training. An effective minimum wage policy is likely to reduce investment in on-the-job training, typically a major channel for investment in human capital in less developed countries, because workers subject to minimum wage constraints would not be able to exchange money for training benefits provided by employers. Not only is the potential for distortions in the allocation of resources large, the extent to which income shares of covered workers could rise may also be small if the relevant elasticities of substitution between unskilled and other workers, or other factors, were relatively high in the typically less sophisticated industries of the less developed countries.

Bibliography

Cotterill, Philip. "Differential Legal Minimum Wages." Paper prepared for the Conference on Legal Minimum Wages, American Enterprise Institute, November 1979.

Cotterill, Philip, and Wadycki, W. "Teenagers and the Minimum Wage in Retail Trade." *Journal of Human Resources* 9 (Winter 1976): 69–85.

Gregory, Peter. "Legal Minimum Wages as an Instrument of Social Policy in Less Developed Countries, with Special References to Costa Rica." Paper prepared for the Conference on Legal Minimum Wages, American Enterprise Institute, November 1979.

Welch, Finis. "Minimum Wage Legislation in the United States." *Economic Inquiry* 12 (September 1974): 285–318.

Welch, Finis, and Cunningham, J. "Effects of Minimum Wages on the Level and Age Composition of Youth Employment." *Review of Economics and Statistics* 60 (February 1978): 140–45.

The Context of Recent Research

Robert S. Goldfarb

The paper by Carolyn Shaw Bell belongs to a literature that has developed rapidly in the last five or six years, and it can best be evaluated by placing it in the context of recent research developments. Six years ago there was some fairly consistent statistical evidence of disemployment effects for teenagers. A number of other important potential effects had not been systematically investigated, or investigators had produced inconclusive or ambiguous results.[1] The following effects seemed to need further investigation:

I. Income distribution effects.

II. Employment and unemployment effects.

a. Effects on adult employment and unemployment.

b. Effects on teenage *unemployment* (while previous employment studies gave relatively consistent results, unemployment studies did not).

c. Studies by race, with special emphasis on explaining black teenage unemployment.

d. Studies providing ways of dealing with problems which affected even the "successful" teenage employment studies: effects of changing coverage and noncompliance, interactions of macroeconomic policy with announced minimum wage changes, and so forth.

e. Substitution effects across types of labor (particularly relevant for analysis of youth differentials in the minimum wage).

III. Effects of minimum wages on education decisions (If increases in minimum wages kept some teenagers in school, by decreasing employment opportunity, this might have important human capital effects.)[2]

IV. Studies setting forth more sophisticated evaluative frameworks

---

[1] Articles discussing the state of the art five or six years ago include Robert S. Goldfarb, "The Policy Content of Quantitative Minimum Wage Research," in *Industrial Relations Research Association Proceedings* (December 1976), pp. 261–68; Finis Welch, "Minimum Wage Legislation in the United States," *Economic Inquiry* 12 (September 1974): 285–318; and Edward M. Gramlich, "The Impact of Minimum Wages on Other Wages, Employment, and Family Incomes," in *Brookings Papers on Economic Activity* 2 (1976): 430–51.

[2] Welch, "Minimum Wage Legislation," suggests that the effect on education is theoretically ambiguous because of the need to finance education through part-time jobs.

for discussing minimum wage policy. For example, some of the early studies seemed satisfied with the assertion that, if the minimum wage raised (lowered) the wage bill, it was a worthwhile (bad) increase; there was no explicit recognition that it might matter who got the increases versus who (that is, poor versus nonpoor)lost the jobs.

The lack of income distribution studies (item I above) seemed particularly crucial since it prevented the narrowing of informed opinion about the usefulness of minimum wage increases. While opponents of such increases could stress teenage disemployment effects, sophisticated advocates of minimum wage increases had a defensible counterargument: "Of course there are negative employment effects from minimum wage increases, but I believe these are relatively small, fall mostly on teenagers and not family heads, and are completely overwhelmed by the increase in wage rates to the working poor, many of whom are family heads. That is, the beneficial income distribution effects completely swamp any minor disemployment effects." In short, a case could have been made for minimum wage increases on the basis of income-raising or "poverty-fighting" effects. So long as such effects were possible, there was a plausible basis for a pro–minimum wage argument.

In the years since 1974, there has been important progress in some of the listed areas. In my opinion—since I was always bothered by the pro–minimum wage income distribution argument—a crucial breakthrough has been with respect to income distribution effects. Terence Kelly and Edward Gramlich,[3] using complementary methods on 1973 and 1974 data from the Current Population Survey (CPS), presented strong evidence that minimum wage increases are unlikely to have much effect on the distribution of income. Gramlich showed that a sizable percentage of any increase is likely to go to families with relatively high average incomes, while Kelly showed that quite large increases in minimum wage rates are unlikely to yield large decreases in commonly used measures of poverty.

Kelly takes a sample of families from the CPS and simulates the effect of a minimum wage increase by raising the wage of each worker earning the minimum wage (or less) up to a new higher minimum. He then recalculates three different poverty indexes (percent in poverty, a dollar poverty gap measure, and a gap measure which weights gains to the very poor more heavily) to see how much the higher minimum has lowered these measures of poverty. The general result is that large increases in the minimum have only small effects on poverty indexes. For example, an increase in the 1973 minimum from $1.60 to $3.50—

---

[3] Terence Kelly, "Two Policy Questions Regarding the Minimum Wage" (Urban Institute Working Paper, February 1976).

that is, a more-than-doubling—lowers each of the indexes less (sometimes considerably less) than 10 percent.

Since both Kelly and Gramlich explicitly ignored disemployment effects in their empirical estimates (indeed, it is not easy to see how they could have been included), the true poverty-decreasing effects might be even smaller than those measured. Those two studies indicated that favorable income distribution effects could not be expected from raising the minimum wage.

Another important area of progress has been the development of more sophisticated frameworks for modeling employment and unemployment effects. In the early 1970s a simple supply and demand diagram was often used to analyze minimum wage effects. More recently, analysts such as Welch, Mincer, and Gramlich[4] have studied the problem in the much more appropriate two (or more) sector context, carefully taking into account the existence of an uncovered sector.

Advances have been made in several other areas since 1974. Several analysts[5] employed a promising method for estimating unemployment effects which seems to avoid some of the earlier studies' difficulties. Instead of estimating a single reduced-form equation to measure the effect of a higher minimum on the unemployment rate, they estimate separate "supply" and "demand" (actually employment and labor force participation) equations, and obtain an estimate of the unemployment effect by taking the difference between demand and supply at the minimum wage. While extremely promising, this technique has not yet been subject to wide enough use and criticism to be sure of its properties. For example, Cagan[6] argues that "Mincer's method seems more reliable than those of other studies, but it could lead to overestimates of the effect of minimum wages. Mincer's estimates may have spuriously incorporated many other influences on young workers which were not allowed for separately." Additional insight into measurement difficulties comes from Gramlich's reminder that previous studies focused on employment rather than hours, and it is conceivable that there is a strong hours effect in addition to any employment effect.

Gramlich presents empirical evidence indicating that there is a reduction in hours. The implicit analytics seems to be that decreases in

[4] Welch, "Minimum Wage Legislation"; Jacob Mincer, "Unemployment Effects of Minimum Wages," *Journal of Political Economy* 84 (August 1976): S87–S104; and Gramlich, "Impact of Minimum Wages."

[5] Mincer, "Unemployment Effects"; and James Ragan, "Minimum Wages and the Youth Labor Market," *Review of Economics and Statistics* 59 (May 1977): 129–36.

[6] Phillip Cagan, "The Reduction of Inflation and the Magnitude of Unemployment," in *Contemporary Economic Problems*, William Fellner, ed. (Washington, D.C.: American Enterprise Institute, 1977): pp. 15–52.

demand may result in hours reductions or employment reductions or both. However, there is an opposing analytical argument suggesting hours could conceivably increase (that is, in some instances full-time employment might be substituted for part-time). Employers must recoup initial per worker hiring costs by paying wages below marginal product. Higher minimums lower the possible wage–marginal product gap; in such a circumstance, more hours per period allow the smaller gap to be offset by a faster recoupment of hiring costs.

Another area of progress has included the effects of noncompliance and noncoverage. Both Gramlich and Ashenfelter and Smith[7] have produced useful examinations of the possibility of widespread noncompliance. Two further developments would be extremely useful here. One would be studies dealing more convincingly with excluding legal noncoverage when measuring noncompliance. A second would incorporate a "correction" for noncompliance in studies of employment effects, or at least explain why, if noncompliance is really so widespread, the employment studies consistently show significant disemployment effects. Is the implication that strong and effective enforcement efforts would greatly increase measured disemployment effects?

Several other developments are worth noting. The question of substitution among classes of labor has received some attention. Welch, in one of several excellent studies of the employment effects of minimum wages, has attempted with Cunningham[8] to estimate substitution possibilities among teenage subgroups. Hamermesh and Grant[9] have also given us an extremely useful review of the state of the entire literature on "labor-labor" substitution (without special emphasis on minimum wages). Another very important development, not primarily concerned with minimum wages, is the emerging literature on the possible "lifetime" labor market implications of employment and unemployment experience as a teenager; two examples are by W. Stevenson and D. Ellwood.[10] A typical study of such lifetime experiences uses the National Longitudinal Survey to relate labor market experience of a particular

[7] Orley Ashenfelter and Robert Smith, "Compliance with the Minimum Wage Law," *Journal of Political Economy* 87 (April 1979): 333–50.

[8] Finis Welch and James Cunningham, "The Effects of Minimum Wages on the Level and Age Composition of Youth Employment," *Review of Economics and Statistics* 60 (February 1978): 140–45.

[9] Daniel Hamermesh and James Grant, "Econometric Studies of Labor-Labor Substitution and Their Implications for Policy," *Journal of Human Resources* 14 (Fall 1979): 518–42.

[10] W. Stevenson, "The Relationship between Early Work Experience and Future Employability," in *The Lingering Crisis of Youth Unemployment*, Arvil Adams and Garth Mangum, eds. (Kalamazoo, Mich.: W.E. Upjohn Institute, June 1978), pp. 93–124; and D. Ellwood, "Teenage Unemployment: Permanent Scars or Temporary Blemishes," Harvard University and National Bureau of Economic Research Working Paper, May 1979.

teenager to labor market performance of that same individual when he is in his twenties. This literature has not yet achieved a consensus view about the carry-over of effects, but the papers produced are increasingly sophisticated. A definitive set of studies would indicate, for example, how seriously any minimum-wage-induced teenage unemployment might affect future adult labor market and earnings prospects. Finally, the very existence of the income distribution studies indicates a growing sensitivity to item IV above; the need to produce more sophisticated evaluative frameworks for discussing minimum wage policy. Gramlich asks another provocative question: "Would those workers directly affected by minimum wage increases 'vote' for these increases; that is, would they be in favor of accepting the chance of higher wages versus higher unemployment represented by the increase?" While this consideration is only one possible item in a complete evaluative framework, it is certainly an interesting one. (Consumer-taxpayer interests, including, but not limited to, any change in transfer payment levels due to changed minimum wages, as well as any broader social concern for employment or income distribution, would also be taken into account in a sophisticated evaluative framework.)

Having briefly reviewed recent progress in minimum wage research, let us turn to Professor Bell's paper, which clearly fits into the "income distribution effects" category. Bell sets out to investigate the relationship between wage rates and income, and especially "the efficiency of . . . minimum wage policy to alleviate poverty." Thus, the paper is closely related to the work of Gramlich and Kelly. In this context, the Bell paper has several positive features. First, her emphasis and data are different from those of Gramlich and Kelly, yet her analysis serves to reinforce their point that the relationship between minimum wage increases and raising the income of low-income families is tenuous at best. Second, Bell presents a much more thorough discussion than either Gramlich or Kelly of the complexity of the relationship between wage levels and income determination. While Gramlich and Kelly focus almost exclusively on empirical evidence, Bell puts considerable effort into explaining *why* the relationship between minimum wage increases and poverty reduction might turn out to be tenuous. For example, besides the more well-known difficulty that low-wage workers may be secondary earners in families with other earners, some of whom may receive high wages, she points out the less well known problem that official poverty levels vary by family size and by other characteristics ("124 different incomes exist for 'the poverty level' "), so that "no money sum of wages can be calculated to be a minimum wage that will provide an income above poverty," without also raising nonpoor incomes significantly. Moreover, since Bell uses more recent data (1978

Current Population Survey) than Gramlich or Kelly, her work shows that the general Gramlich-Kelly conclusions have not changed over time. As she puts it, "What becomes strikingly clear . . . [from the data] . . . is the concentration of low-wage workers in families with incomes above any published poverty level."

On the negative side, one feature of the Bell paper makes it less useful than it might otherwise be. Despite its obvious connection to the earlier studies on income distribution effects, Bell makes very little attempt to relate her work to that of Gramlich and Kelly. Several obvious questions arise in thinking about comparisons. First, are there any economic reasons—changes in welfare programs, aggregate economic activity, and so forth—for expecting somewhat different quantitative results about the elasticity of poverty with respect to minimum wages in 1977 than in 1973? This issue is never even raised. Second, how different are the actual results? Given the conceptual looseness of the connection between wage rates and incomes, do simulations of the effects of a minimum wage increase based on 1977 data produce much smaller or much larger reductions in poverty than Kelly's 1973 simulations? This question is not answered because Bell does not replicate the Kelly simulations, which provide a very direct and revealing way of examining the relation between minimum wage increases and poverty reduction. While Bell is entitled to perform her analysis as she thinks best, it would be of great aid to the reader to know why she chose *not* to redo Kelly's simulations. Is it lack of data? Is she suspicious of Kelly's procedures? Placing her paper much more explicitly in the context of previous research would increase its usefulness.

Let us consider the papers by Gramlich, Kelly, and Bell as a group and ask what gaps in the overall approach future work might attempt to fill. First, the estimates provided do not correct for disemployment effects. Is it possible to produce theoretical or empirical information about the initial income positions of those likely to be disemployed? Notice that this question is of interest only to the extent that one wants more precise estimates of income distribution effects. Noncoverage and noncompliance create similar difficulties when trying to simulate distribution effects. Second, it is sometimes claimed that minimum wage increases result in increases in wages above the minimum. An institutionalist is likely to assert the existence of these "ripple effects" without further ado, while those of the neoclassical persuasion are likely to mumble something about substitution effects in addition. Can convincing estimates of ripple effects be made and incorporated into an exercise similar to Kelly's? A related effect, in the opposite direction, is the lowering of wages in the uncovered sector as job-losers in the covered sector supply themselves to the uncovered sector. Note that, for both disemployment and ripple effects, one might in the absence of good data on the actual effects at least be able to simulate how some plausible sizes and distributions of effects might change income distribution implications. A third gap in current estimates involves the interaction between higher minimum wages and eligibility for government transfer payments. Poverty-reducing effects could either be amplified or lessened by such interactions. (The families of those losing work might qualify for higher payments, while the families of those receiving wage increases might have payments lowered.) Finally, since so many of those affected by minimum wage changes are teenagers, we should consider the effect of a minimum wage change today on the teenager's income earning ability as an adult. Suppose minimum wages raise teenage unemployment, keep some teenagers in school, and change the ability of both teenagers and low-wage family heads to finance education; clearly all sorts of future income distribution implications could flow from this, though it is not easy to see how anyone could get very far predicting changes in future distributions.

Bibliography

Ashenfelter, Orley, and Smith, Robert. "Compliance with the Minimum Wage Law." *Journal of Political Economy* 87 (April 1979): 333–50.

Cagan, Phillip. "The Reduction of Inflation and the Magnitude of Unemployment." In *Contemporary Economic Problems, 1977*, edited by W. Fellner. Washington, D.C.: American Enterprise Institute, 1977: pp. 15–52.

Ellwood, D. "Teenage Unemployment: Permanent Scars or Temporary Blemishes." Harvard University and National Bureau of Economic Research Working Paper, May 1979.

Goldfarb, Robert S. "The Policy Content of Quantitative Minimum Wage Research." In *Industrial Relations Research Association Proceedings*, December 1974: pp. 261–68.

Gramlich, Edward M. "The Impact of Minimum Wages on Other Wages, Employment, and Family Incomes." *Brookings Papers on Economic Activity* 2 (1976): 430–51.

Hamermesh, Daniel, and Grant, James. "Econometric Studies of Labor-Labor Substitution and Their Implications for Policy." *Journal of Human Resources* 14 (Fall 1979): 518–42.

Kelly, Terence. "Two Policy Questions Regarding the Minimum Wage." Urban Institute Working Paper, February 1976.

Mincer, Jacob. "Unemployment Effects of Minimum Wages." *Journal of Political Economy* 84 (August 1976): S87–S104.

Ragan, James. "Minimum Wages and the Youth Labor Market." *Review of Economics and Statistics* 59 (May 1977): 129–36.

Stevenson, W. "The Relationship between Early Work Experience and Future Employability." In *The Lingering Crisis of Youth Unemployment*, edited by

The Unanswered Question: Why Are Minimum Wages Popular with the Poor?

Keith B. Leffler

This volume on minimum wages has examined a host of empirical issues relating to the effects of minimum wages. Various papers were devoted to teenagers. Other papers singled out agricultural workers, domestic service workers, cotton farmers, and residents of the South. The general conclusion (or frequently the supposition) of these studies is that low-income workers as a group are the major victims of minimum wage legislation. While their academic temperament makes economists wont to disagree on any issue, in this case disagreement seems to be limited to the details of econometric estimations. To the noneconomist this must seem a surprising consensus, for poverty group representatives and humanitarian do-gooders consider minimum wages to be a powerful weapon in their arsenal combating low incomes. Yet economic analysis suggests that this weapon serves not the interests of the poor but rather the interests of the relatively well-to-do labor unions and the bourgeois northern capitalists.

Minimum wage legislation is not a recent experiment in the United States. Economic analysis implies that for over fifty years low-income individuals have been fooled as to actual effects of minimum wage laws. Over these same fifty years economists have pointed out the folly of combating poverty by constraining the market wage. Stigler has lamented the continual support of minimum wages by its major victims as one of the clearest failures of economists.[1] Indeed, if we judge ideas by their success in the marketplace, the economic analysis of minimum wages appears to avoid bankruptcy only via government subsidy. In this comment, I would like to suggest that the success of poverty group representatives who support minimum wages and the relative lack of success of economists to influence this policy results not from the inability of the poor to comprehend the law of demand but rather from beneficial distributional effects accompanying minimum wages. Hence, the lack of understanding may rest with the very economists who decry others' lack of understanding.

[1] George Stigler, "Do Economists Matter?" *Southern Economic Journal* 42 (1976): 347–54.

Only a sparse body of research addresses directly the incentives for various lobbies and political representatives to support or oppose minimum wages. The accepted political-economic theory of minimum wages is one based on the intensity of preferences of the benefiting union sector and also those industrial sectors whose technology uses relatively skilled labor. In both cases, consumer substitution toward products produced by firms using low-productivity, low-wage workers is limited by legally elevating the wages paid by these firms. Generally these politically based, pressure-group explanations for the political popularity of minimum wages are specific to the United States. Yet in this session of the conference we have accounts of minimum wages in Central and South America, where the representatives of the low-productivity classes have consistently been political advocates of minimum wages.

The standard analysis of minimum wages is based on relatively simple supply and demand tools. A legislated increase in the wage rate leads to disemployment of low-wage workers. The minimum wage creates the one case in which jobs are truly in short supply. Nearly every introductory text contains a discussion of how goods are rationed when market prices are constrained, yet the details of the nonprice rationing under minimum wages are essentially unexplored by economists.[2] Here I wish to suggest some ways in which the rationing of scarce jobs may lead to redistributions among the low-wage workers and thereby benefit both the representatives of these individuals and the politically relevant low-wage group.

Consider first a common method of competition under price controls—competition in waiting. In the case of employment, the form of a queue is likely to be excessive job search time. The equilibrium cost of queuing will be that which equates the expected gain from obtaining the job to the cost of waiting or searching. Presumably low-wage workers have a continuum of job valuations and waiting costs. Generally, we would expect the cost of waiting to be inversely related to the opportunity costs of working in the minimum wage job. Hence, those with lower opportunity costs will be those most successful in this form of nonprice competition. The differences in opportunity costs can be due to differences in uncovered employment opportunities (for example, theft, drug dealing, legal self-employment, and legislatively excluded employment), schooling opportunities, welfare opportunities, child care, or simply a high subjective value of leisure. Imposition of a minimum wage can therefore alter the form of competition in a way that focuses the gains on those with the worst opportunities. The nonprice

---

[2] While the emphasis upon the unemployment effects on teenagers is certainly related to this issue, the emphasis seems to this reader to result as much from the age distribution of low-productivity workers as from the rationing activity of employers.

competition minimizes the loss to the unemployed in such a manner that calculation of the wage bill before and after the minimum wage need bear no relationship to the cost of the legislation to low-income workers.

Price controls and the resulting shortage of jobs also lower the cost of employers exercising their personal preferences about employee characteristics. In allocating the valuable, scarce minimum wage jobs, employers will favor those workers with personal characteristics that the employer likes. Because of the minimum wage, the cost of discriminating among employees on a nonproductivity basis is reduced. If employers in general have "average" tastes, the favored characteristics of low-income workers will tend to be those favored by society as a whole. Society's willingness to subsidize low-income individuals is likely related to the personal characteristics of the individuals. The "worthy" poor may be those that are hard working (that is, poor because of their endowment rather than because of their tastes), those with families, and those with middle-class tastes. The characteristics favored by employers in rationing the scarce minimum wage jobs may be exactly those characteristics which make one a subsidy-worthy low-income individual.

Minimum wages may be designed to transfer income among the poor. Of course, if desired characteristics could be clearly defined, wage subsidies could be directed to this group. This would not only be unconstitutional, but subject to large policing costs. It seems reasonable to me that employers may have relatively low costs of determining the actual characteristics of the employees and that their discrimination may be such as to maximize the value of a wage restriction to the general voter. Note also that the rationing by employers based on workers' personal characteristics may also favor those that are older and have established communication channels with poverty group representatives. Those of voting age will also be disproportionately favored. Rationing by employers will therefore lead to the benefits of minimum wages accruing to those individuals who are the constituents of the minimum wage proponents.

A final method of equilibrating a market subject to a price control (considered here) is alterations in the characteristics of the transacted good. Indeed, if goods are generally composed of many characteristics, not all of which are explicitly priced, price controls will not lead to shortages or surpluses since adjustment in unpriced, uncontrolled characteristics will equate supply and demand. In the minimum wage case employers can and will alter the working conditions (for example, safety, noise, air conditioning), the level of fringe benefits (for example, coffee breaks, tardiness penalties, sick pay), and also the extent of training provided by the job. In all these cases, competitive equilibrium under a minimum wage constraint can have higher employment and higher consumers' surplus for the low-wage workers than equilibrium in the absence of the wage constraint.[3] While in this case the substantial evidence showing that employment falls with minimum wages indicates the empirical irrelevance of this possibility, the analysis does highlight the dependence of the effects of minimum wages on the methods used to ration the scarce "high" wage jobs.

If economists are to influence minimum wage policy (and the literature suggests this intention), an understanding of the support for minimum wages by the alleged victims of the policy seems crucial. The prevalent supposition that, if only the poor could understand the first law of demand, their substantial support for minimum wages would vanish has likely been detrimental to economic influence. Not only is such a view elitist but also, if incorrect, it will cause skepticism about other related policy advice. In addition, the current tone of economic research on minimum wages, emphasizing the disemployment effects of minimum wages, is probably irrelevant to the support for such policy. While redistributions couched in terms of liberal do-gooding may be palatable to the average uninterested taxpayer, research showing the inconsistency of minimum wages and the general welfare of the poor is of interest mainly to welfare economists. Just as politicians do not maximize social welfare, neither do the leaders of poverty groups maximize the welfare of the society of the poor.

At the present time, minimum wage studies tend to use aggregate data, which obscures redistributional effects within the aggregate. By focusing on individual data, economists can hope to identify the characteristics of the workers retained at the constrained minimum wage. A simultaneous development of a theory of the political power of subgroups of low-income individuals may go far to explain the vociferous support of minimum wages by the spokesmen of the poor.

[3] See Yoram Barzel and Keith Leffler, "Equilibrium When Goods Are Multidimensional and Pricing Is Costly," University of Washington working paper, January 1980, for a general analysis of this proposition. Masanori Hashimoto, "Minimum Wage and Earnings Growth of Young Males," University of Washington working paper, December 1979, provides a specific application to on-the-job training and minimum wages.

A NOTE ON THE BOOK

*The typeface used for the text of this book is
Times Roman, designed by Stanley Morison.
The type was set by
FotoTypesetters Incorporated, of Baltimore.
Thomson-Shore, Inc., of Dexter, Michigan, printed
and bound the book, using Glatfelter paper.
The cover and format were designed by Pat Taylor,
and the figures were drawn by Hördur Karlsson.
The editing was supervised by Carol Rosen and
Claire Theune of the AEI Publications staff.*

Selected AEI Publications

AEI Associates Program

The American Enterprise Institute invites your participation in the competition of ideas through its AEI Associates Program. This program has two objectives:

The first is to broaden the distribution of AEI studies, conferences, forums, and reviews, and thereby to extend public familiarity with the issues. AEI Associates receive regular information on AEI research and programs, and they can order publications and cassettes at a savings.

The second objective is to increase the research activity of the American Enterprise Institute and the dissemination of its published materials to policy makers, the academic community, journalists, and others who help shape public attitudes. Your contribution, which in most cases is partly tax deductible, will help ensure that decision makers have the benefit of scholarly research on the practical options to be considered before programs are formulated. The issues studied by AEI include:

- Defense Policy
- Economic Policy
- Energy Policy
- Foreign Policy
- Government Regulation
- Health Policy
- Legal Policy
- Political and Social Processes
- Social Security and Retirement Policy
- Tax Policy

For more information, write to:

AMERICAN ENTERPRISE INSTITUTE
1150 Seventeenth Street, N.W.
Washington, D.C. 20036